# *Assessing and Correcting Reading and Writing Difficulties*

**Thomas G. Gunning**
*Adjunct Professor, Professor Emeritus*
*Southern Connecticut State University*

**Allyn and Bacon**
*Boston • London • Toronto • Sydney • Tokyo • Singapore*

*Senior Editor:* Virginia Lanigan
*Editorial Assistant:* Kris Lamarre
*Editorial-Production Service:* Omegatype Typography, Inc.
*Manufacturing Buyer:* Megan Cochran
*Cover Administrator:* Jenny Hart

A Viacom Company
160 Gould Street
Needham Heights, MA 02194

Internet: www.abacon.com
America Online: keyword: College Online



**Library of Congress Cataloging-in-Publication Data**

Gunning, Thomas G.
Assessing and correcting reading and writing difficulties / Thomas G. Gunning
p. cm.
Includes bibliographic references and index.
ISBN 0-205-27438-2
1. Reading disability—Evaluation. 2. Reading—Ability testing. 3. Reading—Remedial teaching. 4. English language—Composition and exercises—Ability testing. 5. English language—Composition and exercises—Study and teaching. I. Title.
LB1050.5.G846 1998
372.43—dc21 97-25013
CIP

Printed in the United States of America

10 9 8 7 6 5 4 3 2 1 02 01 00 99 98 97

*For my brothers and sisters, for the love and support they have provided over the years . . .*

*Marguerite Marie Gunning Phelps*
*Mary Evelyn Gunning Hartman*
*Ann Lee Gunning Haire*
*Barbara Maxwell Gunning Buchman (deceased)*
*Paul Walter Gunning*
*Francis Xavier Gunning*
*Mary Kathleen Gunning Arle*
*Joseph John Gunning*

# Contents

# Sample Lessons

# *Preface*

Although grounded in theory and research, *Assessing and Correcting Reading and Writing Difficulties* is, above all else, a practical text. It specifies how to assess students and how to use assessment results to provide effective instruction. Forty sample lessons, described in step-by-step fashion, cover virtually every major skill or strategy. The emphasis is on teaching strategies that students can use independently for improving word recognition, vocabulary knowledge, comprehension, reading in the content areas, writing, and study skills.

One reason low-achieving readers fall behind is that they typically read less than their peers. Realizing this, I have provided numerous suggestions for books that can provide additional reinforcement or that students might want to read for enjoyment. Because low-achieving readers read below their grade level, books that are easy to read yet appealing to older students have been emphasized. Appendix B contains an extensive list of high-interest, low-readability texts. Realizing, too, that low-achieving readers and writers need plenty of practice, I have included numerous suggestions for reinforcement activities. Most chapters also present Exemplary Teaching, a vignette of especially effective instruction, and brief case studies that exemplify the major principles explored in that chapter.

Because there are many approaches to teaching low-achieving readers and writers and various philosophies behind these approaches, this text presents the techniques and practices that seem most promising. Low-achieving readers and writers need explicit instruction. They also need the opportunity to derive satisfaction and enjoyment from reading and writing for real purposes. This text recommends planned, systematic instruction within the context of holistic reading and writing activities.

Since there are many valid ways of teaching reading and writing, the text frequently provides a choice of methods. The chapter on phonics, for instance, explores both holistic and several direct, systematic instructional techniques. Regardless of which technique is selected, emphasis is on providing contextual, functional instruction with many opportunities for real reading and writing.

Today there is an emphasis on collaboration between the classroom teacher and the specialist. At times, specialists use techniques that are different from those used by the classroom teacher, and specialists from different fields might choose different methods. For instance, when working with students who have severe reading problems, the reading specialist might show a preference for a teaching method known as the Fernald tracing technique, whereas a specialist with a learning disabilities orientation might use the multisensory Orton-Gillingham technique. It is important to be acquainted with both techniques in order to choose the approach that is best suited to a given situation, and also to enable you to work knowledgeably and effectively with other professionals.

Chapters 1 and 2 provide an overview of reading and writing difficulties and a summary of the factors that contribute to reading and writing problems. Chapters 3, 4, 5, and 6 present ways of assessing the strengths and weaknesses of low-achieving readers and writers. Since assessment and instruction are often intertwined, additional information on assessment is presented in the chapters on instruction. The focus is on obtaining information that helps in planning an effective program.

The bulk of the text explores techniques for teaching low-achieving readers and writers. Chapter 7 discusses emergent literacy. Chapters 8, 9, 10, and 11 explore methods for improving word recognition and include a chapter on phonics; one on high frequency words; one on dictionary skills and syllabic, morphemic (meaningful word parts), and contextual analysis; and a chapter on developing vocabulary.

Chapters 12, 13, and 14 are devoted to understanding the written word and include chapters on general comprehension, reading in the content areas, and study skills. Chapter 15 explores writing techniques for helping struggling writers. Chapter 16 describes methods for helping students who have severe word-learning problems, and programs for teenage and adult problem readers and students who are still acquiring English. Chapter 17 focuses on materials, voluntary reading, and the use of technology. The book concludes with a chapter on organizing a program for low-achieving readers and writers.

With its broad coverage, detailed lessons, and numerous suggestions for reinforcement, this text will be a practical guide and ready reference as you work with low-achieving readers and writers.

## *Acknowledgments*

I owe a debt of gratitude to Virginia Lanigan of Allyn and Bacon, who saw value in the original, unwieldy manuscript and offered the kinds of suggestions and support that enabled me to pare it down but enrich it. I am also grateful to Kris Lamarre, her capable assistant, who shepherded the manuscript through all the many phases that led up to publication, and to Omegatype for careful copyediting. Many thanks, too, to the anonymous reviewers who offered numerous suggestions that were both thoughtful and valuable.

# *Assessing and Correcting Reading and Writing Difficulties*

# Chapter 1

# Introduction to Reading Difficulties

## *Using What You Know*

This first chapter of this text serves as an overview and introduction to a complex topic: reading and writing difficulties. Before reading the chapter, think about the knowledge that you bring to the topic so you will be better prepared to interact with the information presented. Have you read books or articles on reading and writing difficulties? Do you remember from your school days what steps were taken to help those classmates who struggled with reading? If you are teaching now, think about students of yours who may have difficulty with reading or writing. What problems are they manifesting? How are these students being helped?

After reflecting on your knowledge of the topic, complete the anticipation guide that follows. The anticipation guide is a device that will help you interact with the chapter's main concepts. Most of the statements in the anticipation guide are open-ended and may not have a right or wrong answer. These statements are designed to help you explore your beliefs and attitudes. They can also help indicate topics on which you might need additional information. The anticipation guide is a device that you can use with your students. Suggestions for teaching the Anticipation Guide are presented in Chapter 13.

## *Anticipation Guide*

Read each of the following statements. Put a check under "Agree " or "Disagree" to show how you feel about each one. If possible, discuss your responses with classmates.

| | Agree | Disagree |
|---|---|---|
| **1.** A problem reader is one who is reading below his/her grade level. | ______ | ______ |
| **2.** In most instances, reading problems can be prevented. | ______ | ______ |
| **3.** Most cases of reading difficulty should be handled by the classroom teacher. | ______ | ______ |
| **4.** Low-achieving readers need to have tasks broken down into their component parts. | ______ | ______ |
| **5.** There is no one best approach for working with low-achieving readers. | ______ | ______ |

## *Reading Difficulty Defined*

There are many ways of defining reading difficulty, but the most telling definition was uttered by Awilda, a fourth-grader in a large urban school. When asked how school was going, she replied, "I got trouble with my reading."

Counting the extra year spent in second grade, Awilda had received more than four years of formal instruction in reading. However, despite having average intelligence, she was only reading on an early first-grade level. Although she had a stable personality, a caring family, and dedicated, highly competent teachers, she was reading at a level far below what might reasonably be expected. What's more, Awilda's difficulty was interfering with her functioning both in school and the larger society. She lacked the skills necessary to read the literature, social studies, and science selections typically required of a fourth-grader. Outside of school, she was unable to read the letters her grandmother sent from Houston, use the newspaper's TV guide to find out the evening's schedule, read the ads on cereal boxes, or engage in any of the literacy tasks that fourth-graders might encounter. Worst of all, Awilda's self-esteem was being eroded.

Awilda was manifesting a reading difficulty in two related but different ways. There was a discrepancy between overall intellectual ability and her reading achievement. Although she had average ability, she was reading well below grade level. And her lack of reading ability was interfering with the demands made by her life circumstances. Awilda was evidencing a functional difficulty.

### *Discrepancy Definition*

When considering whether a person has a reading difficulty, the reader's intellectual capacity is frequently taken into consideration. Theoretically, a student should be able to read at a level equal to their intellectual capacity or level of oral language development. Gifted students would be expected to read above grade level because their capacity is above average (Rosenberger, 1992). On the other hand, a student with mental retardation would not be expected to read on grade level because her or his capacity is well below average. Students with below average intelligence are often denied corrective services because it is believed that diminished intellectual functioning is the cause of their reading problem. However, if a student with mental retardation is reading below the level indicated by their listening and/or cognitive ability test, that student is demonstrating a reading problem. A problem reader, then, is one who is reading below intellectual capacity or oral language development.

**Discrepancy** definition of reading disability: a difference exists between the student's ability and achievement. A 5th-grader with the ability of a 7th-grader would be expected to read on a 7th-grade level.

Defining problem readers as those reading below capacity is known as the **discrepancy** definition of reading disorders. Although it is the most widely accepted concept of reading difficulty, it does have some major problems. First of all, there is no agreement on a definition of intellectual ability nor on how to measure it. Gardner (1983), for instance, speaks of many kinds of intelligences: linguistic, musical, logical-mathematical, spatial, bodily-kinesthetic, intrapersonal, and interpersonal. The fairness of intelligence tests has also been called into question (Ysseldyke, 1988). One solution has been to use listening tests as measures of students' potential (Spring & French, 1990). Listening comprehension is the level of material that students can understand when the material is read to them. If a student's listening comprehension is at a fifth-grade level and the student is reading on a first grade level, then there is a four-year discrepancy between capacity and achievement.

However, in both listening and intelligence tests, there is the issue of the confusion of cause-effect. Because they are unable to fully utilize one source of intellectual or language development, poor readers may do less well on verbal intelligence and listening tests (Stanovich, 1991). Through wide reading, verbal abilities such as word knowledge and the ability to use and comprehend language are fostered, so that the reading process actually makes students "smarter" (Stanovich, 1992).

In addition, the dramatic success of a wide variety of intervention programs has called into question the validity of making judgments solely on the basis of measured ability. Indeed, some research suggests that problems in acquiring word recognition skills are remarkably similar for both poor readers of low ability and those of average ability and may be rooted in the same factors (Stanovich & Siegel, 1994). As Allington (1995) comments:

> *We have good evidence that children with low scores on readiness assessments can learn to read along with their peers, but only when provided substantially larger amounts of more intensive instruction than is normally available. . . . While we are able to predict which children will benefit from larger amounts of more intensive instruction, too often we have used this knowledge not to provide that instruction but to categorize and label children. We must move beyond thinking about tests as indicating which children can learn and which cannot and use such indicators to predict how much of what kind of instruction will be needed to develop the literacy of all children. (pp. 6–7)*

**Functional** definition of reading disability: achievement fails to meet a certain standard or interferes with the reader's functioning in or out of school.

## *Functional Definition*

Many programs now use a **functional** definition in identifying problem readers. They simply provide instruction for the lowest achievers in reading. The State of Connecticut, for instance, administers the *Degrees of Reading Power* assessment (Touchstone Applied Science Associates,

1990) to all fourth-, sixth-, and eighth-graders (special education and bilingual students may be excluded). Additional testing and programs of remediation are mandated for students who fail to achieve the cutoff score, regardless of students' cognitive capacity. The federally funded ***Title 1*** programs, (also known as "Chapter 1") which were designed to provide supplementary literacy and math instruction to children living in poverty, typically provide services for students whose scores fall below a certain standard. **Reading Recovery,** a highly successful program designed to boost the reading performance of low-achieving first-graders, provides intensive one-on-one instruction for those students identified as being in the bottom 20 percent of reading achievement. Again, academic aptitude is not a factor. All students within the lowest 20 percent are provided with assistance. Although it may overlook some bright underachievers, the functional approach provides added help for the poorest readers, regardless of any labels that may have been attached to them.

**Title 1** is designed to foster improvement in math and literacy skills in students living in poverty areas.

**Reading Recovery:** intervention program using specially trained teachers working one-on-one thirty minutes a day with first-graders deemed "at risk."

Another way of looking at reading difficulty from a functional approach is to judge whether or not it interferes with the reader's life circumstances. Does it hinder her or him from engaging in reading and writing activities that others in similar circumstances encounter? Awilda was unable to write to her grandparents or complete her school work. For high school students, it might take the form of reading so slowly that they can't keep up with outside reading assignments. For a police trainee it might be the inability to read the department's manuals or write coherent reports. Barr, Blachowicz, and Wogman-Sadow (1995) define a reading problem on the elementary school level as one in which "a student cannot adequately understand the materials used for regular classroom instruction" (p. 9).

In its description of reading disorders, the *DSM IV* (*Diagnostic and Statistical Manual* of Mental Disorders) (American Psychiatric Association, 1994), which is widely used by mental health workers, combines elements of both a discrepancy and a functional definition:

> *A. Reading achievement, as measured by an individually administered standardized test of reading accuracy or comprehension, is substantially below that expected given the person's chronological age, measured intelligence, and age-appropriate education.*
> *B. The disturbance in A significantly interferes with academic achievement or activities of daily living that require reading skills.*
> *C. If a sensory deficit is present, the learning difficulties are in excess of those usually associated with it. (p. E:1)*

Although Part A calls for the use of a standardized reading test, an informal reading inventory would also be acceptable (see Chapter 4). A test of listening comprehension could be substituted for a test of intelligence (see Chapter 6).

In this text the emphasis will be on a combined discrepancy and functional definition of literacy disorders. Keeping in mind the limitations of intelligence and listening tests, it is recommended that one adopt a broad view of ability. Students can manifest ability in a variety of ways: by the thinking and language abilities they display in classroom discussions and discussions with peers, by their ability to solve everyday problems, or by their knowledge of the world around them. One way of estimating students' learning abilities is by teaching them and seeing how much they learn. Many students who have been written-off bloom when provided with the right kind of instruction (Allen, Michalove, & Shockley, 1993; Five, 1992; B. Taylor & Hiebert, 1994).

As a practical matter, using both the discrepancy and functional definitions of reading disorder is necessary because of funding regulations. As noted earlier, *Title 1* and *Reading Recovery* students are chosen on the basis of a functional difficulty. However, students who have learning disabilities, most of whom have literacy difficulties (C. R. Smith, 1994), are selected on the basis of a discrepancy between measured ability and achievement. In addition, research suggests that students who display the greatest discrepancy between listening ability and achievement make the most progress when given additional help (Shany & Biemiller, 1995).

## *Incidence of Reading Problems*

What proportion of the population has a reading difficulty? How many Awildas are there? The best data we have on reading achievement comes from two National Assessment studies (National Assessment of Educational Progress, 1986; Kirsch & Jungeblut, 1986; Lenger, Applebee, Mullis, & Foertsch, 1990), which identified the levels at which nine-, thirteen-, seventeen-year-olds, and young adults were reading. When translated into approximate grade levels as presented in Table 1-1, the data indicate that more than a third of the representative sample of nine-year-olds tested were reading below grade level. Of that number, 7 percent could not cope with easy second-grade material. Approximately, 42 percent of thirteen-year-olds read below a seventh-grade level, with 5 percent of that group reading below a fourth-grade level. On the high school level, the proportion of below-grade readers increases. Some 58 percent of the seventeen-year-olds tested were reading below a mid-high school level, with more than 14 percent of that group functioning below a seventh grade level. Young adults between the ages of twenty-one and twenty-five performed somewhat better. Only 43 percent were reading below a mid-high school level, but 16 percent of these were below a sixth- or seventh-grade level (Kirsch & Jungeblut, 1986).

More recently, measures were used that featured longer passages and required students to construct rather than simply choose responses. From these tests, the National Assess-

**TABLE 1-1 Percentages of Students Reading below Key Levels**

| Age | Below 2 | Below 4 | Below 6–7 | Below H.S. |
|---|---|---|---|---|
| Nine | 7% | 37.5% | — | — |
| Thirteen | 0.2% | 5% | 42% | — |
| Seventeen | 0% | 1.1% | 14% | 58% |
| Twenty-one to Twenty-five | 0% | 4.0% | 16% | 43% |

ment of Educational Progress found that the following percentages of students were unable to function on a basic level, which means that they could not comprehend text at a literal level and relate it to their lives (Williams, Reese, Campbell, Mazzeo, & Phillips, 1995).

| | |
|---|---|
| Grade 4 | 42 percent |
| Grade 8 | 31 percent |
| Grade 12 | 30 percent |

Of course, as discussed earlier, all students reading below their grade level or a certain standard or cutoff score aren't necessarily problem readers. Some may have limited cognitive ability. However, the statistics do suggest the magnitude of the problem. Based on National Assessment and other data, it is estimated that up to 25 percent of the population has some difficulty with reading. Not all of these students have serious problems. Most have a mild to moderate difficulty. They may be functioning a year or two below what might be expected. Only a small percentage have severe problems (Awilda would be classified as having a severe reading problem). Approximately 10 percent of the school population have a mild problem, 12 percent have moderate difficulties, and up to 3 percent have a more serious difficulty (McCormick, 1995; Vellutino et al., 1996). The number of genuinely disabled readers may be as few as five in a thousand (Farnham-Diggory, 1992).

## *The Problem with Using Labels*

*Dyslexia* originally referred to the loss of the ability to read because of damage to the central nervous system but now is used to refer to a serious reading disorder.

A few years ago, I got an urgent phone call from a distraught parent. "I just found out my son has dyslexia," she announced. "What should I do?" It wasn't my first **dyslexia** call; nor was it my last. I receive several a year. The problem with the term is two-fold. First, the term *dyslexia* itself has very little meaning. The term is used by some to mean a serious reading problem, others use it for a spelling problem, and some use it to describe mild or moderate reading problems. The second problem with the usage of that term is that it suggests a neurological condition (D. Johnson, 1993). The term *dyslexia* may be taken to mean that there is something neurologically wrong with the student, which accounts for his problems learning to read. However, the problem may well be in the program. When proper adaptations are made, nearly all children learn, including those whose difficulty may be rooted in a neurological condition. Referring to students who are slow to learn to read as "slow learners," Marie Clay (1993b), the major force behind *Reading Recovery,* explained:

> *What is possible for slow learners is different from what we used to think was possible . . . slow learners are slow learners only because of the ways in which we have tried to teach them. In society and in education we categorize them, and they grow to fit our categories. All we had to do was rearrange the teacher's talents, change the delivery conditions, and provide opportunities to succeed; then, slow learners caught up with their average classmates. (pp. xiii–xiv)*

What is true for the term *dyslexia* also applies to other terms used to label underachieving students: *learning disability, at-risk, corrective,* and *remedial.* As C. Weaver (1994a) explains:

> *Nowadays, students diagnosed as dyslexic or learning disabled are often referred to as students with special needs. I like to think of them simply as "special learners"—and I hope that someday the educational bureaucracy will recognize that* all *learners are unique,* all *are special, and* all *need to be treated and taught accordingly. (p. 501)*

The variability concept is replacing the deficit model. When working with struggling readers and writers, teachers think in terms of matching instruction to needs rather than overcoming deficits.

Being unique, individual students have and always will vary in their reading and writing abilities just as they vary in running, playing basketball, singing, or solving math problems. Some students seem to learn words after seeing them once or twice; others struggle with words they have seen a hundred times or more. Instead of considering struggling readers as being disabled, Roller (1996) believes that we should learn to accept the variability that students display as being normal, and adjust instruction to meet the needs of each student.

Unfortunately, labels seem to be here to stay. Often, in order to receive special services, students must first be labeled as *learning disabled, at risk, special needs, remedial,* or *corrective.* What we need to do is to look beyond the label and see the individual.

## *The Nature of Corrective Instruction*

Corrective instruction comes in many forms. Although specialized techniques are sometimes used, corrective instruction is often simply more individualized application of methods employed in the regular classroom. Corrective techniques can be classified as being part-to-whole, whole-to-part, or interactive.

In a **bottom-up approach** (part to whole), students are taught letters and sounds before being taught to read words. Emphasis is on processing the text rather than making use of the reader's background.

### *Part-to-Whole Approach*

In a **bottom-up** or part-to-whole approach, students learn the nuts and bolts of reading and assemble them into a whole. Proceeding from the bottom of the process, they learn letter sounds and then blend them into whole words, which are then read in brief stories. Incorporating the belief that reading is easier if broken down into its parts and then reconstructed, many corrective programs have taken a part-whole, or bottom-up, approach.

A **top-down approach** (whole to part) emphasizes constructing meaning through the readers' use of their background knowledge and language ability.

### *Whole-Part Approach*

In a **top-down** or whole-part approach, students start at the top of the reading process and proceed downward to letters and sounds. Instruction is initiated by reading whole stories with teacher assistance. Through reading whole stories and by using their knowledge of language patterns, students learn individual printed words and letter-sound relationships.

Whole language is based on a top-down view of reading. Children learn to read and write by being immersed in meaningful literacy activities. Whereas in a bottom-up approach, meaning is constructed by decoding words and assembling sentences and paragraphs, in a top-down approach, meaning is predicted. K. Goodman (1994) refers to reading as being a psycholinguistic guessing game in which the readers use their background knowledge and language ability to predict the meaning of a sentence or passage. Instead of processing the sentence letter by letter, word by word, the reader uses as few cues as possible. For instance, according to this view, seeing the sentence "The sun is shining," readers need not decode *shining* letter by letter. Using their knowledge of what the sun does and the context of the sentence, the reader predicts that the word will be *shining.*

Theorists with a bottom-up approach would posit that the reader would process all or most of the letters of *shining* and get little help from context.

## *An Interactive View*

An **interactive approach** emphasizes that reading is a parallel, simultaneous process. As readers process words, they use language ability and background to construct meaning.

In this text reading is viewed as an interaction between part-whole and whole-part or top-down and bottom-up processes. As Rumelhart (1985) hypothesized in his classic **interactive** model, reading is not linear. We don't proceed from letters to words to meaning in step-by-step fashion. Nor do we proceed from the whole to the part. Rather, we engage in parallel processing so that we simultaneously use knowledge of language as well as contextual and letter-sound cues. Reading is both top-down and bottom-up.

The truth is that readers, especially ones who have serious problems, need to use all the reading processes. Because low-achieving readers often manifest difficulty decoding words (Bader & Wiesendanger, 1986), there is a temptation to focus on lower-level processes, such as sounding out words. However, reading is very much a total language process. The efficient reader simultaneously uses background knowledge, facility with language, ongoing comprehension of a selection, and decoding skills. For instance, when reading the following sentence, Jason, a fourth-grade low-achieving reader who has been receiving intensive instruction in decoding strategies, used a variety of sources to help him decipher the word *cocoa,* which for him was an unfamiliar print form:

If the topic is familiar, readers can make heavier use of background. If the text is unfamiliar, they place heavier reliance on processing text.

After shoveling the snow, grandpa had a cup of hot cocoa.

Because Jason has had experience with hot cocoa, his ability to use the context of the sentence enhances his use of decoding skills so that he is able to process the word faster and more readily that he would have if the word *cocoa* had not been in his listening vocabulary. Top-down processes, including language ability and background knowledge, have made it easier for him to apply lower-level decoding processes. Had the context been weak or had the word *cocoa* simply been in a list, Jason would have had to rely more heavily on decoding.

An **interactive approach** combines systematic instruction in basic word recognition and comprehension strategies combined with much reading of stories, poems, and factual text.

Using a computer analogy, Adams (1990) theorizes that orthographic (letter), phonological (sound), meaning, and context processors all work simultaneously to decode words. However, the way that processors are brought into play is partly dependent upon the nature of the task. As adept readers our decoding skills become so well learned and rapid that they function automatically. There are occasions, however, when bottom-up processes are brought to the fore. Notice how consciously you use decoding skills as you read the following sentence:

Thēz wərdz ar speld fənetiklē.

Did you notice that you had to deliberately sound out each word? With your processes being slowed down, were you also able to notice how you used your knowledge of language and background of experience along with decoding skills to reconstruct the sentence? The key in an interactive approach is to teach and reinforce skills in the context of real reading and writing.

## *A Systems Approach*

Reading and writing problems, especially when severe, affect all aspects of the student's life. Although easily the brightest student in first-grade, Robert was threatened with retention. Robert had serious difficulty learning to associate spoken words with their printed symbols. Despite special assistance, he had learned only a half-dozen words by the end of the year. Unfortunately, he learned to fear reading in the process. By the time he was referred to a university reading clinic, he was refusing to attempt to read. Why try when failure was virtually guaranteed? The wall he had built around himself to prevent further failure was so impenetrable that counseling was required.

Robert's reading problem also manifested itself physically. Complaining of stomach pains, Robert was given a thorough examination. Unable to find a medical cause for the pains, the doctor believed they were caused by stress at school. Even Robert's social relationships were harmed by his reading difficulty. Classmates teased him for his slowness in catching on to reading. Baffled by Robert's difficulty, his family was torn between sympathy for his plight and a suspicion that maybe the source of Robert's problem was lack of effort. Meanwhile, at school, Robert mentally withdrew from all tasks involving reading and writing. He noted that his favorite part of school was "the bus ride home."

Systems approach: looks at all aspects of the student's life and the effect each has upon the student.

Understanding a student's reading difficulty, especially when it is a severe one, means finding out how it affects and is affected by the significant aspects of his life: family, school, and friends. For older low-achieving readers, society at large and the world of work must also be figured into the equation. The understanding must be ecological. For instance, it is important to see how the low-achieving reader functions in her or his classroom. Questions that need to be answered include: How does the student interact in the classroom? How do other students respond to her or him? What changes might be made to improve the student's progress? If the student is in a corrective program, the key question becomes: How might the corrective and regular classroom program be coordinated so as to achieve maximum benefit for the student? How can the classroom teacher and the reading specialist support one another's efforts? How might the home be involved? A comprehensive plan of assistance must take into account how the school, the home, and other institutions might play a role in remediation.

As Bartoli and Botel (1988) note, we need to see the interrelationship of the student with peers, with teachers, with any specialists that might be involved, and with parents. The idea is not to place blame but to see how all systems of learning or nonlearning are working and to integrate the cognitive with the emotional and the social. Under a systems approach, the role of corrective specialist becomes that of a collaborator who works closely with the classroom teacher. Rather than focusing on the causes of the child's failure, the corrective specialist and the classroom teacher work together to adjust the total environment so the student achieves success. The home is also involved in the process, and measures are taken to meet the student's out-of-school literacy needs. In a systems approach, instead of worrying about who did what wrong, emphasis is on getting the child on the right track.

## *Interlocking Aspects of Reading*

In addition to considering the student's literacy activities at home, in school, and in the wider world, a program of correction needs to take into account the five major interlocking aspects of reading: reader, task, text, instructional approach, and situational context (Walker, 1992). At the center of reading is the reader. Reading is a highly personal activity. Each of us brings to reading a unique blend of background, ability, perspective, interests, and proficiency. We interpret a text in the light of who we are and what we know.

Rosenblatt (1978, 1994) explains the interaction between reader and text as being a ***transaction.*** The text is transformed by the reader and the reader, in turn, is transformed by the text. The ease of reading, the degree of interest, the organization of the text, and, the use of illustrations affect the quality of the transaction. The degree of involvement will be minimal if the text is boring, too difficult, or both.

> **Transactional theory:** the reader transforms text through personal perspective, yet is also changed by the text. Meaning is created by the **transaction** between reader and text.

The task is also a key factor. Will the reader be skimming the material, reading it casually, or studying it in preparation for a test? Will the material be read silently or orally? Interacting with the task is the instructional approach used. Some students may respond well to highly structured direct instruction. Others thrive with approaches that focus on student involvement and stress discovery learning. Teachers of low-achieving readers need to ask: What instructional approach works best with this student or group?

All the other factors—reader, text, task, and technique—are affected by the context. Discussions, for instance, are dramatically altered by context. Students who are stone silent in a large group may become very expressive in a small cooperative learning group. (Exemplary Teaching Lesson 1-1 demonstrates how Angela changed when her setting, teacher, and instructional approach were altered.)

**BOX 1-1 Exemplary Teaching: Becoming Empowered**

Although a year older than the other fifth graders in her class, eleven-year-old Angela seemed shy and immature (Five, 1992). Classified as learning disabled, she spent most of her mornings working on academics in a pullout program. In the afternoons, she returned to her classroom. Believing that Angela could benefit from process writing, Cora Lee Five, her teacher, included her in the afternoon writing program. At first, Angela's writing, which she restricted to brief journal entries, was very limited. Angela also refused to take part in writing conferences but did sit near the conference table, where she could overhear what was being said. Through listening in, Angela was slowly drawn into the process. In time, Angela started conferring about her writing with a friend. This was a turning point. Little by little, she began to become involved in the class's activities. Throughout the year Angela's writing skills improved as did her social skills. Angela began taking control of her learning and her life.

As Five noted, by being included in the class's activities, "Angela changed dramatically. The shy, dependent child who had no confidence and no real connection to her classmates and to learning turned into an animated involved girl who thought of herself as a learner" (Five, 1992, p. 25).

## *Principles of Corrective Instruction*

Problem readers are a diverse group. The majority have difficulty decoding; however, there are a number of excellent decoders who have difficulty understanding what they read. Degree of difficulty ranges from mild to severe. Possible causes run the gamut—from inappropriate materials to poor nutrition. Depending on the nature, severity, and source of the problem, programs for low-achieving readers will vary. However, there are a number of basic principles that should be incorporated in any program created to help students who are struggling with reading and writing.

### *Prevention versus Correction*

Prevention is preferable to remediation. However, from 15 to 30% of students who complete prevention programs still need help.

Most cases of reading difficulty may be prevented through early intervention. *Reading Recovery,* an early intervention program of one-on-one instruction designed by Marie Clay (1985, 1993b) and her colleagues in New Zealand, has achieved remarkable success in giving first-graders a second chance to learn to read. The object of *Reading Recovery* is to bring the lowest 20 percent of students in the six-year-old group up to the level of the average readers in the class. In New Zealand, 95 percent of students who participate in *Reading Recovery* are able to reach the average level of reading achievement of their classmates after just twelve to twenty weeks of instruction for thirty minutes a day (Clay, 1991b). In the United States, the success rate is 82 percent of all those who have completed the program (Reading Recovery Program at The Ohio State University, 1995). This does not include participants who move away or don't complete the program because of high absenteeism or other reasons.

Prevention, of course, is vastly superior to remediation. Prevention safeguards self-esteem, eliminates ineffective strategies before they are hardened into habits, and saves limited corrective resources for those who most desperately need it. (Chapter 7 explores

Typically, large-scale studies of a variety of programs include a range, from those that are poorly palnned, to those that are superior. Well-planned programs competently executed generally have encouraging, sometimes dramatic success. A number of such programs are noted in this text.

*Reading Recovery* and other preventive programs.) Prevention also works better than remediation. According to national evaluations of corrective reading programs, on average, only one additional month of achievement is gained for each year spent in a compensatory program (McGill-Franzen & Allington, 1991).

### *Importance of Success*

In reading as in life, nothing succeeds like success. In *Reading Recovery* and other effective programs for low-achieving readers, carefully chosen materials, well-trained personnel, and powerful teaching techniques combine so that success is virtually guaranteed. With success, there is increased effort, and more success. Marjorie Johnson (1966) describes the dawning of hope in a student with a severe reading problem who had spent several weeks laboriously, but successfully, learning a basic reading vocabulary.

> *When Francis first learned that he could read a particular preprimer [beginning reading book] which happened to contain no words which he did not know at this point, he was amazed. It had been a long, hard struggle for him to acquire any immediate recognition vocabulary. His reaction showed both his recognition of his difficulty and his hope for the future—an awareness that he could and would progress. (p. 156)*

### *Building on the Known*

During the period of "roaming the known," the teacher observes the child, asking such questions as: "What does he do well? What strategies does he try? How does he help himself?" (Clay, 1993b, p. 7)

A close corollary of teaching for success is building on what is known. All too often, corrective instruction focuses on what the student doesn't know or can't do. In this text both assessment and instruction will be presented as positive forces. The emphasis will be on building upon what the student already knows. In *Reading Recovery,* for instance, the instructor spends two weeks "roaming around the known." As Clay (1985) advises, "Go over what he knows in different ways until your ingenuity runs out, and until he is moving fluently around this personal corpus of responses, the letters, words and messages that he knows how to read or write" (p. 55).

Building on the known also means taking into consideration the student's background. In today's highly diverse classrooms, students come from a variety of cultures. It is important to use examples with which the student will be familiar. It is important to use materials that incorporate the student's culture and to use discussion and responding styles that the student finds comfortable and familiar. If the student is learning English as a second language, it is important to be aware of the student's language proficiency and to build on that proficiency.

### *Fostering Independence*

The phrase "learned helplessness" is often used to describe low-achieving readers. Having a history of failure, they see themselves as unable to cope successfully with reading and writing tasks. In a study of poor readers, Butkowsky and Willows (1980) found that these students lacked confidence in their reading, had lower expectations of success, and gave up more easily. Poor readers are also more likely to attribute their success to luck (Wigfield & Asher, 1984) and failure to a lack of ability. Since luck and ability are beyond their control, they are inclined to give up too quickly or seek help, rather than rely on their own resources. Relying too heavily on others, their reading development is further stunted and they conclude that they are "helpless."

Often, well-meaning teachers fall into the trap of unwittingly reinforcing learned helplessness. Realizing that a student has limited skills and is struggling, the teacher supplies answers or figures out hard words for him because she feels sorry for him. Over time, some students develop a negative reflex reaction to academic challenges. Upon encountering a difficult word, they immediately lift their heads from the page and look to the teacher for help. Upon answering a discussion question, they study the teacher's face for a sign indicating whether the answer was correct or not. They seldom venture opinions. Browbeaten by a cycle of failure and self-defeating behaviors, they feel like outcasts in the community of readers and writers. In addition to teaching these students strategies, the teacher must also build confidence, instill an openness to taking risks, and a willingness to take responsibility for one's learning.

To foster independence, never do for students what they can do for themselves. A corollary is to never accept anything but the student's best. Accustomed to having substandard work accepted by overly sympathetic teachers, students internalize their lowered expectations. The greatest compliment that a teacher can pay a student is to reject inferior efforts. By accepting only the student's best, the teacher is saying, "I have faith in you." Expectations, of course, need to be realistic.

## *Active Involvement*

Winograd and Smith (1987) state: "fluent readers are purposeful, active, and flexible, while many poor readers are purposeless, passive, and inflexible" (p. 307).

Being an independent learner requires active involvement in the task at hand. Unless the student is actively involved, the most carefully planned program will fail by default. In explaining the success of VAKT, an instructional program which makes use of *v*isual, *a*uditory, *k*inesthetic (sense of movement), and *t*actile modalities, and which was designed for students with the most serious reading problems, M. S. Johnson (1966) notes:

> *Learning take place through purposeful activity. It is an active process. It grows out of reacting to stimuli in a purposeful way. A child using VAKT is participantly involved to a maximum degree. He formulates the ideas to be worked with. They are expressed in his own words. He listens, speaks, writes, and reads to reach his goals. If he failed to involve himself, he suffers the immediate consequence of his lack of involvement in that things do not go well for him—he does not learn what he sets out to learn. (p. 155)*

## *Personalized Instruction*

In addition to providing direct instruction to low-achieving readers, it is important to adapt instruction to meet individual variations in interest and background and in preference for

Gentile and McMillan (1987) found that while some low-achieving readers fought against their difficulties by acting out in class, others used a variety of means to escape reading.

strategies. Some low-achieving learners do best with holistic instruction, others learn best when instruction is parceled out in manageable bits. No one corrective package fits all needs. The structured phonics system that works so well with some low-achieving readers is frustrating to students who prefer a more holistic approach.

### Continuous Assessment

Using feedback from the students and a knowledge of their unique abilities, the teacher is constantly adjusting instruction.

Teaching and assessment should merge. Initial instruction should be based on an assessment that highlights the students' strengths and weaknesses and establishes an appropriate level of instruction. As the instruction proceeds, the teacher is guided by the students' responses. If the materials are too hard or lacking in interest, the teacher obtains more appropriate materials. If students have difficulty applying a strategy, the teacher provides on-the-spot support and guidance.

### A Full Range of Literacy Experiences

Because low-achieving readers and writers often manifest difficulty with subskills such as decoding, poor oral reading, spelling, or handwriting, there is a natural temptation to remedy the deficiency by providing lots of extra practice in the poorly developed skill. As a result, corrective students may end up working on fragmented skills. Instead of reading intriguing trade books or composing imaginative stories, they spend their time filling in blanks on worksheets or reading brief, unrelated selections and answering low-level multiple choice questions.

Graves (1991) describes Billy, a third-grader with a learning disability who put so much effort into his spelling and handwriting that the final product was a badly smudged series of disconnected sentences. While Billy had serious handwriting and spelling problems, what he needed most was a program that encouraged him to express himself. Focusing on the things that he did poorly, Billy failed to see himself as a writer. As far as he was concerned, he had nothing of value to say. An appropriate program for Billy would begin with Billy's concept of himself as a writer. Once he is convinced that he has something to say and begins to express himself on paper, Billy will see the need for conventional spelling and readable handwriting. At that point, Billy will be ready for helpful instruction related to his handwriting and spelling.

As Palincsar and Klenk (1992) note, overemphasizing low-level tasks leads to "impoverished understandings regarding the nature of reading and writing" (p. 212). Students see writing as copying and reading as saying the printed words right. To counteract these erroneous concepts, low-achieving readers need a program that stresses plenty of reading and writing for real purposes.

### Direct, Systematic Instruction

Although it is an essential ingredient, surrounding students with interesting, readable books and intriguing writing and reading tasks is not enough. The skills and strategies that achieving readers soak up through immersion all too frequently escape low-achieving readers un-

One group of poor comprehenders improved so much after instruction in comprehension strategies that their teachers accused them of cheating on content area tests (Pearson, 1986).

less they are provided with explicit explanations and demonstrations. Low-achieving readers and writers need a program of direct, intensive, systematic instruction presented in the context of lots of real reading and writing. In one instance, below-level readers were carefully taught strategies for making inferences, they were soon operating on the same level as the average readers (Hansen and Pearson, 1982).

Direct instruction should not be misinterpreted to mean the fragmented teaching of isolated skills and the use of workbooks and worksheets (Roller, 1996). Direct instruction should be conducted within the context of real reading and writing and should focus on guidance in the purposeful use of strategies.

### *An Integrated Approach*

**Units** help struggling readers organize concepts. When tied together by a common theme, history, geography, reading, writing, art, and even math reinforce each other and result in a broad but thorough knowledge of the unit theme.

Poor readers and writers often have difficulty organizing and relating new knowledge to what they already know. Using a unit or theme approach is one way of helping low-achieving readers form the kind of cognitive connections that adept readers make on their own. By providing varied and sustained experience with key concepts or themes, students develop a depth of understanding. In addition, studying commonalities improves students' cognitive performance. In a study in which low-achieving readers read and discussed a series of passages, those who read passages that developed a common theme showed a greater increase in overall comprehension. They also demonstrated significant improvements in their ability to construct generalizations and to infer the theme when reading about new topics (Palincsar & Klenk, 1992).

### *Wide Reading*

We literally learn to read by reading. As might be expected, poor readers read less (R. Anderson, Wilson, & Fielding, 1988; Mullis, Campbell and Farstrup, 1993). This is partly cause and partly effect. The lack of reading causes deficiencies in the application of skills. However, lack of reading is also an effect of skills deficiency. Because reading is a struggle for them, poor readers read less. Reading less, poor readers fall further behind their more proficient peers. Stanovich (1986) calls this the *Matthew effect,* a situation in which the rich get richer and the poor get poorer. For instance, students who have limited decoding ability get off to a slow start in reading. Not being able to read even the simplest materials independently, they are unable to improve by reading on their own. They can't engage in the kind of wide reading of easy materials that leads to fluency and higher levels of reading.

Unfortunately, not only do poor readers read less on their own; they also have fewer opportunities to read independently in school (Applebee, Langer, & Mullis, 1988): "poor readers presumably have more difficulty reading on their own and, therefore, are less likely to be encouraged to do so" (pp. 38–39).

In order to fully develop their capacities, poor readers need to make up for lost time. They need to read more, not less, than their higher-achieving peers. According to one commercially sponsored study, below-average readers improved two and one half years beyond their present level when they engaged in at least sixty minutes of reading per day over a year's time (Paul, 1996). Actually, one reason some students make slow progress in reading is because they read less. According to Paul (1996), the bottom 25 percent of readers read only one quarter as much as the top 25 percent.

### *Providing Materials with the Appropriate Challenge Level*

Time on task increased from 20% to 50% percent when low-achieving readers were given a text that was one year below their grade level (R. Anderson, 1990).

Allington (1995) comments, "The longer we allow children's development to lag behind that of their peers the more difficult it becomes to accelerate their learning" (p. 8).

If students are to engage in wide reading, reading should be relatively easy. In instructional settings, students apparently do best when they know 95 to 98 percent of the words in the selection (Berliner, 1981; Gambrell, Wilson & Gantt, 1981). Given texts on or close to the appropriate level, poor readers spend more time on task. Achievement also improved. When poor readers know most of the words, they are better able to use context clues and so don't have to overly rely on sounding out the words. They read with more fluency and understanding.

All too often students reading below grade level are given books that are too difficult for them. To help students with the many hard words they encounter in their basal readers or chapter books, the teacher proceeds slowly through the book. Perhaps the group spends an entire week on a single story. As a result, they end up spending a minimum amount of time reading. But, actual reading is what these students need most. Instead of inching their way through a book that is too hard, they should be given lots of books that have the appropriate level of challenge. Examples of easy reading materials will be provided throughout the body of this text and also in Appendix B.

### *A Sense of Community*

Low-achieving readers also need a sense of community. By being accepted and valued in the classroom and in reading and writing groups, low-achieving readers are motivated to try harder. And, of course, they then are better able to learn from their peers. Describing the struggling readers and writers that they had been observing, Allen, Michalove, and Shockley (1993) explain that "Reggie learned how to choose classmates who could really help him read. Lee learned to write initially by copying what his friends wrote; eventually, he became a genuine collaborator, first in the oral composing of the story, and then in the physical writing." (p. 249)

## *Sources of Help for Low-Achieving Readers*

Apart from the classroom teacher, a number of specialists work with low-achieving readers and writers: the reading/language arts specialist, the Title 1 teacher, and learning disabilities specialist. Professionals in migrant and bilingual or ESL education might also be involved (Johnston & Allington, 1991). Why are so many different professionals involved in assisting low-achieving readers? Johnston and Allington state that federal regulations are one probable cause. Two of the major pieces of legislation that provide for corrective services are Title 1 and the Individuals with Disabilities in Education Act (IDEA).

## *Title 1 Legislation*

Title 1 programs are designed to provide economically disadvantaged students with assistance that supplements and supports, but does not supplant, classroom instruction. The program is designed to reduce the gap in achievement between economically disadvantaged students and other students, with particular emphasis on helping the following:

> *Low-achieving children in our highest-poverty schools, children with limited English proficiency, children of migrant workers, children with disabilities, Indian children, children who are neglected or delinquent, and young children and their parents who are in need of family-literacy services. (Title 1 of Improving America's Schools Act of 1994, Sec. 101)*

Far from being a call for a skill and drill approach, the latest version of Title 1 is based on the premise that:

> *All children can master challenging content and complex problem-solving skills. Research clearly shows that children, including low-achieving children, can succeed when expectations are high and all children are given the opportunity to learn challenging material." (Title 1 of Improving America's Schools Act of 1994, Sec. 101)*

The law recommends that students chosen for assistance be provided access to high-quality, regular school programs and be given extra help through extended time activities. Emphasis is on the students' meeting high standards established by individual states and the use of assessment measures aligned with these standards. School-wide programs are also encouraged for schools where at least 50 percent of the children are from low-income families.

## *Individuals with Disabilities Education Act*

Another major source of funding for students with reading and writing difficulties is IDEA (Individuals with Disabilities Education Act), which is a revision of PL 94-142, the Education for All Handicapped Children Act. Under the provisions of IDEA, the number of students identified as being learning disabled, which is the largest category of handicapped children, skyrocketed. Today about 5 percent of the population is said to be learning disabled (C. R. Smith, 1994). Although **learning disabilities** is defined as "a disorder in one or more of the basic psychological processes involved in understanding or in using language, spoken or written" (PL94-142), the disorder most frequently manifests itself as a reading difficulty. Lerner (1991) estimates that approximately 85 percent of students diagnosed as having learning disabilities evidence a reading problem. As a result, often the students who have the severest reading problems are taught by the learning disabilities specialist.

**Learning disabilities:** "disorder in one or more of the basic psychological processes involved in understanding or in using language, spoken or written, which may manifest itself in an imperfect ability to listen, think, speak, read, write, spell, or to do mathematical calculations" (PL94-142).

Despite being in different fields, the corrective services offered by the learning disabilities and the reading specialist may be more alike than different. Based on the concept that learning disabilities have a neurological basis, the learning disabilities field had a distinctly medical orientation. However, this has now given way to an academic approach. In addition, although learning disabilities programs tend to emphasize a bottom-up, parts-to-whole, subskill approach with a heavy emphasis on phonics, there is a discernible shift to more holistic approaches. Actually, corrective programs, regardless of who teaches them, are remarkably similar (Johnston & Allington, 1991; Walsmley & Allington, 1995).

Because of a past lack of coordination between corrective and classroom programs and a concern that pullout programs fragment instruction, current trends are toward collaboration and inclusion (Allington & Shake, 1986). Increasingly, *Title 1* teachers are working within the classroom as are special education teachers. Under the *Regular Education Initiative,* children with learning difficulties, especially those who have moderate problems, are being returned to the regular classroom (Lapp & Flood, 1992). Collaborating with the classroom teacher, the learning disabilities specialist, *Title 1* instructor, or reading specialist functions as a resource person or team member.

## *The Whys of Reading Problems*

Although it is possible to remediate literacy difficulties without knowing their causes, it can help us plan a better program if we know why a student is struggling. For instance, there is a condition known as a word-finding difficulty in which a student has a problem remembering common words. If through a careful assessment, we become aware that a student has that difficulty, there are modifications that can be made in the program that can help the student build word retrieval skills; there are also strategies that we can teach the student that will help him or her cope with this difficulty. The next chapter will take a look at the major factors involved in reading and writing difficulties, to shed light on a vital area in hopes that we might better help the many students who suffer some form of reading or writing disorder.

## *Summary*

According to a discrepancy definition, a problem reader may be defined as one who is reading below intellectual capacity. According to a functional definition, a problem reader may be defined as one whose reading ability is significantly below grade level or whose functioning in one's life situation is hindered by a deficiency in reading ability. Approximately 25 percent of students have a reading problem. However, most of these have a mild or moderate problem. Only about 3 percent have a severe difficulty.

Corrective instruction may be part-whole, whole-part, or interactive. Reading is a parallel rather than a sequential process with four processes working simultaneously: the orthographic, phonological, meaning, and context.

Since reading affects all aspects of one's life, it is advisable to take a systems approach, which considers the reader's functioning in school, in the family, with friends, and—for older, low-achieving readers—in the workplace. Reading instruction also has five interlocking aspects: reader, text, task, instructional approach, and context.

Although the nature and severity of reading difficulty may vary, there are a number of principles that undergird the teaching of problem readers. These include emphasizing prevention, offering a full range of literacy experiences, and providing direct instruction with integrated and personalized approaches. Also helpful is gearing instruction to ongoing assessment, building on the known, fostering independence, demanding active involvement, providing wide reading of material on an appropriate level of challenge, and building a sense of community.

In corrective programs, students are helped by a variety of professionals: classroom teachers, Title 1 personnel, reading/language arts specialists and consultants, learning disabilities specialists, and migrant and bilingual educators. Although taught by professionals from diverse fields, corrective reading programs tend to be similar. Current trends are toward collaboration between specialist and classroom teacher and the provision of corrective instruction within the classroom.

## *Application Activities*

1. Go back to the Anticipation Guide that you completed at the beginning of the chapter. Respond to the items once more. Have you changed your mind about any of the items? If so, what caused you to change your response? Even if your responses stayed the same, your reasons for agreeing or disagreeing may be different.

2. Interview the literacy specialist at a local school. Find out what kinds of help are given to students are who experiencing difficulty with reading.

3. Read "A Case Study of Middle School Reading Disability," (*The Reading Teacher, 49,* February 1996, pp. 368–377), which describes how a sixth grader was provided corrective assistance. What roles did the home, school, and reading clinic play in this successful intervention?

4. Think about the way you process information. Which do you favor, a holistic, part-to-whole, or an interactive approach?

# Chapter 2

# Factors Involved in Reading and Writing Difficulties

## *Using What You Know*

This chapter explores factors involved in the attainment of proficiency in reading and writing. One factor is the ability to pay attention. All other things being equal, students who are better at paying attention become better readers. This doesn't mean that a student who has difficulty paying attention can't or won't become a proficient reader or writer. But it does mean that adjustments might need to be made in the student's program. For instance, allowing students to choose their own books and establishing eye contact when you give directions might help the student better pay attention (Weaver, 1994b).

From your experience, what do you think might be essential factors in the attainment of reading and writing proficiency? What might be some factors that hinder progress? As you mull over these questions, think about possible intellectual, physical, environmental, psychological, and educational causes. Also, think in terms of the stages of reading. What might make it difficult for a beginning reader to make adequate progress? What factors might be associated with a reading problem in the middle grades? In the upper grades?

## *Anticipation Guide*

Read each of the following statements. Put a check under "Agree" or "Disagree" to show how you feel about each one. If you can, discuss your responses with classmates.

| | Agree | Disagree |
|---|---|---|
| **1.** The major cause of reading problems in young children is failure to teach phonics. | ______ | ______ |
| **2.** Reversals can be a sign of a serious reading problem. | ______ | ______ |

3. Deficiencies in auditory processes are more likely to cause reading problems than are difficulties in visual processes. _______ _______
4. Fortunately, most low-achieving readers don't suffer from emotional difficulties. _______ _______
5. The ultimate origin of severe reading difficulty is probably neurological. _______ _______
4. Low-achieving readers need to have tasks broken down into their component parts. _______ _______

## *Interacting Factors in Reading and Writing Difficulty*

Although Josh and Chip were eight years old, both were virtual nonreaders when their parents enrolled them in a special after-school program for underachieving students. Chip was able to read a few words such as *I* and *me* at sight and could write his full name and a few other words. Josh was only able to read the word *I* on the word recognition test that was administered to him and was able to write his first but not his last name. Although the manifestations of their difficulties were similar, the boys had very different backgrounds. Josh was language delayed and neurologically impaired. He had extreme difficulty learning words either through phonics or by memorizing them.

It was easy to see why Josh had failed to learn to read. But Chip was something of a puzzle. Although Chip experienced some difficulty learning new words, he had average intelligence, adequate language development, and no obvious physical, psychological, social, or emotional problems. However, during instructional sessions, Chip gave up easily. If he didn't get a difficult word on the second or third try, he threw up his hands. Because there were so many words he didn't know, he found reading to be very frustrating. Because he was also easily distracted, much of the instructor's time was spent getting and maintaining his attention. While his parents expressed a sincere desire for him to succeed, they didn't back up their words with supportive action. Chip was frequently absent or tardy and often failed to complete assignments, which his parents were asked to supervise. Although showing some limited progress, Chip dropped out of the program.

Realizing that Josh would have difficulty attaining proficiency in reading and writing, his parents had vowed to support him in any way they could. They read to him regularly, conversed with him continuously, took him on frequent trips, and vigorously supported his academic efforts. Friendly and outgoing, Josh set about the task of learning to read with dogged determination. He was never late for his sessions and rarely absent. All assignments were completed. Noting Josh's interest in dogs and cats, the teacher built many of the activities around the topic of pets. Whenever possible, she gave Josh a choice of activities and materials. Working closely together, Josh's special program instructor and classroom teacher supported each other. Josh's progress surpassed the more optimistic predictions.

The same factors that contributed to Josh's success—effort, drive, healthy self-esteem, parental support—were lacking in Chip's situation and so contributed to his lack of success. In addition, the suitability of the instructional programs differed. Josh's teacher built on his interests and gave him choices. However, Chip's teacher had apparently given him

Chip might have been more successful if text, approach, and context had been manipulated until a mix was found that better met his needs.

material that was too difficult, which intensified his feelings of frustration and failure. Moreover, his teacher didn't seem to have effective techniques for handling his distractibility.

As suggested by these two cases, reading difficulty is often the result of a host of interacting factors or contributing causes. These factors may be classified as being cognitive, linguistic, psychological, social–emotional, physical, and educational. Although placed last, educational factors are often key. For instance, had Chip had a more satisfying, more appropriate program, he may have persevered. Perhaps, too, greater efforts could have been made to enlist parental support.

Although each of the major factors will be discussed in isolation, it should be emphasized that often no one factor causes reading problems. In general, it's an interaction of factors (Kibby, 1995).

## *Cognitive Factors*

There are a number of cognitive factors that are possible causes of reading problems. These include overall cognitive ability or ability to learn, memory, associative learning, and the ability to pay attention.

### *Overall Cognitive Ability*

Generally speaking, the brighter the students, the better they read. Cognitive ability affects language development. Students with mental retardation, for instance, are slower to develop language, show a depressed rate of vocabulary development, and have a lower final level of language development (Ratner, 1993). Language development, in turn, places limitations on reading development (Carroll, 1977). Reading requires bringing to a conscious level one's implicit knowledge of language (Menyuk, 1991). Delayed language development may hinder reading development.

Students with very limited language or cognitive ability, for instance, those who have profound retardation, may never learn to read. Students with mental retardation who are classified as being educable, on the other hand, should meet with some success in learning to read but may not progress beyond a second- or third-grade level. Often these students do well with decoding but have difficulty with comprehension. As noted in Chapter 1, student's reading levels should match their level of cognitive or oral language development. An average fifth-grader who can understand fifth-grade selections that are read to her or him should be able to read on a fifth-grade level. A teen with mental retardation who can understand language typical of third-graders should be able to read on a third-grade level. Of course, the relationship between cognitive ability or language development and reading achievement is not one to one. Other factors such as quality of the program, amount of voluntary reading, and motivation of the students enter into the equation (Singer, 1977).

It should also be noted that the relationship between reading and language and cognitive growth is reciprocal. As Ratner (1993) notes, it seems likely that linguistic and cognitive ability develop in parallel. Moreover, reading leads to fuller development in vocabulary and syntax and may also promote greater cognitive efficiency. Our ability to process information is based, in part, on how much we know. Through reading, we acquire a broader base of knowledge, which should foster cognitive growth (West, Stanovich, & Mitchell, 1993).

In addition to general cognitive capacity, there are a number of specific cognitive and linguistic abilities involved in learning to read. These are discussed in the following section.

## *Memory*

To investigate the role that memory plays in reading difficulty, it is important to understand the current concept of working memory. Memory is composed of three essential processes: *encoding, storage,* and *retrieval.* Simply put, outside data are translated into a code (encoded) that is placed into working memory and then long-term memory, from which they can later be retrieved through recall or recognition. The memory process begins when raw data enter the sensory register. The data are only held there for about a second. During that time, attentional processes select from the masses of data entering the sensory register those stimuli that we wish to process further. Stimuli not chosen fade away. Sensory data that have been chosen enter a short-term storage facility known as working memory.

**Working memory:** temporarily holds all the information of which we are conscious, including what has just been perceived and what is being thought.

***Working memory*** "holds all the information that we are currently thinking about or are conscious of at any given time" (W. Gordon, 1989, p. 199). As such, it has a limited capacity depending upon the type of data being held there. Working memory is the system that temporarily stores information during the performance of such cognitive tasks as reading a sentence or working out a math problem in one's head (Hulme & MacKenzie, 1992). Working memory simultaneously stores and processes information and is composed of three subsystems: the central executive, the phonological or articulatory loop, which temporarily stores verbal information, and a visuospatial sketch pad, which temporarily stores visual images (Baddeley, 1992). (See Figure 2-1 for a diagram of working memory.) The central executive decides which information to place in long-term storage and also retrieves information from long-term storage.

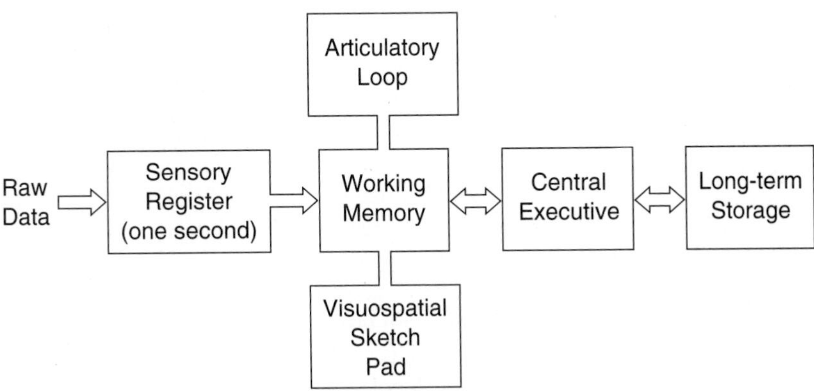


**FIGURE 2-1 Model of Working Memory**

**Phonological coding:** ability to use the sounds in a word to store that word in working and long-term memory and, later, to retrieve that word.

Much of the information that is selected from the sensory register for placement in working memory is translated into a **phonological** or **verbal code.** For instance, if we were to see three words presented visually we will probably remember them by saying them and hearing ourselves say them. That is, they would be verbally encoded. Even if we saw three geometric figures, we would more than likely encode them verbally by saying their names: "circle, square, triangle." New data entering working memory will replace old information. Therefore, we must rehearse the information that we wish to retain, or it, too, will fade away.

To see how working memory operates, try the following experiment (Carlson, 1993). Read the letters below and try to remember them. Look away from the book for a few seconds and then see if you can recite them.

E Q M T B X A

Although we also have memories for smells, tastes, motor movements, and nonverbal sounds, only visual and verbal working memory are included in the model.)

How did you keep the letters in working memory? First of all, you probably verbally encoded the letters by retrieving their names from long-term memory. That is you said the names of the letter. Then you probably rehearsed them. You said them to yourself or said them out loud over and over so you wouldn't forget them. Working memory, then, makes use of information stored in long-term memory as well as information that enters from sensory store. In similar fashion, when you read words at the end of a sentence you relate them to words at the beginning of the sentence (which are stored in working memory). However, you also relate the unfolding meaning of the gist of sentences and paragraphs previously read and now stored in long-term memory and relate it to experiences you have had, which is also information stored in long-term memory. As information is being placed in the articulatory loop, the executive system can retrieve information from other parts of the memory system and form associations so that data from working and long-term memory can be integrated.

How much information can be held in working memory? As a rule of thumb, as much verbal information as the articulatory loop will hold, which is approximately as much as you can say in two seconds (Baddeley, 1992). (In a classic experiment, this averaged out to about seven bits of information, for most people [Miller, 1956].)

Torgesen & Hecht (1996) found a subgroup of children who have difficulty using a phonological code to store letter sounds or words. Because some children have difficulty encoding words and letter sounds into working and long-term memory, they have difficulty retrieving them and experience problems learning phonics and sight words.

Verbal encoding of the typed noted by Baddeley is an essential process in reading. Inefficient verbal encoding may be at the heart of word recognition, comprehension, and vocabulary difficulties. As Brady (1991) notes, "The most striking characteristic of poor readers is the common occurrence of verbal memory problems" (p. 130). When compared with higher-achieving readers, low-achieving readers have more difficulty with remembering a series of letters, words, numbers, and similar verbal tasks. However, according to Brady (1991) low-achieving readers have no difficulty with tasks that required visual rather than verbal encoding. They do just as well as good readers when asked to remember a series of nonsense doodles or photos of unfamiliar people. The difficulty that low-achieving readers have remembering words or a series of verbal items such as digits apparently reflects a deficiency in verbal encoding

(Brady, 1986). Poor readers can code incoming stimuli phonologically, but they do so less efficiently, which impedes both working and long-term memory.

The effects of inefficient phonological encoding can be seen most clearly when students are learning how to decode words. For instance, a student with weak phonological ability may only partially code the word *bug* when he learns it initially. Later, when he encounters the word in print, he may have difficulty retrieving its spoken form because it was stored without adequate phonological cues.

Memory is developmental. As children grow, their capacity to encode, store, and retrieve material increases.

Inefficient use of working memory may also hinder comprehension. Good readers process information more efficiently and also store more information than do poor readers (Daneman & Carpenter, 1980). In addition, better readers pass information into working memory faster (Jackson, 1980). Because the words in the beginning of a sentence are stored in working memory while the rest of the sentence is being processed, an efficient working memory is crucial to comprehension. Otherwise, by the time the reader reaches the end of the sentence, she or he may have forgotten the content of the beginning of the sentence (McCormick, 1987).

## *Associative Learning*

Randall is a nine-year-old third-grader. According to informal reading inventory results, Randall has a listening capacity of grade three. However, Randall is operating on a beginning reading level. He is able to read just a few words at sight and knows initial but not final consonants. When presented with a word-learning test in which he was taught a series of seven words, with each word being presented a minimum of ten times, Randall learned only one word (see the Word Learning Test in Appendix A). Randall doesn't do any better in actual classroom teaching–learning situations. Even when new words are carefully presented in context, he fails to learn them.

When given this same word-learning test, Maria, a ten-year-old fourth-grader who was also reading on a beginning level, learned all seven of the words. However, when retested, just thirty minutes later, Maria was only able to read two of the words. Both Randall and Maria have **associative word learning difficulties.** They have extreme difficulty learning to associate printed words with their spoken equivalents. In kindergarten and first grade, both students, according to their teachers' reports, had difficulty learning to associate letters and their names, and later, letters and sounds. Despite having had excellent teaching, they had made very little progress in reading. The two students have a condition known as specific or primary reading disability. As described by S. Rosner, Abrams, Daniels, and Schiffman, (1981):

**Associative word-learning difficulty:** serious difficulty learning to associate symbols and their spoken equivalents: letters and sounds; written words and their oral equivalents.

> *The dyslexic's major problem is symbolization or association. He experiences basic difficulty in the association of common experiences and the symbols (words) representing them. Since reading is a process of association, difficulty in this area means that the child will frequently encounter many problems in acquiring a sight vocabulary . . . the major presenting symptom is the tremendous difficulty in decoding. (p. 442)*

Associative word learning problems are most likely rooted in phonological coding difficulties and inefficient memory and probably represent the most severe reading difficulty. However, there are several techniques for remediating this deficiency; these are discussed in detail in Chapter 16.

## *Attention*

**Attention:** act or state of directing one's consciousness to stimuli.

Another important condition for learning to read is **attention.** There can be no learning without attention (Simon, 1986). Attention fulfills three functions: screening out irrelevant stimuli, selecting relevant elements, and shifting from one stimulus to another (Robeck & Wallace, 1990).

### *Attention-Deficit/Hyperactivity Disorder*

**Attention-deficit/hyperactivity disorder:** "persistent pattern of inattention and/or hyperactivity–impulsivity that is more frequent and severer than is typically observed in individuals at a comparable level of development" (American Psychiatric Association,1994, p. 78).

A condition that interferes with attention is the somewhat controversial AD(H)D (**attention-deficit/hyperactivity disorder**). According to the DSM-IV (American Psychiatric Association, 1994), the essential feature of AD(H)D is a "persistent pattern of inattention and/or hyperactivity–impulsivity that is more frequent and severer than is typically observed in individuals at a comparable level of development" (p. 78). Indications of inattention include difficulty sustaining attention to tasks in school and at play, not listening or following instructions, not completing tasks that require sustained effort, being easily distracted and forgetful, doing work in a careless fashion, shifting from one unfinished task to another, and losing items. Signs of hyperactivity include not being able to sit still, excessive motion, inability to play quietly, talking excessively, and impulsivity. Impulsivity includes interrupting others, blurting out responses, difficulty waiting in line or waiting for one's turn. Symptoms should occur by the age of seven and should be evident in a variety of situations: at home, at school, and at play. The symptoms should not be the result of anxiety, personality, or other mental disorder and should not be occasioned by a temporary period of stress. One reason that AD(H)D is difficult to diagnose and controversial is that the symptoms are subjective and occur, to a degree, in many students.

Some professionals wonder whether AD(H)D couldn't be controlled by altering the instructional environment and teaching better self-management skills, using medication only as a last resort.

Although most children with AD(H)D will manifest signs of both inattention and hyperactivity–impulsivity, there are three subtypes of AD(H)D: a combined type which includes both inattention and hyperactivity–impulsivity, a predominantly inattentive type (ADD), and a predominantly hyperactive–impulsive type. A list of symptoms for all three types is presented in Table 2-1.

Students who have a serious reading problem also seem to be at greater risk for AD(H)D. In one study of clinically referred ADD students, half had reading problems (Dykman & Ackerman, 1991). However, the two disorders do not seem to be physically related. Students who have severe reading problems are characterized by increased brain activity, especially in areas in the left hemisphere, which are critical for reading, whereas those suffering from attention deficit disorder have a lowered pattern of brain activity (F. Wood, 1994). ADD is additive. It adds to the disabled reader's woes.

**TABLE 2-1 Diagnostic Criteria for Attention Deficit/Hyperactivity Disorder**

A. Either (1) or (2):

(1) Six (or more) of the following symptoms of inattention have persisted for at least six months to a degree that is maladaptive and inconsistent with developmental level:

*Inattention*
(a) often fails to give close attention to details or makes careless mistakes in schoolwork, work, or other activities
(b) often has difficulty sustaining attention in task or play activities
(c) often does not seem to listen when spoken to directly
(d) often does not follow through on instructions and fails to finish schoolwork, chores, or duties in the workplace (not due to oppositional behavior or failure to understand instructions)
(e) often has difficulty organizing tasks and activities
(f) often avoids, dislikes, or is reluctant to engage in tasks that require sustained mental effort (such as schoolwork or homework)
(g) often loses things necessary for tasks or activities (e.g., toys, school assignments, pencils, books, or tools)
(h) is often easily distracted by extraneous stimuli
(i) is often forgetful in daily activities

(2) Six (or more) of the following symptoms of hyperactivity or impulsivity have persisted for at least six months to a degree that is maladaptive and inconsistent with developmental level:

*Hyperactivity*
(a) often fidgets with hands or feet or squirms in seat
(b) often leaves seat in classroom or in other situations in which remaining seated is expected
(c) often runs about or climbs excessively in situations in which it is inappropriate (in adolescents or adults, may be limited to subjective feelings of restlessness)
(d) often has difficulty playing or engaging in leisure activities quietly
(e) is often "on the go" or often acts as if "driven by a motor"
(f) often talks excessively

*Impulsivity*
(g) often blurts out answers before questions have been completed
(h) often has difficulty awaiting turn
(i) often interrupts or intrudes on others (e.g., butts in conversation or games)

B. Some hyperactive/impulsive or inattentive symptoms that caused impairment were present before age 7 years.

C. Some impairment from the symptoms is present in two or more settings (e.g., at school [or work] and at home).

D. There must be clear evidence of clinically significant impairment in social, academic, or occupational functioning.

E. The symptoms do not occur exclusively during the course of a Pervasive Development Disorder, Schizophrenia, or other Psychotic Disorder and are not better accounted for by another mental disorder (e.g., Mood Disorder, Anxiety Disorder, Disassociative Disorder, or a Personality Disorder).

From the American Psychiatric Association, *Diagnostic and Statistical Manual of Mental Disorders,* 4th ed., Washington, D.C.: American Psychiatric Association, 1994, (pp. 83–85).

Zentall (1993) sees ADD as a *bias* rather than a *deficit:* ADD students are biased toward strong stimuli, so a very strong stimulus may hold their attention more fully than it should and neutral or less attractive stimuli are ignored. The student may hone in on an interesting fact and miss the main idea.

Although some professionals question the validity of ADHD (Armstrong, 1996), others state that an estimated 3 to 5 percent suffer from the condition (McBurnett, Lahey, & Pfiffner, 1993), and one estimate runs as high as 10 to 20 percent of the school-age population (S. E. Shaywitz & B. A. Shaywitz, 1993). In addition, there a number of accounts by parents, students, and teachers of students who made dramatic improvements once they were diagnosed as having ADHD and were given effective treatment (Weaver, 1994b).

Even if ADHD were not a valid learning disorder, there are students who do have difficulty paying attention and who are overly-active and impulsive. Some suggestions for working with these students include the following:

- If students may have difficulty with tasks requiring sustained attention, have them read brief rather than lengthy selections or break lengthy selections into segments.
- Use color or boxes or other means to highlight important details. This will call their attention to essential items.
- Plan assignments that involve the students in activities. This will help focus their attention. For instance, creating a web or semantic map or composing a time line would sustain attention better than simply answering questions.
- Provide a variety of interesting practice activities to attract and hold students' interests.
- Provide students with strategies that will help them compensate for their difficulties. For instance, impulsive students do poorly on multiple choice items because they have difficulty delaying a response until they have read all the items (Zentall, 1993). Teach them a test-taking strategy that helps them read and consider all options before responding. Also teach strategies for planning and organizing work to impulsive students, who tend to jump in without thinking ahead.
- Provide structure and remove distractions or competing stimuli so that there is a better chance that students will focus in on relevant stimuli.
- Keep oral directions brief and to the point.
- Provide students with stretch breaks and opportunities to move around.
- Use positive reinforcement. Praise the students for rules followed and activities completed.
- Because ADHD students often respond better to visual stimuli, add visual elements to oral directions. A middle-school teacher in Pennsylvania placed a model on the board to illustrate the steps in organizing assignments. Students were encouraged to compare their work with the model before turning it in. As a result, students' organizational skills improved (Burcham, Carlson, Milich, 1993).

**BOX 2-1 Exemplary Teaching: Fostering Attention**

Although ADHD can conjure up associations of a student who calls out answers, cannot sit still, bounces around the classroom, acts impulsively, and has difficulty getting along with the other children, Randy Lee Comfort (1994), an assessment and remediation specialist, has worked successfully with

**BOX 2-1** *Continued*

these students because she builds on their positive characteristics: their energy, creativity, spontaneity, and humor.

Building on the students' creativity and energy, Comfort involves them in planning goals and the activities needed to achieve those goals. As she explains, "Too often we forget to talk to children about what they want and need; we forget to include them in their own growing up and learning process. Asking a child what kind of help is needed or listening to a student talk about when he or she wants to work on something independently might give teachers and parents clues as to the child's particular learning style" (Comfort, 1994, p. 67). Being involved in the planning also gives the child a sense of being in control.

ADHD children need structure and routine, but they also need choice and independence. As Comfort explains, they become anxious when they don't know the routine, and this increases their activity level. However, they also react to a structure that is too rigid so they need to be able to make choices. ADHD children also do better when the work is intrinsically interesting and involves higher thinking processes. If the work consists of completing low-level worksheets, they tend to rush through it. If the task requires thoughtful responses and is also interesting, then they become more deeply engaged and they are less likely to speed through the activity.

Working with Brad, a bright seven-year-old who couldn't seem to stay in his seat or concentrate on his work, Comfort and Brad set a goal of having Brad work for ten continuous minutes. After that, Brad would be allowed to play for five minutes to get rid of tension that might build up as he worked for ten minutes.

In order to provide challenge and to make the task interesting, Comfort gave Brad a series of answers to word problems. Brad had to create the problems. Brad became so involved in the task, which used his creativity and analytic skills, that he skipped his five-minute break. Given the right kind of situation, Brad's ADHD is minimized.

## *Visual Processing Deficits*

Although auditory and linguistic abilities are more important to reading than visual skills are, visual processing does play a varied, sometimes surprising, role in reading. While linguistic coding and other deficits seem to be a major cause of reading disability, visual perceptual deficits may be complicating factors. There are a number of descriptions by researchers around the world of subtypes of reading disability that include groups who have difficulty learning to read because of visual factors. In addition, there are a number of recent clinical studies that report finding a proportion of low-achieving readers, about 20 percent, who seemed to have visual-perceptual deficits or who had difficulty learning printed forms of words by memorizing them (Watson & Willows, 1993).

### *Reversals*

As commonly used, **reversals** is a generic term that encompasses a number of confusions. These include:

Orientation or rotation errors—*b* for *d* or *p* for *q*
Mirror images—Ǝ for E
Letter sequence or transposition errors—*was* for *saw*

### *A Natural Process*

As students first encounter print, it is natural for them to transpose, rotate, and reverse letters. Beginning at birth, perception develops and matures as the child grows older. Perception is selective. As visual perception develops, a student becomes more adept at searching out critical information in a display. Perception also becomes more differentiated. Thus, the child becomes better able to detect slight differences between *m/n, b/d,* and other easily confused letter pairs (Gibson & Levin, 1974).

At four years of age, children make a high proportion of mirror image and rotation errors (Gibson, Gibson, Pick, & Osser, 1962). But in a sense these aren't errors at all for a young child. Real objects don't change their identity when their position in space is altered. A chair is a chair whether it is upright, upside down, or lying on its side. However, depending on its orientation, a letter formed with a vertical line and a circle can be a *b, d, p,* or *q*. Rotation errors, then, are natural. More than half of all kindergartners make these errors, with right–left rotation errors (*b/p*) posing special problems (Gibson & Levin, 1974).

The discrimination of graphic features is an ability that continues to develop through the age of eight. By age eight, most students make few mirror image or rotation errors. However, low-progress readers may continue to make transposition and rotation errors beyond the age of eight if they are still learning beginning reading skills. They may simply be going through the stages of letter and word discrimination that younger readers have already completed. In addition, according to Vellutino and Scanlon (1988), low-achieving readers make more reversal errors because their decoding skills are weak, and they are therefore less analytical in their processing of printed words. In their research, students taught to use an analytical strategy made very few reversal errors.

Some classic confusions also seem to be memory rather than perceptual problems. Younger and low-achieving readers often confuse letter pairs such as *b* and *d* that have a very similar appearance. However, this confusion, when it persists, isn't because they can't see the difference between a *b* and a *d.* They can't remember whether the symbol they see is a *b* or a *d.*

As far as sequencing errors are concerned, Gibson and Levin (1974) believe these may be caused by the manner in which novice readers process words. Inexperienced readers proceed letter by letter (h-o-p), whereas more mature readers use patterns of letters to read words (h + op). Because they process words letter by letter, rather than in chunks, poor readers are more likely to mix up the order of the letters.

## *Delayed or Faulty Directionality*

Although most children, learn to process print naturally and with little difficulty, Marie Clay (1991a) discovered students who continued to have problems processing print in proper order for at least a period of three years. Persistent errors in processing print may be caused by a faulty or slow developing sense of **directionality.** Clay speaks of the child developing "sensory postural awareness of one side as being different from the other" as being necessary to develop directionality (1991a, p. 116). Our sense of left and right and up and down grow out of motor explorations (Kephart, 1966). As children reach to the left and to the right, and up and down, they develop an internal sense of directional-

> **Directionality:** ability to detect left, right, up, and down consistently and automatically.

ity. If the development of that sense is delayed or disturbed, students may have difficulty perceiving letters in a consistent left-to-right order and so transpose letters.

In summary, rotating or transposing letters is a natural part of learning how to process print. In most instances, they are not a factor in reading disability. Although often equated in the popular press with letter transpositions and visual deficits, most cases of reading disability seem to spring from auditory language deficits. "Far from being a visual problem, dyslexia appears to be a limited facility in using language to code other types of information" (Velluntino, 1987, p. 34). However, if reversals persist beyond the age of seven or eight, despite careful instruction, they may be a sign of an underlying disorder in directionality (Harris & Sipay, 1990).

If students do manifest directional difficulties, observe and decide which of the following is the most probable description of the situation:

- The student is a novice reader and writer and is still learning to process print in a consistent manner. There is evidence that reversals or other signs of directional confusion are decreasing.
- Despite extended instruction and practice, there is continued evidence of directional errors. However, most of the errors have to do with substitution of *d* for *b* or *p* for *q* or other easily confused items. These suggests a memory rather than a perceptual problem.
- Despite extended instruction and practice, there is continued evidence of directional errors. These errors involve confusing the order of letters in words, syllables in words, or words in sentences. Older low-achieving readers may make subtle transposition errors, such as mixing up the order of syllables in multisyllabic words, thus reading "enmentjoy" for *enjoyment* (Robeck & Wallace, 1990). If they persist, errors such as these may indicate an underlying processing problem.

### *Corrective Measures*

Although in most instances poor readers simply outgrow orientation and sequencing errors, their progress is aided by good teaching practices, which stress consistent movement from left to right. These include:

- When reading from the board, chart paper, or a big book, emphasize that you read the words from left to right.
- When drawing objects on the board or decorating a wall, proceed from left to right.
- Insofar as possible, arrange and present displays from left to right.
- Using a chart with arrows or other devices, stress the need to form letters in a consistent fashion. For instance, when presenting the letter *t,* emphasize drawing the initial stroke from top to bottom and the second stroke from left to right. If students sometimes cross the *t* from left to right and at other times right to left, they are opening themselves up to directional confusion.
- Physical activities. Directionality grows out of our physical sense of left and right. Plan a wide variety of games and activities, such as the Hokey Pokey, that foster development of that internal sense.

For those few children who continue to have difficulty with letter orientation and sequencing, try the following:

*Tracing.* Tracing, especially if supervised, helps children with both orientation and directionality.
*Keyboarding.* Encourage the use of word processing programs or even ordinary typewriters. The slower, more deliberate selection of letters aids proper sequencing.
*Context.* Always have students check their reading to make sure it makes sense. Children should be alerted to make adjustments when they read sentences like "I have on pets" for "I have no pets" or "I saw sad" for "I was sad."
*Sounding Out.* Encourage the use of sounding out along with context. Students are less likely to read "I saw sad" if they are using initial consonants or, preferably, all the letters in a word along with context to help them decode words. When such an error does occur, ask if the sentence makes sense and also ask them to tell what letter *saw* begins with so that they can see that, both semantically and phonologically, their response is wrong.
*Mechanical Aids.* Encourage the use of finger pointing and markers if they help. Although discouraged when used by more capable readers because it is believed to foster word-by-word reading, finger pointing can be a helpful aid for novice readers.

### Other Visual Processing Deficits

Poor readers may have difficulty shifting from one fixation to the next (Lovegrove & Williams, 1993).

Although reversals may not be an important factor for most students who have a reading disability, there are a number of visual processing deficits that may play a more prominent role. In a review of the literature on visual processing of good and poor readers, Willows, Kruk, and Corcos (1993) found that low-achieving readers are slower at processing information visually. Younger low-achieving readers also had difficulty recognizing word shapes. Apparently this was due to their failure to note distinctive features in the words. The difficulties arose from an inadequate initial analysis of the forms rather than from failure to remember them. However, a visual-memory deficit was also found in some young low-achieving readers. Willows, Kruk, and Corcos (1993) state:

*If some disabled readers have delays or deficits in their visual processing abilities, such weakness could be a factor in their apparent difficulties differentiating between similar looking letters and words; especially in analyzing and remembering the orthographic patterns in words and in processing letters and words at a rapid rate in text. (p. 282)*

## Language Factors

Deficits in oral language are a major characteristic of low-achieving readers. According to Wiig (1994), approximately 70 to 80 percent of learning disabled students—most of whom have reading problems—have language disorders. In the preschool years, these students may be delayed in language development—a condition that is almost always a precursor of a delay in reading development. They may have difficulty following a story, show little interest in verbal activities, and have difficulty with word retrieval, (e.g., remembering the names of objects). Syntax may be similar to that of a younger child. Verbal concept development is also delayed. Upon entering school, they may not be able to name colors, letters, or days of the week.

Although these children may be able to function adequately in their home and play environments, the classroom places increased communication demands on them. They have difficulty with more complex syntactical structures and have difficulty with comparative, spatial, and temporal concepts. Difficulties with these concepts may be based in cognitive deficits. If children have difficulty perceiving relationships, they will have a problem understanding these same relationships when expressed in words. Likewise, children who have difficulty generalizing and are concrete in their thinking have restricted understanding of vocabulary words and will have difficulty understanding figurative language and multiple meanings of words (Wiig & Semel, 1984).

### *Articulation Difficulties*

Speech articulation problems may also contribute to reading difficulties. Students may experience increased difficulty learning letter–sound relationships for sounds they are having difficulty forming, for instance. However, reading and speech should not be confused. Just because the child is not able to articulate a sound, doesn't mean that the child can't perceive that sound or can't make sense of words in which the sound appears. When working with students who have articulatory or other language problems, it is best to consult with the school's speech and hearing specialist. Many children with articulation problems also have concurrent language disorders (Ratner, 1993).

Additional language difficulties that might contribute to a reading difficulty include poor phonemic awareness, inadequate automatized rapid naming, and deficient word finding.

### *Phonological Factors*

A widely accepted theory of reading disability holds that a major cause is a subtle phonological deficiency (Vellutino, 1987). The deficiency includes difficulty with **phonemic awareness,** which involves detecting separate sounds in words, and phonological coding deficits, which is a slowness or difficulty in using the sounds of a word to help remember that word and was discussed earlier. Students who are deficient in phonemic awareness have difficulty dealing with language in an abstract way. For instance, although they can understand the word *hat* and use it in normal conversation, they are unaware that *hat* is composed of three sounds: /h/, /a/, /t/. These students might also have difficulty identifying initial consonants in words or even detecting rhyme. Not being able to perceive individual sounds in words, these students are unable to match up letters with sounds and are also unable to learn phonics.

> **Phoneme:** smallest unit of sound that distinguishes one word from another. **Phonemic awareness:** the ability to detect the separate phonemes in a word: /b/ /a/ /t/.

> After intensive training using taped speech and computer games, students who evidence a slower processing rate improved dramatically (Tallal et al., 1996).

Difficulty with phonemic awareness may be rooted in temporal processing deficits (Tallal et al., 1996). For some students, the ability to perceive certain rapidly articulated speech sounds, such as the consonants

/b/, /d/, /t/, /p/, may be slower than average. These children might have difficulty, for instance, discriminating between *ben* and *den.* However, when the speech is artificially modified so that it is slowed down and the problem consonants are also articulated in a slightly louder tone, the children's ability to discriminate improves markedly. (See Chapter 7 for a fuller discussion of phonological factors.)

## *Rapid Automatized Naming*

**Rapid automatized naming:** ability to name letters, numbers, colors, or objects quickly with a minimum of cognitive effort.

Slowness in naming numbers and letters is a sign of a slowness in underlying processes and could hinder decoding.

Even when students do have adequate phonemic awareness, they may have difficulty naming or processing language rapidly and automatically. Many poor readers are slower at such **rapid automatized naming** tasks as naming a series of random numbers or letters (Wolf, 1991). Poor readers are also slower in reading words in lists and text Biemiller (1977–1978). Slowness in naming in low achieving readers persists into adulthood. Long after low-achieving readers are 100 percent accurate in naming letters and numbers, their speed at doing so remains less than that of high-achieving readers (Samuels, 1994).

## *Word Finding*

A process related to but on a higher level than speed of naming of familiar objects and symbols is word retrieval or word finding. Deficiencies in word finding affect comprehension and higher-level word recognition skills, such as using context.

Burly, good-humored, and talkative, ten-year-old Mel was reading on a first-grade level, despite having average ability. In addition to his obvious reading disability, Mel's speech was marred by "you knows," hesitations, and roundabout expressions for common words. He referred to the carpet on the classroom floor as "the thing you walk on." It wasn't that the word *rug* or *carpet* wasn't in his vocabulary. Mel simply couldn't retrieve *rug* or *carpet* from his store of words. When the teacher said, "Do you mean rug?" Mel quickly responded, "Yes. The rug."

All of us have difficulty finding the right word on occasion—whether it be the name of a co-worker's spouse, a technical term, or a distinctive word that would be especially appropriate for a special situation. However, Mel's difficulty is ongoing and frequent. His word finding difficulty interferes with reading and writing as well as speech. Although Mel's difficulty is so severe that it is noticeable to even the casual observer, many students suffer from less obvious forms of word finding.

**Word-finding** difficulty: persistent slowness or inability to generate a word to name a specific object, event, and idea, even though the word is in the speaker's vocabulary.

A **word-finding** deficit is defined as "a problem in generating the specific word that any given situation, stimulus or sentence context evokes" (Snyder & Godley, 1992, p. 16). Symptoms of word-finding difficulty include frequent pauses, circumlocutions or roundabout language, repetitions, misuse of nonspecific words such as "things," "stuff," frequent use of expressions such as "you know" or "I can't think of the word," and the frequent use of *ums* and *ahs* and similar meaningless sounds (Snyder & Godley, 1992). Frequent "I don't knows" when called upon to answer in class can also be a sign of word finding difficulty. The "I don't know" may mean that the student can't think of the words to express the answer.

Wolf and Goodglass (1986) compared low- and high-achieving readers with similar *receptive* vocabularies. When shown a picture and asked to supply a label or word for it, low-achieving readers had more difficulty.

Seen in children with brain damage and students who have learning and communication disorders, word-finding deficits have until recently been the responsibility of the communication disorders and/or learning disabilities specialists. However, a growing body of research indicates that there is a strong relationship between deficits in word finding and reading disability. Just as some problem readers have difficulty with the automatic naming of numbers and letters, some also have difficulty retrieving words (Wolf and Goodglass, 1986).

Students with word-finding difficulties may have difficulty using picture and text clues. Stumped by the word *penguin,* Sandy was encouraged by her teacher to use the story's illustration, which showed a *penguin,* to help her decode the word. Unable to retrieve the name of the pictured animal, Sandy finally responded with the word *bird.* Deficient word-finding ability had hampered her use of a picture clue. Her use of other contextual clues will also be hampered by word-finding difficulties. Encountering a difficult word, she will be less able to predict what word might logically fit the sense of the sentence, because retrieving words from her mental storehouse is both slower and less accurate. However, this doesn't mean that students with word-finding difficulties shouldn't use context. Ironically, although hampered in the use of context, they rely on context more heavily than students who have no difficulty retrieving words. Since context provides added clues, it aids in the retrieval of words.

Had Sandy used phonics along with picture clues, she would have had a better chance of retieving the word.

***Working with Students Who Have Word-Finding Deficits***

Students with word-finding deficits need help in two broad areas, storage and retrieval. *Storage* refers to the placement of items in long-term memory. It's a little like storing file folders containing data in cabinets. Storage capacity is virtually limitless. Billions of pieces of data can be stored and the system still has room for more. However, retrieval is another question. Retrieval has to do with finding the stored bits of information.

Word finding can be improved by enhancing both storage and retrieval. Increasing storage means expanding students' vocabulary. The more words children know the more they can retrieve. Vocabulary can be expanded by adding totally new words and by adding new meanings to words already known. Storage is strengthened as new words and new meanings are added and relationships among stored words are established.

Establishing relationships among words also aids retrieval. If new words, for instance, are organized by category or some other fashion, they are easier to retrieve. It's easier to remember these items: *okra, collards,* and *kale* if they are categorized as "green vegetables."

***Word-Finding Strategies***

Retrieval is facilitated through the use of cues. The cue might be a category name (it's a member of the cat family—*tiger*) or a function (it's used to pound nails—*hammer*). In reading, context may be used. (What word would make sense here?) Letter clues might also be used (it begins with an *l*—*lettuce*). Of course, teachers won't always be around to provide retrieval cues, so students should also be taught strategies to help them cope with their difficulty in retrieving words. Students are taught to use alternate words when they are unable to retrieve a word and to use reflective pausing (German, 1992). Alternate words might include synonyms (*auto* for *car*), a more general word (*game* for *checkers*), or a descriptive or functional phrase (*the train car that runs on tracks* for *light rail* or *trolley*). Reflective pausing is especially useful for students who are fast but inaccurate word retrievers. When pausing, students should be using one of the cues mentioned above to help them retrieve the desired word.

Remembering the text will also be a problem for students with word-finding difficulty since there is a greater chance they will be unable to retrieve the words encapsulating key concepts or events in the text. Having difficulty retrieving the necessary words, students with word-finding deficits will be less likely to join in class discussions of the selections that they've read; if they do join in, they may not always be able to express the information they have garnered from their reading.

***Compensatory Programming***

Traditionally, the speech therapist or communication disorders specialist works with students who have word-finding difficulty. However, there are a number of steps that you can take to help these students compensate for their difficulties.

- In discussions, provide more clues and additional wait time. Keep in mind that these students may know more than they can say. (Remember how you felt taking a test and getting items wrong when you knew the date or name or word but couldn't remember it until after your test paper was turned in). Students with retrieval problems may experience these feelings on an almost ongoing basis.
- Before reading, provide an overview of the selection or give a preview of the story. Place key words from the story on the board. Prominently displaying semantic maps and webs helps prepare students for the story. They also help cue retrieval during the reading of the selection and during the subsequent discussion.
- Stress the use of phonics in decoding unfamiliar words. Hampered in their use of context clues, these students should be taught to use phonics as a compensatory device. However, use of phonics should be integrated with context.
- Adjust evaluation procedures. Students with retrieval problems may have special difficulty with tests of expressive vocabulary that involve having the students retrieve words. They may also have difficulty with tests that require them to supply dates, names, and terms. Consider using a multiple choice format with these students, since this lessens retrieval requirements.

Speed may be a factor in word-finding difficulty. Students with word-finding difficulties may successfully retrieve a word, but may take longer to do so. Excessive pausing and overuse of *ahs* and *uhs* indicates a slowness in locating a word in the mental storehouse.

## *Social and Emotional Factors*

Although gifted, Florence had difficulty learning to read in first grade. Seeing her friends learn with relative ease, she wondered why she couldn't make sense of the words on the page. The words that she had worked so hard to learn on Monday were forgotten by Tuesday. A naturally outgoing, confident child, she became withdrawn as her concept of herself as a competent learner plummeted. Within a few months, she gave up trying. She had acquired a condition known as learned helplessness.

According to Seligman (1975), **learned helplessness** is the response manifested by people who believe they are unable to exert any influence over a situation. Feeling that her

**Learned helplessness:** children believe, based on repeated failures, that their efforts to learn will be ineffective and they must rely on others to help them.

efforts to learn to read were futile, Florence gave up trying. Instead of attempting to read the easy story books that her teacher gave her, she persuaded a friend or her mother to read them to her. When she came across a word she couldn't read, instead of trying to work it out, she immediately asked another student or the teacher for help. Believing that she couldn't learn to read became a self-fulfilling prophecy for Florence. Because she had judged her efforts to be futile, Florence no longer worked on reading, learned less, and fell further behind, thus confirming her feelings of defeatism.

## *Fight or Flight*

Social and emotional maladjustment can be the cause of a reading problem or an effect or a mixture of both. In Florence's case, learned helplessness was an effect of a reading difficulty, but in time it became a cause of her continued lack of progress. Being asked to read caused obvious stress in Florence. Students who have serious reading difficulties often display a fight or flight reaction to escape the stress caused by having to engage in a behavior that they find virtually impossible. Students who adopt a fight reaction are soon noticed because they engage in confrontational or disruptive behavior, or they may simply refuse to read. They may criticize the reading material, complaining that it's a stupid book. They may say that reading is boring or deny having a reading problem. The student may refuse to begin an assignment, yell, or even have a tantrum (Gentile & McMillan, 1987). The purpose behind the behavior is to avoid reading at all costs. For the aggressive problem reader, being chastised, kept after school, or sent to the principal's office is preferable to reading.

The behaviors of students who exhibit a flight reaction are generally more subtle and more socially acceptable than those engaged in by the fight group. Instead of criticizing reading and displaying outward signs of anxiety, the students turn inward. They engage in self-criticism, blame themselves for their failure to read, become withdrawn and silent, and may escape into daydreams. When they do engage in reading activities, they adopt a learned helplessness approach and frequently seek help from peers and teachers.

## *Developing a Sense of Self-Efficacy*

Whether through fight or flight, students with negative associations with reading avoid it—or if they do read, they engage in the task with less intensity. Students are more likely to undertake an activity such as reading or writing if they have a sense of self-efficacy. Bandura (1977) describes **self-efficacy** as students' belief in their ability to complete a task successfully. When judging their abilities as readers and writers, students consider four factors:

**Self-efficacy:** belief in oneself as a learner.

1. Progress as readers and writers,
2. Observational comparison, or how students feel their performance compares with that of others in the class,
3. Social feedback, or direct or indirect performance feedback provided by teachers, peers, or family; and
4. Physiological states, which are the feelings students have as they read or write. (Henk & Melnick, 1995)

Through observation and careful questioning, you can get a sense of students' perception of themselves as readers. When observing, watch for signs of avoidance behavior, failure to complete tasks, or quitting a task when it becomes difficult. Some questions that you might ask include:

- What do you like best about reading?
- What do you like least?
- Is reading easy or hard for you?
- Does anything give you trouble in reading? If so, what?
- Do you feel peaceful when you read?
- Do you feel anxious when you read?
- How do you feel about reading aloud? Why do you feel that way?
- How would you compare your reading with that of others in the class?
- Is reading getting easier or harder?
- What do you do if you are reading a book and it has a lot of hard words?

If there is a problem with the student's sense of self-efficacy, Henk and Melnick (1995) recommend that teachers take the following steps:

> (a) devise more meaningful and considerate ways to communciate reading process to their students,
> (b) modify their current classroom oral reading practices,
> (c) revise their grouping techniques,
> (d) pay closer attention to the reading materials they assign,
> (e) become more sensitive to indirect signals they send to children regarding their reading performance,
> (f) counsel the class and parents about constructive feedback or
> (g) strive to make the children more physically and mentally comfortable during the act of reading (p. 474).

> Students' self-efficacy is enhanced when the learning task is perceived as being doable, the text is on the appropriate level, instruction is clear and well-organized, and students feel comfortable.

Success breeds success. What students need above all else to build a sense of efficacy is a history of success. The tasks which students successfully complete must be at the proper level of challenge. Tasks that require too much effort or are judged to be very easy do not build a sense of self-efficacy. As Bandura (1977) comments, "To succeed at easy tasks provides no new information for altering one's sense of self-efficacy, whereas mastery of challenging tasks conveys salient evidence of enhanced competence" (p. 201). In reading, this means providing students with materials that they can handle. It also means carefully teaching strategies and making sure that students have ample opportunity to apply those strategies independently. Students lacking an adequate sense of self-efficacy need to see that they can successfully use strategies on their own. "Independent performance, if well executed, produces success experiences, which further reinforce expectations of self-competency" (Bandura, 1977, p. 202).

Strategy instruction is especially effective when students see the value of the strategy and understand when and where to apply it (Schunk & Rice, 1987). Praise and feedback also help. However, feedback should be specific. "I like the way you used context to figure out those hard words" is a more effective form of feedback than the general comment, "You're doing great." Both effort and ability should be praised. "You're really working hard," should be complemented by, "You really know what you're doing" or "You caught on fast." After an erroneous response, help the student see what she might do to achieve a successful experience: "You weren't able to sound that word out or find a part that you know, but try saying *blank* for the word and reading to the end of the sentence. Read the whole sentence again and then see if you tell what word might be placed in the blank."

In summary, self-efficacy can be enhanced by group and individual goal setting, careful teaching with emphasis on building independence in use of strategies, positive expectations, using peers as models, and providing positive feedback. It also helps if you have high expectations and convey these to the class and involve students in creating an instructional context. Having materials and instruction on the proper level of challenge is also important.

### *Parental Pressure*

Undue parental pressure to perform may also adversely affect the disabled reader. On the one hand, parental support is important as the child learns to read and write. The child sees that parents value achievement and, in response, works hard, taking necessary risks, giving up play for work, and generally taking responsibility for learning. However, if undue pressure is added, the child may judge that "if I don't do well, Mom and Dad will be angry with me." If the pressure is increased even more, the child may see failure as catastrophic, thus creating in the child a genuine fear of failure (Bricklin, 1991). Under intense fear of failure, the child may engage in avoidance behavior or even give up trying, reasoning that if you don't try, you don't really fail.

> Ironically, undue fear of failure leads to behaviors that cause failure (Bricklin, 1991).

### *Helping Students Overcome Negative Behaviors*

Children with serious emotional and adjustment problems should be helped by the school social worker, psychologist, and other appropriate professionals. In addition to the suggestions of mental health workers, try the following measures when working with students whose academic self-esteem is deficient.

- Provide a stable, caring learning environment. Be positive. Build on the students' strengths, rather than focusing on their weaknesses. Supply clear instructions and establish orderly, consistent routines and high, but realistic, expectations. Be accepting of individual differences. Through example and instruction, teach mutual respect. Value each individual because of who he or she is, not because of what he or she does.
- Handle oral reading with care. Oral reading practices that discourage low-achieving readers include: asking them to read difficult passages or orally read parts in difficult plays; having them read books that are beneath their maturity level; frequently correcting them or allowing other students to correct them; and stopping them from reading but assigning a better reader to continue with their part or to help them (Gentile &

McMillan, 1987). On the other hand, don't exclude low-achieving readers from oral reading activities, but see to it that they are adequately prepared. Working with a disabled reader whose oral reading was dysfluent, Bradley and Thalgoot (1987) found that when the student read a selection silently before reading it orally, his rate of reading doubled and the number of misread words was significantly reduced. The student also seemed more relaxed and involved. In contrast, when reading orally at sight in the classroom, he mumbled the words, made frequent errors, and appeared both anxious and embarrassed.

- Acknowledge difficulties. When students evidence obvious fight or flight reactions, judiciously acknowledge the difficulty and the emotion behind it. "You don't seem to like reading group," or "You seem to have a difficult time choosing a book to read" or "Tests seem to make you nervous." These acknowledgements need to be expressed "in an emotionally accepting way" (Bricklin, 1991, p. 212). The acknowledgment shows that you care and gives the child the opportunity to talk about the difficulty. Once the difficulty is acknowledged, steps can be taken to remedy it through encouragement, use of strategies, or, for more serious problems, sessions with a mental health professional.
- Promote independence. Don't fall into the trap of providing unneeded assistance for students who have learned helplessness. As noted in Chapter 1, a general principle of remedial education is never to do for the students anything that they can do for themselves. Don't sound out a word that a student can sound out for herself. And if she can't sound out the whole word, encourage her to sound out as much as she can and then build on that. If she can't recall an important fact from a selection she read, encourage her to go back and find it. Teach students strategies that they will be able to apply independently. Although they may need guidance in the beginning, gradually lead them to a stage of independence. Also redirect questions that indicate a lack of independence, especially if asked by students who are overly dependent (Glazer, 1991). For instance, if a student asks, "Should I read this again?" redirect the question so that the student must exercise her own judgment. Ask: "Would you like to read it again," or "Do you think you need to read it again?" If the student asks, "Which book should I read?" redirect that to "Which book would you like to read?"
- Give students choices whenever possible. Allow them to select books and stories to read and to choose activities. Involve them in setting up classroom rules and procedures. If involved, they'll put more of themselves into their work. And you're also telling them that their thoughts and judgments are important. This will boost their self-esteem and give them a sense of control over their lives.

In many instances, students' mental health takes a turn for the better once they begin to make progress in reading. Feeling good about themselves, they try harder and do better, which leads to even more success. It is the beginning of a very positive cycle. But some students have such severe emotional problems that professional intervention is needed before they can make progress. For instance, a student who is deeply depressed may need mental health assistance before she or he is able to invest energy in improving reading skills or even take an interest in schooling. While it is always a good idea to work collaboratively with other professionals, when teaching deeply disturbed students, it is essential.

## *Physical Causes*

In a holistic assessment, it is important to take a look at the student's mental and physical condition. Neurological and health factors, as well as vision and hearing, need to be considered.

### *Neurological Factors*

The most severe instances of reading difficulty—and, perhaps, some less severe cases—are caused or complicated by variation in neurological development, including subtle damage or changes in neurological organization that may not be readily apparent. Based on autopsies of low-achieving readers and sophisticated imaging studies, neuroscientists have found several differences in the structure and functioning of brains of low-achieving readers (Rosen, Sherman, & Galaburda, 1993; Wood, 1994). Recent research on the brain and reading also indicates that many parts of the brain are dynamically involved in reading. As Riccio and Hynd (1996) comment: "It is clear that there is no unitary neurological factor that results in dyslexia. Rather, the research to date suggests a combination of structural or functional differences" (p. 11).

Mysterious as well as complex, the brain is organized in ways that may seem strange to us. For instance, the part of the brain responsible for sequencing letters also controls rhythmic activities (Luria, 1970). An awkward gait may be accompanied by letter reversals.

### *Hearing Impairments*

In the past, most children with serious hearing problems were taught in residential schools or day schools that had special full-time programs. Today, more and more students are being taught within the regular classroom. This is due to a change in philosophy and advances in technology and techniques. With inclusion, it is important that the classroom teacher and reading specialist have a basic understanding of hearing difficulties.

#### *Degree of Physical Loss*

Hearing loss is measured in terms of pitch and intensity (Meyen & Skrtic, 1988). Sound waves vibrate. The number of vibrations or cycles per second is the sound wave's pitch or **frequency,** which is measured in a unit known as **Hertz.** The higher the frequency, the higher the Hertz. Humans are sensitive to sounds in the 20 to 20,000 Hertz range, but testing is generally done in the 125 to 8,000 range, which encompasses speech frequencies. There may be loss across all frequencies or a loss in specific frequencies.

In addition to measuring pitch, the intensity or loudness of sounds is also assessed. The higher the **decibel** the louder the sound. A whisper is 20 decibels, conversation about 55–60, heavy traffic 90, and thunder 120. Losses from 20 to 60 db are classified as mild, 60 to 80 are severe, and 90 or above profound.

**Frequency:** number of sound waves emitted per second.

**Hertz** (Hz): unit of measurement for sound waves. One hertz equals one cycle or sound wave per second.

**Decibel:** unit for measuring loudness of a sound.

### *Extent of Impairment*

While hearing loss can be measured in terms of frequencies and decibels, the extent of impairment is dependent upon a number of factors. These include age of loss, age of intervention, and type of communication input (Meyen & Skrtic, 1988). Generally speaking, the earlier the loss, the more profound its impact. Children who lose their hearing before acquiring speech are much more seriously impaired, than those whose loss occurred after the acquisition of language. However, early intervention, which could include use of an assistive device, such as a hearing aid or a special microphone used by the teacher; special teaching; and training of parents can significantly lessen negative effects. The use of sign language and other means of communication also have a positive impact.

### *The Reading Teacher's Role*

While severe and profound cases of hearing impairment are generally handled by speech and hearing specialists, you can help by noting children who seem to have undetected hearing difficulties and referring them for testing, by making appropriate program adjustments, and by collaborating with the speech therapist. Having deficits in vocabulary, syntax, and figurative language, hearing impaired students generally lag significantly behind in reading comprehension. They may also be deficient in their knowledge of story structures and so would experience difficulty comprehending narratives. Corrective students who are hearing impaired or who lost but regained hearing because of **otitis media,** which is an inflammation of the middle ear and is a fairly common and sometimes persistent and recurring condition in young children, might be expected to evidence language deficits and so need additional assistance.

**Otitis media:** inflammation of the middle ear—a fairly common and sometimes persistent and recurring condition in young children.

Signs of a possible hearing problem include talking too loudly or too softly, poor articulation, asking to have directions repeated, difficulty listening, and frequent ear infections. An observational checklist of possible symptoms is presented in Table 2-2. It is especially important for teachers of young children to be on the lookout for signs of otitis media.

### *Auditory Screening*

Hearing can be screened with an audiometer. Although they are generally administered by the school nurse or a speech and hearing specialist, in some school systems and university reading clinics, the reading teacher conducts the screening for hearing loss. An **audiometer** produces sounds called pure tones at a range of frequencies and decibels. Listening through earphones, students signal when they hear the target sound. The student's performance is charted on an **audiogram,** which shows how well the students hears in her left and right ears at the crucial speech frequencies of 125, 250, 500, 1,000, 2,000, 4,000, and 8,000 Hz. The audiogram in Figure 2-2 shows the performance of Natalie, a ten-year-old disabled reader. X's are used to indicate hearing in the left ear, O's hearing in the right ear. Ability to hear at 15 decibels or lower is adequate. If a loss higher than that is detected, a referral should be made. Note that Natalie shows some loss beyond 20 decibels in both ears at the higher frequencies of 1,000, 2,000, 4,000, and 8,000. She was referred to an audiologist for testing.

**Audiometer:** used to measure the ability to hear sounds of varying levels of loudness and at various frequencies.

**Audiogram:** graph that shows the results of a hearing test.

**TABLE 2-2 Observation Checklist: Signs of Possible Hearing Problem**

| | |
|---|---|
| Faulty pronunciation or other speech difficulties | ________ |
| Poor spelling | ________ |
| Frequent requests to repeat directions and questions | ________ |
| Lack of attention | ________ |
| Inappropriate responses | ________ |
| Focusing on speaker's lips | ________ |
| Earaches | ________ |
| Frequent rubbing of the ear | ________ |
| Unnatural pitch of the voice | ________ |
| Cupping ear or turning ear towards speaker | ________ |
| Complaints of ringing or buzzing in ear, dizziness, or closed feeling in the ear | ________ |
| Sores in ear or discharge | ________ |
| Frequent sore throats, colds, or tonsillitis | ________ |

Audiometers are relatively easy to use and can detect students who need further testing by trained specialists. Some cautions are in order, however. Testing should be done in a quiet area, preferably a soundproof booth. Audiometers are precise machines, so their calibrations should be checked periodically. It is also important to become familiar with testing procedures and the operation of the machine before actually using it with students. There is a possibility of damaging a child's hearing should the tester inadvertently send a pulse of sound to a student's ears at 110 decibels, the "loudest" setting on most machines.

### *High Frequency Loss*

**High frequency hearing loss:** one in which students can hear low frequency sounds but not high frequency sounds such as /f/, /s/, /th/.

One type of impairment that sometimes evades detection is a **high frequency hearing loss.** Students can hear sounds in the lower range, which includes most consonants and the vowel sounds. However, they are unable to hear certain consonants, such as /f/, /s/, and /th/, which are at the higher end of the range (Harris & Sipay, 1985). Since these children can hear most speech sounds and can understand some words, their impairment may escape detection, especially if only a few consonants are involved. However, since they miss some words, these students find school confusing and, of course, have special difficulty learning letter–sound relationships.

Because her hearing impairment was subtle, Mandy's high frequency loss was not detected until she entered school. As a result, her vocabulary was limited as were her general background of knowledge and concepts. Once Mandy's impairment was discovered, she was fitted with a hearing aid and given special help by the speech therapist.

Mandy acquired a fairly substantial sight vocabulary, but she experienced difficulty learning decoding skills, and her comprehension was poor. Decoding skills showed an improvement when her reading teacher began using a modified version of a pattern approach. Through careful testing, the speech therapist had been able to determine what sounds Mandy could hear and which she still had difficulty with. She taught those patterns that were composed of sounds that Mandy could hear. Working with the speech therapist, she also devised techniques in which she was able to show Mandy how high frequency sounds,

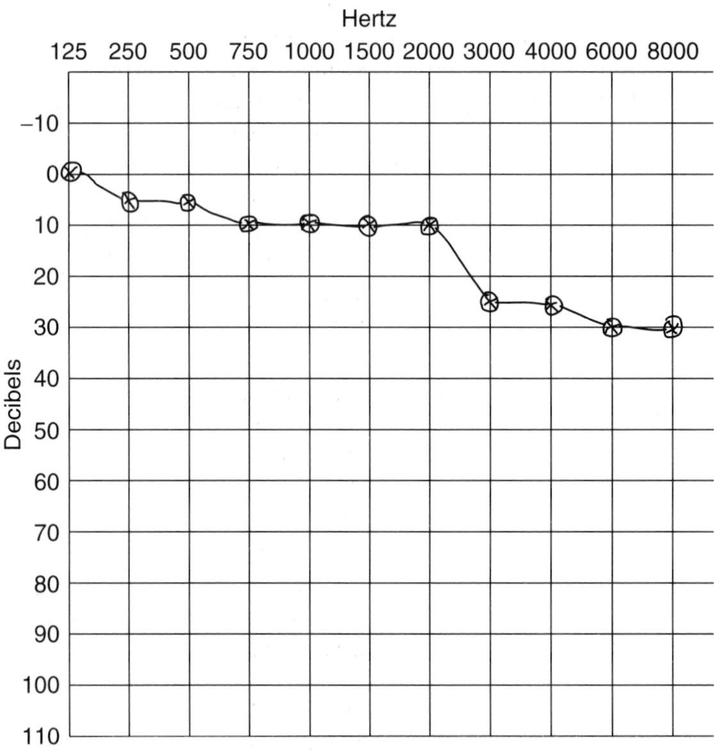


**FIGURE 2-2 Audiogram**

the ones she couldn't hear, were formed. In a sense, she added a step to her phonics lesson. In order to compensate for Mandy's hearing impairment, she helped Mandy form difficult-to-hear sounds with her mouth. Mandy's teacher also helped Mandy with her writing. Because Mandy was overly concerned with spelling, she did virtually no writing. Mandy's writing consisted of a sentence or two of the plainest of prose devoid of all embellishment and elaboration. Encouraged by her teacher to spell as best she could, Mandy was finally convinced to try invented spelling. Little by little, her pieces grew in content and quality of expression. Wide reading and lots of discussion helped expand Mandy's meager background.

## *Vision Impairments*

Although poor vision is rarely a cause of poor reading, blurred, fuzzy, or strained vision can certainly add to the problem. Vision is both structural and functional. In order to have correct vision, our eyes need to be properly shaped. However, having properly shaped eyes is not enough. It is possible to have a vision system that is physically perfect but still have vision problems. Vision is functional, a learned act. Through experience, humans literally learn to see. Because of the physiology of the eyes, we should see two objects. However, we learn to fuse dual images into one.

Vision is initiated when light rays from an object enter the cornea and pass through the lens. The lens bends the rays so that they are focused on the retina. An optic nerve connects the retina with the visual cortex, which interprets the signal. In order for the light rays to be focused on the retina, the eye must be properly shaped. If the eyeball is too long, light rays fall in front of the retina resulting in nearsightedness or **myopia.** If the eyeball is too short, light rays fall behind the retina, resulting in farsightedness or **hyperopia. Astigmatism,** a third major structural defect, results from an irregular curvature of the cornea and causes a blurred or misshapen image. All three of these conditions can be corrected with lenses.

**Myopia:** condition in which the light rays fall in front of the retina so that distant objects are not seen clearly.

**Hyperopia:** condition in which the light falls behind the retina so that close objects are not seen clearly.

**Astigmatism:** irregularity in the cornea that causes blurred vision.

**Accommodation:** automatic focusing of the lens.

**Convergence:** automatic adjustment of the pointing of the eyes in order to maintain clear vision.

**Strabismus:** muscular imbalance of the eyes so that the eyes point in different directions.

**Amblyopia:** suppression of vision in one eye. Because that eye is not used it becomes weakened. Lost vision can be restored through stimulating the affected eye IF detected early enough.

### *Accommodation and Convergence*

Acuity of vision is not sufficient, however. The student's eyes must also function in such a way that she or he can see a single object at all working distances. Accommodation and convergence mechanisms must work in tandem. In **accommodation,** the shape of the lens is adjusted according to the distance of the target object. In **convergence,** a group of six pairs of muscles move the eyes so that they focus on the object. As an object gets closer, for instance, the lenses contract and the eyes turn inward.

Two visual conditions that contribute to reading difficulties include **strabismus,** which is a condition in which the eyes are misaligned and point in different directions (American Academy of Ophthalmology, 1984, 1990), and insufficient convergence, which means that the eyes are not fixating on the same spot at near point. Because these conditions strain the visual system, eyes may become tired, with resulting redness, itching, and burning. A headache may ensue. For some students reading also may be disturbed. They may experience:

> *letters and words that appear to overlap, letters and lines that appear to be crooked, parts of words that disappear, letters that become unclear, and problems with finding the next line of print. (Aasved, 1989, p. 192)*

### *The Special Case of Amblyopia*

Although eight-year-old Amy passed her **Snellen test,** frequent complaints of headaches and squinting alerted her teacher to a possible vi-

**Snellen chart:** used in vision test, with rows of letters, each row's smaller than the last. The chart is placed 20 feet from the viewer.

sion problem. An examination by a vision specialist revealed a serious problem. Amy had amblyopia, which can be caused by strabismus. Vision in her right eye was 20/20. However, vision in her left eye was 20/100. Amy could see at 20 feet what people with average vision could see at 100 feet. Suppressing vision because of a lack of coordination with the right eye, the left eye had lost much of its power through disuse. Glasses and patching of the strong eye were prescribed. Patching of the stronger eye would force the weaker eye to go back to work.

Amy was fortunate. According to Jobe (1976), amblyopia is best treated when the child is young. When untreated until the age of eight or nine, there is danger of a complete loss of vision in the weaker eye. However, after months of patching, Amy's vision improved. Vision in her left eye was restored to 20/50.

### *Color Vision*

When the class was reading *Little Blue and Little Yellow* (Lionni, 1959), which explains how colors can be mixed to form new ones, Raphael seemed confused. Later, a visual exam revealed that Raphael is unable to distinguish the colors yellow and blue. The ability to see color ranges from those who can distinguish all hues, to those who see only one color. In between are those who have difficulty detecting one or more of the primary colors: red, green, and blue. Most people who are color blind confuse red and green and are said to have red-green color blindness. However, some color-blind persons may also confuse blue and yellow. To them, blue is green, and yellow appears to be pink. A few color-blind persons are achromatic, and see only white and shades of gray including black. An inherited, x-linked trait, color blindness is far more prevalent among boys. About one boy out of twenty has some degree of color blindness. However, only about one girl out of every two hundred is color blind (Carlson, 1993).

It is important to be aware of children's ability to see color. Color blindness cannot be corrected and does not directly affect reading. However, it can be a source of confusion when teaching students how to read color names or when reading stories such as *Little Blue and Little Yellow* in which color figures prominently, or when materials are color coded. Children who are color blind should be aware of their condition and should be taught strategies for adapting to it.

### *Screening Vision*

While working with students, you might inquire as to whether they have had a vision exam and whether glasses were prescribed. Often, students don't wear their glasses.

Although poor vision is usually not a cause of reading problems, it can make reading and related learning activities, such as copying from the board, more difficult. Therefore, it is important for the school to screen students for possible vision problems. Sometimes, signs of difficulty are obvious. The student holds the book too close or too far, or squints when copying from the board. Other signs are more subtle: tilting the head or covering one eye when reading, headaches or nausea after reading, or frequent tearing or redness in the eye. A list of symptoms is presented in Table 2-3.

**TABLE 2-3 Vision Checklist**

| | |
|---|---|
| Reddened eyes or lids | ______ |
| Frequent sties | ______ |
| Frequent tearing | ______ |
| Squinting | ______ |
| Headaches | ______ |
| Eyes turn in or out | ______ |
| Burning or itching sensation in eyes after reading or writing | ______ |
| Rubbing eyes while reading or writing | ______ |
| Excessive blinking while reading or writing | ______ |
| Double vision | ______ |
| Closing or covering one eye while reading or writing | ______ |
| Tilting head while reading or writing | ______ |
| Holding printed material too close | ______ |
| Frequently changing distance between eyes and printed material | ______ |
| Difficulty copying from board | ______ |
| Skipping or rereading lines | ______ |
| Omitting words | ______ |
| Using finger to keep his or her place | ______ |
| Difficulty writing on lines when writing or staying in lines when coloring | ______ |
| Writing with ragged left margin | ______ |
| Writing or doing math problems crookedly on page | ______ |

Adapted from: *Your Child's Vision Is Important* (pp. 10–11) by C. Beverstock, 1991, Newark, DE: International Reading Association.

The school nurse or a visiting vision specialist typically screens students. However, sometimes there is no provision for screening, so the reading specialist may want to screen students, especially those who have reading problems. Even when the school does screen students, the reading specialist may want to double-check results, especially if the screening used only the Snellen Chart, which fails to assess how well the eyes work together. Ekwall and Shanker (1988) found that half the problem readers taught at the University of Texas at El Paso Reading Center had visual problems that had gone undetected in school screenings.

The most widely used of the screening tests, the **Snellen Chart,** assesses distance vision. Placed 20 feet from the person being tested, the Snellen Chart has rows of letters of gradually decreasing size. (For those who can't read letters, an illiterate E is used. Instead of naming a letter, the students shows in which direction the open lines of the E are pointing.) The top row can be read at a distance of 200 feet by a person who has normal vision. Other distances are 100, 75, 50, 40, 30, 20, and 15. The norm or standard is being able to read the letters on the row marked 20 feet. One is then said to have 20/20 vision. The Snellen Chart is especially effective at detecting myopia, astigmatism, and, sometimes, hyperopia (Jobe, 1976).

**Stereoscopic Screening Devices.** Because the Snellen test neglects binocular function and tests vision only from far points, some professionals prefer a stereoscopic instrument, which tests both eyes working together and tests at near and simulated far points. The Keystone Telebinocular Visual Survey (Academic Therapy), for instance, tests the following functions: usable vision at near and far point, fusion at near and far point, coordination of eyes at far and near point, depth perception, color perception, and simultaneous vision. Other stereoscopic screening tests include the School Vision Tester (Bausch and Lomb), the Sight Screener (American Digital), and Titmus School Vision Tester (Titmus).

### *Making Referrals*

Vision is a technical area. Reading teachers are not expected nor should they attempt to diagnose visual problems. However, they should be prepared to make referrals. There are two specialists who deal with vision problems: the ophthalmologist and optometrist. An ophthalmologist is a medical doctor who specializes in diseases of the eye. Ophthalmologists may emphasize far-point vision and structural and physical aspects of vision. Ophthalmologists can prescribe medications and perform or recommend surgery or other medical treatment.

Optometrists generally receive four years of post-college training in vision. They tend to stress near-point tests and often take a functional approach to vision. Some optometrists, for instance, offer visual training for students who seem to have difficulty with such occularmotor tasks as reading along a line of print or whose eyes seem to skip lines. When making referrals, it is customary to provide a choice of three or more professionals so as to avoid favortism or conflict of interest.

### *Visual Training*

As noted earlier, there is more to vision than just acuity. Vision is a learned act. Although children may start kindergarten as early as age four, vision doesn't mature until about the age of seven and one-half. Young children tend to be far-sighted. However, school demands a wide range of visual activities. Years ago, noted child developmental researchers Ilg and Ames (1965) claimed that the following visual skills should be required for reading: ability to focus and point eyes together as a team, speed of perception, accuracy in looking from one object to another, ability to sustain focus at the reading distance, and eye-hand coordination. The authors recommended training for those found to be deficient in visual skills. They felt that for many children, visual therapy—that is being taught how to move, focus and fixate the two eyes so that they coordinate properly—is essential for efficient visual development.

Now, three decades later, visual training is controversial (Casbergue & Greene, 1988), but its effectiveness has not been disproved. One conclusion that is clear is that visual training in isolation is ineffective. Visual training must be combined with instruction in reading and writing in order to have an impact. By and large, low-achieving readers and writers will improve in reading and writing when given careful instruction in these areas and lots of opportunities for practice and application. If students do evidence problems maintaining their place or sweeping their eyes across a line of print, steps can be taken to ease visual tasks. For one, the student can be

> At one time using a marker was discouraged, but one should be recommended for students who would benefit from its use. Older students might use a six-inch ruler or similar device.

shown how to use a marker. Clearly designed books with large print might be used. Periods of reading and writing might be interspersed with activities that involve far-point vision so as to give the child's near-point visual mechanism a rest. Copying from the board might be kept to a minimum as the shifting from far to near point and back again makes maximum demands on the accommodation/convergence systems. Use of big books and chart stories, on the other hand, should be stressed because these make use of the child's far-point vision.

### *The Role of Visual Defects in Reading Problems*

Based on thorough visual and academic assessments administered to 2,590 students in Bergen, Norway, no cause–effect relationship between visual deficits and reading or spelling problems was noted (Aasved, 1989). Both good and poor readers had a variety of visual conditions that needed correcting. The author concluded that most children with eye problems do not have a reading problem. However, this doesn't mean that vision should be neglected. A visual difficulty could add a burden to a student's learning problem.

## *Physical Health*

Kevin's case demonstrates the importance of an interactive approach. The first step in helping Kevin would be encouraging his family to make sure he was well rested.

Seven-year-old Kevin was having difficulty learning to read. Although in the second grade, he still was operating at a beginning reading level. Observation indicated that Kevin was inattentive and seemed to lack energy. Kevin was also frequently absent due to colds and other minor illnesses. When questioned by his teacher, Kevin revealed that he stayed up late at night watching TV. Sleepy and irritable the next day, he had little energy to devote to the strenuous task of learning to read. His progress was further hampered by his frequent absences, which caused him to miss crucial instruction. Tragically, Kevin's reading difficulty was caused by inadequate care.

Unfortunately, more and more children are receiving substandard care. In a three-year-study by a blue-ribbon panel of experts and leading citizens, it was determined that the quality of child care in the United States has deteriorated dramatically. Approximately one child in every five lives in poverty (Carnegie Corporation, 1994). The number of children raised in foster care has increased by more than half from 200,000 to nearly half a million. More than half of the mothers of children under one year of age are working outside the home, as compared to fewer than one in five in 1960. The number of children born to unmarried mothers and being raised in single-family homes has also risen dramatically. There is also an increase in child abuse, homelessness, and violence in the lives of children. These factors are having a negative impact on the emotional and cognitive development of children and, of course, on their reading and writing development.

### *Asthma and Other Chronic Illnesses*

Also on the increase is asthma. Between 6.7 and 12 percent of children have asthma (Celano & Geller, 1993). There is some evidence that low-achieving readers have a greater incidence of asthma and other allergic conditions (Hugdahl, 1993). Asthma and other chronic illnesses can impede progress in reading in one of five ways: increased absenteeism, side effects of medication, lessened ability to engage in learning activities because of the effects of the illness, interference from anxiety and other emotional facts caused by the illness, and teachers' or parents' perceptions that the student is too fragile to engage in learning activities (Celano & Geller, 1993).

Research suggests that students who have asthma don't necessarily experience greater difficulty with reading. However, asthma may combine with other factors, such as low socioeconomic status and behavior problems, and then impede progress in reading (Celano & Geller, 1993).

Educational programs designed to help children better understand and manage asthma can help improve school performance. When planning programs for these children, it would be helpful to involve health care professionals and parents. Providing instruction in management and consulting with parents and health care professionals are effective procedures for working with any youngster who has a chronic health problem. The child's reading and writing difficulties should be considered in the total context of all of the child's needs.

## *Educational Factors*

Educational factors are at the heart of many instances of low achievement in reading. On the basis of a longitudinal study, Vellutino et al. (1996) concluded that experiential and instructional deficits were at the heart of the reading difficulties of the middle-class students studied. All but 3 percent of students classified as being disabled readers made substantial progress in a carefully planned instructional program. Factors that contribute to poor performance include failure to gear instruction to the needs of the student. Unfortunately, as a group, poor readers spend less time reading silently, do more oral reading, are asked a greater proportion of lower-level questions, are given fewer prompts, and less time to answer (Barr & Dreeben, 1991; Allington, 1983).

> Goodman (1982) comments, "Coping with school texts, especially in upper elementary and secondary grades, is a problem that most troubled readers face even as they are improving in their ability and self-confidence."

Using inappropriate materials, especially materials that are too difficult, is also a major educational factor in reading difficulty. In her longitudinal study of poor readers, Juel (1994b) found that, on average, these students could only read about 50 percent of the words in their beginning readers. From first- through fourth-grade, they were only able to read between 70 and 80 percent of the words in their basal readers. In fourth grade, the average poor reader was able to read just 74 words out of a 100. In other words, for four years these youngster were forced to read materials that were far too difficult for them. It is small wonder that they disliked reading. When interviewed in fourth grade, 26 out of 29 expressed a distaste for reading. When asked whether they would rather read or clean their rooms, 40 percent opted for cleaning. Poor pacing, inadequate classroom management, and failure to develop independence are other factors that contribute to reading problems (Harris & Sipay, 1990).

Struggling readers may have difficulty coping with today's basals. Although enriched by the greater use of children's literature, today's basal readers, at least on the first-grade level, are far more difficult than yesterday's texts. On average, they introduce nearly twice as many words, between 1,680 and 1,824 in 1993 programs vs. 962 in the 1986/1987 programs (Hoffman, et al., 1994). In addition to being more diverse, words are longer and harder to decode. There are a great number of words with advanced phonic elements and a higher proportion of multisyllabic words. In addition, sentences are longer and more complex. Moreover, some instructional practices recommended in today's basals may work to the detriment of struggling readers. In the past, it was suggested that students be grouped by reading level. Many of today's basal manuals suggest that the whole class read the same story. Although the teacher may provide additional assistance to the poorest readers, the material may still be too difficult for them.

### *Need for Balanced Instruction*

Lack of effective instruction is also a major factor in reading difficulty. Although benefiting from immersion in print, many emergent readers require systematic instruction in phonological awareness and letter knowledge (Pinnell & McCarrier, 1994). Later, they need direct instruction in decoding, comprehension, vocabulary, and study skills. As Richek, Caldwell, Jennings, and Lerner (1996) comment, "Although the typical student often learns word recognition and comprehension strategies from extensive reading, low-achieving students may need direct, sequenced lessons" (p. 7). However, the program should be balanced. An overemphasis on phonics or oral reading can be detrimental (Allington, 1984). Students need ample opportunity to apply skills so there should be an emphasis on reading a variety of materials. As Goodman (1982) notes, "Readers in trouble are more likely to be the victims of too much skill use than not enough" (p. 89). What they need, Goodman explains, are "opportunities to read and write, and most of all, the experience of success." They need to realize that "the easiest things for them to read are going to be the very ones they have the most interest in, the most background for, and that they get the most pleasure from" (p. 90).

Poor instructional planning can also be a factor in reading problems. As noted earlier, a small percentage of students who participate in *Reading Recovery* prove to be difficult to accelerate. Observations undertaken to note instructional factors that foster or hinder progress found that the major factor associated with a lack of success was failure to plan daily lessons. Other negative factors included not using consistent, specific language; not demonstrating enough; and not noting whether a student had gained control of a skill in a variety of contexts (Lyons, 1995).

## *Social and Cultural Factors*

In many ways reading and writing are social activities. When we talk about a book we have read or ask a friend to explain a passage or, as members of a club, draft a letter to the editor, we are working with others to construct and create meaning. In schools, students read to each other, discuss books in small and large groups, work with a partner in reading, and share their writing in small and large groups. Students' learning is dependent, in part, upon their role in the group, how the group perceives them, and how effectively they operate in the group. Unfortunately, students who are poor readers are frequently rejected by their classmates (Richek, Caldwell, Jennings, Lerner, 1996). Feeling rejected, they become passive, stop participating, and fail to get help from their peers. Motivation and sense of self-efficacy also suffer. As noted in Chapter 1, building a sense of community in which everyone is valued is essential for all students, especially those who are struggling.

Learning may also be impeded if instruction fails to reflect the cultural diversity of today's students. Although the social nature of learning is being increasingly recognized, in many classrooms emphasis is on individual achievement and individual response. In the typical classroom the teacher poses a question, students raise their hands, and the teacher selects one child to respond. However, in some cultures responding is a group activity. In Hawaii, for instance, children use a method of responding known as story talk in which two or more students respond at the same time. Using story talk, students provide enriched responses that focus on the important elements of the selection that has been read. When teachers unfamiliar with story talk structure discussions so that one student responds at a time, discussions falter and the teacher spends much of the time trying to get the students to wait their turn.

Most schools have typically fostered a competitive atmosphere (D. Johnson & Johnson, 1994). However, in many cultures, learning is cooperative. For instance, overall, both African American and Mexican American students perform better when they work in cooperative groups (Sharan, 1985). Students also do better when materials reflect their cultural heritage and when the reading and writing activities in which they engaged are ones that are important in their cultures. It is all too easy to underestimate the rich heritages that students from diverse cultures bring to the school (Taylor & Dorsey-Gaines, 1988).

## *Economic Factors*

Poverty is on the increase. It is now 20 percent and rising. By the year 2000 as many as 40 percent of children will have spent at least one year on welfare (Cunningham & Allington, 1994). Although many poor children do quite well in school, poverty frequently impedes reading and writing achievement.

A recent study of 790 welfare families revealed that more than half the mothers had poor reading and math skills (Lewin, 1996). Although, for the most part, the mothers provided homes that were safe and orderly, interviewers indicated that there was little cognitive stimulation for the children. Only a small percentage of the mothers read to their youngsters. The children, who were aged three to five, performed poorly on tests of basic concepts, such as knowing colors, shapes, and directional words like *under* or *behind.* When children have not been read to and don't have a grasp of such basic concepts as colors when they start school, they are more likely to experience difficulty with reading and writing. Fortunately, family literacy programs have been successful in developing the language and literacy skills of both parents and children (Philliber, Spillman, & King, 1996). (See Chapter 18 for more information about family literacy programs.)

Although teachers want the best for their students, they may structure instruction for the poorest readers in such a way that their growth is unintentionally limited. In her study of fifth-graders, Anyon (1980) found that schools in poverty areas emphasized more rote learning, less student involvement, and lowered expectations when compared with schools in more affluent areas. Students in poverty areas are also less likely to be taught comprehension strategies and may not be asked to do out-of-class readings because the teachers judge they would not do them (Garcia, Pearson, & Jimenez, 1994). However, when poor and middle-class students are given similar reading instruction, their achievement is similar.

## *Summary*

Reading problems are often the result of a host of interacting factors or contributing causes. Possible factors include cognitive, visual perceptual, linguistic, emotional, physical, educational, social, cultural, and economic factors. Having adequate intelligence is not a guarantee that one won't have a reading problem. Specific cognitive factors, such as memory, associative learning and attention, apparently play roles in reading disorders. While deficits in memory can affect reading in a variety of ways, inefficient verbal coding may be at the heart of word recognition, comprehension, and vocabulary deficiencies. Related to and possibly caused by inefficient verbal encoding is a deficit in associative learning. A deficiency in associative learning is characteristic of students who have the most serious reading difficulties.

Students who have difficulty paying attention have difficulty learning. As many as 50 percent of students diagnosed as having the somewhat controversial condition, attention deficit disorder, have reading problems. Although auditory processing deficits seem to lie at the heart of many reading disorders, visual processing difficulties can contribute to the problem.

Deficits in oral language are a major characteristic of low-achieving readers. These deficits may take the form of articulation problems, auditory discrimination and phonological difficulties, deficiencies in vocabulary, syntax, and knowledge of story grammar, slowness in rapid automatized naming, and slowness in word retrieval.

Failure to learn to read can be both a cause and effect of social and emotional problems. A multidisciplinary approach should be used when working with students who have social/emotional problems.

Reading difficulties can be rooted in physical factors or intensified by them. Both vision and hearing should be screened. Poor health does not necessarily adversely affect reading development. However, chronic conditions such as asthma, when combined with factors such as poverty, may hinder progress in reading.

Educational factors are at the heart of many instances of low achievement in reading. Inappropriate materials, poor pacing, lack of effective instruction, and overuse of skill and drill may lead to reading problems.

Failure to provide for the social nature of learning and the diversity that exists in today's classrooms can impede growth in reading. Poverty can also be a barrier to progress in reading and writing development.

## *Application Activities*

**1.** To get a concrete sense of a severe reading difficulty and what its effect might be, read the case study cited below. As you read, ask: What are the possible causes of Peter's difficulty? How was his difficulty treated? McCormick, S. (1994). A nonreader becomes a reader. *Reading Research Quarterly, 29,* 157–176.

**2.** Read *Success At Last! Helping Students with AD(H)D Achieve Their Potential* by C. Weaver (Ed.) (Portsmouth, NH: Heinemann, 1994), or another text about attention deficit disorder.

**3.** Choose one of the possible causes of reading difficulty and investigate it in more detail.

# Chapter 3

# Overview of Assessment

## *Using What You Know*

Have you ever had the feeling, after taking a test, that the test wasn't a valid indicator of your knowledge, that you really knew more but the test did not allow you to show it, or that the test seemed unfair because it asked questions about topics not covered in the class? This chapter looks at some basic principles of assessment. It also looks at a number of different kinds of tests and the ways in which tests and other assessment devices can be chosen and used so as to provide the most accurate and useful information.

## *Anticipation Guide*

Read each of the following statements. Put a check under "Agree" or "Disagree" to show how you feel about each one. If you can, discuss your responses with classmates.

| | Agree | Disagree |
|---|---|---|
| **1.** In assessment, how a student gets an answer is more important than whether the answer is right or wrong. | ______ | ______ |
| **2.** Most tests don't yield useful information because they distort the reading/writing process. | ______ | ______ |
| **3.** In general, informal tests are better than formal ones. | ______ | ______ |
| **4.** One of the best ways to assess a student is to teach him or her in a weak area and see how much and how well she or he learns. | ______ | ______ |
| **5.** Time spent assessing low-achieving readers would be better spent instructing them. | ______ | ______ |

## *Principles of Effective Assessment*

Tracy, a fourth-grader, was a puzzle. She had above-average academic ability, and her word recognition skills were superior. She could read multisyllabic words with ease. Her oral reading was smooth and expressive. However, her comprehension was surprisingly poor. On both informal and formal tests, she missed all but the easiest questions. The test results revealed that Tracy had a comprehension problem, but they didn't suggest any reasons for Tracy's problem, nor were there any suggestions in the results as to the best way to teach Tracy. The testing had been static. It provided the end product of Tracy's reading achievement and academic ability, but it provided no information about the processes Tracy used. It didn't indicate what Tracy needed in order to perform adequately. Nor did it suggest how much help Tracy might need. Also missing was information about other important aspects of Tracy's performance: How did she respond to classroom instruction? Were there some kinds of tasks that she enjoyed or found easier than others? How did she feel about herself as a learner? What was her relationship with her classmates? What was her family life like? Was her family supportive of her efforts in school?

> Although assessment and instruction are placed in separate sections in this text, in practice, the two are blended. Assessment should be an integral part of all instruction.

What Tracy required was an assessment that was both interactive and dynamic. An **interactive** assessment considers both top-down and bottom-up factors. It also postulates that the reader changes as the task changes. For instance, the student who daydreams her way through a science article may read a biography of her favorite sports star with intense interest. An interactive approach to assessment recognizes that five major factors have to be considered: the reader, the text, the techniques being used, the reading or writing task involved, and the situational context in which the reading or writing is performed (Walker, 1992). The student who is lost in a large group situation may do quite well when taught in a small group. A student who responds negatively to a technique that is teacher directed might be more positive when taught by a method that relies more heavily on student input.

> Standards for assessment endorsed by the International Reading Association and National Council of Teachers of English (IRA/NCTE Joint Task Force on Assessment, 1994) stress that the primary purpose of assessment is to improve teaching and learning.

Because reading and writing are such complex activities, the assessment must also be multidimensional. It should include the following areas: general cognitive ability; other cognitive processes, such as memory and associative learning; the ability to use independent learning strategies in decoding, comprehension, and study skills; vocabulary knowledge; writing; spelling; and handwriting. Language development and physical factors, such as overall health, vision, and hearing, as well as home and school factors should be considered. Being holistic and interactive, the assessment needs to consider the interplay among the factors and how they affect each other. For instance, chronic ear infections may impair hearing, which may make learning phonics more difficult. This, in turn, lowers the student's self-esteem as a learner, which reduces effort and achievement.

Assessment also needs to be realistic. The best assessment is that which is closest to the skill or strategy in its actual use in the classroom (Meltzer, 1993). For instance, the *Informal Reading Inventory,* which is presented in Chapter 4, is one of the most effective assessment devices because it involves actual oral and silent reading and oral retellings or the oral answering of questions, which is similar to the way reading is conducted in the classroom.

## Dynamic Assessment

Assessment must reflect changing academic demands as students move up through the grades and encounter higher-level comprehension and study tasks.

Assessment must also be dynamic. It should not just measure what the student can do now, it should also predict the student's potential for change. For instance, two students may both do poorly on a test of word reading ability. Although their scores may be identical, their potential for learning the words might be very different. But how does the teacher know this? The solution is to teach the students a sampling of the unknown words and to carefully note what each student required in order to learn them. You might do this in a number of ways. First, select the words to be taught. You might choose from those missed on the test, seven words of medium difficulty. Teach the words by using a sight or memory approach. Place the words on cards. Display a word and ask the student to read it. If the student is able to read it, say the word and have the student repeat it. Point out distinctive features of the word, and use it in a sentence. Each time you say the word, point to it. Then present the next word in the same way. After all the words have been presented, shuffle them, and present them again in the same way they were presented the first time. Keep a record of the number of words that the student is able to read correctly. See how many trials it takes the student to learn all seven words, but set a limit of approximately ten trials so that the student doesn't become frustrated. If the student learns all the words in a few trials, then you can infer that the student has good word-learning ability and should make rapid progress.

If the student has difficulty with the task, try other teaching approaches. Use a phonics or word-building approach as explained in Chapter 8. In a dynamic assessment you don't just find out what the student doesn't know, you explore the student's level of knowledge, the amount of instruction needed to teach the element, and, in some instances, the way in which the student learns best. Dynamic assessment answers the all-important question: How does the student learn? What must be done in order for the student to learn? As such, instruction is linked to assessment.

Dynamic assessment is based on Vygotsky's view of learning (Haywood, Brown, & Wingenfeld, 1990), which holds that children learn higher level concepts through their interactions with peers and adults (Vygotsky, 1978). Vygotsky suggested that in addition to measuring student's current functioning level, we should also assess how well the child might do if helped by an adult. The difference between what a child can do on his own and what the child can do with the assistance of an adult or more knowledgeable peer, is known as the **zone of proximal development.** This is what is measured in dynamic assessment.

**Zone of proximal development:** difference between what students can do on their own and what they can do under the guidance of an adult or more knowledgeable peer.

In a sense, dynamic assessment provides a more realistic estimate of students' potential because it yields information about their learning ability. As Feurstein, Rand, and Hoffman (1979) have shown in their research, lack of knowledge may be mistaken for lack of ability to acquire that knowledge. Dynamic assessment has the potential for providing a more accurate, fairer estimate of learning ability in children who may not have had adequate opportunity to learn because of an impoverished home life or substandard schooling.

**Administering a Dynamic Assessment**

In general, administering a dynamic assessment involves the following steps:

*Step 1: Gather Baseline Data*

Administer the test the way it is normally given. This will provide baseline data.

*Step 2: Teach and Record*

Provide assistance or instruction so that the student can reach an acceptable level of performance on the task or a sample of the task. Record the amount and type of help required to reach an acceptable level.

*Step 3: Retest*

Give the original test once again and chart improvement from first to final testing. Degree of change suggests the extent to which students will benefit from instruction.

*Step 4: Evaluate Intervention*

Note the student's response to your assistance. What helped? What didn't? Is the student able to apply or use in new context what she or he learned? Also note any difficulties the student had during the learning trials. Then describe the conditions and procedures most likely to improve the skill or strategy tested (Haywood, Brown, & Wingenfeld, 1990; Haywood,1993).

Dynamic assessment is time-consuming. But for students with severe reading problems, dynamic assessment could mean finding techniques that work. "In such cases, the cost of dynamic assessment may be much less than the cost of *not* finding the answers to important educational questions" (Haywood, Brown, & Wingenfeld, 1990, p. 417).

## *Assisted Testing*

In assisted testing you ask: "How much help and what kind of help do I have to provide in order for a student to perform successfully?" You start off by giving a little assistance and then increasing it until the student can respond correctly.

Assisted testing is an easy-to-apply form of dynamic assessment in which students are given cues or prompts to see how much help they need in order to respond correctly (D. Johnson, 1993). At first, provide an easy cue. Then gradually provide more substantial cues until the student is able to respond correctly, or you run out of prompts. Based on the cues that you've given, determine what the student already knows or can do and what she or he would need to know in order to be able to perform successfully. For instance, on a test of word recognition, the student responded "I don't know," to many of the words. Going back over a sampling of the missed words, the teacher first asked the student if there was any part of a missed word that she knew. If that didn't work, the teacher covered up the first portion of the word and had the student read the second portion. Then uncovering the second portion, the teacher had the student read that, combine the two parts, and read the whole word. For instance, for the word *morning,* the student said she could not read any parts. But when the teacher covered up all but the *or,* the student had no difficulty reading it. When *m* was uncovered, the student was able to add *m* to *or* to form *mor* and then, reading the *ing*, added it to *n* and combined all the elements into the word *morning*. With similar help, the student was able to decode a number of the multisyllabic words that she had gotten wrong on the first pass through. The teacher concluded that the student knew the elements that the words were composed of, but needed help locating known elements in multisyllabic words and then reconstructing the words.

On the basis of the initial testing the teacher would have concluded that the student simply couldn't handle polysyllabic words. Using assisted testing, she could see that the student had some knowledge of multisyllabic words. The teacher also had discovered a way of helping the student learn what she needed to know in order to be more successful decoding polysyllabic words. Figure 3-1 shows an analysis of the dynamic testing of the student, including recommendations for future instruction.

**Title of Assessment:** *Basic Reading Inventory, Graded Word Lists B*

**Original Results**

| Level | Number Correct |
|---|---|
| *pp* | *20/20* |
| *p* | *19/20* |
| *1* | *17/20* |
| *2* | *17/20* |
| *3* | *10/20* |

*Did well with single-syllable words but had difficulty with multisyllabic words.*

**Retest Results**

| Level | Number Correct |
|---|---|
| *pp* | *20/20* |
| *p* | *20/20* |
| *1* | *19/20* |
| *2* | *19/20* |
| *3* | *16/20* |

*Was able to read 11/17 multisyllabic words previously missed.*

**Assistance Provided**

*Showed student how to look for familiar word parts in words she had difficulty with and use those familiar parts to reconstruct whole word. Needed four prompts.*

**Recommendations**

*Needs to be taught multisyllabic patterns, especially the less common ones. Needs more instruction in use of decoding strategies. Stress application of strategies.*

**FIGURE 3-1 Dynamic Assessment Analysis**

## Level of Knowledge

Finding a student's knowledge level provides a realistic starting point. Often we assume that problem learners have no knowledge in a particular area and we waste time reteaching what they already know.

When assessing students, also try to determine their level of knowledge. If they can't respond on a higher level, move to a lower level. In the Durrell Analysis of Difficulty (Durrell & Catterson, 1980), alphabet knowledge is tested on five levels. The highest level requires students to write the letters of the alphabet. If the students can't do that, they are asked to identify a series of letters. Failing to do that, students recognize letters by choosing from four letters the one that the teacher says. Students who can't do that are asked to match letters from memory. For example, shown the letter *m,* which is then removed from sight, the student picks the *m* from a series of four letters. The lowest level is a straight match. The students, while looking at the letter *m,* select its match from a series of four letters. The point of having these levels is to find out where the students are in terms of alphabet knowledge so that instruction can proceed from there.

All too often, when students miss an item or a series of items, we assume they have no knowledge in that area. However, using a level of knowledge approach, we retest until we determine on what level the students are operating. For instance, if a student can't read the word *where* on a test of word reading, the task could be made into one of recognition rather than recall by saying the word *where,* and then having the student pick it out from among two or three other words.

Also vary the mode of response. If students are unable to write a summary, perhaps they can give one orally. If students have difficulty with certain questions, you might reword them. Perhaps, they were too vague or too complex (D. Johnson, 1993).

## Trial Teaching

Also known as diagnostic teaching (Walker, 1992), **trial teaching** is based on the information yielded by an assessment. It works best if the assessment has been dynamic because a dynamic assessment provides insight into the student's learning processes. Constructing hypotheses based on an analysis of assessment data, you, in cooperation with the student, construct a tentative approach that you feel will work best. You also carefully monitor the instruction to make necessary changes in approach, materials, setting, pacing, or any other aspect of the situation. As Lipson and Wixson (1991) note, diagnostic teaching is "thoughtfully planned" and contains "our best guesses" about what may work for a particular student (p. 74).

Fittingly, the first step in trial teaching is to consult with the student. Discuss with the student the results of the assessment and explain that there are several ways of helping her or him and that you—teacher and student—will be trying out different ways of teaching and different materials to find out which works best (Roswell & Natchez, 1989). Depending on the skill or strategy being taught, the student is invited to choose materials and, in some instances, activities. Using your strongest hypothesis, try out one or more instructional procedures. If one doesn't work out, try another.

See Chapter 6 in this text for more information on trial teaching.

Diagnosis doesn't stop with dynamic or assisted testing or even trial teaching. It's an ongoing process. As Doris Johnson (1993) notes, "It goes on forever." In assessment, you

Assessment should emphasize the students' strengths so that these provide a foundation for instruction.

create a hypothesis and evaluate it through testing, including dynamic testing, observation, trial teaching, and carefully monitoring the student's performance. In a sense, every lesson that you teach should be a trial or diagnostic one.

**Essential Steps in the Assessment Process**

As adapted from Kibby (1995), the assessment process consists of six essential steps.

*Step 1.*
Establish an estimate of the levels on which the student is operating.

*Step 2.*
Gather and evaluate information about students' reading/writing strengths and weaknesses.

*Step 3.*
Assess and evaluate students' teaching–learning situation. Through dynamic testing and trial teaching, determine under what circumstance students learn best. Also assess the home situation.

*Step 4.*
Evaluate materials used in the students' program.

*Step 5.*
Integrate information and design a long-term program.

*Step 6.*
Continually assess and evaluate the program and make modifications as necessary. In general you will be asking the following questions:

- On what levels are students functioning?
- What are the students' potential for growth?
- What are the students' strengths and weaknesses in reading and writing?
- What are the students' most immediate or most essential needs in reading and writing?
- What would be the most effective materials for these students?
- Under what circumstances and in what setting would these students learn best?
- What are the most effective techniques or approaches for teaching these students?
- Are there any physical, psychological, social, or other factors that need to be addressed in order for students to do their best?
- How might the home, larger community, and school work together to help students?

To answer these questions you will need assessment instruments, which are devices for gathering information about students' performance.

## *Authentic Assessment*

Every child can learn, given the right kind of instruction, materials, tasks, and situation. The purpose of assessment is to determine the optimal learning circumstances for a particular student.

Given an interactive transactional theory of reading, which is based on the premise that students use both top-down and bottom-up processes to construct meaning, it follows that assessment should involve the kinds of reading and writing tasks that students are called on to perform in and out of school—reading whole books, studying texts, and writing stories or letters. Although the term *assessment* might conjure up visions of tests, testing is just one way of getting information about students' reading and writing performance. You will also use observations, interviews, questionnaires, and samples of students' work. In addition, student records and portfolios can provide insight into the students' reading and writing experiences and capabilities. Portfolios, which are collections of samples of students' writing and reading, are especially rich sources of information.

This chapter will provide an overview of tests frequently used in literacy assessment and and some basic measurement concepts. Chapter 4 will explore the informal reading inventory and related tests. Chapter 5 will focus on gaining insight into students' reading and writing processes using observations, interviews, questionnaires, work samples, and formal and informal tests.

## *Tests*

Although many traditional reading tests have been recently modified to reflect a more holistic view of reading, most aren't very effective measures of students' ability to construct meaning. While many of the newer group-reading tests feature longer passages, including some drawn from children's books, they don't require students to create meaning. Rather, they provide students with a series of multiple choice items so that they select rather than create responses. In addition, higher-level skills are neglected. Furthermore, group tests generally assess the product rather than the process of reading. Tests results may indicate the percentage of answers correct, or compare students with others who have taken the test, but they don't generally provide insight into the strategies students use to respond to test items.

There are some encouraging improvements in group-reading tests. For instance, the fourth edition of the *Stanford Diagnostic Reading Tests* includes three supplementary devices designed to provide insight into processes used by readers: a reading strategies survey designed to determine which strategies readers use; a reading questionnaire that probes interests, attitudes, and background knowledge; and a story retelling section in which students summarize what they have read. In addition, major tests makers have introduced a number of **performance-based** measures. In performance assessment, students "demonstrate their level or competence or knowledge by creating a product or response" (Hiebert, Valencia, & Afflerbach, 1994, p. 11). In a performance-based test known as *Goals* (Harcourt), students respond to text by writing an answer, completing a diagram, or drawing a picture. In the CTB Performance Assessment (CTB/McGraw-Hill), students working in groups use many written sources of information to construct a written response to a problem or situation.

**Performance-based measures** require students to complete tasks similar to those in the school or out-of-school environment. Examples: writing an essay after reading a literary selection or assembling a portfolio of one's written work.

Despite their shortcomings, the traditional group tests of reading and writing are predominant. If results of group tests are available and interpreted with care, they can provide useful information. They can function as screening devices. Low scores on group tests can indicate possible problems. Individuals with low scores might be given individual assessments. Low scores by groups of students in key areas such as comprehension or vocabulary development might suggest the need for changes in the instructional program or materials.

## *Norm-Referenced versus Criterion-Referenced Tests*

### *Norm-Referenced Tests*

**Norm-referenced test:** the performance of students is compared to that of a norming or sample group.

Group tests of reading and writing generally fall into one of two categories: norm-referenced or criterion-referenced. In a ***norm-referenced test,*** students are compared with a sample of others who are in the same grade or are the same age. The score indicates whether students' performance is average, above average, or below average. Scores are commonly reported in one or more of the following ways:

**Percentile rank:** the most used score for norm-referenced tests of reading and writing.

- Raw score is the total number correct. It has no meaning until transferred into a percentile rank, grade equivalent, or other score.
- *Percentile rank* indicates where a student's score falls on a ranking of percentages from 1 to 99. A percentile rank of 10 indicates that the students did better than 10 percent of the norm group. A rank of 50 is average and indicates that the student did better than 50 percent of the norm group. Percentile rank is the most frequently used norm score. However, percentile ranks are not equal units. A percentile rank of 80 does not mean that the student did twice as well as a student with a percentile rank of 40. Therefore, percentile ranks should not be added, subtracted, divided, or multiplied, or used for subtest comparison.
- Grade-equivalent scores characterize performance as being equivalent to that of other students in a particular grade. A grade equivalent score of 6.2 indicates that the student answered the same number of items as the average sixth-grader in the second month of that grade. The grade equivalent score does not indicate at what level the student can read. A score of 6.2 does not mean that a student is reading on a sixth-grade level. Grade-equivalent scores are most meaningful when the test students have taken is at the right level and the score is not more than a year above or a year below average. Grade-equivalent scores are misleading and easily misunderstood and so should be used with care (Gunning, 1996).
- Normal curve equivalents (NCEs) place students on a scale of 1 through 99. The main difference between NCEs and percentile ranks is that NCEs represent equal units and so can be added and subtracted and used for comparing performance on subtests.
- Stanine is a combination of the words *standard* and *nine* and describes a nine-point scale. The stanines 4, 5, and 6 are average points, with 1, 2, and 3 being below average and 7, 8, and 9 above average. Stanines are useful when making comparisons among subtests.
- Scaled scores are a continuous ranking of scores from the lowest levels of a series of norm-referenced tests through the highest levels—from kindergarten or first grade through high school. Scaled scores, which range from 000 to 999, are useful for tracking long-term growth.

Many of the scores provided for a norm-referenced test are based on the concept of the normal curve. According to this concept, if a large number of people took a test and the scores were depicted graphically, most of the scores would fall in the middle. As scores fell more and more above or below average, there would be fewer cases so that a bell shaped curve would be formed as in Figure 3-2. A line drawn through the middle would depict the average or mean score. In addition to having a mean, scores have a standard deviation. The standard deviation indicates the degree of deviation from the mean. The more the scores vary, the higher the standard deviation. Because of the shape of the curve, about 68 percent of the cases fall within one standard deviation above or below the mean. Close to 96 percent fall within plus or minus two standard deviations. And nearly 100 percent fall within three standard deviations. Figure 3-2 shows standard deviations and how norm-referenced test scores relate to the normal curve and to each other. Also shown are scores from two intelligence tests: the Wechsler scales and the Stanford-Binet. Both have a mean of 100, but the Wechsler scales have a standard deviation of 15 and the Stanford-Binet has a standard deviation of 16.

**Criterion-referenced test:** student performance is measured against a standard. A typical standard of performance on a criterion-referenced comprehension test is 75%.

### *Criterion-Referenced Tests*

Instead of comparing students with each other, a practice that fosters competition, **criterion-referenced tests** compare students' performance with a criterion or standard. On measures of comprehension, a typical criterion is 75 percent. On measures, such as knowledge of the letters of the alphabet or initial consonants, the criterion might be set at

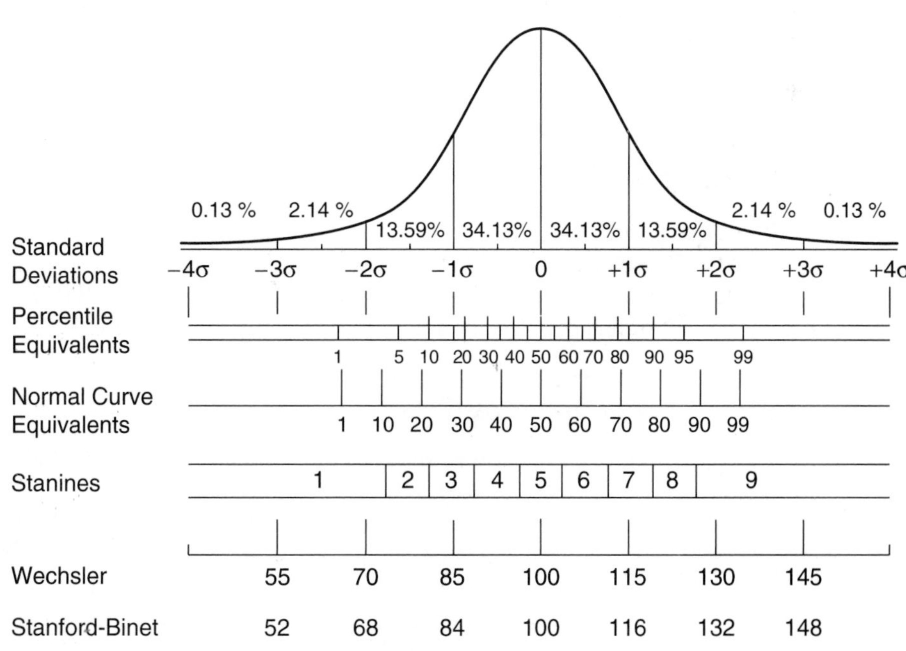


**FIGURE 3-2 Comparison of Norm-Referenced Scores**

100 percent. One problem with criterion-referenced tests is that the standard is set arbitrarily. For instance, no one actually tries out the test with a representative group of students to set what a reasonable criterion or standard might be. However, criterion-referenced tests, since they indicate how well students did on specific reading and writing tests, provide information that can be used to plan instruction.

**Benchmark:** standard of performance against which students' achievement might be assessed. An end-of-first-grade benchmark might be the ability to read an excerpt from a Frog and Toad book with 95% word recognition and 75% comprehension.

**Benchmarks.** One form of criterion-referenced assessment is the benchmark. The **benchmark** is a description of a key task that students are expected to perform. For instance, in one intervention program for struggling readers, the benchmark is that they be able to read a children's book entitled *A Kiss for Little Bear* (Minarik, 1961) (Hiebert, 1994). Benchmarks need not be tied to a specific book but might be stated in more general terms:

- Uses context and phonics cues to decode difficult words
- Can read fourth-grade material and retell the main events or details in the selection

### *Survey versus Diagnostic Tools*

Reading tests can also be categorized as being survey or diagnostic. Survey tests typically provide an overview of general comprehension and word knowledge. Diagnostic tests assess a number of areas or assess key areas in greater depth. The *Stanford Diagnostic Reading Test,* one of the best known of the group diagnostic tests, assesses comprehension, reading or listening vocabulary, word analysis skills, and, at higher levels, the ability to scan. A list of survey and diagnostic tests is presented in Tables 3-1 and 3-2.

### *Individual Tests*

In addition to group tests, there are a number of individual survey and diagnostic tests. There is the *Gray Oral Reading Test,* that assesses only oral reading. Also there are tests such as the *Slosson Oral Reading Test* and the reading subtest of the *WRAT (Wide Range Achievement Test)* that only test the ability to read orally lists of words.

### *Formal versus Informal Tests*

**Standardized test:** assessment tasks and administration are carefully specified so that anyone taking the test does so under similar conditions. The term *standardized test* is also used to mean a norm-referenced test.

Tests can also be categorized as being formal or informal. Formal tests are **standardized.** They are designed to be given according to a standard set of circumstances. These tests have sets of directions, which are to be followed exactly. They may also have time limits. All norm-referenced tests are standardized. The advantage of formal standardized tests is that typically they have been constructed with care and tried out on hundreds or thousands of students.

Informal tests generally do not have a set of standard directions, so there is a degree of flexibility in how they are given. In fact, the main

**TABLE 3-1 Survey Reading Tests: Norm-Referenced**

**Group Tests**

| Name | Publisher | Grades | Skill Areas |
|---|---|---|---|
| California Achievement Test (CAT) | CTB/McGraw-Hill | K–12 | comprehension, vocabulary |
| Comprehensive Test of Basic Skills (CTBS) | CTB/McGraw-Hill | K–12 | comprehension, vocabulary |
| Degrees of Reading Power | Touchstone | 1–College | comprehension |
| Gates–MacGinitie Reading Test | Riverside | K–12 | comprehension, vocabulary |
| Iowa Tests of Basic Skills (ITBS) | Riverside | K–8 | comprehension, vocabulary |
| Iowa Tests of Achievement and Proficiency | Riverside | 9–12 | comprehension, vocabulary |
| Metropolitan Achievement Tests | CTB/McGraw-Hill | K–12 | comprehension, vocabulary |
| Nelson–Denny | Riverside | 9–13 | comprehension, vocabulary, reading rate |
| Stanford Achievement Test | CTB/McGraw-Hill | K–12 | comprehension, vocabulary |

**Individual Tests**

| Name | Publisher | Grades | Skill Areas |
|---|---|---|---|
| Kaufman Test of Educational Achievement (K-TEA) | AGS | 1–12 | comprehension, decoding |
| Peabody Individual Achievement Test Revised (PIAT-R) | AGS | K–12 | comprehension, letter and word recognition |

advantage of informal tests is their flexibility. They may be designed to assess almost any skill or area, and may be tailor-made for any population. Informal tests are typically constructed by teachers. Their disadvantage is that they may not be constructed with sufficient care, and their reliability and validity may be unknown. One of the most widely used assessment devices in the field of literacy is the informal reading inventory, which is explored in the next chapter.

## *Evaluating Assessment Devices*

**Reliability:** the consistency of an assessment device. It is the degree to which the device would yield similar results if given to the same person or group again.

### *Reliability*

In order to be useful, assessment devices must be both reliable and valid. A reliable device is one that yields consistent results. For a test, ***reliability*** means, that if students retook the test they would get approximately the same score. For an observation guide, it means that if two or three observers were rating the same student at the same time,

**TABLE 3-2 Diagnostic Reading Tests**

| Name | Publisher | Grades | Skill Areas |
|---|---|---|---|
| **Group Tests** | | | |
| California Diagnostic Reading Test (CDRT) | CTB/McGraw-Hill | 1–12 | comprehension, vocabulary, decoding, reading speed, study skills |
| Stanford Diagnostic Reading Tests (SDRT) | Harcourt | 1–13 | comprehension, vocabulary, decoding, scanning |
| **Individual Tests** | | | |
| Diagnostic Assessment of Reading with Trial Teaching Strategies | Riverside | 1–6 | comprehension, decoding, oral reading, reading levels, listening capacity, trial teaching |
| Diagnostic Reading Scales-Revised | CTB/McGraw-Hill | 1–7+ | comprehension, oral reading, word reading, reading levels, decoding |
| Durrell Analysis of Reading Difficulty | Harcourt | 1–6 | comprehension, oral reading, word reading, decoding, reading levels, letter knowledge, spelling, visual memory |
| Gates-McKillop-Horowitz Reading Diagnostic Tests | Teacher's College | 1–6 | comprehension, oral reading, word reading, decoding, auditory discrimination, blending, spelling, written expression |
| Woodcock Reading Mastery Tests-Revised | AGS | K–13 | comprehension, vocabulary, word reading, decoding, letter knowledge, visual-auditory (associative) learning |

their ratings would be similar. In the rating of essays, it means that a single rater would give the same essays similar ratings if she or he rated them on different occasions, or that the scores given by different raters to the same piece of writing would be similar.

### *Validity*

**Validity:** degree to which an assessment device measures what it intends to measure; also, the degree to which the results can be used to make an educational decision.

**Validity** means that a device measures what it says it measures, such as vocabulary, comprehension, rate of reading, attitude toward reading and so forth. It also means that the device will provide information that will be useful in making an instructional decision, deciding, for instance, whether students' comprehension or word recognition is adequate or if a program or approach is working (Farr & Carey, 1986). Moreover, the way a skill or strategy is assessed should be dictated by the way it was taught and the materials used. If students were taught to write brief summaries of informational text using their science books, then a multiple choice test that only requires them to select from four options the best summary of a brief, narrative piece would not be valid.

**Correlation coefficient:** statistical measure that expresses in mathematical terms the degree to which two variables are related.

For commercially produced tests, information about a test's reliability and validity are generally contained in the test administration or technical manual. Reliability is expressed as a **correlation coefficient.** A correlation coefficient can range from 0, which means no relationship, to 1, which means a perfect relationship, and can be positive or negative. For making decisions about a group, a correlation of .8 is adequate. However, when making individual decisions, a correlation of .9 is desired.

Validity may also be expressed as a coefficient of correlation. One way of indicating the validity of a new reading test, for instance, is to compare students' performance on the new test with their performance on an established test or some other criterion. The correlation should be high but not too high. A correlation of .9, for instance, would indicate that the tests are so closely related that they seem to be measuring the same thing, so what's the purpose of the new test? This type of validity is known as *statistical* or *concurrent validity.* Some tests also have *predictive validity.* That is, they predict how well a student will do on a related task at some later date. For instance, tests of alphabet knowledge and phonemic awareness given in kindergarten can be used to predict how students will do in reading in first grade. They would typically have correlations as high as .5 or .6, indicating a strong relationship between these factors and later success in reading.

Test makers also frequently include descriptions of construct and content validity. *Construct validity* is the degree to which a test relates to a theory or construct. The construct on which a test of phonological awareness is based is the theory that phonological processes are essential for the acquisition of reading skill. This theory is supported when students who have high scores in phonological awareness do well in reading. *Content* or *curricular validity* is the degree to which the content of a test reflects reading or tasks as they are taught in the schools. The best way to judge content or curricular validity is to see how close a match there is between what you teach and what the test assesses.

## *Standard Error of Measurement*

**Standard error of measurement:** estimate of the difference between the obtained score and what the score would be if the test were perfect.

In judging the quality of a test, it is also important to know the **standard error of measurement** (SEM). The SEM is a statistical estimate of the amount that a test score might vary if the test were given again and again. Although tests yield a particular score, that score should be thought of as a range of likely scores. For instance, if a norm-referenced test has a SEM of 5 percentile points and you got a score of 50, that means that if you retook that test there is a two-thirds (one standard deviation) chance that your score would fall between 45 and 55, which is plus or minus one SEM.

### *Fairness*

Tests, of course, should also be fair. As the Joint Task Force on Assessment (1994) notes, "Because traditional test makers have all too frequently designed assessment tools reflecting narrow cultural values, students and schools with different backgrounds and concern often have not been fairly assessed" (p. 41).

For additional information about tests, see the *Twelfth Mental Measurements Yearbook* (Conoley & Impara, 1995). This and previous yearbooks contain critical reviews of virtually all of the major tests of reading and writing.

## *Functional Level Assessment*

When group tests are used, struggling readers are often unfairly assessed. It is a widespread practice to administer the same norm-referenced or criterion-referenced test to an entire class, even though there may be a wide range of reading ability in that class. For instance, a seventh-grade student reading on a second-grade level would find a typical seventh-grade test to be extremely frustrating. Moreover, the test would yield misleading results. Norm-referenced tests have a bottom. As soon as the students answer a question or two on a seventh-grade level test, they might earn a grade-equivalent score of 3.5 or so. With a little bit of lucky guessing, students might achieve a grade equivalent score of fourth-grade or higher. Thus, the teacher might assume that the student can read on a fourth- or fifth-grade level, so that the results are that student has materials that are too difficult. In addition, the experience of taking a test that is far too difficult can be be very demeaning and discouraging.

The solution is to assess students on the level at which they are functioning (Gunning, 1982). For a seventh-grader reading on a second-grade level, this means giving the student a test that actually has second-grade material on it. If the material is too juvenile for the student, then you might use a test designed for older students or adults who are reading on a second-grade level. Another possible solution is to select a test that assesses a wide range of reading levels.

## *Summary*

An interactive process, assessment should consider the reader, the text, the techniques being used, the reading or writing task involved, and the context in which the reading or writing is performed. Assessment should also be dynamic. Through instruction provided after initial testing, or through trial or assisted teaching, it should attempt to discover what the student's true learning potential is and how the student learns best.

Assessment devices should be authentic. They should reflect the kinds of reading and and writing tasks that students undertake in and out of school. Because they consist mainly of brief passages and multiple choice items, traditional group tests have limited authenticity.

There are many different kinds of reading and writing tests. Tests can be norm-referenced or criterion-referenced. Norm-referenced tests compare a student's performance with that of a sample or norm group. Although they are most often reported in percentile ranks, test performance can also be expressed in stanines, normal curve equivalents, scaled scores, or grade equivalents. Criterion-referenced tests compare students' performance with a criterion or standard, which may be a percentage of answers correct, or a benchmark such as being able to read a book on a certain level. Tests can also be classified as being group or individual, survey or diagnostic, formal or informal. Some categories overlap. For instance, a test can be both criterion- and norm-referenced.

Tests are expected to meet standards of reliability and validity. A reliable test is one that yields the same approximate score if taken over and over again. A valid test is one that measures what it says it measures. In order to be valid, a test should also provide useful information for an educational decision. Kinds of validity include concurrent or statistical, predictive, curricular or content, and construct. Tests are not precise measures but have a standard error of measurement, which can be used to estimate the scores that a person would achieve if he took the same test over and over.

## *Application Activities*

**1.** Start a collection of sample informal and formal tests and other assessment devices that you might use. Also collect ideas for assessing students in reading and writing.

**2.** Examine a norm-referenced or criterion-referenced test. Note the skills being tested and the way they are being assessed. What does this suggest about the content validity of the test? What information does the testmaker provide about reliability, validity, and fairness? What suggestions, if any, does the test publisher give for using test results?

Chapter 4

# Placing Students: The Informal Reading Inventory and Related Measures

## Using What You Know

Have you ever had to read a book that was simply too difficult for you? How did you feel? How would you feel if, day after day, you were asked to read books that were too hard for you? What do you think might be the overall effect on your attitude and your progress? One of the most important decisions that you will make as a literacy teacher is matching students with materials that have an appropriate level of challenge. One of the best devices for placing students is the informal reading inventory or devices modeled on the inventory. A simple but powerful device, the inventory consists primarily of a series of selections that gradually grow more difficult.

## Anticipation Guide

Read each of the following statements. Put a check under "Agree" or "Disagree" to show how you feel about each one. If possible, discuss your responses with classmates.

| | Agree | Disagree |
|---|---|---|
| **1.** Although subjective, informal tests are more useful than formal tests. | ______ | ______ |
| **2.** When estimating a student's reading level, the most important factor is the ability to read words. | ______ | ______ |

3. When estimating a student's reading ability, silent reading performance is more important than oral reading. ________ ________
4. For most students, group tests provide adequate data about reading performance. ________ ________
5. Analyzing a student's errors is one of the best ways of diagnosing a reading difficulty. ________ ________

## *The Informal Reading Inventory*

**Informal reading inventory:** a series of passages that gradually increase in difficulty, used to assess oral reading and comprehension.

When properly administered and interpreted, the **informal reading inventory** (IRI), yields much of the information about a student that the reading teacher needs. Although it only takes about thirty minutes to administer, the informal reading inventory indicates the student's reading level and approximate level of language development. It provides insight into word analysis and comprehension strategies, background knowledge, work habits, and interests. Once you are familiar with the IRI, it can be used as a framework with which to observe and interpret students' reading behavior.

One of the most valid and reliable measures of reading, the IRI is the basis for a number of commercially produced diagnostic assessments as well as the running record, which is an essential ingredient in **Reading Recovery,** and the technique of miscue analysis, an important element in whole language assessment. Like many important developments in other fields, the IRI is simple and sensible. In its original form, administering an IRI was like having a customer try on shoes. The teacher had a series of graded readers and tried them on for size until finding the one that fit just right—neither too easy nor too difficult.

As originally conceived, inventories were constructed by teachers. Typically, IRIs were created using passages from basal readers. In keeping with the spirit of using children's books to teach reading, it is also possible to construct an inventory based on a series of children's books that increase in difficulty. (Instructions for creating an inventory can be found in M. Johnson, Kress, & Pikulski's (1987) *Informal Reading Inventories* 2nd ed. Teacher-constructed inventories are more valid because they reflect the types of materials you actually use in your class. Because of the time involved in creating an inventory, many teachers use commercially produced IRIs. Most commercial inventories range from a **preprimer** level through grade eight. However, the *Bader Reading and Language Inventory, Burns & Roe, Ekwall/Shanker,* the *Flynt-Cooter,* and the *Informal Reading-Thinking* inventories extend up through grade eleven or twelve, which makes them especially useful with older students. There are also specialized inventories such as *Reading Evaluation Adult Diagnosis* (Colvin & Root, 1982), which is distributed by Literacy Volunteers and contains an inventory designed for adults. A listing of commercial inventories is presented in Table 4-1.

Until recently, first-grade books were classified into five levels of difficulty: preprimer 1, preprimer 2, preprimer 3, primer, grade 1 reader.

Procedures for administering and interpreting inventories vary. The procedures presented in this text are drawn from those described in *Informal Reading Inventories* (Johnson, Kress, & Pikulski, 1987), which is a widely used, highly respected source.

**TABLE 4-1 Commercial Inventories**

| Name | Publisher | Grades | Skill Areas |
|---|---|---|---|
| Analytic Reading Inventory | Woods & Moe | Grades 1–8 | |
| Bader Reading and Language Inventory | Bader | Grade 1–12 & adult | Also assesses phonics, language, spelling, and emergent literacy. |
| Basic Reading Inventory | J. Johns | Grades 1–8 | |
| Classroom Reading Inventory | N. Silvaroli | Grades 1–8 | Forms C and D can be used with older readers. |
| Ekwall/Shanker Reading Inventory | Ekwall/Shanker | Grades 1–12 | |
| Informal Reading-Thinking Inventory | Manzo/Manzo/McKenna | Grades 1–11 | Includes assessment of prior knowledge and higher-level comprehension. |
| Flynt-Cooter Reading Inventory for the Classroom | Flynt & Cooter | Grades 1–12 | Features longer pieces, retellings, picture reading and an observation guide to assess emergent reading. |
| Informal Reading Inventory | Burns & Roe | Grades 1–12 | |
| Qualitative Reading Inventory | Leslie & Caldwell | Grades 1–8 | Features longer pieces and retelling procedures. |
| Stieglitz Informal Reading Inventory | Stieglitz | Grades 1–8 | Assesses emergent literacy and prior knowledge. |

One problem with testing older low-achieving readers is that the easiest passages in most inventories are written for young children and would be both demeaning and boring for older students. However, the *Classroom Reading Inventory* (Silvaroli, 1994) has four forms, two of which contain passages, even at the easiest levels, that are appropriate for older students. Forms A and B are designed for elementary school students. Form C is meant for students in junior high, and Form D is designed for assessing high school students and adults. Even at their easiest levels, Forms C and D present selections that deal with cars, sports, and other mature topics. The *Bader Reading and Language Inventory* also has a form designed for older students and one created for adults.

The *Bader Reading and Language Inventory* has a third form specifically designed for adult readers. It ranges from preprimer through grades 11–12.

The typical IRI, whether teacher-created or commercially produced, consists of two major components: graded word lists and graded passages. The graded word lists consist of separate lists of ten to twenty words on a preprimer through an eighth- or twelfth-grade level. The passages consist of a series of graded selections beginning at preprimer level and extending to eighth, ninth, or twelfth grade. Generally, there are two passages at each level, one to be read orally and one to be read silently. Some inventories provide only an oral passage and, to save time, some teachers omit the administration of the silent reading passages in inventories that assess both oral and silent reading. However, omitting silent reading passages lessens both the validity and reliability of the IRI. Moreover, in some students, there is a marked difference between performance on oral and silent reading passages.

Besides the comparison of oral and silent reading performance, other important information is lost when the administration of the silent reading passage is omitted. The teacher is unable to observe the strategies that a student uses when reading silently and is unable to gauge silent reading speed. The teacher also misses the opportunity to note whether the students finger point, subvocalize, or engage in other similar behaviors that may be symptomatic that the material is too difficult and/or the readers are inefficient.

Administering the inventory is fairly straightforward. The inventory is administered individually and begins with the student being asked to read the words on the word lists, starting with the easiest list. Using the results of the word list administration, the teacher locates a probable starting point for the reading of the graded passages. Beginning with passages where comprehension and word recognition are virtually flawless, the student continues to read until the material is obviously too difficult. As the student reads, the teacher carefully observes the student's comprehension, word recognition, use of strategies, oral language development, and how he or she handles the testing situation. The better the observation, the greater the insight obtained.

## *The IRI as a Placement Device*

A primary purpose of the IRI is to obtain placement information. The teacher needs to know what level of material is most likely to produce optimum results. This is especially crucial for low-achieving readers, who tend to be given materials that are too difficult for them, a condition that leads to frustration and makes it impossible for them to apply a balanced set of reading strategies (Clay, 1985).

The IRI yields four levels: independent, instructional, frustration, and listening capacity. As its name suggests, the **independent level** is the point at which students can read on their own, without any help from teachers, parents, or peers. They recognize at least 99 percent of the words and comprehension is nearly perfect. At the **instructional level,** students can read at least ninety-five out of one hundred words and they recall at least 75 percent of what they read. If given instructional assistance, they can read with confidence and competence. At the **frustration level,** the material is simply too difficult for the student to read, even with assistance. Students miss ten or more words out of a hundred and/or remember only half of what they read. Students may exhibit lip movement during silent reading, may be easily distracted, or may engage in hair twisting, grimacing, or other stress-signaling behaviors (Johnson, Kress, & Pikulski, 1987).

Once a student has reached the frustration level, the teacher reads the inventory selections to her or him in order to assess the student's ability to understand written language when decoding isn't a factor. The highest level at which the student can understand 75 percent of the material that is read to her or him is the **listening capacity.**

Although guidelines vary somewhat, the most accepted standards for the four levels are presented in Table 4-2. Powell (1971) and others have argued for lower standards and/or standards that vary according to

**Independent level:** level of material that a student can read with at least 99% word recognition and 90% comprehension.

**Instructional level:** level of material that a student can read with at least 95% word recognition and 75% comprehension.

**Frustration level:** level of material where a student's word recognition is 90% or less **or** comprehension is 50% or less.

**Listening capacity:** level of material that a student can understand with 75% comprehension when it is read to him or her.

**TABLE 4-2 Informal Reading Inventory Standards**

| Level | Word Recognition in Context | | Comprehension |
|---|---|---|---|
| Independent | 99% | (and) | 95% |
| Instructional | 95% | (and) | 75% |
| Frustration | 90% | (or) | 50% |
| Listening Capacity | | | 75% |

grade levels. However, as noted in Chapter 1, research indicates that students do best when they can cope with at least 95 to 98 percent of the words (Berliner, 1981; Biemiller, 1994; Gambrell, Wilson, & Gantt, 1981). Indeed, Enz (1989) found that relaxing IRI standards resulted in a deterioration of both achievement and attitude. Students placed according to higher standards spent a greater proportion of time on task, had a higher success rate, and had a more positive attitude toward reading.

## *Administering the Word Lists Tests*

The graded word lists provide a starting point for administration of the graded passages. They also yield valuable information about a student's ability to recognize words immediately and to use word-level processing strategies to decode words that are not immediately recognized. In a sense, the task is artificial because in actual reading words are generally encountered in running text, thus providing the opportunity to use context. Since the words in the word lists tests are presented in isolation, students have no recourse but to use word analysis strategies; so this brief, but important, test provides excellent insight into a student's ability to use phonics, syllabic analysis, and other word-level decoding skills.

The *Flynt-Cooter Reading Inventory* uses brief sentences that gradually increase in difficulty rather than lists of words to establish a starting point.

In order to get the most information from word lists tests, they should be given in a timed (flash) and an untimed (analysis) administration. In a timed administration, each word is flashed for a second, so that the student is assessed on her or his ability to pronounce words immediately, without recourse to decoding. The student should be seated to the side of you and should be reading from her or his copy. Use a second copy for marking, but keep that on your desk or a clipboard.

Using two three-by-five cards, flash each word for a second as shown in Figure 4-1. A word is flashed by pulling down the card in the left hand while keeping the card in the right hand in place for one second. As the word is being exposed, it is important that the card in the right hand be held steadily and not dragged down, preventing the student from getting a clear, unobscurred look at the word. To make sure that the word is exposed for a second, but no longer, say, "One thousand," to yourself and then snap the opening closed by pushing down the card in the right hand. Continue to flash the words in this fashion until the student misreads a word or is unable to read a word within one second. At that point, record the student's response in the flash column and open up the cards so the student can then analyze the word she or he missed. The student is then encouraged to use word-analysis skills to try to figure out the word. The student's response is recorded in the untimed column, and testing is resumed. Continue testing until the student misses half the words under the flash

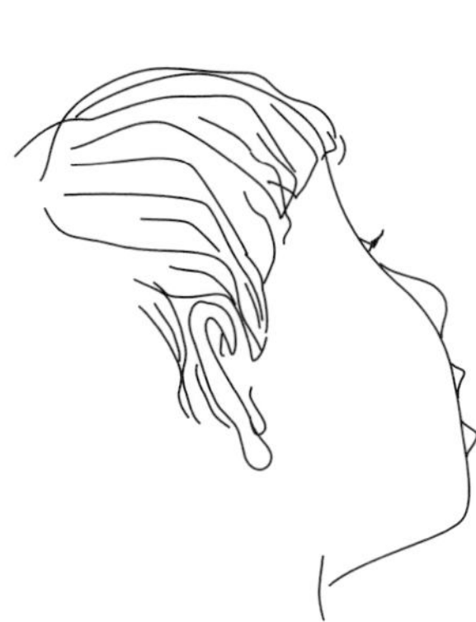

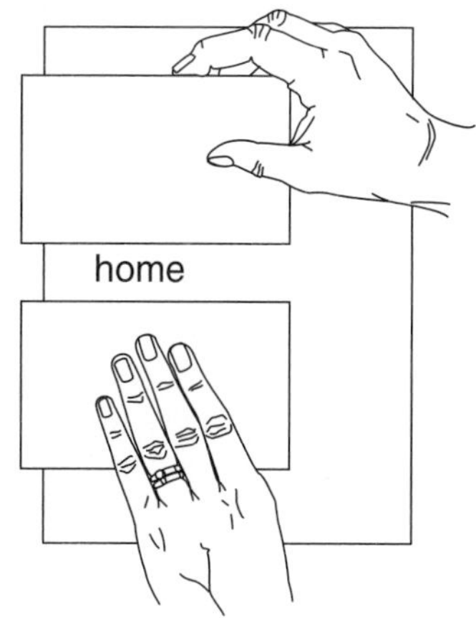


**FIGURE 4-1**

condition on two consecutive levels. Extending the testing to a level where the student is meeting difficult words provides you with the opportunity to observe the student's word-analysis skills in isolation in full operation.

When the student makes an error, record her or his performance. If the student mispronounces or substitutes a word, write the mispronunciation or substitution. If the student says, "I don't know," write *dk* in the blank. Write *o* if the student makes no response. A check indicates a correct response. (However, to keep the test moving, you need not record checks in the flash column until later. Since you don't need to write anything in the flash blank unless the student fails to respond or makes an error, you can assume that the blanks that haven't been written in are correct items.)

If a student reads correctly a word that she missed on flash, then place a check in the untimed column. If a student makes the same mistake, record it with a check with a tail. If the student gives a second mispronunciation or substitution, one that is different from the first, record that. It is important to record a student's errors because they provide information about the kinds of elements he has mastered and those with which he is having difficulty. A list of symbols used to mark the word lists test is presented in Figure 4-2. A marked word lists test is presented in Figure 4-3.

| | Flash | Untimed | | |
|---|---|---|---|---|
| saw | ✓ | | ✓ | (Correct response). |
| then | *they* | | *they* | (Substitution. The substitution is written on the line). |
| wet | *we* | ✓ (with tail) | ✓ (with tail) | (Made same error on untimed as on flash). |
| was | *dk* | *dk* | *dk* | (Said, "Don't know."). |
| boy | *0* | *0* | *0* | (No response). |

**FIGURE 4-2 Word-Lists Test Marking Symbols**

| | Flash | Untimed |
|---|---|---|
| 1. me | ✓ | |
| 2. get | ✓ | |
| 3. home | ✓ | |
| 4. not | *no* | ✓ |
| 5. he | ✓ | |
| 6. tree | *tee* | ✓ |
| 7. girl | ✓ | |
| 8. take | *tack* | ✓^ |
| 9. book | ✓ | |
| 10. milk | *more* | *my* |
| 11. dog | ✓ | |
| 12. all | ✓ | |
| 13. apple | ✓ | |
| 14. like | ✓ | |
| 15. go | ✓ | |
| 16. farm | ✓ | |
| 17. went | *when* | ✓ |
| 18. friend | *dk* | *dk* |
| 19. about | *above* | ✓^ |
| 20. door | *do* | *dot* |
| Percent correct: | *60%* | *75%* |

**FIGURE 4-3 Performance on Word List Test**

Before giving the word lists test, explain its nature and purpose. Say, "I am going to ask you to read some words for me. At first, I will only show you the word for a second because I want to see how well you can read words without needing time to figure them out. If you are unable to read a word in one second, then I will give you time to figure it out. That will help me to see how you figure out words. As you go through the lists of words, they will become harder, but do the best you can."

Because they only test the student's ability to pronounce printed words, word lists should not be used to obtain students' *reading* levels. However, they are useful for estimating sight vocabulary.

### *Interpreting the Results of the Word Lists Tests*

After the entire inventory has been administered, analyze the results, beginning with the words in isolation, the word lists tests. First, make a gross comparison between performance on the flash list and performance on the untimed list.

The flash score represents the student's ability to recognize words automatically, without resorting to decoding them. The untimed score indicates the student's ability to use phonics, syllabication, and morphemic analysis to decode words not recognized immediately. A high flash score indicates a high sight or immediate recognition vocabulary. An improved analysis score is a gauge of decoding ability. The larger the difference between the two scores, the greater the decoding ability. However, a very large difference may indicate that the student has few words that she or he can recognize at sight and so must sound out nearly all words. This can be a problem. If too much of a student's working memory is taken up by word analysis, too little will be left for comprehension (Samuels, 1989). What does the performance shown in Figure 4-3 suggest about the student's sight vocabulary and decoding skills?

After making a global analysis of a student's ability to recognize words at sight versus his ability to decode words, examine the kinds of words that were read correctly and those that were read incorrectly. Choose from the following questions those that apply to the student you have tested. The questions address gradually increasing levels of difficulty. The first questions are most appropriate for novice readers. The latter questions are more suitable for advanced readers.

- What parts of the word can the student read? Beginning? Middle? End?
- Can the student read beginning consonants? Can the student read ending consonants?
- Can the student pronounce short-vowel patterns (cat, pet)?
- Can the student read double-letter long-vowel patterns (goat, rain)?
- Can the student read final-*e* long-vowel patterns (wave, home)?
- Can the student read *r*-vowel patterns (car, chair, here, store, sir)?
- Can the student read other-vowel patterns (choice, how, crawl, brook, spoon)?
- Can the student read multisyllabic words?
- Does the student's difficulty pronouncing words seem to be caused by a lack of familiarity with the words in oral language? Is this essentially a vocabulary problem?

## *Administering the IRI Passages*

Some informal reading inventories use longer passages to reflect the kinds of sustained reading that students actually do. The disadvantage is that these inventories take longer to administer.

To determine the students' starting point for reading the oral and silent passages, locate the student's last perfect performance on the flash list. The starting point for the passages is the level below the last perfect performance. If the student's last perfect performance on flash was fourth grade, begin testing at the third-grade level. If you suspect a comprehension problem, you might start at an even lower level (Johnson, Kress, & Pikulski, 1987). Looking at Sheila's scores (Figure 4-4), you can see that her starting point would be grade two.

As conceived by Betts (1946), the IRI is modeled on the directed reading activity (guided reading lesson), except that the emphasis is on evaluation rather than instruction. A second major difference is that one passage at each level will be read orally without any preparation. Normally, passages are read silently before being read orally. The steps in administering the inventory, which, except for assessing listening comprehension, are similar to those in a traditional reading lesson include: preparing for reading a passage, assessing background knowledge, setting a purpose for reading, reading of passage, retelling of

Word-Lists Scores

| Level | Flash | Untimed |
|---|---|---|
| PP | 100 | 100 |
| P | 100 | 100 |
| 1 | 100 | 100 |
| 2 | 100 | 100 |
| 3 | 100 | 100 |
| 4 | 75 | 90 |
| 5 | 50 | 60 |
| 6 | 40 | 50 |

**FIGURE 4-4 Sheila's Test Results**

passage or answering questions about the passage, oral rereading of a selected segment of the silent passage (optional), and assessing listening comprehension.

Before students read the oral passage, explain the test and its purpose. Explain that they will be reading a series of stories (articles). State that you will be taking notes on their reading so that you can get some information on how they read. Tell them that after they read the passage, you will ask them to answer some questions (or retell the story or article in their own words).

***Preparation for Reading a Passage***

Ask a question or two about the title, topic, or illustration to explore briefly the student's knowledge of the topic. Before reading a selection about possums, you might direct the student's attention to the illustration of a possum and ask him what the picture shows. If there is no response, this might indicate a lack of background information about possums. To verify this, you might asks the student what she or he knows about possums. As the student responds, evaluate the depth and accuracy of her or his background knowledge. Since reading is very much a matter of bringing meaning to a page or activating schema, it is important to have an estimate of the quality of the student's store of information. However, in the preliminary discussion make sure that you don't give away major ideas or key vocabulary in the passage to be read. As part of a discussion, set a purpose for reading. This might be a general purpose, such as, to find out more about the topic, or it may be more specific. Most commercial inventories contain a preliminary discussion and/or purpose-setting question. In the *Basic Reading Inventory* (Johns, 1994), for instance, the student is asked to read the title and tell the examiner what she or he thinks the passage will be about.

Once the purpose has been set, have the student read the selection aloud to answer the purpose question. As the student reads aloud, use a series of symbols to describe her or his reading behavior. Note mispronounced words, omitted and inserted words, asking for help, correction of errors, hesitations, repetitions, misread punctuation, word-by-word reading, inaccurate intonation, head movement, finger pointing, and other behaviors that might yield insight into the manner in which the reader processes print. Symbols for each of these behaviors are presented in Figure 4-5.

As students read orally, note their fluency. Fluency is the smoothness with which students read. A fluent reader groups words into meaningful phrases and reads with appropriate expression.

**Quantitative errors**

| | |
|---|---|
| the angry cat (angry crossed out, *orange* written above) | Mispronunciation (Substitution) |
| the angry cat (angry crossed out) | Omission |
| the (angry) cat (angry circled) | Asked for word |
| the ^ angry cat (*big* inserted) | Insertion |
| the angry cat (angry crossed out, *angle* ✓ written above) | Self-correction (not counted as an error) |

**Qualitative errors**

| | |
|---|---|
| the \| angry cat | Hesitation |
| the angry cat (the underlined) | Repetition |
| the angry cat *w x w* | Word-by-word reading |
| The angry cat hissed⊗ And away ran the dog. | Omitted punctuation |
| This is your cat. ↑ | Rising inflection |
| Is this your cat? ↓ | Falling inflection |
| *HM* | Head movement |
| *FP* | Finger pointing |

**FIGURE 4-5 IRI Oral Reading Symbols**

As a practical matter, only uncorrected mispronunciations, omissions, insertions, and words supplied by the teacher count as errors. Repetitions and hesitations and other behaviors provide qualitative information about the student's reading. If a student reads so rapidly that it is difficult to record all his errors, then focus on noting those misreadings that count as errors. You may also record any other behavior that would shed light on the student's reading. In the sample marked-up inventory selection in Figure 4-6, the examiner included a comment in which the student stated that he likes animals. This information about the student's interests will come in handy when selecting materials.

### *Comprehension Check*

After the student has read the passage, comprehension is checked. The traditional procedure for assessing comprehension of an IRI selection is to ask comprehension questions.

The Pet Shop

*Commented, "I like all kinds of animals."*

Maria really wanted a little dog. One day she went with her parents to the pet shop. They looked at the fish, turtles, parrots, and many kinds of dogs. Maria and her parents saw one nice puppy that acted very lively. It looked like a small bouncing black ball of fur. The puppy was a fluffy black poodle. It jumped around in its cage. When Maria petted the puppy, it sat up and begged. Maria and her parents laughed because the poodle looked so cute. They decided to buy the poodle. After all, who could resist such a nice dog.

*par-rots* *lively ✓* *little* *fat* *barked* *rest*

**FIGURE 4-6 Sample Informal Reading Inventory Performance**

From *Basic Reading Inventory*, Sixth Edition, by J. L. Johns, 1994, Dubuque, IA: Kendall/Hunt Publishing Company. Used with permission.

Students' responses to questions should be recorded so you can take time later to examine any responses about which you are unsure. If the student has not supplied enough information for you to make a determination as to whether the answer is right or wrong, you can ask the student to tell you more. However, do not supply any clues or hints. After scoring the comprehension responses, analyze them in terms of their quality. Were they complete? Was additional information volunteered? What level of language did the student demonstrate as she or he answered questions.

> **Retelling:** process of recounting orally or in writing a story or an information piece. The purpose of a retelling is to assess comprehension.

As an alternative to asking questions, you might check comprehension by requesting a retelling. In a **retelling,** a student is asked to recall a selection in her or his own words. Generally, the teacher uses a guide that indicates the main points that should be covered in a retelling. Figure 4-7 presents a sample retelling guide from the *Qualitative Reading Inventory* (Leslie & Caldwell, 1995).

The major advantage of the retelling procedure is that students reconstruct the piece according to their personal interpretations. The teacher is provided with the opportunity to observe how the students organize their retellings and what kind of information they recall or choose to include. A retelling also shows what the reader inferred or added to the selection (Irwin & Mitchell, 1983). For more information on retellings, including sample questions, refer to pp. 103 to 105.

***Setting/Background***

_____ John Chapman was born
_____ in 1774
_____ He became a farmer
_____ and grew crops.
_____ John liked
_____ to grow
_____ and eat apples.
_____ People were moving west.
_____ Apples were a good food
_____ for settlers to have.

***Goal***

_____ John decided
__5__ to go west.
_____ He wanted
__3__ to plant apple trees.

***Events***

_____ John got many seeds
_____ from farmers
_____ who squeezed apples
_____ to make a drink
_____ called cider.
_____ He left
_____ for the frontier.
_____ He planted seeds
_____ as he went along.
_____ He gave them away.
_____ John walked miles.
__6__ He crossed rivers
__7__ and went through forests.
_____ He was hungry
_____ and wet.
_____ He had to hde
__8__ from Indians
_____ unfriendly Indians.
__9__ His clothes were torn.
_____ He used a sack
_____ for a shirt
_____ and he cut out holes
_____ for the arms.
__11__ He wore no shoes.

***Resolution***

_____ John's fame spread.
__1__ He was nicknamed
__2__ Johnny Appleseed.
_____ Settlers accepted seeds
_____ gratefully.
_____ Thanks to Johnny Appleseed
__12__ trees grow
__13__ in many parts
_____ of America.

Other ideas rcalled including inferences

4 *lived in Massachusetts*
10 *didn't give up*

**FIGURE 4-7 Retelling Scoring Sheet Sample**

From: *Qualitative Reading Inventory-II* by Lauren Leslie and JoAnne Caldwell. Copyright © 1995 by HarperCollins College Publishers. Reprinted by permission of Addison-Wesley Educational Publishers, Inc.

Since students are not allowed to look back at the passage when answering comprehension questions, recall skills, as well as understanding, are being tapped.

Since asking questions and requesting a retelling both have distinct advantages, you might assess comprehension by doing both. First, have the student provide a retelling. Then ask questions about any essential information not included in the retelling or follow-up probes.

### Administering Silent Reading Passages

Immediately after discussing the oral passage, administer the silent reading passage on that same level. After administering the third-grade oral passage, for instance, have the student read the third-grade silent passage. Do not administer all the oral passages at once and then the silent passages.

Just as was done when administering the oral passage, background should be explored in preparation for reading the passage and a purpose should be set. The student should be directed to read the passage silently. As the student reads silently, make notes on his behavior. Using the symbols presented in Figure 4-8, indicate lip movement, head movement, finger pointing, and vocalization. Also note any words for which the student asks for assistance. (You may supply a word if the student asks for it, but if that word is part of the answer to a comprehension question, the student is not given credit for the answer even if he gets it correct. The rationale is that the student wouldn't have gotten the answer without the help you supplied.) At the conclusion of the silent reading, request a retelling or seek answers to traditional questions as you did for the oral passage.

Since the student has already read the passage silently, the oral rereading should be more fluent than the reading of the oral passage at that level.

### Oral Rereading

Although not included in most commercial inventories, a valuable activity is to plan an oral rereading of a portion of the passage that is to be read silently. This rereading accomplishes three aims. It provides:

> *(1) a gauge of the student's ability to skim for the relocation of specific information; (2) a measure of ability to read for a specific purpose and to stop when that purpose has been satisfied; and (3) an index of the ability to profit from previous silent reading of the material, and thus improve the fluency of oral performance over oral reading at sight at the same level of difficulty (M. Johnson, Kress, & Pikulski, 1987, p. 35).*

The oral rereading should be marked in the same manner as the oral selection was. A comment should also be placed on the teacher's copy to indicate how successfully the student reread the passage in question.

| | |
|---|---|
| HM | Head movement |
| LM | Lip movement |
| FP | Finger pointing |
| SV | Subvocalization |
| PC | Use of picture clue |

**FIGURE 4-8 Symbols for Silent Reading**

Rate of reading and fluency are not identical. Rate of reading is speed of reading and doesn't consider whether words are grouped into phrases and read with expression.

### *Rate of Reading*

Another valuable piece of information that the inventory can yield is the rate of reading. The rate at which a student reads can provide insight into her or his fluency. Slow reading can be a sign that decoding is taking an excessive amount of time or the student may be reading word by word. Or it may be an indication that the student processes information slowly. Another possibility is that the student may be very anxious about remembering all the details in a selection and may believe that the best way to foster comprehension and retention is to read very slowly. Slow reading, especially among older students who have adequate decoding skills, is often a sign of an underlying problem.

Once students have mastered basic decoding skills, oral reading should match the student's rate of speaking (the average rate of speaking is 125 words per minute) and, beyond grade two, silent reading speed should surpass rate of oral reading. To assess rate of reading, use a stop watch but be unobtrusive. Students might feel pressured if they see that they are being timed.

A slow rate of reading on independent and instructional level material suggests that the student's reading is not fluent (Rasinski & Padak, 1996).

Approximate average rates of reading for both oral and silent selections in grade one through seven are presented in Table 4-3. (from Powell, cited in Lipson & Wixson, 1991). In seventh grade and beyond, students' rate of silent reading is approximately 200 to 250 words per minute (Harris & Sipay, 1990).

### *Reaching the Frustration Level*

Students continue reading oral and silent passages until they reach their frustration level. The frustration level is the point at which students have a score of 90 percent or below on the word recognition of the oral passages or comprehension is 50 percent or less. If students have acceptable word recognition but comprehension is 50 percent or below, test at the next highest level to make sure that the students have truly reached their frustration levels. Because of a lack of interest or inadequate background in a specific topic, students' comprehension may temporarily dip but rebound on a higher level selection.

### *Establishing Listening Capacity*

Once students have reached the frustration level, they stop trying to read the inventory selections, and you begin reading the passages to them. The object is to locate the highest level at which students can understand printed materials, once the barriers posed by

**TABLE 4-3 Median Rates of Reading**

| Instructional Reading Level | Oral Reading | Silent Reading |
|---|---|---|
| Grade 1 | 55 | 55 |
| Grade 2 | 85 | 85 |
| Grade 3 | 115 | 130 |
| Grade 4 | 135 | 155 |
| Grade 5 | 145 | 185 |
| Grade 6 | 150 | 205 |

Because listening develops faster in the primary grades than reading does and some students have difficulty processing oral language, listening levels must be interpreted with care (Sticht & James, 1984).

translating print have been removed. Two selections at each level are read to students in order to find the highest point at which students can understand 75 percent of the material. Again, be prepared for dips in performance. Do not stop as soon as the student reaches the 75 percent mark. Even if the performance slips below 75 percent, test at the next level. Listening comprehension may rebound.

Obtaining a listening capacity level yields important information. The expectation is that students will be able to read up to their listening capacity level. The listening-capacity task is an approximate measure of overall receptive language development. Students whose instructional level is below their listening comprehension level are judged to be reading below their potential. Average students can typically grasp listening materials at their grade level. Below-average students generally have a listening level that is below grade level, and above-average students generally are able to comprehend material that is above their grade level. Note the scores presented in Table 4-4. Although all three students whose scores are reported in the table are in the same grade and have differing instructional levels, none is classified as a problem reader because all are reading up to their listening capacities. Jonathan, the first youngster, has a listening level of grade two but also is reading at a grade-two level. Jonathan's language development would seem to be below average. Maxine's instructional level of grade four, which is at grade level, matches her listening level. Maxine's language development is apparently average. Benjamin, on the other hand, has an instructional and listening level of grade eight. His scores suggest superior language development.

As with the oral and silent passages, background should be explored and purposes set before the listening passages are read to students. For testing purposes, use the passages that the student has not yet read. However, if these are too hard, read easier passages from alternate forms. In the majority of cases a student's listening capacity will match or exceed the instructional level. However, some students have listening difficulties and will do even worse on a listening comprehension test than they do on a reading test. They may have depressed listening scores because of emotional or attentional problems. A small percentage have difficulty processing information presented orally. For these students, it may be necessary to read passages to them that are below their instructional level. To get a measure of receptive language development in instances where the listening capacity test doesn't seem to be working out, administer the *Peabody Picture Vocabulary Test* or a similar instrument.

## *Interpreting Inventory Results*

Informal reading inventories do much more than just give reading levels. Because IRIs include a variety of lengthy selections and duplicate, in a controlled setting, the act of

**TABLE 4-4 Performance of Three Fourth-Graders on an IRI**

| | Johnathan | Maxine | Benjamin |
|---|---|---|---|
| Independent | 1 | 3 | 4 |
| Instructional | 2 | 4 | 8 |
| Frustration | 3 | 5 | 6 |
| Listening Capacity | 2 | 4 | 8 |

reading, they provide an excellent opportunity for insightful, in-depth observation. To interpret an inventory, begin with the most general information, the levels. The listening comprehension level provides information about the student's cognitive ability and language development. The higher the student's listening comprehension, the more fully developed are his language and cognitive abilities. Listening comprehension that is significantly above grade level indicates better-than-average potential. Now take a look at the instructional level. Some students may have a range of instructional levels. Remember that a student is instructional if her word-recognition-in-context scores fall between 95 and 98 percent and comprehension is between 75 and 89 percent. Note Angela's levels in Figure 4-9. Her instructional levels are grades two and three. Angela's basic instructional level, which is the highest level at which she meets the criteria, is grade three. Her immediate instructional level is grade two. That's the level at which the student begins to show needs. In deciding at which level to place Angela, a number of factors need to be considered. If Angela is older, it might be better to place her in the higher levels, since that would make it easier to obtain materials that are age-appropriate. If Angela seems insecure and gives up easily, it would be advisable to place her in lower level materials, so she wouldn't feel overwhelmed.

Name *Angela* ____________ Age ____________

Date ____________

Grade ____________ School ____________ Examiner ____________

**Informal Reading Inventory Summary Sheet**

| **Word List Scores** | | | **Passage Scores** | | | | |
|---|---|---|---|---|---|---|---|
| | | | Word Recog. | Comprehension | | | Listening |
| Level | Flash | Untimed | in Context | Oral | Silent | Avg. | Capacity |
| PP | 100 | — | | | | | |
| P | 100 | — | | | | | |
| 1 | 90 | 100 | 99 | 100 | 90 | 95 | |
| 2 | 85 | 90 | 98 | 80 | 90 | 85 | |
| 3 | 75 | 85 | 95 | 80 | 70 | 75 | |
| 4 | 60 | 70 | 89 | 60 | 50 | 55 | |
| 5 | 50 | 60 | | | | | 80 |
| 6 | 40 | 50 | | | | | 80 |
| 7 | | | | | | | 50 |
| 8 | | | | | | | |
| 9 | | | | | | | |

**Levels**

| | |
|---|---|
| Independent | 1 |
| Instructional | 2–3 |
| Frustration | 4 |
| Listening Capacity | 6 |

**Summary of Needs**

*Difficulty with main idea questions and multisylabic words.*

**FIGURE 4-9 Sample IRI Levels**

An examination of the levels yields other valuable information, too. They provide an estimate of the degree of discrepancy between ability and achievement in reading. For instance, the greater the difference between listening capacity and instructional level, the more serious the problem. Note that Angela is reading three years below her listening capacity. Although both Orlando and Maria, whose levels are presented in Figure 4-10, have the same instructional level and are in the same grade, Orlando apparently has the more serious problem. With a listening capacity of 7, Orlando is five years below capacity whereas, Maria with a listening capacity of 5, is only three years below capacity.

Another comparison that should be noted is the magnitude of the difference between the instructional and the frustration levels. There is a buffer between the instructional and frustration level that is at least 5 percent in word recognition and 25 percent in comprehension since the criteria for the instructional level is at least 95 percent word recognition and 75 percent comprehension but 90 percent word recognition or 50 percent comprehension for the frustration level. The greater the distance between the instructional and frustration levels the more likely it is that the student will make rapid progress because this indicates a gradual, rather than a steep, drop off in skills.

Take a look at Orlando's and Maria's instructional and frustration levels. Orlando's word recognition score takes a nose dive after he reaches the instructional level at grade two. His 86 percent word recognition score at grade three indicates that he will need lots of work in that area to bring word recognition up to an acceptable level. Maria's scores, on the other hand, taper off. With a little work, she should be able to bring up those 91 and 93 percentages to the 95 percent level.

After comparing levels, take a look at the student's scores in the two major areas assessed: word recognition and comprehension. Is there a discrepancy between the two? Is word recognition high but comprehension low or vice versa? Or do both dip as the selections get harder, which would be the typical pattern? Once you have a global sense of the student's

| | Orlando | Maria |
|---|---|---|
| Independent | 1 | 1 |
| Instructional | 2 | 2 |
| Frustration | 3 | 4 |
| Listening | 7 | 5 |

| Level | Word Recognition in Context | Average Comprehension | Word Recognition in Context | Average Comprehension |
|---|---|---|---|---|
| PP | — | | — | |
| P | 100 | 100 | 100 | 90 |
| 1 | 99 | 90 | 98 | 90 |
| 2 | 95 | 80 | 96 | 80 |
| 3 | 86 | 60 | 93 | 70 |
| 4 | — | — | 91 | 60 |
| 5 | — | — | 90 | 60 |
| 6 | | | | |
| 7 | | | | |
| 8 | | | | |

**FIGURE 4-10 Comparison of IRI Levels**

reading performance, make an in-depth analysis of major areas, noting, of course, that reading is a holistic act so that ultimately information from all areas will need to be integrated.

> If the student's performance on the word lists and oral passages portions of the IRI has been carefully analyzed, this should provide a wealth of information on word-analysis abilities so that it may not be necessary to give a separate phonics test.

### *Word Recognition*

Keeping in mind the information gathered from an analysis of the word lists tests, analyze the student's performance on word recognition in context. Is the student's percentage of word recognition in context higher at each level than her or his percentage of words recognized in isolation in the untimed condition? Was the student able to read some words in context that she or he had missed in isolation? Because of the availability of clues, most students are better able to recognize words in context than in isolation.

On the other hand, there are a few students whose word recognition skills are actually worse in context. These students have poor decoding skills. Deciphering words is a struggle for them. Given words in isolation, they are forced to apply their weak phonics skills. However, given words in running text, they overuse context, which is easier for them to apply than their weak phonics skills. If there is a picture available, they may use that, too. Overrelying on pictorial and verbal context and failing to use the decoding skills they possess, they actually miss some words that they could read in isolation if they tried. They need to learn to use context along with phonics, not instead of phonics. They also need to have their phonics skills strengthened, with ample opportunity to apply them so they become automatic.

Also observe the processes the student uses to decode words that posed problems. Did the student process the word sound by sound, saying "c-r-u-n-ch" for *crunch*? Did the student use chunks of the word saying "un-run-crunch" or "run-crunch"? And what about the integration of strategies? Ideally, students should be making balanced use of the three language system to decode words. These include the graphophonic, syntactic, and semantic. As you examine a student's errors, ask yourself the following questions:

- When the student encounters a difficult word, what does she or he do?
- Does the student try to sound it out?
- Does the student use verbal context?
- Does the student use picture cues?
- Does the student ask for help or give up without trying to work out the difficult word?
- Are student's miscues (misread words) meaningful?
- Does the student monitor her or his reading? Does the student self-correct when the text isn't making sense or the word decoded doesn't fit? Self-corrections indicate that the student is reading for meaning and is monitoring her or his reading, and so are a positive sign. Self-correction of minor miscues, however, could indicate an over-concern with pronunciation. Good readers tend not to correct minor miscues that don't have an effect on the meaning of the passage (Y. Goodman, 1992).
- What strategies does the student use to correct an error?

At this point, take a look at the qualitative markings on the inventory. Slow or word-by-word reading, frequent hesitations, and repetitions are signs that the student is having difficulty with decoding. Take a little time, too, to examine the student's mastery of the "content" of phonics. What word-analysis elements was the student able to use? With what word-analysis elements did the student have difficulty? Using the list of word-recognition skills presented earlier in the chapter, examine the student's word recognition in context performance. What phonic (consonants, consonant clusters, single vowels, vowel combinations, short vowels, long vowels, other vowels), syllabic, or morphemic elements (prefixes, suffixes, roots) was the student able to use? With which did she or he have difficulty?

### *Comprehension*

Comprehension is affected by a number of factors including language development, cognitive ability, background of experience, word recognition, and appropriate use of strategies. A good starting point for assessing comprehension processes is to look at the preparatory portion of each of the oral and silent selections. What background of information did the student bring to the selection?

If the student has answered traditional questions, analyze responses. What kinds of questions did the student answer best? What kinds of questions posed problems? Note in particular what the student's performance was on key questions and hypothesize what this implies about underlying cognitive processes. Literal questions, those whose answers are directly stated in the story, require selection and retention of details. Inferential questions and questions that require drawing a conclusion may require that a student integrate comprehension of details and background knowledge. Vocabulary questions hinge on word knowledge and, depending upon the nature of the item, the ability to use context. Main-idea questions involve the ability to organize or categorize details and draw a conclusion as to what the main idea is. Instead of simply noting how many details, main idea, or inferential questions the students answered, take note of the basic comprehension processes that these responses suggest. Ask: How is the student processing printed information? What are the student's strengths? What are the student's weaknesses?

### *Supplementary Questions*

To get a more complete look at the student's use of comprehension strategies, supplement the administration of the IRI with key questions about the use of strategies. After administering the comprehension portion of the IRI, ask such questions as: What do you do before you read an article or story? (Students should be surveying the text, predicting, setting purposes.) What do you do as you read? What do you think about? (Students should be selecting important details, organizing and evaluating information, relating new information to old, creating mental images.) What do you do if there is a part that you don't understand? (Students should be rereading, or, perhaps, using graphic cues.) What do you do after you read? (Students should integrate new and old information, evaluate information, and think about how the new information might be applied or used.) To get a fuller look at a student's use of strategies, you may wish to supplement the administration of the IRI with an administration of a think-aloud, which is discussed in Chapter 5.

### *Shortcomings of IRIs*

Despite the obvious utility, IRIs have their shortcomings. If not given by trained professionals or if the professional doesn't heed the standards, they may yield inflated levels (Enz, 1989). If selections are unappealing, require backgrounds that students don't possess, or contain questions that are ambiguous or which can be answered without reading the selection, then they may yield erroneous results (Lipson & Wixon, 1997). Many of these short-

Composed primarily of selections from children's books, today's basals are more difficult at the lower levels than were former basals. Commercial IRIs may overestimate the difficulty level of material that students can read.

comings can be overcome by trying out several inventories and selecting the one that you feel gives the best results. Also, as you become familiar with an inventory, you learn its strengths and weaknesses, and can take steps to compensate. You may find that the sports selection on level four penalizes students who know little about sports but motivates reluctant readers who like sports to do their best and often reveals hidden strengths. In addition, levels yielded by an inventory should be thought of as estimates. Observe students' actual performance reading their texts and make adjustments as necessary.

## Miscue Analysis

**Miscues:** oral reading responses that differ from the expected responses. The term *miscues* is used instead of *errors* because miscue theory holds that they are not random mistakes but are attempts by the reader to make sense of the text. By examining miscues you will gain insight into the reader's decoding processes.

Miscue analysis, which is a way of examining and interpreting students' oral reading errors, is based on the premise that not all oral reading mistakes are equal or even negative. For instance, if a student substitutes the word *car* for *automobile* in the sentence, "The automobile in the showroom window caught my eye," he is demonstrating that he is reading for meaning, since *car* is a synonym for *automobile.* The word **miscues** rather than *errors* is used "to avoid the negative connotation of errors (all miscues are not bad) and to avoid the implication that good reading does not contain miscues" (K. Goodman, 1969, p. 12).

As noted earlier, according to K. Goodman, the reader draws on three basic sources of information: graphophonic or phonics, syntactic, and semantic, which includes the sum total of the reader's background of knowledge. By comparing miscues to the original text, we can gain insight into the reader's processes. For instance, we can surmise whether the reader is using a balanced strategy or is overusing graphophonic strategies or fails to use semantic cues. The promise of miscue analysis is that it provides insight into the reading process (K. Goodman, 1974). At "the same time it provides a window on the strategies and language cueing systems that readers control, it provides teachers with information about how the reading process works" (Y. Goodman, 1992, p. 20).

### Adapted Miscue Analysis

Originally designed for research purposes, reading miscue analysis can be time-consuming. Because of this, you may want to use the simplified miscue analysis procedures described below. To further save time, it is recommended that the procedures be used in conjunction with the oral reading passages of an IRI. If miscues from an IRI are used, select only those miscues that occur at the independent and instructional levels and on any passages that occur between the instructional and frustration levels. Do not choose miscues from the frustration level. As material becomes too difficult, both good and poor readers tend to overuse graphophonics cues because they aren't able to read enough words to use context.

When analyzing miscues, don't include errors at the frustration level (90% or below). When students cannot read many words in a passage, they have difficulty using context and overrely on phonics.

On a sheet similar to the one in Figure 4-11, make a list of the student's miscues. List twenty-five, if you can. If there are fewer than twenty-five, list as many as are available. But remember the fewer the miscues, the less dependable the conclusions that you can draw from the data. Next to each miscue, write the word that was misread, the actual text. Then compare the miscue with the text. Assess whether the miscue fits the sense of the selection. Ask: "Is the miscue meaningful? Does it fit the sense of the selection?" If so, put a check (✓) in the first column. If not, put a minus (–).

Next, determine whether the miscue is graphically similar. A miscue is graphically similar if at least half the graphic elements in the miscue are the same as those in the text. Note in the next two columns whether the beginning, middle, and end of the miscue is similar to the beginning, middle, and end of the text word. If the word has only two graphemes (*he, bee*), assess only the beginning and the end. A two-grapheme word, would be similar

| Miscue | Text | Semantic Similarity | Graphic Similarity | Degree of Graphic Similarity Beg. | Mid. | End | Self-corrections | Non-words |
|---|---|---|---|---|---|---|---|---|
| 1. be | beyond | – | – | ✓ | – | – | ✓ | |
| 2. wild | wide | ✓ | ✓ | ✓ | – | ✓ | | |
| 3. milk | Mike's | – | ✓ | ✓ | – | ✓ | | |
| 4. letter | leather | – | ✓ | ✓ | – | ✓ | | |
| 5. his | him | – | ✓ | ✓ | ✓ | – | | |
| 6. out | up | ✓ | – | – | – | – | | |
| 7. was | were | ✓ | – | ✓ | – | – | | |
| 8. title | titles | ✓ | ✓ | ✓ | ✓ | ✓ | | |
| 9. books | book | ✓ | ✓ | ✓ | ✓ | ✓ | | |
| 10. covers | covered | ✓ | ✓ | ✓ | ✓ | – | | |
| 11. full | fell | – | ✓ | ✓ | – | ✓ | | |
| 12. men | mean | – | ✓ | ✓ | – | ✓ | | |
| 13. talking | taking | – | ✓ | ✓ | – | ✓ | ✓ | |
| 14. out | ought | – | ✓ | ✓ | – | ✓ | | |
| 15. de-shed | demolished | – | ✓ | ✓ | – | ✓ | | ✓ |
| 16. schap | scrap | – | ✓ | ✓ | – | ✓ | | ✓ |
| 17. wreaked | wrecked | – | ✓ | ✓ | – | ✓ | | ✓ |
| 18. being | be | ✓ | ✓ | ✓ | | – | | |
| 19. collection | collectors | – | ✓ | ✓ | ✓ | – | | |
| 20. budding | building | – | ✓ | ✓ | | ✓ | | |
| 21. a | one | ✓ | – | – | – | – | | |
| 22. Claude | Claudia | ✓ | ✓ | ✓ | ✓ | – | | |
| 23. five | fife | – | ✓ | ✓ | ✓ | – | | |
| 24. tree | three | – | ✓ | – | ✓ | ✓ | ✓ | |
| 25. dis-tor | destroy | – | ✓ | ✓ | ✓ | – | | ✓ |
| Totals | | 45% | 85% | | | | 3 | 4 |

**Figure 4-11 Miscue Analysis of a Fourth-Grader's Reading**

if one of the graphemes was the same. A three-grapheme (*goat, red*) word would be similar if two of the three graphemes were the same.

After assessing a miscue for graphic similarity, note whether it was self-corrected. Self-corrected miscues do not count as errors on an IRI but provide valuable information about a student's reading processes, and so are included in the analysis. In the next column, note whether the miscue is a nonword. Production of nonwords is significant because it indicates a failure to read for meaning and suggests the overuse of decoding.

After filling in each column, tally the check marks and convert the total in each column to a percentage. Note which strategies the student is using. A high percentage of meaningful miscues and self-corrections indicate the use of context. A high percentage of graphically similar words indicates the use of graphophonics strategies. Compare percentages to determine whether strategies are being used in balanced fashion. Is there an overreliance on meaning or sounding out? Does one strategy area seem to be weak?

If phonics is a problem area, examine the columns to see which elements are being used. Most poor readers fail to use the middles of words because they have difficulty with vowel correspondences. Some overrely on initial consonants. Reexamine the miscues and see if you note any particular needs in phonics or structural elements.

Most important of all, as you analyze the data, set up tentative hypotheses that would describe the current state of the student's reading development and some steps that might be taken to foster the student's growth in literacy. As you administer additional assessment measures or work with the student, be prepared to amplify and revise your hypotheses.

For more information on miscue analysis, see Goodman, Y. M. & Marek, A. M. (1996).

Examine the sample miscue analysis in Figure 4-11. This is an analysis of the reading performance of Madeline, a fourth-grader who was receiving special help because of comprehension problems. The percentages tell the story. Madeline's miscues were graphically similar 85 percent of the time but only fit the context 45 percent of the time. In addition, she only self-corrected 12 percent of her miscues. It is clear from even a quick survey of the results that Madeline is neglecting context clues. Note that she produced four nonwords, a further sign that she doesn't always read for meaning.

A program for Madeline would emphasize reading for meaning and monitoring one's reading so the student is constantly asking: "Does this sound right? Does this make sense? What word would fit here?" Madeline also needs to integrate the use of context with her deciphering skills. With help from context, she should have been able to figure out words like *leather* and *wrecked.* Although she overrelies on sounding out, Madeline needs some instruction in the use of word-analysis skills. She does well with single-syllable words but has difficulty with multisyllabic words. Vocabulary knowledge may also be a factor. She may have missed *demolished* because it is not in her listening vocabulary.

## *Running Records*

An ingenious adaptation of the informal reading inventory and miscue analysis, **running records,** are a quick, easy assessment of a student's oral reading behavior. Like the miscue analysis, running records are designed to reveal the processes the student is using to read text.

**Running record:** an oral reading assessment with a dual purpose: determine (1) whether the material being read is on the appropriate level, and (2) which strategies the reader uses to decode hard words.

*When the performance is less than perfect, there are opportunities to record the work done by the child to get it right, to puzzle it out. This reveals something of the process by which the child monitors and corrects his own performance. When he encounters something new we can observe how he approaches the novel thing, and what he learns from the encounter. (Clay, 1993a, pp. 21–22)*

Unlike miscue analysis, running records are quick and easy to administer, and no special material is needed. Generally, the student is given material felt to be on his instructional level and asked to read orally. As with other assessment procedures, the purpose of the running record is explained to the youngster. As the student reads, the teacher records the student's performance, using the symbols presented in Figure 4-12.

Although running records are typically recorded on a blank sheet of paper, they may be recorded on a photocopy of the text that the student is reading (Learning Media, 1992).

A blank sheet of paper may be used to record a student's performance on a running record. Two lines of words and symbols are used to indicate each line of text. For most reading behaviors, the student's performance is written on the top line. The bottom line is left blank and later, after the running record has been administered, is filled in with the words from the text. A check mark is written on the top line to indicate words read correctly. Substitutions are also written on the top line. If a student sounds out a word, that is indicated by using lower case letters: *p-e-t.* Uppercase letters are used to indicate words that the student has spelled out (*L-I-O-N*). Insertions are indicated by writing the insertion above the line and a dash below it. Omissions are recorded by writing a dash above the line. The letters *SC* indicate a self-correction, *T,* being told the word, and *A,* an appeal for help. The letter *R* symbolizes a repetition with a line and arrow used to indicate the extent of the repetition.

In general, you should take a neutral stance when assessing oral reading. Be supportive and encouraging but don't give assistance, as it will invalidate your results. Although as a teacher your natural inclination is to provide instruction, when you are assessing you need to see what students can do on their own. Occasionally, however, students may make so many errors in a passage that they need to be redirected. This can be accomplished by asking them to "Try that again." If you resort to this intervention, which should be used sparingly, bracket the text in question and label it "TTA" for "try that again."

On some occasions, a student may be blocked by a key word that she or he is unable to decode but which is important to the sense and the flow of the passage. For instance, it might be the word *cheetah* in an informational piece about cheetahs. Unable to decode the word, the student will be blocked from using background knowledge to process the text. For this type of situation, you may tell the student the word, but code your assistance with a "T" to indicate "told word," and count it as an error.

As in the IRI, substitutions, omissions, insertions, appeals for help and being told a word are counted as errors. Self-corrections are not counted as mistakes. A repeated error, saying *there* for *this,* counts each time it occurs but a proper noun, no matter how many times mispronounced, counts as only one error.

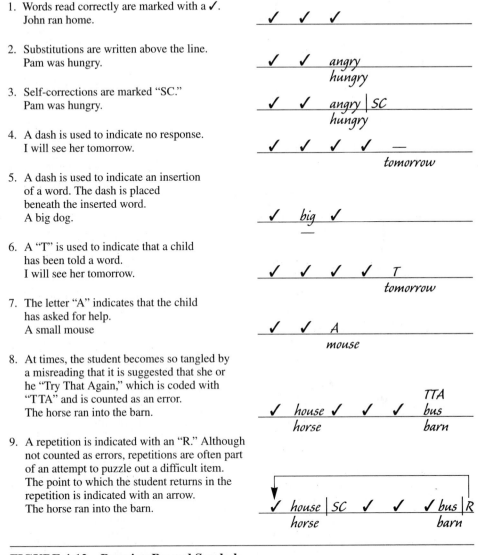

| Symbol | Example |
|---|---|
| 1. Words read correctly are marked with a ✓.<br>John ran home. | ✓ ✓ ✓ |
| 2. Substitutions are written above the line.<br>Pam was hungry. | ✓ ✓ angry<br>hungry |
| 3. Self-corrections are marked "SC."<br>Pam was hungry. | ✓ ✓ angry \| SC<br>hungry |
| 4. A dash is used to indicate no response.<br>I will see her tomorrow. | ✓ ✓ ✓ ✓ —<br>tomorrow |
| 5. A dash is used to indicate an insertion of a word. The dash is placed beneath the inserted word.<br>A big dog. | ✓ big ✓<br>— |
| 6. A "T" is used to indicate that a child has been told a word.<br>I will see her tomorrow. | ✓ ✓ ✓ ✓ T<br>tomorrow |
| 7. The letter "A" indicates that the child has asked for help.<br>A small mouse | ✓ ✓ A<br>mouse |
| 8. At times, the student becomes so tangled by a misreading that it is suggested that she or he "Try That Again," which is coded with "TTA" and is counted as an error.<br>The horse ran into the barn. | TTA<br>✓ house ✓ ✓ ✓ bus<br>horse barn |
| 9. A repetition is indicated with an "R." Although not counted as errors, repetitions are often part of an attempt to puzzle out a difficult item. The point to which the student returns in the repetition is indicated with an arrow.<br>The horse ran into the barn. | ✓ house \| SC ✓ ✓ ✓ bus \| R<br>horse barn |

**FIGURE 4-12 Running Record Symbols**

After scoring the running record, calculate the percentage of errors. Divide number of errors by number of words in the selection and subtract from 100 percent. Using more lenient standards than the IRI, guidelines for running records are presented in Table 4-5. The instructional level for word recognition, for instance, is 90–94 percent, rather than the 95–98 percent required by IRI standards. Note that only word recognition is included in the standards.

**TABLE 4-5 Running Record Standards**

| Text | Word Recognition |
|---|---|
| Easy | 95–100% |
| Instructional | 90–94% |
| Hard | 80–89% |

## *Analyzing Miscues in a Running Record*

Just as with the informal reading inventory, it is important to code students' miscues and self-corrections when analyzing a running record. Note for each miscue and self-correction the cue or cues being used. To interpret the student's oral reading, Clay (1985) suggests that the teacher examine every error and ask, "Now what made him say that?" (p. 21). As you analyze miscues, ask yourself: "Is the student using meaning? Does the miscue made sense? Is the student using syntax? Does the miscue fit grammatically? Is the student using visual cues? Does the miscue fit the graphic construction of the word? Does it begin and/or end with the same sound? Does it have the same vowel sound?" Code the miscues, "M" to indicate use of meaning, "S" for syntax, and "V" for visual (phonics). Or students might be using two or even three strategies so you would code the miscue "MV, SV, SM," or "SVM." Also note whether the student engages in cross-checking, that is, using one type of cue to support another. For instance, a student reads "The dog were barking" for "The dogs were barking." Noting that *dog* doesn't fit with *were,* the student went back to the beginning of the sentence and saw that *dog* ends in an *s* and self-corrected by adding *s* to the noun. A syntactic cue alerted the student that she had misread, but a visual cue, the *s* at the *end* of dogs, was used to verify her correction so the item should be coded "SV."

Using running record procedures, you focus on what the students can *do* because you mark each word read *correctly.*

Look for a pattern. One or two miscues in the meaning category would be inconclusive. In order to obtain a sufficient number of miscues on which to base a valid conclusion, students should read a passage of about one hundred words or more. The passage should be challenging but not overwhelming. As the text becomes too difficult, students' skills disintegrate so the examiner would get a false impression of their reading. At the maximum, students should be making no more than one error for every ten words read. For a thorough analysis of student's use of strategies, you might try a running record on an easy, medium, and difficult selection, but not one in which the student's error rate exceed 90 percent. You might also compare a student's performance on a new story with one that has been previously read. Note the running record displayed in Figure 4-13. What strategies does the student seem to be using?

As you become familiar with the running record technique, you can make more detailed analyses of strategies used. This would be especially true in the visual category. Note, for instance, whether a student seems to sound out words letter by letter or is chunking sounds. Is the student breaking down a word like rat in r + a + t, or is the student chunking sounds so that she or he analyzes it as r + at. Is he using the first letter and combining that with context or is he attempting to use larger sections of the word?

Note how effectively and efficiently strategies are being used. Ask: Are any strategies being overused or used inappropriately? Are meaning strategies used when visual strategies

**The Elves and the Shoemaker**

| | | E | S | *Cues Used* E | *Cues Used* SC |
|---|---|---|---|---|---|
| The shoemaker was very poor. | ✓ T ✓ ✓ ✓ / shoemaker | 1 | | M S V | M S V |
| He had just enough leather | ✓ ✓ ✓ every letter / enough leather | 2 | | M S (V) / M (S)(V) | M S V / M S V |
| to make one more pair | ✓ ✓ ✓ ✓ \| poor / pair | 1 | | M S (V) | M S V |
| of shoes. | ✓ ✓ | | | M S V | M S V |
| He cut out the leather | ✓ ✓ ✓ ✓ letter / leather | 1 | | M (S)(V) | M S V |
| for a new pair of shoes, | ✓ ✓ ✓ poor SC ✓ ✓ / pair | | 1 | M S (V) | (M)(S) V |
| and then he went to bed. | ✓ ✓ ✓ ✓ ✓ ✓ | | | M S V | M S V |
| He was soon fast asleep. | ✓ ✓ ✓ first SC ✓ R / fast | | 1 | M (S)(V) | (M) S V |

**FIGURE 4-13 Sample Running Record**

For more information on running records, see: Clay, M. M. (1993a).

are called for or vice versa? To what extent are strategies being used in a balanced, integrated fashion?

As you assess, consider the student's stage of development. Overattention to one or another cue source is very common for brief periods of time in students' development. It is quite common for students just getting the hang of letter–sound relationships to devote an overabundance of effort to them, even to the extent that meaning is lost as attention is exhausted by the process of decoding words.

## *Comparing IRI, Miscue Analysis, and Running Record*

All three instruments, the IRI, miscue analysis, and running record, play a role in assessment. The IRI is the most versatile of the three and the easiest to administer and interpret. The IRI is also the best of the three instruments for placing pupils and, when interpreted with care, can provide a wealth of information about the student's reading process.

The more specialized miscue analysis provides extensive information about the way in which the student processes printed language, information that can be used to plan a program of instruction. However, in an interview with Mellor and Simons (1991), K. Goodman warns that miscue analysis is of no value unless it is rooted in an understanding of its underpinnings.

> *A key thing is that miscue analysis isn't any use at all unless you have some sense of the theoretical context and the view of language and reading that's involved. If you try to use it from a clinical, medical, diagnostic point of view, a miscue is just another name for an error, and all you're preoccupied by is what the kids are doing wrong so that you can get them to stop doing it. (Mellor & Simons, p. 100)*

Running record, a direct descendant of miscue analysis, is most valuable as an ongoing indicator of strategies that students are using and as a check on the suitability of materials they are reading. Easy to administer, the running record is a useful, practical instrument; but because of its focus on decoding, it works best with students who are operating on the earlier levels of reading.

The major benefit of the IRI, miscue analysis, and running record is that they provide a peek into students' reading processes. Using an IRI perspective whenever you examine students' reading performance, you would be mentally estimating whether the material they are reading is on their independent, instructional, or frustration level. From a miscue analysis or running-record perspective, you would be asking: What cues is the student using to process print? As Y. Goodman notes:

> *Once you are aware of what is involved in miscue analysis, you are always listening with what I call a "miscue head"; you have the scheme of miscue analysis in your head. Sometimes, working with students whose strategies are not very efficient, you may need to do a very full, complete miscue analysis, but if kids are developing appropriately, it's not necessary to use a miscue inventory because you know that they're using the strategies in an appropriate way, and you just keep monitoring it yourself. (Mellor & Simons, 1991, p. 100)*

## *IRI-Based Tests*

A number of reading assessment instruments are based on the concept or embody some of the major features of an IRI. These include oral reading tests, group reading inventories, cloze and modified cloze tests, and word-opposites and word-lists tests.

### *Oral Reading Tests*

As their title suggests, oral reading tests do not include the assessment of silent reading. As such, they are quicker to administer, but are less valid because they neglect silent reading, and less reliable because they assess the student on just one passage for each level instead of two. One advantage of oral reading tests is that many of them are norm-referenced and standardized so they may be used in situations that demand validated instruments, such as in pre- and post-testing for an experimental or government-funded program.

### *Gray Oral Reading Test*

One of the earliest reading tests, the *Gray Oral Reading Test* (GORT) was first published in 1917 but has been revised many times over the years. Consisting of a series of brief selections that gradually increase in difficulty from a beginning level to a college level, the GORT measures comprehension and speed and accuracy of oral reading. Although it includes a miscue analysis, the GORT's use of short, artificial passages and multiple-choice questions limits its appeal.

Oral reading tests are also found in a number of diagnostic batteries including: the *Durrell Analysis of Reading Difficulty,* the *Diagnostic Assessments of Reading with Trial Teaching Strategies* (DARTTS), the *Gates-McKillop-Horowitz Reading Diagnostic Tests,* and the *Spache Diagnostic Reading Scales.*

## *Word-Lists Tests*

To save time, teachers and diagnosticians sometimes administer word-lists tests instead of IRIs. As discussed earlier, a word-lists test consists of a series of words in isolation that gradually increase in difficulty. There is a close correlation between the ability to pronounce words in isolation and overall reading (Manzo & Manzo, 1993). However, since they require only the ability to pronounce words, these tests neglect comprehension and may report misleading levels for students who are superior decoders but poor comprehenders or vice versa. In a comparison of commercial and teacher-made IRIs with the reading subtest of the WRAT (*Wide Range Achievement Test*), which only requires the pronouncing of isolated words, the WRAT yielded estimates that were one to two grade levels above the estimates yielded by IRIs (Bristow, Pikulski, & Pelosi, 1983). The two most popular word-lists tests are described below.

### *Slosson Oral Reading Tests (SORT)*

This test presents twenty words at each grade level from preprimer through grade twelve. The student is only required to pronounce the words and does not have to know their meanings. Standardized and norm-referenced, the Slosson yields grade equivalents, percentile ranks, and stanines.

### *Oral Reading Subtest of the WRAT*

Similar in format to the SORT, the WRAT also assesses reading through the pronunciation of isolated printed words. The WRAT is frequently administered by school psychologists.

## *Group Inventories*

Because of the time involved, it may be impractical to administer individual IRIs. However, you may choose to administer a group reading inventory. Information about constructing and administering group reading inventories can be found in *Informal Reading Inventories* (2nd ed.) by Johnson, Kress, & Pikulski, (1987). Some reading series contain group reading inventories. There are also two standardized tests that function as group inventories: the *Metropolitan Reading Achievement Tests* and the *Degrees of Reading Power.*

### *Metropolitan Reading Achievement Tests*

Most standardized, norm-referenced tests of reading are not designed to provide reading levels. Even though a test may yield grade equivalents—3.2, 5.2, and so forth—these scores do not tell on what level students are reading. A grade equivalent score of 3.2 simply means that the test taker got the same number of answers correct as the average third-grader who took the test in the second month of the school year. One shortcoming to these tests is that the students could have achieved their scores by lucky guessing. They may not even have read any third-grade material on the test.

As of now, the only traditional, norm-referenced test designed to yield placement information is the Metropolitan. It provides an instructional level that indicates the level of material that a student should be able to handle. A group test of this type works best if the student is given the proper level. For instance, if a sixth-grader is reading on a primary level, then he should be given a primary-level test. If given the test designed for average sixth-graders, his score will be invalid. Through guessing, he may well end up with an instructional level that is well beyond his abilities (Gunning, 1982). However, when properly administered, the Metropolitan yields instructional levels that are comparable to those obtained with IRIs (Bristow, Pikulski, & Pelosi, 1983).

> Still another option for obtaining reading levels is to construct and administer a traditional cloze test.

### *Degrees of Reading Power (DRP)*

The Degrees of Reading Power is the only group standardized test designed primarily to provide an instructional level. A modified cloze test, the DRP has no questions. Composed of a series of passages that gradually increase in difficulty, the DRP assesses overall reading ability by having students choose from among five options the one that best completes a portion of the passage from which words have been omitted. Each passage has nine deletions.

As in a classical IRI, the passages gradually increase in difficulty and encompass a wide range of difficulty so that slow, average, and superior readers' ability may be adequately assessed. Instead of yielding a grade-level score, the instrument provides a DRP score. The DRP score indicates what level of material the student should be able to read. A complementary readability formula is used to indicate the difficulty level of books in DRP units. The basic intent of the DRP is to match students with books that are on their levels (see pp. 467 to 469 for information on using DRP scores to match students with books on the appropriate level).

## *Minicase Study*

Mike, the new boy in third grade, was something of a puzzle. Although he had been in the class for three weeks, he hadn't made any friends. The other children didn't pick on him, but they didn't seek him out for inclusion in their games.

Quiet and undemanding, Mike was easily overlooked in the hustle and bustle of the classroom. Although Mike did well with math calculations, he had difficulty with any activity that required reading or writing. Because he was struggling with his third-grade basal reader, the school's reading specialist gave Mike an IRI.

The source of Mike's reading difficulties soon became obvious. According to the word-lists tests, Mike's ability to recognize words at sight or immediately was adequate up through the preprimer grade level. Although he did better with word recognition in context, Mike's instructional level turned out to be first grade. Actually, Mike was able to read second-grade material with 80 percent comprehension, but his word recognition was only 85 percent. Having a rich background of information, Mike was able to make maximum use of context to reconstruct the story.

Mike also had excellent listening comprehension. When selections were read to him, Mike was able to answer at least 75 percent of the comprehension questions up through the seventh-grade level. This suggested that Mike had highly developed oral language and cognitive abilities.

Based on the IRI results and the classroom teacher's observations, Mike was provided additional assistance with word-recognition skills. The program included systematic instruction in phonics and in the use of context clues, with heavy emphasis on applying those skills by reading lots of books and other materials on the appropriate level. Writing also became a prominent part of the program.

In order to build on Mike's excellent cognitive and oral language skills, he was encouraged to listen to books on tape and to view informational CD-ROM programs. Mike was also placed in a cooperative learning group composed of students who were especially friendly and outgoing. After a slow start, Mike made rapid progress.

## *Summary*

Widely used, the informal reading inventory, IRI, consists of graded word lists and oral and silent passages that extend from the preprimer through the eighth- or twelfth-grade level. The IRI yields four levels: independent, instructional, frustration, and listening capacity. The independent level is the point at which the student's word recognition is 99 percent and comprehension is 90 percent. Figures for the instructional level are 95 percent word recognition and 75 percent comprehension. The frustration level is reached when word recognition slips to 90 percent or below, or comprehension is 50 percent or less. After a student has reached the frustration level, selections are read to her or him. The listening capacity, which provides an estimate of the level of material that a student could handle if she or he had the necessary processing skills, is the highest point at which the student can understand 75 percent of the material that is read to her or him.

When carefully analyzed, inventories are a rich source of information about a student's reading behavior. Miscue analysis, which can also be used with an IRI or a running record, builds on the concept of the IRI and yields information that opens a window to the strategies that the student is using and the reading process itself. In miscue analysis, an attempt is made to determine to what extent contextual and graphophonic cues are used.

Built on the concept of miscue analysis, the running record is an efficient way to assess students' oral reading. Used extensively in *Reading Recovery,* the main objectives of running records are to make sure students are reading on the appropriate level and to provide insights into they strategies they are using as they decode words.

A number of other tests are modeled on the format or purpose of the IRI. These include oral inventories, word-lists tests, group inventories, and cloze (fill-in-the-blank) tests.

## Application Activities

1. Compare two of the inventories mentioned in this chapter. Pay particular attention to the quality of the selections and questions. Which inventory seems to be better? Why?
2. Administer an informal reading inventory. Using the modified miscue analysis recommended in the chapter, analyze the inventory results. Based on this analysis, what strategies are used by the student you tested? What might be done to improve this student's reading?
3. Administer a running record to a student in a primary grade. Analyze the results and answer these questions: Was the text that you used on the appropriate level of difficulty? What strategies did the student seem to be using? What seemed to be the student's greatest strengths and weaknesses?

# Chapter 5

# Assessment of Reading and Writing Processes

## *Using What You Know*

This chapter complements the previous one on informal reading inventories, miscue analyses, and running records. It continues to look into ways in which reading and writing problems are assessed and analyzed and to provide techniques for assessing critical areas, such as decoding and comprehension, in more depth. It also discusses ways of assessing such related areas as spelling and writing. In addition, it goes beyond formal and informal tests and looks at other ways of gathering information.

What do you know about assessing reading difficulties? In addition to knowing at what level the student is reading, what else would you wish to know if you were teaching a student with a reading difficulty? How would you go about gathering that data in order to get the most useful information in the shortest amount of time?

## *Anticipation Guide*

Read each of the following statements. Put a check under "Agree" or "Disagree" to show how you feel about each one. If you can, discuss your responses with classmates.

| | Agree | Disagree |
|---|---|---|
| **1.** The most useful way to gather information about reading and writing processes is through observation. | ______ | ______ |
| **2.** Decoding is the most important reading area to assess. | ______ | ______ |
| **3.** When testing decoding skills, it is better to use real words rather than nonsense words. | ______ | ______ |

4. Having students retell a story is a better way to assess comprehension than asking them questions about the selection. ________ ________
5. If a student has good comprehension, you don't need to test decoding or vocabulary skills. ________ ________

## *Reading Processes: Decoding*

Having insight into a student's decoding processes will help you decide on the most promising approaches to use when instructing the youngster and determine what kinds of instruction the student might need. In the previous chapter, you learned how to interpret the results of word-lists tests and word recognition in context on informal reading inventories and also how to interpret running records. Through interviews, observation, and occasional informal questions, you can verify findings and gain additional information about the student's decoding processes.

> By asking students to tell you how they figured out a hard word, you are helping them become more aware of their thought processes.

As students read aloud, note the processes that they are apparently using. Note, first of all, whether they seem to have strategies that are effective. Do they use context? When they decode a word, do they sound it out letter by letter (B + e + n) or do they attempt to put large elements together (B + en). Do they integrate context and sounding out? Do they try another pronunciation when the word they have reconstructed doesn't make sense?

After students have successfully decoded a difficult word, ask them how they figured out the word; or, as they are unsuccessfully attempting to decode a word, ask what you might do to help them. For students who have serious decoding and word-learning problems, you might use the interview presented in Figure 5-1. It isn't necessary to ask all the questions listed. Simply ask those that seem most pertinent.

Name of Student ______________________________

Date ______________

Age ______________ Grade ______________ Reading Level ______________

**Word Identification Interview**

1. How do you feel about reading?
2. Is reading hard?
3. What do you think makes reading hard?
4. What is the hardest thing for you to do in reading?
5. Why do you think that it's hard for you to learn words?
6. What is the hardest thing about learning words?
7. What would make it easier?
8. What do you do when you come across a hard word?
9. What makes it hard to figure out words?
10. What kinds of words are the hardest to learn?

**FIGURE 5-1**

If you want to find out what phonic elements a student knows, administer the *Word Patterns Survey* in Appendix A. The *Survey* consists of sixty words that include most of the major word patterns found in single-syllable words. If students do poorly on the *Word Patterns Survey* and don't seem to know initial consonant correspondences, administer the *Beginning Sounds* test, also found in Appendix A. If students do well on the *Word Patterns Survey,* administer the *Syllable Survey* in Appendix A to see how well they can decode multisyllabic words.

## *Reading Processes: Comprehension*

Comprehension can be assessed in a variety of ways. In addition to administering and analyzing an informal inventory, observing students in a discussion in class, noting students' performance on teacher-made comprehension tests or on end-of-book-unit tests provide an overall sense of a student's ability to comprehend what has been read. Group standardized norm-referenced tests, such as the *Metropolitan, Iowa, Gates-MacGinitie, California,* or *Stanford,* or other similar measures, provide overall measures of comprehension. As noted in Chapter 3, guessing is a factor in most norm-referenced tests since they generally have a multiple-choice format; in light of this, the tests are measures of recognition of information rather than recall or construction of meaning. A better test of comprehension is the informal reading inventory or a similar measure, since guessing does not play a factor, and the students must construct their responses.

### Retellings

As noted when discussing informal reading inventories, an excellent way to assess comprehension is to arrange for a student to read a selection of the type typically read in class and then request a retelling. To use a retelling to probe comprehension of an expository piece, try the following procedures:

#### *Step 1: Provide Material*

Provide a student with expository material on his level. The material shouldn't be so hard that is frustrating, but it should be challenging so that you can observe what strategies the student uses to read difficult materials.

#### *Step 2: Observe Student Reading*

Observe the student to see if he does anything before reading. Watch to see if he gets an overview of the selection, uses the title, headings, or illustrations, or simply dives right in. As the student reads, note whether he looks at illustrations, uses the glossary, or rereads.

#### *Step 3: Have Student Retell*

Have the student retell the selection. To elicit a retelling, start off with open-ended questions, so students have complete freedom to formulate their responses. For an informational selection, ask such questions as: "Tell me in your own words as much information as you can from the selection that you just read." Or, "Tell me what you learned from the selection." If the student doesn't provide sufficient information, ask, "Can you tell me more about what you just read?" Note the quality and organization of the retelling. Is the student able to restate the main idea of the selection or provide a summary? Are most of the major points included in the retelling? Does the student seem to have an adequate understanding of the information? Does the student relate

*continued*

**Retellings** *Continued*

the information to her personal life or other information that she possesses?

*Step 4: Ask Follow-Up Questions*

If the student was not able to retell the selection adequately, then ask follow-up or probing questions designed to assess how well the main idea and supporting details were comprehended. Ask: "What was this selection mostly about? What important details did the author include in the selection?" If the student has difficulty, provide assistance, but note what kinds of help are needed and how much help is required. Also try to gain insight into the student's reasoning processes so that you have a sense of what kind of help will be effective. If you are working with a group, you might have them write a summary of a brief expository piece.

**Questions** mold responses into a certain form. **Retellings** provide insight into the processes students use to construct meaning and organize information.

After analyzing retellings, reflect on what this information tells you about students' reading-thinking-speaking processes and their ability to organize, integrate, and evaluate.

A retelling of a piece of fiction would take a somewhat different format and would be structured around the main elements of a story: setting, characters, plot, goal, story problem, and theme. After the student has read the selection, ask him to retell it. For a younger student you might say something like, "Pretend I have never heard this story. Tell it to me." If necessary, use prompting questions, such as the following:

| | |
|---|---|
| Setting: | Where did the story take place?<br>When did it take place? |
| Characters: | Who are the main characters in the story?<br>What can you tell me about them? |
| Problem(s): | What problem(s) did the main character have to solve? |
| Goal: | What is the main character's goal?<br>What is she trying to do? |
| Plot: | What are the main things that happened in the story? |
| Outcome: | How was the story problem resolved? |

In assessing a retelling, ask such questions as:

- Are major events or ideas highlighted?
- Are appropriate inferences made about characters and events?
- Is the retelling accurate?
- Is information from the selection integrated with the student's background of information?
- Does the student evaluate information?
- Does the student use the author's organizational pattern?
- What does the retelling reveal about the student's oral language development and presentation style?

To make the assessment of a retelling more efficient and more accurate, list the main elements from an informational piece or story to check off as students mention them. You might use numbers to indicate the sequence of items included in the retelling. Put a "1" next to the plot element that the student mentioned first, a "2" next to the second element mentioned, and so forth. Code items with a *p* that were mentioned as a result of probing. (A sample retelling scoring sheet was presented in Figure 4-7.) Also note the overall completeness and quality of the retelling.

Because of difficulties with expressive language or other problems, some students may have difficulty retelling a story even though they fully comprehend it. Careful use of probes should help you discover to what extent students understood a piece. Using the levels of difficulty–concept of assessment, start with a request for a retelling. If the student is unable to retell the selection, use probes. If the student has difficulty with probes, ask recognition-type questions in which the student only has to recognize or select the right answer: "At the end of the story, did the dog return to its first owner, find a new home, or join a pack of wild dogs?" The idea is to find out at what level the student understands the selection and in what format she or he is best able to respond. Students who have adequate comprehension but encounter difficulty in retelling should be taught how to retell a story. If it is not possible to obtain individual retellings, you might arrange for students to create written retellings.

A written retelling assesses students' ability to construct meaning from what they have read and organize that in written form. Poor readers are typically penalized when written responses are required (Simmons, 1990).

## *Think-Alouds*

A key component in comprehension is the appropriate use of background knowledge when reading text. Poor comprehenders may read in bottom-up fashion focusing on decoding rather than understanding the passage, or they may overrely on background knowledge and insert their own information for what the text actually conveyed. One way to determine how students are processing text is to use a think-aloud. As its name suggests, a **think-aloud** involves having readers discuss what is going on in their minds as they read. This reveals processes that the readers use. Think-alouds can be brief and informal. For instance, during a discussion of a selection, you might ask questions similar to the following:

**Think-alouds:** readers or writers describe their thought processes as they read a selection or compose a piece.

- *What was the selection mainly about?*
- *How did you get the main idea of the selection?*
- *What were you thinking about as you read the selection?*
- *What do you think will happen next in the selection? What makes you think so? (Gunning, 1996)*

To conduct a more formal think-aloud, use a selection that is one hundred to two hundred words in length. Mark off sections of the text where you want the students to stop and discuss their thought processes. This could be after each sentence or after brief segments of text. Ask questions designed to reveal students' thought processes. These might include the following:

- **Before Reading**
  What do you think this selection might be about? What makes you think so?
- **During Reading** (after reading each marked-off segment)
  What was going on in your mind as you read the selection? What were you thinking about? Were there any parts that were hard to understand? What did you do when you came across parts that were hard to understand? Were there any hard words? What did you do when you came across hard words?
- **After Reading** (after reading entire selection)
  Tell me in your own words what this selection was about.

If students haven't engaged in thinking aloud, they may be reluctant to do so or may tell you what they think you want to know. To get students used to the idea, model the process. Tell them to take time every once in a while to think about what they are doing. This will get them used to noticing their thinking and, if done before you conduct a think-aloud, it should enhance the richness of the think-aloud. Think-alouds are also more productive if the student feels secure and accepted (P. Johnston, 1992).

Think-alouds can focus on aspects of reading. Wade (1990) created think-alouds to assess students' ability to predict, read flexibly, and integrate text information with background knowledge.

As students think aloud, record their responses word for word. Then analyze their responses. Note behaviors listed below (these strategies are discussed in Chapter 12). Then come to conclusions about the effectiveness of the strategies that the student is using and the extent to which the student is monitoring for meaning.

- Made predictions
- Revised prediction or conclusion based on new information
- Considered information previously read
- Made inferences
- Drew conclusions
- Made judgments
- Visualized or created images
- Paraphrased
- Summarized
- Constructed questions
- Reasoned about reading
- Monitored for meaning
- Noted difficult words
- Noted confusing passages
- Reread difficult sections
- Used illustrations as an aid
- Used context or other decoding skills

If possible, think-alouds should be used with actual school texts. One advantage of using think-alouds with actual school texts is that it increases the validity of the procedure and also increases the possibility that the results can be used to plan a program of intervention (Myers & Lytle, 1986). Myers and Lytle have constructed think-alouds specifically for use with low-achieving readers. They use passages that are fifteen to twenty sentences in length and retype the passage so each sentence is on a separate line. Sentences are uncovered one by one. After reading a sentence, students are asked to tell what they were thinking about or what event went through their minds as they were reading. Particular emphasis is placed on having the students tell what is going through their minds when they encounter difficult sentences because it is at this point that insights into their way of processing difficult text are garnered.

Caroline, a fourth-grader, was referred to a university reading clinic because she was having difficulty comprehending what she read. Through administering a Think-Aloud Protocol Analysis, Myers and Lytle (1986) found that she used a number of strategies including paraphrasing, inferring, and elaborating on the text by adding information and visualizing. However, Caroline failed to monitor for meaning with the result that she sometimes failed to comprehend difficult passages and wasn't aware of her lack of comprehension.

Building on Caroline's strengths, the teacher affirmed her use of strategies and overall comprehension with the result that Caroline increased the use of her strategies and seemed more confident about her reading. She was also shown how to monitor her comprehension so she could take corrective action when she did not understand a passage. Strategies such as predicting and creating hypotheses about the reading were also demonstrated.

## *Questionnaires and Interviews*

> A good example of a well-designed questionnaire is The Elementary Reading Attitude Survey in the May 1990 issue of *The Reading Teacher.*

Another way of getting information about reading processes is through questionnaires or interviews. Some questions that might be asked include the ones listed in the comprehension interview presented below. Of course, all these questions wouldn't be asked in one sitting. First, you would determine which area or areas of comprehension you want to explore and then choose or compose questions designed to tap into these areas. The three boldfaced questions are the most open-ended. Encourage students to respond to these. If more information is desired, ask the probing questions listed under each boldfaced query.

**Before Reading**

**What do you do before you read?**

Do you read the title and headings?

Do you look at the pictures?

Do you predict what the selection might be about?

Do you ask yourself what you know about the topic?

Do you plan how you are going to read the selection—fast, medium, or slow?

**During Reading**

**What do you do while you're reading?**

Do you think about what you're reading?

Do you stop every once in a while and ask yourself what you've read so far?

Do you picture in your mind the people, events, and places that you are reading about?

Do you make up questions in your mind as you read?

Do you imagine that you are talking to the author as you read?

**What do you do if the passage is confusing?**
Do you read it again?
Do you just keep on reading?
Do you try to get help from photos or drawings?
**What do you do if you run into a hard word?**
Do you use context to try to figure it out?
Do you try to sound it out?
Do you use a dictionary or a glossary?

**After Reading**

**After reading the selection, what do you do?**
Do you think about what you've read?
Do you do something with the information that you've learned?
Do you compare what you've just learned from your reading with what you already know?

A less formal way to assess students' use of strategies is to include some of these questions in pre- and post-reading discussions. An easy way to assess the difficulty students might be having with text—especially text that they're reading on their own—is to have students jot down the locations of words or passages that are posing problems or simply to place a sticky note under a difficult word or confusing passage (Gunning, 1996).

To enhance the validity and reliability of observations, determine which behaviors you wish to observe, for how long, and under what conditions. Construct an observation checklist so you can focus on target behaviors. Schedule several observations.

### *Observations*

Direct observation is also a valuable source of information about comprehension and other processes. Although observations may be made at any time, some situations provide especially rich sources of information. In a reading conference or a group discussion of a selection, note the level of comprehension, the degree of interest and involvement, the grasp of strategies, and the immediate needs of students. During a period of voluntary reading, observe the kinds of books students select to read and the interest with which they read. In cooperative groups, note how students interact. During writing workshop, note how students approach their writing and how they use their time. It is especially helpful to observe students as they encounter a difficult word or confusing passage: What strategies do they use? How successful are they at applying these strategies?

Since memory is fleeting and deceptive, it is helpful to keep a record of observations. A checklist is useful for recording observations because it helps us to focus on key areas. You might also compose anecdotal records.

**Anecdotal record:** recording of an incident or behavior that provides information about a student.

### *Anecdotal Records*

An **anecdotal record** is the recording of an event that sheds some light on the student's reading/writing behavior. An anecdotal record may be very brief but should contain a summary portrayal of the event, the time, date, names of persons involved, and a description of the setting. In addition to providing information about comprehension and other reading processes, anecdotal records may be used to obtain data about interests, attitudes, strategy use, work habits, interaction with others, or other elements of the program. Records might be kept daily, weekly, or monthly. It is helpful to take records of the same type of behavior in a variety of situations. For instance, a student might achieve excellent comprehension under some circumstances but evidence poor comprehension under others. When making anecdotal records, include a number of observations so that you don't form a conclusion based on limited data. Also take note of successful efforts as well as unsuccessful ones. There is a tendency to stress the failures and omit the successes, but this results in an inaccurate portrayal (Bush & Huebner, 1979).

An anecdotal record is a recording, not an evaluation of behavior. In an anecdotal record, you tell what the student did, not how you feel about the behavior. For instance, the statement, "Fred was lazy today" is an evaluative statement whereas the statement, "Fred wrote only one page in the thirty-minute writing period and refused to read" is a description of Fred's behavior.

In addition to being an accurate description of behavior, an anecdotal record should also describe the setting in sufficient detail "to give meaning to the event" (Thorndike & Hagen, 1977, p. 525). If the record includes an interpretation or evaluation of the event, that should be kept separate from the description of the event. The interpretation might be placed in parentheses. Presented in Figure 5-2 are a series of anecdotal records. What do they reveal about the student? How might this information be used in planning instruction for the student?

> A convenient way to take anecdotal records is to summarize the behavior on a sticky note and, later post it in a notebook set aside for keeping anecdotal records.

In order for anecdotal records to be used effectively, they should be reviewed periodically and summarized. Teachers should look for developmental trends or patterns. Strengths and weaknesses should be noted and used as a basis for gaining insight into the student's learning and planning instruction (Rhodes & Nathenson-Mejia, 1992).

Anecdotal records are especially useful for observing behaviors in which there is a social interaction, but may be used in any situation in which there is overt, recordable behavior that may have some significance for the learning process. For low-achieving readers, such situations might include: their working in reading or writing groups or conferences, their using strategies in reading and writing, their general work habits, their behavior during voluntary reading periods, their interactions in cooperative groups, their strategies used in studying informational text, and their behavior when encountering an unknown word or confusing passage.

## *Vocabulary Knowledge*

Assessment of vocabulary may not require additional testing. You can get some sense of students' listening and speaking vocabularies by noting the kinds of words that they use in their conversations with you and the quality of their responses to questions. How does their use of words compare with the demands of the situation? Is it adequate? Is it more than adequate? Is it less than satisfactory? If the vocabulary portion of an individual intelligence

Student: *Marcia* Date: *10-11*

*During reading workshop, Marcia listened to Three Billy Goats Gruff on tape. I asked her if there were any books that she wanted to take home but she said no and said that all the books in the room had too many hard words. I told her that I had some new books that she might like because they didn't have so many hard words. I showed her Have You Seen My Cat?, The Good Bad Cat, Cat on the Mat, and Let's Get a Pet. After looking over the books, she chose Have You Seen My Cat?, which I share-read with her.*

Student: *Marcia* Date: *10-12*

*Marcia rushed in this morning and claimed she could read Have You Seen My Cat? Relying heavily on pictures, she was able to retell the story. Marcia asked if she could take another book home and chose Cat on the Mat. I share-read it with her. I asked her to point to words as I read them, which she did.*

Student: *Marcia* Date: *10-14*

*When Marcia returned Cat on the Mat, she said she would like to read it to me. She was able to read it, but continued to use pictures to help her. However, she was obviously using the print. She only used the pictures when she had difficulty with a word. She asked if she could take Let's Get a Pet home. She said that she was getting a pet and wanted to see if the book had any good ideas.*

**FIGURE 5-2 Anecdotal Record**

test has been given, check to see how the students performed. If there still seems to be a need for vocabulary testing, you might administer the *Peabody Picture Vocabulary Test* or another receptive test of vocabulary. Some diagnostic tests also assess vocabulary. The DARTTS (Riverside), Gates-McKillop-Horowitz (Harcourt), and the first two levels of the Stanford Diagnostic Reading Test (Harcourt) assess listening vocabulary. Also look at the informal reading inventory results. How did the students do with items that involved difficult vocabulary? How did they do on the word-lists tests? Were they able to pronounce the difficult words? Did they mispronounce some of the multisyllabic words in such a way that suggests that they aren't a part of their listening vocabulary?

Note students' reading vocabulary as well as their listening and speaking vocabularies. There may be words in their listening or speaking vocabularies that they don't recognize in print. Most norm-referenced tests contain a reading vocabulary subtest. Generally, vocabulary and comprehension scores are comparable. When vocabulary is high, comprehension is high. When vocabulary is low, comprehension is low. A high-vocabulary, low-comprehension score suggests that the student has the potential to read better, but is not using it. The cause could be an attention problem, weakness in strategy use, or difficulty seeing relationships among words or ideas. A low-vocabulary, high-comprehension score suggests that the student has a language difficulty or might be still learning English. Students who are still acquiring English may have a wealth of background to bring to a selection and so are able to answer a number of comprehension questions, but their English vocabulary is limited because they lack extended experience with the language.

## *Writing: Assessment of Writing*

More than any other subject, writing lends itself to assessment. The product is there for all to see and can be analyzed in many different ways. However, although an analysis of the final product will yield important information, it is also important to examine the process of writing. Combining product and process information provides a fuller understanding of your students as writers, and so helps you to plan the best possible program for them. In your evaluation, include an assessment of the teaching techniques that you have used.

### *Role of Students*

Include students as an integral part of the evaluation process. Evaluation starts with the assessment of needs and the setting of goals. Discuss with students their goals for the writing program and discover what their needs are. These goals and needs don't have to be expressed all at one time, and will change as the students' writing ability changes. An opportune time to discuss goals and needs is when examining the student's writing portfolio. You might ask such questions as:

- What kinds of writing do you do in school?
- What kinds of writing do you do outside of school?
- How do you feel about writing?
- What do you like about writing?
- What do you like best about writing?
- What is hard for you in writing?
- What kinds of writing would you like to learn to do better?

### *Assessment Techniques*

#### *Observations*

Observe students as they write. How do they go about choosing topics? About what kinds of topics do they like to write? What kind of pre-planning do they do? How much effort do they put into composing? What are their work habits like? How do they go about revising and editing?

As you hold conferences with students, note strengths and needs. Also note strengths and needs during discussions and sharing. Keep a chart similar to the one shown in Figure 5-3. Also keep anecdotal records on actions and events that offer special insight into the student as writer.

| Student | Date | Subject | Status | Strengths | Needs | Plans |
|---|---|---|---|---|---|---|
| Alberto | 1/9 | Letter to friend | 2nd draft | Lots of information | Show interest in other person | Ask person questions |
| Georgia | 1/9 | New sister | 1st draft | Warm tone | Weak beginning | Work on beginning |
| Latisha | 1/9 | Grandmother | planning | Interesting personality | Examples of courage & kindness | |
| Raphael | | Editorial: rats | | | | |
| Stephanie | | Dancing Contest | | | | |

**FIGURE 5-3 Writing Conference Notes**

### *Journals*

Students' journals provide insight into their writing. Journal entries may include a description of the topics they have explored, some of the struggles they have had with their writing, and some of their achievements as writers. Of course, the journal itself might show how the students' writing has changed. Are the selections longer? Are they more specific and purposeful? Are they more alive?

## *Evaluating Pieces of Writing*

How should a piece of writing be assessed? Should it be evaluated holistically, according to the general impression that it makes? Or, should it be analyzed element by element, including content, style, originality, and mechanics? As you will see in the next two sections, both holistic and analytic approaches have merit.

**Holistic scoring:** process of assessing compositions on the basis of an overall impression of the piece.

**Rubric:** overall description of standards, often accompanied by example pieces, for assessing a composition holistically.

### *Holistic Scoring*

In ***holistic scoring,*** the teacher reacts to the piece as a whole, rather than being unduly influenced by any one of the major elements of writing. The piece is assessed in terms of its overall effectiveness: Does it work? Is it convincing or moving? To score a piece holistically, you might compare it to three anchor pieces that have already been rated as being good, fair, or poor. Determine which of the three pieces the composition being assessed is most like. You should also use a written **rubric** as a guide. The rubric contains a description of key elements that would most closely characterize a good, fair, and poor piece. A sample holistic-scoring rubric is presented in Figure 5-4.

| | Level 4 | Level 3 | Level 2 | Level 1 |
|---|---|---|---|---|
| *Content* | Develops topic clearly and fully. Develops main point with interesting examples or ample detail. | Develops topic clearly. Uses several examples or details. Examples or details are adequate to develop topic but lack originality or interest. | Develops topic with examples or details. Doesn't use enough examples or details to be convincing. Some details may not pertain. | Topic is not clearly developed. Does not use details or examples to develop topic, or uses details or examples that are not related to the topic. Statement of topic may not be clear. |
| *Organization* | Shows a definite pattern of organization. All elements clearly relate to main topic and are in proper sequence. Uses signal words or other devices to show how ideas are related. Piece has a natural flow. | Shows a definite organizational pattern. Details are in proper sequence. Uses some signal words to indicate organization. Piece lacks a natural flow. | Shows some sense of organization. Details generally relate to main idea. However, may not show how details relate to each other and main idea. May include extraneous details. Fails to use signal words or other organizational devices. | Fails to develop a main idea. Details do not relate to main idea. |
| *Sentence Structure* | Uses varied sentence structure. Includes complex and compound as well as simple sentences. Sentences are grammatically correct. | Uses some complex sentences but primarily uses simple or compound sentences. Makes few sentence errors. | Uses simple sentences primarily. Sentences are brief and lack development or expansion. Includes run-ons and sentence fragments. | Sentences are brief and inadequately developed or may contain one or two very long sentences connected with a series of *and*s. Many sentence fragments and run-ons. Inadequate use of adjectives and adverbs. |
| *Word Choice* | Word choice is appropriate and varied. Uses vivid words. Use of advanced vocabulary. | Word choice is appropriate and varied. Uses words typical of average student. | Word choice is generally appropriate but lacks variety and vividness. | Uses limited stock of words. Some words may be inappropriate. |
| *Mechanics* | No or very few errors in use of basic mechanics. | Few errors in spelling, punctuation, or capitalization. | Shows a grasp of rudimentary mechanics: capitalization of first word in sentence and correct use of end punctuation but has several spelling, punctuation, or capitalization errors. | Numerous errors in rudimentary mechanics. |

**FIGURE 5-4 Holistic Scoring Rubric for Expository Prose**

**Analytic scoring:** process of scoring compositions through a consideration of major features of the pieces.

### *Analytic Scoring*

While holistic scoring is an excellent device for gaining an overall impression of a piece of writing, **analytic scoring** helps the teacher note specific strengths and weaknesses in the student's writing. When using analytic scoring with writers who have difficulties, it is best to focus on a few essential features that you have been emphasizing rather than noting all the errors in a piece. This provides a framework for both you and the student and helps keep the struggling writer from becoming disheartened. A sample analytic-scoring guide is presented in Figure 5-5.

## *Using Portfolios to Assess Writing*

**Portfolio:** collection of pieces of writing, or other work samples, lists of books read, test results, and other data.

Although originally designed primarily as a way of assessing writing, ***portfolios*** are also used to assess progress in reading and in content areas. Modeled on the artist's portfolio, the student's portfolio is designed to house a sampling of the student's work. As such, it displays the breadth of her or his work and shows development over time. Portfolios serve the following purposes:

To assess the processes a subject uses, include samples from various stages of a project. For writing, include pre-writing sheets, first draft, revisions, and final copy.

1. By assembling a portfolio and periodically examining it, students see how they have grown and developed as writers, what their strengths are, and in what areas they need to work.
2. Portfolios provide teachers with a means of assessing the growth of their students so they can plan activities to foster further growth. They also give teachers a deeper understanding of the way students develop as writers.
3. Portfolios can help parents better understand the development of their children's abilities. They can see areas in which their children have grown and areas in which they need additional work. Seeing how their children have developed is more meaningful to them than numerical or letter grades.

Physically, portfolios can be a folder, an oversize manila envelope, a small box, or an accordion folder. Contents can range from rough drafts through finished copies, to videotapes of an enactment of an original drama. In order to fulfill their promise, portfolios have to be carefully planned. There are five steps to using portfolios: establishing goals, deciding on indicator tasks, establishing standards, managing portfolios, and evaluating (Paris, 1993).

### *Steps to Using Portfolios*

Poor writers do better on portfolio assessment than on test compositions. Portfolios provide them with the time they need to do their best work (Simmons, 1990).

*Step 1: Establishing Goals*

As with any evaluation, you must first establish goals. These will be overall goals for your program and individual goals or objectives for each student. If you have constructed an IEP (Individual Education Plan required for students who are assigned special education services) or if students in your class have such plans, that could be one source from which objectives can be drawn.

Student's name ______________________ Date ____________

| | Analytic Scores | | | |
|---|---|---|---|---|
| | poor | fair | good | superior |
| *Content* | | | | |
| Opinion is clearly stated. | ____ | ____ | ____ | ____ |
| Has reasons and examples to back up opinion. | ____ | ____ | ____ | ____ |
| Reasons and examples are convincing. | ____ | ____ | ____ | ____ |
| Ends with forcefully stated conclusion. | ____ | ____ | ____ | ____ |
| *Organization* | | | | |
| Reasons are logically ordered. | ____ | ____ | ____ | ____ |
| *Style* | | | | |
| Opinions and proof are convincingly stated. | ____ | ____ | ____ | ____ |
| *Mechanics* | | | | |
| Each sentence begins with a capital letter. | ____ | ____ | ____ | ____ |
| Correct end punctuation has been used. | ____ | ____ | ____ | ____ |
| Words are spelled correctly. | ____ | ____ | ____ | ____ |
| *Sentence Structure* | | | | |
| Sentences are written correctly. | ____ | ____ | ____ | ____ |
| Sentences are fully developed. | ____ | ____ | ____ | ____ |
| Uses variety of sentence patterns. | ____ | ____ | ____ | ____ |
| *Word Choice* | | | | |
| Uses varied vocabulary. | ____ | ____ | ____ | ____ |
| Uses words correctly. | ____ | ____ | ____ | ____ |
| Imaginative use of words. | ____ | ____ | ____ | ____ |

**FIGURE 5-5 Analytic Score for an Opinion/Proof Paragraph**

*Step 2: Deciding on Indicator Tasks*

Once you have decided on your goals, you must select indicator tasks that you will be able to use to tell whether or not the goal has been reached. For instance, if one goal is to increase students' ability to write expository prose, then samples of expository writing could be used as a basis for assessing that goal.

*Step 3: Establishing Standards*

You need to decide what counts as an adequate performance. For example, what qualities must an expository essay meet before you can say that a student's performance is adequate? As noted earlier, a type of standard frequently used in the assessment of writing and other literacy tasks is the rubric. Rubrics can be composed for individual literacy tasks and also for the portfolio as a whole.

To examine a portfolio, have the student explain it to you. Ask: "What is your favorite piece of work?" Or "What does the portfolio show about your progress as a reader and writer?"

*Step 4: Managing Portfolios*

Portfolios can get out of hand. They can become a warehouse for a student's work, including virtually every piece of writing he or she has done. So that you and the student can focus on what's important, portfolios should include only key samples of work. A portfolio is not the same as a writing or a reading folder. The writing folder might contain virtually everything the student has written, including works in progress and lists of possible topics. The portfolio can be more selective, including only samples of the student's work. These samples are chosen because they can be used as indicators of progress toward one or more of the goals that have been specified. Samples from the beginning, middle, and end of the instructional period should be included so that progress can be assessed. In addition, some of the samples should include rough drafts as well as finished copies. Encourage students to include samples of work done out of school in addition to work done in school. If students are composing poems, taking part in a play put on by a community group, reading books on their own, or engaged in other significant literacy activities outside of school, this should be noted in their portfolios. Both teacher and student should agree on a system for deciding upon which pieces of writing or other work samples are to be included in the portfolio. The student may want to include only her or his best pieces. However, you may want to select a variety of pieces so that the portfolio reflects multiple aspects of the students' literacy development. You might adopt a system in which the student chooses a third of the pieces to be included, you choose a third, and you mutually agree on a third. Whichever system you choose, the student should be involved in the process.

A checklist or summary sheet placed on the inside cover or other suitable spot should provide an overview of the contents of the portfolio. Students should also provide statements in which they list their goals, the activities undertaken to reach their goals, and a reflection on their progress on meeting their goals. Students might also note continuing needs and future goals and plans for meeting those needs and reaching those goals. Some teachers use the three-column chart presented in Figure 5-6 to help students reflect on their progress (Hansen, 1987). These charts were designed for writing folders but could be used in portfolios as well.

To build students' sense of self-efficacy, demonstrate how much they have improved. Examine pieces written at different times of the year that show a progression.

As Farnan, Flood, and Lapp (1994) note, portfolios promote students' monitoring of their progress in literacy development. This is especially important for low-achieving readers and writers, who are often passive recipients rather than active, involved participants.

> *When students document and reflect on their progress, they can gain insights about their learning often denied to students. Through these insights, students can develop strategies that*

| Things I can do well | Things I'm working on | Things I plan to learn |
|---|---|---|
| *Write a letter*<br><br>*Capitalize, use periods and question marks* | *Writing pieces that explain or tell how to do something*<br><br>*Spelling*<br><br>*Better sentences* | *How to write interesting beginnings*<br><br>*How to write better endings* |

**FIGURE 5-6 Portfolio Reflection**

> *will give them a sense of control over their future learning and an opportunity to overcome feelings of learned helplessness. (p. 308)*

*Step 5: Evaluating Portfolios*

Both teacher and students evaluate the contents of the portfolio. Portfolio conferences should be held at least four times a year (Farr & Farr, 1990), but may be held more frequently, especially if you are working one-on-one or with small groups of low-achieving readers and writers.

## *Assessing Writing Samples*

If a portfolio is not available, the next best source of information is to obtain writing samples. Samples can be obtained in a number of ways. You might give students a drawing or photo and ask them to write a story about it. For young students, you might supply the following prompt: Ask them to draw a picture of something that they like to do. Then have him write a story about the picture. This prompt could also be adapted for use with older students. Omitting the drawing portion, you might ask them to tell about things they like to do, including hobbies and sports and other interests.

Another prompt that might be used with students of varying ages is to have them write a letter telling about themselves. Picture prompts might be used to elicit narrative tales. Prompts from topics such as those listed below might elicit a variety of narratives, informational, or persuasive pieces:

My Favorite Book
The Most Important Person in My Life
How to Make My Favorite Sandwich
The Importance of Taking Care of Our Home, the Earth
Why We Should or Should Not Build a Station in Space
Why Cats Make Better Pets Than Dogs (or vice versa)
What I Would Do If I Had a Million Dollars

If possible, obtain two or three samples of students' writing. Also try to obtain pieces written for varied purposes. When obtaining the samples, emphasize that students should do their best but should not worry about handwriting or spelling. Because you want to obtain an estimate of what the student can do independently, do not provide help with spelling or mechanics.

Analyze the writing samples along a variety of dimensions ranging from content to handwriting. When analyzing the samples, start with the highest-level aspect—content—and work down to the lowest-level aspect—handwriting. Areas that might be assessed are listed below:

| | |
|---|---|
| **Content** | Does the piece have a main idea or theme?<br>How well developed is the main idea or theme? |
| **Organization** | How well organized is the piece?<br>Do all the details support the main idea?<br>Are the details in their proper order? |
| **Sentence Structure** | How well structured are the sentences?<br>Are there a variety of sentences?<br>Are the sentences well developed? |
| **Word Choice** | What is the quality of the word choice?<br>Are a variety of words used?<br>Are words used correctly?<br>Is there an attempt to use language in an imaginative way? |
| **Mechanics** | Has correct style been used?<br>Is the capitalization, punctuation, spelling, and usage correct? |
| **Handwriting** | How legible is the handwriting?<br>Is the handwriting readable?<br>Are all the letters correctly formed?<br>Is spacing between words and letters accurate? |

As students write their sample pieces, observe their performance. Note whether they spend time planning or revising. Note, too, how much effort they put into their into their writing.

Commercial tests might also be used to assess writing achievement. One of the best known writing tests is the Test of Written Language-2 (TOWL-2). The TOWL-2, which is designed for students from age seven through seventeen, assesses the mechanics of writing, sentence combining, spelling, and the ability to write a story. (For additional information on the assessment of writing, see Chapter 13.)

## *Spelling*

> Although poor spellers can be good readers, the reverse is almost never true. Poor readers are virtually always poor spellers.

Research conducted by Henderson (1990) and his colleagues indicates that spelling develops in stages. By knowing what stage a student is in, the teacher can build on that knowledge and teach spelling and decoding more effectively. However, in order to understand the developmental stages of spelling, it is important to understand the basic principles of spelling development.

Spelling is based on three principles: alphabetic, within-word, and meaning (Henderson & Templeton, 1986). On its most primitive level, English spelling is alphabetical. Letters represent sounds. In the word *hat,* for instance, the letters *h-a-t* represent the sound /h/, /a/, /t/. However, there are a large number of words in which there isn't a one-to-one relationship between a word's letters and sounds. The within-word pattern principle means that spelling is frequently determined by the patterning of letters within a word. For instance the *e* marker at the end of a word indicates that a vowel is long rather than short, as in *hat/hate.*

When students correctly spell words they have misread, they may not be analyzing the words in their reading. They may be creating a pronunciation on the basis of a quick look.

According to meaning, the third principle, words that have similar meanings have similar spellings, even if their pronunciations differ. For instance, the italicized letters in the following word pairs have different pronunciations even though the letter in each pair is the same: compe*t*e/compe*t*ition, ser*e*ne/ser*e*nity. Spellings have been kept the same to show the similarity in meanings. As students' knowledge of spelling develops, they learn first the alphabetic principle, then the within-word principle, and, finally, the meaning principle.

## *Stages of Spelling*

Based on the alphabetic, within-word, and meaning principles, spelling development is divided into five broad stages: prephonemic, letter-name, within-word pattern, syllable juncture, and derivational constancy.

In the prephonemic stage, children haven't grasped the alphabetic principle. They don't realize that letters represent sounds.

### *Prephonemic*

The student in this stage does not use the alphabetic principle. The student may create letter-like forms, use a mixture of letters and numbers, or just use letters. However, the letters do not represent speech sounds.

### *Letter Name*

The student's writing incorporates the alphabetic principle. In the earliest stages, a single letter may represent a whole word: *K* for *car.* Later, the student represents the first and last consonant sounds: *KR* for *car.* As the student progresses, she or he begins using vowels. Long vowels are spelled with letter names: *FET* for *feet, BOT* for *boat.* Fortunately for the inventive speller, the names of the long vowels incorporate their sounds. Because short-vowel sounds are not incorporated by a distinctive set of letters, many inventive spellers use the letter name for the long vowel that is formed in approximately the same place in the mouth as the short vowel they are attempting to spell. Say "ay," the long-vowel sound for "A" and "eh," the short-vowel sound for "A" and you will notice that both are very close in their place of articulation. Since short *e* is articulated in approximately the same place as long *a, bed* is often spelled as *bad* in the letter-name stage. This is known as the "close to" tactic. Other "close to" spellings include spelling short *i* with an *E* (*BET* for *bit*), short *o* with an *I* (*TIP* for *top*), and short *u* with an *O* (*COT* for *cut*) (Read, 1971).

Students in the letter-name stage rely not only on how words sound but also on how the sounds feel as they are articulated. /v/ feels like /f/ so *love* is spelled *LF* (Bear et al., 1996).

For some consonant spellings, the spelling–sound connection is not apparent at first glance. For instance, *tr* is frequently spelled *ch* as in *CHAN* for *train* and *dr* may be spelled *JR* as in *JROM* for *drum.* To see why these spellings are logical from the student's point of view, listen carefully as you say *chain* and *train.* Did you notice that the beginning sound of train is very similar to the beginning sound of chain? And if you say *chree,* it sounds like *tree* (Temple, Nathan, Temple, & Burris, 1993). In similar fashion, the *d* in *dr* has a /j/ sound, so *drop* may be spelled *JRUP* or simply *JUP.* During this stage, spellings with nasal sounds such as *m* and *n* are omitted when they occur before a consonant so that *bump* would be spelled *BUP.* At the end of this stage, students begin to spell regular short-vowel words (*hat, pet*) correctly.

### *Within-Word Pattern*

Through encountering standard spelling in books and other printed matter in their environment, children begin to notice certain spelling conventions: the consonant cluster at the beginning of *train* is spelled with *tr; e* at the end of a word is a marker for a long vowel (*rake*), and so forth. They begin to use visual features in addition to sound features to spell words and enter the within-word pattern stage. Their spelling is no longer solely based on sound. Although their spelling is not always correct (they may spell *rain* as *RANE*), it is becoming more standard and incorporates such features as final *e* markers and double vowel letters to spell long vowel sounds. As students progress in this stage, they learn to spell most single-syllable words accurately.

> The key understanding in the within-word pattern stage is that words are not spelled by sound alone. Orthographic patterns such as final *e* (*brave*) and digraphs (*plain*) must be incorporated.

> The key characteristic of the syllable juncture stage is applying knowledge about spelling single-syllable words to spelling multisyllabic ones; for instance, knowing when to double the final consonant when adding inflectional endings (*hop + ed = hopped*).

### *Syllable Juncture*

With additional experience with print, students begin encountering multisyllabic words. They have a firm grasp of single-syllable patterns, but now must be able to apply their knowledge to multisyllabic words. Students learn when to double the final consonant or drop final *e* when an ending such as *ing* is added (*dropping* or *taking*).

> In the derivational-constancy stage, focus is on meaningful elements rather than sound elements. Students break up words into prefixes, suffixes, and roots rather than syllables.

### *Derivational Constancy*

In this stage, students apply the principle of meaning. Words that have similar meanings have similar spellings even though pronunciations may be different. From a phonemic point of view, a better way to spell *sign* would be *SIN*. However, the *g* is retained to maintain the semantic connection among *sign, signal,* and *signature* (Venezky, 1965). Other examples include: *compose/composition* where the long *o* in the second syllable of *compose* becomes the short *o* in the second syllable of *composition* and *contribute-contribution* with the short *i* in the second syllable of *contribute* becomes a schwa in the second syllable of *contribution* (Ganske, 1993). A chart of the major stages of spelling can be found in Figure 5-7.

As the description of the phases of spelling suggest, learning to spell is a constructive conceptual process. Through the experience of reading and writing words, students create

| | |
|---|---|
| *Prephonemic*<br>*zq* | Use of random letters to spell words. Letters have no relation to sound. |
| *Letter-Name*<br>*td, tod* | Letters represent sounds. In early stage, an initial or an initial and a final consonant may be used to represent the whole word. Later, long-vowel sounds are spelled with their letter names, and short-vowel sounds are spelled with the long-vowel letter formed closest to the place where the short vowel is articulated. At end of stage, regular short vowel words are spelled correctly. |
| *Within-Word Pattern*<br>*tode, toad* | Realizes that there is a visual component to spelling. Thus, a final *e* or another vowel letter would be added to *tod* (toad) to signify the long *o* sound. At the end of this stage, most single-syllable words would be spelled correctly. |
| *Syllable-Juncture*<br>*planning* | Students begin to form hypotheses about how to spell multisyllabic words. They become aware of dropping final *e* or doubling the final consonant when adding certain endings. |
| *Derivational-Constancy*<br>*sign, signal* | Students realize that words with a common derivation and meaning have similar spellings even if the pronunciations vary. |

**FIGURE 5-7 Spelling Stages**

hypotheses about the way words are spelled and then test them. In the letter-naming phase, for instance, students conceive of spelling as being a process of writing one letter for each sound. In the within-word pattern phase, they realize that the pattern of a word, and not just its individual sounds, must be considered when the word is being spelled.

For a more thorough analysis of children's spelling, use the *Developmental Spelling Analysis* (Ganske, 1993).

Since spelling is constructive, conceptual, and progresses through various phases, it is important that spelling instruction match students' level of word knowledge (Henderson & Templeton, 1986). Vowel markers or the doubling rule for consonant-vowel-consonant words (*hopped, planning*), for instance, would be too difficult conceptually for students who are still grappling with letter-name phonics. They might be able to memorize words like *hate* or *planned* but they wouldn't grasp the underlying principles that determine their spellings. Words should be presented that fit children's developmental levels so they can discover and make use of the underlying regularity of the language.

## *Determining the Spelling Stages*

Although designed for elementary school students, the *Elementary Spelling Inventory* can be used with older, poor spellers who are operating on an elementary school level.

Spelling stages can be assessed by observing the kinds of spellings students create. You can also give a screening test to assess students' spelling development. One such test is presented in Table 5-1. *The Elementary Spelling Inventory* (Bear & Barone, 1989) presents twenty-five words that gradually grow more difficult. Start with the easiest item for each student and continue testing until the words are obviously too difficult. Encourage students to spell the words as best they can. Before

## TABLE 5-1 The Elementary Spelling Inventory (with Error Guide)

| Stages | Early Letter Name | Letter Name | Within-Word Pattern | Syllable Juncture | Derivational Constancy |
|---|---|---|---|---|---|
| 1. bed | b bd | bad | bed | | |
| 2. ship | s sp shp | sep shep | sip ship | | |
| 3. drive | jrv drv | griv driv | drieve draive drive | | |
| 4. bump | b bp bmp | bop bomp bup | bump | | |
| 5. when | w yn wn | wan whan | wen when | | |
| 6. train | j t trn | jran chran tan tran | teran traen trane train | | |
| 7. closet | k cs kt clst | clast clost clozt | clozit closit | | |
| 8. chase | j jass cs | tas cas chas chass | case chais chase | | |
| 9. float | f vt ft flt | fot flot flott | flowt floaut flote float | | |
| 10. beaches | b bs bcs | bechs becis behis | bechise beches beeches beaches | | |
| Stages | | | Within-Word Pattern | Syllable Juncture | Derivational Constancy |
| 11. preparing | | | preparng preypering | preparing prepairing preparing | |
| 12. popping | | | popin poping | popping | |
| 13. cattle | | | catl cadol | catel catle cattel cattle | |
| 14. caught | | | cot cote cout cought caught | | |
| 15. inspection | | | inspshn inspechin | inspecshum inspecsion inspection | |
| 16. puncture | | | pucshr pungchr puncker | punksher punture puncturec | |
| 17. cellar | | | salr selr celr seler | seller sellar celler cellar | |
| 18. pleasure | | | plasr plager plejer pleser plesher | plesour plesure | pleasure |
| 19. squirrel | | | scrl skwel skwerl | scqoril sqrarel squirle squirrel | |
| 20. fortunate | | | forhnat frehnit foohinit | forchenut fochininte fortunet | fortunate |
| Stages | | | Within-Word Pattern | Syllable Juncture | Derivational Constancy |
| 21. confident | | | | confadent confedint confedent confadent conphident confiadent confiedent confendent confodent confident | |
| 22. civilize | | | | sivils sevelies sivilicse cifillazas sivelize sivalize civalise civilise civilize | |
| 23. flexible | | | | flecksibl flexobil fleckuble flecible flexeble flexibel flaxable flexibal flexable | flexible |
| 24. opposition | | | opasion opasishan opozcison opishien opasitian | opasition oppasishion oppisition | oposision oposition opposition |
| 25. emphasize | | | | infaside infacize emfesize emfisize imfasize ephacise empasize emphasise | emphisize emphasize |

Note: The Preliterate Stage is not presented here.
Adapted from *Reading Psychology 10* (3), 1989, pp. 275–292, by Donald Bear and Diane Barone. 

giving the test explain its purpose. Tell students that you want to find out how they spell words. Explain that some of the words may be hard but they should do their best to spell as much of each word as they can. Say each word, use it in a sentence, and then say the word once more.

Graded lists of spelling words can be found in the *Classroom Reading Inventory* (Silvaroli, 1994) and *My Kid Can't Spell* (Gentry, 1997).

To estimate students' stage of development, carefully analyze their spelling in terms of the major characteristics of each stage. For instance, students would be in the early letter–name stage if they were representing whole words with one or two consonant letters, as long as those letters were intended to represent sounds. They would be in the late letter–name stage if they were beginning to represent long vowels with single letters, containing the vowels' names. They would be in the within word–pattern stage if they used two vowel letters or a final *e* to represent long-vowel sounds. Students might also show signs of being in two stages at the same time or moving back and forth between stages. An error guide designed to help you determine students' spelling stages is also presented in Table 5-1. Verify the results of the *Elementary Spelling Inventory* by analyzing spellings that appear in students' writing. Misspellings are better indicators of stages, because words correctly spelled might be ones that the student has memorized without understanding the basic principles behind correctly spelling the words. For instance, a student could memorize the spelling of *like* without realizing that the final *e* marks the *i* as being long (Schlagal, 1992).

Spelling stages should not be thought of as a biological unfolding. Although some cognitive maturity is needed, instruction and opportunity to learn are critical factors.

Figure 5-8 shows the performance of a student on the *Elementary Spelling Inventory.* What stage is he in?

To further assess students' spelling, examine their written pieces and observe them during the writing process to see whether or not they are able to detect spelling errors and to go about correcting them. Also assess the student's ability to learn to spell. Choose five words from the ones that the student has misspelled and ask the student to study them because she or he will be tested on them. Note how the student goes about studying the words. Retest the student on the words and note how effective her or his study techniques were.

## *Handwriting*

Although often associated with severe reading difficulty, poor handwriting tends to be neglected in programs of remediation. Perhaps because there are higher-level skills that need remediating, handwriting is given a low priority, although a low-level skill, deficient handwriting can lead to lowered grades and lowered self-concept. Written work that is not neat or legible is frequently downgraded and is also a constant reminder to the student and his teachers of his other learning difficulties.

**Dysgraphia** is a neurological condition in which the person loses the ability to write. A dysgraphic student can read but has difficulty writing.

Although a low-level skill, handwriting is a complex task (Bain, 1991). Poor handwriting may reflect poorly developed motor skills, deficient visual or kinesthetic memory, or **dysgraphia,** which is a disorder that occurs between the visual memory system and the motor system (Bain, 1991; Johnson & Myklebust, 1967).

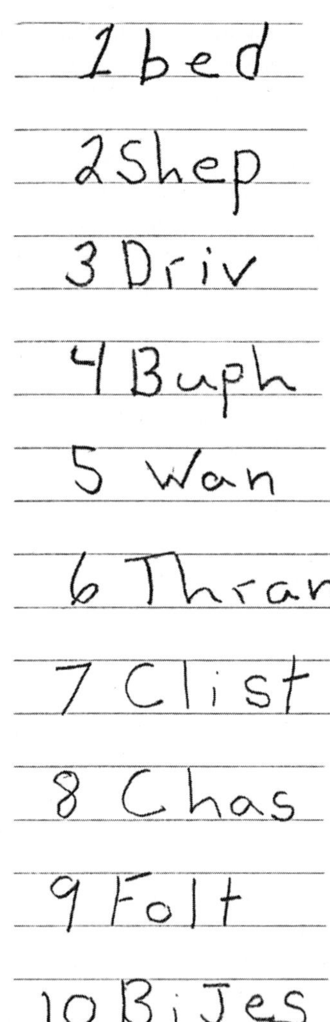


**FIGURE 5-8 Student's Performance on Elementary Spelling Inventory**

Since handwriting disorders may be manifested in many ways, observation is an important element in their assessment. Because different tasks make different demands, the student should be observed in a variety of situations: copying from material on his desk, copying from material on the board, composing a piece, and—if older—taking notes. Posture, grip, handedness, quality of writing, and speed of writing should be noted; and the product of the student's writing should be compared with a standard piece of writing (Bain, 1991; Rowell, 1992). If appropriate, both manuscript and cursive writing should be compared.

Observation of handwriting is important because this can lead to a better understanding of a handwriting deficiency. Slowness in copying from the board, for instance, may be caused by inattention, by forming letters one at a time rather than as part of a group, by poor visual memory which requires the student to check the board for each new letter that is being copied (Bain, 1991). It could even be caused by a lack of automatized skill in letter formation so that the student has to look several times at a single letter that is being copied to see how it is formed.

Scales for assessing quality of handwriting are available from publishers who distribute handwriting material such as, Zaner Bloser, Scott-Foresman (D'Nealian). Cursive writing may be assessed on the Handwriting Scale of the Test of Written Language (TOWL) (PRO-ED) or The Test of Legible Handwriting (TOLH) (PRO-ED). The TOLH assesses the readability of handwriting, manuscript or cursive, in grades two through twelve.

## *Assessing Study Skills*

> In preparation for assessing students' study skills, determine what skills and work habits they will need in order to complete assignments and prepare for tests.

Lack of adequate study skills is a major reason for referring older students for corrective help. Study skills may be diagnosed through observation, interviews, questionnaires, and by subtests of standardized tests. One way to assess the effectiveness of study skills is to see how well students do on quizzes, tests, and assignments that require home preparation. If students are doing poorly, you might conduct an interview to determine the source(s) of the difficulty. Since effective studying involves habits, attitudes, and motivation as well study strategies, your interview should cover all these areas. Because students may tend to tell you what they think you want to hear, ask questions in an open-ended fashion. Sample interview questions are presented in Figure 5-9.

> Study skills consist of strategies students might use to help them learn and retain information: outlining, notetaking, reading to retain information.

To save time, pick from the group of questions in Figure 5-9 the ones that are most pertinent. Also feel free to add questions, and reword questions to fit the needs of your students. If you are working with groups of students and don't have time for individual interviews, hold a group discussion on the topic. Often, students will be more open with their peers than they will be with their teachers. A checklist of study strategies is presented in Figure 5-10.

In order to see whether students possess study strategies, observe them as they use study strategies in the class. You might stage a study session in which they prepare for a test on a brief informational passage, study vocabulary words, memorize dates or facts, or study a list of spelling words. For more information on assessing and teaching study skills, see Chapter 14.

I'm going to ask you some questions about the way you study. Your answers will help me understand how you study, so that I should then be able to give you suggestions for improving the way you study.

1. Which subject is your hardest to study for?
2. What makes that subject hard for you to study?
3. Which subject is easiest to study for?
4. What makes that subject easy for you to study?
5. What do you do when you are studying and there is something that you don't understand?
6. What do you do to try to help you remember the material you have studied?
7. How do you know when you have studied enough?
8. What do you think could be done to improve your studying?
9. What kinds of tests do your teachers give?
10. What's the best way to study for a test in which you have to fill in blanks?
11. What's the best way to study for a multiple choice test?
12. What's the best way to study for an essay test?
13. Where do you study?
14. What supplies do you have in the place where you study?
15. When do you study?
16. Do you study at the same time each day?
17. How long do you study?
18. Do you listen to the radio or a CD or tape player or watch TV while you are studying?
19. Do you take breaks during your study periods? If so, when and for how long?
20. Do you ever study with other students? If so, do you find that helpful?
21. Which of your school books do you have to study the most? Pretend that you are studying for a quiz on a short section of this book. Show me how you would study for the quiz.

**FIGURE 5-9 Study Strategies and Habits Interview**

| | | | |
|---|---|---|---|
| 1. Does the student use SQ3R (see Chapter 14 for explanation of SQ3R) or some other study approach? | usually | sometimes | never |
| 2. Does the student clarify difficult concepts or passages? | usually | sometimes | never |
| 3. Does the student take notes on her or his reading? | usually | sometimes | never |
| 4. Does the student outline important information? | usually | sometimes | never |
| 5. Does the student organize the information into a semantic map or another type of graphic organizer? | usually | sometimes | never |
| 6. Does the student rehearse the information by saying it over and over again, visualize the information, or use some other strategy for remembering it? | usually | sometimes | never |
| 7. Does the student integrate material from notes and text? | usually | sometimes | never |
| 8. Does the student self-test herself or himself on the material? | usually | sometimes | never |
| 9. Does the student take adequate notes in class? | usually | sometimes | never |
| 10. Do study efforts manifest themselves in the student's earning higher grades? | usually | sometimes | never |

**FIGURE 5-10 Checklist of Study Strategies**

## *Summary*

Both decoding and comprehension processes can be assessed in greater detail through the administration of formal and informal tests, observations, questionnaires, and think-alouds. The emphasis should be on gaining insights into the processes that the student is using. For comprehension, retellings generally yield more information than asking questions. However, if students have difficulty with retellings because of language processing or other problems, then answering questions would be a more appropriate means of assessment.

Vocabulary knowledge can be assessed through observation and informal or formal tests. Writing can be assessed through examination of portfolios and obtaining and analyzing writing samples. A developmental spelling inventory can be administered and analyzed to estimate what stage students are in, and to see how this data might be used to plan spelling and word analysis instruction. The effectiveness of the methods students use to study spelling words can be assessed by providing them the opportunity to study five words that they misspelled and then giving a retest. Diagnostic and placement spelling tests are also available. Handwriting can be assessed informally or with the aid of commercial scales.

Study skills, a leading area for referrals for corrective help for older students, should also be assessed. Questionnaires, interviews, observations, and an analysis of content area–test results are among the methods that can be used to assess study skills.

## *Application Activities*

1. Focusing on one aspect of behavior, observe a student and compose an anecdotal record. If possible, observe the student on three different occasions. Then compare the records. What conclusions can you draw?

2. Examine one or more of the tests presented in this chapter. Note what the test is measuring and its format. Note, too, its strengths and weaknesses.

3. Read Marie Clay's *An Observation Survey of Early Literacy Achievement* (Portsmouth, NH: Heinemann, 1993). Which of the assessment measures described in her book do you feel are most useful? Why?

# Chapter 6

# Assessment of Cognitive, School, and Home Factors

## *Using What You Know*

This chapter looks at the ways of assessing students' cognitive and related capabilities: academic aptitude, memory, attention, and associative learning, which includes the crucial ability to learn printed words. Because of the interactive nature of assessment, personal, home, and school factors are also explored. What has been your experience with intelligence and other tests of cognitive abilities? What might be some effective ways for gathering information about personal, home, and school factors as they affect reading and writing development?

## *Anticipation Guide*

Read each of the following statements. Put a check under "Agree" or "Disagree" to show how you feel about each one. If you can, discuss your responses with classmates.

| | Agree | Disagree |
|---|---|---|
| **1.** The main problem with intelligence tests is that no one knows exactly what intelligence is, so it can't be measured accurately. | ________ | ________ |
| **2.** Tests of listening capacity are more equitable measures of one's ability to learn to read than are tests of intelligence. | ________ | ________ |
| **3.** Questionnaires and interviews lack validity because people are inclined to tell the questioners what they want to hear. | ________ | ________ |
| **4.** Parents are reliable sources of information about their children. | ________ | ________ |
| **5.** The best way to gain insight into students' reading problems is to talk to them. | ________ | ________ |

## *Assessment of Capacity*

One of the most basic questions asked in an assessment is what is the student's aptitude for reading? Or, to ask the question in another way, given optimum development—one in which any reading deficiencies might be remedied—on what level should the student be reading? There are three main ways to assess a student's capacity: administer a test of academic aptitude, obtain the student's listening capacity, or provide the student with the opportunity to learn and see how she or he does.

What we call *intelligence* is the result of interaction between heredity and environment. The richer the environment, the more fully our mental capabilities are developed (Carnegie Corporation, 1994).

Because of past misuse and misinterpretation, the testing of intelligence is highly controversial. Intelligence tests have been criticized for favoring some cultures over others, with the result that members of some groups were believed to obtain artificially low scores. Today's tests are constructed with greater sensitivity and are carefully screened for items that are culturally biased. However, as Carlson (1993) notes, "Unfortunately, the problem of cultural bias has not been solved. Even though questions with obvious cultural bias are no longer incorporated into intelligence tests, different experiences can lead to different test-taking strategies"(p. 448). In addition, intelligence tests reflect not only innate ability but also the opportunity to develop that ability. Students who come from environments where there is limited interaction with adults may have depressed scores. And, of course, motivation is a factor. Students who try harder often achieve more.

Intelligence tests sample those behaviors that the author of the test believes manifest cognitive ability. Different authors use different items so that the same student taking three different tests might get three different scores. In some instances, there might be significant differences among the scores. Most intelligence tests are really measures of academic aptitude. They measure such behaviors as vocabulary development, background information, ability to see likenesses and differences, ability to complete verbal and figural analogies, ability to complete patterns, and other similar abilities which are good predictors of school performance (Salvia & Ysseldyke, 1988). However, intelligence tests fail to include items that assess practical problem solving abilities, which may be a good predictor of how one does in life.

Sternberg (1985) concludes that there are three main areas of intelligence: componential, experiential, and contextual. Componential intelligence includes verbal ability and deductive reasoning. Experiential intelligence refers to the ability to handle novel situations or problems and to learn from experience. Contextual intelligence refers to the ability to adapt to the environment, to find one's place in the environment, and to shape the environment to fit one's needs. In other words, intelligence involves the ability to plan and organize one's life.

Gardner (1983) theorizes that intelligence encompasses seven areas: linguistic, musical, logical–mathematical, spatial, bodily–kinesthetic, intrapersonal, and interpersonal.

Human abilities are varied and can be manifested in many ways. When assessing students' abilities, we need to look at a broad range of ability. We need to see how the students handle life's challenges and problems as well as how they handle academic challenges and problems.

Intelligence tests are biased against poor readers in at least two ways. Beyond the primary grades, group-intelligence tests may involve reading. Unless students can read the test items with relative ease, they may be unfairly penalized. Scores will reflect both reading and intelligence.

Neville (1965) states that a valid performance on a group-intelligence test requires at least a fourth-grade reading level. Even on individual intelligence tests, which require no reading, low-achieving readers may be penalized. For instance, poor readers typically read less, which restricts their ability to learn new vocabulary and build background of information—two areas which are frequently assessed by intelligence tests (Stanovich, 1991). Carlson points out:

> *Another problem with intelligence tests is that they may lead low-scoring students to underestimate themselves. Children who discover that they have scored poorly on an intelligence test are likely to suffer feelings of inferiority and may become disinclined to try to learn, believing that they cannot. (1993, p. 448)*

Low scores may also lead teachers to believe that students cannot achieve. Believing this to be so, they may not challenge them sufficiently or give them as rich a program as they should. As Carlson (1993) comments, "Clearly, schools should use intelligence tests with great caution. If the results are not themselves used intelligently, such tests are actually harmful" (p. 418).

## *Role of Intelligence Tests*

Despite their obvious limitations, intelligence tests can play an important role in the assessment of reading problems, if results are interpreted with the awareness of the above limitations. For one thing, intelligence tests provide an indication of the extent of a student's reading difficulty. They may also indicate potential. Problem readers, especially if they have retreated into themselves, may be judged to have lesser cognitive ability. For instance, Frank, an eight-year-old reading on a first-grade level, spent much of his time daydreaming, and seldom spoke in class. That, together with his unkempt appearance, created the impression of a student who had average or low-average ability. However, when tested, Frank achieved a score of 141, which put him in the top one percent of the population. Realizing that Frank was intellectually gifted and that his reading problem was even more severe than it seemed since Frank should have been reading far above grade level, Frank's teacher obtained additional services for him.

> Frank meets the functional and discrepancy definitions. He was reading below grade level and was unable to handle his school texts. Achievement was also below ability.

As a practical matter, most intelligence testing is conducted by a school psychologist. However, knowing the contents of the major intelligence tests and what scores on subtests signify puts you in a position where you can make use of that information. If analyzed carefully, information about the student's performance on specific elements on an intelligence test can shed light on the student's reading difficulty and can be used to plan a program of remediation.

> Interpreted with caution, individual intelligence tests can provide insights into students' cognitive functioning and so can be used to plan a more effective intervention.

## *Wechsler Scales*

The most popular of the intelligence tests are the *Wechsler Scales*, which define intelligence as the "overall capacity of an individual to understand and cope with the world around him" (Wechsler, 1974, p. 5). Although conceiving of intelligence as being global and multifaceted,

Wechsler created scales that included a number of subtests. The *WISC-III* (*Wechsler Intelligence Scale for Children III*), which can only be administered by a qualified examiner, is designed for students between the ages of six and sixteen. In addition to obtaining an estimate of a student's overall functioning intelligence level, the teacher can, by examining performance on subtests, determine a student's relative strengths and weaknesses in several crucial areas. A description of each subtest and its relevance is presented below:

### Verbal Scale

**Information:** The subject is asked questions about general knowledge. Measures how well the subject has interacted with the environment and recalls information. Since poor readers are cut off from one source of information, their scores may be somewhat depressed. A low score suggests a need to build a background of information.

**Comprehension:** Students tell what they would do in a variety of social situations. The subtest measures common sense and social judgment. Since school-type learning isn't being assessed, poor readers are not penalized.

**Arithmetic:** Requires students to solve arithmetic problems mentally. It measures ability to pay attention and concentrate and remember the elements that need to be manipulated. Poor readers frequently do badly in those areas and so, tend to do badly on this test.

**Similarities:** The subject tells how two items are alike. This subtest measures the ability to form concepts. Poor readers can do well on this subtest. A low score suggests the need to teach thinking skills such as noting similarities and differences and categorizing.

**Vocabulary:** Subjects are asked to define words. This subtest measures students' store of concepts and is generally considered to be the best assessment of academic aptitude. Older low-achieving readers may have somewhat depressed scores because they are cut off from one avenue of learning new words: reading. Scores, however, should not be too depressed because there are many ways, besides reading, of learning new words. A low score suggests a need to develop vocabulary.

**Digit Span:** Subjects say a series of numbers forwards and backwards. This subtest measures attention, concentration, and working memory. Because poor readers may have problems in one or all three of these areas, they tend to do poorly on this subtest.

### Performance Scale

**Picture Completion:** The subject is asked to identify the missing part in a picture. The subtest measures attention to detail and the ability to differentiate between essential and nonessential elements. Poor readers are not penalized on this subtest.

**Picture Arrangement:** The youngest subjects assemble three-piece puzzles. Older subjects arrange cut-up pictures in order so that they tell a story. This subtest measures the ability to see sequential, cause-effect, and other relationships and the ability to plan. Poor readers can do well on this subtest.

**Block Design:** Students use blocks to reproduce a design. The subtest measures nonverbal concept formation and the ability to detect and construct relationships. Poor readers are not penalized on this subtest, but students with neurological impairments may do poorly.

**Object Assembly:** Subjects assemble puzzles. This subtest measures the ability to see visuo-spatial relationships. Poor readers can do well on this subtest.

**Coding:** The subject associates the code that goes with a symbol and writes it in a blank. The subtest measures the ability to make, remember, and record associations. Because some low-achieving readers may have difficulty making associations, they may do poorly on this task.
**Mazes** (alternate subtest): Using a pencil, subjects make their way through a maze. This measures the ability to plan ahead. Poor readers are not penalized on this subtest.

Students with learning problems may evidence "scatter." Often, they have some surprisingly low scores and miss easy items but get difficult items correct.

As a group, poor readers tend to do poorly on the Information, Arithmetic, Digit Span, and Coding portions of the test. As Galvin (1981) notes, the latter three have in common paying attention to, and keeping in memory, abstract symbols, an area in which poor readers often have difficulty.

Wechsler scales have a standard deviation of 15. Since 68% of the population have a score of 100 + or – one standard deviation, this means that 68% have an IQ score of between 85 and 115. Some 14% have an IQ of between 115–130. Another 14% have scores that fall between 70–85. Only 2% have scores above 130 and 2% have scores below 70.

## *Stanford-Binet*

The *Stanford-Binet,* which is based on the earliest intelligence test, one devised for French children in 1905 by Albert Binet, was most recently revised in 1985 and assesses the following areas: verbal reasoning, comprehension, quantitative reasoning, abstract/visual reasoning, and short-term memory. The *Stanford-Binet* can only be given by a qualified examiner.

**Verbal Reasoning:** The subject defines vocabulary words, answers questions that require judgment and common sense, explains why a series of pictures are absurd, and explains why series of three of four objects are alike and why one of the four is different.
**Quantitative Reasoning:** The subject answers questions that involve counting, detecting the next number in a series, and constructing equations.
**Abstract/Visual Reasoning:** The subject reproduces geometric patterns, copies designs, selects or constructs the answer to matrices, and constructs paper designs.
**Short-Term Memory:** The subject identifies or duplicates patterns of beads, repeats sentences, repeats digits forwards and backwards, and recognizes a series of objects previously displayed.

## *Slosson Intelligence Test*

Unlike the *Stanford* and *Wechsler Scales,* which can only be given by qualified examiners, the *Slosson* may be administered by teachers, counselors, and reading specialists.

Although originally modeled on an early edition of the *Stanford-Binet,* the *Slosson Intelligence Test Revised* (SIT-R) has fewer items and is quicker and easier to give. The *Slosson Intelligence Test Revised* is a screening device designed to measure verbal intelligence. The six domains assessed in the SIT-R are similar to the verbal subtests of the *Wechsler Scales* and the *Stanford-Binet,* Fourth Edition, and include: four verbal tests: vocabulary, general information, similarities and differences, and comprehension. The *SIT-R* also includes a subtest of quantitative reasoning and a subtest of auditory memory.

Results of the *Slosson* or any other intelligence test should be interpreted with care, keeping the narrow scope and limitations of the instrument in mind. The *Slosson* is brief and emphasizes verbal abilities. Because it has a large number of vocabulary and information items, items that are more likely to be developed in enriched mainstream environments, results should be interpreted in the light of the students' opportunity to learn.

### *Peabody Picture Vocabulary Test*

The *Peabody Picture Vocabulary Test* is frequently used as a measure of receptive vocabulary rather than of academic ability.

Another test that can be administered by teachers and reading specialists is the *Peabody Picture Vocabulary Test.* Sometimes used as a test of verbal ability, the *Peabody* measures only one aspect of intelligence, receptive vocabulary (Salvia & Ysseldyke, 1988). The *Peabody* measures vocabulary by having the student point to the picture that best represents the meaning of the word that the examiner says. Because it only requires the student to point to a picture, the *Peabody* works especially well with students who are shy or are withdrawn or who have difficulty expressing themselves. The Peabody can be used to detect difficulties in word-finding abilities. Since they don't have to recall or retrieve words but only need point to the pictures that represent words, students who have difficulty retrieving words stored in their mental dictionaries do relatively well on the *Peabody.* However, these same students would have difficulty with a test like the *Boston Word Naming Test,* which requires subjects to supply names for pictures.

Easy to administer, the *Peabody* can be given to people between the ages of two and one-half and forty. Because the *Peabody* was designed to test "subjects who have grown up in a standard English-speaking environment" (Dunn & Dunn, 1981, p. 2), it may yield erroneous results if administered to those with hearing difficulties, non-native speakers of English, or to those who have in some other way not had a full opportunity to learn standard English vocabulary.

As noted in Chapter 3, tests of listening can also be used to estimate students' potential. Tests of listening from an IRI can be used, or you might also use a test of listening vocabulary in which words and possible definitions are read to a student, and the student marks the correct definition. Tests of this type can be found on some levels of the *Stanford Achievement Tests* and the first two levels of the *Stanford Diagnostic Reading Tests.* The *DARTTS* and other individual diagnostic reading tests feature listening vocabulary tests in which the student supplies definitions for target words that are read by the examiner. One advantage of a listening test is that it doesn't pigeonhole students into a particular cognitive category as an intelligence test does. Another measure of ability is to provide students with opportunities to learn under optimum conditions and see how they do.

## *Assessment of Memory*

Working memory may be assessed through both verbal and nonverbal tests. Auditory working memory can also be assessed by having students repeat a series of words, sentences, or nonsense syllables or orally recall a series of pictured objects. A popular test for working memory is digit span, which involves having the student repeat a series of digits forward or in reverse. Digit span is one subtest given on the *Weschler Scales.* To see if there is a possible memory problem, you should compare the student's scaled score on Digit Span with scores on the other subtests to see if there is a significant difference. Each of the subtests on the *Wechsler* yields a score between 1 and 20, with 10 being an average score. Since the scores are all on the same scale, they can be compared. However, only a difference of 3 or more points is considered to be significant.

If *Wechsler* scores aren't available, you can administer digit span items from the Slosson. To use these items to assess auditory memory, simply regroup them and ask them, one series at a time, starting with the shortest span of numbers and working up to the highest number. Administer digits forward and then digits reversed. To analyze performance, note the highest age level at which the student was able to repeat all the digits. Memory for sentence items, which involves having the student repeat sentences, can also be regrouped, administered, and analyzed in the same way that digit span items were. Other sources of auditory memory items include the following two subtests of the *Detroit Tests of Learning Aptitude,* 3rd Edition (American Guidance Service):

**Sentence Imitation** The student repeats sentences that gradually increase in length.

**Word Sequences** Students repeat a series of unrelated words. A useful comparison is to see whether students do better with Word Sequences or Sentence Imitation. Are they able to use the sense and structure of the sentences in Sentence Imitation to remember more words?

*The Detroit Tests of Learning Aptitude* also have a test of visual memory, which is described below.

**Design Sequences** In Design Sequences, students choose from a set of six cubes, each of which contains five shapes, the ones that are the same as those presented by the examiner before being hidden from view. Since the figures are nonsense shapes, the student would have difficulty using a name to help him remember the shapes, and so visual memory is being tapped. A useful comparison would be to contrast visual and verbal memory. Many low-achieving readers apparently have difficulty using a verbal code to help them store and/or retrieve items but do fine with visual memory.

Attention and concentration are also involved in memory tasks. Students may have difficulty with a memory task because they are tired, are feeling anxious, are distracted by a problem that is bothering them, or are having difficulty paying attention or concentrating for some other reason.

## *Associative Word Learning*

Of all the diagnostic areas mentioned so far, associative word learning is probably the most crucial. Associative word–learning difficulty is the defining characteristic of a severe reading difficulty. All the students with the most serious reading problems that I have encountered have had a serious, dramatic unmistakable problem in this area.

Difficulty learning the printed forms of words is the major hurdle faced by students who have the severest reading problems.

Associative word learning can be diagnosed in many ways. One indication of a problem in this area is a noticeable difficulty learning letter names, letter sounds, and sight words. Poor performance on the word-lists tests of the IRI despite ample opportunity to learn is a possible sign of an associative word–learning problem. To assess a student's word-learning ability, uses a procedure similar to that employed for dynamic testing. Gather seven words that are in the student's listening vocabulary but which she doesn't recognize in print (these could be seven words that she missed on the word-lists test). Pre-testing to make sure that the student can't read the words, see how many presentations it takes before the student learns all seven words. However, stop after ten presentations so that the student doesn't become too frustrated. Note the number of words known at the last presentation. Then retest thirty minutes later and then the next day to assess delayed recall. (A Word Learning Test is presented in Appendix A.)

To assess word-learning ability, also note the student's performance when new words are presented. How many words does he learn? How many does he retain?

The average student will learn all seven words within ten trials and will be able to recognize most, if not all, the words thirty minutes later and the next day. Students with associative word–learning difficulties may only learn one or two words in ten trials; but, even if they do learn them all in the ten trials, they will be able to recognize only one or two thirty minutes or a day later. These same students will also do poorly on other tests of associative learning that use visual symbols. Additional tests of associative learning can be found on the *Woodcock-Johnson Cognitive Abilities Battery* (Riverside) and are listed below:

**Visual-Auditory Learning:** The student learns to associate familiar spoken words with symbols in the context of a story.
**Memory for Names:** The student learns to associate nonsense names with drawings of space creatures.

Your assessment of word learning abilities should be dynamic. After you have assessed the student's word learning abilities, try teaching words missed. Use several approaches and see which one works best. However, do not teach the words until after the student has had the follow-up test, which is one day after the original testing

## *Word-Finding*

As indicated earlier, word-finding difficulties can be diagnosed by comparing performance on a test of receptive vocabulary, such as the *Peabody,* with a test such as the *Boston Naming Test* or *One-Word Vocabulary Test,* both of which require the students to supply the words being tested. An instrument specially designed to diagnose word-retrieval difficulties is the *Test of Word Finding* (Riverside). The *Test of Word Finding* assesses the student's ability to name pictured nouns (*nest*) and verbs (*painting*), categories (*birds*), descriptions (*What part of your face is used to smell, has two openings, and is below your eyes?*) The ability to complete sentences is also tested. (*A bird lays eggs in a* _______.)

Word finding can also be assessed through observation. A word-finding observation checklist is presented in Figure 6-1.

| | | | |
|---|---|---|---|
| 1. Does the student use roundabout phrases (the thing that you cut with)? | rarely | sometimes | often |
| 2. Does the student frequently answer "I don't know" when you believe that she or he does know the answer? | rarely | sometimes | often |
| 3. Does the student frequently pause or use "ums" and "ahs" when speaking? | rarely | sometimes | often |
| 4. Does the student frequently say "I forgot" "I can't remember" or "I can't think of the name of that"? | rarely | sometimes | often |
| 5. Does the student frequently use vague or general words such as "that boy," "that place," or "something" rather than the specific name of the person, place, or object? | rarely | sometimes | often |

**FIGURE 6-1 Observation Guide for Word-Finding Difficulties**

If you do suspect that a student has a word-finding difficulty, involve the speech therapist. The speech therapist will be in a better position to evaluate the student's overall language ability and might work with the student if the student turns out to have a word-finding difficulty. The speech therapist might also give you assistance as you plan a program for the student.

## *Assessing the Instructional Situation*

In an interactive assessment, the student's instructional situation should be observed and analyzed. At the Reading Clinic at Southern Connecticut State University, students who have severe reading problems may receive services for two or even three years. Having a different student-teacher for each semester, they may have as many as six instructors over a period of three years. The amount of progress that students make varies from instructor to instructor, sometimes to a considerable degree. Although all the instructors are well trained and carefully supervised, each has a different personality and a unique style of interacting. Each has different preferences in materials and teaching approaches. When students have exceptional teachers, they generally make exceptional progress.

Although the teacher is the most important factor in determining the amount of progress, other essential elements include amount of instructional time, how the time is used, the degree to which the student is actively involved, the type of materials used, and the kinds of activities pursued. In general, time spent on actual reading—including voluntary reading—and writing has a greater payoff than time spent on worksheets. Students also benefit more when instruction is pegged to their interests and abilities. Overall, the instructional situation has an enormous impact on students' learning and is particularly crucial for low-achieving readers.

If you are assisting a student but are not his or her classroom teacher, explore the student's school situation as part of your assessment. Talk to the student's teachers. Get an overview of the major tasks that the student is expected to complete and an assessment of the student's performance. Ask about the student's strengths and weaknesses in key subject areas. Ask, too, about the student's work habits and overall adjustment. Invite the student's teacher(s) to provide any insight they might have about the student's difficulty with reading and writing. Find out what kinds of approaches have been used with the student. Balanced programs seem to work best. The student may have been in a program that didn't provide systematic instruction in crucial skills or in a program where there were insufficient opportunities for application. In particular, try to find out what kinds of activities and materials work particularly well and which don't. Observe the student on two or more occasions during reading and writing sessions. If the student attends subject-matter classes, observe those. If the student is receiving special help, arrange for a conference with the specialist and observe the student working with the specialist. In addition to conducting observations and interviews, evaluate the student's ability to cope with her or his school books (Broaddus & Bloodgood, 1994). Ask the student how textbooks are used. Does the student read them in class or is he expected to read them independently at home? If read at home, is the student provided with some sort of study guide? If read in class, are they read silently or are they read aloud?

Have the student indicate what chapter the class is on in each text and then read a portion of the next chapter. In IRI test style, assess whether or not the texts are on the student's instructional level. Also note the strategies the student uses to comprehend the text.

Assess the student's home assignments and how they are handled. Find out if the student makes a note of homework assignments so he knows what to do. If the student does, ask to see a record of the assignments. Note whether the record of the assignments is clear. If the student doesn't keep a record, ask the student how she or he remembers what the homework assignments are. Also find out whether the student completes assignments on a regular basis (Meltzer, 1993).

## *School Records*

According to the Family Educational Rights and Privacy Act (Buckley Amendment, PL 93-380, 1974), schools may not release information from school records without parental permission. When requesting information, it is advisable to obtain a written release from parents.

School records can be a valuable source of information, especially if the student has been tested extensively, or if the school keeps a portfolio. If you are not working in the student's school, you need to get written parental permission to examine records. All information should be kept confidential. Pertinent information includes the following:

- Attendance: Spotty or sustained attendance can interfere with learning.
- Retentions: Students who spent a year in a transition class or who were retained in first-grade or another grade may have a more serious problem than those who were not, because they have had an additional year of schooling.
- Grades: Look at overall performance and areas of strength and weakness.
- Performance on Achievement and Aptitude Tests: Look at all areas, not just reading and writing. Sometimes a student will show strengths in areas like math or art, where reading and writing are not as important.
- Special Help Given: If the student has been given help and is still having difficulty, it may indicate a more serious problem exists.
- Transfers: Moving from school to school can cause gaps in the students' learning.

## Case History

When obtaining a case history, interview both parents together, if possible. Maintain a nonjudgmental, professional attitude.

In order to get a fuller understanding of the student's background, it is important to obtain a case history from the parents or other primary caregivers. A case history will provide a backdrop for interpreting test results and other data. The focus of the history is on obtaining data about the biological and environmental factors that affect the student's physical, emotional, social, and cognitive development (Abrams, 1988). To obtain needed information, the following six areas should be explored:

1. Family constellation and student's role within the family.
2. History of the mother's pregnancy, and her child's birth, and infancy.
3. Developmental milestones, such as the age at which the student sat up, crawled, and walked, with special emphasis on language development. Major developmental milestones are listed in Table 6-1. The sequence of these milestones is the same for all children. Children coo and babble and then say single words before they speak in sentences. However, there is enormous variation within each stage. For instance, although most children speak in two-word phrases or sentences by about the age of two, some normal children may not do so until they are three or four (Lenneberg, cited in Stewig & Nordberg, 1995). A delay in reaching developmental milestones may not be significant in and of itself. However, a pattern of late development takes on more significance, especially when accompanied by other indicators of slow development and learning problems.
4. Medical and psychological history, with emphasis on factors that might influence reading and writing development.
5. School history with emphasis on elements that might have an impact on reading and writing development (Abrams, 1988).
6. Personal adjustment.

**TABLE 6-1 Developmental Milestones**

| | |
|---|---|
| Lifts head | 2 months |
| Coos | 4 months |
| Babbles | 6–9 months |
| Sits without support | 6 months |
| Stands alone | 11 months |
| Walks | 12 months |
| Says one or more words | 12 months |
| Scribbles randomly | 18 months |
| Speaks in two-word sentences | 24 months |
| Speaks in three-word sentences | 36 months |
| Makes word-like scribbles | 36 months |
| Writes letters but letters do not represent sounds | 48–60 months |
| May attempt invented spelling in which letters represent sounds | 48–72 months |

If parents express feelings of guilt about their children's learning problems, explain that they should not blame themselves but should focus on working to improve their children's reading and writing.

A case history should be obtained from both parents or the student's primary caregivers. The interview should be held in a relaxed, private setting. Take a few minutes to put the parents at ease and also explain the purpose of the interview: that you wish to obtain information that will give you a total picture of their child so that you can reach a fuller understanding of their child's reading and/or writing difficulty. Explain that it is important for you to gain an understanding of the problem from their perspective. In order to obtain a maximum amount of information, questions should be asked in open-ended fashion. Sample questions are listed in the following sections.

### *Family Factors*

*Can you tell me about your family? Who lives in your home? What are the names and ages of the other children? Have any of your other children had problems in school? Did you or your spouse have any difficulty in school?*

### *Pregnancy*

*How would your describe your pregnancy? Did you experience any illnesses during your pregnancy? Did you take any medications? How would you describe the birth? Did you have any difficulties or complications?*

### *Early Years and Overall Health*

*What was _______ like as an infant? Was _______ easy or difficult to care for? What kinds of childhood illnesses did _______ have? Has _______ ever had her/his eyesight or hearing checked? Did she/he have any high fevers? Did _______ ever have any convulsions? Were there any head injuries? Did _______ ever lose consciousness? How would you describe _______ health now? Is _______ on any medication now? How much sleep does _______ get each night? Does she/he have any difficulty sleeping? How would you describe her/his appetite? Does she/he eat most foods? Does she/he eat breakfast? Has _______ ever been diagnosed as being hyperactive or having an attention deficit disorder?*

Parents can provide valuable insights into their child's attitude towards school, response to different kinds of instruction, and self-feelings as a learner.

### *Developmental Milestones*

*Did you keep any records telling when _______ talked or walked? At what age did _______ sit up? At what age did _______ crawl? Stand? Walk? Say first word? Say first sentence? How would you describe _______ speech as she/he was growing up?*

### *Early Language and Literacy Development*

*What language or languages are spoken in the home? What language does _______ use at home? Did _______ play with pencils and crayons? Did _______ try to write? Did*

*_______ have favorite storybooks? Did anyone read to her/him? Did _______ ever pretend to read to you, to teddy bears or dolls, or to younger children? Did _______ watch TV? How often did she/he watch? What kinds of shows did she/he like best? As a young child did _______ ever ask questions about signs? Did _______ ever ask you how to write her/his name or other words? Did _______ try to write before going to school?*

### *School History*

*What can you tell me about _______ reading/writing difficulty? How do you see the problem? What do you think is the cause of the problem? When did you first notice that _______ had a difficulty? What has been done to help _______ solve the problem? What else, if anything, do you think should be done? Does _______ like school? What are _______ favorite subjects? Which subjects does she/he like least? Did _______ attend preschool? Kindergarten? In what ways have you or other members of the family tried to help _______? How is _______ school attendance? About how many days a year does _______ miss? Has _______ ever missed a long period of schooling because of illness or other reasons?*

Questioning parents about the students' homework can yield valuable information about the student's study strategies and habits.

### *Home Factors*

*Do you or anyone else in the family try to help _______ with homework? About how much homework does _______ have each evening? Where does _______ do homework? Do you take _______ to the library? If so, how often? Do you buy books or magazines for _______? Do you read to _______? Did you read to _______ when she/he was younger? Do you like to read? About how much reading do you do each day? Do you subscribe to any newspapers or magazines? What plans do you have for _______? What plans does _______ have for herself/himself? What does _______ plan to be when she/he grows up?*

### *Interests/Personal Adjustment*

*How does _______ get along with the other children at school? Does _______ belong to any clubs or teams? How does _______ spend her/his free time? Does _______ like to read? How much time does _______ spend reading each week? About how many books would you say _______ read last month? Does _______ have any hobbies or other interests? How does _______ get along with the children in the neighborhood? How does _______ get along with the other members of the family? Is there anything else you would like to tell me about _______?*

The questions do not have to be asked in order. Rather, you should follow the natural flow of the interview. When asked a health question, parents may get into the area of school history because the child got sick in school. To get the most information, follow the parent's lead. Rearrange questions as the situation dictates. Also spend added time in those areas that seem to have the most bearing on the particular student you are examining. If chronic illness is a major factor, for instance, spend additional time discussing the student's medical background. Also, keep in mind that parents are not always objective. Some information may be omitted or distorted. And some information, such as the age of some of the developmental milestones, may not be remembered accurately. If parents have medical or developmental records, these should be consulted. All information should, of course, be kept confidential.

### *Using Questionnaires*

If you are unable to interview parents or school personnel, you might use a written questionnaire to obtain information. Although interviews are more effective in eliciting information, using a questionnaire is better than obtaining no information at all. Since school personnel are busy, questionnaires should be succinct. Because some parents of poor readers and writers may also have experienced difficulty with reading and writing, parent questionnaires should be easy to read and easy to answer. Sample questionnaires are presented in Figures 6-2 and 6-3.

## *Students' Views*

Students' responses can help you determine assessment/instructional priorities. If students say the words make reading hard, look into their decoding skills or the difficulty level of the reading material.

An essential element in the assessment is to obtain the students' views of their reading and writing. How do they think they are doing? What kinds of skills would they like to learn? What kinds of help, if any, would they like to have? Some possible questions that might be asked are listed below. Choose the questions that seem most appropriate. Also feel free to add questions. Instead of using a formal interview fashion, ask the questions in an informal, conversational style.

By asking children what they would like to learn to do in reading and what would help them to become a better reader, you involve them in setting goals.

- What are your favorite school subjects? Why?
- Are there any subjects that are hard for you? What makes them hard? What might make them easier?
- What things are easy for you in reading?
- What things are hard for you in reading?
- What kinds of things would you like to learn to do in reading?
- What would help you to become a better reader?
- Do you read on your own at home?
- What kinds of things do you like to read?
- What are your favorite books?
- Who are your favorite authors?

All of the above questions can also be asked about writing. Responses can be supplemented by observational data and other information that you obtain about the students and their perception of reading and writing.

Name of child ______________________ Date of birth ______________________
Name of school ______________________ Grade in school ______________________
Mother's name ______________________ Occupation ______________________
Father's name ______________________ Occupation ______________________

Names and ages of brothers and sisters

______________________________________________________________

Main language spoken in home ____________ Other languages spoken in home ____________
How would you describe your child's overall health?

______________________________________________________________

Does your child now have any major illnesses?

______________________________________________________________

Has your child had any major illness or had any accidents that caused an injury?

______________________________________________________________

Does your child wear glasses? _____ When was the last time your child's eyes were checked?

______________________________________________________________

Has your child ever had any difficulty with hearing? ______________________
When was the last time your child's hearing was checked? ______________________
Has your child ever repeated a grade or been placed in a transitional class? ______________
What difficulty does your child have in reading or writing?

______________________________________________________________

______________________________________________________________

When was this difficulty first noticed?

______________________________________________________________

______________________________________________________________

Has the school tried to help your child? If so, how?

______________________________________________________________

______________________________________________________________

Except for help that you have given, has your child been helped outside of school? _____ If so, how?

______________________________________________________________

______________________________________________________________

Have you tried to help your child? If so, how?

______________________________________________________________

______________________________________________________________

Has your child been tested for a learning problem? If so, what kind of testing was done?

______________________________________________________________

______________________________________________________________

Is your child in any special programs for children with learning problems?

______________________________________________________________

______________________________________________________________

Has your child missed a lot of time from school? _____ If so, please describe.

______________________________________________________________

______________________________________________________________

What does your child like to do when not in school?

______________________________________________________________

______________________________________________________________

What special interests or hobbies does your child have?

______________________________________________________________

______________________________________________________________

Is there anything else that you can tell us that would help us to understand your child's reading or writing difficulty?

______________________________________________________________

______________________________________________________________

**FIGURE 6-2 Parent Questionnaire**

Name of student ______________________ Grade ____________ Date __________
Name of school ______________________ Teacher ______________________
School Address ______________________________ Phone ____________

1. Student's reading level ______________________
2. Name and level of materials now being used ______________________
3. Results of standardized tests ______________________
4. Results of IEP or other special assessments ______________________
5. Grades for last marking period ______________________
6. Results of vision test ______________ Hearing test ______________
7. Description of speech or behavior problems, if any ______________________
8. Any extended or frequent absences ______________________
9. Grades repeated or placement in a transition class ______________________
10. Description of any extra special or extra help given ______________________

Classroom teacher's or specialist's description of the child's problem in reading or writing and suggestions for helping the child.

______________________________________________

______________________________________________

Is the child now being considered for special placement or retention? If so, please describe.

______________________________________________

______________________________________________

**FIGURE 6-3 School Questionnaire**

## *Reading Expectancy*

**Reading expectancy:** estimate of the level at which a student should be reading, based on tests of academic aptitude, listening capacity, or estimated ability to learn.

An assessment should include some indication of the level at which the student should be reading. This is the student's **reading expectancy.** As a general principle, students should be able to read up to their cognitive or linguistic capacity. Tests of cognitive ability such as the *WISC-III, the Stanford-Binet,* or the *Slosson,* can be used to estimate a student's reading capacity. The higher the score on these tests, the higher the student's reading expectancy. As a rough rule of thumb, to get a measure of expectancy, subtract 5.6 from the student's mental age (5.6 is the average age at which students start kindergarten). If the test doesn't give a mental age, then you can calculate that by multiplying the student's chronological age by the test's standard or IQ score. Thus a nine-year-old with an IQ of 133 would have a mental age of 12 (1.33 × 9) and a reading expectancy of 6.6. (11 years, 12 months minus 5 years, 6 months). The student would be expected to be able to read on a sixth grade level. Still, another way to calculate reading expectancy is to use the following formula: (IQ/100 × years of reading instruction + 1 = Reading Expectancy) (Bond, Tinker, Wasson, & Wasson, 1994). Using this formula, the student's reading expectancy would be grade 5 (133/100 × 3 + 1 = 5), so this formula gives a more conservative estimate. In calculating years in school, begin with first grade, not kindergarten, even though there may have been some formal reading instruction in kindergarten. If a student repeated a grade or spent an extra year in a transition class, that should be included when calculating years in school.

When calculating reading expectancy, also consider opportunity to learn. A very bright first grader, for instance, who has a reading expectancy of 4.0, might not have had sufficient exposure to reading for this to be a realistic expectation.

Technical procedures are sometimes used to determine reading expectancy, reading achievement, and whether there is a significant gap between the two. For a student to be classified as being learning disabled because of a reading difficulty, there must be a substantial discrepancy between the student's measured ability and reading achievement. In Connecticut, there must be a difference of 1.5 standard deviations (Spear-Swerling & Sternberg, 1996). This means that if a student achieved an average score of 100 on the *Wechsler Scales,* which have a standard deviation of 15 points, then his achievement on a standard measure of reading, also having a standard deviation of 15, would have to be 77.5 or lower.

### *Listening Capacity*

When determining a reading expectancy, consider several sources of information. Use an IQ score if available and also the listening level yielded by the informal reading inventory.

As noted earlier, it isn't necessary to administer a test of cognitive capacity to obtain a measure of a student's reading expectancy. There are also a number of measures of language development that might be used to gauge a student's reading expectancy. The simplest of these is a test of listening capacity. The informal reading inventory, which was covered in detail in the previous chapter, yields a listening level. This is obtained by reading stories to students and finding the highest level at which the students can understand 75 percent of the questions asked about a selection that has been read to them. If a third-grader reading on a first-grade level obtains a listening level of grade five, that is the student's reading expectancy. Other sources of language capacity are listening vocabulary subtests found in some norm-referenced group tests and some individual diagnostic tests as noted in Chapter 5. The grade equivalent yielded by these subtests is an estimate of the student's reading expectancy.

## *Summarizing the Data*

Once you have assembled all the data from your assessment, it is important to organize the information so that trends can be noted and comparisons made. Use a form similar to the one in Figure 6-4 to help you group data about reading in one block, data about spelling and writing in another, data about emergent literacy in a third, and so on. Suggestions for placing data are presented in Figure 6-5.

After placing the data in blocks, examine each of the blocks in terms of the first one, which summarizes the student's estimated cognitive ability, listening capacity, and reading expectancy. Looking at the reading block, for instance, note how the student is doing in terms of reading expectancy or listening capacity. Is the student reading above or below reading expectancy or listening capacity? Looking at the writing and/or spelling block, note whether performance is above or below the student's estimated capacity or expectancy. After examining each block in this way, make comparisons among the blocks. How do writing and spelling compare with reading or word analysis? Also look for strengths and needs. Examining the categories at the bottom of the page, note major findings from the case study. These might include long-term illnesses, grades repeated, or indications of extra help given at school. Including only the most essential information, such as reading level, reading expectancy or listening capacity, major strengths and needs, summarize the data. However, hold off on making recommendations until you have conducted a **trial-teaching** lesson.

**Trial teaching:** use of sample lessons to determine which instructional approaches are most effective, based on assessment data.

Name *Robert Lawlor* Date of Birth *4-19-86* Grade *3* Date *3-10-97*

| Cognitive | IRI & Other Rdg. Tests | Word Recog. | Emergent | Spelling/ Writing | Oral Language | Assoc. Lrng. | Memory | Ach. Tests |
|---|---|---|---|---|---|---|---|---|
| *WISC 110* | *Ind. pp* | *F U* | | *1–50* | *Seems* | *Word Lrng* | *Digits 8* | *Stanf.* |
| *High* | *Inst. p* | *pp 75 85* | | *2–20* | *adequate* | *Imm-7/7* | *Arith 9* | *Rdg. 10 P.R.* |
| *Comp-13* | *Frus. 1* | *p 65 75* | | *Letter* | | *Delayed-6/7* | | *Math 40 P.R.* |
| *Vocab-12* | *List. 5* | *1 50 55* | | *name* | | | | *Lang 11 P.R.* |
| *Low* | | *2 40 40* | | *stage* | | | | |
| *Block-7* | *Stan.* | *Word* | | *writing* | | | | |
| *Obj-7* | *Tot.-10 P.R.* | *patterns—* | | *sample—* | | | | |
| Listening Capacity | *Comp-11 P.R.* | *diff* | | *very* | | | | |
| | *Wd.St. 9 P.R.* | *with* | | *rudimen-* | | | | |
| *5* | *Vocab. 9 P.R.* | *long* | | *tary* | | | | |
| | | *vowels* | | | | | | |
| Reading Expect. | | | | | | | | |
| *5.4* | | | | | | | | |

**Case History Highlights**

*Repeated 1st grade*
*Lagged in overall motor & lang dev*
*Emotional outbursts*
*Likes sports*

**Screenings**

*Vision—squints & holds book close*

**Trial Teaching**

*Responded best to whole-part teaching of word analysis skills*

**Summary**

*High/avg ability*
*Possible diff with memory & attention*
*Signif behind in reading, writing, & spelling*

**Recommendations**

*Use easy-to-read sports books*
*Use whole-part approach to word analysis*
*One-on-one instr*

**FIGURE 6-4 Case Summary**

Note: P.R. stands for percentile rank.

| | |
|---|---|
| *Cognitive Ability* | Give results of IQ test. Note high and low scores on subtests or areas in which student did well and areas in which student did poorly. |
| *Listening Capacity* | Note listening capacity from IRI. |
| *Reading Expectancy* | Use IQ or listening test or both to estimate reading expectancy. |
| *Reading Achievement* | List IRI levels. Give results of other reading tests, think-alouds, or observations of reading. |
| *Word Recognition* | Give results of word-lists tests. Provide information from the Word-Patterns Survey, Syllable Survey, the Word-Identification Interview, think-alouds, and observations. |
| *Writing/Spelling* | Give results of the Elementary Spelling Inventory, a test on graded lists of spelling words, and examination of writing samples and portfolio. |
| *Oral Language* | Provide test results of vocabulary assessment or other language measures and note observational data. Include word finding data, if this area was assessed. |
| *Assoc. Learning* | Provide results of Word-Learning Test. Note results of symbol learning tests and observations. |
| *Memory/Attent.* | Note results of tests of memory and attention. |
| *Emergent* | If pertinent, note knowledge of concepts of print, letter knowledge, phonemic awareness, and beginning sounds. Note interest in reading and writing and awareness of the purposes of reading and writing. |
| *Case History* | Note both major positive and negative factors. Note school situation. |
| *Screenings* | Note hearing, vision, health or other screenings. |
| *Trial Teaching* | Briefly describe trial teaching and note results. |
| *Summary* | Indicate reading expectancy; reading, writing and spelling levels; major strengths, weaknesses, and needs. |
| *Recommendations* | Suggest type of assistance (small group, one-on-one), major areas of needed instruction, and possible techniques or approaches and possible materials. Also recommend needed screenings. |

**FIGURE 6-5 Suggestions for Filling Out the Case Summary**

## Applying Trial Teaching

Once you have assembled all your assessment data, except for trial teaching, reflect upon the data and construct hypotheses as to what the student's major strengths and weaknesses are and what might be the best way to instruct the student. To test out your hypotheses, arrange for a trial-teaching lesson, as explained in Chapter 3. A trial-teaching lesson consists of the following steps:

### *Step 1: Plan*

Based on an analysis of assessment data, construct hypotheses and plan tentative techniques for teaching one or two key strategies. Assemble materials on the appropriate level of difficulty that you think would be appealing to the student.

### *Step 2: Explain to Student*

Inform the student of the results of the assessment in a concrete but positive way. Emphasize strengths and note that many bright students have difficulty with reading. Explain to the student the techniques that you will be using and how they will help her or him.

## Applying Trial Teaching *Continued*

### *Step 3: Present Choice*

Give the student a choice of materials and activities.

### *Step 4: Implement, Assess, Adjust*

Implement the technique and assess its effectiveness and also the student's reaction to it. Make adjustments as necessary.

### *Step 5: Discuss with the Student*

Discuss the effectiveness of the technique, activities, and materials with the student. Explain to the student that this session shows that she or he is a capable learner and should make progress using this and similar techniques. Invite the student's suggestions and implement them as fully as possible.

## Exemplary Teaching: Trial Teaching

Maria, a fifteen-year-old ninth-grader, was reading on a fourth-grade level despite having average ability as indicated by a WISC administered by the school psychologist. Her listening level indicated adequate language development. Based on the results of the listening comprehension score, Maria was reading five years below her capacity.

During interviews with teachers, Maria's parents, and Maria, it was revealed that Maria disliked school in general, and reading in particular. During her interview Maria stated that she hated reading because it was boring and she couldn't see any sense in reading all that dumb stuff. When the examiner looked over the texts from content-area subjects, she could see that they were all written at or above grade level, which was well above Maria's fourth-grade reading ability.

During the trial-teaching session, the examiner explained to Maria that she could understand ninth-grade stories and articles that were read to her. This meant that she was a bright person and had a good vocabulary and knew lots of things. The examiner also explained to Maria that she was good at reading one-syllable words, but because she had difficulty reading words that had two or more syllables, she would have a hard time reading ninth-grade books.

Looking frustrated, Maria said she had been taught all the syllable rules but they didn't help much. The examiner explained that she had a special way of teaching multisyllabic words, one she had used to help other bright students who had trouble with long words. She showed Maria how she could use her knowledge of single-syllable words to read multisyllabic words. Writing the words *side, beside, divide, decide,* and *provide* on the chalkboard, she helped Maria use her knowledge of *side* to read *beside, divide, decide,* and *provide.* Maria had missed both *provide* and *decide* during her testing.

Sensing that Maria had a negative attitude towards traditional classroom material, probably because she had been given texts that were too hard for her, the examiner displayed an array of easy-to-read novels, the local newspaper, and *Action* (Scholastic), a magazine written on a third- through fifth-grade level. Maria found *Action* to be appealing, especially after reading the cover selection and seeing that it wasn't too long nor too hard to read.

Based on Maria's reactions, a program was planned in which she was taught high frequency syllable patterns and shown how to use her knowledge of single-syllable words to decode multisyllabic words. Patterns introduced were drawn from materials that she was reading so that she would see the value of learning the skill and apply it in the context of real reading. She was also provided with high interest materials on a fourth-grade level of difficulty. Because her content-area texts were too difficult for her, tapes were made so she could read along with the tapes. A variable speed tape recorder was obtained so she could set the reading speed at a comfortable pace. Because she was so far behind, she was given help in the classroom and also after school by the reading specialist. By year's end, Maria was able to handle sixth-grade material. Her attitude towards school also showed a marked improvement, as did her grades.

Upcoming chapters explore materials, methods, and settings for corrective instruction. You will be better able to plan an intervention program after reading the rest of the text.

## *Making Recommendations*

Make recommendation on the basis of the assessment data and trial teaching. Recommendations might include suggestions for level of help—one-on-one, small group, regular classroom—and for the approach that might be taken—language experience, reading workshop, and so forth. Recommendations might also be provided for major needs—comprehension of main ideas, application of study strategies, ability to read short-vowel patterns, or ability to decode multisyllabic words, for instance. Possible teaching techniques, especially if these have been tried and shown to be successful, should be listed. The recommendations should answer the key questions established in Chapter 3.

- On what level is the student functioning?
- What is the student's potential for growth?
- What are the student's strengths and weaknesses in reading and writing?
- What would be the most effective materials for this students?
- Under what circumstances and in what setting would this student learn best?
- What are the most effective techniques or approaches for teaching this student?
- Are there any physical, psychological, social, or other factors that need to be addressed in order for students to do their best?
- How might the home, larger community, and school work together to help the students?

# *Professional Reports*

When sharing results, emphasize the student's strengths and the practical steps that the parents or teacher might take to help the child.

Reading specialists, along with psychiatrists, psychologists, communication disorders specialists, and other professionals are called upon to summarize the results of their assessments and make appropriate recommendations. Although they differ from profession to profession, these reports or case studies have a number of commonalties. In terms of style, they are typically written in formal English and attempt to be both objective and conservative. Care is taken to base conclusions and recommendations on test data and observations. Since these reports may be used to place students, obtain additional services, or plan a program of remediation, they should be complete, clear, and precise. Although the reports should embody a professional tone, they should be free of jargon and written in clear, simple language so they may be understood by parents and others outside the profession, as well as school principals, school counselors, and other professionals. Technical terms should be used with care, and, if used, should be explained. For instance, instead of saying, "Mario had difficulty with vowel digraphs," state that "Mario had difficulty with words like *rain* and *bean*

When constructing reports, avoid judgmental language. Instead of "Frank was lazy during the testing sessions," say, "Frank needed encouragement to continue working."

The focus of an assessment will change depending on the stage the student is in. For beginning readers, decoding might be the emphasis. For more advanced readers, focus might be on study skills.

Some assessment reports also include a listing of tests administered along with test scores on the first page. This provides the person reading the report with an overview of the test results.

The assessment outline is a sample and should be adapted to fit your situation. Include categories that may have been left out; delete areas that you do not assess.

in which two letters are used to spell the vowel sound." Instead of talking about a student's independent level, translate this into a phrase that a nonspecialist would understand, "Level at which Mario can read on his own, without any help from the teacher."

### *Content of the Assessment Report*

The content of the assessment report will vary, depending upon the complexity of the case and the extent of the assessment procedures. A diagnostic report may range from two or three pages to twenty or more. However, the reports written by reading specialists for schools are generally brief.

Although the assessment report may include information about the student's health, interests, social and psychological adjustment, school record, cognitive abilities, vision, and hearing, the emphasis should be on reading and writing and the kinds of programs that would seem to work best with the student. Presented below is an outline for a full report. Reports vary somewhat in both format and content so the outline should be adapted.

I. Identifying Information (on cover sheet)
   A. Student's name
   B. Date of birth and chronological age at start of assessment
   C. Sex
   D. Grade in school
   E. Name of school
   F. Examiner and place of assessment
   G. Dates of assessment

II. Reason for Referral and Summary of Observations (on inside pages)
   A. Name, age, grade, school, reason for referral
   B. Test-taking behavior, best-liked and least-liked tasks
   C. Results of interview about reading/writing problems, interests, and vocational plans

III. School History
   A. Summary of progress in school
   B. Achievement in specific subjects
   C. Results of achievement and other tests
   D. Attendance, repeated grades
   E. Description of classroom program
   F. Notes on special placement or special help given
   G. Classroom and special placement observations

IV. Results of Assessment
   A. Physical
      1. Vision
      2. Hearing
      3. Other
   B. Cognitive
      1. Academic aptitude
      2. Memory
      3. Associative learning
      4. Auditory and visual discrimination
   C. Reading achievement
      1. Word recognition
      2. Informal reading inventory levels
   D. Emergent reading—if applicable
   E. Special phonics testing
   F. Writing
   G. Spelling
   H. Handwriting
   I. Results of dynamic testing and trial teaching

V. Summary of Assessment
   A. Highlights of cognitive testing
   B. Highlights of reading achievement and other testing
   C. Conclusions

VI. Recommendations
   A. Setting and approach
   B. Major needs to be addressed
   C. Ways in which school can be supportive
   D. Ways in which parents can be supportive

VII. Description of Intervention (if applicable)
   A. Setting, approach
   B. Major needs that were addressed
   C. Skills/strategies taught
   D. Techniques used
   E. Materials employed
   F. Evaluation of progress

(A sample assessment report can be found in Appendix D.)

## Assessment: An Ongoing Process

Assessment should be ongoing and continuous. Whenever a student is engaged in a learning activity, assess the activity. How does the student cope with the activity? Which activities cause difficulty? Which are done with ease? What factors are hindering the student's progress? What factors are accelerating progress? What changes might be made to improve the student's chances for success? For instance, one student was struggling with a word-pattern approach, but began making progress when taught by a sound-by-sound approach. Apparently, his phonemic awareness was weak, and he needed added instruction in letter–sound relationships. Later, building on his improved phonemic awareness and solid knowledge of letter–sound relationships, he did quite well with a pattern approach. Another student, who made excessive word identification mistakes when reading prose, did much better when given short, easy poems to read (Bloodgood & Broaddus, 1994). Chances are that even the most comprehensive assessment wouldn't yield this information. This is the kind of data that continuous assessment, and trying out different approaches and materials is most likely to reveal. The important thing is to ask two questions as you work with the corrective reader: How is this approach/material/setting working? If it isn't working out, what might work better?

## *A Multidisciplinary Approach*

A reading problem, especially one that is severe, can have many causes, and can affect many aspects of a student's life. It is important to involve other professionals, parents, and the individual student in the process of assessment and remediation. The school psychologist can shed light on cognitive and affective factors and, perhaps, provide help with the emotional aspects of the problem. The speech therapist can test language abilities and provide help with articulation, word finding, and other difficulties. The Learning Disabilities specialist can test in math and cognitive processing areas. The nurse can provide insight into health issues and screen for auditory, visual, or health problems. Working collaboratively with other professionals is not just an excellent way to obtain a full array of information on a student, it is also an excellent way to enlist needed support.

## *Minicase Study*

Although nine-year-old David had adequate word-recognition skills, his comprehension was very poor. To worsen matters, David was uninvolved with reading and writing. When it came time to read and write, David couldn't seem to concentrate. The slightest distraction would cause him to lift his eyes from the page. His teacher wondered if he had an attention deficit disorder (Freppon, 1994).

Because of his puzzling lack of achievement, David was referred to a university reading clinic. Since traditional tests weren't providing needed information, a variety of other assessment devices were used. Through interviews, think-alouds, and observations, the instructor determined that David didn't see much purpose in reading and writing, except to keep the teacher happy. He didn't read or write voluntarily, and didn't have a favorite story or book.

To David, reading was primarily a matter of saying the words. When the instructor gave him a story with rearranged words to read, David focused so much on getting the words right that he failed to notice that the selection didn't make any sense.

Based on information obtained through a broad-based assessment, a program was planned for David. The program emphasized reading and writing for real purposes. David was encouraged to read books that had a genuine appeal to him, and he wrote about things that mattered. Unhappy about the school playground, David was encouraged to write about the situation. David also created cartoon strips, which he shared with his mother. David read favorite books with his instructor, mother, and other students. In time, David began to focus on reading for meaning. He also began to understand the purposes of reading. As he grew to understand the purposes of reading, he started taking control of his reading. He was able to use strategies, such as predicting upcoming story events and monitoring for meaning, to improve comprehension.

## *Summary*

A student's literacy capacity can be assessed through administering an intelligence or a listening test. Focusing as they do on academic aptitude, and encompassing tasks that all students may not have had an equal opportunity to learn, intelligence tests need to be interpreted with care and should be supplemented by observation of what the student can actually do. The most popular intelligence tests are the *Wechsler Scales,* whose subtest scores can be analyzed to yield diagnostic information. Only qualified personnel can administer the *Wechsler Scales;* however, reading professionals may administer the *Slosson Intelligence Test* and the *Peabody Picture Vocabulary Test,* a measure of receptive vocabulary.

Specific areas of cognitive functioning that should be assessed in a thorough assessment include memory and associative word learning. If a student is showing symptoms of word-finding difficulty, this area should also be assessed.

As part of an interactive assessment, the student's school situation should be observed. If possible, observe the student in reading and writing and content-area classes. Also interview the student's teachers and analyze school records. If it isn't possible to interview teachers, ask the school to complete a concise questionnaire. A case history obtained by interviewing the student's parents provides a backdrop for interpreting other assessment data. To determine whether a student has a reading disorder and the degree of severity, if there is a disorder, it is essential to establish where the student should be in terms of reading achievement. In general, students are expected to read up to their capacity as indicated by an IQ test, a listening test, or an oral vocabulary test. If possible, complement test and observational data by conducting condensed trial-teaching lessons in a key area.

Reading professionals may be expected to summarize assessment data in a professional report. Such a report follows the same general style and format of that in a psychological report.

## *Application Activities*

1. Talk to a school psychologist or a reading specialist about the kinds of measures that she or he administers. Discuss the value and limitations of the measures.
2. Complete an assessment and write a professional report based on your findings. If time and circumstances permit, write a full report. If not, write a mini-report based on a reading assessment that focuses on informal reading inventory results.

# Chapter 7

# Emergent Literacy and Early Intervention Programs

## *Using What You Know*

Emergent literacy, which encompasses both reading and writing, acknowledges that all students come to school with some experience with reading and writing. Emergent literacy refers to those early reading and writing behaviors that ultimately emerge into conventional literacy. What might be involved in making the transition from the informal literacy activities engaged in at home to a formal introduction to reading and writing? How might the literacy backgrounds of students differ? What difficulties might students encounter, especially those who are at risk because of poverty or other factors, as they enter into reading and writing programs? What might be done to alleviate these difficulties? What kinds of early-intervention programs might be effective in helping students who otherwise might experience failure in their attempts, to learn to read and write?

## *Anticipation Guide*

Read each of the following statements. Put a check under "Agree" or "Disagree" to show how you feel about each one. If you can, discuss your responses with classmates.

| | Agree | Disagree |
|---|---|---|
| **1.** Children learn to read and write in much the same way as they learn to speak. | ________ | ________ |
| **2.** Early interventions should not be started too soon because some students may simply need more time to mature. | ________ | ________ |
| **3.** For at-risk students, a structured emergent literacy program works best. | ________ | ________ |

4. Older students just learning to read and write may need to go through the same stages of learning to read and write as average kindergartners and first-graders do. ________ ________
5. Direct instruction in phonics should be an essential element in early-intervention programs. ________ ________

## Changing Concepts of Emergent Literacy and Intervention

At one time, young children were not given corrective help in reading and writing until they reached second grade. Reading and writing were thought to require readiness, which was seen as a natural, biologically based process akin to walking, a "neural ripening" (Gesell, 1925). It was believed that, like walking, the perceptual and cognitive factors underlying reading could not be hurried. According to the maturational concept, the best course was thought to be to wait for the child to develop, to mature. Children weren't given extra help until they had been in school for a year or two.

The maturational concept of readiness gave way to an interactionist view, which held that readiness could be enhanced by providing instruction. Thus, readiness programs were created. The purpose of these programs was to supply instruction that would foster the children's development and provide them with the prerequisite skills needed for formal reading instruction. Providing children with reading instruction before they were ready for it was thought to be potentially harmful emotionally and might also be a cause of later reading failure.

### A New Concept of Beginning Literacy

Over the past decade, the concept of readiness has given way to the concept of emergent literacy; with this, the concept of delaying corrective help until the student has demonstrated failure has been replaced, mercifully, with the concept of early intervention. According to Sulzby (1989), ***emergent literacy*** can be described as "the reading and writing behaviors of young children that precede and develop into conventional literacy" (p. 84). In reading, these behaviors might range from leafing through a picture book to reading a repeated phrase or, in writing, from drawing or scribbling to composing a message in invented or even conventional spelling.

> **Emergent literacy:** reading and writing concepts and behaviors of young children that develop into conventional reading and writing (Sulzby & Teale, 1991).

While emergent literacy recognizes that all students who come to school have some knowledge of and experience with reading and writing, that knowledge and experience can vary enormously. Some students will be able to write their names, recognize most of the letters of the alphabet, and, perhaps, read a few words. A few, about one in a hundred, will be able to read on a level comparable to that of the average second- or third-grader. On the other end of the continuum, some will not be able to write their names or recognize any letters. A few will never have held a book or a pencil. As Gillet and Temple (1994) comment:

> *Four out of five children make a host of useful discoveries about print before and during kindergarten. From being read to, from reading back favorite storybooks,*

*and from attempting to make messages with pencils, these children pick up a range of concepts about print that enable them to grow as readers and writers with the help of normal tutelage. One out of five children are not so fortunate, however. These children do not have their early print concepts in place when they begin first grade, and things do not go well for them. (p. 58)*

## An Environment That Fosters Literacy

**Literacy-rich classroom:** one in which children have many opportunities to read to themselves and each other and to write using invented and/or conventional spelling.

To foster literacy, Morrow (1994) suggests setting up centers of learning. These may incorporate content areas or may be devoted to particular activities such as reading, writing, and viewing.

Being developmental, emergent literacy is a natural outgrowth of learning oral language and is fostered in much the same way as oral language is fostered, though interaction with adults and peers. In the classroom this means providing a literacy-rich environment in addition to instruction. On the surface, a literacy-rich environment is one in which the student is surrounded by the tools of literacy: books, signs, posters, labels, paper, envelopes, and writing instruments of every kind, including typewriters, word processors, and rubber stamps. On a deeper level, a literacy-rich environment is more than an impressive display of the artifacts of literacy; it is one in which "a thoughtful teacher capitalizes on opportunities to focus on . . . print and make children aware of its various functions in real contexts" (Learning Media, 1991, p. 55). For the teacher, a key element in a literacy rich environment is reading to students.

### Benefits of Reading Aloud

Some children will enter kindergarten having been read to for 1,000 to 1,700 hours (Adams, 1990). Others will never have been read to by anyone. Yet, according to the Commission on Reading, "The single most important activity for building the knowledge required for eventual success in reading is reading aloud to children" (Anderson, Hiebert, Scott, Wilkinson, 1985, p. 23). Reading aloud to a child builds background of experience, vocabulary, syntax, and comprehension (Dickinson & Smith, 1994). It also builds an acquaintance with literary language and a sense of story so that students have a framework for understanding narratives.

Reading aloud to students is a vital element in a literacy program for low-achieving readers. Hampered in their ability to read, they are cut off from one source of developing language and background.

There are literally thousands of books that would be appropriate to read to students. The important point is to read books that both you and the students enjoy. It's also a good idea to include informational books so that you build background as you build language.

How a book is read has a bearing on how much students benefit. Students seem to benefit most when the book is given an introduction, read through without much interruption, and then discussed fairly thoroughly (Dickinson & Smith, 1994). An important component of the discussion is "child involved analytical talk" (p. 117). Child involved analytical talk includes analyzing characters or events, predicting events, making connections between events or characters in the story and events and people in the listeners' lives, talking about words and their meanings, summarizing portions of the story, evaluating the story, and clarifying comments students make about the story (Dickinson & Smith, 1994).

The following read-aloud lesson incorporates principles just discussed, which lead to increased development of vocabulary, overall language, and comprehension.

**Read Aloud Lesson**

*Before Reading*

Read the title and display the cover and encourage students to predict what the story might be about. Have them justify their predictions. Introduce any concepts that might hinder students' comprehension of the story. Have students read the story to compare their predictions with what actually happens.

*During Reading*

Clarify any elements that might be confusing. Also check students' predictions, and when appropriate, encourage them to make new predictions. However, emphasize the story itself. Do not allow long discussions to interrupt the flow of the story.

*After Reading*

Discuss students' predictions. Have them compare their predictions to what actually happened in the story. Discuss events in the story and characters. Have students justify and explain their responses so that they are analyzing the text and the language of the story. For instance, after reading *Anansi Goes Fishing* (Kimmel, 1992) and after discussing the main events of the story, ask why Anansi went to the justice tree. Also ask why the tree is called a "justice tree" and why the judge didn't believe Anansi. Discuss why Anansi didn't speak to Turtle for a long time. Talk over, too, the good that came out of the story and the meanings of some of the difficult words: *disgrace, justice, judge, warthog.* Also have students relate characters and events to their own lives.

## *Fostering Emergent Literacy*

Within the context of holistic reading and writing activities and being read to, students grow in literacy. While many children may develop literacy naturally, with a minimum of instruction, low-achieving readers and at-risk students need direct instruction in addition to numerous opportunities to engage in reading and writing. Areas in which direct instruction would be especially important are concepts about print, phonological awareness, letter knowledge, and knowledge of beginning consonant correspondences.

## *Concepts about Print*

Even though they may have been in school for a while and have had experience with reading and writing in their homes, low-achieving readers may not have acquired essential **concepts about print.** These include the following:

**Concepts about print:** basic understanding about written language—printed words represent spoken words, are composed of letters that represent sounds, are read from left to right, etc.

**Book-Orientation Concepts**

Locating the front and back of a book
Recognizing the function of the cover and title page
Recognizing the function of print and pictures

**Print-Direction Concepts**

Reading from left to right
Reading from top to bottom

**Print Concepts**

Understanding that words can be written down and read
Recognizing a letter, a word, and a sentence
Understanding that printed words are composed of letters
Understanding that words are composed of sounds
Understanding that letters represent sounds
Being able to point to separate words in print and match these with words that are being read by oneself or another
Understanding the difference between uppercase and lowercase letters
Understanding the function of punctuation marks

*The Bader Reading and Language Inventory* contains several tests for assessing emergent literacy, including one for noting separate words in a sentence.

Above all, students should understand that reading is a meaningful act. Reading isn't primarily a task involving translating letters into sounds but is mainly a matter of constructing understanding.

Some of the print concepts are interdependent. For instance, students' concept of words and their ability to form letter–sound relationships are apparently related. One device students use to follow a line of print is the ability to use initial consonants. In fact, being able to segment and pronounce or spell initial consonants seems to be a prerequisite for following a line of print by pointing to each word with one's finger (Morris, 1992). Knowing initial consonants apparently helps students locate the beginnings of words. Being able to fingerpoint, in turn, seems to contribute to further development of letter–sound relationships. Once students were able to detect individual words, they were then able to note the functions of final, and later, medial letters.

### *Informal Assessment of Concepts of Print*

To informally assess students' concepts about print, give the child a copy of *Brown Bear, Brown Bear, What Do You See?* by Bill Martin (1983) or a similar book. Ask a series of questions that probe the student's knowledge of print conventions: "Have you ever seen this book? What do you think this book might be about? How can you tell what a book is about? What do you do with a book?" Opening to a page that has an illustration and text, say, "I'm going to read this page to you. Where should I start reading? (Lipson & Wixson, 1997). Point to the first thing I should read. (Note whether the child points to print or an illustration and whether the child points to the first word.) Now I'm going to start reading. Point to each word as I read it." (Read two facing pages of text slowly. Note whether the child can point to each word as you read it. Note, too, whether the child goes from left to right, makes a return sweep, and goes from top to bottom and from the left page to the right page.) Pointing to a line of print, ask, "How many words are in this line?" Pointing to a word, ask, "How many letters are in this word? Can you read any of the words?" After assessing the child's knowledge of print, note the child's overall level of development, and fill in the Concepts about Reading section of the Observation Guide presented in Figure 7-1.

### *Writing Sample*

As part of your assessment of the child's emergent literacy, ask the child to write her name. If the child seems hesitant, encourage her to write it as best she can. If she can write her name, then ask her to write any additional words that she knows. Also ask the child to write

Student's Name ______________________ Age ______________________
Date ______________________ Native Language ______________________

Put a check (✓) in the blank if satisfactory, minus (–) if has a need in that area, and plus (+) if advanced. Comments may also be written on the blanks.

*Oral language*

Can express self clearly ______________________
Asks questions when necessary ______________________
Uses a vocabulary appropriate for age ______________________
Uses sentence structure appropriate for age ______________________
Listens to and understands stories ______________________
Can retell a story ______________________
Can follow oral directions ______________________
Can converse effectively with peers ______________________
Can converse effectively with teacher ______________________

*Concepts about reading*

Understands the main purpose of print ______________________
Recognizes environmental print ______________________
Can name the letters of the alphabet ______________________
Can point to each word as a line of print is read ______________________
Can detect individual sound in words ______________________
Can detect rhyme ______________________
Can detect beginning sounds ______________________
Can read own name ______________________
Recognizes some words in print ______________________

*Interest in reading*

Responds to being read to ______________________
Shows an interest in books ______________________
Pretends to read books ______________________
Attempts to read books ______________________
Asks questions about words, letters, or pictures in books ______________________

*Writing*

Understands the functions of writing ______________________
Writes or draws stories, letters, or lists ______________________
Uses invented spelling ______________________
Uses writing to communicate ______________________
Can write name ______________________

*Attitude and work habits*

Wants to learn to read and write ______________________
Can work independently ______________________
Is able to sustain attention ______________________
Can work with others ______________________
Is willing to experiment and risk making mistakes ______________________
Has confidence in own ability ______________________

**FIGURE 7-1 Emergent Literacy Observation Guide**

a story. Ask her to write a story telling about games that she likes to play or other things that she likes to do. Encourage her to write as best as she can or to write the way she usually does. (Accept drawing, scribbling, letterlike symbols, and other forms of written expression.) Note the child's overall level of development. With this information, complete the Writing section of the Observation Guide.

In addition to observing the child's performance on the structured reading and writing observations, note whether she understands the functions of reading and writing. As you observe, ask: "Does the child enjoy listening to stories? Is she able to retell a story? Does she enjoy browsing through books? Does she attempt to read or retell a story from a book? Does she attempt to write? Does she write for a variety of purposes: to tell a story, to send a message, make a list?" For additional suggestions for assessing young students, see Marie Clay's *An Observation Survey of Early Literacy Achievement.*

## *Developing Literacy Concepts*

Literacy concepts are best developed through an immersion in reading and writing activities. As you read books to children, point out the cover, the front of the book, the title, and the author's name. Discuss illustrations as you read. As you write messages or lists of names or schedules on the chalkboard, reinforce appropriate literacy concepts. Display and discuss signs, labels, notes, letters, announcements, and students' writing. Also use techniques such as shared reading.

### *Shared Reading*

**Shared reading:** technique in which the teacher reads aloud from a big book or other enlarged text and students follow along. It is used to introduce concepts of print and high frequency words.

In a **shared reading,** you read an enlarged text as students follow along. In subsequent rereadings of the text, students join in the reading. Enlarged text may take the form of commercially produced big books, big books that you create yourself, poems or songs written on the chalkboard, or experience stories written on large sheets of paper or on the chalkboard. Because the text is enlarged, the class can follow along as you read a selection. This procedure can be used to introduce or reinforce nearly any skill or understanding in early reading from the concept of going from left to right to the reading of words, phrases, and sentences. Listed below are procedures for conducting a shared reading activity (Gunning, 1994a).

Prepare students for a shared reading by discussing the cover illustration and the title and, if you wish, some illustrations from the text. Based on a discussion of the cover (and text illustrations) and the title, have them predict what the selection might be about. Set a purpose for reading. If students have made a prediction, the purpose might be to compare their predictions to what actually happened in the text.

As you read the selection, run your hand under it, pointing to each word as you say it so students get the idea of going from left to right and that there is a one-to-one match between the spoken and the printed word. Stop and clarify difficult words and concepts. Discuss interesting parts and have students evaluate their predictions, revising them if they see fit.

After students have read the selection, discuss it with them. Begin by talking over their predictions. Also try to relate the selection to experiences that students may have had. Try to elicit responses to the characters and situations portrayed, asking such questions as: "Do you know anyone like the main character? Has anything like this ever happened to you?"

During a second reading of the text, point out and discuss words, letters, punctuation marks, and other elements of print. During this second reading, encourage students to join in and read parts that they can handle. This may be a repeated word or phrase or whole sentence. If the book is a popular one, schedule several rereadings. Each time, the students should take more responsibility for the reading.

As a follow-up, students may want to listen to taped versions of the big book, or read regular-size versions to a partner. Depending on the student's development, this may be a pretend reading, a retelling based on pictures, or a genuine reading.

### *Concept of Separate Words*

One of the most essential print concepts for students to learn is that each printed word represents one separate spoken word. One way of developing a concept of separate words is through voice pointing. Beginning readers often memorize stories that have been read to them over and over again or use the illustrations in highly predictable books to "read" a text. Although they seem to be reading the words on the page, actually they are reciting a memorized story or constructing a story based on the picture. This is especially true of students who are experiencing difficulty learning to read. To convey the concept of separate words and to teach children to begin to take note of the details of individual words, point to each word as the class share reads a story and encourage the children to look at each word as you point to it. When you come to a repeated line of text such as, "Are you my mother?" slow down the pace, very deliberately point to each word, and make sure that the students say the word as you point to it. Have a volunteer read the repeated sentences, pointing to each word as he does so.

As individual students are reading a predictable book with you, occasionally have them point to each word as they read it. Also request finger pointing whenever you feel that a student is reciting a memorized sentence rather than really reading it. Besides helping to build a concept of separate words in a sentence, it helps students notice the details of printed words and to learn some printed words incidentally. After all, if students aren't looking at words as they read on their own or through shared reading, or aren't looking at the right words, then they won't learn anything about the makeup of the words.

## *Students' Writing*

To further foster the development of literacy concepts, encourage students to write. In the past, children were discouraged from writing, except for copying, until they had been taught how to form letters of the alphabet and were taught how to spell some words. As a result, their writing was limited to words that they could spell and whose letters they could form. The current concept of writing is that it is a developmental ability that has its roots in language, starts with scribbling, and evolves into drawing and ever more complex representations, including the use of random letters, **invented spelling,** and, eventually, con-

**Invented spelling:** intuitive spellings that students create before being introduced to conventional spelling, or as they are learning to spell.

ventional spelling (Calkins, 1994; Temple, Nathan, Temple, & Burris, 1993).

As they progress, children create or invent a system of representing sounds that, in the early stages, might use a letter or two to represent a whole word such as *lion* (which might be spelled *LN*) but which becomes increasing accurate. Through invented spelling, children explore the nature of the spelling system and advance in their ability to spell and to decode printed words. (See pp. 188–190 for additional information about the stages of spelling.)

Daily writing activities in which invented spelling is encouraged foster development in both reading and writing. Initially, the writing activities might start with drawing a picture and then writing a story about the picture. Other writing activities include describing trips and memorable events, writing pieces telling about themselves and others, composing lists, writing notes and letters, creating fictional pieces, and keeping a journal.

Unfortunately, many low-achieving readers have had negative experiences with writing and may be extremely reluctant to write. Having had their erroneous spelling corrected on many occasions, they may also be unwilling to try invented spelling. Part of fostering a willingness to write is the approach that one takes. Sulzby and Barnhart (1992) suggest incorporating three elements in your approach. First, accept whatever form of writing children choose to use, whether this be drawing or scribbling or using random letters. Second, make your request simple. Say, "Write a story" or "Write a letter to your mother." Third, be reassuring. Say, "It doesn't have to be like grown-up writing. Just do it your own way" (p. 126). You might even model some of the forms of writing that novice writers choose.

After a student has written his piece, have him read it back. If the writing is not decipherable, some teachers choose to write a translation beneath the child's writing so they have it for later reference. As the student reads her or his piece, note how she reads it. If the student is reading a story, does it sound like storybook reading? Does a friendly letter sound and look different from a story? As the student reads, does she attend to the symbols that she wrote? How close is the match between the symbols that the student wrote and the reading?

In general, students should be encouraged to write every day. One good way to start is to have them draw a picture and then write a story about it. The picture actually helps them to encapsulate their thoughts so they can better structure what they want to write.

Foster a variety of writing activities: stories, letters, lists, signs, advertisements, and announcements. Strike a balance between providing topics or story starters and having children choose what they want to write about. Also strike a balance between the writing children generate on their own and dictated pieces that are created through a language-experience approach.

## *Language-Experience Approach*

**Language-experience** approach: a single student or group dictates a story which is scribed by the teacher and then used to teach reading and writing.

In a **language-experience approach,** students discuss an experience that they have had, such as a trip to a farm, getting a new classroom pet, the arrival of a baby brother and so forth, and then dictate a story about the experience. Through careful questioning, the teacher may structure the story, but the language of the piece should be the students' own. The story can be one that is created by the group or one that the student dictates to the teacher or an aid. After it has been written, the teacher reads the story back as the student follows along. The student is invited to make any changes that he wishes. After changes have been made, the teacher reads the story and the student joins in much the same way as a shared-reading lesson is conducted.

Because they incorporate their own experiences and own language, many low-achieving readers and students learning to speak English find language-experience stories easier to read than texts composed by others. Another advantage of the language-experience approach is that it can be used with students of all ages and is an excellent method of instructing older novice readers. For more information on the language-experience approach, see Chapter 6. A sample language-experience story is presented in Figure 7-2.

Use conventional spelling when scribing a student piece. To avoid confusion between your mature writing and students' emerging form, you might explain that you use grown-up writing when you write down their stories and that someday they will use grown-up writing too. But it's okay for them to write the way other students do.

## *Shared Writing*

**Shared writing:** differs from language experience because both the teacher and the student share in composing the piece. In interactive shared writing, students do some of the physical writing of the story.

Modeled on shared reading, shared writing is a collaborative process in which both teacher and students take part in composing, scribing, and reading a piece of writing (Pinnell & McCarrier, 1994). Just as in traditional language experience, the class writes about experiences they have had or books that have been read to them. Often a shared reading of a favorite book forms the basis for the class's writing. If their writing is to be based on a story, the story is read several times so that they have a firm grasp of the plot and become familiar with the language of the story.

A story-based piece of writing can take a number of forms. After hearing Goldilocks and the Three Bears, one class created a labeled drawing of the interior of the three bears' home. Another class, after hearing a version of Tolstoy's *The Enormous Turnip,* summarized it by creating a mural in which each character had a completed speech bubble.

Whatever form the written piece takes, students play an active role in deciding the content. For instance in creating the mural for *The Enormous Turnip* (Domanska, 1969), each student drew one of the characters in the tale and, in a conversation bubble drawn by the teacher, decided what the character would say. One student decided that his character would say, "One, Two, Three, Pull" (Pinnell & McCarrier, 1994).

*Hermit Crabs*

*Hermit crabs are sneaky.*
*They do not have homes of their own.*
*They steal shells from snails.*
*Then they make their homes in the shells.*

**FIGURE 7-2 Language-Experience Story**

In addition to suggesting content, students also participate in the writing. The teacher encourages students to spell or actually scribe initial consonants, parts of words, or even whole words. One strategy that these novice writers are encouraged to use is knowledge of the spellings of their names. For instance, Tiffany was able to supply the first letter of *turnip* because *turnip* begins like *Tiffany,* and Paul was able to supply the first letter of *pull.* Another student who knew how to spell the word *ten,* used her knowledge of that word to form the word *hen.* Students may tell the teacher what letter(s) to write or may actually write them in the piece. A written piece can be a combination of teacher and student handwriting. Finished pieces are placed on the walls. Using a pointer, the teacher share reads the pieces. As students become familiar with the pieces, they are encouraged to read the walls.

The students' names are also placed on the wall in alphabetical order so these can be used to help with the spelling of words. Lists of color, number, and other common words are placed on the wall. Students are encouraged to use these lists and also stories placed on the wall to help them with pieces that they write independently. Because shared writing is a group project, stories are written in standard spelling. When students write independently, they use invented spelling. However, often their writing contains conventional spellings drawn from lists and stories on the walls.

In shared writing, the teacher emphasizes basic concepts of print. For instance, after adding a word to a story, the teacher goes back and reads the portion of the sentence that has been written so far. Focused on the details of the writing of a word, students may have lost the gist of the sentence. Going back over what has been written helps the students keep the story in mind and also helps them make a one-to-one match between written and spoken words. After, for example, adding "pulled" to "The Cat," the teacher rereads all that has been written of the sentence: "The cat pulled." After the word *the* has been written, the teacher reads, "The cat pulled the" and after *turnip* has been added, the teacher reads, "The cat pulled the turnip."

Here is sample dialog to show how shared writing might be implemented. It is based on work by Martin (1995). After reading *All I Am* (Rowe), students discuss things they can do. The class decides to compose a shared story telling what they can do.

*Robert:* "I can sing."

*Teacher:* "How shall we write that in our story?"

*Tanya:* "Robert can sing."

*Teacher:* (pointing to spot on chalkboard) "Robert, will you write your name here?"

*Teacher:* (pointing to and reading "Robert") "What goes next?"

*James:* "can"

*Teacher:* "How does *can* begin? Who has a name that begins like *can*?"

*Carmelita:* "I do."

*Teacher:* "How does your name begin?"

*Carmelita:* "With a *c*. My name begins with a *c*."

*Teacher:* "Can you write a *c* here?" (Judging that the class does not know the sound of the short *a,* she adds an *a* and reads /ca/.) "What do we need to add to /ca/ to make *can*?"

*Class:* "*n*"

*Teacher:* "Who can add an *n*?"

*Nina:* "I can."

*Teacher:* (after *n* has been added) reads while pointing to each word as she says it, "Robert can. What can Robert do?"

*Class:* "Sing"

*Teacher:* "How does *sing* begin? Whose name begins like sing?" (Getting no response) "How about *Sandra*? Does sing *begin* like *Sandra*?"

*Teacher:* "Sandra, can you make an *s* here?"

*Teacher:* Adds *ing* to *s* and reads, "sing. Robert can sing. Is this right? Is this what we wanted to write?"

### *Handwriting*

Even though they may have been in school for several years, low-achieving readers may not have learned how to form correctly all of the letters of the alphabet. As they explore writing, students will naturally learn aspects of letter formation. Displaying a large model alphabet and individual alphabet cards will help. However, they may also benefit from direct instruction. (See Chapter 13 for suggestions for teaching handwriting to older students whose handwriting skills are deficient.)

## *Phonological Concepts and Reading*

Upon entering school, the average child has a command of some 6,000 words and has mastered the basics of a breathtakingly complex language system. They would have no difficulty distinguishing between the statements: "I stepped on my cat" and "I stepped on my hat," even though the two statements differ by only a single speech sound. When communicating, children are operating on automatic pilot and are attending to the meaning of what they hear and say, rather than the structure of their utterances. However, reading demands that students be able to deal with the structure of language in an abstract way. For instance, students must be able to abstract the beginning sounds of words before they can learn that *b* represents the sound /b/ as in the beginning of *ball.*

In conversation, students aren't aware that words have separate sounds. They may not even have a concept of what a word is or may not be able to tell how many words are in a sentence. "What did you say?" may seem like a single speech event to them: "Whatyasay?" Without being able to detect the separate words in a sentence, students won't be able to match up printed words with their spoken equivalents.

Although most students learn the necessary phonological skills with little difficulty, a significant number do have problems in this area. Clay (1991) found that a large percent-

Speech sounds, or phonemes, vary according to their environment. The sound of /p/ in *pat* is not the same as the sound of /p/ in *tap.*

age of six-year-olds who were having difficulty learning to read could not detect the separate sounds in words. Juel, Griffith, and Gough (1986) found that most of the children who had difficulty learning to decode in first grade had been deficient in phonemic awareness when they entered first grade.

Metalinguistic ability: the ability to think of language as an object itself: to think of words as words and speech sounds as speech sounds.

What makes detecting the sounds of a word like *sun* or *cat* so difficult? First of all, students aren't used to dealing with language on an abstract or metalinguistic level. **Metalinguistic** ability requires that the child deal with the form as well as the content of language. Even at age six, students may simply lack the cognitive development needed to think on a metalinguistic level. Speaking of tasks that require the manipulation of beginning sounds, Harris and Sipay comment, "The ability to abstract a beginning sound from a spoken word and compare it with the beginning sound of another word is a cognitive ability that many five- and six-year-olds have not yet developed. In Piaget's terms, it requires 'decentration'" (p. 42).

**Decentration:** cognitive operation in which a child has the ability to consider two or more aspects of an object or event at the same time.

**Decentration,** which is a hallmark of the stage of concrete operations, means that a child must be able to consider two aspects of a situation at that same time. In language, the child must realize that *cat* represents an animal and is a word composed of sounds. Watson (1984) posits a decentration lag for those who have difficulty noting sounds in words. Some students who perform normally on general language measures are slow to develop decentration ability, which, in turn, slows down development of phonemic awareness, which, in turn, blocks progress in reading. These students would need additional experience with phonemic awareness activities.

The linguistic properties of speech sounds also make them more difficult to discriminate. Speech sounds are not articulated separately. For instance, the word *hat* is not articulated "h-a-t." Nor is it perceived as three sounds. The word *hat* is spoken as one continuous flow of sound. Its sounds are formed and perceived more or less simultaneously. Because of a speech phenomenon known as coarticulation, the lips form /h/ and at the same time the tongue articulates an /a/ and glides into a /t/. The /h/, /a/, and /t/ overlap and form a single pulse of sound (in Liberman and Shankweiler, 1991). This is an advantage for the listener. It speeds the perception of speech. However, coarticulation makes detecting individual sounds difficult.

Phonemic awareness goes beyond merely noting separate sounds in words. It requires mentally holding onto and manipulating sounds in words (Gentry & Gillet, 1993).

Detecting rhyme and noting syllables in words is easier than perceiving individual sounds. About half of the five-year-olds tested in one study could perceive syllables in words, but only one child in five in that age group could isolate separate sounds. (I. Liberman, Shankweiler, Fischer, & Carter, 1974). By age six, most children can isolate syllables in words, but one child in six still had difficulty segmenting a word into its individual phonemes (Sawyer, 1988). The ability to segment words into individual phonemes develops last.

## *Assessing Phonemic Awareness*

Phonemic awareness can be assessed in a variety of ways: by having the student tell how many sounds are in words, or by deleting a sound from a word: taking /k/ from *cat,* for instance, or by deleting and substituting /p/ for /w/ to make *pet* from *wet.* A fairly straightforward but reliable instrument for assessing phonemic awareness is the *Yopp-Singer Test of Phoneme Segmentation.*

### *Segmentation Tasks*

The *Yopp-Singer Test,* which is shown in Figure 7-3, consists of twenty-two single-syllable words. The teacher says each word aloud and then asks the student to say each of the word's sounds. For instance, when the teacher says "keep," the student is expected to respond /k/, /e/, /p/.

General directions for administering the test are provided in Figure 7-3. Unlike most tests, feedback is provided. If the student gives the correct answer, the teacher says, "That's right." If the answer is incorrect, the teacher says the word and its separate sounds: "cat: /k/, /a/, /t/." Only responses in which the student provides all the word's sounds are scored as correct. However, the student's attempts should be recorded as these could provide insight

**Yopp-Singer Test of Phoneme Segmentation**

Student's name________________________________ Date________________

Score (number correct)___________

Directions: Today we're going to play a word game. I'm going to say a word and I want you to break the word apart. You are going to tell me each sound in the word in order. For example, if I say "old," you should say "/o/-/l/-/d/." (*Administrator: Be sure to say the sounds, not the letters, in the word.*) Let's try a few together.

Practice items: (*Assist the child in segmenting these items as necessary.*) ride, go, man

Test items: (*Circle those items that the student correctly segments; incorrect responses may be recorded on the blank line following the item.*)

| | | | |
|---|---|---|---|
| 1. dog | ____________ | 12. lay | ____________ |
| 2. keep | ____________ | 13. race | ____________ |
| 3. fine | ____________ | 14. zoo | ____________ |
| 4. no | ____________ | 15. three | ____________ |
| 5. she | ____________ | 16. job | ____________ |
| 6. wave | ____________ | 17. in | ____________ |
| 7. grew | ____________ | 18. ice | ____________ |
| 8. that | ____________ | 19. at | ____________ |
| 9. red | ____________ | 20. top | ____________ |
| 10. me | ____________ | 21. by | ____________ |
| 11. sat | ____________ | 22. do | ____________ |



**FIGURE 7-3 Yopp-Singer Test of Phoneme Segmentation**

From Yopp, H. (1995). A Test for Assessing Phonemic Awareness in Children. *The Reading Teacher,* 49, pp. 20–29.

A score of 15 or higher on the *Yopp-Singer* is an indication that apparently students have adequate phonemic segmentation ability.

into a student's performance. A partially correct answer, for instance, shows that the student has some segmenting ability. The average kindergartner is able to segment half the items. Students who correctly segment most or all of the words are judged to be proficient. Those who only segment one or two words or none at all, may need intensive work in this area (Yopp, 1995). Although designed to be administered to kindergartners and first-graders, it can also be given to older students who are having difficulty learning to read.

***TALS (Test of Awareness of Language Segments)***

*TALS* (Sawyer, 1987) tests phonemic awareness and also awareness of longer chunks of language. It assesses a student's ability to segment sentences into individual words, long-spoken words into syllables, and short-spoken words into individual phonemes. To make the task of segmenting concrete, the student uses blocks or chips to indicate segments. To indicate the two phonemes in *see,* for instance, the student puts a block in place and says "sss" and then puts another next to it while saying "eee". Having three levels, the test does a better job of indicating the stage of a student's segmenting ability. Although designed primarily for children between the ages of 4 ½ and 7, *TALS* has been used with older disabled readers and adults.

***Beginning Sounds***

Phonemic awareness can also be assessed informally by having students sort picture cards according to beginning sound (Johnston, Juel, & Invernizzi, 1995). Provide the students with fifteen picture cards that depict three different beginning sounds. Choose sounds that are relatively easy to discriminate and which are very different from each other such as /s/, /m/, and /h/. Introduce the task by presenting a model picture for each beginning consonant sound: *sun, moon,* and *hat.* Put sun at the top of the table or desk and explain: "This is a picture of the sun. Sun begins with a sss sound." Pointing to the other cards, say, "Put all the cards whose names begin with sss as in *sun* under the picture of the sun." Putting the picture of the moon next to the picture of the sun, say, "This is a picture of the moon. Moon begins with mmm. Put all the pictures whose names begin with mmm as in *moon* under the picture of the moon." Holding up a picture of a hat, explain, "This last picture shows a hat. Hat begins with a hhh sound." Place the picture next to that of the moon and explain, "Put all the pictures whose names begin with hhh as in *hat* under the picture of the hat."

To make sure the student understands what to do, sort three sample cards. Holding up the picture of the numeral 6, say, "This is a picture of a sssix. Where does sssix go?" Also place the pictures of the mop and hand. Give help as needed with the samples, but then direct students to place the rest of the cards on their own. First, however, make sure that the student can name all the cards.

If students are unable to perceive most of the beginning sounds, they probably need work with language play and similar activities as described in the section to follow. You might also back up and assess their ability to detect rhyme, which is easier to detect than initial sounds. Rhyme can also be informally assessed through the use of sorting. Students might sort three groups of pictures that include the following: hat, cat, rat, bat; car, jar, star; ring, wing, king, swing, string.

## *Techniques for Building Phonological Skills*

Although a large number of phonological skills have been identified, only the following are apparently crucial for the development of reading: identifying the separate words in a sentence, detecting rhyme, identifying the separate sounds in a word, detecting beginning sounds (and eventually matching these with the letters that represent them), and blending sounds (combining /s/ and /at/ or /s/, /a/, /t/ to form the word *sat*).

One way to foster overall phonological awareness is through natural activities such as word play and listening to rhymes, riddles, puns, jokes, songs, and stories that call attention to words as words and sounds as sounds. When students play with language, instead of just listening to the meaning, they are drawn to words and sounds as abstract units of language.

### *Rhyme*

A good place to begin the development of phonological skill is with rhyme. An enjoyable way to develop the concept of rhyme is to read nursery rhymes and other rhyming tales to students. At first, just read and discuss the rhymes so that students build a kind of subconscious storehouse of rhyming knowledge. Maclean, Bryant, and Bradley (1987) found that children who knew nursery rhymes were better at detecting rhyme and learned to read faster than children who lacked that knowledge. For older students, who might perceive nursery rhymes as being too babyish, substitute humorous verses or jump rope rhymes similar to the following:

When you're old and think you're sweet
Pull off your shoes
And smell your feet.

As students become familiar with rhyming pieces, stress the rhyming elements. As you develop a concept of rhyme, also build the language used to talk about rhyme: *same, sounds, rhyme, words* and so forth.

### *Sorting Rhymes*

Sorting is also an excellent way to reinforce the concept of rhyme. In sorting, students group objects or pictures whose names rhyme. If possible, begin with objects. Objects are more concrete than pictures and less likely to be misinterpreted. Using toys and dollhouse furniture, assemble sets of objects similar to the following: boat, coat, goat; bug, mug, rug, plug. Display two boxes, one with a toy bug in front of it and one with a goat in front of it. Tell students that they will be putting the objects that rhyme with *bug* in the bug box and those that rhyme with *goat* in the goat box. Sort one or two objects as examples. Holding up a rug from a doll house or a small piece of rug, say its name, emphasizing the *ug* portion, then say "*Rug* rhymes with *bug*. Both have an *ug* sound, so I'll put it in the bug box."

> Another way of sorting rhymes is to give each child a picture card. In a pocket chart, place the example cards (cat, goat) and have students come up and place their picture cards under the example cards with which they rhyme (Gentry & Gillet, 1993).

Once students understand what they are to do, have them sort the objects. Have them name the object, tell which of the two boxes it should be placed in, and why. After all the objects have been sorted, have students name the objects in each box and note that all the objects rhyme.

Also have students sort pictures. Some pictures that might be used in sorting rhymes include: bat, cat, hat, rat; nail, pail, sail, snail; cake, rake, snake; bed, bread, sled; car, jar, star; king, ring, string. Pictures are sorted in much the same way as are objects. Select a picture to serve as a model for each rhyming pattern and have students place rhyming pictures underneath.

Students can work individually, in pairs, or in small groups. After a sort has been completed, have students say the name of each picture in a category. If students are slow or hesitant, discuss any questions they might have and ask them to sort again. If students have completed a sort under your guidance, have them sort the items a second time for additional practice.

Also use the following activities to teach or reinforce the concept of rhyme:

- Call attention to rhyming sounds in nursery rhymes and rhyming tales.
- When reading rhyming lines, read all but the last word and have students suggest a word to complete the couplet.

  Twinkle, twinkle, little star,
  How I wonder what you _______.
  Up above the world so high,
  Like a diamond in the _______.
- Hold up an object (or picture of an object) and have students chose from a display another object whose name rhymes with the name of the object you are holding. Holding up a stuffed cat, for instance, have students say "cat." Then have them choose from a display of a ball, a hat, and a box, the one that rhymes with *cat.*
- Give students a single word and have them supply words that rhyme with it. Have them supply rhyming words for *cat, hill, cake,* for instance.
- Have students sort objects whose names rhyme: can, toy van, toy man; bat, toy cat, toy rat; toy house, toy mouse; toy rake, rubber snake, toy cake; toy goat, toy boat, coat.
- Have students tell which word in a group doesn't rhyme: *hat, soap, cat; goat, bell, coat.*

> If students have difficulty segmenting single sounds, have them note the syllables in words, which is an easier task. Show students how to clap for each syllable in a series of multisyllabic words that you say.

### *Sounds in Words*

To introduce the concept of sounds in words—which is phonemic awareness because a phoneme is an individual speech sound—play this game with students. Pointing to a picture of a goat, ask, "Is this a /g/?" When the class says, "no," agree and explain, "That's right. I didn't say all of the word's sounds. I said, 'Is this a /g/?'" Then say, "Is this a /g/, /ō/?" (emphasize each sound). Explain that no, this is not a /gō/. It doesn't have enough sounds. Next, ask, "Is this a goat?" Once again, carefully enunciate all three sounds /g/, /ō/, /t/. When the class says, "yes," explain that they are right. *Goat* has three sounds and you said all three of them. Present *sun* and *cat* and other three-sound words in this same way.

> **Elkonin technique:** method that teaches phonemic awareness by having students put tokens in boxes to show how many sounds a word has.

### *Elkonin Technique*

To further reinforce and also to extend the concept of sounds in words, use the **Elkonin technique** (Elkonin, 1973). Through the use of sound boxes, Elkonin sought to "materialize" the analysis of a word into its component sounds (phonemes). Children are given a picture of an object whose name contains two or three sounds. Underneath the picture appear boxes that match the number of sounds the picture's name contains. One block is drawn for each sound. For the word *cat,* three blocks would be drawn, one each for /k/, /a/, /t/. Three boxes would also be drawn for the word *goat.* Although goat has four letters, it has only three sounds: /g/, /ō/, /t/. Students indicate the number of sounds in a word by placing a marker in the box for each sound they hear. Figure 7-4 shows Elkonin boxes.

**Elkonin Technique Lesson**

*Step 1: Demonstrate*

Showing the child the drawing and the boxes, demonstrate the task and explain its purpose and importance. As you say the word, stretch out its sounds to enhance the child's perception of them. Place a marker in the first box as you say the first sound, place a marker in the second box as you say the second sound, etc. Demonstrate until the child seems to grasp the task. Then guide the child through several words.

*Step 2: Help*

Give the child a drawing of a hat, the sun, or other three-sound words. The number of boxes should equal the number of sounds in the word, not the number of letters. Direct the child to say the word and listen carefully to the sounds that she hears. She puts a marker in the box when she hears a sound. For the word *hat,* the child says "hat," slowly and deliberately, and then says /h/, putting a marker in the first box as she does so, says /a/, again putting a marker in the second box as she does so, and says /t/, again putting a marker in the third box as she does so. The student then says the whole word.

*Step 3: Success*

Eventually the student should be able to indicate the number of sounds in words without the aid of boxes.

Also use naturally occurring opportunities to point out the sounds of words. As you write the day's date, messages, or students' names on the chalkboard, say each sound as you write the letter(s) that represents it. As you write the name *Bob,* for instance, say /b/, /o/, /b/. Then discuss the number of sounds in *Bob.* Also read books to students that focus on the sounds of language. At this level, the focus is on detecting sounds in words. That's why students put markers rather than letters in the boxes. As students learn letter–sound relationships, they can put letters rather than markers in the boxes.

***Playing with Sounds***

To further develop students' implicit knowledge of the sounds of language, sing songs and read books to them that play with language. For instance, read *Jamberry* (Degan, 1983), a humorous picture book in which the word *berry* is used to form dozens of words:

One berry
Two berry
Pick me a blueberry.

Hatberry
Shoeberry
In my canoe berry.

# Sounds in Words

**Say the word that names the picture. Put a marker in the first box as you say the first sound of the word. Put a marker in the second box as you say the second sound of the word. Put a marker in the third box as you say the third sound of the word.**

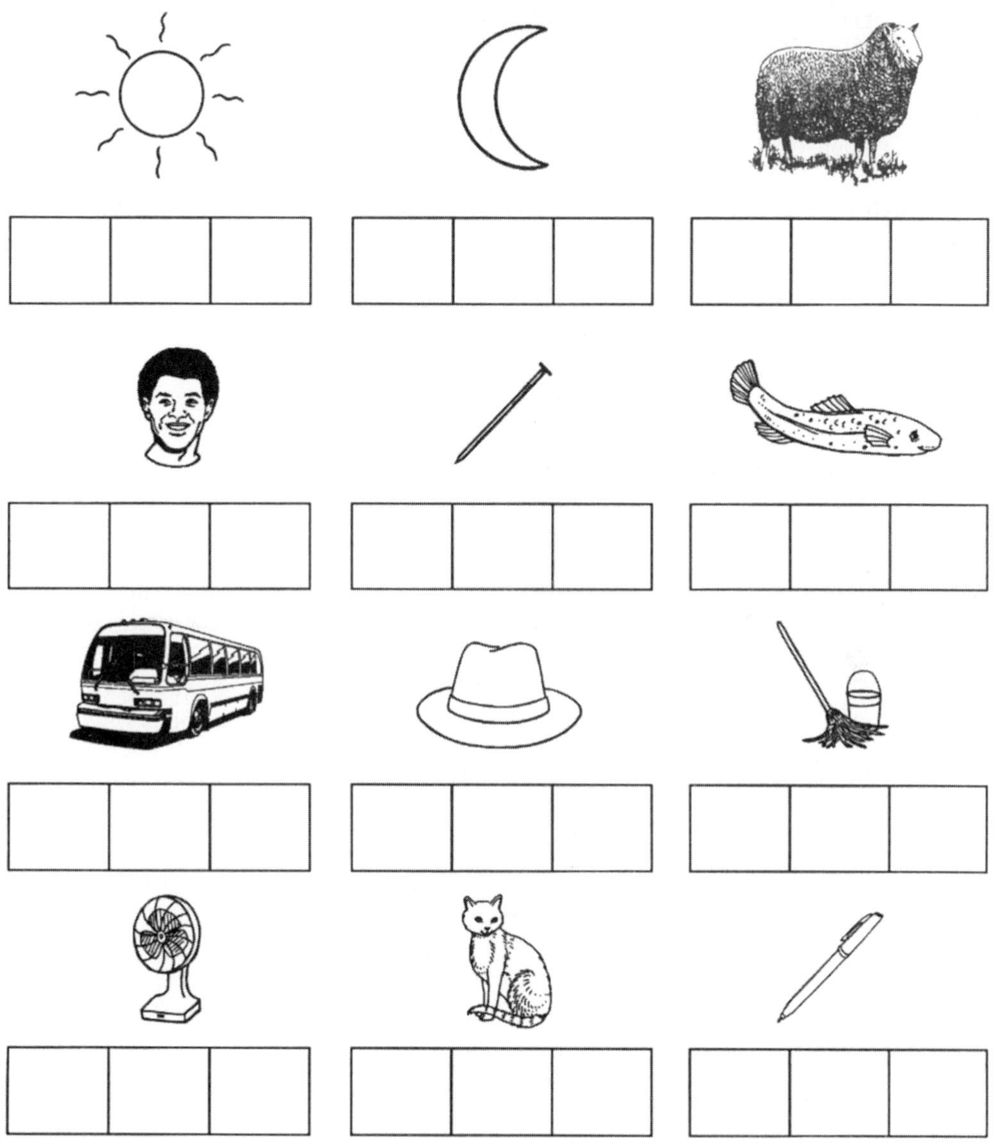

**UNIT TWO: Phonemic Awareness** **Lesson Five: Segmenting Words into Speech Sounds** Page 7

**FIGURE 7-4 Elkonin Boxes**

From *Word Building: Beginnings* by T. Gunning, 1994. New York: Phoenix Learning Resources. Reprinted by permission of Galvin Publications.

As you read the book, have the students clap out the rhythm of the piece—one clap for each syllable. After discussing the tale, ask students to form *berry* words, the sillier the better. Other children's books that play with language include:

Geisel, T. (1991). *Mr. Brown Can Moo! Can You?* New York: Random House.
Geisel, T. (1979). *Oh Say Can You Say?* New York: Random House.
Hutchins, P. (1976). *Don't Forget the Bacon.* New York: Morrow.
Hutchins, P. (1976). *Follow That Bus.* New York: Knopf.
Lunn, C. (1990). *A Buzz Is Part of a Bee.* Chicago: Children's Press.

### *Riddles*

Read riddles and jokes to students, especially those that involve a play on word sounds. Discuss riddles that call attention to sounds in words. For instance,

What kind of key can climb a tree?
A mon-**key.**
What kind of pet can play in a band?
A trum-**pet.**
What kind of vegetable can take you for a ride?
A **cab**-bage.

> Another book to introduce beginning sounds is *The Story of Z* (Modesitt, 1990), in which the letter Z leaves the alphabet. As you read this book aloud, highlight the missing sound and discuss beginning sounds in words.

### *Beginning Sounds*

Once students have demonstrated some ability to deal with language on an abstract level, as evidenced by their ability to detect rhyme and play with and manipulate sounds, introduce the concept of beginning sounds. A delightful way to do this is through reading Dr. Seuss's *There's a Wocket in My Pocket* (1974), which combines rhymes and perception of beginning sounds.

After reading the text, discuss the rhymes and the words that Dr. Seuss made up. Lead students to see that Dr. Seuss made up his silly words by changing the first sound of a real word: *pocket—wocket.* Supply real words and help students create silly words by changing the first sound. In the exercise below, students change the first sound in the last word in each sentence.

There's a _______ in my book.
There's a _______ in my lunch box.
There's a _______ in the room.
There's a _______ on my desk.
There's a _______ on the bus.

Also use names to convey the concept of beginning sounds. Ask students if you are *Ms. _eynolds.* When they say no, and say you are *Ms. Reynolds,* ask them what was missing from *_eynolds.* Lead them to see that the beginning sound was missing, that you are Ms. RRReynolds, drawing out initial /r/. Go around the room and ask: Is this *_am*? Is this *_eth*? Is this *_uis*? Have students add the beginning sound to each name. Repeat the child's name, stretching the initial sound as you do so, "SSSam."

Follow the same procedure with objects or pictures of objects: Is this an *_ail* (nail)? Is this an *_en* (pen)? Is this an *_ook* (book)? Is this an *_orse* (horse)? If students have difficulty with this task, drop down to a lower level, one that requires only sound discrimination. For instance, holding up a real object or a picture, ask the following questions.

(Holding up a pen) Is this a pen or a ten?
(Holding up a pan) Is this a pan or a tan?
(Holding up a hat) Is this a hat or a bat?
(Holding up a ball) Is this a ball or a tall?

To further reinforce the concept of beginning sounds, choose a book that lends itself to this activity such as *Morris and Boris* (Wiseman, 1959). Discuss how *Morris* and *moose* begin in the same way. Also read alliterative tales or alphabet books to students. If reading the *s* page of an alphabet book that contains a number of items that begin with /s/, discuss how all the items begin with the same sound. Emphasize the /s/ in each word so that students can clearly hear it. Say the sound in isolation and in the context of a whole word. Talk about the sound of /s/ as in *sun*. Discuss students' names that begin with /s/: *Sam, Sarah, Sandy.*

When introducing initial sounds, there is a tendency to supply the letter that represents the sound. However, doing so may distract the child from the task, which is perceiving sounds.

Also read alliterative verses and sing alliterative songs. Discuss the names of common objects that begin with /s/ and create a bulletin board of objects whose names begin like *sun*.

Have students complete words whose names begin with *s*. Pointing to a sandwich ask, "Is this an _andwich?" Have the class say what the object is and tell what sound they had to add to make the word *sandwich.*

During the normal course of the day's activities, take advantage of naturally occurring opportunities to reinforce awareness of beginning sounds: if it's a *Monday* in *May,* discuss how Monday and May begin with the same sound. If discussing animal sounds, note that cows make a *moo* sound.

Calling attention to the way sounds are formed can also help students learn to detect beginning sounds, especially when the means of articulation is readily detectable. For instance, have students say "mmm" and discuss how the lips are used to make this sound. Realizing how phonemes are articulated helps lay a conceptual foundation for phonemic awareness (Lindamood & Lindamood, 1975). Using articulatory movements to explore sounds may help students who have difficulty perceiving them auditorially (Torgesen, 1994).

### *Other Activities*

- Have students sort objects or pictures whose names have the same beginning sound. Follow the same procedures that you followed for sorting rhymes.
- Say a rime (part of a word that follows the initial consonant or cluster) and have students make as many words as they can by adding initial consonants. For instance, say "*-eep.*" Students might say, *beep, deep, jeep,* and so forth. As an alternative, say a word and have students make new words by changing the first sound of the word so that *cat* becomes *bat, hat, pat, sat,* etc.
- Give the rime of a word and a clue. Have students guess what the word might be. Say, "ay." Monday is a _ay. Give me some money. _ay me. Feed this to a horse. _ay.

- Detecting the missing sound. Ask the student to identify a sound that has been deleted. Tell the child: "Say 'sat.' Now say 'at'. What sound is missing in *at* that you said in *sat*?" (J. Rosner, 1975).

Phonemic awareness apparently enjoys a reciprocal relationship with reading (Perfetti, 1992; Perfetti, Beck, Bell, & Hughes, 1988). Thus, adults who have never learned to read are lacking in phonological awareness (Alegria & Morais, 1991). While some awareness of sounds in words is necessary for the acquisition of initial reading skills, experience with initial reading tasks further develops phonemic awareness. You do not have to wait to introduce letter–sound relationships, sight vocabulary, and other beginning reading skills until children have mastered phonemic awareness. As long as students have at least some ability to detect sounds in words, they may be instructed in actual reading skills.

## *Letter Knowledge*

A key prerequisite to learning to read is knowing the letters of the alphabet. If students don't know the identity of *s*, then they will not be able to associate it with the sound it represents. If they confuse *m* and *n*, they may assign the sound of /n/ to /m/ and vice versa. The learning of letter–sound relationships will be greatly hindered. While it is not essential for students to learn the names of the letters, it can be helpful. Knowing the name of a letter aids memory. Students who know the names of the letters are better able to learn letter–sound relationships (Ehri, 1983). According to Murray, Stahl, and Inez (1993), "Identifying letter names is a suboperation in the task of learning letters sounds" (p. 5).

### *Assessing Letter Name Knowledge*

To test students' knowledge of letter names, give the Letters Name Test presented in Appendix A. If students are unable to name the letters when they are shown them, drop down to a lower level of knowledge. Say the name of a letter and have students pick it out from a series of four letters in a row.

### *Teaching Letter Names*

Children learn the letters of the alphabet by contrasting distinctive features rather than by memorizing shapes (Gibson, Gibson, Pick, & Osser, 1962). Distinctive features include curves, slants, and whether lines are open or closed. To foster the learning of distinctive features, it is important that letters be presented in such a way that one can be compared with another so that students can note how *t* differs from *d* or *l* differs from *t*. It is best, however, not to present easily confused letters such as *b* and *d* or *p* and *q* at the same time.

A logical starting point for teaching letter names is with students' own names. If students know any letters at all, chances are these are the letters used to spell their names. Write the names of students on the board and discuss the letters that make up their names. Note names that begin with the same letter. List and discuss, for example, names that begin with *B* or *T*. If students can't write both their first and last names, this is a good time to teach that skill. At this point, you might also want to review correct letter formation, if necessary. Often low-achieving readers incorrectly form some letters or form them inconsistently. Forming letters consistently builds perceptual and organizational skills. Because poor readers often have difficulty remembering visual–verbal material, it might be helpful if you supplied them with copies of the alphabet that they might paste in their notebooks and refer to as needed. (See Chapter 15 for additional suggestions on handwriting instruction.)

One of the best ways to reinforce knowledge of letter names is to surround students with examples of letters and reasons to use them. Display a model alphabet and have available old typewriters, computers, stamp sets, letter stencils, magnetic and felt letters, and a wide assortment of writing instruments and paper. Encourage students to experiment with the alphabet and to play alphabet games. Also encourage wide writing with invented spelling. Most important of all, read and discuss alphabet books and encourage students to read these texts. Simply reading alphabet books to students seems to increase their letter knowledge and their sensitivity to sounds in words (Murray, Stahl, & Inez, 1993). Other activities that might be used to reinforce letter knowledge include the following:

- Using a magnetic letter board, mix several examples of the letter being taught with letters that have already been learned. Don't mix letters that are similar in form, *m* and *w*, for example. Have students assemble all the examples of the target letter, all the *s*'s, for example (Clay, 1993b).
- Help students create an alphabet book. Set aside twenty-six pages in a composition book. As students learn a letter, write that on the appropriate page in upper and lowercase form. Write a model word that begins with the letter so that students can see the letter in the context of a word and also begin to get a sense of the sound that the letter represents. Have students paste in or draw an illustration of the model word.
- Use environmental print. This is an especially useful approach if you work with older students, who would see environmental print as being mature. Bring in cereal boxes, milk cartons, and other items containing labels. Have students "read" the labels and identify the letters that make up the labels.
- Develop letter knowledge as a natural part of your routines. As you list names or write messages on the board, spell out the words and names. Also surround students with the tools of writing so that they are encouraged to experiment with writing and make discoveries about the alphabet as they do so. One especially useful device is to load talking software, such as *Dr. Peet's Talk/Writer* (Hartley) into your computer so that when a key is pressed it says the name of the key's letter. Later, as students move into letter sounds, the software's operation can be changed so that when a key is pressed, the sound of the letter, rather than its name, is spoken.

> Children can make essential discoveries about letter–sound relationships through their attempts to write. Children "reinvent writing and thereby make it their own" (Ferreiro, 1986, p. 37).

## *Invented Spelling*

Encourage experimentation with writing and spelling. Through their attempts at spelling, students are providing themselves with a valuable analysis of letter–sound correspondences. Invented spelling also opens a window onto the child's processing of letter relationships. By examining samples of a student's invented spelling, it is possible to estimate where a student is on the path to understanding the alphabetic system. Does the student understand that words are composed of letters? Does the student realize that letters can be used to represent sounds? Does the student know some basic letter–sound correspondences? If so, which ones? (See Chapter 5 for additional information about spelling development. See Figure 5-5 for a chart of stages of spelling development.)

## *Early Intervention Programs*

Children who experience difficulty in the early stages of reading do learn. Unfortunately, what they most often acquire from the experience are ineffective strategies and a concept of themselves as a nonlearner. Speaking of delaying instruction until the child has experienced failure, Marie Clay (1985) notes, "The difficulties of the young child might be more easily overcome if he had practised error behavior less often, had less to unlearn and relearn, and still had reasonable confidence in his own ability" (p. 10).

### *Reading Recovery*

Programs of early intervention are both more effective and less expensive in terms of time, money, and emotional damage, than are traditional corrective programs. The best known of the early intervention programs is *Reading Recovery.*

Growing out of her observations initiated in 1962 of how children in New Zealand learn to read, Marie Clay and several colleagues made an intensive two-year study of procedures used by teachers working one-on-one with low-achieving readers. After a year of observing, discussing, and piloting promising techniques, a set of procedures was established and refined.

The plan of the program is to accelerate children's progress by providing intensive one-on-one instruction, thirty minutes a day, five days a week for a period of twelve to twenty weeks. The intent is to develop students' skills and abilities so that they can function as well as the average child in their class. In New Zealand, this was accomplished for 95 percent of the students who took part in the program (Clay, 1991). In the United States, the recovery rate is approximately 81 to 88 percent. Student mobility and absenteeism were the major reasons why a higher percentage of students did not meet the program's standards (Dunkfield, 1991; Lyons & Beaver, 1995; Smith-Burke & Jaggar, 1994). However, most of those who didn't meet the criterion of success still made encouraging gains.

#### *A Reading Recovery Lesson*

A typical thirty-minute reading recovery lesson includes the following components:

**Reading of Familiar Books.** The child rereads two or more familiar books. The purpose of this rereading is to build fluency and confidence. It also gives the child the chance to apply previously taught strategies, such as using context or letter–sound relationships. Because the books have been previously read, the child should find that it is easier to apply the strategies.

**Rereading of Previous Day's Book and Taking a Running Record.** As the child reads the book orally and, generally, without any help from the teacher, a running record is taken.

In a running record, which is somewhat similar to the administration of the oral selection of an informal reading, both of which were explained in Chapter 3, the teacher makes note of words successfully read and also errors or miscues. An analysis of the running record provides an assessment of the child's progress but, more importantly, yields information about the kinds of strategies the student is using. Is the student using verbal or pictorial context? Is the student using phonics? Is the student monitoring the reading so that miscues are corrected? At the end of this segment, the teacher praises the student for the quality of the reading, notes an instance or two when she effectively applied strategies, and points out one or more instances in which a strategy that wasn't used could have been applied or an instance where she might apply a strategy more effectively.

### *Working with Letters*

While reviewing the child's rereading or whenever else appropriate, the teacher and student can build words together, using magnetic letters and a metal board. The magnetic letters might be used to help the child see the similarities in pattern words (*cat, hat, sat*), note *s* or *ed* endings, or focus on the sequence of letters in a sight word. Magnetic letters are also used to present the make-and-break technique in which students construct, break apart, and reconstruct common word patterns (Clay, 1993b).

### *Writing a Story*

One of the basic assumptions of *Reading Recovery* (Clay, 1991) is the concept that reading and writing are closely related and that writing can be used as a means for understanding reading. Depending upon her or his competence, the child is asked to dictate or write a one- or two-sentence story or message with the teacher's help, if necessary. The piece might be related to a previously read book, some event in the child's life, or another topic of interest. A notebook or looseleaf binder containing unlined paper turned sideways is used. The student tells the story to the teacher, who jots it down on a separate piece of paper so the story isn't forgotten or distorted. The teacher repeats the story exactly as the student dictated it, and the student writes as much of the story as she or he can on the bottom page. The top page functions as an instructional or practice page. Here the student attempts to write words she or he is unsure of. The teacher may provide assistance by drawing Elkonin boxes and coaching the student as she or he fills in the letters of the target word. If the student knows just one or two letters in the word, the initial and final consonants, for instance, the student might write those in the appropriate boxes. The teacher would help the student fill in the rest of the boxes. The teacher might also write words here, if the student has little or no chance of successfully writing them. A sample story is presented in Figure 7-5.

After the story has been written by the child on the bottom or story page and it has been read and reread, the teacher rewrites it on a strip of tagboard. The sentence is then cut up and the student reassembles it and reads it. Reassembling the sentence fosters comprehension and knowledge of syntactic structures. The cut-up sentence is placed in an envelope so the student can practice reading it at home.

### *Reading a New Book*

The culmination of a *Reading Recovery* lesson is the reading of a new book. Reading a new book has been placed last on the schedule, so that the child can apply and integrate strategies introduced in the earlier part of the lesson. New books are carefully chosen and

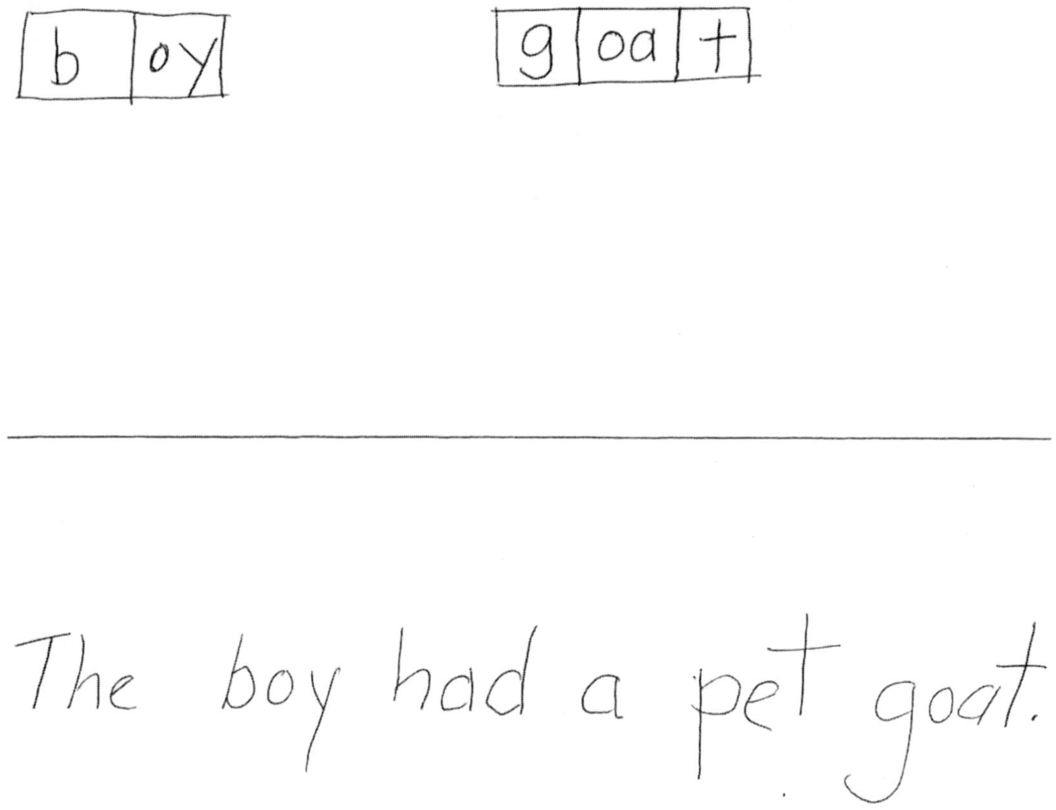

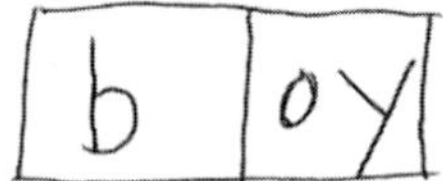


**FIGURE 7-5 Sample Story**

A key feature of *Reading Recovery* is the lists of hundreds of children's books grouped by level of difficulty.

introduced. If a variety of books are available, the child takes part in the selection process. Books provided by the teacher present some challenge, but not too much. Students should know at least 90 percent of the words in the text (although this text advocates a 95 percent standard). Having previewed the book in terms of the child's capabilities, the teacher "walks" through the book with the child, pointing out the title and author, and using illustrations to get an overview of the text. The child is invited to relate the text to other books he has read or relevant experiences that he has had. The teacher may recite from the text unfamiliar terms, expressions, or syntactic structures. These may be pointed out in the text and the student may be asked to repeat them (Clay, 1991). The basic purpose of this orientation is to prepare the child for a successful reading of the text. The new book may be reread if there is time. It is read the next day during which time the teacher prepares a running record of the child's reading. Because introducing a book is a highly effective technique and can be used in any program, an adapted version of this procedure is presented in the box to follow.

In a storybook introduction or text walk, the teacher provides a scaffold so that students can get more out of the story and are better able to use strategies.

## Introducing a Book

*Step 1: Analyzing the Text*

Analyze the text. Note concepts, background information, words, or language structures that might be barriers for the prospective reader. In the book, *The Hungry Giant* (Cowley, 1980, 1990), the word *bommy-knocker* would be unfamiliar. To understand the story, the reader would need to have a concept of a giant and background information about bees, beehives, and honey.

*Step 2: Introducing the Title and Topic*

Introduce the title and the topic of the text to the student. Help the student relate the topic to her own background of experience. Do not dwell on the title as this will detract from the main purpose, which is a successful reading of the text. When introducing *The Hungry Giant,* read the title to the student and ask her to point to the giant on the cover. You might note that the giant is angry because he is hungry.

*Step 3: Highlighting the Story*

Text walks can be more extensive as the selections increase in difficulty.

Walk the student through the story page by page so that she has an overview of the tale. Knowing the gist of the story and who the main characters are, the student will be better able to use contextual and other clues to achieve a successful reading. As you walk the student through the story, preview words, concepts, and language structures that you think she might have difficulty understanding. Paraphrase key portions of the text that contain difficult items. Then help the student point out these items. For instance, after paraphrasing the first page, in which the unfamiliar word *bommy-knocker* is used, ask the student to point to the bommy-knocker in the illustration and tell how a bommy-knocker might be used. Then ask the student to point to the word *bommy-knocker* on the page. Also have the student point to *bread, roared,* and *giant,* which are words that would be in her listening–speaking vocabulary, but which she might have difficulty reading. As you walk through the text, paraphrasing the story, have the student point out other words that might be hard for her to read: *people, butter, honey, everywhere,* and *beehive.* To build necessary background, briefly discuss with the student what a beehive is and the fact that bees make honey and keep it stored in a beehive. Do not display the last page. Instead, ask the students to tell what they think will happen when the giant smashes the beehive with his bommy-knocker. Although the student will know most of the story before she reads the book, she will still have the enjoyment of finding out how the story ends.

*Step 4: Reading the Story*

As the student reads the story, note whether the selection seems to be on the appropriate level and also analyze the student's performance to see what strategies she is using and which strategies she might need to improve. Encourage the student to read the story on her own, but provide guidance and support as needed. If the student has difficulty with the word *with* in the sentence, "Get me some honey, or I'll hit you with my bommy-knocker," prompt the use of context. Have the student read "blank" for the unknown word *with* and then reread the sentence and use context to see what word would make sense there (these strategies are described in detail in Chapters 9 and 10).

For additional examples of a text walk, see Clay, M. M. (1991), "Introducing a new storybook to young readers" in *The Reading Teacher, 45,* 264–272.

*Step 5: Discussing the Story*

Discuss the story. Start with the student's purpose for reading, which was to find out what happened when the giant hit the beehive with his bommy-knocker. Discuss, too, what the people did when ordered to bring the giant food and why they brought him a beehive.

*Step 6: Skill/Strategy Instruction*

Praise the student for her use of strategies: "I like the way you used the meaning of the story to help you read *with.*" Call attention to strategies that might need

*continued*

**Introducing a Book** *Continued*

introducing or refining. "You read this word," (pointing to *zoomed*) "as *ran*. The word *ran* makes sense in the story. But what letter does *ran* begin with? What letter does this word begin with? What word that begins with *z* might make sense here?"

*Step 7: Rereading*

Encourage the student to dramatize the story. You might take the part of the people while the student takes the role of the giant.

*Reading Recovery* has been adapted for use with groups. Students read and discuss the same book and do group rather than individual writing.

Although carefully constructed and featuring a host of proven teaching techniques, the **Reading Recovery** lesson owes its success to the teacher. Within the framework of the *Reading Recovery* lesson, there are a variety of strategies that the teacher might present, a number of materials that might be used, and a number of teaching techniques that might be employed. Based on a careful observation of the child's ongoing performance, the teacher must make minute-by-minute decisions about questions to be asked, strategies to be emphasized, and activities to be undertaken. If the child stumbles on a word, for instance, the teacher must note how the child is operating and decide whether to ask a question that leads the child to use context or one that leads to the use of letter–sound relationships or both phonics and context. Perhaps, magnetic letters might be used to help the child decode the word.

Making effective instructional decisions requires a teacher who has an in-depth knowledge of how a child learns to read, how to observe and diagnose, and how to instruct. *Reading Recovery* requires well-prepared teachers.

## Other Intervention Programs

### Early Intervention in Reading

Although *Reading Recovery* is the best known and most carefully documented of the early intervention programs, there are a number of others that also attempt to prevent, rather than remediate, reading problems. One inexpensive but highly effective preventive program is Early Intervention in Reading (EIR). Although it uses many of the techniques that makes *Reading Recovery* so successful, EIR can be implemented in the classroom by the classroom teacher (B. Taylor, 1992). The assistance of a part-time aide is recommended, but even that can be optional. The program is designed for use with the five or six lowest-achieving students, as determined by the classroom teacher and a screening test that assesses knowledge of the alphabet, phonemic awareness, initial consonant sounds, and ability to read high-frequency words.

Students are taught holistically, with phonemic awareness and word identification and other skills and strategies being presented in the context of reading children's books. To reinforce phonemic awareness, for instance, the teacher selects four or five words from a story that has just been read and models how to segment the words into their separate sounds and then blends them into words. For example, *hen* would be segmented /h/, /e/, /n/ and, later, blended into "hen." Students also box four or five words from the story. "Box-

EIR is presented in four levels. In Level A, students read books that range in length from forty to sixty words. In Level B, length is sixty to ninety words, Level C, fifty to one hundred and fifty, Level D, one hundred to two hundred.

ing" a word means that a word is segmented phonemically into a series of Elkonin boxes. However, instead of putting markers in the boxes, the word's letters are written there. For the word *pet, p* is placed in the first box, *e* in the second, and *t* in the last. Since the letter(s) that represent each sound are placed in the boxes, students are learning letter–sound relationships at the same time that phonemic awareness is being reinforced. Essentially, phonics is being taught through a spelling approach and reinforced through reading and writing, since students also compose sentences using their words.

Stories are taught in three-day cycles. Here is an adapted version of how a typical three-day cycle might be implemented. On the first day, the teacher reads the selection from a big book or chart. As the teacher reads, he runs his hand under the words so students can follow along. During subsequent readings, the teacher selects four or five words that can be used to demonstrate a skill or strategy that he wishes to teach. These might be four words that begin with the consonant *s,* four words that contain the *-at* pattern, five high-frequency words, or five words that illustrate how context might be used to identify or verify a word.

By the end of first grade, 72 percent of the EIR students, were reading at a preprimer level or better. By the end of grade two, 72 percent were reading on grade level.

On the second and third days, the selection is reread. The teacher encourages use of previously learned strategies or teaches new ones. Students box words and write a sentence about the selection they have read. Students are also given individual copies of the enlarged text, which they read to the teacher or an aide. The goal is to have the students read the book with 93 percent accuracy by the end of the third day. Students move on to the next booklet even if they haven't reached that level. After day three, the children take the booklet home to read to their parents.

The program is economical in terms of time. The teacher only works with the group fifteen to twenty minutes a day. However, if aides or volunteers are available, students read their books to them individually for five to ten minutes a day. The aides or volunteers must be trained to encourage the student to use previously taught strategies to identify difficult words. Word identification is reinforced primarily by teachers asking questions which guide students in their use of appropriate word-identification strategies: "What would make sense here? How does the word begin?" Students reread the book three, four, or even more times to an aide to achieve fluency.

### *Boulder Project*

Using a similar approach, Hiebert (1994) also created a successful intervention program. Her program emphasizes building phonemic awareness, using word patterns (*-at, -en*), repeated readings of predictable books, especially those that reinforce patterns, writing sentences in journals, and taking books home. Teachers work daily with groups of three to six children for twenty to twenty-five minutes. Hiebert (1994) also recommends continued assessment through the use of running records.

Although more economical, group instructional programs achieve a success rate of about 70 percent as compared to the 81 to 88 percent success rate of *Reading Recovery* in the United States. That is, 70 percent of the lowest-achieving students attained sufficient success by end of grade one to profit from regular classroom instruction, and, therefore, stand a good chance of getting off and staying off the corrective track. Students who still needed assistance were continued in the program through second grade. By end of second grade, 87 percent of the students were reading on or above grade level.

Two teachers tried out an adapted form of the program in third grade (Hiebert, 1996). This program included reading easy chapter books such as the Henry and Mudge and Ronald Morgan series, learning word patterns and decoding strategies, and writing. The students met in small groups of no more than seven for twenty to thirty minutes four times a week during independent reading time. The children were instructed by the regular classroom teacher. All of the students made encouraging progress. Two thirds were reading at or above grade level by year's end.

In addition to one-on-one tutoring, *Success for All* coordinates its efforts with the regular reading program and also attempts to eliminate obstacles to learning, such as poor attendance.

### *Success for All*

Another promising program that stresses prevention rather than remediation is *Success for All* (Slavin, Madden, Karweit, Dolan, & Wasik, 1994). More extensive than *Reading Recovery, Early Intervention in Reading,* or the *Boulder Project, Success for All* encompasses grades one through three. Focusing on prevention and intensive intervention, *Success for All* includes the following features:

**Reading Tutors.** Students who need assistance are provided one-on-one instruction for twenty minutes a day. Informal reading inventories are used to identify students in need of tutoring.

**Sustained, Direct Instruction.** Tutoring sessions are complemented by ninety-minute periods of sustained, direct instruction. During these sessions, tutors instruct whole groups. The instructional period begins with reading high-quality children's literature to the children followed by discussion. Using a technique called STAR, students listen to, retell, and dramatize children's literature. In its early stages, the program features systematic instruction in decoding skills, extensive reading of easy books, and repeated oral reading with a partner. In later stages, through cooperative learning, students learn to predict and summarize. Decoding skills are extended, vocabulary development is fostered, and writing is encouraged. Students are also expected to read on their own twenty minutes a night. Twice a week "book club" sessions are held to share outside reading. Books are discussed and presented through dramatization, puppet shows, and so forth. Other features include:

**Continuing Assessment.** Each student's progress is assessed at least once every eight weeks. As a result of these assessments, needed adjustments are made in the program. Additional testing, such as vision and auditory screening, might also be recommended.

**Family Support Team.** Two social workers and a parent liaison supply programs of parent education that include suggestions for helping students and supporting their successes. The team also provides help when behavior or other problems interfere with the child's education.

**Leadership.** One of the keys to the success of the program is effective leadership. Working with the principal, a program facilitator helps with the planning and implementation of the program and coordinates the efforts of teachers and support staff.

## *Model Program for Early Intervention*

Intervention programs need not be expensive. Effective programs have been conducted by classroom teachers who provided additional assistance to those who needed it.

Based on a review of the research, a careful look at successful group-intervention programs, and practical experience, a program for group intervention should include the following:

- Beginning assessment to find out where students are. This should include alphabet knowledge, ability to segment words into sounds and/or identify beginning sounds, knowledge of letter–sound relationships, and knowledge of high-frequency words. Your own judgment should also be a factor.
- Instruction in small groups of three to five.
- Instruction should cover phonological awareness (rhyming, segmentation, identification of beginning sounds), decoding (initial consonants and patterns), high-frequency words, and essential conventions of print. Each session should include a five- to ten-minute lesson on a consonant, pattern, or other element that appears in the text to be read. Because students don't always apply skills, have them examine in the selection to be read sentences containing words that incorporate the element that has been taught. This should be done in preparation for a reading of the selection.
- Shared reading of big books or charts.
- Reading and rereading of books that reinforce the pattern or other element that has been taught. These books should be on the appropriate level of difficulty. Students should be able to read them with 95 percent accuracy. In order to achieve this high level of performance, books should be carefully and thoroughly introduced using the *Reading Recovery* procedure for introducing a book which was described earlier. This introduction (text-walk) would include introducing difficult words and concepts before students read the book. This should be done in addition to the word analysis lesson.
- During oral rereadings of the text and as the opportunity arises, students should be guided in the use of word analysis and comprehension strategies. Word-analysis strategies should include using pronounceable word parts, analogy, context, and—in some cases—letter-by-letter sounding out (see Chapters 9 and 10 for a full discussion of these strategies). Students should also be monitoring for meaning.
- Students should be provided with as many opportunities as possible to read one-on-one with the teacher, an aide, a volunteer, or even an older student. Helpers should receive training so they are able to guide the student in the use of strategies.
- Students should read independently as much as possible. This could include rereading familiar books or reading easy books for the first time. Students should take books home to read or reread on a daily basis.
- The program should have a writing component. Students might write, with your guidance, a single sentence about a book that they read, as in *Reading Recovery.* The sentence would be cut up and taken home to be put together and read to parents.
- Parents should be involved. Parents need to understand the program so that they can support their children's efforts by listening to them as they read books and their segmented sentences.

- The program needs ongoing assessment. Running records are an excellent device for observing the student's use of strategies and to check the difficulty level of the material. Since this is a time-consuming procedure, you might conduct a running record once a week and assess brief segments of text. Other assessment devices include observing students and filling out an observation checklist (an observation checklist for word analysis strategy use can be found in Chapter 4), quizzing students on patterns and higher-frequency words that have been previously taught, and evaluating writing samples.
- Keep the program structured. Students feel more secure when they have a routine to follow. However, don't be so structured that you lose sight of students' individual needs (Barnes, 1996–97).

### *Instructional Routine for an Intervention Program*

A typical routine for a twenty-five- to thirty-minute group session might include the following activities:

1. Rereading of a familiar book (five minutes)
2. Word study (five to ten minutes in which a new pattern, initial consonant, or other element is presented)
3. Introduction and reading of a new book (ten minutes)
4. Writing a sentence (five minutes)

Although studies of group early-intervention programs are encouraging, approximately 30 percent of the students selected for these programs fail to make adequate progress. These students, who make up approximately 6 percent of the total school population, may need more extensive assistance and one-on-one help with a highly trained professional. Chapter 14 contains suggestions for working with students who have the most serious reading problems.

## *Minicase Study*

Jan's performance was puzzling. Although a seven-year-old second-grader, she was still struggling to learn initial consonants. She had learned a series of alliterative sentences for each consonant. If you asked her the sentence for /m/, she would reply, "Mighty Mack made a muddy mess." And when she saw the letter *m,* she would say "mmm." All of this led Jan's teacher to believe that Jan had mastered initial consonants. However, Jan was unable to apply this knowledge. For instance, when Jan encountered the word *man* in a story, she responded with a very elongated "mmmm" and then said "dog."

Through rote memory, Jane had learned to associate /m/ with the letter *m* and could recite the alliterative sentence but could not manipulate individual sounds in words. Thus, when she saw the word *man,* she was unable to manipulate the sound /m/ and produce a word that began with /m/. When told by the teacher, "I am going to take the "kuh" away from *cat.* What word do I have left?" Jan replied "can." When told, "I am going to add /s/ to *ay,* what word will I make," Jan was unable to respond.

In an informal survey, Jan was able to supply sounds for all of the consonant letters except *z* and *y.* However, this knowledge was built on a very weak foundation, one that did not include adequate phonemic awareness. Because Jan's previous program had consisted primarily of isolated drill work, it was decided to present phonemic awareness and related skills primarily through the shared reading of easy, highly-predictable children's books. After reading *Have You Seen My Cat?* (Carle, 1987) or *Brown Bear, Brown Bear, What Do You See?* (Martin, 1983) the sounds of key words in those books were discussed.

Rhymes, short poems, and word-play games were a regular part of the program. Jan was also encouraged to use invented spelling. Progress was slow and labored. However, the teacher noted that Jan responded with animation and enthusiasm to games. A colleague recommended a board game entitled *Road Racer* (Curriculum Associates). A fairly typical board game, *Road Racer* has a raceway composed of initial consonants and clusters. Printed on the dice—there are ten of them—were common rimes: *-at, -ame, -et.* The idea was to roll the dice and create words by combining the initial consonant element with the phonogram. Forming words in this way involved manipulating sounds and was exactly the skill with which Jan had difficulty.

Jan's eyes lit up when the teacher introduced the game. Using a modified set of rules, the teacher read the rimes and asked Jan what sound needed to be added to make the target word. For instance, if the *et* rime turned up, the teacher read *et* and asked Jan to tell what sound would need to be added to *et* to make *pet.* Jan was far more successful with the game than she had been with any of the other devices or techniques that had been tried. She still needed hints and missed an item here and there. But excited by the challenge of the game, she put forth maximum effort. Animated by the fun of the game and flush with success, Jan attacked her lessons with increased vigor and renewed insight into the language's sound system and was able to apply this knowledge to her reading of beginning level books. At long last, Jan was on the roadway to literacy.

## *Summary*

Although the concept of emergent literacy recognizes that all children come to school with some experience with reading and writing, the quantity and quality of this experience varies enormously. Because of limited literacy experiences or slow progress, at-risk learners should be directly taught literacy skills in the following areas: concepts of print, phonological awareness, and letter knowledge. These are taught within the context of holistic reading and writing activities and reading aloud to students.

Concepts of print that should be taught include understanding the purpose of print and being able to identify the basic parts of a book and the basic units of print, especially letters, words, and sounds. A crucial understanding for emergent readers is being able to point to separate words as they are read aloud.

A major cause of reading disorders is a deficiency in phonological awareness. In order to read, students must be able to detect separate words, syllables, and sounds. They should also be able to note words that rhyme, and perceive beginning sounds. Playing with words, listening to rhymes, riddles, and alphabet books, and engaging in a variety of reading and writing endeavors are key activities for teaching necessary phonological skills. However, in addition to direct instruction and experiences, students apparently also need a degree of cognitive maturity in order to attain needed phonological awareness.

Letter knowledge can be presented through alphabet books, immersion in print, explicit instruction, writing, and a variety of other techniques. Students experiencing difficulty learning to read and write should be encouraged to write using invented spelling if they are unable to spell conventionally. Invented spelling, and writing in general, foster growth in phonemic awareness, concepts of print, writing, letter–sound relationships, and spelling.

A variety of early intervention programs have achieved encouraging success. The major advantages of early intervention programs include preventing the learning of erroneous concepts and eliminating the emotional damage that often accompanies failure.

## *Application Activities*

1. Read Marie Clay's *Reading Recovery: A Guidebook for Teachers in Training* (Portsmouth, NH: Heinemann, 1993), which describes *Reading Recovery* in detail. What principles or techniques from *Reading Recovery* might you adapt for use in your teaching?

2. Observe a *Reading Recovery* or other early intervention program in your area. What are the main elements of the program? Which of these elements might you be able to use in your teaching?

3. Make a list of five children's books that might be appropriate for a shared reading lesson.

4. Plan a shared reading or language experience lesson. If possible, teach the lesson and evaluate its effectiveness.

5. Analyze five samples of young children's writing. What stages are the children in? What does an analysis of their writing indicate about their knowledge of letter–sound relationships?

# Chapter 8

# Teaching High-Frequency Words

## *Using What You Know*

High-frequency words are also known as "sight words." The term *sight words* is a confusing one and has at least three meanings. It refers to words like *the, is,* and *that,* which occur with very high frequency. It also refers to words like *of* and *one* that can't be learned through phonics but would need to be memorized and learned by sight. *Sight words* also refers to the concept that some words may be recognized at sight or immediately. Based on these multiple meanings of the term *sight words,* how do you think they should be taught?

## *Anticipation Guide*

Read each of the following statements. Put a check under "Agree" or "Disagree" to show how you feel about each one. If possible, discuss your responses with classmates.

| | Agree | Disagree |
|---|---|---|
| **1.** The easiest way for beginning readers to learn words is simply to memorize them. | ________ | ________ |
| **2.** The best way to practice recognizing printed words quickly is through wide reading. | ________ | ________ |
| **3.** Phonics does not work well with high-frequency words like *when* and *is.* | ________ | ________ |
| **4.** Flashing words on cards or computer screens is a good way to increase speed of recognition. | ________ | ________ |
| **5.** Students who confuse words like *where, what,* and *when* and read one for the other need to be taught to be more careful. | ________ | ________ |

## *The Nature of High-Frequency Words*

What are the most difficult words for reading-disabled students to learn to read? Ironically, the shortest, most frequently occurring words pose the most serious problem for many students. Compared to decoding *were, was,* or *where,* the words *rhinoceros* and *elephant* are a breeze. Compensating for their length by their distinctive spelling and specific meanings, *rhinoceros* and *elephant* are relatively easy to learn to read. After one or two presentations and a few encounters in a text, many students have these words mastered for life. After dozens, maybe hundreds of presentations, and countless encounters, some students still stumble over *was, were, where,* and *are.*

Unfortunately, many of the most frequently occurring words in the language are abstract or are lacking in meaning, serving only as function words in a sentence (*the, of, with*), lack a distinctive appearance, and so are easily confused with other words (*will, with, what*), and may have a spelling that gives little or no clue to their pronunciation (*one, of*). In order to teach students to read **high-frequency words,** it is important to understand the stages students go through as they learn to read words. Major word-learning stages are described below.

> **High-frequency words,** commonly known as **sight words,** are the 200 or so most frequently occurring words in printed English.

## *Stages in Learning to Read Words*

Readers' processes change as they become more skillful. From emergent literacy through mature reading, the developing reader seems to go through three stages: logographic, alphabetic, and orthographic (Ehri, 1994).

### *Logographic Stage*

In the logographic stage, which corresponds to the "letter name" stage in spelling, readers directly connect certain visual aspects of a word with its meaning. These visual features do not involve letter–sound relationships and may not involve letter identities. The word *McDonald's* is recognized because golden arches are in the background, not because the child realizes that McDonald's starts with an *m.* The word *look* might be remembered because the *o*'s in the middle of the word look like eyes. Since the connections are arbitrary and fail to grow out of an understanding that letters represent sounds, they are easily forgotten or confused or may result in the youngster producing a synonym for the target word. The student might read "see" for the word *look.* As Ehri (1992) explains:

> **Logographic** stage: students learn words by memorizing their shapes or other distinctive features.

> Because the visual cues are connected to meanings rather than pronunciation, readers may produce synonyms rather than one specific word when they read spellings. Thus word reading during this phase is not very reliable or accurate. (p. 125)

Major characteristics of this stage include:

- Student can read a few high-frequency words.
- Student uses word length, shape of the word, or similar cues to remember words.

- Learning words at this stage requires many exposures (McCormick, 1995).
- Student's miscues are generally meaningful. Student might substitute *plane* for *jet* because the focus is on using meaning cues rather than letter–sound cues. As students reach the end of the stage, they may balk at attempting to read words they don't recognize at sight. Beginning to realize that letters represent sounds, but unable to make full use of that information, students may stop responding (Biemiller, 1970).
- Not having made the connection between letters and sounds, the student may spell words with random letters. *Ball* might be spelled *WOF.*
- Poor readers remain in this stage longer and may overrely on picture and meaning cues.

## *Alphabetic Stage*

The alphabetic stage in reading corresponds to the letter–name stage in spelling. In both students make growing use of letter–sound relationships.

As novice readers begin to learn letter identities and letter–sound relationships, they enter the alphabetic stage (which corresponds to the "letter name" stage in spelling), which is also known as cipher reading, and begin to use this knowledge to make connections between the letters in words and their sounds. They note that the *b* in *boy* stands for /b/, *cat* ends with a *t,* which represent the sound /t/. Novices may not make all the necessary letter–sound connections in a word. They may only associate the first or first and last letter with speech sounds. Even so, reading is more accurate and more reliable in this stage because the connections are between letters and the sounds they represent, not between a word's meaning and an arbitrary visual feature. Confusion continues to arise, however, especially if the youngster is not using all the letters in the word. In time, the novice learns to use all of the letters in a word and uses these to make more accurate and more reliable connections between letters and sounds.

Major characteristics of this stage include:

- The student uses letter–sound relationships to decode unfamiliar words.
- Students may analyze words sound by sound: r-a-t.
- Students can read more words.
- Students can learn words more easily because they use the relationships between a word's letters and its sounds to help them remember words.
- Students may overemphasize phonics and produce words that are graphically similar to the target words but which don't fit the sense of the selection: *bad* for *bank.* Overly focused on sounding out, students may also produce nonsense words: *hep* for *help.* In time, students integrate the use of phonics and context so that they produce fewer non-words or words that don't fit the sense of the selection (Biemiller, 1970).
- Students' spelling reflects their growing knowledge of letter–sound relationships. At first, they may use just initial consonants to spell words (F for *fire*). Later, they add final consonants (FR for fire) and, later still, vowel letters (FIR for *fire*).

## *Orthographic Stage*

In the orthographic stage, which corresponds to the "within-word" pattern stage in spelling, students use more sophisticated print units to make associations between print and sound. For instance, the reader may use final *e* as a sign that the vowel sound in *cape* is /ā/ rather

The orthographic stage corresponds to the within-word pattern stage in spelling. Students use their knowledge of patterns, rather than single letters, to read and spell.

than /a/. Instead of reading *goat* as /g/ + /ō/ + /t/, the reader clusters the word into longer units and may read *goat* as /g/ + /ōt/.

Major characteristics of this stage include:

- Recognizing natural units in words, students use longer units to decode words. The word *ranch* might be decoded: *ran-ranch* or *an-ran-ranch.*
- Students use knowledge of such orthographic features as final *e* (*cape*) or two vowels coming together (*goat*) to decode words.
- In their spelling students begin using orthographic information. They add final *e* and use double vowel letters to spell vowel sounds.

Students taught by a phonics method may move into the alphabetic stage faster, whereas those taught by a holistic method may remain in the logographic longer (Cohen, 1974–75).

According to Ehri (1994), as a student processes words, connections are created between letters and sounds. In time, these connections solidify so that the student does not have to process *cat* /k/, /a/, /t/ or /k/, /at/ but seeing the letters triggers the memory of the word. It isn't necessary to translate the word's letters into sounds. Repeatedly meeting the word in print, and processing it forges the necessary link between the visual representation of the word and retrieving that word, including its meaning and pronunciation, from memory. Through practice, the recognition process becomes automatic. Gough, Juel, and Griffith (1992) explain the process somewhat differently. They theorize that even known words are analyzed letter-by-letter or letter group-by-letter group. However, access speed increases as a result of meeting the word in print many times so that even though words are analyzed element by element this is done so rapidly as to be virtually instantaneous.

Noting that some students were experiencing difficulty applying phonics strategies, Gaskins et al. (1996–1997) revised the word-attack program so that students were taught to fully analyze words. To learn the word *will,* students noted the sounds in the word /w/, /i/, /l/ and matched these with the letters that represent the sounds *w, i, ll.*

Regardless of how the process is explained, the end result is the same. In time, nearly all the words that expert readers encounter in print are read as "sight" words. They are recognized just about instantaneously. A key point here is that, except for the rote learning of a limited number of begining reading words and a few irregularly spelled words, words are not learned by sight. In order to make the connections necessary to have a word recognized automatically, it is important to process the word's letter–sound relationships, unless, of course, the word is irregularly spelled. Otherwise, the connections made will be arbitrary and easily forgotten.

There is another reason for using phonics cues to help students remember high-frequency words. Students with the most serious reading problems have great difficulty retrieving the pronunciation of printed words. Using phonics cues should not only strengthen connections, it will also provide these students with a strategy for pronouncing words when retrieval fails them. Most children learn high-frequency words even if the instruction only provides visual cues or repetition. What they apparently do is to create their own letter–sound connections. However, many low-achieving readers fail to make these connections and so need instruction.

Except for words like *of* and *one,* all words should be taught through a phonics approach so that connections are made between letters and sounds.

## *How High-Frequency Words Are Learned*

Because their spellings don't do a good job of indicating the sounds they represent, some high-frequency words, such as *of, you, was,* and *they,* don't lend themselves to a decoding approach. These words are taught in a logographic or paired-associate fashion. Students learn the words by associating the spoken words with visual features. In addition, there are other words that do have predictable pronunciations, but they incorporate advanced phonic elements: *which, each, how.* Because these words occur with high frequency, it is difficult to read even the simplest of selections without encountering them. Therefore, they are often introduced in paired-associate or logographic fashion in the earliest stages of reading.

Novice readers can and do learn words through a sight or logographic approach. However, the number of words that they can learn in this way is limited to about forty (Gough & Hillinger, 1980). At that point, the system begins to fall apart. The learner runs out of distinctive features by which to remember each word. In addition, with many high-frequency words being similar in appearance, they are easily confused because the "visual cues selected are not unique to individual words" (Ehri, 1994, p. 326). Words are also hard to fix in memory because the cues used to establish the associations are arbitrary. The cues have no relationship to the sounds that the letters in the words represent.

Once students have reached the alphabetic stage, high-frequency words, insofar as possible, should be taught through a phonics approach. When taught through a decoding approach, they are easier to learn and remember. Most high-frequency words are completely regular: *and, in, that, it, at, this, but.* Their pronunciations can easily be predicted from their spellings. Except for a very few words, words like *of, one, on,* even the irregular words are mostly predictable. For most of them, the vowels are irregular: *was, from, some.* However, their initial and final letters can be used to determine beginning and ending sounds: *have, said, find, word.* Not taking advantage of these regularities deprives students of a means of learning high-frequency words. For instance, disabled and novice readers typically confuse the *wh* words: *who, what, when, where, why, which.* However, *when* is completely regular. When presenting the word *when,* help students see the familiar word part *en* in *when* by relating it to *ten* or *pen* or other known *-en* words. *Which* is also completely regular and could be related to words like *itch, pitch,* or *witch.* Although not completely regular, *what* can be distinguished from the other *wh* words because it ends in *t. Why* is also completely regular. Relate it to *by, cry,* or other words that end in *y* = /ī/. *Who* which incorporates the less frequent correspondence wh = /h/ and has an irregular spelling for its vowel sound, is more problematical. One way of teaching *who* would be to present it with other high frequency words that incorporate the *o* = /o͞o/ correspondence: *do, to, two.*

> Even though students have learned words through phonics, they should be given many opportunities to meet the words in the context of stories, songs, verses, etc.

## *High Payoff of High-Frequency Words*

The High-Frequency List presented in Table 8-1 consists of the 200 words that most frequently appear in books and other materials read by school children (Zeno, Ivens, Millard, & Duvvuri, 1995). These 200 words would make up approximately 50 percent of the words

**TABLE 8-1 High-Frequency Words**

| | | | | |
|---|---|---|---|---|
| 1. the | 41. which | 81. made | 121. also | 161. name |
| 2. of | 42. their | 82. over | 122. around | 162. should |
| 3. and | 43. said | 83. did | 123. another | 163. home |
| 4. a | 44. if | 84. down | 124. came | 164. give |
| 5. to | 45. will | 85. way | 125. three | 165. air |
| 6. in | 46. do | 86. only | 126. word | 166. line |
| 7. is | 47. each | 87. may | 127. come | 167. mother |
| 8. you | 48. about | 88. find | 128. work | 168. set |
| 9. that | 49. how | 89. use | 129. must | 169. world |
| 10. it | 50. up | 90. water | 130. part | 170. own |
| 11. he | 51. out | 91. little | 131. because | 171. under |
| 12. for | 52. then | 92. long | 132. does | 172. last |
| 13. was | 53. them | 93. very | 133. even | 173. read |
| 14. on | 54. she | 94. after | 134. place | 174. never |
| 15. are | 55. many | 95. word | 135. old | 175. am |
| 16. as | 56. some | 96. called | 136. well | 176. us |
| 17. with | 57. so | 97. just | 137. such | 177. left |
| 18. his | 58. these | 98. new | 138. here | 178. end |
| 19. they | 59. would | 99. where | 139. take | 179. along |
| 20. at | 60. other | 100. most | 140. why | 180. while |
| 21. be | 61. into | 101. know | 141. things | 181. sound |
| 22. this | 62. has | 102. get | 142. great | 182. house |
| 23. from | 63. more | 103. through | 143. help | 183. might |
| 24. I | 64. two | 104. back | 144. put | 184. next |
| 25. have | 65. her | 105. much | 145. years | 185. below |
| 26. not | 66. like | 106. good | 146. different | 186. saw |
| 27. or | 67. him | 107. before | 147. number | 187. something |
| 28. by | 68. time | 108. go | 148. away | 188. thought |
| 29. one | 69. see | 109. man | 149. again | 189. both |
| 30. had | 70. no | 110. our | 150. off | 190. few |
| 31. but | 71. could | 111. write | 151. went | 191. those |
| 32. what | 72. make | 112. used | 152. tell | 192. school |
| 33. all | 73. than | 113. me | 153. men | 193. show |
| 34. were | 74. first | 114. day | 154. say | 194. always |
| 35. when | 75. been | 115. too | 155. small | 195. looked |
| 36. we | 76. its | 116. any | 156. every | 196. large |
| 37. there | 77. who | 117. same | 157. found | 197. often |
| 38. can | 78. now | 118. right | 158. still | 198. together |
| 39. an | 79. people | 119. look | 159. big | 199. asked |
| 40. your | 80. my | 120. think | 160. between | 200. going |

Adapted from *The educator's word frequency guide* by S. M. Zeno, S. H. Ivens, R. T. Millard, & Duvvuri, 1995, Brewster, NY: Touchstone Applied Science Associates.

in continuous text. The first word, *the,* would occur about 2 percent of the time. Because high-frequency words play such an important role, they should be introduced periodically along with the patterns. Presented in the next section is a sample lesson for direct instruction in high-frequency words. The approach taken to introduce sight words will depend, in part, on the students' stage of development and the nature of the words. Students in the alphabetic or orthographic stages can be guided to use their knowledge of letter–sound relationships to learn sight words as long as they are at least partly regular.

## *Direct-Teaching Approach*

The direct-teaching technique is adapted from an approach devised by Bryant, Kelly, Hathaway, and Rubin (1981). It emphasizes repetition and context, and, in its adapted form, the use of phonics to help the student make solid, lasting connections between printed words and their spoken equivalents. A carefully structured, thorough technique, it has been effective with students who had considerable difficulty learning high-frequency words.

### High-Frequency Word Lesson

*Step 1: Selecting Words to Be Taught*

> If the meanings of any of the words are unknown, discuss them. However, don't spend time developing meanings for words that are already in the students' listening vocabulary.

Choose between four and six words for instruction. Words chosen should be ones that students will meet in a basal-reader selection, children's book, or other reading material that they are about to read. The words should also be ones that appear more than once in the piece, are important to the piece, and will probably occur in other selections. Words such as *for* and *from* that are easily confused should not be presented at the same time. Print the words on 3 × 5 cards. To avoid wasting time with words that are already known, pretest students by holding up each card and asking them to read it. Discard words known by nearly everyone. Step 2 shows how the words *old, wore, green, hat, man* might be introduced.

*Step 2: Presentation in Isolation*

First, reconstruct each word sound-by-sound or pronounceable element-by-pronounceable element so that students establish and later learn to recognize familiar parts in words. Here's how the high-frequency word *old* might be presented. Write *old* on the board. Ask if anyone can read it. If no one can, build on any knowledge of letters or letter–sound relationships that students have. If students are in the alphabetic or orthographic stage and know the letters o-l-d and the sounds they represent, then ask students if there is any part of the word that they can say. If there are parts of the word that are familiar, have them read and use the familiar parts to reconstruct the word. If the word is totally unfamiliar, cover it up except for its vowel and reconstruct the word sound by sound. For the word *old,* cover up the *l* and *d,* and ask students to say the sound that *o* stands for. Give help if necessary. After students read *o,* uncover the *l* and have students read *ol,* giving help as necessary. After students have read *ol,* uncover the *d,* have students say what sound it stands for, and have them read *old.* Supply assistance as needed. Then ask each student to read the word. If a student misses the word, reconstruct it with him, having the student read "o-ol-old" as you uncover the word's letters. If students are in the logographic stage, emphasize the appearance and spelling of the word, especially the first letter.

> Using phonics to teach high-frequency words teaches students a reliable way of recognizing the words, and provides a means by which the words can be stored in memory.

Present the word *wore* in the same way. If students are in the alphabetic or orthographic stage, begin instruction with *or* and then build the word by adding final *e* (note that this *e* doesn't change anything) and then *w.* For *green,* start with *ee* and add *n* so that you have formed the ending portion of the word, then *r,* and finally, *g.* For *hat* start with *a* and add *t.* For *man,* relate it to the known word *an.* Here students read *an.* Then add *m* and have the word *man* read. After this initial presentation of the words, print them on cards, if you haven't already done so, and present them once

*Continued*

**High-Frequency Word Lesson** *Continued*

more. Continue presenting the words until students are able to read each one within one second on two consecutive presentations.

*Step 3: Presentation in Context*

Present the words in phrases or short sentences. The phrases might include two or more of the high frequency words and should be cumulative. Phrases for the words *old, wore, green, hat, man,* for example, might be introduced as follows:
*old hat*
*old green hat*
*wore an old green hat*
*The man wore an old green hat.*
The phrases and sentences should be presented until students can read all of them fluently.

*Step 4: Application*

Introduce the selection from which the high-frequency words were drawn. Discuss the title and key illustrations. Assist students in finding and reading the target high-frequency words in the selection. Have them read the entire sentence in which the target high-frequency word appears. Then after setting a purpose for reading based on a discussion of the title, key illustrations, and high-frequency words, have students read the selection silently. During or after the follow-up discussion of the story, have students once again read the story sentences in which the high-frequency words appeared.

*Step 5: Review*

The next day, go over the words in isolation and in phrase and sentence context. Also provide review sessions for high-frequency words learned in previous sessions. Focus on words that continue to cause difficulty. Provide a variety of opportunities for students to apply their growing knowledge of high-frequency words by completing the practice activities presented later in this chapter. Keep in mind that the best way to build a high-frequency vocabulary is to have students read lots of easy materials. A list of books containing high-frequncy words is found in Table 8-2.

## *Indirect Teaching Techniques*

An efficient way of presenting high-frequency words would be to teach patterns that incorporate these words. Present *he, be, me, we, see;* or *at, that;* or *way, may, day.*

### *Shared Reading*

An excellent device for introducing and reinforcing high-frequency words, shared reading is a way of helping low-achieving readers read whole selections that they wouldn't be able to read on their own. Instead of being limited to books on their reading level, which may be simplified or lacking in appeal, low-achieving readers are given access to more mature, more interesting materials.

If you are working with groups, use a big book or write the selection on the chalkboard or story paper, or show it on an overhead projector so that everyone can see the words. If working one-on-one, a regular-size book can be used. Introduce the text, share read it with students, and discuss it with students in the way that was suggested in Chapter 5. During a second reading of the text, invite the students to read along with you. If the text has repeated phrases, stop as you come to these and have the students as a group or individual volunteers read them. Pay particular attention to the high-frequency words you wish students to learn. During the reading of the text make sure that you point to each word as it is being read and that students look at the word as you point to it so connections can be made between printed and spoken words. In addition to share reading and highlighting them in context, also have students read high-frequency words in isolation so that they can concentrate on each word's

## TABLE 8-2 Books Containing High-Frequency Words

**Level 1: Picture Reading**

Pictures illustrate all of the text. Generally one or two words label the picture: a drawing of an elephant is shown and the word *elephant* appears under it.

Bruna, D. (1984). *Animal book.* Los Angeles: Price/Stern/Sloan.
Burningham, J. (1985). *Colors.* New York: Crown.
Burton, M. R. (1989). *Tail toes eye ears nose.* New York: Harper.
Cohen, C. L. (1986). *Three yellow dogs.* New York: Greenwillow.
Hoban, T. (1972). *Count and see.* New York: Macmillan.

**Level 2: Caption**

Pictures illustrate most of the text. Often, the text is a frame, which is a repeated sentence or phrase that varies by one or two words. The subject or verb varies but the rest of the sentence stays the same: The dog sat on the mat. The tiger sat on the mat. The elephant sat on the mat. The illustration may depict the part of the sentence that changes.

Bernal, R. (1989). *Night zoo.* Chicago: Contemporary.
Brown, C. (1991). *My barn.* New York: Greenwillow.
Burningham, J. (1984). *Wobble pop.* New York: Viking.
Cameron, A. (1994). *The cat sat on the mat.* Boston: Houghton Mifflin.
Gomi, T. (1991). *Who hid it?* Brookfield, CT: Millbrook Press.
Kalan, R. (1978). *Rain.* New York: Greenwillow.
Keyworth, C. L. (1986). *New day.* New York: Morrow.
McMillan, B. (1993). *Mouse views, what the class pet saw.* New York: Holiday House.
McMillan, B. 1989). *Super Super Superwords.* New York: Lothrop, Lee & Shepard.
McMillan, B. (1983). *Here a chick, there a chick.* New York: Morrow.
Maris, R. (1983). *My book.* New York: Puffin.
Rathmann, P. (1994). *Good night, Gorilla.* New York: Putnam's.
Tafuri, N. (1984) *Have you seen my duckling?* New York: Greenwillow.
Tafuri, N. (1986). *Who's counting?* New York: Greenwillow.
Wildsmith, B. (1983). *Cat on the mat.* New York: Oxford.
Wildsmith, B. (1983). *What a tail.* New York: Oxford.

**Easy Sight Word Level**

Illustrations generally depict much or at least some of the text. There are usually 1–2 lines of text. The number of different words used in the selection ranges from 10 to 35.

Anderson, P. (1987). *Time for bed the babysitter said.* Boston: Houghton Mifflin.
Barton, B. (1994). *Where's the bear?* New York: Mulberry.
Beck, I. (1992). *Five little ducks.* New York: Holt.
Berenstain, S. & Berenstain, J. (1968). *Inside outside upside down.* New York: Random.
Berenstain, S. & Berenstain, J. (1968). *Bears on wheels.* New York: Random.
Carle, E. (1971). *Do You Want to Be My Friend?* New York: Harper.
Casey, P. (1994). *My cat Jack.* Cambridge, MA: Candlewick.
Christelow, E. (1989). *Five little monkeys jumping on the bed.* New York: Clarion.
Clarke, G. (1992). *Old McDonald had a farm.* New York: Lothrop, Lee & Shepard.
Florian, D. (1988). *A winter day.* New York: Greenwillow.
Ginsburg, M. (1972). *The chick and the duckling.* New York: Macmillan.
Gomi, T. (1977). *Where's the fish?* New York: Morrow.
Greene, C. (1982). *Snow Joe.* Chicago: Children's Press.
Grindley, S. (1987). *Four black puppies.* New York: Lothrop, Lee & Shepard.
Hutchins, P. (1968). *Rosie's walk.* New York: Macmillan.
Kraus, R. (1970). *Whose mouse are you?* New York: Macmillan.
Martin, B. (1967). *Brown bear, brown bear, what do you see?* New York: Holt.
Namm, D. (1990). *Little Bear.* Chicago: Children's Press.
Peek, M. (1987). *Roll over!* Boston: Houghton Mifflin.
Rascha, C. (1993). *Yo! Yes!* New York: Orchard.
Reese, B. (1979). *Little dinosaur.* Provo Utah: Aro.
Reese, B. (1979). *Sunshine.* Provo Utah: Aro.
Tafuri, N. () *Early morning in the barn.* New York: Greenwillow.
Titherington, J. (1986). *Pumpkin pumpkin.* New York: Mulberry.
Williams, S. (1989). *I went walking.* San Diego: Harcourt.
Winder, J. (1979). *Who's New at the Zoo?* Provo, UT: Aro.
Wolcott, P. (1974). *The cake story.* Reading, MA: Addison-Wesley.

distinguishing features. As in the direct instruction lesson, lead students to see the pronounceable word parts or letter sounds in the high-frequency words so that they will have additional memory pegs.

As an extension, invite students to read the text with a partner or on their own. If taped versions of the text are available, also have students read along as they listen. If the text is a favorite, arrange for additional rereadings from time to time.

After students seem to have a grasp of the high-frequency words, place the words on cards and have students read them. Individual words might be recorded on 3 × 5 cards and put on rings, in envelopes, or filed in small boxes known as ***word banks.*** The words would then be available for sorting and other reinforcement activities. The sentences in which the high-frequency words appear might be placed on sentence strips so that students see the words in context as well as in isolation. Choose additional practice activities from those listed later in this chapter.

**Word bank** is a collection of words that students have learned or are in the process of learning. They are used in a variety of reinforcement activities.

## *Singing High-Frequency Words*

As a variation on shared reading, have students sing songs that contain high-frequency words. In addition to being motivational, songs are easier to process because of repeated refrains and the element of rhyme. Sing the song or play a recorded version of it, pointing to each word as it is sung. During the second singing, have students sing along. During a third singing, you might sing the main stanzas while students sing the refrain.

As a follow-up, have students sing the words as they follow along with a taped version of the song. As they sing, they should be pointing to the words they are singing. The following sets of tapes and books are especially well done.

*Down by the Bay.* Raffi. New York: Crown (1987).
*Kids Songs 1.* Cassidy, N. Palo Alto, CA: Klutz Press (1988).
*Kids Songs 2.* Cassidy, N. Palo Alto, CA: Klutz Press (1989).
*One Light, One Sun.* Raffi. New York: Crown (1987).
*Shake My Sillies Out.* Raffi. New York: Crown (1987).
*Wheels on the Bus.* Raffi. New York: Crown (1987).

## *Experience Stories*

As explained in the previous chapter, an experience story recounts in writing an event in the students' lives, such as a trip to a farm, getting pet hamsters for the classroom, or the arrival of a baby brother. The story might also be based on a piece the students have read or a classroom discussion. Dictated by the students and written by the teacher, the experience story becomes the students' reading material. High-frequency words naturally appear in all experience stories. By choosing certain topics, you can ensure that special high-frequency words will find their way into the story. If, for instance, you want to reinforce the high-frequency words *like* and *do,* you might have the class dictate a piece on the topic, "Things I Like to Do." Because it is based on the children's experiences and written in their language, the experience story is readily understood and usually easy to read, especially for students who are still learning to speak English.

### Constructing an Experience Story

*Step 1: Introducing the Experience Story*

Students discuss the experience they have had. In the discussion, you draw out the children's ideas.

*Step 2: Writing the Experience Story*

Through questioning you help children frame their experience. You might say, for instance, "Let's write a story about our visit to the recycling center so that we can share it with others. What should we call our story?" Write the title that the children suggest: "Our Trip to the Recycling Center." As you write each word, say it so students match the written and spoken form. After writing the title, read it, running your hand under each word as you do so. After writing and reading the title, have students suggest a good beginning sentence, a second sentence, and so on. As with the title, read each word as you write it and then read each completed sentence. After writing the whole story, read the story once more. Ask the students if the story says what they want it to. Ask students if they want to make any changes or add any details.

*Step 3: Rereading the Story*

Read the story once more. Invite the students to read along with you. Stop before high-frequency words that you want to reinforce and invite the class or individual volunteers to read them.

> Richek, Caldwell, Jennings, & Lerner (1996) describe a student who took ten weeks to learn eight sight words. The student may have had an associative word–learning problem of the type described in Chapter 6.

*Step 4: Using Sentence Strips and Word Cards*

Some students may simply memorize the story or use context to such an extent that they aren't attending to the printed words. This step is designed to have them focus on the printed forms of the words. After students are familiar with the target words and sentences in the story, create tagboard strips containing the sentences. Mix up the order of the sentences and have students rearrange the sentences in correct order. If available, use a pocket chart to hold the sentence strips. If you are working with a group of students, you may want to duplicate the story and cut it into strips so that each student has a series of sentences to manipulate. Once students have arranged the sentences in their personal copies of the story, you can have a volunteer read the sentence that goes first and place the tagboard version at the top of the pocket chart and continue until all the sentences have been placed as in Figure 8-1. The story is then read and checked to make sure sentences are in the right order. Students then compare their reconstructions with the one in the pocket chart. If you are working with older students and pocket charts seem too juvenile, have them rearrange ordinary strips of papers on their desks.

After students have reassembled the sentences in the story, cut the first sentence into individual words and have students reassemble it. Then proceed to the other sentences.

*Step 5: Reading the Experience Story to Others*

Copy the story from the board, duplicate it, and distribute it to students. Have them read it to a partner. Once they can read the story with a degree of fluency, they may take it home and read it to their brothers and sisters, parents, and grandparents.

*Step 6: Adding Words to the Word Bank*

Words that students have learned to read are added to their word banks. These words can be identified by having students underline words they can read or you can test them by putting the words on 3 × 5 cards and asking students to read them. Words that are partially known or that are not identified consistently and words that are not known but that you feel are important, could be set aside for additional instruction.

You might have students keep two word banks (McCormick, 1995). Words that the student knows could be placed in a word bank entitled "Words I Can Read." Words that the student is still learning could be placed in the "Words I Am Learning" word bank.

*Step 7: Providing Additional Practice*

Review the words in the word bank on a daily basis if possible. Sorting and assembling words into sentences make excellent practice exercises. If your time is limited, you might have pairs of students test each other on their words and complete other practice activities.

**The Big Splash**

| We went to see the dolphins. |
|---|
| We got soaked! |
| The dolphins jumped high. |
| We sat in the first row. |
| They made a big splash when they landed. |

**FIGURE 8-1 Scrambled Sentences**

***Individual Experience Stories***

Individual experience stories are composed in much the same way as group stories. However, individual stories allow you to personalize the words being introduced. Individual stories can be illustrated and compiled into a booklet. The booklet may be taken home and, later, placed in the class library.

## *Predictable Books*

**Predictable books** are easy to read because they contain elements that enable the reader to read the print: repeated phrases, rhyme, and illustrations that depict much of the print.

Using a technique that is a combination of shared reading and language experience, Bridge, Winograd, and Haley (1983) used predictable books to develop high-frequency vocabulary in students reading at a beginning level. **Predictable books,** as their name suggests, are texts that have repeated elements or are told in such a way that after reading or hearing a portion of the text, it is easy to predict what the rest of the text will say. Some traditional examples include *The Gingerbread Man, The Three Little Pigs, Goldilocks.* Table 8-2 contains a number of predictable books.

Selecting a book that contains words that you want to teach, read the book to students, and, then reread it, encouraging students to join in. You might read a big book version, if available, so that students can follow along.

After students have read a predictable text, cover the pictures and ask students to read the text. This gives them the experience of using phonics and context rather than relying on picture clues.

After several rereadings, the story is placed on a chart. In this version, there are no illustrations, so students are forced to focus on the words. (Finding it so much easier, some poor readers read pictures, instead of text, and so miss out on the opportunity to develop a high frequency vocabulary.) With your help, if necessary, the students read the story in its chart form. Having duplicated portions of the story, cut it into sentences and distribute them to students just as you did with the experience story. Students match the sentences to sentences on the chart. If a pocket chart is available, they might retell the story with their sentences, placing the first sentence in the first pocket and so on. Later, sentences are cut up into individual words and matched to words in the chart story. Students can then reassemble the sentence by arranging the words in the proper order.

**Exemplary Teaching: Getting Help from Other Professionals**

Having a serious word learning problem, Marvin stumbled over the word *the* every time he encountered it. Being the most frequently appearing word in printed English, *the* makes up two percent of the words in running context. One out of every fifty words that Marvin encountered was *the.* His teacher tried every trick she knew—tracing, reading easy story books, creating mental images of *the*—but nothing worked. Attempting to read one easy story book, Marvin encountered and misread *the* eight times. When he did attempt to pronounce *the,* he invariably pronounced it as though it began with just the letter *t.* In discussing Marvin's difficulty during a collaborative meeting of several professionals concerned with his learning problems, the communication disorders specialist suggested trying a technique that she used to help children who had articulation problems. She advised, "Tell Marvin that *th* makes the tongue and teeth sound and that when he sees *th,* he should put his tongue between his teeth and say 'the.'" The technique worked. After a few reminders from his teacher, Marvin mastered *the.* It soon became one of the few words that he never missed.

## *Using Holistic Programs*

In addition to individual predictable books, there are several series of books that were designed to foster reading development through the presentation of high-frequency words in predictable books written on a variety of levels of difficulty. Several of these series are listed in the section to follow.

- **Ready to Read** (Richard C. Owen): Designed to provide students in New Zealand with a graded series of children's books from the emergent-literacy stage through the early-reading and fluency stages or approximately the level reached at the end of second grade. Books at the emergent stage make maximum use of pictures, repetitive structures, short sentences, and easy vocabulary. They provide an opportunity for even the poorest of readers to interact successfully with real books.
- **Story Box** (Wright Group): *Story Box* is a whole language reading program that ranges from the emergent to the early fluency level, which is approximately second grade. Books in Level 1, the emergent level, are arranged in sets A through G, which gradually increase in difficulty. Each set contains eight titles for a total of fifty-six titles.
- **Literacy 2000** (Rigby): Literacy 2000 is a whole language program designed for students in the emergent literacy and early fluency stages. The core of the program is a series of one hundred books arranged in two stages. The books gradually increase in difficulty from books that contain a single sentence or phrase per page to ones that contain five or more sentences per page.
- **Sunshine at Home** (Wright Group): Although designed for use by parents, this forty-book set of emergent literacy–reading books might also be used in the classroom and clinic. Each book contains three selections. Gradually growing in difficulty, the series

is arranged in four sets of ten books each. The series reinforces a group of ninety-eight high-frequency words. Words introduced in earlier levels are reinforced in later levels. A Spanish version is also available.

- **Reading Corners** (Dominie Press): Series of eight-page booklets designed to reinforce high-frequency sentence patterns. In the easiest texts, a full-page illustration is accompanied by a one-sentence caption that incorporates a basic sentence pattern: I like ________. Here is ________. I have ________.
- **Read More Books** (Dominie Press): Designed for emergent readers, these twelve-page informational books are written around themes (People at Work, At the Store, Where Do You Live?) or language patterns (I can__,Yes, No). Four-color photos on the left-hand page are accompanied by one- or two-line captions on the right-hand page.
- **Ready Readers** (Modern Curriculum Press): Designed for the primary grades, Ready Readers consist of two hundred booklets ranging in length from eight to twenty-four pages. Booklets are arranged in five levels of difficulty from beginning reading to the level usually achieved at the end of first grade.
- **Little Red Readers** (Sundance): Series of forty sixteen-page booklets on five graduated levels ranging in difficulty from beginning reading to an end-of-first-grade level. On the easiest levels, includes such patterns as: The lion got on the train. The bear got on the train.
- **Word Books** (Phoenix): Series of small books written at five levels which are based on the number of different words used in each book: 10, 20, 30, 40, or 60. Both English and Spanish versions are available. Some titles are also available in big book form.

### *Creating Little Books*

In addition to acquiring pattern books, you might create your own. The books might incorporate a particular theme: People in My Family, Foods I Like, Things I Can Do, Holidays, or a particular pattern: I can ___, I see___, I like ___, ___ got on the bus (Johnston, Juel, Invernizzi, 1995). You might create these on your own or recruit help from your students.

The books might be illustrated with pictures that you draw, pictures from a desktop-publishing program, or student-drawn illustrations. Since instructional time is limited, be careful that students don't spend an excessive amount of time creating illustrations. You might also create open-ended books and have students complete them by placing words in the blanks. For instance, they might complete five "I can ___." or "I like ___." sentences.

### *Read-Along Technique*

Obtain an easy book, one in which the student has an obvious interest. If the book does not have an accompanying audio-tape, create one. Have the student follow along as the taped version is read. The student might read a book such as *Brown Bear, Brown Bear, What Do You See?* (Martin, 1983), which has only thirty-two different words, or *The Cake that Mack Ate* (Robart, 1986), which has just thirty different words. Start with shorter books and work up to longer ones. Students can read along with the tape until they are able to read the book on their own (Chomsky, 1978). This may require as many as twenty read-alongs. As students acquire a broader sight vocabulary and begin to acquire decoding skills, fewer rereadings will be required.

## Building Fluency

Although the activities described so far help to introduce high-frequency words, they also build accuracy of recognition and fluency. Before students can recognize words rapidly or automatically, they must first achieve accuracy (Samuels, 1994). Low-achieving readers may take longer to achieve accuracy than higher-achieving readers. By one estimate, students may require thirty-five or more exposures to a word before learning it, with the slowest students needing almost three times as many exposures as the brightest students (Gates, 1931). Provide ample practice so that the words are recognized accurately. Once students can recognize words accurately, emphasize speed so that words are recognized instantaneously, and fluent reading is fostered. Although one characteristic of fluent reading is processing words at an acceptable rate, fluency also entails reading in meaningful phrases and with appropriate expression. Model fluent reading when reading to students. Explain that as you read, you group words into meaningful phrases and read with expression. The following suggestions and activities are designed to develop rapid word recognition and fluent reading.

### Wide Reading

Some low-achieving readers decode or attempt to decode every word they meet. They are able to read high-frequency words, but they are unable to read them as sight words. They seem to need to take time to sound them out. As a result, their reading is slow and laborious. These students may not have had enough time to practice newly learned skills or words, or phonics and oral reading may have been overemphasized so much that they believe the purpose of reading is to pronounce written words correctly. Stress meaning by asking students to retell selections or answer questions about them and reduce the amount of oral reading.

Fluency can also be fostered by having students read a wide variety of easy books. As they read books in which nearly all the words are known, their ability to recognize the words faster should increase. Students, especially if they are younger, might also be encouraged to read the same books a second, a third, or even a fourth time.

### Repeated Readings

**Repeated reading:** reading a text over and over to achieve fluency.

Another technique for achieving fluency is through **repeated reading.** One way of learning high-frequency words is to read the same story over and over again. Often poor readers stumble over their text, especially when they encounter words that are easily confused, such as *what, where,* and *when.* Repeated reading gives them the opportunity to achieve accuracy. At the same time, through providing practice, it fosters instantaneous recognition of high-frequency words or fluency. The box to follow gives an example for presenting a lesson in introducing repeated readings.

**Repeated Readings Lesson**

Lipson and Wixson (1997) report that rereading a text is a favored activity among low-progress readers. It provides them with the opportunity to master the text.

*Step 1: Introducing Repeated Readings*

Explain the procedure to students. Tell them that they will be reading a short selection over and over again so that they will learn to read faster and better.

*Step 2: Selecting a Passage*

Select or have the student choose short, interesting selections of approximately one hundred words.

*Step 3: Obtaining an Initial Timing*

Obtain baseline data on the selections. Have the students read them orally. Time the readings and record the number of words read incorrectly. If students take more than two minutes to read the selection and make more than five errors out of a hundred words (not counting missed endings), the selections are too hard. If students make only one or two errors and read the selection at eighty-five words per minute or faster, the selection is too easy.

*Step 4: Rereading*

Go over the students' miscues with them. Help them read these words correctly. Then direct them to reread the selections until they feel they can read them faster and more smoothly. Practice can take one of three forms: a) reading the selection to oneself; b) listening to an audiotape while reading the selection silently and then reading the selection without the aid of the tape; c) reading the selection to a partner.

Choral reading, in which the group reads together a speech, poem, or play, promotes fluency and fosters participation of the poorest readers.

*Step 5: Evaluating the Reading*

The students read the selections to you or to a partner. The number of word recognition errors and reading speed are noted. The students are informed of their progress. A chart, as in Figure 8-2, might be constructed to show the degree of improvement. The goal is to have students read at least eighty-five words per minute. Students should practice until they reach that criterion. Word recognition errors should also decrease. However, do not insist upon 100 percent word recognition. Insisting upon perfection in word reading sends the wrong message to students. It makes them think that reading is a word-pronouncing rather than a meaning-making activity. It also impedes fluency. Afraid of making a mistake, students will slow their reading rate (Samuels, 1979).

***Variations on Rereading***

Repeated readings foster fluency by providing practice with easy materials. This goal can also be achieved by having students read lots of easy books.

Selections can be reread on a less formal basis. The evaluation may also be informal. Instead of working with a teacher, students may work in pairs. However, model the procedure first. One student reads and attempts to reach criterion while the other tracks her or his progress on the chart shown in Figure 8-2. Then they switch roles. Show students how to time the reading and count errors. To simplify the charting procedure, have students check one hundred-word samples only. The reader may actually read a lengthier selection but only one hundred words are used for charting progress. Students may speed through a selection to beat the clock. Encourage students to read at a normal pace. Stress that the goal is to meet the criterion, not set a world record.

If you read the same words over and over, you will read faster and better. On this sheet, show how long it took you to read 100 words. Blacken one block for each 10 seconds of time you took. For the first time that you read the story, blacken the blocks under number 1. For the second time, blacken the blocks under number 2, and so on. Write down the number of mistakes that you make on the lines at the bottom.

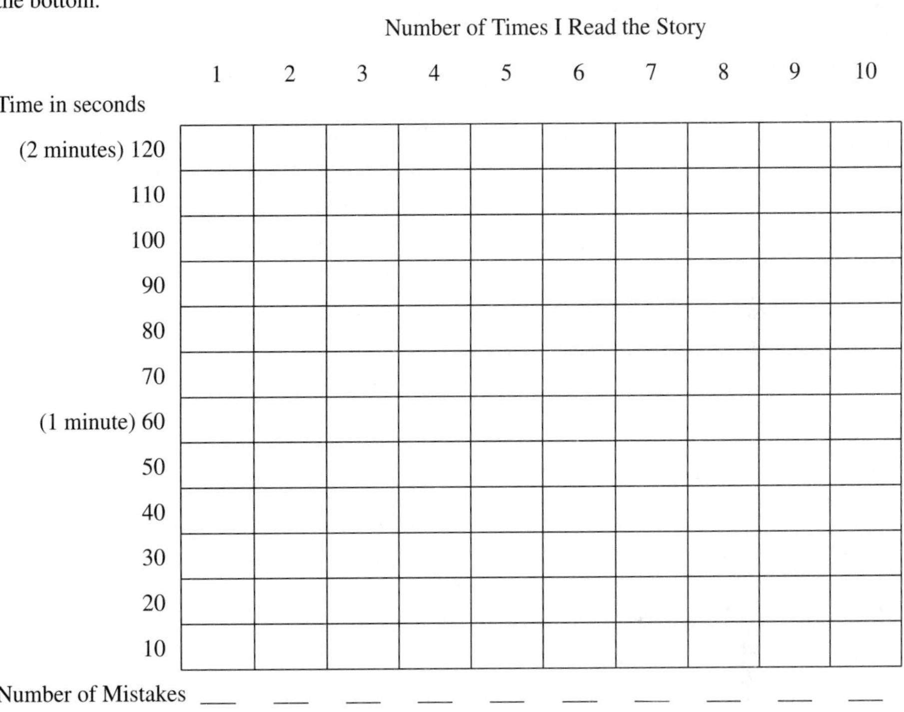

Number of Times I Read the Story

| Time in seconds | 1 | 2 | 3 | 4 | 5 | 6 | 7 | 8 | 9 | 10 |
|---|---|---|---|---|---|---|---|---|---|---|
| (2 minutes) 120 | | | | | | | | | | |
| 110 | | | | | | | | | | |
| 100 | | | | | | | | | | |
| 90 | | | | | | | | | | |
| 80 | | | | | | | | | | |
| 70 | | | | | | | | | | |
| (1 minute) 60 | | | | | | | | | | |
| 50 | | | | | | | | | | |
| 40 | | | | | | | | | | |
| 30 | | | | | | | | | | |
| 20 | | | | | | | | | | |
| 10 | | | | | | | | | | |
| Number of Mistakes | ___ | ___ | ___ | ___ | ___ | ___ | ___ | ___ | ___ | ___ |

**FIGURE 8-2 Speed of Reading Chart**

Occasionally, use a song or a poem instead of a typical reading selection. Because of their rhythm, some narrative poems and songs lend themselves to a speedy reading.

## *Carbo Recorded-Book Method*

One way of increasing the ability of students to recognize words automatically is to have them read along as the same story or brief book is read repeatedly. An excellent way of providing these repeated readings is through taped stories. However, taped stories typically move along at the pace of normal speech. This may be too rapid for the listener to match printed and spoken words. When a student reads along with a tape, the tape speed should be at about the same rate as the student can read orally. Otherwise, comprehension may suffer. You may wish to record books for students who are struggling to increase their fluency. In choosing books to record, select those that are interesting and which students will be able to understand when they hear them read aloud. When recording books, read with expression but read slowly enough so that students can follow along. You might read the text at about 85 to 100 WPM and then have students play it back using a tape recorder that has a speed regulator (Shany & Biemiller, 1995). As you encounter words or expressions that might be unfamiliar, pause before and after reading them so that students will have time to process the difficult words or phrases (Carbo, Dunn, & Dunn, 1986).

Reading along with tape-recorded or CD-ROM stories can be a highly effective way to foster fluency and comprehension (Shany and Biemiller, 1995).

Record small amounts of text from two to five minutes on each side of a tape. Gather short articles, brief chapters, poems, or other short pieces to record. In preparing audiotapes, begin the recording by announcing title and author. Clearly describe the point where reading will start. Signal when it is time to turn a page and announce when the reading has been completed (Carbo, Dunn, & Dunn, 1986). Produce recordings of readings with increasing length and difficulty.

Encourage students to read along with the taped selection several times, until they feel they can read it on their own. Have them attempt to read it without the tape, note difficult parts, and then have them listen to the tape once more and reread the text to brush up on parts that posed problems. Students can work alone or in pairs. If working in pairs, they can read to each other after practicing with the tape.

Reading poems and plays is an excellent way to build fluency. Both naturally lend themselves to repeated readings.

Sometimes word-by-word reading persists despite your best efforts. If word-by-word reading persists, you might consider having students read selections in which phrases are marked so that they have practice reading in meaningful chunks. As always, stress comprehension. Don't overemphasize fluent reading,or students might focus on sounding good instead of constructing meaning.

## *Additional Practice Activities for High-Frequency Words*

### *Words on the Wall*

An excellent device for reinforcing high-frequency words is to create a word wall. About five or so new words are added each week (P. M. Cunningham & Allington, 1994). Words are drawn from newly taught patterns, basals, trade books, experience stories, and real-world materials that students are reading. They are words that students are sure to encounter many times in their reading and writing. The words may be accompanied by a sentence or picture clue or may be displayed alone. Words displayed alone might be presented in such a way that distinctive features or configurations are highlighted. For instance, *where* can be distinguished from *were* by the *h* that sticks up.

Words are arranged on the wall in alphabetical order by first letter so that students can find them rapidly. When adding words to the wall, be sure to discuss any parts that students can already say or any distinctive features that the word might have and any cues that students might use to help them remember the word or distinguish it from other words: "You can tell that h-e-a-r means to listen because it has an ear in it." Also discuss the word's meaning if it is unknown or vague.

Each day, if possible, review items on the word wall. You might have students find all the animal words, for instance, or locate the opposite of *on, old,* and *dark* or note words that incorporate a newly learned pattern. When words have been mastered, remove them.

## *Sight-Word Commands*

Create a series of cards that contain commands composed primarily of high-frequency words. When the command is displayed, the class carries it out. Commands might be just for fun, or they may be functional. Some possible commands include: Count to three. Hold up a piece of paper. Put up one hand. Put up both hands. Line up in the front of the room. Sing a song. Sit down. Stand up. Stand on one foot.

## *Read the Label*

Label appropriate items in your class. Label the light switch with an *on* and an *off,* for example. When writing directions, try to use high-frequency words: "Put blocks here. Put toys in the box." Introduce the sign, label, or set of directions. Read it for students, pointing out each word as you do so. Then have students, as a group, read the item along with you. Also encourage individual volunteers to read the item. From time to time, review the item. Some possible functional high-frequency word signs, labels, and directions include the following:

| | |
|---|---|
| In | Pull |
| Out | Walk. Don't run. |
| Up | Mrs. Doyle's Room |
| Down | Pet Corner |
| Push | Book Corner |

> In pantomime, pairs of students are given a series of five to eight words that can be pantomimed: *walk, run, fly, jump, throw.* One student pantomimes the words. The second holds up the high-frequency word being pantomimed.

## *Forming Words*

To help students become aware of the letters that make up a high-frequency word, have them use magnetic letters to spell out high-frequency words that have been introduced. Make duplicate cards for high-frequency words and cut apart the extra cards into individual letters, then have students reconstruct the words. Store the pieces for each word in its own envelope.

## *Forming Phrases and Sentences*

From a big book selection, experience story, or other source, copy a sentence that contains several high-frequency words onto oak tag. (If you are working with a large group, you might photocopy the sentences.) Cut the words apart and place them in an envelope. Have students arrange the words so they form a sentence. This builds sentence sense and comprehension while providing practice with high-frequency words.

## *Sorting*

Using their bank of high-frequency words, have students sort their words. They might group them semantically: all the color words, all the number words, all the action words. Or they might group them structurally or phonemically: all the words that begin with *s,* or all the words that end with the *at* pattern.

## *Audiovisual Aids*

### *CD-ROM Read Alongs*

A high-tech approach to introducing and reinforcing high-frequency words is that of CD-ROM read alongs. The presentation features graphics, which include animation, still pictures, or movie clips; background music and sound effects; and an oral reading of the story. As the story is being read, the text is highlighted so that the viewer can read along. If students wish, they can click on a word and have it pronounced. The viewer can even control the pacing of the reading so that the selection can be read at a slower than normal rate as in the Carbo recorded-book technique. CD-ROM books can be especially helpful for youngsters who are still learning to speak English.

Another piece of software, *Bailey's Book House* (Edmark), introduces a series of high-frequency words along with other beginning-level reading skills. In addition to pronouncing the words, it presents them in sentences and uses animated sequences to illustrate each word's meaning. To illustrate *in* and *out,* for example, it shows a dog in and out of a dog house. It also provides practice in using high-frequency words by helping the student compose a story.

### *Videos with Words*

A number of children's videos use a bouncing ball to draw attention to the words of a song so that the viewers can sing along. Have students sing along with the tapes. Once they feel they know the words to the song, they can turn down the volume and then attempt to sing along. If they have difficulty, they may turn up the volume and practice some more. Sing-along tapes that you might use include the following:

*Sing-Along Songs: Heigh-Ho.* Walt Disney. Burbank, CA: Buena Vista Home Video.
*Sing-Along Songs: Zip-A-Dee-Doo-Dah.* Walt Disney. Burbank, CA: Buena Vista Home Video.
*Sing-Along Songs: You Can Fly!* Walt Disney. Burbank, CA: Buena Vista Home Video.
*Sing-Along Songs: The Bare Necessities.* Walt Disney. Burbank, CA: Buena Vista Home Video.
*Sing-Along Songs: Fun with Music.* Walt Disney. Burbank, CA: Buena Vista Home Video.
*Sing-Along Songs: Under the Sea.* Walt Disney. Burbank, CA: Buena Vista Home Video.
*Sing-Along Songs: Disneyland Fun.* Walt Disney. Burbank, CA: Buena Vista Home Video.

## *Games*

#### *Concentration*

Players attempt to match up from memory as many pairs of high-frequency words as they can. This provides good practice in having students describe easily confused words.

**Materials.** Six to twenty pairs of cards on which matching sets of two high-frequency words have been printed are needed for this game. Construction paper or oak tag might be used. If use construction paper, you may want to use different colors to indicate different levels of difficulty.

**Directions for Playing.** Start out with a small deck of six to eight pairs and work up to a larger deck of up to twelve to twenty pairs. Shuffle the cards and lay them out with the high-frequency words face down. Players take turns trying to match up pairs. A player turns over a card, reads it, and attempts to locate its match.

If a player makes a match, he removes that pair and places it in front of him. He continues to make matches until he turns over a card that doesn't match. At that point, the player to his right takes a turn.

The game is over when all the cards have been matched. The winner is the player who made the most matches. Hint: Use words that are challenging but not too difficult. Players should be on approximately the same level.

***Fish***

Players obtain sets of four of the same card. The player with the most sets wins. Each player is dealt five cards. Cards that are left over are placed in the center of the playing area.

**Materials.** Sets of eight to twelve cards containing high-frequency words. Make four copies of each card.

**Directions for Playing.** The person to the right of the dealer takes the first turn. Looking over her cards, she selects one for which she would like to build a set. She then chooses the player that she believes might have a card in that set. If she wants to make a set of *I* cards, for example, she says, "Billy, give me all your *I's.* She holds up the card for all to see as she makes her request. If he has *I's,* Billy surrenders them. The original player then can request the same card from other players or ask for another card that matches one she has in her hand. Her turn continues as long as she successfully obtains cards. If a player does not have a requested card, he says, "I don't have any *I's.* Go fish." The dealer then picks a card from the pile in the center. If she happens to pick the card she requested, she gets another turn. Otherwise, she loses her turn.

Whenever a player gets a set of four cards, he announces that he has a book. He reads the word for which he has a set and places the book face up in front of him. The game continues until all the cards have been made into books. When the cards in the Go Fish pile have all been taken, then players simply skip the "Go fish" part of the game.

The game continues until all the cards have been placed in books. The winner is the one with the most books. Hint: The game has the most benefit when the words are challenging but not impossible and the players have approximately the same level of high frequency–word knowledge.

Students, especially those who are struggling with reading and writing, need to sees signs of progress. You might use a thermometer,

> Once students reach the alphabetic stage they use letter–sound clues to learn words. However, they can be provided with reinforcement activities that are more visual than auditory or vice versa or which are kinesthetic: tracing words, assembling sentences, pantomiming words.

ladder, football field, or simple graph to represent number of words learned. On the graph in Figure 8-2, the student colors in one block for every ten words learned.

If despite your best efforts, students can't seem to learn high frequency words, they may have a serious word learning problem. They may need to be taught with a multisensory approach such as VAKT, which is described in detail in Chapter 14. To test for a serious word learning problem, administer the Word Learning Test contained in Appendix A.

## *Minicase Study*

Although he was eight-and-a-half and about to enter third grade, Peter could only read four words: *I, a, and, but,* two of which—*I* and *a*—were pronounced the same as the letters that spell them. Peter also lacked any systematic knowledge of phonics (McCormick, 1994). Because Peter obviously needed many exposures to learn words and was in a logographic phase of learning words, an approach known as Multiple Exposures/Multiple Context was used. The core of the program was a series of very easy readers. Since the series had the same characters and setting, many of the words were repeated from book to book. Before reading a segment of the book, Peter was given a pre-test on the text. Words difficult for him were taught using puzzles, magnetic letters, games, cloze, and other activities that helped him to focus on the graphic features of the word, and also enabled him to encounter the words in multiple contexts. Once Peter had mastered the words, he read the text from which they had been drawn.

During the next session, Peter reread the text and was then pre-tested on the next book, and the cycle began once more. After Peter began making significant progress, direct instruction in phonics was introduced, and it soon became evident that Peter was entering the alphabetic phase of reading. As the months passed, Peter was given direct instruction in increasingly complex word identification skills, including decoding multisyllabic words, reading prefixes and suffixes, and using context. Accompanying intensive, carefully planned instruction was ample opportunity for guided practice and independent application. In one four-week period, Peter read thirty-three trade books. In fact, the key to Peter's success, might just have been the stress placed on sustained reading of materials on his level. After three-and-a-half years of instruction, Peter was able to read on a seventh-grade level.

## *Summary*

Easy, high-frequency words, such as *was, of, the,* which are known as "sight words," are among the most difficult to learn to read. Because their spellings don't always adequately represent their sounds (*of, one*), or they are presented before students have learned the phonic elements necessary to decode them (*how, look*), they are taught through a logographic or paired-associate method. However, only about forty words can be learned in this way because the learner runs out of ways of creating distinguishing cues, and the cues themselves are arbitrary. In actuality, most words are fully or partially regular. If feasible, high-frequency words should be learned through phonics because this makes it possible for the student to use letter–sound cues to remember them.

A direct approach to teaching high-frequency words incorporates phonics, repetition, and reading the words in the context of real stories. Indirect approaches to teaching high-frequency words include shared reading, language experience, predictable books, and composing sentences.

High-frequency words have a high payoff in reading. The 200 highest-frequency words comprise about 50 percent of the words in running text. In order to make reading fluent, it is important that these high-frequency words be recognized immediately. Procedures that promote fluent reading include wide reading of books and rereading familiar material. There are also a number of games and activities and devices, including CD-ROM software, that can be used to promote accuracy and fluency in the reading of high-frequency words.

## Application Activities

1. Using the direct-teaching approach, plan a lesson teaching a series of high-frequency words. If possible, teach the lesson and evaluate its effectiveness.
2. Read five or more predictable books listed as being appropriate for the teaching of high-frequency words.
3. Add five books to the list of predictable books suggested as being appropriate for teaching high-frequency words. If you are working with young children, choose books that would be appropriate for them. If you are working with older students, choose books appropriate for their maturity level.
4. Examine and try out CD-ROM software that might be used to reinforce high-frequency words. What is your assessment of the software?
5. Try out one of the games or other activities for reinforcing high-frequency words. Assess its value.

# Chapter 9

# Teaching Phonics

## *Using What You Know*

Because our speech sounds can be represented by letters, we can write and read anything that can be spoken. Unfortunately, large numbers of students have difficulty learning phonics, the system of letter–sound relationships that enables them to translate printed symbols into meaningful language.

What has been your experience with phonics? What do you do when you encounter an unfamiliar name or a word that you have never seen before? How do you decipher these words? Do you know any students who have difficulty decoding words? How might they be helped? What role do you think phonics should play in a program for low-achieving readers?

## *Anticipation Guide*

Read each of the following statements. Put a check under "Agree" or "Disagree" to show how you feel about each one. If possible, discuss your responses with classmates.

| | Agree | Disagree |
|---|---|---|
| **1.** Inadequate instruction in phonics is a major cause of reading failure in the early grades. | ______ | ______ |
| **2.** An effective way to learn phonics is through spelling. | ______ | ______ |
| **3.** Vowel spellings are so irregular that instruction should focus on consonants, especially in the early stages of learning to read. | ______ | ______ |
| **4.** The easiest way to decipher a printed word is to decode it sound by sound. | ______ | ______ |
| **5.** Problem readers should learn phonics through reading rather than through formal instruction. | ______ | ______ |

## *Phonics and the Poor Reader*

Unless suffering from aphasia or a similar impairment, children learn to understand and speak their native language with little difficulty. By the time they reach school age, they have mastered the basic syntax of the language and have acquired a speaking vocabulary of several thousand words. Despite this incredible achievement, as many as one in four of these students will experience significant difficulty learning to read. Why? For the majority of them, it will be the alphabetical nature of printed language.

One reason reading is more complex than speech is because the reader must translate printed symbols—the letters of the alphabet—into their spoken equivalents. The average student is expected to master the basics of phonics by the end of second grade (Anderson, R., Anderson, C., Hiebert, Scott, & Wilkinson, 1985). For a significant percentage of students, this is a very difficult task, one that is so poorly mastered that it remains a stumbling block to effective reading for many years or, in some cases, a lifetime. Failure to master phonics or related word-analysis skills is easily the number one cause of reading problems. In a longitudinal study that followed fifty-four students from first through the fourth grade, Juel (1988, 1994b) found that of the twenty-four children who remained poor readers through all four grades, twenty-two were poor decoders and had, in fact, failed to reach the level of decoding achievement of average second-graders.

In addition to a generalized difficulty with processing words phonologically, poor readers have a variety of specific difficulties learning and using phonics. As a group, low-achieving readers are slower learning phonics, rely on smaller units of sound, have difficulty applying phonics, tend to overrely on phonics, and fail to integrate context clues with their use of phonics (Adams, 1990).

Poor readers may also scan words less efficiently. In her study of beginning readers, Cohen (1974–75) found that poor readers tend to use fewer letter cues. For instance, they may process only the word's first letter or first and last letter. They may fail to process the medial vowel, even though the medial vowel is known. As she notes, "One might say that the poor reader is confused with vowel sounds, but there are too many instances where it is more likely that the poor reader simply made a quick judgment based on first letter cue" (p. 647). Making judgments based on an incomplete scan could be developmental. As Cohen notes, according to the Piagetian concept of decentering, younger children make judgments based on a single perception. However, as children develop cognitively, they are able to use successive elements in a word. Responding on the basis of an incomplete scan of a word's letters could also be due to an impulsive style. Some poor readers may respond too quickly, without looking at all the letters (Gaskins, Ehri, Cress, O'Hara, & Donnelly, 1996–1997).

### *Example of Decoding Difficulty*

As discussed in Chapter 4, it isn't necessary to give a phonics test to detect decoding difficulties. Problems show up on informal reading inventories in both the graded word lists and oral reading passages of the test. Take a look at Figure 9-1, which shows Rachel's performance on the graded word list of the *Basic Reading Inventory* (Johns, 1994). Pay particular attention to the untimed column. This shows the number of words that Rachel, who has just started third grade, was able to read when given time to apply decoding skills.

| | Flash | Untimed |
|---|---|---|
| 1. me | ✓ | |
| 2. get | go | ✓ |
| 3. home | here | her |
| 4. not | no | ✓ |
| 5. he | ✓ | |
| 6. tree | ✓ | |
| 7. girl | ✓ | |
| 8. take | to | ✓ |
| 9. book | boy | barn |
| 10. milk | more | my |
| 11. dog | ✓ | |
| 12. all | ✓ | |
| 13. apple | dk | dk |
| 14. like | lick | ✓ |
| 15. go | ✓ | |
| 16. farm | for | fine |
| 17. went | when | we |
| 18. friend | dk | dk |
| 19. about | dk | dk |
| 20. door | do | down |
| Percent correct | 35 | 45 |

**FIGURE 9-1 Performance on Word List Test**

Looking at word recognition on both the word-lists test and oral reading passages provides a more valid assessment because most students do better when reading words in context.

Appendix A contains the Word Pattern test, which assesses students' ability to read major word patterns. This test can be used to establish a starting point for phonics instruction.

A comparison of the timed and untimed columns shows that Rachel was only able to sound out two words that she didn't recognize at sight or automatically. An examination of the words missed indicates that she is able to use initial consonants to decode words but fails to use consistently medial vowels and final consonants. An examination of her performance on the oral reading passages and classroom observations confirms this conclusion and also suggests that she overuses context and picture clues and underuses decoding strategies. Although in third grade, Rachel has failed to master rudimentary decoding skills and strategies. She needs a systematic program that follows the principles and techniques presented in this chapter.

## *A Theory of Decoding*

In order to correct decoding deficiencies, it is necessary to understand what processes students use to decode words and construct a theory that accounts for these processes. Instruction should grow out of the theory. Decoding is a complex operation in which several processes interact. According to K. Goodman (1974, 1984), one of the founders of whole language, three cueing systems are used to process text: syntactic, semantic, and graphophonic (phonics). For instance, if the word *barked* were unknown in this sentence, "The dog barked at me," readers would use their knowledge of the world and the way language is used and, perhaps the initial consonant in the word *barked,* to predict the identity of the word *barked.* Their syntactical knowledge would intuitively tell them that a verb was needed. Their awareness of the meaning of the sentence and their past experience with dogs and their knowledge that *b* represents a /b/ sound would help them to conclude that the word is *barked.* Because of the utility of the cues, the readers would not have to process all the letters in the word *barked.*

Based on an extensive review of the research, Adams (1990) also theorizes that the reader uses interacting cues. Using a computer analogy, she concludes that there are four processors at work: orthographic, meaning, context, and phonological as is shown in Figure 9-2. The orthographic processes letters, which are translated into speech sounds by the phonological processor. The meaning processor assigns an identity or meaning to the series

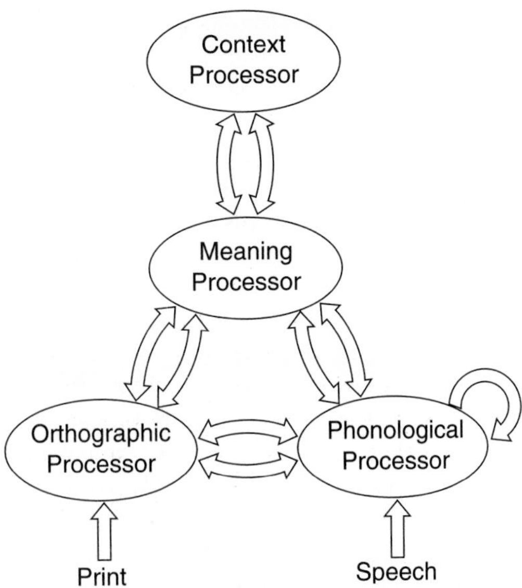


**FIGURE 9-2 Modeling the Reading System: The Four Processors**

Source: Adams, M. J. (1990). *Beginning to read: Thinking and learning about print, A summary.* Prepared by S. A. Stahl, J. Osborn, & F. Lehr. Champaign, IL: Center for the Study of Reading, University of Illinois.

Top-down views of reading describe decoding as being a sampling/predictive process. The reader identifies part of a word (often just the first consonant) and then, based on the context, predicts what the whole word is. Bottom-up and interactive theories hold that all or most of the letters in a word are processed.

of sounds translated by the phonological processor. This meaning is fed into the context processor, which constructs a continuing understanding of the text. However, communication among processors is two-way. Working in parallel fashion, the processors both send and receive information. Information from context, for instance, can speed up the other three processors and vice-versa. And when information from one processor is weak, the other processors work extra hard. For instance, when one encounters a word like *produce,* which can have different pronunciations, functions, and meanings, the context processor aids the meaning and phonological processors in assigning a meaning and pronunciation. In this explanation, both the orthographic and phonological processes play a larger role than they do in Goodman's model. In Adams' view, readers process all or most of the letters of the words they read. Blending aspects of both theories, it would seem that readers use phonics and context cues in parallel fashion and that most, if not all, of a word's letters are processed. In keeping with this view, this text will emphasize the use of both phonics and context.

## Principles of Teaching Phonics

The key to teaching phonics to poor readers is to use an approach that is systematic and which fits the needs of individual learners. Ample reinforcement in the form of extensive reading is also essential. In all too many programs, students are given large doses of phonics but little opportunity to apply decoding strategies. Extensive reading is required for students to incorporate strategies to the point where they become automatic.

This text recommends early, systematic instruction in phonics along with application in context. Context speeds the use of phonics, but does not replace it.

Care also needs to be taken that phonics is not overemphasized to the detriment of comprehension. Students may become so focused on sounding out words that they fail to read for meaning. Ironically, this cuts them off from context clues, a very valuable source of information about the identity of printed words. And it may also create a comprehension problem. Even when working on word-recognition difficulties, the ultimate aim should be to have students read for meaning.

For those who need it, there should be some instruction in phonics every session, accompanied by opportunities to apply what was learned by reading books or other materials that incorporate the element presented.

Realizing that students are deficient in phonics, teachers may spend lengthy periods instructing students in word-analysis skills so that the students can "catch up." While direct instruction in phonics is essential for poor readers, a little phonics instruction goes a long way. A brief period of direct phonics instruction should be complemented by fairly lengthy periods of reading or other forms of application. As a rule of thumb, ten or fifteen minutes of phonics instruction a day is probably plenty. This is approximately the amount of time that a number of highly successful intervention programs spend on word recognition (Hiebert & Taylor, 1994). The best way for low-achieving readers to "catch up" is through extra reading.

It goes without saying that the skills taught should be those that are incorporated in the selection to be read. For instance, a good time to present the *-at* pattern would be when students are about to read a text such as a *Cat on the Mat* (Wildsmith, 1982). The skills taught should also be skills that the student needs to know.

## *The Content of Phonics: Consonants*

Although there are only twenty-six letters in the alphabet, there are approximately forty-one speech sounds in English. These include twenty-five consonant and sixteen vowel sounds. Many of these sounds can be spelled in more than one way. English vowels are notorious for the many ways in which they can be spelled. However, if you look at the list of consonant sounds and their spellings in Table 9-1, you can see that most have only one spelling. The consonant /b/, for instance, is regularly spelled *b* as in *baby.* Even the consonant /f/, which is one of the most variable consonant elements, is generally spelled *f*; it is only rarely spelled *ph* (photo) or *gh* (laugh). Because consonants are less variable than vowels in their spellings, they are usually presented first in most phonics programs. Coming in initial position as they do in many words, consonant letters also provide more essential and more usable cues than vowels. Also, in children's invented spelling, consonants are the first letters to appear (Read, 1971).

**TABLE 9-1 Consonant Spellings**

| Sound | Spelling: Initial | Spelling: Final | Model Word |
|---|---|---|---|
| /b/ | **b**oy | tu**b**, tu**be** | **b**all |
| /d/ | **d**ay | ha**d** | **d**og |
| /f/ | **f**ive, **ph**one | li**fe**, gra**ph** | **f**ish |
| /g/ | **g**ate, **gh**ost, **gu**ide | ba**g** | **g**oat |
| /h/ | **h**en, **wh**o | | **h**at |
| /hw/ | **wh**en | | **wh**ale |
| /j/ | **j**eep, **g**iant | ga**ge**, bri**dge** | **j**ar, **g**iraffe |
| /k/ | **c**ap, **k**ing, **qu**it, **ch**aracter | ba**ke**, tra**ck**, a**che** | **c**at, **k**ey |
| /l/ | **l**ittle | we**ll** | **l**ion |
| /m/ | **m**e | a**m**, ti**me**, hy**mn**, to**mb** | **m**an |
| /n/ | **n**ew, **gn**aw, **pn**eumatic | | **n**ail |
| /p/ | **p**age | to**p** | **p**en |
| /r/ | **r**ead | | **r**ing |
| /s/ | **s**ide, **c**ent | bu**s**, pa**ss**, ra**ce** | **s**un |
| /t/ | **t**ail | ba**t**, hoppe**d** | **t**en |
| /v/ | **v**an | bra**ve** | **v**ase |
| /w/ | **w**et, **wh**eel | | **w**agon |
| /y/ | **y**es, on**i**on | | **y**o-**y**o |
| /z/ | **z**oo | say**s**, pri**ze**, qui**z** **z**ebra | |
| /ch/ | **ch**urch, **c**ello | ha**tch**, ques**t**ion | **ch**air, fu**tu**re |
| /sh/ | **sh**e, **s**ugar, **Ch**icago | | **sh**oe |
| /th/ | **th**ink | ba**th** | **th**umb |
| /*th*/ | **th**at | ba**the** | **th**e |
| /zh/ | a**z**ure, ver**s**ion | | |
| /ŋ/ | | si**ng** | ri**ng** |

Note: "Initial" and "final" refer to words *or* syllables.

## *Approaches to Teaching Consonants*

**Explicit (synthetic) phonics:** presents phonic elements in isolation and synthesized into whole words. Thus *t* = /t/, *e* = /e/, and *n* = /n/ would be taught as separate elements and then blended to form the word *ten.*

The two major approaches to teaching phonics are the explicit and implicit, which are sometimes termed the synthetic and analytic. In the **explicit** approach, students are taught isolated sounds and then blend the sounds together to create a word. In deciphering the word *hat,* the student would say "huh-ah-tuh" and then blend the sounds into "hat." A major problem with an explicit approach is that it distorts sounds. Consonant sounds can't be spoken in isolation without distorting them (try saying *l* without making a vowel sound). In addition, blending sounds to form a word is a difficult task for many readers.

**Implicit (analytic) phonics:** presents letter–sound relationships within the context of a whole word. The correspondence *t* = /t/ is taught as *t* represents the sound heard at the beginning of *ten.*

By far the more popular, the **implicit** approach teaches phonics in the context of whole words and is the method espoused in most of the best-selling basal systems. It is also favored three to one by the directors of university clinics (Bader & Wiesendanger, 1986). In an implicit approach, students aren't taught that *h* makes a "huh" sound, but are told that *h* makes the sound heard at the beginning of *hat.* The major disadvantage of the implicit approach is that it is somewhat circuitous. For *m* = /m/, students are required to think about the sound they hear at the beginning of the word *moon* and abstract it from that word. Although it results in a distortion, it is easier to identify the sound of *m* as being "mmm."

Novice readers may process words sound by sound (/h/ + /e/ + /n/), but gradually learn to chunk sounds (/h/ + /en/).

Because it breaks down phonics into its smallest elements, explicit phonics is frequently used in corrective materials and programs. However, because of the distortion and the difficulty of blending, readers may not recognize the word that they have sounded out. The best way to resolve this problem would be to use elements of both explicit and implicit phonics. For instance, in teaching *m* = /m/, refer to *m* as the letter that stands for "mmm" as in *moon.* In this way, you are presenting the correspondence in isolation *and* in context. Students encounter the correspondence in a real word but also hear it alone. Hearing the consonant pronounced in isolation is especially important for poor readers because some students have difficulty abstracting sounds from words, detecting the /m/ in *moon,* for instance. The following sample lesson combines the best features of an explicit and an implicit approach.

### *Combined Approach to Teaching Consonant Correspondences*

**Consonant Correspondence Lesson**

*Step 1: Auditory Perception*

Hold up a series of objects or pictures of objects whose names begin with *s:* saw, six, socks, seal, sandwich. Have students say the name of each object. Repeat the names of all the objects, emphasizing the initial sound as you do so. Lead students to see that the words all begin with the same sound. Present the sound both in isolation and in the context of a word. (Although saying the sound in isolation

## Consonant Correspondence Lesson *Continued*

> Adjust instruction for students who are not native speakers of English. Students whose first language is Spanish may have difficulty perceiving the consonant sounds /b/, /v/, /k/, /j/, /z/, /sh/, /th/, and /ch/. Spend extra time developing perception of these sounds and stress the use of context.

distorts it, some youngsters have difficulty detecting a sound in the context of a word.) Say that *saw, six, socks, seal,* and *sandwich* begin with the sound /s/ as in *sun.* If any members of the class have first names that begin with *s,* ask them to raise their hands. Help the class determine whether or not the names do actually begin with *s.*

If students have difficulty detecting initial sounds, try asking silly questions that focus on *s.* Holding up a sock, ask, "Is this a lock? Is this a rock?" Lead students to see that *lock* and *rock* begin with the wrong sounds and must be changed to /s/ to make *sock.* Other silly questions might include the following: "Is this a wheel? (holding up a picture of a seal). Is this a bun?" (holding up a picture of the sun).

### *Step 2: Letter–Sound Integration*

Write the name of each of the objects from Step 1 on the board: *saw, six, socks, seal, sandwich* and *sun.* Read each name and have students tell with which letter each of the words begins. Lead students to see that the letter *s* stands for the sound /s/ heard at the beginning of *saw, six, socks, seal, sandwich* and *sun.* (Create a model word for *s* = /s/. A model word is one that would most likely be a part of the students' listening vocabulary and is used to illustrate a correspondence such as s = /s/. Most model words are easy to depict so they can be accompanied by an illustration. A good model word for *s* = /s/ would be *sun.* Place the model word along with an illustration on a consonant chart. If students forget the sound that a letter represents, the model word accompanied by its picture can be used as a reminder. Tell students if they forget what sound *s* stands for, they can use the Consonant Chart to help them.)

### *Step 3: Guided Practice*

Have students read sentences that contain easy *s* words: *I see the sun. I see Sam.* With the class read labels and signs that contain *s* words, as in the examples listed below.

Salt
For Sale
Soda
Seven Up

### *Step 4: Writing the Target Letter*

> After presenting a few consonants, introduce a vowel or two so students can see how real words are formed and begin to use their skills to read words.

Review the formation of *s,* upper and lowercase. Encourage students to write sentences or stories that contain *s* words.

### *Step 5: Application*

Have students read stories and real world materials that contain easy *s* words. Easy picture books that feature *s* words include *Have You Seen My Cat?* (Carle, 1973) and *Brown Bear, Brown Bear, What Do You See?* (Martin, 1973). If students' skills are too limited for independent or guided reading, use shared reading of big books or create experience stories that contain the target consonant correspondence.

## *Other Consonant Elements*

After learning most of the initial consonant correspondences, students are introduced to consonant digraphs, final consonants, and consonant clusters.

## *Consonant Digraphs*

**Digraph:** two letters that represent one sound, as in *sh* for *ship.* A trigraph consists of three letters representing one sound, as in the *igh* spelling of long *i* in the word *sigh.*

**Consonant digraphs** (*di* = "two", *graphs* = "letter") are correspondences in which single consonant sounds are represented by two letters, as in *shore.* Note that in *shore* two letters are used to spell the initial consonant sound, but in *sure* a single consonant letter is used to spell the beginning consonant sound. Although the beginning sounds in both *shore* and *sure* have the same pronunciation, *shore* contains a digraph but *sure* doesn't. Common digraphs are listed in Table 9-2.

Digraphs are taught in the same fashion as single consonant-letter correspondences are. However, you may want to point out to students that sometimes single sounds are spelled with two letters.

## *Final Consonants*

Final consonant correspondences are generally introduced after most initial-consonant and consonant-digraph correspondences have been taught. Final consonant correspondences can be confusing. For instance, although initial *r, w,* and *y* represent consonant sounds, final *r, w,* and *y* are used to spell vowel sounds (*or, snow, wow, cry, holly*). Sounds represented by spellings may also change. *S* at the beginning of a word represents /s/ but may represent /s/ or /z/ at the end of a word: *bus, has.* However, at least one correspondence, final *c* = /s/, is easier to decode than initial *c* = /s/. Although initial *c* may represent /k/ or /s/ as in *can* and *city,* final *c* is generally accompanied by an *e* that marks the letter as representing /s/, as in *ice* and *face.*

**Cluster:** two or more letters representing two or more sounds, such as the *sc* in *scale* and the *scr* in *scream.* Clusters are also referred to as *blends.*

### *Consonant Clusters*

As their name suggests, ***clusters*** (sometimes known as blends) are composed of two or more letters, but unlike digraphs they represent two or more sounds, as in the *st* (/s/, /t/) in *stop* or the *spl* (/s/, /p/, /l/) in *splash.* Poor readers experience significant difficulty with clusters. Knowing the individual consonant correspondences that make up a cluster doesn't

**TABLE 9-2 Consonant Digraphs**

| Digraphs | Examples |
|---|---|
| ch = /ch/ | **ch**ildren, **ch**ur**ch** |
| ck = /k/ | tra**ck,** sa**ck** |
| gh = /g/ | **gh**ost, **gh**etto |
| gu = /g/ | **gu**ess, **gu**est |
| gh = /f/ | lau**gh,** rou**gh** |
| kn = /n/ | **kn**ow, **kn**ot |
| ng = /ŋ/ | ri**ng,** bri**ng** |
| ph = /f/ | **ph**onics, **ph**easant |
| sh = /sh/ | **sh**op, **sh**ell |
| th = /th/ | **th**ink, **th**umb |
| th = /*th*/ | ***th***is, ***th***at |
| wh = /hw/ or /w/ | **wh**eel, **wh**eat |
| wr = /r/ | **wr**ong, **wr**ite |

guarantee they will be able to decipher it. Although they may be able to read *nail* and *sail,* they stumble over *snail.*

When teaching consonant clusters to poor readers, build on what they already know. Most clusters are composed of *s, l,* or *r* combined with other common consonant letters. A list of clusters is presented in Table 9-3. When introducing a cluster, review the known correspondences that make up the cluster. Before introducing *sp,* for instance, review initial *s* and *p.* Then use a word building technique. Write the words *pot, pin,* and *park* on the chalkboard. Have students read each word. Then ask what letter you would have to put in front of *pot*

**TABLE 9-3 Consonant Clusters**

| | Initial | | Final |
|---|---|---|---|
| **L** | | | |
| bl | **bl**anket, **bl**ue | ld | go**ld**, so**ld** |
| cl | **cl**am, **cl**oud | lf | wo**lf**, she**lf** |
| fl | **fl**ower, **fl**oor | lk | mi**lk**, wa**lk** |
| gl | **gl**ass, **gl**ad | lt | be**lt**, bo**lt** |
| pl | **pl**ate, **pl**ay | | |
| sl | **sl**ide, **sl**ap | | |
| **R** | | | |
| br | **br**ush, **br**ead | — | |
| cr | **cr**ab, **cr**ack | — | |
| dr | **dr**um, **dr**eam | — | |
| fr | **fr**og, **fr**ee | — | |
| gr | **gr**apes, **gr**ay | — | |
| pr | **pr**etzel, **pr**ize | — | |
| tr | **tr**ee, **tr**unk | — | |
| **S** | | | |
| sc | **sc**arecrow, **sc**out | — | |
| sch | **sch**ool, **sch**edule | — | |
| scr | **scr**eam, **scr**ub | — | |
| shr | **shr**ew, **shr**ink | — | |
| sk | **sk**unk, **sk**y | | de**sk**, ma**sk** |
| sl | **sl**ide, **sl**ed | — | |
| sm | **sm**ile, **sm**ell | — | |
| sn | **sn**ake, **sn**eeze | — | |
| sp | **sp**oon, **sp**in | | wa**sp**, gra**sp** |
| spl | **spl**ash, **spl**inter | — | |
| spr | **spr**ing, **spr**ead | — | |
| st | **st**ar, **st**and | | ve**st**, ma**st** |
| str | **str**ing, **str**eet | — | |
| squ | **squ**irrel, **squ**are | — | |
| sw | **sw**ing, **sw**eep | — | |
| **Others** | | | |
| tw | **tw**elve, **tw**ig | ct | a**ct**, effe**ct** |
| qu | **qu**een, **qu**ick | mp | ju**mp**, la**mp** |

to make the word *spot.* After adding the *s,* read the word stressing the /s/ and /p/. Point out that spot begins with an *s* and *p.* Ask volunteers to read the word. Have *spin* and *spark* formed in this same way. After all the words have been read, point out that *sp* stands for the sound heard at the beginning of *spot.*

To provide additional practice with *sp,* dictate a series of *s* and *sp* words to students. Have them write the beginning letter or letters. You might dictate words like *soon, spoon, sank, spank, send* and *spend.* As students write the beginnings of the words, tell them to say the sounds slowly so they can hear whether to write just an *s* or an *sp.* After students have attempted spelling the beginning of a word, write the whole word on the board and have students read it.

Students might also sort words containing *sp* or other clusters. The sort could take a number of forms. Initially, students might sort words according to whether they begin with a single consonant sound or a cluster of sounds Students might then sort words according to which cluster they begin with.

Share read with students selections that contain *sp* words and have students complete a variety of practice exercises. Most important of all, have students read and write stories that contain *sp.* Easy picture books that contain *sp* words include *Spot Goes to the Circus* (Hill, 1986) and *More Spaghetti I Say* (Gelman, 1977).

### *Confusing Consonants*

Two consonant letters that offer special difficulty are *c* and *g* since they can represent two sounds each (*c* = /k/ (*can*), *c* = /s/ (*cent*); *g* = /g/ (*girl*) and *g* = /j/ (*gym*)). When teaching these consonant letters, present the most frequently occurring correspondences in each pair first (*g* = /g/, *c* = /k/). Later, present the less frequently occurring correspondence (*g* = /j/, *c* = /s/). Teaching the following generalizations might also be helpful:

- The letter *c* stands for /k/ when followed by *a, o,* or *u: can, cot, cub.*
- The letter *c* stands for /s/ when followed by *e, i,* or *y: cent, city, cycle.*
- The letter *g* often stands for /g/ when followed by *a, o,* or *u: game, gone, gun.*
- The letter *g* often stands for /j/ when followed by *e, i,* or *y: general, giant, gym.*

For low-achieving readers, who typically don't do well applying generalizations, it would be more helpful to teach them that *g* and *c* each represent two sounds /g/ as in *goat* or /j/ as in *giant* and /k/ as in *cat* and /s/ as in *city.* When they are reading a word beginning with *g,* they should try the /g/ sound first and if that doesn't work, try the /j/ sound. If reading an unfamiliar word beginning with *c,* they should try the /k/ sound first and, if that isn't right, try the /s/ sound. When a group of second-graders who had been taught the generalization encountered the sentence, "We went to the city to catch a train," most read it as "We went to the kitty to catch a train" (Gunning, 1988b). Had they been taught to try alternate pronunciations and to use both phonics and context, there is a better chance that they would have read the sentence accurately. It also would have helped if reading for meaning had been stressed.

To help build awareness of the major sounds that letters represent, create a consonant chart similar to the one in Figure 9-3. The chart depicts major consonant letters and the major sounds these letters represent. When students encounter a letter or letter combination for which they are unable to produce a sound, they can refer to the chart. The chart would

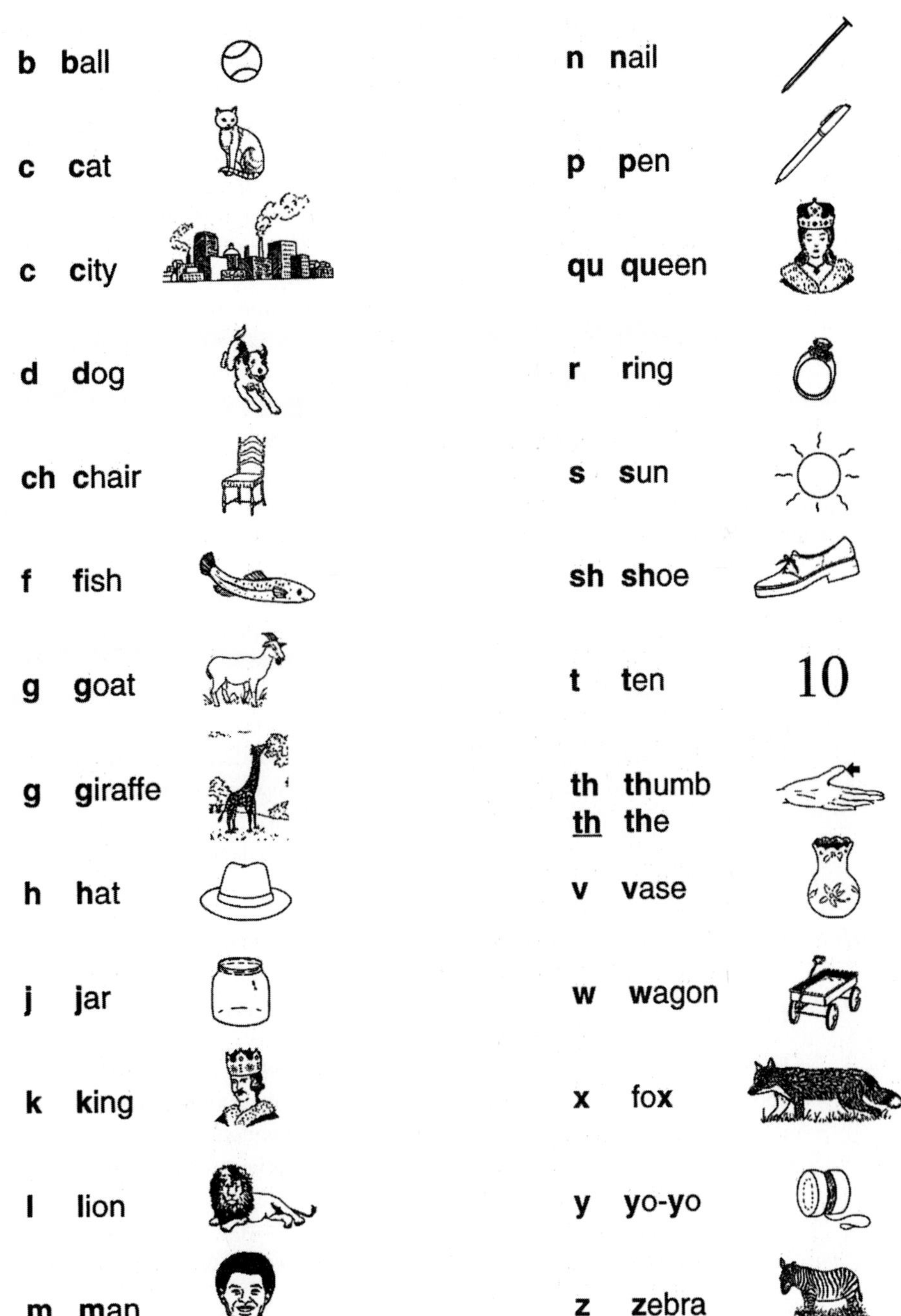


**FIGURE 9-3 Consonant Chart**

From: *Word Building Book A with Predicatable Stories* by T. Gunning, 1996. New York: Phoenix Learning Resources. Reprinted by permission of Galvin Publications.

be especially helpful for deciphering letters that represent multiple sounds. The chart clearly indicates, for example, that *c* represents two distinct sounds as does *g*. After a correspondence has been introduced, add it to the chart. For students who have difficulty remembering initial consonant correspondences, a consonant chart can be a very useful aid, one that fosters both learning and independence.

### Sequence of Teaching Consonants

Consonant correspondences can be taught in any order, but frequency of occurrence and ease of learning should be considered when determining which elements should be taught first. Many low-achieving readers have difficulty with auditory discrimination and perception. Therefore, it's best to start with /s/, /m/, /f/, /r/, /n/, or /w/. These sounds are known as ***continuants,*** which means that they are articulated with a continuous stream of breath. Being articulated in this way makes them easier than stop consonants to detect. These continuants also occur with a high degree of frequency. A suggested scope and sequence for both consonants and vowels is presented in Table 9-4. The sequence is based on the frequency with which the correspondences appear and their estimated level of difficulty (Gunning, 1975).

**Continuant:** speech sound produced by releasing a continuous stream of breath: /f/, /j/, /l/, /m/, /n/, /r/, /s/, /v/, /w/, /ch/, /sh/, /th/, /*th*/, /wh/, /zh/. Continuants are easier to say and detect in isolation.

Although in most programs, consonants are typically taught before vowels and short vowels are taught before long vowels, it is recommended that consonants and vowels be taught together and that easy long-vowel patterns (he, no) be presented before short vowels. After presenting four or five initial consonant correspondences, introduce some easy long vowels, and, as additional consonant correspondences are introduced, gradually present short vowel patterns. If the introduction of consonants and vowels are integrated in this fashion, then it will be possible to form words from elements that have been taught and also to use knowledge of both consonants and vowels to decode words.

## Reinforcement Activities for Consonant Correspondences

### Using Children's Books

Perhaps the best way to provide additional instruction and reinforcement with consonant correspondences is to use children's books. Alphabet books are especially appropriate for introducing and/or reinforcing consonant correspondences, as are books that are alliterative. Some books that would be especially appropriate for providing practice with consonant correspondences are listed below.

Chess, V. (1979). *Alfred's Alphabet Walk.* New York: Greenwillow. Scenes are described with alliterative phrases.

Eastman. P. D. (1974). *The Alphabet Book.* New York: Random House. Each letter is accompanied by alliterative phrases.

Geisel, T. S. (1973). *Dr. Seuss's ABC.* New York: Random House. Each letter is accompanied by a humorous alliterative story.

Kellogg, S. (1987). *Aster Aardvark's Alphabet Adventures.* New York: Morrow. Each letter is accompanied by an alliterative story.

**TABLE 9-4 Sequence for Teaching Vowels and Consonants**

Preparatory Level: Letter Names, Phonemic Awareness

Level 1

High-Frequency Initial Consonants

| | | |
|---|---|---|
| s = /s/ | r = /r/ | d = /d/ |
| m = /m/ | l = /l/ | c = /k/ |
| f = /f/ | b = /b/ | p = /p/ |
| h = /h/ | t = /t/ | n = /n/ |

Easy Long Vowels
-e, -ee = /ē/ (he, me, see)
-o = /ō/ (no, so, go)

Lower-Frequency Initial Consonants and *y*

| | | |
|---|---|---|
| g =/g/ | r = /r/ | z = /z/ |
| w = /w/ | c = /s/ | x = /ks/ |
| j = /j/ | g = /j/ | |
| j = /k/ | y = /y/ | |

High-Frequency Initial Consonant Digraphs

| | |
|---|---|
| ch = /ch/ | th = /*th*/ |
| sh = /sh/ | wh = /hw/ or /w/ |
| th = /th/ | |

Short Vowels
a = /a/ (hat)
e = /e/ (pet)
i = /i/ (sit)
o = /o/ (not)
u = /u/ (but)

Level 2

Final Consonants
High-Frequency Initial Consonant Clusters
L clusters: bl, cl, fl, gl, pl, sl
R clusters: br, cr, dr, fr, gr, pr, tr
S clusters: sc, scr, sk, sl, sm, sn, sp, st, str, sw
Other clusters: tw, qu, ct, mp

Long Vowels: Final-e Marker
a-e = /ā/ (br**a**v**e**)
e-e = /ē/ (th**e**s**e**)
u-e = /ū/ (f**u**s**e**)

Long Vowel Digraphs and Trigraphs
ai/ay = /ā/ (r**ai**n, h**ay**)
ee = /ē/ (tr**ee**)
ea = /ē/ (s**ea**l)
oa = /ō/ (g**oa**t)
ow = /ō/ (cr**ow**)
igh = /ī/ (n**igh**t)

Level 3

Advanced Consonant Correspondences
ti = /sh/ (na**ti**on)
ssi = /sh/ (mi**ssi**on)
ch = /sh/ (**ch**ef)
ch = /k/ (**ch**aracter)

R-Vowel Correspondences
ar = /ar/ (st**ar**)
er = /er/ (h**er**)
ir = /er/ (s**ir**)
ur = /er/ (t**ur**n)
or(e) = /or/ (f**or**, st**ore**)
air = /air/ (ch**air**)
ear = /eer/ (d**ear**)
eer = /eer/ (d**eer**)

Other-Vowel Correspondences
au/aw = /aw/ (**au**to, cl**aw**)
al = /aw/ (b**al**l, w**al**k)
oo = /oo/ (l**oo**k)
oo = /o͞o/ (f**oo**d)
oi/oy = /oy/ (b**oi**l, b**oy**)
ou/ow = /ow/ (**ou**t, c**ow**)
ue, ew = /o͞o/ (tr**ue**, gr**ew**)

Level 4
Multisyllabic Patterns

Note: The teaching of consonant and vowel correspondences should be integrated. After introducing four or five consonants, introduce easy long vowels and, gradually, short vowels as additional consonants are taught.

## *Additional Practice Activities*

To help students remember letter–sound relationships, superimpose an object whose name contains the letter's sound. For instance, *s* written in the form of a snake: the letter *c* curled around a cup.

The following activities can be used to provide added reinforcement for *s* = /s/ or whatever correspondence is being taught.

- Using magnetic or letter cut-outs, have students form *s* words.
- Students read a number of alphabet books and note the different words used to illustrate *s*.
- Students find and read *s* words in sign and food labels.

- Students create their own alphabet books.
- Students write as many *s* words as they can think of.
- Create an alphabet zoo. As a correspondence is introduced, add animals whose names begin with the target correspondence: *seal, salamander, salmon, sardine, sunfish.*
- Encourage students to use context and knowledge of *s* = /s/ to help them decode unfamiliar words that begin with *s*. However, once vowels have been introduced, encourage the use of all the word's letters and sounds.

## *The Content of Phonics: Vowels*

There are fewer vowel than consonant sounds. There are approximately sixteen vowel sounds in English. Table 9-5 shows twenty-one vowel sounds because these include vow-

**TABLE 9-5 Vowel Spellings**

| Vowels Sounds | Examples | Model Word |
|---|---|---|
| *Short Vowels* | | |
| /a/ | hat, batter, have | cat |
| /e/ | ten, better, bread | bed |
| /i/ | fit, little, remain | hit |
| /o/ | hot, bottle, father | mop |
| /u/ | cup, butter | bus |
| *Long Vowels* | | |
| /ā/ | made, nail, radio, hay, flavor | cake |
| /ē/ | he, see, seal, sunny, turkey, these, neither | tree |
| /ī/ | smile, night, pie, spider | bike |
| /ō/ | no, hope, grow, toad, gold, roll, local | goat |
| /ū/ | use, music | mule |
| *Other Vowels* | | |
| /aw/ | ball, walk, paw, song, caught, thought, off | saw |
| /oi/ | joy, join | boy |
| /o͞o/ | zoo, blue, grew, fruit, group, two, | moon |
| /oo/ | took, could, push | book |
| /ow/ | owl, south | cow |
| /ə/ | ago, telephone, similar, opinion, upon | banana |
| *R Vowels* | | |
| /ar/ | car, charge, heart | star |
| /air/ | fair, bear, care, there | chair |
| /eer/ | ear, cheer, here | deer |
| /ir/ | sir, her, earth, turn | bird |
| /or/ | for, four, store, floor | door |

Short vowels are the most frequent (cat, pet, hit, hot, cut). Long vowels "say their own name" (cake, sheep, like, boat, use). R vowels are affected by *r* (car, fair, for, hear, wire). "Other" vowels fall into none of these categories: (paw, box, look, too, cow.)

els affected by *r.* Technically speaking, *r* vowels are not separate entities. However, they pose special problems for readers and so are treated as distinct elements.

Vowel correspondences are said to be irregular because a vowel sound may have a number of different spellings. However, although a vowel sound may have a dozen or more spellings, only three or four of those spellings would be major. For example, long *i* has more than ten spellings: *pine, night, bayou, aisle, height, geyser, lie, coyote, dye, aye, eye* (Mish, 1993) but is most often spelled *i-e, -igh,* or *-y* as in *line, night,* or *try.* Only major spellings of vowels are presented in Table 9-5.

## Vowel Generalizations

Although English vowel sounds can be spelled in approximately 200 ways, the great majority of vowel spellings are covered by five generalizations (Gunning, 1975). These are listed below.

### Short-Vowel Generalization

A vowel is short when it is followed by a consonant: (*bat, sit*). This generalization also applies to multisyllabic words. A vowel in a multisyllabic word is usually short when followed by two or more consonants: (*batter, bitter*). More than one word out of every four follows this generalization.

Poor readers often have difficulty applying generalizations; provide practice in applying words that incorporate generalization.

### Open-Syllable Generalization

A vowel is long when it comes at the end of a word or syllable: *no, na tion, e qual.* This generalization only occurs in about one word out of every five.

### Final e–Marker Generalization

A vowel is long when followed by a consonant and a final silent *e* marker: *cane, time.* This generalization applies to about one word in every twenty.

The most frequent of the vowel sounds is schwa, which is the unaccented vowel sound heard in the second syllable of *sofa.*

### Unstressed-Syllable Generalization

A vowel is given a schwa pronunciation when it occurs in an unaccented syllable: *a bout, di vide.* This generalization occurs in nearly one word out of five. The problem with applying the rule is that the reader would only be able to tell that a syllable is unstressed by pronouncing it.

### Digraph Generalizations

About one out of every six vowel sounds is spelled with two or more letters (Gunning, 1975). However, digraph generalizations have been suffering from bad press for more than twenty years. At one time, there was a generalization that stated, "When two vowels go walking, the first one does the talking." As a blanket generalization, this one doesn't work very well. For one thing, there are many vowel combinations that don't spell long-vowel sounds: *ou (out),* and *ea (bread),* for example. And some digraphs represent a variety of sounds. The digraph *ea,* for instance, represents at least six sounds: *bread, eat, earn, steak, dear,* and *bear.* However, a number of vowel digraphs do occur with a high degree of frequency and consistency. These include the following:

Since *ow* might represent a long *o* sound (tow) or the /ow/ sound (cow), students need to apply the *meaning* test. If they try one pronunciation and that does not result in a meaningful word that fits the context, they should try the other pronunciation.

| | | | |
|---|---|---|---|
| ai/ay = /ā/ | paid/pay | oa = /ō/ | boat |
| au/aw = /aw/ | cause/saw | oi/oy = /oi/ | boil/boy |
| ea = /ē/ | beak | oo = /o͞o/ | soon |
| ea = /e/ | bread | oo = /oo/ | book |
| ew = /o͞o/ | flew | ou/ow = /au/ | out, town |
| ee = /ē/ | see | ow = /ō/ | snow |
| ie = /ē/ | field | | |

Although vowel correspondences are basically regular and fall, for the most part, into five spelling patterns, there are a number of exceptions. Because of this, students should be taught a flexibility strategy. They need to know that many individual vowel letters and vowel digraphs can represent more than one sound. They should also know what those vowel sounds are. Then if they try one pronunciation and that doesn't work out, they should try another.

One device that helps students deal with the variability of English spellings is a vowel decoding chart such as the one presented in Table 9-6. The decoding chart lists spellings and then gives the vowel sounds most frequently represented by those spellings. The vowel decoding chart lists high-frequency vowel spellings such as *ea* that may represent more

**TABLE 9-6 Decoding Chart for High-Frequency Variable Vowel Patterns**

| Vowel Spelling | Corresponding Sound |
|---|---|
| b**ea**d | /ē/ |
| br**ea**d | /e/ |
| br**ea**k | /ā/ |
| **ea**r | /ēr/ |
| b**ea**r | /air/ |
| f**i**nd | /ī/ |
| w**i**nd (moving air) | /i/ |
| r**o**ll | /ō/ |
| d**o**ll | /o/ |
| w**oo**d | /oo/ |
| f**oo**d | /o͞o/ |
| l**o**st | /aw/ |
| m**o**st | /ō/ |
| c**ow** | /ow/ |
| cr**ow** | /ō/ |

than one sound. Infrequently occurring items like the vowel spellings of *said, says,* and *friend* are not listed.

> Homographs demonstrate the need to integrate sounding out and context. You can't assign an accurate meaning and pronunciation to words like *lead, produce, wound, bow* until you see how the word is used in context.

Here is an example of how students might use the chart. Coming across the word *own,* the student reads, John had his own /own/ (rhymes with *town*) money. Realizing that /own/ is not a word and the sentence doesn't make sense, the reader searches for *ow* on the chart. Noting that *ow* can also have long *o* in addition to an /ow/ pronunciation, the student constructs the word *own* (/ōn/). The student sees that own (/ōn/) is a real word and also makes sense in the sentence. Like other strategies, this one should be modeled and reinforced with guided practice and application. As students learn alternative pronunciations for spellings, they should gradually learn to apply the flexibility strategy without the help of the chart.

## *Approaches to Teaching Vowels*

Vowels may be taught implicitly, explicitly, or in a pattern, or word-building approach. A typical lesson has the same five steps as that of a consonant correspondence lesson. In a way, vowels are easier to teach because vowels can be pronounced in isolation without distortion. Here is how short *o* might be taught in an inductive implicit lesson.

### *Vowel Correspondence Approach*

#### Vowel Correspondence Lesson

*Step 1: Auditory Perception*

Hold up a *pot,* a *mop,* and a *sock.* Have students name each of the objects. Ask students what is the same about the words, *pot, mop,* and *sock.* Lead them to see that all three words have an /o/ sound. Discuss other words that have an /o/ sound: *hop, stop, clock.*

*Step 2: Letter–Sound Integration*

Write *pot, mop,* and *sock* on the chalkboard, saying each word as you do so. Point out the *o* in each word and lead students to see that the *o* makes the /o/ sound heard in *pot, mop,* and *sock.* Have students individually and as a group read the words. Discuss other words that have the sound of /o/. Ask if there is anyone in the room whose name has an /o/ sound: *Tom* or *Rob,* for example. If so, write their names on the board. Read the names and have the class read them.

*Step 3: Guided Practice*

Share read a big book, experience story, song or rhyme, or other piece that has a number of short *o* words. Stop when you come to a short *o* word and invite the class to read the word.

*Step 4: Application*

Have students read easy books such as *Who Is Who?* (McKissack, 1983,) or one of Eric Hill's *Spot* books, or other pieces that contain short *o* words. Easy-to-read books that reinforce vowel correspondences are listed in Table 9-7.

## TABLE 9-7 Books That Reinforce Vowel Patterns

**Short-Vowel Patterns**

*Short a*

Allen, J. (1987). *My first job.* Aro Publishing.
Antee, N. (1985). *The good bad cat.* Grand Haven, MI: School Zone.
Carle, E. (1987). *Have you seen my cat?* New York: Scholastic.
Hawkins, C. & Hawkins, J. (1983). *Pat the cat.* New York: Putnam.
Moncure, J. B. (1981). *Word Bird makes words with cat.* Elgin, IL: The Child's World.
Wildsmith, B. (1982). *Cat on the mat.* New York: Oxford.
Ziefert, H. (1988). *Cat games.* New York: Puffin.

*Short e*

de Rubertis, B. (1997). *Penny Hen.* New York: Kane.
Gregorich, B. (1984). *Nine men chase a hen.* Grand Haven, MI: School Zone Publishing Company.
Snow, P. (1984). *A pet for pat.* Chicago: Children's Press.

*Short i*

de Rubertis, B. (1997). *Bitty Fish.* New York: Kane.
Greydanus, R. (1988). *Let's get a pet.* Mahwah, NJ: Troll.
Wang, M. L. (1989). *The ant and the dove.* Chicago: Children's Press.

*Short o*

de Rubertis, B. (1997). *Foxy Fox.* New York: Kane.
McKissack, P. C. (1983). *Who is who?* Chicago: Children's Press.
Moncure, J. B. (1981). *No! no! Word Bird.* Elgin, IL: The Child's World.

*Short u*

de Rubertis, B. (1997). *Lucky Duck.* New York: Kane.
Foster & Erickson (1991). *The bug club.* Hauppauge, NY: Barron's.
Gregorich, B. (1984). *The gum on the drum.* Grand Haven, MI: School Zone Publishing Company.
Lewison, W. C. (1992). *Buzzz said the bee.* New York: Scholastic.
McKissack, P. & McKissack, F. (1988). *Bugs!* Chicago: Children's Press.
Petrie,C. (1983). *Joshua James likes trucks.* Chicago: Children's Press.
Ziefert, H. (1987). *Nicky upstairs and down.* New York: Puffin.

*Short-Vowel Review*

Boegehold, B. D. (1990). *You are much too small.* New York: Bantam.
Kraus, R. (1971). *Leo, the late bloomer.* NewYork: Simon & Schuster.

**Long-Vowel Patterns**

*Long a*

de Rubertis, B. (1997). *Janey Crane.* New York: Kane.
Neasi, B. J. (1984). *Just like me.* Chicago: Children's Press.
Oppenheim, J. (1990). *Wake up, baby!* New York: Bantam.
Raffi. (1987). *Shake my sillies out.* New York: Crown.
Robart, R. (1986). *The cake that Mack ate.* Toronto: Kids Can Press.
Stadler, J. (1984). *Hooray for Snail!* New York: Harper.

*Long e*

Bonsall, C. (1974). *And I mean it, Stanley.* New York: Harper.
de Rubertis, B. (1997). *Zeeley Zebra.* New York: Crane.
Greene, C. (1983). *Ice is . . . whee!* Chicago: Children's Press.
Hutchins, P. (1972). *Good night, Owl!* New York: Macmillan.
Shaw, N. (1986). *Sheep in a jeep.* Boston: Houghton Mifflin.
Ziefert, H. (1988). *Dark night, sleepy night.* New York: Puffin Books.
Ziefert, H. (1990). *Follow me!* New York: Puffin Books.

**TABLE 9-7** *Continued*

*Long i*

de Rubertis, B. (1997). *Tiny Tiger.* New York: Crane.
Gelman, R. G. (1977). *More spaghetti I say.* New York: Scholastic.
Hoff, S. (1988). *Mrs. Brice's mice.* New York: Harper.
Ziefert, H. (1987). *Jason's bus ride.* New York: Random House.
Ziefert, H. (1987). *A new house for Mole and Mouse.* New York: Puffin.
Ziefert, H. (1984). *Sleepy dog.* New York: Random House.

*Long o*

de Rubertis, B. (1997). *Joey Goat.* New York: Kane.
Hamsa, B. (1985). *Animal babies.* Chicago: Children's Press.
Oppenheim, J. (1992). *The show-and-tell frog.* New York: Bantam.
Schade, S. (1992). *Toad on the road.* New York: Random.

*Review of Long Vowels*

Matthias, C. (1983). *I love cats.* Chicago: Children's Press.
Parish, P. (1974). *Dinosaur time.* New York: Harper.
Phillips, J. (1986). *My new boy.* New York: Random House.
Ziefert, H. (1985). *A dozen dogs.* New York: Random House.

**R and Other Vowel Patterns**

*R Vowels*

Hooks, W. H. (1992). *Feed Me!* New York: Bantam.
Penner, R. (1991). *Dinosaur babies.* New York: Random.
Wynne, P. (1986). *Hungry, hungry sharks.* New York: Random House.

*/aw/ Vowels*

Oppenheim, J. (1993). *"Uh-oh!" said the crow.* New York: Bantam.
Oppenheim, J. (1991). *The donkey's tale.* New York: Bantam.

*/$\overline{oo}$/ Vowels*

Blocksma, M. (1992). *Yoo Hoo, Moon!* New York: Bantam.
Brenner, B. (1990). *Moon boy.* New York: Bantam.
Wiseman, B. (1959). *Morris the moose.* New York: Harper.

*/oo/ Vowels*

Platt, K. (1965). *Big Max.* New York: Harper.

*/ow/ Vowels*

Lobel, A. (1975). *Owl at home.* New York: Harper.
Oppenheim, J. (1989). *"Not now!" said the cow.* New York: Bantam.
Siracusa, C. (1991). *Bingo, the best dog in the world.* New York: Harper Collins.

*/oy/ Vowels*

Marshall, J. (1990). *Fox be nimble.* New York: Pufffin.

*Review of R and Other Vowels*

Brenner, B. (1989). *Annie's pet.* New York: Bantam.
Brenner, B. (1992). *Beavers beware.* New York: Bantam.
Hopkins, L. B. (1986). *Surprises.* New York: Harper.
Marshall, E. (1985). *Four on the shore.* New York: E. P. Dutton.
Marshall, E. (1985). *Fox on wheels.* New York: E. P. Dutton.
Milton, J. (1985). *Dinosaur days.* New York: Random House.
Rylant, C. (1987). *Henry and Mudge: The first book.* New York: Bradbury Press.

## Pattern Approach

A popular approach to teaching phonics is to present elements in patterns or phonograms. In a linguistic spelling-pattern approach, students learn both vowel and consonant elements by contrasting pattern words. The words *pet, wet, set,* and *jet* might all be presented at the same time. The teacher reads these words, spells them, and has students spell and read them. Students are also directed to contrast the words, noting, for instance, how *pet* and *wet* have a common element but differ. A major problem with the linguistic pattern approach has been the use of contrived reading material. However, patterns may be presented through an approach known as word building. This approach takes advantage of the regularity of a pattern approach, is based on the way students actually decode words, and espouses natural rather than artificial language.

## Word-Building Approach

Because it actively involves students in constructing words, the most effective way to introduce patterns is through a word-building approach (Gunning, 1995). In a word-building approach, beginning consonants are added to vowel patterns (*h + e = he, sh + ow = show*) and vowel-consonant patterns (*h + at = hat, g + et = get*). Research suggests that patterns have a more stable pronunciation and are easier to learn, especially when they are broken up into their onset and rime (Adams, 1990; Glushko, 1979; Goswami, 1986, 1988; Goswami & Bryant, 1992; Santa, 1976–1977). The ***rime*** is the rhyming part of the word, the part that begins with a vowel (*-et*). The ***onset*** is the word's initial consonant or consonant combination (*g-*). From a linguist's point of view, onset and rime seem to be the natural parts of a word or syllable (Tremain, 1992). A list of common rimes and words containing those rimes is presented in Table 9-8.

> The **rime** is the part of the word that begins with the vowel. It is the portion that rhymes. The *o* in *no,* the *ip* in *trip,* and the *eam* in *stream* are rimes.

> The **onset** is the part of the word that precedes a vowel. It could be a consonant (*t + eam*), digraph (*th + eme*), or cluster (*st + eam*).

The word-building approach also fits in with the way students naturally decipher printed words. When they attack unknown words, both achieving and problem readers seek out pronounceable word parts (Hardy, Stennett, & Smythe, 1973; Glass, 1976; Gunning, 1988a). Encountering the word *trust,* students might read it as "us-rus-trust". The word *chip* might be read as "ip-chip". Except for the final *e,* second-graders who were observed attacking unfamiliar words made little use of phonics generalizations and rarely sounded out words letter by letter, even though half the students had been taught by an explicit phonics approach. Most sought out and used pronounceable word parts (Gunning, 1988a).

When initiating the word-building approach, it is best to begin with long rather than short vowels because long vowels have stronger, more distinctive sounds which are easier for students, especially low-achieving readers, to perceive. A good choice would be long *o* or long *e* because words can be formed by simply adding an initial consonant (*go, no, so; be, he, me*). If your students have a Spanish language background, long *o* is the better choice because both Spanish and English have a long *o* sound which is spelled with the letter *o.* The box shows how a word-building lesson might be structured.

> Because long vowels are easier to discriminate than short vowels, this text recommends starting with the long vowels before presenting short-vowel patterns: *-e* (*he, me, we, she, be*), *-ee* (*bee, see, tree*), and *-o* (*go, no, so*).

## TABLE 9-8 Major Word Patterns

Short Vowels

| **-ab** | **-ack** | **-ad** | **-ag** | **-am** | **-amp** | **-an** | **-and** | **-ang** | **-ank** |
|---|---|---|---|---|---|---|---|---|---|
| cab | back | bad | bag | *ham | camp | an | and | bang | *bank |
| tab | jack | dad | rag | jam | damp | can | band | gang | sank |
| *crab | pack | had | tag | slam | *lamp | fan | *hand | hang | tank |
| | sack | mad | wag | swam | stamp | man | land | *rang | blank |
| | *tack | *sad | drag | | | *pan | sand | sang | thank |
| | black | glad | *flag | | | tan | stand | | |
| | crack | | | | | plan | | | |
| | stack | | | | | than | | | |
| **-ap** | **-at** | | **-ed** | **-ell** | **-en** | **-end** | **-ent** | **-ess** | **-est** |
| cap | at | | bred | *bell | den | end | bent | guess | best |
| lap | bat | | fed | fell | hen | bend | dent | less | nest |
| *map | *cat | | led | tell | men | lend | rent | mess | pest |
| tap | fat | | red | well | pen | mend | sent | bless | rest |
| clap | hat | | shed | yell | *ten | *send | *tent | *dress | test |
| slap | pat | | *sled | shell | then | tend | went | press | *vest |
| snap | rat | | | smell | when | spend | spent | | west |
| trap | sat | | | spell | | | | | chest |
| wrap | that | | | | | | | | guest |
| **-et** | **-ead** | | **-ick** | **-id** | **-ig** | **-ill** | **-im** | **-in** | **-ing** |
| bet | dead | | kick | did | big | bill | dim | in | king |
| get | head | | lick | hid | dig | fill | him | fin | *ring |
| jet | read | | pick | kid | *pig | *hill | skim | *pin | sing |
| let | *bread | | sick | *lid | wig | kill | slim | sin | wing |
| met | spread | | click | rid | twig | pill | *swim | tin | bring |
| *net | thread | | *stick | skid | | will | | win | sting |
| pet | | | thick | slid | | chill | | chin | thing |
| set | | | trick | | | skill | | grin | |
| wet | | | quick | | | spill | | skin | |
| | | | | | | | | spin | |
| | | | | | | | | thin | |
| | | | | | | | | twin | |
| **-ink** | **-ip** | **-it** | | **-ob** | **-ock** | **-op** | **-ot** | | **-ust** |
| link | dip | it | | job | dock | cop | dot | | bust |
| pink | lip | bit | | mob | *lock | hop | got | | dust |
| *sink | rip | fit | | rob | rock | *mop | hot | | just |
| wink | tip | *hit | | sob | sock | pop | lot | | *must |
| blink | zip | kit | | *knob | block | top | not | | rust |
| clink | chip | sit | | | clock | chop | *pot | | trust |
| drink | flip | knit | | | flock | drop | shot | | |
| stink | *ship | quit | | | knock | shop | spot | | |
| think | skip | split | | | | stop | | | |
| | trip | | | | | | | | |
| | whip | | | | | | | | |
| **-ut** | **-ub** | **-uck** | **-ug** | **-um** | **-ump** | **-un** | **-unk** | **-us(s)** | |
| but | cub | *duck | bug | bum | bump | bun | bunk | *bus | |
| cut | rub | luck | dug | hum | dump | fun | hunk | plus | |
| hut | sub | cluck | hug | yum | hump | gun | junk | us | |
| nut | tub | stuck | mug | *drum | *jump | run | sunk | fuss | |
| shut | club | struck | *rug | plum | lump | *sun | shrunk | muss | |
| | scrub | truck | tug | | pump | spun | *skunk | | |
| | | | chug | | thump | | stunk | | |
| | | | | | stump | | | | |

*Possible model words

*Continued*

**TABLE 9-8** *Continued*

Long Vowels

| **-ace** | **-ade** | **-age** | **-ake** | **-ale** | **-ame** | **-ape** | **-ate** | **-ave** | **-ail** |
|---|---|---|---|---|---|---|---|---|---|
| *face | fade | age | bake | pale | came | ape | ate | *cave | fail |
| race | *made | *cage | *cake | sale | game | *cape | date | gave | jail |
| place | grade | page | lake | tale | *name | tape | *gate | save | mail |
| space | shade | rage | make | *scale | same | scrape | hate | wave | *nail |
| | trade | stage | rake | | tame | grape | late | brave | pail |
| | | | take | | blame | shape | mate | | sail |
| | | | wake | | shame | | plate | | tail |
| | | | flake | | | | skate | | snail |
| | | | shake | | | | state | | trail |
| | | | snake | | | | | | |

| **-ain** | **-ay** | | **-eel** | **-ea** | **-each** | **-eak** | **-eal** | **-eam** | **-ean** |
|---|---|---|---|---|---|---|---|---|---|
| main | bay | | feel | pea | each | *beak | deal | team | *bean |
| pain | day | | heel | sea | beach | leak | heal | *dream | lean |
| rain | *hay | | kneel | *tea | *peach | peak | meal | scream | mean |
| brain | lay | | steel | flea | reach | weak | real | stream | clean |
| chain | may | | *wheel | | teach | creak | *seal | | |
| grain | pay | | | | bleach | sneak | squeal | | |
| *train | say | | | | | speak | steal | | |
| | way | | | | | squeak | | | |
| | gray | | | | | | | | |
| | play | | | | | | | | |

| **-eat** | **-ee** | **-eed** | **-eep** | **-eet** | | **-ice** | **-ide** | **-ile** | **-ime** |
|---|---|---|---|---|---|---|---|---|---|
| eat | *bee | deed | beep | *feet | | *mice | hide | mile | *dime |
| beat | see | feed | deep | meet | | nice | ride | pile | lime |
| neat | free | *seed | *jeep | sheet | | rices | side | *smile | time |
| *seat | knee | weed | keep | sleet | | lice | wide | while | chime |
| cheat | tree | bleed | peep | sweet | | twice | *bride | | |
| treat | | freed | weep | | | | slide | | |
| wheat | | speed | creep | | | | | | |
| | | | sleep | | | | | | |
| | | | steep | | | | | | |
| | | | sweep | | | | | | |

| **-ine** | **-ite** | **-ive** | **-ie** | **-ind** | **-y** | | **-o, -oe** | **-oke** | **-ole** |
|---|---|---|---|---|---|---|---|---|---|
| fine | bite | dive | die | find | by | | go | joke | hole |
| line | *kite | *five | lie | kind | guy | | *no | poke | mole |
| mine | quite | hive | pie | *mind | my | | so | woke | *pole |
| *nine | white | live | *tie | blind | dry | | doe | broke | stole |
| pine | | drive | | | fly | | hoe | *smoke | whole |
| | | | | | *sky | | toe | spoke | |
| | | | | | try | | | | |
| | | | | | why | | | | |

| **-one** | **-ope** | **-ose** | **-ote** | **-oad** | **-oat** | **-ow** | **-old** | | **u-e** |
|---|---|---|---|---|---|---|---|---|---|
| bone | hope | hose | *note | load | boat | bow | old | | use |
| cone | nope | *nose | vote | *road | coat | low | cold | | fuse |
| *phone | *rope | rose | quote | toad | *goat | tow | fold | | *mule |
| shone | slope | chose | wrote | | float | blow | hold | | huge |
| | | close | | | | glow | *gold | | |
| | | those | | | | grow | sold | | |
| | | | | | | slow | told | | |
| | | | | | | *snow | | | |

**TABLE 9-8** *Continued*

| Other Vowels and R-Vowels | | | | | | | | | |
|---|---|---|---|---|---|---|---|---|---|
| **-all** | **-aw** | **-au** | | **-oss** | **-ost** | **-ought** | | **-oil** | **-oy** |
| *ball | caw | fault | | boss | cost | ought | | *boil | *boy |
| call | jaw | caught | | loss | *lost | *bought | | soil | joy |
| fall | paw | taught | | toss | frost | fought | | | toy |
| hall | *saw | | | *cross | | broug | | | |
| wall | claw | | | | | | | | |
| small | draw | | | | | | | | |
| | straw | | | | | | | | |
| **-oud** | **-our** | **-out** | **-ound** | **-ow** | **-own** | | **-ood** | **-ould** | |
| loud | our | out | bound | ow | down | | good | *could | |
| *cloud | *hour | *shout | found | bow | gown | | hood | would | |
| proud | sour | scout | hound | cow | town | | *wood | should | |
| | flour | spout | mound | how | brown | | stood | | |
| | | | pound | now | clown | | | | |
| | | | *round | plow | *crown | | | | |
| | | | sound | | | | | | |
| | | | wound | | | | | | |
| | | | ground | | | | | | |
| **-ook** | | **-air** | **-are** | **-ear, ere** | | **-ar** | **-ark** | **-ard** | **-art** |
| *book | | fair | care | *bear | | *car | bark | *card | art |
| cook | | *hair | hare | pear | | far | dark | guard | part |
| hook | | pair | share | there | | jar | mark | hard | *chart |
| look | | chair | scare | where | | star | park | | smart |
| took | | | spare | | | | *shark | | |
| shook | | | *square | | | | spark | | |
| **-ear** | **-eer** | | **-or** | **-orn** | **-ort** | | | | |
| *ear | *deer | | *or | born | *fort | | | | |
| dear | cheer | | for | *corn | port | | | | |
| fear | steer | | nor | torn | sort | | | | |
| hear | | | more | worn | short | | | | |
| near | | | sore | | sport | | | | |
| year | | | tore | | | | | | |
| clear | | | wore | | | | | | |

## Word-Building Lesson

*Step 1: Adding the Onset (Initial Consonant)*

Write the letter *o* on the board and ask for a volunteer to identify it. Explain to students that the letter *o* says its own name: /ō/. Point to the letter *o* and have students say its sound. Tell students that you want to form some words. Ask them to tell what letter needs to be placed in front of *o* to make the word *go.* (It's helpful, but not necessary, if students have learned initial consonants.) If no one is able to respond correctly, tell the class that the letter *g* when put in front of *o* spells *go.* Have volunteers read the word. Directly under the word *go,* write another *o.* Ask students to tell what sound *o* makes and what letter should be placed in front of

It is possible to start Word Building before students have learned consonant correspondences. However, it works better if students know at least ten consonant correspondences.

*Continued*

**Word-Building Lesson** *Continued*

*o* to make the word *no.* After *no* has been formed, have students tell how *no* is different from *go* and read both words. Introduce *so* in the same way. Encourage volunteers to read the whole list of words.

*Step 2: Adding the Rime (Vowel Pattern)*

When presenting pattern words, limit the number introduced to five or six. Focus on the highest-frequency words and words that students will meet in upcoming selections.

To make sure that students have a thorough grasp of both key parts of the word—the onset and the rime—present the consonant and have students add the vowel. Writing *g* on the chalkboard, ask students to say the sound it stands for (saying consonant sounds in isolation distorts them, but it helps students, especially those who are having difficulty detecting individual sounds in words, make the necessary connection between letters and sounds). Then ask them to tell what you would add to /g/ to make *go.* Adding *o* to *g,* say the word sound by sound and then as a whole. Pointing to *g,* say /g/; pointing to *o,* say /ō/. Running your hand under the whole word, say "go." Present *no* and *so* in the same way and have students read all three words.

*Step 3: Mixed Practice*

Realizing that they are learning words that all end in the same way, students may focus on the initial letter and fail to take careful note of the rest of the word, the rime. After presenting a pattern, mix in words from previously presented patterns and have these read. For instance, after presenting the *o* pattern, you might have students read the following words: *he, so, say, see, go, me, no, way* (assuming that *-ay* and *-e* patterns have been taught). This provides students practice in processing both the onset and the rime and also reviews previously presented patterns.

*Step 4: Introducing the Model Word*

Choose one of the pattern words to be a model word. Select a word that has a high frequency, is easy, and—if possible—which can be depicted. For the long *o* pattern, you might choose *no,* which could be depicted by the universal sign for *no,* a circle with a diagonal slash, or *go,* which could be depicted by a traffic signal that has turned green. Post the model word on a model words chart. An illustrated chart of model words for high-frequency short-vowel patterns is presented in Figure 9-4. (For a more complete listing of model words, see the pattern words in Table 9-8. Possible model words are marked with an asterisk.) Create a model words chart for your class. After a pattern has been introduced, add its model word to the chart. If students forget the pattern, they can refer to the model words chart.

*Step 5: Guided Practice*

Keep a close relationship between the phonics you teach and the phonics students need; preview an upcoming selection and choose a new phonics element they have not mastered.

On the chalkboard write sentences using the new words. Read the sentences to students but pause before new words and have students read them. Display signs using the new words or take a walk and examine signs that use the new words: No Smoking, No Parking. Share read a book that contains a number of *o* words. Sorting activities also provide excellent reinforcement. After being introduced to *-o, -oe,* and *o-e* patterns, students might be asked to sort them. This helps them to note differences in patterns and to generate their own conclusions about how the patterns are spelled.

*Step 6: Application*

Phonics programs for corrective readers are typically heavy on instruction and practice and light on application, with countless hours being spent on workbook pages. Actually, what corrective students need most is the opportunity to apply skills to real reading. Irene Gaskins (personal communication, December 2, 1993) found that the best indicator of success in the Benchmark Program, a word-analysis program for low-achieving readers, is *extension.* Extension is the application of a pattern to a difficult word. To apply a correspondence that was just taught, choose a selection that contains a number of words that fit the target pattern. Walk students through the selection. Discuss the title and illustrations, clarify unfamiliar concepts, point out and read to them difficult words (they should follow along

**Word-Building Lesson** *Continued*

with you in their books). Place particular emphasis on words that follow the pattern you just introduced. Note a sentence or caption that contains a pattern word and ask them to find the pattern word and point it out to you. If the sentence or caption is not too difficult, have them read it as well. For younger students, a book such as *No, No, Joan* (Issacsen-Bright & Holland, 1986) would be an excellent choice. With just one line of print per page and with each page illustrated, this book could be read by students with a minimum of help from you. Through repeated readings, students could learn to read the book fluently, even though their skills might be minimal. Older students and adult novice readers might be encouraged to read the book aloud to a younger student or child so they don't feel that they are doing something babyish. Or they might be helped to read an easy book that is on their level of maturity.

Students might also create experience stories using their new words. They might write about places to which they like to go, for example; or a time when they felt *so* happy or *so* sad; or what life might be like if there were *no* TV or *no* cars. (See Figure 9-5 for an overview of a word-building lesson.)

An interactive approach to decoding combines sounding out, meaning, and familiarity. For instance, *vat* is harder to decode than *cat* or *fat* because *vat* occurs less frequently and would not be in some students' listening vocabularies.

### *Presenting Short Vowel Patterns*

Short vowels seldom appear alone; in most instances a short vowel is followed by a consonant. Therefore, when presenting short vowels, it is important that the vowel be followed by a consonant so that students learn to see natural units. In presenting short *e,* for instance, you might write *et* on the chalkboard, and have students add letters to make *get, let, set,* and *wet.* You could, of course, present a larger number of words containing *et.* However, covering too many words may diminish the student's retention. It's better for the student to focus on a few words and learn them well (Clay, 1985). Lead the students to see that when *e* is followed by a consonant, it generally makes an /e/ sound. Also provide opportunities for mixed practice. For instance, after presenting the *-et* pattern, mix *et* words in with words from a previously presented pattern such as *-ed.* Besides being a good review of the *-ed* pattern, this trains students to use all the word's letters in their decoding processes. Otherwise, students might say the first word in a series of pattern words and then just use the initial consonant to say the rest. If students fail to use all the letters when reading on their own, they may misread *bed* for *bet* or *led* for *let,* etc.

**Exemplary Teaching Lesson 9-1: Building on the Known**

In assisting Marilyn, a second-grader who had been recommended for corrective help because she was a "nonreader," Ms. Marshall, the school's reading teacher, implemented a variation of the word-building technique. Hoping to capitalize upon the knowledge that Marilyn already possessed about written language, she asked her to write any words that she knew. In addition to her name, Marilyn was able to write *cat* and a few other easy words.

Using the word *cat* as a base, Ms. Marshall helped Marilyn build a number of *-at* words: *bat, hat, sat,* and *rat.* During a shared reading of *The Cat in the Hat* (Geisel, 1958), Ms. Marshall paused before the *-at* words and invited Marilyn to read them. Ms. Marshall then introduced Wildsmith's (1982) *Cat on the Mat.* With a little help, Marilyn read the text and asked if she could take it home to read to her mom and dad. She wanted to show them that she had become a reader.

## Model Words

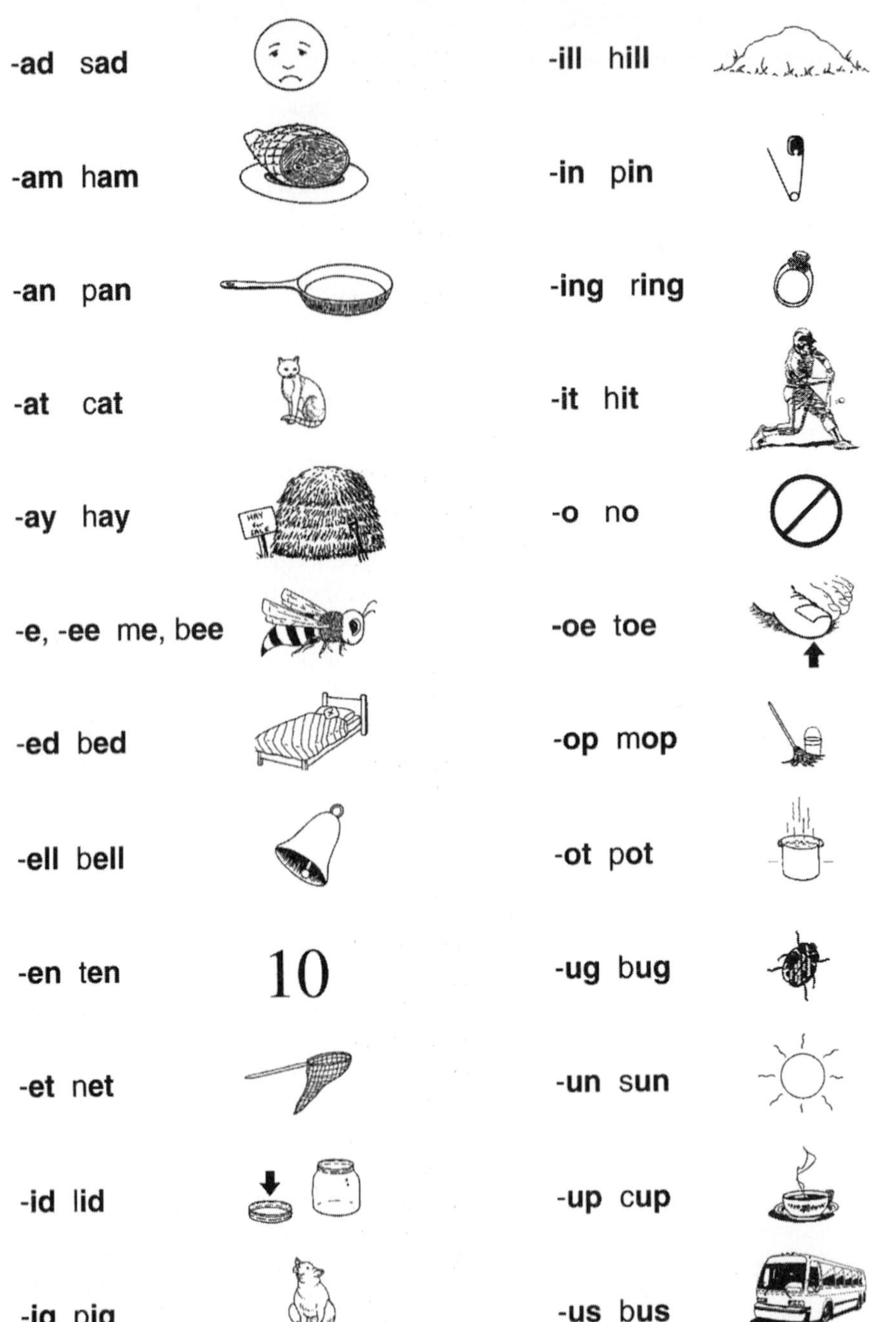


**FIGURE 9-4 Model Words**

From: *Word Building Book A with Predicatable Stories* by T. Gunning, 1996. New York: Phoenix Learning Resources. Reprinted by permission of Galvin Publications.

Step 1: Add the onset. Show teacher adding *g* to *o* on the chalkboard.
Step 2: Add the rime. Show teacher adding *o* to *g*.
Step 3: Provide mixed practice. Teacher is pointing to words on chalkboard as students read them: *no, he, so, see, go.*
Step 4: Introduce the model word. Teacher is writing *no* on the board next to universal sign for *no.*
Step 5: Provide guided practice. Teacher is conducting shared reading with a big book.
Step 6: Apply the pattern. Students are reading books on their own.
Step 7: Extend the pattern. Teacher is writing *goat* on the board.

**FIGURE 9-5 Steps in a Word-Building Lesson**

## *Make-and-Break Technique for Introducing or Reviewing Patterns*

Systematic phonics can make an excellent approach even better. *Reading Recovery* students made more rapid progress when given added phonics (Iverson & Tunmer, 1993).

As an alternative to word building or along with it, you might use the make-and-break technique to introduce patterns. In this approach, students construct, break apart, and reconstruct common word patterns (Iverson & Tunmer, 1993). Choosing the word *and,* for instance, the teacher makes the word with magnetic letters, says the word, and has the student say it. The teacher then jumbles the letters and has the student reassemble the word and say it. This is repeated until the student is able to construct and say the say word with ease. The teacher then puts an *s* in front of *and,* explaining that the word now spells *sand.* The student says the word. The letter *s* is removed, and the teacher explains that the word now says *and.* The student is asked to make the word *sand,* read it, and then make the word *and.* This process is repeated with *band* and *hand.*

## *Whole-Part-Whole Approaches*

Many of the phonics lessons presented have proceeded from the part to the whole. The correspondence or pattern has been presented and then it has been applied within the context of a whole story. However, some practitioners prefer starting with the whole, breaking the whole into parts, and reading a whole selection (Trachtenburg, 1990). Any of the lessons that have been presented can be adapted to start with the whole. For instance, if you were presenting the *-eep* pattern, you might begin by share reading with the class a big book version of *Sheep in a Jeep* (Shaw, 1986). After reading the text and discussing it, point out the *-eep* words. Read the sentences in which the *-eep* words appear. Then proceed to build words using *-eep* as the base just as you would in a word building lesson.

Whole-part-whole approaches might work especially well with students who have had negative experiences with intensive phonics programs. Having failed with his school system's isolated phonics program, which consisted primarily of skills instruction and worksheets, James objected vehemently when his mother attempted to help him with the sheets. "I can't read those," he cried. Having been given too heavy a dose of phonics, James had learned very little about letter–sound relationships. James should be provided a holistic view of reading through the use of easy predictable books or other techniques. Once James has a sense of what reading really is, he might be presented phonics through a holistic children's book technique. To acquaint James with the *-oad* pattern, for instance, share read with him books like *Toad on the Road* (Schade, 1992) or *Railroad Toad* (Schade, 1994). During a rereading of the books, point out and discuss the *-oad* words. Having provided a holistic, successful experience with the *-oad* pattern, the teacher might then build the *-oad* pattern through word building or the make-and-break technique or both. Because it is non-threatening and allows the student to generate her or his own conclusions about patterns, sorting would also be an excellent extension activity for James.

## *Sequence of Teaching Vowels*

Which vowel correspondences should be introduced first? Typically, short vowel correspondences are taught first. These have more predictable spellings and occur with higher frequency. Most often short vowel sounds are spelled CVC (consonant-vowel-consonant), e.g. with the vowel letter that typically represents that sound preceded and followed by a consonant (*cat, pen, tip, pot, tub*). However, this is also the type of sequence that many low-achieving readers have already encountered and have had difficulty with. You might give them a fresh start by presenting some of the easier long vowel correspondences first.

As noted earlier, long vowels are easier to perceive auditorially and, if you introduce only the simplest patterns (go, no, so; bee, see; be, he, me, we, she) are easier to learn to read and spell. Save the final *e*-spellings (hope, note) and digraph-plus-final-consonant spellings (road, coat) until later. A suggested sequence for both vowel and consonant correspondences is presented in Table 9-4. The sequence is based on frequency of occurrence of elements and ease of learning but should be adapted to fit the particular needs of your students. The ultimate determining factor for the sequence of introduction should be the phonics knowledge that your students already possess and their need to know. For instance, if they are about to read a science story about the need for *bees,* then by all means present the *ee* spelling of /ē/.

## *Reinforcement Activities*

### *Using Sorting to Foster Phonics Knowledge*

Sorting helps students discover principles about the way the spelling system works and involves higher level thinking skills as students categorize items.

As noted earlier, an appealing but powerful way to help children discover basic principles of word construction is through sorting. Through sorting, children categorize words according to sound, spelling, meaning, or a combination of features. At the most basic level, pictures can be sorted according to beginning or rhyming sounds. On more advanced levels, words can be sorted according to the spelling patterns they incorporate or the meanings of the words' affixes. Through sorting, students examine each word's features and decide into which category it falls. Thus, they construct their own understanding of the underlying principles that they use to sort words. These principles are clarified and refined in discussions.

So that students receive maximum benefit from this activity, they should only sort words that they can already read or write (Bear, 1995). A good source of words to be sorted would be students' word banks. If the words are familiar, students can then focus on similarities and differences in the structure of the words. Although they may be able to read *hop, mop,* and *top,* students may not have noticed that they all rhyme or that they all follow a CVC pattern. Sorting helps students to construct understandings such as these.

The kinds of sorting activities in which students engage should be determined by their stage of spelling development. Students should also start with simple activities before moving onto more complex ones. Students in the early letter-name stage, for instance, might sort pictures before moving into sorting words. They might then sort words according to beginning consonant. However, they might start with just two easily distinguished categories, such as /m/ and /s/.

Sorts can be open or closed. In a closed sort, students are given the criteria for sorting. In a closed sort of short-*a* patterns, for instance, students would be given a card with the word *cat* on it, a *pan* card, a *bag* card, a *sad* card. Students would then be asked to sort words according to whether they fall in the *-at* (*cat*) pattern, the *-an* (*pan*) pattern, the *-ag* (*bag*) pattern, or the *ad* (*sad*) pattern. In an open sort, students would be given a dozen or so short-*a* cards and asked to sort them. When engaged in open sorting, students have the option of creating a miscellaneous pile (that's a pile of items that don't seem to fit anywhere else). It is important to discuss with students their rationale for sorting words, especially when sorts are open. Knowing why students sort the way they do helps you to better understand their thinking and their decoding development (Bear, 1995). Presented below is a sample lesson using a closed sort format.

**Sorting Patterns by Sound**

*Step 1: Setting Up the Sort*

Set up two or more columns as in Figure 9-6. At the head of each column, place an illustration of the pattern to be sorted. For the *-at, -an,* and *-am* patterns, you might use an illustration of a *cat,* a *pan,* and a *ham.*

*Step 2: Explaining and Modeling Sorting*

If students are not familiar with sorting, explain it to them. Tell them that they will be placing word cards in the *cat, pan,* or *ham* column. If a word rhymes with *cat,* it will be placed in the *cat* pattern, if with *pan,* in the *pan* column, if, with *ham,* in the *ham* column. Shuffle the cards and show how you would sort them. Reading the *van* card, you would say, "Van. Let's see does *van* rhyme with *cat*? No. The ending sound is not the same. Does *van* rhyme with *pan.* Let's see: *van–pan,* they both have the same *an* sound." Sort one or two more words or until students have caught onto the idea.

*Step 3: Sorting of Cards by Students*

Distribute the cards to be sorted. These can be cards that you have made. You could also ask students to make cards. Cards can be sorted as a group or individual activity. In a group activity, an easy way to sort cards is to place the criterion cards in the middle of a table and divide up the cards to be sorted among the students. Students then take turns placing their cards in one of the criterion columns. As students place cards, they should read the words on the cards or name the illustrations on them and explain the basis for their sorting: *hat* has an *-at* sound and rhymes with *cat.* Quickly and simply correct

*Continued*

**Sorting Patterns by Sound** *Continued*

mistakes in sorting. For example, if a student places *tan* in the *cat* column, say *tan* rhymes with *pan* so it goes in the *pan* column (W. Barnes, 1989). A very simple sort entails deciding which items are placed in a one-column sort. For instance, given some cards that rhyme with *cat* and some that don't, students could decide which ones should be placed under *cat*. (Temple, Nathan, Temple, Burris, 1993). At first, students' sorting should be guided. After they have grasped underlying principles and can sort fairly accurately, they can sort independently or with partners or in small groups.

*Step 4: Discussion*

If you haven't already done so, discuss students' responses. The discussion should help students form a generalization about their sorting. You might ask, "Why did you put all the words in this pile?" If a student who has been working independently has missorted a word, you can take one of a number of steps (W. Barnes, 1989).

- Use the missorted word as a basis for sorting. For instance, if the student placed *fence* in the long-*e* column when words were being sorted by long or short *e*, then ask the student to place all the words under *fence* that have an /e/ sound as in *fence*. Make sure, of course, that the student is accurately reading *fence*.
- Ask the student if there are any words that she wishes to change. One problem with this approach is that an unsure student might make wholesale changes of words that are placed correctly.
- Point to the missorted word and ask, "Why did you put that one here?" This gives students a chance to explain their reasoning and also provides the teacher with information about the student's reasoning processes so that the proper kind of assistance can be supplied. Maybe the student missorted a word because he or she was misreading it or was sorting words on the basis of spelling when they should have been sorted on the basis of sound.

*Step 5: Application*

Have students identify words that extend the sort. If students have sorted *-at, -an,* and *-am* words, they might add words such as *Pat, Sam,* and *tan* to the sort. An excellent source of application words would be those that appear in students' reading and writing (Invernizzi, Abouzeid, & Gill, 1994).

Because sorting involves dealing with words in isolation, students need ample opportunity to apply skills by doing lots of reading and writing.

To extend the sort, you might move up to the next level. For instance, you might give students *-ad, -ag,* or *-ap* words and have them engage in an open sort. This will help them discover how each pattern is spelled. Be careful not to move into higher level sorts too quickly, however. As W. Barnes (1989) notes:

> Many teachers ask why a word sort is not mastered the first time it is attempted. The answer is that some children have difficulty generalizing new classifications cognitively. The process is not immediate. Correct and consistent sorting may take place after four or five sessions, but not after the first. (p. 301)

## *Secret Messages*

In addition to being a fun activity, secret messages are designed to provide students with practice in manipulating onsets and rimes or other word-analysis elements (Education Department of Western Australia, 1994). A flexible exercise, secret messages can be geared to virtually any level of competence. Secret messages are formed primarily by adding or deleting parts of words. Once students become proficient at solving secret messages, they can be invited to compose their own.

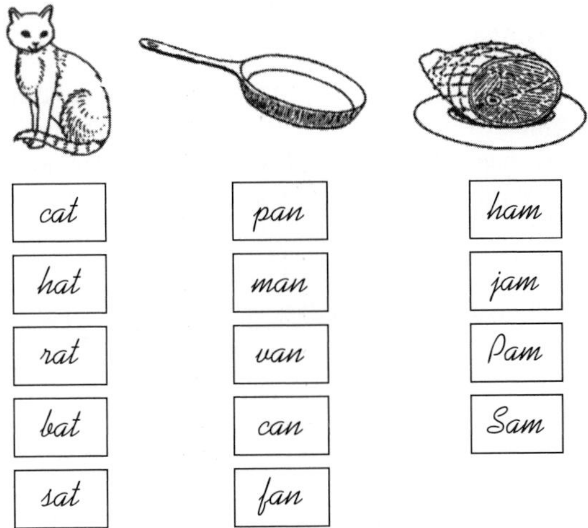


**FIGURE 9-6 Word Sort by Pattern**

Secret messages should be created in such a way that new elements being substituted for old elements have the same sound as the old elements. For instance, taking the *h* from *hash* and substituting *m* so as to make *mash* is acceptable. But substituting *w* for *h* in *hash* would not be since the *ash* in *wash* is not pronounced in the same way as the *ash* in *hash*. Secret messages should also fulfill a specific instructional objective. The first sample secret message is designed to reinforce the *at* pattern. The second was planned to provide practice with initial consonant clusters.

### Secret Message A

1. Take the ***H*** from ***hats*** and put ***C*** in its place. __ __ __ __
2. Take the ***t*** from ***to*** and put ***d*** in its place. __ __
3. Take the ***h*** from ***hot*** and put ***n*** in its place. __ __ __
4. Take the ***b*** from ***bike*** and put ***l*** in its place. __ __ __ __
5. Take the ***b*** from ***bats*** and put ***r*** in its place. __ __ __ __

__ __ __ __  __ __  __ __ __  __ __ __ __  __ __ __ __.

### Secret Message B

1. Add ***F*** to ***lying.*** __ __ __ __ __ __
2. Take ***c*** from ***cakes*** and put ***sn*** in its place. __ __ __ __ __ __
3. Take ***g*** from ***give*** and put ***l*** in its place. __ __ __ __
4. Take ***t*** from ***tin.*** __ __
5. Take ***f*** from ***free*** and put ***t*** in its place. Add ***s*** at the end. __ __ __ __ __

__ __ __ __ __ __  __ __ __ __ __ __  __ __ __ __  __ __  __ __ __ __ __.

## *Using Writing to Reinforce Phonics*

Through writing, students can make important discoveries about letter–sound relationships. Students who are at a rudimentary stage of spelling development should be allowed to use invented spelling. If a student has difficulty spelling a word, have her or him sound it out. Ask questions such as these: "What sound do you hear at the beginning of *bat*? What letter makes the 'buh' sound? What sound do you hear next? Say the word slowly: 'baaaat.' What sound do you hear at the end of *bat*? What letter makes that sound?"

A good way to reinforce pattern words or another element that has been introduced is to have students write a brief story using some of the pattern words. Have students write the story and then, if necessary, help the student with any words containing the target element that might have been misspelled. As always, give students credit for what they did correctly. Here is an example of how a teacher helped a student who wrote *got* for *goat.* She used the miscue as a mini-lesson in applied phonics:

> I see that you wrote *g-o* for the *go* sound in *goat* and that you wrote a *t* for the ending sound of *goat.* That's very good. But the *o* sound in *goat* is spelled *oa* like this (teacher writes and carefully enunciates *goat*). The sound /ō/ is often spelled with an *oa.* If this is how I write *goat,* how might I write *boat*?

## *Assembling Words*

When working with large groups and/or as in alternative to using magnetic letters, have the group assemble letters to make words using procedures adapted from P. Cunningham (1991). Letter cards can be purchased or created by cutting up file folders. To keep the letters organized, place them in separate bags, one bag for each letter.

Distribute a few letters at a time so that students aren't overwhelmed with possible choices. Choose letters that reinforce familiar patterns and correspondences. To reinforce short *e,* for instance, you might distribute the following letters: *e, m, n, t, p.* Before having the words formed, tell students that they will be making words that have a short *e,* which is /e/ as in the word *ten.* Then say a short-*e* word, one that students are familiar with, and have students assemble the word with their letters. Say the word in a sentence to make sure that you and the students have the same word in mind. Also have students repeat the word. Assemble the letters to form a word for one or two examples. If students have difficulty, emphasize the separate sounds of the word: /t/, /e/, /n/. Using a larger version of the letter cards, have a volunteer form the word on the chalkboard ledge or pocket chart.

After a word has been formed and its correct spelling demonstrated, make sure each student has correctly formed the word. Also write the word on the chalkboard. Words to be formed might include *men, ten, pen, met, net, pet.* Make sure that all the words that you ask students to form are in their speaking vocabularies. After all words have been formed, discuss which ones rhyme, which ones begin with the same sound, and so forth.

## *Word Wall*

As noted in Chapter 8, putting words on the wall helps students to remember them. After a pattern has been introduced, place one or more of the pattern words on the wall. Arrange them

Being on the wall, the words are readily available for quick review. Troublesome words can be reviewed daily.

alphabetically by pattern. The *-ab* pattern would be placed first, followed by the *-ack, -ad* patterns, and so forth. Because the words are on the wall, they can be used as a kind of dictionary. If students want to know how to spell a pattern or high-frequency word, they can find it on the wall. Review wall words periodically, using the following or similar activities:

- Find as many animal names, color words, number names as you can.
- Pantomime an action (sit, run) or use gestures to indicate an object or other item (pan, hat, cat, pen) and have students write the word and then hold it up so you can quickly check everyone's response. Have a volunteer read the word and point to it on the word wall. Before pantomiming the word, tell what pattern the word will be in: the *cat* pattern. To make the task a bit more challenging and to get students to analyze the ending letters of patterns, tell students that the word will be in one of two patterns: the *at* or the *an* pattern.

On the wall, place pattern words, high-frequency words, color words, names of the months, compound words, or any other words with which students are working.

- Have a secret word (P. Cunningham & Allington, 1994). Select a word from a pattern, and jot it down on a sheet of paper but don't reveal its identity. Have students number their papers 1–5. Give a series of five clues as to the identity of the word. After each clue, students write down their guess. The object of the activity is to guess the word on the basis of the fewest clues. The clues might be as follows:

1. The secret word is in the *at* pattern.
2. It has three letters.
3. It is an animal.
4. It can fly.
5. Into the cave flew the _______.

- After supplying the five clues, show the secret word (*bat*) and discuss students' responses. See who guessed the secret word first.

## *Making Words*

Making Words is an excellent way to review a pattern or a series of related patterns.

Making Words is a hands-on manipulative activity in which students put letters together to create words and provides excellent reinforcement for word-building patterns. Beginning with two-letter words and extending to five-letter or even longer words, students assemble approximately a dozen words (P. Cunningham & J. Cunningham, 1992). The last word that the students assemble contains all the letters that they were given. Here's how it works. Students are given the cut-out or magnetic letters *a-d-n-s-t* and are asked to do the following:

- Use two letters to make *at.*
- Add a letter to make *sat.*
- Take away a letter to make *at.*
- Change a letter to make *an.*
- Add a letter to make *Dan.*

- Change a letter to make *tan.*
- Take away a letter to make *an.*
- Add a letter to make *and.*
- Add a letter to make *sand.*
- Now break up your word and see what word you can make with all the letters (*stand*).

### *Poems and Verses*

Poems can reinforce a variety of patterns ranging from simple short *a* patterns to multisyllabic ones. Some easy-to-read collections include *Surprises* (Hopkins, 1987) or *Soap Soup* (Kuskin, 1991).

Overusing their decoding skills or, perhaps, struggling so hard to decode words that meaning is neglected, poor readers often ignore substitutions that don't fit the sense of the sentence. Because of its rhythm and rhyme, poetry is harder to misread. The interrupted flow created by a miscue is more noticeable and more likely to be corrected. Some poor readers' mistakes seem due more to carelessness or an inexact style of reading than a lack of skill. But poetry demands an exact reading. Having students read verses is a fitting way for them to experience accuracy in their reading (Bloodgood & Broaddus, 1994). Poetry can also be used to promote fluency since poetry is meant to be read over and over again.

## *Pronounceable Word Part and Analogy Strategies*

Tied in to the word-building instructional technique are the pronounceable word part and analogy strategies. As noted earlier, the word-building technique takes advantage of students' natural tendency to seek out pronounceable word parts by highlighting them. However, students also need a specific strategy which helps them to apply decoding skills. This is especially true of corrective readers because one of their major characteristics is a difficulty in taking control of their learning. Corrective readers need to be taught to use what they know to analyze apparently unknown words. Here is how the strategy works.

### *Pronounceable Word Part Strategy*

Rob, an eight-year-old corrective student, is baffled by the word *slop* even though he knows the phonogram *op* and several words that begin with *sl.* The teacher asks Rob is there is any part of the word that he can say. Rob looks over the word, says "op," and then says "slop." The teacher's questioning helped direct Rob to a word part that he knew. Using the known element as a base, he was able to reconstruct the entire word. This step in the strategy is known as seeking out known or **pronounceable word parts.** Later, Rob has difficulty with the word *tick.* Rob is unable to locate any pronounceable parts so the teacher assists him by covering up the *t.* Rob reads "ick" and then "tick". Although the teacher provides help when needed, the objective is to have the student apply the strategy independently. Here is how the strategy might be taught.

Pronounceable word parts are chunks of words that naturally lend themselves to being pronounced, such as *an* or *ran* or *bran* in the word *branch.*

## Teaching the Pronounceable Word–Part Strategy

### *Step 1: Assessing Strategy Usage*

Observe students as they encounter printed words whose meanings they know but which they cannot pronounce. Note the strategies they use and how successfully they are able to apply them. Discuss strategies for decoding words. Tell students that all readers, even you, run into difficult words. Ask students how they go about figuring out hard words. As you introduce strategies, build on what students know. Help them fit new strategies in with ones they are using.

> Some disabled readers may first read words sound by sound. They should gradually be encouraged to "chunk" sounds.

> When prompting the use of the pronounceable word–part strategy, ask students if there is any part of the word they can say. Do not ask them to "look for the little word in the big word." Often there is none, but there is usually a pronounceable word part.

### *Step 2: Introducing the Strategy*

Explain to students that words that might appear difficult often contain parts that can be sounded out. Explaining that they will be learning a strategy called pronounceable word parts, model the strategy. Show how you might look for and use a known word part to help you sound out a word. After you have worked out the pronunciation of a word, show how you would check your reconstruction by seeing if your pronunciation was that of a real word and also seeing if the word fit the context of the sentence. Explain to students that when seeking out pronounceable word parts, there is no one correct way to do it. In the word *bench,* for instance, *en* might be the familiar word part for some students. For others, the familiar word part might be *ben.* Do not ask students to look for the "little word" in the big word. For one thing, many big words don't contain little words. For another, using word units might make it more difficult to pronounce the entire word. Finding *hop,* the little word in *chop*, would actually make it harder to work out the pronunciation of *chop.*

### *Step 3: Guided Practice for Pronounceable Word Parts*

Provide guided practice with the strategy. Have students seek out known word parts in the following or other words that contain elements familiar to your students. Pointing to each word, ask: "Is there any part of this word that you can say?"

ranch lunch spend sting stump

As students attempt to apply the strategy, provide assistance. If they are unable to find a pronounceable word part even though the target word has one, cover up all of the word except the pronounceable word part and encourage them to say the part that is uncovered and use that part to reconstruct the whole word. For instance, if a student who knows the word *hen,* balks at *tent,* cover up all but the *en* and encourage the student to pronounce it. After *en* has been pronounced, uncover the initial *t* and have the student pronounce the *t* and then *ten.* Uncover the final *t,* have the student pronounce it, and then ask the student to read the whole word. Be sure to affirm students' efforts with specific comments: "I like the way you looked for a part of the word that you could say and then used that to help you figure out that hard word. "

Do not encourage the use of the strategy with words like *of* or *you* or *wash* or other words that are irregular and so don't lend themselves to this strategy. Encourage the use of context for these words. If it is obvious that a student can't work out a word, tell the student the word, or ask, "Could that word be ________ (you supply the target word)?" (Clay, 1993b).

As part of your instruction, inform students that the pronounceable word part strategy will not always work. For instance, pronouncing the *ow* in *knowledge* or *ash* in *squash* won't help much.

*Continued*

**Teaching the Pronounceable Word–Part Strategy** *Continued*

Students need to learn to check their constructions to make sure they are real words that fit the context. If not, they should try alternative pronunciations.

Application of the pronounceable word–part strategy should be part of instruction in patterns. Once students have learned the *-en* pattern, they should use *-en* to help them read difficult words that contain this element.

*Step 4: Application*

Before students read a selection, highlight some words that you feel they may have difficulty with. If they can't pronounce them, have students seek out pronounceable word parts and see if they can construct the words' pronunciations. Emphasize the need to check to see that the word they construct is a real word and fits the story context. During reading, remind students to use the pronounceable word part strategy if they encounter graphically unknown words. Supply help as needed. After reading, discuss words that students successfully decoded. Talk over the processes that they used to decipher the words so they become more fully aware of how the strategy works.

*Step 5: Review*

Review the pronounceable word strategy from time to time. Whenever a new word pattern is introduced, provide students with opportunities to note that pattern in words. For instance, after *-at* has been presented, have students note *at* in words such as *chat, flat, patch,* and *rattle.* Encourage students to bring to class examples of encounters with newly taught patterns and instances where they were able to work out the pronunciation of words by using the pronounceable word part strategy.

## *Analogy Strategy*

Although natural, effective, and relatively easy to teach, the pronounceable word–part strategy doesn't always work. When it doesn't work, students should try an analogy or comparison–contrast strategy. Research suggests that the analogy or comparison–contrast strategy is relatively easy to teach (Ehri & Robbins, 1992) and is highly effective (P. Cunningham, 1979; Gaskins, Gaskins, & Gaskins, 1991). Here is how the ***analogy strategy*** works. While reading a sports story, Rob encounters the word *tame,* a word that is in his listening vocabulary but which he has never seen in print. Neither urging Rob to look for a familiar part nor covering up the *t* helps. Knowing that Rob can read the word *name,* the teacher uses an analogy strategy. She asks Rob if the word looks like any word that he knows. If Rob is unable to think of an analogy word, she may refer him to a list of analogy words known as the Model Words List (see Figure 9-4), or she might supply the analogy word. The teacher carefully prints the word *name* and immediately under it the word *tame.* She asks Rob to read the first word, which he does with ease. Noting that *tame* is similar to *name,* Rob reads it, too. If he had still been unable to read *tame,* the teacher would have used known *t* words (*to, toy*) to help him decode the initial consonant and then blend the two elements. Here is how the analogy strategy might be taught.

The **analogy strategy** is a method in which students work out the pronunciation of a hard word by comparing it to a known word.

To use the analogy strategy, students must first think of a word that is like the word with which they are having difficulty and compare the known word to the unknown one.

### Teaching the Analogy Strategy

*Step 1: Introduction of the Analogy Strategy*

Explain to students that sometimes they may not be able to find a word part that they can pronounce. Tell them that if this happens, they should try to think of a word they know that is similar. Model the strategy for them. For instance, show them how they could use the word *rain* to help decode *chain* or the word *him* to decode *trim.* Stress the need to see if the reconstructed word is a real one.

*Step 2: Guided Practice*

Provide a number of words that may be new to students but which are analogous to known words. Have students use the known words to figure out the new ones. For instance, students might use the known words *pen* and *hit,* to decipher *when, bent, spend, quit,* and *split.*

*Step 3: Practice and Application*

Have students integrate the analogy and pronounceable word–parts strategy and apply them, as needed, to unfamiliar words in stories and articles. Post a list of model words similar to that presented in Figure 9-4 so that students can use these in case they can't think of an analogy word. To guide students in their use of the pronounceable word–parts or analogy strategies, post a set of directions for using the strategies, model their use, and provide ample opportunity for practice and application. Whenever students encounter difficulty with a word, encourage them to apply the strategies. A sample set of instructions for using the strategies is presented in the section "How to Figure Out Hard Words." You may want to reword the instructions to fit the level of your students.

*Step 4: Review*

Review the analogy strategy from time to time. Encourage students to bring to class examples of encounters with newly taught patterns and instances where they were able to work out the pronunciation of words by using the pronounceable word part or analogy strategy.

## *How to Figure Out Hard Words*

Listed below is a series of steps that students might take when confronting a word that is unfamiliar in print.

The pronounceable word–part strategy is placed first because it is less intrusive to the flow of reading and because it's faster and easier to apply than analogy or contextual strategies.

1. See if there is any part of the word that I can say. If I can't say any part of the word, go to 4.
2. Say the part of the word I know. Then say the rest of the word. If I can't say the rest of the word, go to 4.
3. Ask: "Is the word I said a real word? Does it make sense in the story?" If not, try again or go to 4.
4. Is the word like any word I know? Is it like one of the model words? If not, go to 6.
5. Say the word. Is it a real word? Does it make sense in the story? If not, try again, or go to 6.
6. Say "blank" for the word. Read to the end of the sentence. Ask myself: "What word would make sense here?"

Although context is listed last in the list of steps, it might be placed first, if that fits in better with your students' level of development or the reading approach that you favor. The pronounceable word–part strategy was placed first because it's the easiest and fastest strategy to use. In addition, research suggests that phonics strategies work more often than contextual ones do (McCormick, 1995).

To foster independence, review strategy use from time to time, provide lots of practice and application opportunities, and use prompts liberally.

Students should practice saying and eventually memorize the steps of the decoding strategies. In an experiment in which low–achieving readers rehearsed the steps of a strategy by saying the steps aloud and then to themselves, they did much better than a group who were simply taught the strategy. Affirming responses so that students could see they were successfully using the strategy also increased performance (Schunk & Rice, 1993). A listing of strategies and prompts that the teacher might use to elicit strategy use is presented in Table 9-9.

### *Scope and Sequence of Analogy Words and Patterns*

Word Building can be used with any age student, including adults. Words within each pattern can be varied so that older readers are presented with more mature words.

Presentation of the patterns will vary according to the reading ability of the students and their oral language development. Younger students who are struggling with beginning reading skills would be presented with the easiest patterns: *cat, hat, fat; pet, wet.* Words introduced would be restricted to those generally known by primary-age pupils. Older students who are functioning at a beginner-reader level might also need to learn basic patterns such as *-at.* The main difference in presentation would be in choice of words to be introduced. Having more extensive vocabularies, older readers might be able to handle more difficult words within each pattern: *chat, vat, slim* and *whim,* for instance. A suggested sequence for introducing word-building patterns is presented in Table 9-10.

Rate of introduction of patterns will vary. In the beginning, introduce only one pattern at a time and work on it until students seem to have a firm grasp of it. As students catch onto the concept of the patterns, you may be able to present two or three at a time. This is especially true if students have some phonics skills but need a systematic review. This does not mean that all low-achieving readers should be taught all the patterns. Give students credit for what they know. They are dismayed when retaught skills that they have already mastered. An IRI, observation, and/or the Word Pattern Survey contained in Appendix A could be used to establish a starting point for instruction.

## *Other Word-Analysis Programs*

In addition to the word-building teaching technique and pronounceable word–part or analogy strategy programs described in this text, there are three other programs that are based on a pronounceable unit or analogy strategy. In order of length of existence, these are the Glass Analysis (Glass, 1976), P. Cunningham's compare/contrast program (1978), and Benchmark word identification program (Gaskins, Gaskins, & Gaskins, 1991; Gaskins, Ehri, Cress, O'Hara, & Donnelly, 1996–1997).

The Glass Analysis program is available from Easier to Learn, Garden City, NY.

Presenting 117 vowel and two consonant clusters, Glass Analysis is designed to help students see and say pronounceable word units (*at, ide* or, *ue*) in the context of whole words. Glass's thesis, which is based

**TABLE 9-9 Student Strategies and Teacher Prompts**

| Strategy | Student Behavior | Teacher Prompt |
|---|---|---|
| Picture Clue | Student uses illustration to help her/him guess what an unfamiliar word might be. | What does the picture show? You said, "dog." Does the picture show a dog? |
| Context | Student uses sense of sentence or passage to guess identity of the unfamiliar word. Student may reread sentence because it doesn't sound right or make sense. | What word would make sense here? What word would fit here? Say "blank" and read to the end of the sentence. Can we say it that way? |
| Initial Consonant Plus Context | Student uses sense of story and initial consonant | What word that begins with *b* would fit in here? What would you expect to see here? The word you said is *toy*. What letter does *toy* begin with? What letter does the word in the story begin with? |
| Pronounceable Word Part | Seeks a part of the word she or he can say and builds word. For *branch,* says "an-ran-bran-branch." | Can you say any part of that word? |
| Analogy | Compares unknown word to a known one. Compares the unknown word *vet* to *net.* | Is that word like any word you know? Is it like any of the model words? |
| Sound by Sound | Works out a word by saying it sound by sound: "buh-ah-tuh." | What is the first sound? The next sound? The next? Can you put all the sounds together? |
| Onset + Rime | Works out a word by saying the onset then the rime: "buh+at." | Can you say the first part of the word? Can you say the second part? Can you say the whole word? |
| Crash | Student says sound of first letter, then puts first two letters together, and keeps on saying sounds until he can say the word: "c-cr-crash." | Teacher writes letters on board. Child says sounds represented by accumulating letters until he recognizes the word. For *crash,* the teacher writes *c, cr, cra, crash.* |
| Cross-checking | Student uses a semantic cue to check use of a phonics cue or vice-versa. Child uses context to read the word *wagon.* | How did you know the word was *wagon*? |
| Monitoring/ Checking | Student makes error. Prompt directs attention to locating error or correcting a sentence that doesn't sound right or make sense. | You made a mistake on that page. Can you find it? Try that again and think what would make sense. Try that again and think what would sound right. |
| Affirmations | Student applies a strategy. | I like the way you tried to work that out. I like the way you used context. I like the way you went back and corrected that sentence. How did you know it was *wagon* and not *toy*? How did you figure that word out? |
| Starter Prompt | When all else fails, supply the word in question form so the student begins to think about what strategies she or he might use. | Would *toy* fit here? Do you think it looks like *toy*? |

Note: Many of the strategies are adapted from Clay, M. (1993). *Reading Recovery: A guidebook for teachers in training.* Portsmouth, NH: Heinemann.

**TABLE 9-10 Word-Building Scope and Sequence**

*Preparatory*

Phonemic awareness
letter knowledge
initial consonant correspondences

*Level 1*

Easy long-vowel patterns: -e (he), -ee (bee), -o (no)
Short-vowel patterns

*Level 2*

Long-vowel patterns

*Level 3*

Other-vowel patterns: -oy (boy), -ou (out), -ain (pain), -oo (book), oo (soon), and r-vowel patterns

Most of Glass's patterns are incorporated in the word-building patterns or model words, which can be found in Table 9-8.

on a study of achieving readers (Glass & Burton, 1973), is that skilled readers do not decode individual letters but automatically cluster groups of letters that represent pronounceable sound units. The purpose of his program is to train students to recognize these units rapidly and respond with the group of sounds they represent. The approach requires the student to read isolated words and respond to two key questions: What letters make a particular sound? What sound does a particular cluster of letters make? The compare/contrast programs and the Benchmark Word Identification program have been set up to help students decode both single-syllable and polysyllabic words and are discussed in the next chapter.

## *Balanced Use of Decoding Strategies*

An analysis of the performance of low-achieving readers suggests that those who use strategies make progress. Those who don't, make very limited progress.

In addition to pronounceable word part and analogy strategies, there are a number of others that can be used to decipher words. These include: using picture clues, using context, using the initial letter of an unknown word, sounding out a word letter-by-letter, using phonics rules, using a picture glossary or picture dictionary, asking for help, or simply skipping the word altogether. Often, strategies are combined. For instance, sounding out the initial letter of a word may be combined with a picture clue or context or both.

Strategy use may be inefficient or inappropriate. Using pictures clues is an early strategy that should give way to some form of using context and phonics clues. However, being deficient in higher level decoding strategies, some poor readers continue to overuse picture and context clues. Because they overuse picture and context clues, they fail to develop other, more useful strategies.

Strategies should be directly taught, but careful instruction needs to be accompanied by extensive opportunities for applying strategies. After being taught a strategy, students need to be guided in its proper application. Their efforts also need to be affirmed with specific praise.

The degree to which students make progress is also a reflection of the teacher's guidance. Decoding instruction must go beyond teaching students a series of short-vowel patterns or consonant clusters. The instructor must teach students what to do when they encounter an unknown short-vowel or consonant cluster word. That instruction cannot be limited to a few lessons or review sessions. It should include prompts that the teacher uses when the students encounter difficult words.

## *Using Prompts to Foster the Use of Balanced Decoding Strategies*

Julia, a seven-year-old second-grader reading on a primer level, misread the sentence "The light is red now" from Dr. Seuss's *Go, Dog, Go* as "The little is red new." Analyzing the misreading, the teacher realized that while Julia had made use of initial consonants (*little* and *light* and *new* and *now* begin with the same consonant sound), she ignored other sources of information. For instance, an illustration at the top of the page clearly shows a stop light that has turned red, and in previous portions of the story, green and red lights have been mentioned. Apart from these picture and textual clues, Julia's knowledge of language should inform her that a noun would follow the article *the.* Her general knowledge of the world as well as her knowledge of language would also indicate that the sentence didn't make sense.

In a way, Julia had failed to make adequate use of all three cueing systems. Her miscues didn't fit syntactically, semantically, or visually, except for the beginning sound. Through careful questioning or ***prompts*** the teacher can lead Julia to the use of the semantic, syntactic, or phonic cueing strategies that would help her rectify her misreading. Theoretically, the following prompts might have been used:

> **Prompts** are statements that teachers make in order to guide students to use a strategy. When students balk at a word, give them a chance to apply a strategy on their own. If they need guidance, supply a prompt.

- Semantic: Does that sentence make sense? What would make sense here?
- Syntactic: Does that sound like real language? What would sound right here?
- Phonic: *Little* begins with an *l,* but how does it end? How does this word end? (teacher points to *light*) Can you think of another word that has *i-g-h-t*? What sound does it make? (Earlier in the story, Julia had correctly read *night.* Using this as an analogy, she might be led to work out the word *light.*) Or you could try a pronounceable word part strategy and ask: "Is there any part of this word that you can say?"

When choosing which prompt to use and therefore which cueing system to emphasize, you need to consider a number of factors. You need to ask, "What prompt is most likely to lead to a correct response? Which prompt will provide the greatest payoff in terms of helping students cope with difficult words in the future?" You also need to consider the student's development in reading. What strategies has she mastered? What strategies is she strug-

> While picture clues might be fostered during the logographic and early alphabetic stages of reading, phonics and contextual clues should gradually replace them.

> **Cross-checking** is the use of one strategy to verify the results of another. For instance, a student uses context to verify that the word she sounded out makes sense.

gling to learn? Although the pronounceable word–part approach is frequently a good strategy to start off with because it is simple, direct, and easy to apply, a better choice for Julia might be to supply semantic prompts. First and foremost, students need to see that reading should make sense. A semantic prompt (What word would make sense here?) would be a reminder of that fact. Since Julia neglected to relate *light* to the known word *night,* a phonic cue might be used as a ***cross-check.*** After the student supplies *light* on the basis of semantic cues, ask her if *light* begins with an *l* and ends with a *t.* Ask her if she can think of another word that ends in i-g-h-t. If she remembers *night,* have her say the word and compare *light* to this known word.

The nature of the text being read also has an effect on strategy choice. For instance, Tiffany, a third-grader, had difficulty with the sentence, "The bear fell from the tree." Since Tiffany was stuck on *from,* she hadn't read the phrase "the tree." Noting that *from* is "irregular" and believing that having more context would aid Tiffany, the teacher requested that Tiffany reread the beginning of the sentence, say "blank" for the unknown word, read to the end of the sentence, and then see if she could tell what the word might be. After rereading the entire sentence, Tiffany had no difficulty identifying *from.* As a cross-check, the teacher asked Tiffany to tell what letters *from* begins with and what sounds these letters stand for. Noting some hesitancy and remembering that Tiffany had stumbled over other words that contained initial clusters such as *fr,* the instructor planned future lessons on clusters.

> Do not pose riddle-like prompts: "It rhymes with *shoots.* You wear these on your feet" (boots). Use a prompt that leads to strategy use: "What would make sense here? Can you say any part of that word?"

In the following excerpt from a lesson, notice how Regie Routman prompts a meaning strategy in one situation and a deciphering strategy in another.

*Jason:* "When Jamaica arrived at the park, it was almost super time but she still had a few . . ."

*Routman:* "Keep going."

*Jason:* ". . . to play."

*Routman:* "It's the end of the day. Is it *super* time? Does that make sense? Think about what would make sense."

*Jason:* "It was almost *supper* time but she still had a few minutes to play."

*Routman:* "Good for you. I like the way you looked at how the word began and put in what made sense" (Routman, 1991, p. 140).

Notice that Routman did not jump in and correct Jason. Instead, she prompted him to "go on" and read the rest of the sentence. This provided him with the opportunity to correct his miscues on his own. Seeing that he did not do so, she followed up with a prompt which led him to reread the text, make one self-correction, and supply the word that he had skipped (minutes). Rereading the sentence is crucial since in the original reading much of the student's attention was diverted to word identification matters. In his second reading, his focus was on meaning so he was able to make effective use of context.

> To gain insight into students' strategy use, occasionally ask them to tell how they figured out a hard word. You might ask: "How do you know that word was "numb?"

A second student, Meredith, had difficulty with the word *stains.* Remembering that Meredith had correctly read the word *rain* in a previous selection, Routman prompted the analogy strategy. After Routman wrote the known word *rain* on a small chalkboard that she kept with her, she invited Meredith to read it, which she did with ease. Writing *stains* on the chalkboard, Routman asked, "How does it start?" and pronounced the *st* to "put the sound in her ear." Meredith was able to transfer her knowledge of *-ain* to *stain* and read the word correctly (Routman, 1991, p. 140).

The pronounceable word–part strategy might also have been used in this situation. Routman could have asked: "Is there any part of this word that you know?" This would have given Meredith a more direct strategy to use, one that is easier to apply since it doesn't necessitate retrieving an analogy word. If the strategy didn't work, then it would have been time to go to the analogy strategy.

> If you are not sure which is the best prompt to use with a student, enlist the students' input by asking: "What would help you figure that word out?"

Choice of strategies is also determined, in part, by the student's cognitive processing abilities. Tiffany has difficulty remembering words and may miss the same word every time it appears in a story. In one story, Tiffany repeatedly missed the word *chance.* Hoping to provide some hook which would help Tiffany retrieve *chance* the instructor asked Tiffany if there were any part of *chance* she could say. Tiffany recognized the *an,* added *ch* to it, said "chan" and then was able to read *chance.* In subsequent encounters with *chance,* Tiffany was able to use this strategy when she failed to recognize *chance.*

### *Crash*

Sometimes, the best strategy is a very direct one known as "crash." When a student fails to attempt to decode a word that seems to be within his range of skills, the teacher writes the word in cumulative fashion on the chalkboard, inviting the student to read what she has written: c-cr-cra-crash. The student is often able to read the word before it has been written in its entirety (Clay, 1993b).

## *Fostering Self-Correction*

In reading, as in life, errors provide opportunity for growth. When a student misreads a word, don't immediately supply a correction. Let the student read to the end of the sentence or perhaps the paragraph. Often, reading additional text will indicate to the student that a miscue has been made and she will reread the text correctly. If not, supply a prompt that will lead her to self-correct: "Does that sound right? Does that make sense?"

If a student's misreading was partially correct, bring that to the youngster's attention. To confirm a student's use of context, you might say, "The word *dog* fits the sense of the sentence. Dogs do howl. But the word begins with a *w.* What word that begins with a *w* might fit there?"

Only provide prompts after a reasonable interval and when it seems likely that the student will benefit from some help, and then only give as much help as is needed to nudge the student onto the right path. Use the least intrusive prompt possible. Prompts for frequently used strategies are listed in Table 9-9.

In most programs, context prompts, such as asking the student to say "blank" and read to the end of the sentence are provided first. However, based on personal experience teaching low-achieving readers and observations of dozens of teachers using prompts with a wide variety of problem readers, I have found that pronounceable word part and analogy strategies are faster and more productive. Research also suggests that, overall, a phonics strategy works best (McCormick, 1995). But your choice of prompts will also depend on the nature of the text. Context would be the best choice for decoding *through* in the sentence, "The cat ran through the house." Context is excellent and the word *through* does not lend itself to a pronounceable word part or analogy strategy. However, the pronounceable word part strategy would seem to be the best strategy for identifying the word *drum* in the sentence "I have a drum," since context is weak and the pronounceable word part *um* would be known to most students.

Poor readers often have difficulty with hard words even though these were carefully taught them. Avoid making such statements as "you know this word. We just had it." Provide, instead, whatever prompts you feel would be most helpful.

Sometimes, despite your careful prompting, the student seems unable to make use of any of the strategies. Provide the correct response in question form. For example, instead of simply telling her or him that the unknown word is *goat* ask, "Would *goat* fit here?" Then discuss why *goat* is appropriate. This actively engages the student and points out strategies that she or he might use in the future (Clay, 1993b).

Self-correcting is a sign of a good reader. It means the student realizes that meaning is the ultimate aim of reading. It also means that the reader actively monitors his reading to make sure that it makes sense. When students self-correct without your help, reinforce this behavior by using such comments as: "I like the way you corrected that mistake. That's what good readers do." From time to time, ask students how they made a self-correction or figured out a hard word: "How did you know to change *green* to *grin*? How did you figure that word out?" These questions provide insight into the processes students are using. Because students are called upon to explain what processes they are using, it leads them to a deeper understanding of the strategies and helps them generalize the strategies to other situations (Clay, 1993b).

## *Balanced Strategies*

To build independence, occasionally ask students to decide for themselves what strategy they might apply. Ask "How might you figure out that word?"

Because decoding words is so difficult for them, some poor readers overuse context clues. This is especially true when they are asked to read material that is too hard for them. Other poor readers overuse phonics. Having poor decoding skills, they may have been drilled and skilled in phonics to such an extent that they view reading as primarily a matter of saying the right sounds. Students need to learn to balance their use of strategies. Two lists follow which provide tips about what to do when students are relying too heavily on one strategy.

***When Students Overuse Phonics Cues***

To help students who overuse phonic cues, try the following:

- Make sure the material they read is on the appropriate level. Students should know at least 95 percent of the words. If the reader encounters too many unknown words or decodes too slowly, she or he loses the sense of the selection and will resort to the overuse of phonics.
- Stress reading for meaning. Spend extra time building background. As you build background, list key words on the board so students will be familiar with them and will be primed to read them when they are encountered in the selection. Have purposes set before the student reads.
- Stress silent reading. Oral reading can lead to a preoccupation with correct pronunciation of words rather that the construction of meaning.
- Construct a series of cloze or modified cloze exercises in which students complete stories that have had words deleted. Demonstrate cloze by modeling how you would go about filling in the blanks. Emphasize the need to use context clues and to read beyond the blank. After doing a few exercises cooperatively, have students complete some selections on their own. Be sure to discuss the completed exercises.

***When Students Overuse Context Clues***

Students may overuse context cues for a variety of reasons. Their phonics skills may be weak, they may be holding onto strategies that worked with highly predictable books but aren't appropriate for more mature materials, or they may not be demanding a high degree of accuracy from their reading. To build a more balanced use of phonics strategies, try the following:

- Make sure that materials are on an appropriate level of difficulty. Some students overuse context clues when they don't have the skills necessary to decode a large proportion of the unfamiliar words that they encounter.
- Take several running records or IRI samples of a student's oral reading. Note whether decoding skills are adequate. If not, work to improve weak skills and teach missing ones, making sure that students have plenty of opportunity to apply skills.
- Encourage wide reading of easy materials. Poor readers often need extra practice in order for their skills to become automatic.
- Before students read a selection, review key phonics patterns that appear in the piece so students will be better prepared to use needed phonics skills.
- Review the phonics strategies for attacking unknown words. When students are stumped by a word, ask: "What can you do to help you figure out that word? Are there any parts that you can say? Is the word like any word that you know?"

## *Means to an End*

Phonics is a means to an end. The ultimate aim of decoding is to enable students to read independently. To accomplish that goal, decoding instruction must be functional and contextual. Skills taught should be directly related to selections that students are about to read.

And students should have ample opportunity to put their skills to work by reading a wide variety of children's books, periodicals, and real world materials.

## *Minicase Study*

Despite being tutored by the *Title 1* teacher over a period of two years and having an excellent classroom teacher, Alfredo was making very limited progress. Referred to a university reading clinic, testing revealed that Alfredo, who would soon be celebrating his ninth birthday, was only able to read a dozen or so words. At school, Alfredo had been subjected to several intensive phonics programs, which obviously didn't work. The clinic instructor decided to try a more holistic approach. High-frequency words were taught in the context of easy children's books. After each session, Alfredo took home a set of five or six cards containing new words. At home he studied the words.

Despite intensive studying and completing many activities with the words, Alfredo still experienced difficulty learning new words. Often he would stumble over words like *and* and *that,* which had been introduced and carefully reviewed. Words that were known one week were forgotten the next. Sometimes, by the end of a session, he had forgotten the words that had been taught at the beginning of the session. Encountering the words over and over again just didn't seem to help Alfredo. He seemed to need some type of mechanism that would help him remember the words.

Word building and the pronounceable word–part and analogy strategies were introduced to Alfredo. Progress was slow but steady. Encountering the word *that,* Alfredo balked and looked to the teacher for help. Realizing that the *at* pattern had been introduced to Alfredo, the teacher had Alfredo try the pronounceable word–part strategy. "Is there any part of that word you can say?" she asked. Recognizing *at,* Alfredo was then able to add *th* and say the whole word. Sometimes, Alfredo needed additional guidance. Alfredo was unable to recognize any part of the word *silly* even though he had just studied the *ill* pattern the day before. Covering up all of the word except *il,* the teacher asked Alfredo if he could say that word part. After Alfredo read "*ill,*" the teacher had him add *s* and read *sill* and then read the whole word. Two pages later, Alfredo failed to recognize *silly.* However, when his teacher asked him if there was any part of the word he could say, he was able to read *sill* and then the whole word. As time passed and with lots of guidance and opportunities for application, Alfredo became more proficient at using the pronounceable word–part and other word recognition strategies. He became more confident and began to rely on himself rather than simply giving up or asking the teacher for help. As he put more effort into his work, he learned more. Although he still had a lot of catching up to do, with the help of word building and several carefully taught and well-practiced word recognition strategies, Alfredo had become a reader.

## *Summary*

The forty-one speech sounds of American English can be spelled in more than 200 ways. However, most consonant sounds have only one or two spellings, and most vowel sounds have only three or four common spellings. Despite this regularity, many low-achieving readers have difficulty learning how to decipher words. A program that is systematic, related to their specific needs, and which provides ample opportunity for reinforcement and application should help.

A number of approaches can be used to teach phonics: explicit, implicit, pattern, and word-building. Because it combines the best features of the other three approaches and gives students a "fresh start," the word-building approach is recommended. Although in most programs, consonants are typically taught before vowels, and short vowels are taught before long vowels, it is recommended that consonants and vowels be taught together and that easier long-vowel patterns be presented before short vowels.

Low-achieving readers need to be taught strategies for deciphering unknown words. These strategies include seeking out pronounceable word parts and using analogy. Context should be an integral part of any strategy that is used. Using appropriate prompts, the teacher should guide students in the use of varied but balanced strategies to decode words. Ultimately, students should apply these strategies independently.

## *Application Activities*

1. Examine the phonics component of two sets of materials designed for low-achieving readers. How are the phonics elements taught? Is there adequate provision for reinforcement and application?

2. Make a list of five children's books, stories, articles, or other materials that you might use to reinforce and apply a particular phonics element.

3. Observe a beginning reader. What skills has the student apparently mastered? What skills does the student need? What strategies does the reader use to decipher difficult words?

4. Create two phonics lessons, one using the word building approach, and one using the implicit, explicit, or pattern approach. If possible, teach the lessons. Which one seemed more effective? Why?

5. To see how the analogy approach works, view the video tape *Teaching Word Identification,* which is part of a six-tape series, *Teaching Reading: Strategies from Successful Classroom* (Center for the Study of Reading, 1991) in which several sample lessons are taught. Write a brief description of the program and an assessment of it. What are its strengths? What are its weaknesses?

# Chapter 10

# Syllabic, Morphemic, and Contextual Analysis and Dictionary Strategies

## *Using What You Know*

The previous two chapters have explored ways of learning single-syllable words. This chapter examines strategies for identifying polysyllabic words through syllabic, morphemic, and contextual analysis, and dictionary usage. Both phonic and syllabic analysis strategies primarily involve some form of sounding out. In this chapter word-identification techniques that rely on meaning-based strategies are also introduced. These include morphemic analysis—which is the analysis of meaningful units of words (prefixes, suffixes, and roots)—context clues, and dictionary strategies. How useful do you find these strategies in your reading? Do you sometimes divide words into syllables in order to sound them out? Do you try to use prefixes, suffixes, and roots to help you figure out unknown words? Do you use context clues? The dictionary? If so, how do you use them?

## *Anticipation Guide*

Read each of the following statements. Put a check under "Agree" or "Disagree" to show how you feel about each one. If possible, discuss your responses with classmates.

| | Agree | Disagree |
|---|---|---|
| **1.** Most older low-achieving readers have been taught how to use word-analysis strategies but fail to apply them. | ______ | ______ |
| **2.** Except for phonics, the most valuable word-analysis strategy is the use of context clues. | ______ | ______ |

**3.** In most instances, context doesn't provide adequate clues for the identification of a difficult word. ________ ________

**4.** Using roots and prefixes and suffixes to figure out the meanings of new words is of limited value. ________ ________

**5.** Because it is so difficult for struggling readers to use, the dictionary is the least useful of the word-identification strategies. ________ ________

## *Syllabic Analysis*

As they progress through the grades, most students eventually learn phonics and may even become adept at deciphering single-syllable words. However, a significant number have difficulty applying their knowledge of phonics to multisyllabic words. Carmen is a fairly typical example of a student who has this deficiency.

Reading has never been easy for Carmen. In first grade, while most of her classmates learned sight words after just a few repetitions and seemed to catch on to phonics effortlessly, Carmen had to struggle to catch up. Now in fourth grade, Carmen has long since mastered phonics but has fallen behind once more. Despite working extra hours on her assignments, she can't seem to keep up with all the reading in science and social studies that she is required to do. Concerned, her classroom teacher administered an informal reading inventory. A copy of her performance on the IRI's word lists test is presented in Figure 10-1 What do the test results show?

As you can see from the words she misread, Carmen has learned her phonics lessons well. She was able to read virtually all of the single-syllable words. However, she has difficulty applying her phonics knowledge to multisyllabic words. Note that Carmen was unable to read a number of multisyllabic words that should have been easy to decode. For instance, she can read *mess* and *cape* but stumbled over *escape,* which incorporates the sounds of both these words. She also misread *discover* although she can read *miss, glove,* and *her.* And she misread *carpenter* and *passenger,* although she can easily read *car, pen, her,* and *pass.* She also had difficulty with words like *adventure* and *vacation,* which contain word parts such as *-ture* and *-tion,* which are only found in multisyllabic words. Carmen's syllabication skills, which are sometimes known as syllabic analysis, are weak. Carmen is not alone. Difficulty decoding multisyllabic words is a major problem for many older problem readers.

## *Approaches to Teaching Syllabic Analysis*

> **Syllabic analysis:** breaking of a word into syllables, pronouncing each syllable, then blending the syllables to pronounce the whole word. Used to enable people to read unfamiliar multisyllabic words.

There are two major ways to teach ***syllabic analysis:*** through traditional rules and a pattern approach. These two approaches are not mutually exclusive and so may be used to support each other. Whichever approach is used to teach syllabication, its mission must be kept firmly in mind. In reading, the purpose of syllabication is to break a word into smaller, more manageable units so that each of these can be sounded out, and then put back together to form a whole word. To accomplish

| | Flash | Untimed | | Flash | Untimed |
|---|---|---|---|---|---|
| 1. friend | ✓ | | 1. brief | ✓ | |
| 2. moment | moo | movie | 2. special | dk | dk |
| 3. squawk | ✓ | | 3. passenger | pass | passed |
| 4. mess | ✓ | | 4. settler | ✓ | |
| 5. entrance | en | enter | 5. wreck | ✓ | |
| 6. through | ✓ | | 6. discovery | dis | discuss |
| 7. calm | ✓ | | 7. cause | ✓ | |
| 8. glove | ✓ | | 8. invitation | dk | dk |
| 9. carpenter | car- | carpet | 9. distant | disease | ✓ |
| 10. vacation | dk | dk | 10. stroll | ✓ | |
| 11. beast | ✓ | | 11. escape | 0 | exit |
| 12. howl | ✓ | | 12. famous | ✓ | |
| 13. frighten | ✓ | | 13. adventure | 0 | advice |
| 14. nature | dk | dk | 14. breathe | bread | breath |
| 15. cape | ✓ | | 15. pilot | pile | ✓ |
| 16. country | county | ✓ | 16. judge | ✓ | |
| 17. fruit | ✓ | | 17. claim | ✓ | |
| 18. sly | ✓ | | 18. several | 0 | seven |
| 19. meal | ✓ | | 19. squirt | ✓ | |
| 20. absent | 0 | above | 20. voyage | dk | dk |
| Totals | 65 | 70 | Totals | 45 | 50 |

**FIGURE 10-1 Carla's IRI Results**

this, it isn't necessary for students to break the word at the syllable's exact boundaries. For instance, it doesn't make any difference whether readers divide the word *inspector* into *in-spec-tor* or *in-spect-or* or *ins-pec-tor.* As long as their analysis of the word enables them to pronounce it, that's all that counts.

## *Rules Approach to Syllabication*

Since so many of them are poor decoders, low-achieving readers are generally discouraged by the sheer length of polysyllabic words. Seeing a long word, they immediately give up. What they need is instruction that both builds their confidence and shows them how to handle multisyllabic words. Since they may already have been taught syllabication and failed to learn it adequately, they also need a fresh approach. Even if you are using a traditional-rules approach, you can give it a new look by using animal names to illustrate generalizations as is done in the following box. If you are working with older students, you might try a sports motif.

## Concept of Syllables Lesson

### *Step 1: Introducing the Concept of Syllables*

To introduce (or reintroduce) the concept of syllabication, say the names of some common animals, while emphasizing the separate syllables. Have students tell you how many parts the animal names have. You might also have the class clap for each syllable in a word. Say the following or similar names. If you have pictures of the animals, point to them as you say their names. Some animal names that you might use include the following:

| | |
|---|---|
| cat | monkey |
| yak | lizard |
| ostrich | elephant |
| tapir | hippopotamus |

### *Step 2: Presenting Visual Syllables*

Once students grasp the idea of syllables on an auditory level, write the names of the animals on the board. Point to each syllable while saying it. Have students say the syllables along with you. Start with two-syllable animal names and work up to longer syllables.

### *Step 3: Presenting Generalizations*

> Animal names are used as examples of syllable generalizations to make the presentation of generalizations more interesting and memorable. Use ordinary words or another category of words, if you wish.

When students have a firm grasp of the concept of visual syllables, introduce the traditional syllable generalizations, but use the names of animals, sports teams, or other interesting words to make the generalizations come alive. Listed below, in approximate order of difficulty, are the major syllabication generalizations and animal names that might be used to illustrate the generalizations. You might also use an animal name to characterize each generalization. Thus, *catbird* syllables refer to compounds; *tiger* syllables refer to single consonants occurring between vowels; *rabbit* syllables refer to double consonants occurring between vowels.

<u>Compound (Catbird) Words</u>
A compound word forms separate syllables.

| | |
|---|---|
| bobwhite | catbird |
| nighthawk | ricebird |
| killdeer | jellyfish |
| blackbird | glowworm |
| waxwing | ladybug |
| starfish | glassfish |

<u>Affix (Anteater) Words</u>
Prefixes and affixes usually form separate syllables.

| | |
|---|---|
| anteater | snowy owl |
| sidewinder | golden plover |

<u>Double Consonant (Rabbit) Words</u>
When two consonants are placed between two vowels, the word is usually divided between the two consonants.

| | | |
|---|---|---|
| panda | gibbon | turkey |
| otter | monkey | raccoon |
| possum | penguin | rabbit |

> There are a fair number of exceptions to this generalization: *robin, lizard.*

<u>Single Consonant (Tiger) Words</u>
When a single consonant is placed between two vowels, the consonant usually goes with the syllable to the right.

| | |
|---|---|
| tiger | spider |
| tapir | zebra (*br* forms a single cluster) |

<u>Final *le* (Turtle) Words</u>
Final *le* usually attaches to the preceding consonant to form a separate syllable.

| | |
|---|---|
| turtle | beetle |

### *Step 4: Practice and Application*

Practice and application should involve actually reading and/or writing words that follow the generalization that has been introduced. Having students divide words into syllables or count the number of syllables in a word is of little value because both exercises can be performed without actually reading

*Continued*

**Concept of Syllables Lesson** *Continued*

Exact syllabic division would only be required in writing or typing when dividing words at the end of a line.

the words. In addition, you don't want to emphasize exact syllable division, since approximate division works just fine in most instances. The best practice and application is to have students read selections that contain words that follow the pattern that has been introduced. Other profitable practice activities are described below.

- When introducing new multisyllabic vocabulary words, instead of saying the words, invite students to attempt to use their skills to pronounce them.
- Seek out books and magazines that phonemically respell words. Show students how to use the phonemic respellings. As part of the post-reading discussion, have students pronounce the words or read the passages in which they appear. For instance, the **Reading Rainbow** book, *Dinosaur Time* (Parish, 1974) respells the names of dinosaurs and would provide excellent practice for students just learning how to apply syllabication skills.
- Have the class sing song lyrics. Song lyrics are typically divided into syllables. Sources of songs for elementary school children include the following:

Fox, D. (1991). *Songs of the wild west.* New York: Simon & Schuster.

Glazer, T. (1990). *The Mother Goose songbook.* New York: Bantam.

Johnson, J. W. & Catlett, E. (1993). *Lift every voice and sing.* New York: Walker.

Krull, K. (1992). *Gonna sing my head off: American folk songs for children.* New York: Knopf.

Raffi. (1989). *The Raffi everything grows songbook.* New York: Crown.

## *Pattern Approach to Syllabication*

The **pattern** approach starts with a single-syllable word and shows how multisyllabic words are related to it. The word *let* is used as a basis for reading *letter, lettuce, settle, metal.*

Although syllabic generalizations can be useful, a more concrete method of teaching syllabication is to present high-frequency syllabication patterns. Presenting patterns helps students detect and learn to use pronounceable word parts within multisyllabic words. For instance, instead of presenting the open syllable (tiger) generalization, introduce a group of long *i,* multisyllabic words that fit the pattern. If possible, include a one-syllable known word as a contrasting element so that students can more readily identify the familiar elements in each multisyllabic word as in the following:

| | |
|---|---|
| tie | diner |
| tiger | miser |
| spider | |

Reading *tie* should help students read *tiger,* which should help them read *spider* and so on. This is actually an extension of word building to multisyllabic words. A listing of major multisyllabic patterns is presented in Table 10-1. The patterns are sequenced in approximate order of difficulty and frequency of appearance (Gunning, 1994c). The compound word pattern is presented first because this seem to be the easiest multisyllabic pattern to learn. The schwa *a* (*above, alone*) pattern is introduced next because it occurs with a very high frequency. Several other high-frequency patterns follow: *en* (*open*), *er* (*better*), *it* (*kitten*). Short-vowel, long-vowel, and other vowel patterns are then presented.

## TABLE 10-1 Common Syllable Patterns

Compound-Word Pattern

| **some** | **day** | **out** | **sun** |
|---|---|---|---|
| **some**one | **day**light | **out**side | **sun**up |
| **some**time | **day**time | **out**door | **sun**down |
| **some**thing | **day**break | **out**line | **sun**fish |
| **some**how | **day**dream | **out**grow | **sun**light |
| **some**where | | **out**field | **sun**beam |

Schwa-a Pattern

| **a** | **a** | **a** |
|---|---|---|
| **a**go | **a**round | **a**gree |
| **a**way | **a**long | **a**gain |
| **a**lone | **a**live | **a**gainst |
| **a**wake | **a**part | **a**mong |
| **a**sleep | **a**bout | **a**cross |

High-Frequency Patterns

| **en** | **o** | **er** | **ar** | **at** | **it** | **in** |
|---|---|---|---|---|---|---|
| **pen** | g**o** | h**er** | c**ar** | m**at** | s**it** | w**in** |
| o**pen** | a**go** | und**er** | g**ar**den | m**at**ter | s**it**ter | w**in**ter |
| hap**pen** | **o**ver | ev**er** | sh**ar**pen | b**at**ter | b**it**ter | w**in**dow |
| **en**ter | br**o**ken | nev**er** | f**ar**mer | ch**at**ter | k**it**ten | d**in**ner |
| tw**en**ty | sp**o**ken | oth**er** | m**ar**ker | cl**at**ter | k**it**chen | f**in**ish |
| pl**en**ty | fr**o**zen | farm**er** | p**ar**tner | sc**at**ter | p**it**cher | |
| **miss** | **un** | **be** | **re** | **or** | **a** | **y** |
| **mis**ter | **un**der | **be**came | **re**mind | **or**der | p**a**y | sun |
| **sis**ter | **un**til | **be**side | **re**port | m**or**ning | p**a**per | sunn**y** |
| wh**is**per | h**un**ter | **be**low | **re**ward | c**or**ner | b**a**by | funn**y** |
| **mis**take | th**un**der | **be**gin | **re**fuse | f**or**ty | f**a**mous | dust**y** |
| ten**nis** | h**un**dred | **be**long | **re**ceive | bef**ore** | f**a**vorite | shad**y** |
| **ey** | **ble** | **i** | **ur** | **um** | **ic(k)** | **et** |
| turk**ey** | a**ble** | t**i**e | f**ur** | s**um** | p**ick** | l**et** |
| donk**ey** | ta**ble** | t**i**ger | f**ur**ry | s**um**mer | p**ic**nic | l**et**ter |
| monk**ey** | ca**ble** | sp**i**der | h**ur**ry | n**um**ber | att**ic** | b**et**ter |
| mon**ey** | bub**ble** | t**i**ny | t**ur**key | p**um**pkin | n**ick**el | l**et**tuce |
| hon**ey** | mum**ble** | t**i**tle | t**ur**tle | st**um**ble | p**ick**le | s**et**tle |
| | | Fr**i**day | p**ur**ple | tr**um**pet | ch**ick**en | m**et**al |
| **et** | **im** | | | | | |
| tick**et** | sw**im** | | | | | |
| pock**et** | sw**im**mer | | | | | |
| rock**et** | ch**im**ney | | | | | |
| buck**et** | l**im**it | | | | | |
| magn**et** | **im**prove | | | | | |
| jack**et** | s**im**ple | | | | | |

*Continued*

**TABLE 10-1** *Continued*

Short-Vowel Patterns

| **ab** | **ad** | **ag** | **an** | **ang** | **ap** | **ent** |
|---|---|---|---|---|---|---|
| cab | sad | bag | can | anger | nap | went |
| cabin | saddle | baggy | candy | angry | napkin | event |
| cabbage | paddle | dragon | handy | tangled | happy | prevent |
| rabbit | shadow | wagon | handle | | happen | cement |
| habit | ladder | magazine | giant | | captain | invent |
| absent | address | magnet | distant | | chapter | experiment |

| **el** | **ep** | **es(s)** | **ev** | **ea = /e/** | **ea = /e/** | **id** |
|---|---|---|---|---|---|---|
| yell | pep | less | seven | sweat | treasure | rid |
| yellow | pepper | lesson | several | sweater | measure | riddle |
| elbow | peppermint | address | never | weather | pleasure | middle |
| elephant | September | success | clever | feather | pleasant | hidden |
| jelly | shepherd | yesterday | every | leather | threaten | midnight |
| welcome | separate | restaurant | level | meadow | wealthy | |

| **ig** | **il** | **ob** | **oc(k)** | **od** | **ol** | **om** |
|---|---|---|---|---|---|---|
| wig | pill | rob | doc | cod | doll | mom |
| wiggle | pillow | robber | doctor | body | dollar | momma |
| giggle | silver | problem | pocket | model | volcano | comma |
| signal | silly | probably | chocolate | modern | follow | common |
| figure | building | hobby | rocket | product | holiday | comment |
| | | gobble | hockey | somebody | jolly | promise |

| **on** | **op** | **ot** | **age** | **ub** | **uc(k)** | **ud** |
|---|---|---|---|---|---|---|
| monster | shop | rot | cabbage | rub | luck | mud |
| monument | shopper | rotten | bandage | rubber | lucky | buddy |
| honest | chopper | gotten | damage | bubble | bucket | study |
| honor | popular | bottom | message | stubborn | chuckle | puddle |
| concrete | opposite | bottle | baggage | subject | success | huddle |
| responsible | copy | robot | garbage | public | product | sudden |

| **uf** | **ug** | **up** | **us** | **ut** | **uz** |
|---|---|---|---|---|---|
| stuff | bug | pup | muss | but | fuzz |
| stuffy | buggy | puppy | mustard | button | fuzzy |
| muffin | ugly | supper | muscle | butter | puzzle |
| suffer | suggest | upper | custom | clutter | muzzle |
| buffalo | struggle | puppet | customer | flutter | buzzer |
| | | | discuss | gutter | buzzard |

Long-Vowel Patterns

| **ade** | **aid** | **ail** | **ale** | **ain** | **ate** | **ea** |
|---|---|---|---|---|---|---|
| parade | maid | mail | male | obtain | hesitate | sea |
| invade | afraid | detail | female | explain | hibernate | season |
| lemonade | raider | airmail | | complain | appreciate | reason |
| centigrade | | | | retain | hibernate | beaver |
| | | | | | | eagle |
| | | | | | | easily |

**TABLE 10-1** *Continued*

Long-Vowel Patterns *(continued)*

| **ea** | **ee** | **e** | **i = /ē/** | **i-e = /ē/** | **ide** | **ire** |
|---|---|---|---|---|---|---|
| **eat** | b**ee** | s**e**e | rad**i**o | magaz**ine** | s**ide** | t**ire** |
| **ea**ten | b**ee**tle | s**e**cret | eas**i**er | submar**ine** | bes**ide** | ent**ire** |
| b**ea**ten | n**ee**dle | f**e**ver | per**i**od | gasol**ine** | div**ide** | requ**ire** |
| rep**ea**t | ind**ee**d | f**e**male | spaghett**i** | vacc**ine** | dec**ide** | adm**ire** |
| l**ea**der | succ**ee**d | **e**ven | apprec**i**ate | limous**ine** | prov**ide** | ump**ire** |
| r**ea**der | | **e**qual | happ**i**ness | pol**ice** | | |
| **ize** | **ise** | **ive** | **ope** | **one** | **u** | **y** |
| pr**ize** | w**ise** | dr**ive** | h**ope** | ph**one** | **u**se | tr**y** |
| real**ize** | surpr**ise** | arr**ive** | antel**ope** | teleph**one** | m**u**sic | repl**y** |
| recogn**ize** | exerc**ise** | al**ive** | envel**ope** | microph**one** | h**u**man | suppl**y** |
| memor**ize** | adv**ise** | surv**ive** | telesc**ope** | xyloph**one** | m**u**seum | den**y** |
| apolog**ize** | disgu**ise** | beeh**ive** | | | | magnif**y** |

Other-Vowel Patterns

| **al** | **au** | **au** | **aw** | **oi** | **oy** | **ou** |
|---|---|---|---|---|---|---|
| **al**so | c**au**se | c**au**tion | dr**aw** | p**oi**nt | j**oy** | r**ou**nd |
| **al**ways | s**au**cer | f**au**cet | **aw**ful | p**oi**son | enj**oy** | ar**ou**nd |
| **al**ready | **au**thor | s**au**sage | **aw**esome | disapp**oi**ntment | destr**oy** | ab**ou**t |
| **al**together | **Au**gust | d**au**ghter | dr**aw**ing | n**oi**sy | r**oy**al | ann**ou**nce |
| **al**though | **au**tumn | **au**ditorium | cr**aw**ling | av**oi**d | l**oy**al | am**ou**nt |
| w**al**rus | **au**dience | | str**aw**berry | m**oi**sture | v**oy**age | |
| **ou** | **ow** | **oo** | **ove** | **u** | **ook** | **oot** |
| m**ou**ntain | p**ow**er | t**oo** | pr**ove** | S**u**e | b**ook** | f**oot** |
| f**ou**ntain | t**ow**er | bamb**oo** | pr**ov**en | s**u**per | b**ook**store | f**oot**ball |
| surr**ou**nd | fl**ow**er | shamp**oo** | impr**ove** | st**u**dent | workb**ook** | f**oot**print |
| comp**ou**nd | all**ow** | cart**oo**n | appr**ove** | st**u**dio | c**ook**b**ook** | f**oot**step |
| th**ou**sand | all**ow**ance | racc**oo**n | rem**ove** | tr**u**ly | l**ook**out | baref**oot** |
| | | ball**oo**n | m**ove**ments | t**u**na | | |
| **ood** | **ul(l)** | **ul(l)** | **tion** | **tion** | **sion** | **ture** |
| h**ood** | b**ull** | f**ull** | ac**tion** | ques**tion** | conclu**sion** | fu**ture** |
| neighbor**hood** | b**ull**dozer | cup**ful** | addi**tion** | men**tion** | confu**sion** | na**ture** |
| child**hood** | b**ull**etin | help**ful** | sta**tion** | sugges**tion** | occa**sion** | adven**ture** |
| g**ood**ness | b**ull**frog | care**ful** | inven**tion** | exhaus**tion** | explo**sion** | crea**ture** |
| w**ood**en | b**ull**y | | informa**tion** | indiges**tion** | persua**sion** | |

## A Lesson in Teaching Syllabication Patterns

### *Step 1: Teaching the Patterns*

Explain the importance of being able to read multisyllabic words. Tell students that you will be teaching them three patterns, *-en, o-,* and *-er,* that will help them to read hundreds of multisyllabic words.

### *-en* Pattern

Write *pen* on the board and have students read it. Then write *open* directly under *pen.* Write the separate syllables of *open* in contrasting colors or underline them so students may discriminate them more

*Continued*

## A Lesson in Teaching Syllabication Patterns *Continued*

easily. Say the syllables as you write them. Then have students read *open*. Contrast *pen* and *open*. Present the following words in the same way: *happen, enter, twenty, plenty*. Write the words under each other so they may be contrasted. Point out that *ten* is the model word for the *-en* pattern. Later, if students have difficulty with a word containing an *-en* syllable, encourage them to say each part of the word or as many parts as they can and then reconstruct the word. If necessary, they can use *ten* or other model words to help them.

**o- Pattern**

Write *go* on the board and have students read it. Write *ago* on the board. Write the separate syllables in contrasting colors or underline them. Say the syllables as you write them. Then have students read the word. Contrast *go* and *ago*. Present *over, broken, spoken,* and *frozen* in the same way. Point out that *no* is the model word for the *o-* pattern. Later, if students have difficulty with a word containing an *o-* syllable, encourage them to say each part of the word or as many parts as they can and then reconstruct the word. If necessary, they can use *no* or other model words to help them.

**-er Pattern**

Write *her* on the board and have students read it. Then write *under* beneath it. Write separate syllables in contrasting colors or underline them. Say each syllable as you write it. Contrast *her* and *under*. Present *ever, never, other,* and *fewer* in this same way. Later, if students, have difficulty with a word containing an *-er* syllable, encourage them to say each part of the word and reconstruct it.

### *Step 2: Guided Practice*

The purpose of guided practice activities, such as combining syllables to form words, is to help students become aware of high-frequency syllables.

Have students use pronounceable word parts or the model words to read the following: *stolen, token, woven, opener*. Remind them that the words they construct must be real ones. If they analyze a word and it does not seem to be real, they should try again. Also have students complete reinforcement exercises. Sample exercises include the following:

A. Form words by combining two of the three parts in each line.

| | | |
|---|---|---|
| wo | ven | ver |
| ken | spo | ker |
| ker | to | ken |
| len | ler | sto |

B. Underline the word that best fits the sense of the sentence.

1. The car locks are (frozen, chosen).
2. The door is (open, over).
3. Have you ever seen a four-leaf (chosen, clover)?
4. You will need a (stolen, token) for the bus.
5. This coat has been (frozen, woven) from fine wool.

C. Students read signs or labels that contain pattern words.

Cocoa
Frozen Foods
Open
Buy Tokens Here
Photo Shop

D. Have students create a sentence or story using as many of the key words as they can.

### *Step 3: Application*

Provide students with frequent opportunities to make use of this strategy by reading basal stories, trade books, periodicals, and real world materials.

### *Step 4: Expansion of Patterns*

Expand the *en* pattern to include *tend* and *tent*. Write ten on the board. Then show how *-en* is a part of other words.

| | |
|---|---|
| ten | ten |
| tent | tend |
| rodent | tender |
| moment | fender |

**A Lesson in Teaching Syllabication Patterns** *Continued*

*Step 5: Review*

From time to time, review the patterns and model the process of using them. When students encounter difficult words, encourage them to seek out pronounceable word parts or use the model words to help them decode the words. Provide assistance as needed.

One way of deciding which syllable patterns to introduce is to examine the materials students are about to read, note which multisyllabic words would probably be unknown, then present the patterns they embody.

## *Pronounceable Word–Part and Analogy Strategies Applied to Polysyllabic Words*

Teaching syllable patterns is a useful activity in itself. It introduces words that students might have difficulty recognizing in print. However, the true value of teaching syllable patterns is that they can be used as a basis for providing students with strategies that will enable them to decode most multisyllabic words. If students have already mastered single-syllable patterns, they can build on this knowledge to attack multisyllabic words. Basically, instruction will consist of showing students how to use what they already know to attack unfamiliar words. The pronounceable word–part and analogy strategies, introduced in Chapter 9 as strategies for decoding single-syllable words, are also effective when used to decode polysyllabic words (P. Cunningham, 1978, 1979). Using the knowledge they gained through studying syllabication generalizations and/or patterns and through experience coping with multisyllabic words, students should try to pronounce an unfamiliar multisyllabic word syllable by syllable. In general, students would pronounce the first syllable by seeking out the pronounceable word part, then go on to the second syllable, and so on. For the word *sudden,* the student might decode it "ud-sud, en-den, sudden." Or the student might simply decode it as "sud, den, sudden." Often the pronunciation of the first syllable will trigger pronunciation of the whole word so that students might pronounce it as "sud-sudden" or "ud-sud, sudden." (However, if unable to pronounce the first syllable, they might try their luck with a subsequent syllable. They may be able to pronounce enough syllables so that they are able to reconstruct the word, or pronouncing the medial or ending syllable may trigger the pronunciation of the entire word.)

The key to developing strategy use is to provide many opportunities for students to apply them.

If the pronounceable word–part strategy doesn't work, then students should try the analogy strategy. When used with multisyllabic words, the strategy works much the same way as it does with single-syllable words. However, instead of making just one comparison, it may be necessary to make two or three. Here is how it works. A student stumbling on the word *gander* uses the analogous words *fan* and *her* to sound it out. The word *locate* is sounded out by comparing its two syllables to *go* and *hate.*

The strategy doesn't work all the time. There are some syllables for which no analogies can be found. In addition, the pronunciation of a sound unit is often altered when it is found in a syllable, especially one that is unaccented. For instance, the *re* in *refer* is no longer analogous to *he* because the long *e* has become a short *i* (ri-fur). Students need to be taught to make adjustments in pronunciation when applying this strategy. In making comparisons, students can think up their own analogy words or can use the analogy (model) words presented in the Word Patterns List (Table 9.8) in the previous chapter. Here is how students might be taught the pronounceable word–parts/analogy strategy to decipher multisyllabic words.

For many students who have difficulty with multisyllabic words, it is partly a problem of confidence. They encounter lengthy words and give up. Students need to be encouraged to use their skills.

***Teaching the Strategies***

Explain why it is important to be able to read multisyllabic words. Tell students that even the most difficult words usually have some parts that they can pronounce. Show how you would use known word parts or syllables to pronounce an unfamiliar word, perhaps a name that you had never seen. Then explain that if you didn't see any pronounceable word parts, you would use a comparison strategy. That is, you would see if there were any word parts that were similar to words you know. Show, for example, how you might use the known words *pick* and *him* to pronounce *victim.*

As students encounter difficult multisyllabic words, help them to apply the pronounceable word–part and analogy strategies, along with context, so that ultimately they apply these strategies independently. Your aid could take the form of a guiding question such as: "Are there any parts of the word that you can say? Can you say the first part? The next part? Can you put the word together? If you don't see any parts that you know, can you see if any of the word's parts are like any words that you know? Is the first part like any word that you know? Is the second part like any word you know?" At times your guidance might need to be highly directive. For instance, if a student has been taught the *-o* pattern and has trouble with *frozen* and is unable to note any known parts in the word, you might cover up all but the *fro* and have the student say "fro" (if the student can't read *fro,* cover up all but the *o* and have the student read "o-fro"). Uncover *zen* and have the student say "zen" (if the student can't read *zen,* cover up the *z* and have the student read "en-zen") and then put both parts together and see if it is a real word and fits the context of the selection. If the student is unable to read *fro* or *zen,* you would use the analogy strategy and have the student compare *fro* to the model word *no* and compare *zen* to the model word *ten.* Give students as much guidance as they need, but gradually lead them to the point where they can decode independently. Listed below is a series of steps that students might take when confronting a multisyllabic word that is unfamiliar in print.

1. Say each part of the word or say as many parts as I can.
2. If I can't say a part, think of a word that is like the part I can't say and then try to say that word part. (If I can't do 1 or 2, then go to 5.)
3. Put the parts together to make a word.
4. Ask: "Is this a real word? Does it make sense in the story?" (If not, try again or go to 5.)
5. Say "blank" for the word. Read to the end of the sentence. Ask myself: "What word would make sense here?"
6. If nothing else works, I can use the dictionary.

Two programs that provide instruction in the use of multisyllabic words are *Megawords* (Educators Publishing Service, 31 Smith Place, Cambridge, MA 02138, 800-225-5750) and *Word Building: Book D* (Phoenix Learning Resources, 2349 Chaffee Dr., St. Louis, MO 63146, 800-221-1274).

### *Implementing a Systematic Program*

On a regular basis, introduce a set of pattern words and show how these might be used to decipher multisyllabic words as in the sample lesson. It is recommended that the pattern words be introduced in sets of three. One or two sets might be introduced each week depending upon the needs of the class and the amount of instructional time available. A listing of pattern words was presented in Table 10-1. The patterns are listed in the order in which they might be introduced. Although there are more than 200 syllable patterns, only about 100 of these occur with a high degree of frequency. The patterns listed were chosen on the basis of frequency of occurrence and ease of learning. However, add or delete patterns to fit the needs of your students.

## *Additional Syllabic Analysis Programs*

There are a number of other programs for decoding multisyllabic words. In addition to word building, two of the most carefully constructed are the compare/contrast and the Benchmark methods. Both programs are similar to word building. However, both word building and Benchmark offer a more intensive program than does compare/contrast.

### *Compare/Contrast*

Based on her research with low-achieving readers, P. Cunningham (1978, 1979) concluded that training students to use a **compare/contrast strategy,** in which they decode unfamiliar words by comparing and contrasting them with familiar words, enhances students' ability to attack both single-syllable and multisyllabic words. The following five-step strategy was created for deciphering multisyllabic words (Cunningham, 1978).

**Step 1.** Students begin compiling a store of known words that contain elements frequently appearing in multisyllabic words: *he, went, her, can, car.* Students are then given a group of two-syllable words: *barber, serpent, panther, banner,* and so forth. They match up their known words with the two-syllable ones and attempt to pronounce them.

**Steps 2.–3.** Students accumulate additional cards containing known words: *in, at, then, it, is, let, fish, sun, big, and.* They then practice matching them up with and pronouncing two-syllable words: *hermit, blister, punish, misspent,* and so forth.

**Step 4.** Students are taught to use their entire stock of fifteen known words to seek analogous segments in multisyllabic words.

**Step 5.** Students attack words containing three or more syllables.

The Benchmark program can be obtained from the Benchmark School, 2107 N. Providence Rd., Media, PA 19063.

### *Benchmark Word Identification Program*

Specifically designed for low-achieving readers, the Benchmark Word Identification Program was developed over a period of five years at the Benchmark School (Media, Pennsylvania), a school founded to assist students in grades one through eight who have serious reading disorders. Approximately twenty minutes each day is devoted to the program. The Benchmark Word Identification Program is divided into two parts: beginning and intermediate (Gaskins, Gaskins, & Gaskins, 1991; Gaskins, Ehri, Cress, O'Hara, & Donnelly, 1996–1997). In the beginning program students are introduced to a series of key words that represent high-frequency patterns. These key words are then used to help students decode unknown words. For instance, the key word *it* would be used to help students read *bit* and *mitt.* In the intermediate component, students use key words developed in the primary program to figure out multisyllabic words. For instance, students might use the key words *grab* and *it* to decode the word *rabbit.* In all, students learn 120 key words.

**Exemplary Teaching Lesson: Attacking Multisyllabic Words**

Megan, a student at the Benchmark School in Media, Pennsylvania, is stumped by the word *envelope.* She seeks help from her teacher, Mrs. Marjorie Downer. Instead of simply telling her the word, Mrs. Downer asks, "What did you try?" "Context," Megan responds. The question helps Mrs. Downer ascertain what strategies Megan is using. It is also a subtle reminder that the student should attempt to decode words on her own.

Seeing that context didn't help, Mrs. Downer asks Megan if she can find the first chunk in the word. Megan identifies the *e-n.* Mrs. Downer urges Megan to identify a pattern word on the wall that incorporates *e-n.* Listed on the wall are 120 pattern words that can be used by students to help them work out the pronunciation of most words.

Megan locates *ten* and uses it to help her pronounce the first syllable *en.* Mrs. Downer then leads Megan to find the two pattern words that are analogous to the next two chunks or syllables in *envelope.* Megan uses these to pronounce the last two syllables. Putting all the chunks together, Megan is able to construct the word *envelope.* Megan then reads the word in the context of the sentence to make sure that it makes sense. Although focusing on a word-analysis problem, Mrs. Downer makes sure that meaning is always paramount (Center for the Study of Reading, 1991, pp. 13–14).

## *Morphemic Analysis*

Unless you are in the medical field, the word *hemacytometer* is probably unfamiliar to you. However, there's a good chance that you can figure it out without referring to the dictionary. The form *meter* is already familiar to you. And if you compare *hemacytometer* to *hemophilia, hemoglobin,* or *hemorrhage,* you can see that *hem* refers to blood. The root *cyt* may seem unfamiliar, but if you think of *cytoplasm* or *cytology,* that may help you infer that *cyt* means "cell," so a hemacytometer is simply a device that measures blood cells.

**Morphemic analysis:** identification of the meaningful parts of a word to derive the meaning of an unknown word. A **morpheme** is the smallest meaning-bearing unit in a word. The word *untimely* has three morphemes: *un-time-ly.*

Although the English language contains nearly a million words and is growing by leaps and bounds, a vast number of both its technical terms and general words have been constructed by joining roots or adding affixes to roots. **Morphemic analysis,** which is the study of meaningful word parts, such as compound words, roots, prefixes, and suffixes, can help low-achieving readers recognize hundreds of words. It can also help them learn and remember words. It's easier to learn *chronology* if you can relate it to *chronic* and *chronometer.* And if you forget what *chronology* means, you can use your knowledge of the combining form *chron* and context to help you figure it out.

Some morphemic forms are difficult to detect, occur infrequently, or aren't very helpful. For instance, the root *lab* means "carry" but it is not obvious how knowing this meaning would help a reader figure out the words *laboratory, collaborate,* or *elaborate.* However, many affixes and roots, such as *un-, pre-, -less, -ful, port-,* and *mono-,* occur frequently, are fairly easy to detect, and have a limited number of meanings. These are the ones that should be emphasized. According to Nagy and Anderson (1984), about 60 percent of the new words a reader meets contain morphemic units that provide clear, usable clues to the word's meaning. Another 10 percent give helpful but incomplete clues.

Morphemic units are especially helpful in the content areas. There are thousands of technical terms that have been formed by combining morphemic units: *translucent, cardiovascular, zoology, ecology, hemophilia, invertebrate, stratosphere,* and *epidermis.*

## *Teaching Morphemic Elements*

Morphemic elements should be taught inductively and should build on what students know. For instance, students should use their knowledge of *pedal* to derive the meaning of *pedestrian, biped, pedicure, pedometer.* By noting the use of *ped* in all five words, the students should also be able to derive a meaning for the morphemic form *ped.* Also present related forms at the same time: *podiatrist, tripod, gastropod,* so that students can see relationships among the words.

### *Making Connections*

When presenting morphemic units, group them in some way. When teaching *mono,* also teach *uni* and other number prefixes. Present opposites. When introducing *anti,* teach *pro.* Also teach *less* and *ful* together (Dale & O'Rourke, 1971).

Make connections whenever possible. For instance, in a chapter entitled "Below and Above Earth's Surface" in an easy-to-read geography series (Lefkowitz, 1990), the following technical terms are taught: *atmosphere, stratosphere, ionosphere,* and *hemisphere.* If students are led to see the common elements in the words, they will better understand them, remember them longer, and if they forget their meanings, will be able to use morphemic units to decode the words. Lead them to see that *sphere* means *ball* so that *atmosphere, stratosphere,* and *ionosphere* are layers of gas that form balls that surround the Earth. Note, too, the meanings of the morphemic forms: *atmo* (air), *strato* (layer), *iono* (electrically charged). When discussing *hemisphere,* lead students to see that *hemi* means "half," so that a *hemisphere* is "half a ball."

After teaching *hemi,* you might relate it to *demi* and *semi,* since they have similar meanings and also discuss words in which these morphemic forms appear: *demigod, demitasse, semicircle, semicolon, semidetached.*

In addition to making connections between elements being taught, make connections between morphemic elements and students' current reading needs. In a geometry unit

After students have learned a morphemic unit, show them how they can use this knowledge to derive the meanings of new words. After learning *tri,* students derive the meaning of *trifocals, trilingual,* or *trigraphs.*

focusing on angles, introduce the morphemic forms that students will encounter: *polygon, heptagon, hexagon, octogon, pentagon, quadrilateral, triangle.* Lead students to see the meaning of *gon* (angle) and the meaning of the other morphemic forms. Have students do an illustrated web of the words. Also discuss some everyday uses of the morphemic forms. What would the building called the Pentagon look like? How many sides would it have? How many events are there in the pentathalon? As an extension, you might study other morphemic forms that indicate number (*mono-, uni-, bi-, di-, dec-,* etc.) or spend additional time with *poly* since this is a frequently occurring morphemic unit and is easy to understand.

Before assigning students a selection, scan it to see if any of the potentially difficult words contain morphemic elements that might be taught. And when teaching difficult words, be sure to include an explanation of morphemic forms or, better yet, help students note and build on morphemic forms that they already know. For instance, when teaching the word *arthropod,* ask students if there is any part of the word that they know. Chances are students will know *pod.* If not, discuss the meaning of *pod* as in *tripod.* If no one knows *arthro,* write the word *arthritis* on the board and discuss its meaning. Lead students to see that the morphemic form *arthr(o)* means joints and that arthropods are animals that have jointed appendages. When teaching *invertebrates,* after having introduced *vertebrates,* help students see that the *in* in *invertebrates* means "not" so that an *invertebrate* is an animal that does not have a vertebra or a backbone. Follow the same procedure with the *exo* in *exoskeleton.* By following this procedure, you are adding to students' understanding of the words and you are teaching them to recognize important morphemic units.

The key to teaching morphemic units is to build students' awareness of these elements in words so that when they encounter a difficult word, they see if they can figure out its meaning by analyzing it morphemically. Just as you teach students to seek out pronounceable word parts when applying phonics or word building, you now teach them to seek word parts whose meanings they know. By teaching morphemics, you move students from the level of sound units to meaning units. Because of this new focus, students start noticing the meaningful components of words.

### Prefixes

A **prefix** is a morpheme placed before a word or root that changes the word's meaning, as in *un*afraid or *pre*view.

Although **prefixes** are easier to learn than suffixes because there are fewer of them and their meanings are more concrete, they don't become an important factor in students' reading until they are reading second- or third-grade material. Common prefixes are listed in Table 10-2 in approximate order of difficulty.

When teaching prefixes, teach them inductively and, if possible, have students derive the meaning of a prefix through analyzing known words: *unhappy, unafraid, unknown.* When teaching *pre,* for instance, lead students to derive its meaning by discussing its effect in the following words: *preview, prepay, pretest.* In your instruction and practice activities,

**TABLE 10-2 Common Prefixes**

| Prefixes | Meaning | Examples |
|---|---|---|
| *Easy Prefixes* | | |
| un- | (not) | **un**friendly |
| un- | (opposite) | **un**pack |
| under- | (under) | **under**ground |
| dis- | (not) | **dis**belief |
| dis- | (opposite) | **dis**agree |
| re- | (again) | **re**read |
| re- | (back) | **re**pay |
| im- | (not) | **im**polite |
| in- | (not) | **in**expensive |
| ir- | (not) | **ir**responsible |
| pre- | (before) | **pre**winter |
| sub- | (under) | **sub**marine |
| tri- | (three) | **tri**color |
| *Intermediate Prefixes* | | |
| anti- | (against) | **anti**war |
| bi- | (two) | **bi**cycle |
| co- | (with) | **co**captain |
| deci- | (one tenth) | **deci**meter |
| en- | (forms verb) | **en**circle |
| ex- | (out, out of) | **ex**haust |
| ex- | (former) | **ex**-owner |
| hemi- | (half) | **hemi**sphere |
| inter- | (between) | **inter**state |
| ir- | (not) | **ir**regular |
| micro- | (small) | **micro**scope |
| mid- | (middle) | **mid**night |
| milli- | (one thousandth) | **milli**meter |
| mis- | (not) | **mis**understanding |
| mis- | (bad) | **mis**behavior |
| mono- | (one) | **mono**rail |
| multi- | (many) | **multi**purpose |
| non- | (not) | **non**fiction |
| poly- | (many) | **poly**syllabic |
| semi- | (half, part) | **semi**sweet |
| trans- | (across) | **trans**oceanic |
| pro- | (for) | **pro**-union |
| sub- | (under) | **sub**way |
| super- | (above) | **super**sonic |

focus on having students develop a metacognitive awareness of prefixes as meaningful units. Students may not perceive *un* as being a separate element in words like *unhappy* or *unknown,* and so, would not seek out these elements when deriving the meanings of difficult words that contain the prefix *un.*

### Introducing Prefixes Lesson

*Step 1: Introducing the Concept of a Prefix*

Read the portion of the *Humpty Dumpty* chapter in Lewis Carroll's (1969) *Through the Looking Glass* which talks about unbirthdays. Discuss what an *unbirthday* might be and how it is different from a birthday. Also discuss what an *uncola* might be. List other *un* words on the chalkboard: *unafraid, unhappy, unclear.* Have students tell how *un* changes the words and tell what *un* means. Note than *un* is a prefix and that prefixes are placed at the beginning of words and change the words meanings. Note, too, that a prefix forms a separate syllable.

*Step 2: Guided Practice*

Have students read individual words that contain the prefix *un* and tell what each word means. Also encourage students to complete cloze (fill-in-the-blank) exercises with *un* words or read brief passages that contain *un* words. Students might also illustrate *un* words (*unhappy, unlucky*) or create their own *un* words.

*Step 3: Application*

Have students read materials that contain the prefix *un.* As part of the application step, ask students to use their knowledge of *un* to derive the meanings of new words. Encourage students to use a strategy similar to the one they used for decoding difficult words. However, instead of looking for word parts they can say, students should look for word parts they know.

*Step 4: Extension*

Discuss the fact that *un* can also mean "opposite" as in *undo* and *unpack.*

As you introduce prefixes, inform students of prefix pitfalls (White, Sowell, & Yanagihara, 1989). The first is that many prefixes have more than one meaning. For instance, the prefix *in* can mean "not" as in *incapable* or "lack of" as in *inexperience.* Sometimes an apparent prefix is not a prefix at all. The word *indifference,* for instance, is derived from the Latin word *indifferentia.* Sometimes a prefixed word is not quite the sum of its apparent parts. The true meanings of *unbending* and *uncalled-for* would be hard to infer if just the words themselves were examined. The presence of prefix pitfalls means that prefixes need to be taught with care and students need to integrate morphemic analysis and context clues.

## *Suffixes*

A **suffix** is a morpheme added to the end of a word or root that changes or adds to the meaning of the word, as in care*ful* or fear*less.*

There are two kinds of **suffixes**—inflectional and derivational. Inflectional suffixes have a grammatical function, indicating subject–verb agreement (rabbit *hops*), present participle *-ing* (*singing*), past tense *-ed* (*planned*), past participle *-en* (*written*), comparisons (*sooner, soonest*), plural *-s* (*cats*), and adverbial *-ly* (*suddenly*) functions.

Derivational suffixes either change a word's part of speech or function. Many suffixes form nouns: *-ance* (*resistance*), *-dom* (*freedom*), *-tion* (*action*). A number of others form adjectives -(*i*)*al* (*jovial*), *-ary* (*honorary*), *-ic* (*geographic*), *-ous* (*joyous*).

Don't waste time with inflectional suffixes. Even if students are dropping endings, they generally learn to self-correct on their own.

Do not spend a lot of time teaching inflectional suffixes. If students are reading for meaning and using their sense of the language, they will usually automatically supply the necessary inflectional endings. Besides, generally speaking, little or no meaning is lost if students omit inflectional suffixes as they read. Since low-achieving readers are lagging behind, you need to focus on instructional techniques that have the greatest payoff.

Derivational suffixes are another matter. They should be taught directly and reinforced periodically. When teaching students to apply knowledge of suffixes, it's also a good idea to review prefixes. Many words that have suffixes also have prefixes (White, Sowell, & Yanagihara, 1989). Derivational suffixes begin appearing in students' reading material in grade two. The suffixes *-en, -er* can be found on that level. In grade three, the following suffixes appear with a fair amount of frequency: *-able, -ible, -ful, -ness, -y,* and *-tion* (Gunning, 1996). A good time to teach suffixes would be when students are reading on a third-grade level or when suffixes are appearing in their reading material with some regularity. Suffixes are listed in Table 10-3 in approximate order of difficulty. You may want to stress the following suffixes because they occur with the highest frequency: *-er, (t)ion, -able, -al, -y,* and *-ness* (White, Sowell, & Yanagihara, 1989). Suffixes should be taught inductively, with stress placed on application. Suffixes and other morphemic elements should be taught on a systematic basis and also when there is a need.

Some suffixes have three or four or more definitions, and these definitions may be abstract. For instance, the suffix *ic* is listed as having nine meanings in *Webster's New Collegiate Dictionary* (Mish, 1993). These definitions have been combined and simplified for Table 10-3. Because many suffixes have multiple, sometimes abstract, definitions, it is important that students see many examples of the target suffix in use. Examples need to be used to convey the sense of the suffix. For instance, seeing the suffix-containing words *artistic, comic, historic,* and *poetic* in the context of sentences and whole selections will do a better job of helping students understand the suffix *-ic* than will abstract definitions.

When teaching suffixes, show students how the spelling of the base word or root might be affected. Adding suffixes can change spellings in one of three ways:

1. *consonant doubling:* sunny, runner
2. y *to* i: penniless, reliable, happily, apologize
3. *omitted final* e: hoping, activity, official, cubic *(White, Sowell, & Yanagihara, 1989).*

Show students that they may have to mentally restore the letters that were removed or changed when the suffix was added. Otherwise, they may not recognize the **penny** in *penniless* or the **active** in *activity.*

A **root** is the morpheme that remains after all the affixes have been removed. *Sing* is the root for *singer, singing,* and *sings.* The root is also the historical source of a word.

## *Roots*

The most complex of the morphemic elements is the root. A **root** is the part of a word that is left when all the affixes have been removed. It may be a word (the *help* in *unhelpfully*) or a portion of a word (the *ceive* in *receive*) (McArthur, 1992). Common roots are listed in Table 10-4. (The list contains both roots and elements known as combining forms. To avoid unnecessary distinctions, both combining forms and roots are referred to as "roots.") Although there are hundreds of roots, only the most frequently occurring and most useful elements have been included. For a more complete listing, see *The Reading Teacher's Book of Lists* (Fry, Kress, & Fountoukidis, 1993).

**TABLE 10-3 Frequently-Occurring Suffixes**

| Suffixes | Meaning | Examples |
|---|---|---|
| *Easy Suffixes* | | |
| -en | (made of; having) | gold**en** |
| -er | (one who) | farm**er** |
| -or | (one who) | inspect**or** |
| -able | (is, can be) | believ**able** |
| -ible | (is, can be) | vis**ible** |
| -ful | (full of; having) | thank**ful** |
| -ness | (having) | ill**ness** |
| -tion | (act of) | imagina**tion** |
| -y | (being; having) | chill**y** |
| *Intermediate Suffixes* | | |
| -age | (forms nouns) | mile**age** |
| -al | (being; having) | accident**al** |
| -an, -ian | (having to do with; of) | Americ**an**, Ital**ian** |
| -ance | (state of) | import**ance** |
| -ary | (forms adjectives) | summ**ary** |
| -ence | (state of or quality of) | obedi**ence** |
| -ial | (of; having to do with) | adverb**ial** |
| -ian | (one who is in a field; one who) | music**ian**, guard**ian** |
| -ic | (of; having) | histor**ic** |
| -ify | (make) | terr**ify** |
| -ish | (having the quality of) | fool**ish** |
| -ist | (a person who) | motor**ist** |
| -ity | (state of) | activ**ity** |
| -ize | (make) | memor**ize** |
| -ive | (being) | secret**ive** |
| -less | (without) | hope**less** |
| -ment | (state of) | enjoy**ment** |
| -ous | (having) | danger**ous** |

## A Lesson in Teaching a Root

### *Step 1: Conveying the Nature and Importance of the Element*

> Because it deals with long, difficult words, morphemic analysis is the kind of learning experience that builds students' sense of self-worth because it teaches them to handle long, difficult words.

Before presenting the element, explain to students what roots are and show how they will help them to become better readers. Place some lengthy words containing roots on the board and model the process of pronouncing the word and deriving its meaning. For instance, putting *polychromatic* on the board, explain what a root is, and underline *chrom.* Then show how you would translate the root and the affixes into their meanings (*poly* = "many," *chrom* (at) = "color," *ic* = "having") and come up with the overall meaning of the word: "having many colors." Note that words are like puzzles and often we can solve their meanings by thinking about and putting their parts together.

### *Step 2: Introducing the New Element*

Build on whatever knowledge students might have of the new element. Present words with which they are likely to be familiar. By analyzing these words, help

**TABLE 10-4 Frequently-Occurring Roots**

| Roots | Meaning | Examples |
|---|---|---|
| *Easy Roots* | | |
| graph | (writing) | auto**graph** |
| tele | (distance) | **tele**scope |
| port | (carry) | **port**able |
| saur | (lizard) | dino**saur** |
| phon | (sound) | micro**phon**e |
| vid, vis | (see) | **vid**eo, **vis**ion |
| astro | (star) | **astro**naut |
| bio | (life) | **bio**graphy |
| *Intermediate Roots* | | |
| aud | (hearing) | **aud**ible |
| auto | (self) | **auto**biography |
| -ology | (study of) | ge**ology** |
| cred | (believe) | in**cred**ible |
| chrono | (time) | **chrono**meter |
| dict | (say) | pre**dict** |
| duct | (lead) | con**duct** |
| geo | (earth) | **geo**graphy |
| loc | (place) | **loc**ation |
| manu | (hand) | **manu**al |
| ped | (foot) | **ped**estrian |
| scrib, script | (writing) | in**scrib**e, manu**script** |
| therm | (heat) | **therm**os |

## A Lesson in Teaching a Root *Continued*

them derive the meaning of the element. For the root *bio,* discuss *biography* and *biology* and the common item *bio.* Help them to see that *bio* means "life" or "living." Help students determine the meanings of *biographer, biohazard, biotechnology,* and *biochemistry.* Note that it is sometimes necessary to check the meanings you derive through analysis with definitions given in the glossary or dictionary.

When presenting an affix or root, encourage students to suggest other words in the same "family" (Mason & Au, 1990).

### *Step 3: Guided Practice*

Have students read signs or articles containing *bio.* For instance, they might read a label that contains the word *biodegradable.* Or they may read a selection about *biofeedback.* After the selection has been read, have students explain what they think these *bio* words mean and how they derived these meanings.

### *Step 4: Application*

Step 4 is the key step. As students encounter new words containing morphemic elements that they know, help them to apply their knowledge by using the known part or analogy strategies. For instance, when students encounter the word *biorhythm,* ask them to see if there are any parts of the word whose meaning they know. If they recognize *rhythm* but not *bio,* use an analogy strategy. Compare the *bio* in *biorhythm* to the *bio* in *biology* and *biography* and help them derive the meaning of *bio* and the whole word. After they have derived a tentative meaning, they should test it out in context to see if it fits.

## Contextual Analysis

What are a student's chances of deriving the meaning of a word from context? According to Herman, Anderson, Pearson, and Nagy (1987) the odds are about one in four to nearly one in two if the student is a competent reader and the context is such that it is possible to derive the meaning of the unfamiliar word. However, the odds plummet to a dismal one in ten to one in twenty if the student is a less able reader. For one thing, less able readers know fewer words and their knowledge of the words that they apparently know is less extensive than that of more capable readers. Their backgrounds of experience are also less fully developed. All of this makes it more difficult for them to apply context clues. For instance, five out of sixteen fifth-grade low-achieving readers were unable to use context clues to arrive at the meaning of *gaucho* in the following sentence because they didn't know what a cowhand is: "Gauchos, the cowhands of South America, learned to chase the birds or cow ponies" (Shefelbine, 1990, p. 91). One student thought that cowhands were a kind of pony; another thought that *cowhands* referred to the front feet of a cow. Students can't use **contextual analysis** if the target word and key words in the context clues are unknown.

**Contextual analysis** is the use of verbal clues from a sentence or passage in order to derive the meaning of an unknown word.

Poor readers also have difficulty deriving meanings from context when the target word represents a new concept rather than a new label for an old concept. For instance, deriving the meaning of *infuriated* from context would be relatively easy because it is a label for the familiar concept: *anger.* On the other hand, deriving *fungus* from context would be difficult because it represents a new concept.

Although low-achieving readers may have a more difficult time deriving word meanings from context, they gain proportionately more when taught how to use context clues. Apparently, achieving readers don't gain as much because they already have strategies for using context clues. The research also highlights the importance of providing students with reading material that is on the appropriate level. Students can't use context clues to derive the meanings of difficult words if they can't understand the context clues because the context clues also contain unknown words. Background is also a factor. Students are better able to use context clues when reading about a familiar topic. Since the topic is familiar, they can then use their background knowledge to help figure out the meaning of an unfamiliar word. To improve students' ability to use context clues as they read a particular passage, background, concepts, and key vocabulary words needed to understand the passage should be developed (Shefelbine, 1990).

An informal survey of difficult words in children's books and periodicals revealed the authors only supplied usable context clues about one-third of the time.

When carefully taught how to use context clues, students do improve. In one study, students nearly doubled their ability to derive the meanings of words from context (Jenkins, Matlock, & Slocum, 1989). Before instruction, they were only able to use context one time out of ten. After instruction, they were able to use context successfully nearly two times out of ten. Doubling the rate of effective context use would have a dramatic effect on students' vocabularies. For instance, it is estimated that average readers meet approximately 20,000 new words in their reading each year. If they are only able to use context effectively one out of ten times, then they will become acquainted with 2,000 new words a year. However, if they double the effectiveness of their use of context, then they will double the amount of new words they acquire (Jenkins, Matlock, & Slocum, 1989).

The payoff is enormous. However, in order to improve students' ability to use context clues, instruction needs to be significant. Students given only limited training did not improve.

### *A Two-Stage Process*

To assess students' ability to use context clues, observe them as they encounter a word whose meaning is unknown. What do they do? How successful are they at using context?

Applying context is a two-stage process. In the first stage students hypothesize or make their best guess as to the meaning of the target word. They use all available clues and combine those with their background knowledge to construct their guess. For many students, the process ends here. However, there should be a second stage in which students check their guesses to see if they fit, and, if they don't, they revise their guesses.

The first stage, constructing a meaning involves three subprocesses: selective encoding, selective combination, and selective comparison (Sternberg, 1987). In the selective encoding stage, students seek out information that will help them derive a meaning for the unfamiliar word. They ask themselves: "Are there any clues to the meaning of the hard word in the sentence in which it appears? Are there any clues in the sentence or sentences that come before it? Are there any clues in the sentence or sentences that come after it?"

Using selective combination, students integrate all relevant clues, asking, "What do all the clues suggest about the meaning of this word? The student then incorporates selective comparison into the process, asking: "What past experiences have I had, or what do I know that might help me guess the meaning of this word?" At that point the student constructs a meaning for the word. To check their conjectures, students use a strategy known as SCANR, which is the second stage of using context. SCANR is an acronym that means:

For younger or less able students, simplify or reword the explanation of the SCANR acronym.

**S**ubstitute a word or expression for the unknown word.
**C**heck the context for clues that support your idea.
**A**sk if substitution fits all context clues.
**N**eed a new idea?
**R**evise your idea to fit the context. (Jenkins, Matlock & Slocum, 1989, p. 221)

**Steps for Using Context**

Here are steps students can follow and a series of questions they can ask that incorporate both stages of the encoding-checking process.

*Step 1: Seeking Clues (Selective Encoding)*

Students read the entire sentence, saying "blank" for the unknown word. They then look for clues that might help them guess the meaning of the unknown word. If the clues in the sentence are inadequate, students look at earlier and later sentences.

*Step 2: Combining Clues (Selective Combination)*

Students put all the clues together.

*Step 3: Using Background Knowledge (Selective Comparison)*

Students add background knowledge to the clues they have assembled and construct a tentative definition or meaning.

*Continued*

**Steps for Using Context** *Continued*

*Step 4: Trial Substitution*

Students substitute the tentative word or phrase for the unknown word.

*Step 5: Checking the Substitute*

Students check the context to see if the substitute word or phrase fits all the cues.

*Step 6: Revision*

If the substitute word or phrase doesn't fit, students revise the substitute and try another word or phrase.

## *Types of Context Clues*

Periodically display a word that has such explicit context that it is possible to derive its meaning. Encourage students to use the clues to construct a meaning for the word. Discuss the processes they use.

There are a number of different kinds of context clues, some being easier to use than others. Context clues, such as explicit definitions and synonyms, are easier to use than those that require making inferences (Carnine, Kameenui, & Coyle, 1984). And, of course, the number of clues makes a difference. Some difficult words are accompanied by multiple clues. Distance also has a bearing on the use of context clues. The closer the clue to the target word, the easier it is to use the clues. When instructing students, especially younger ones, start with easier clues. Also focus on words that have near, rather than distant, context clues. The next section lists some frequently occurring context clues (Sternberg, 1987).

### *Definition*

Quite often, authors supply definitions for difficult words, especially technical terms used in science and social studies. In some instances, the definition is detailed and conceptual, far better than what might be found in a dictionary. In many cases, however, the definition is concise and appears as an appositive directly after the difficult word. An extended definition for a *walker,* which is a key word in the story, is provided in the following passage: "What's a walker?" Donna asks. "It's a light metal frame that helps people walk," Mrs. Price says. "It has four legs, and handles for you to hold. When you take a step, you put the walker in front of you" (Cameron, 1990, p. 16).

To spotlight the use of context clues, encourage students to bring in examples of instances where they were able to use context clues to get the meaning of an unfamiliar word.

### *Synonyms*

Except for directly stated definitions, synonyms seem to be the easiest context clue. Synonyms are especially easy when they appear close to the difficult word (Carnine, Kameenui, & Coyle, 1984). In the following sentence, a student can use the synonym *snout* to derive an approximate meaning for *proboscis:* "The housefly has a long snout or *proboscis*" (Steele, 1990a, p. 15).

### *Comparison–Contrast*

Comparison-contrast context clues are sometimes signaled by *not, but, however,* or *even so.* The words *even so* in the following excerpt indicate that the *lepidoptera's* ability to fly huge distances contrasts with the fact that it is *fragile,* and so suggests an approximate meaning for *fragile:* "Lepidoptera are *fragile* creatures. Even so, some of them can fly huge distances, or migrate to warmer climates" (Steele, 1996, p. 18).

As students encounter hard words in rich contexts and aren't using clues, encourage them to do so.

***Function Indicators***

Sometimes, the reader can tell what a word means by noting what the difficult word does. By noting the function of the *incinerator* in the following passage the reader can get a fairly clear sense of what it is: "The chassis oven, as well as the cab ovens, are heated with the help of the plant *incinerator* located out on the receiving dock. Freightliner burns all its scrap paper, lumber, and cardboard boxes in the *incinerator*" (Nentl, 1983, p. 35).

***Example***

One or more examples of the target word are provided. This makes it possible for the reader to examine the example(s) and infer the meaning of the target word. The following passage, which includes *vegetarian,* gives a number of examples of foods that a vegetarian diet might include: "Some birds have a mostly *vegetarian* diet. They eat seeds, fruit, berries, nuts, grasses, shoots, waterweeds, and leaf buds" (Steele, 1991, p. 13).

From time to time review and model the process of deriving the meaning of a word from context.

***Experience***

The target word may label or describe a common experience. Using his background of experience, the reader can often infer meanings. Through real or vicarious experience, the reader can infer the meaning of *remote* by noting the lack of transportation and communication in the setting described in the following excerpt: "In very *remote* parts of the word there may be no roads or railroad, and the land may be covered with jungle, swamp, desert or snow. The only way that villagers or expeditions can keep in touch with the outside world is by air" (Steele, 1990b, p. 13).

***Pictorial Clues***

Encourage students to use illustration clues to get the meanings of unfamiliar words. In a geography text for low-achieving readers (Abbye & Donahue, 1993), *assembly line, prairie, plateau,* and other key words are explained with pictures. When preparing students to read a passage, point out pictorial clues and stress the need to read captions to get the benefit of the clues. Often pictorial clues are far superior to verbal ones.

## *Using the Dictionary*

Before they use their dictionaries, encourage students to survey them so that they become familiar with the wealth of information that a dictionary contains.

Although an essential tool, especially for low-achieving readers, the dictionary is badly neglected. However, the dictionary is the single-most powerful source of self-help for low-achieving readers. Once they have acquired a minimum of reading skill, low-achieving readers can use the dictionary to build their reading vocabulary. For most low-achieving readers, lack of an adequate vocabulary is a major hindrance to proficient reading.

For the poorest of readers, it will be necessary for you to assist with the use of the dictionary. The student will be an apprentice dictionary user, gradually learning from your example and instruction how to use this important tool. At first, students may not be able to do much more than say in which part of the dictionary a word will be found and examine pictures that illustrate a word being looked up. In time, students will take increasing responsibility until they are able to use the dictionary on their own.

For students reading on a beginning or basic level, obtain picture dictionaries or have students create their own. Also investigate the possibility of using electronic dictionaries. These are motivational and they also take the drudgery out of looking up words. Best of all, some of them pronounce the word being looked up and provide a spoken definition. If the books that students are using have glossaries, use them. Glossaries are easier to use than dictionaries because they have fewer words and fewer definitions.

When choosing an easy dictionary, there is a tradeoff. Although easier to use, it will cover fewer words so students may occasionally attempt to look up a word and find that it isn't there.

Dictionaries vary greatly in complexity. As a practical matter, students are unable to handle dictionaries until they are able to read on a third-grade level (Halsey & Morris, 1977). It's virtually impossible to write definitions at an easier level than that. Below that level, students would need to use picture dictionaries, simplified glossaries, or CD-ROM dictionaries such as *My First Incredible Amazing Dictionary* (Dorling Kindersley), which uses spoken words and illustrations to explain 1,000 words). So that students won't become frustrated in their attempts to use the dictionary, obtain one that is as close to the students' reading level as possible. For an eighth-grader reading on a third-grade level, this would mean using a beginning dictionary. Along with ease of reading also consider maturity. Select a beginning dictionary that isn't obviously designed for primary students. Analyze the dictionary. Look for ease of use, definitions that are readable and understandable, and the generous use of illustrations. Or obtain an electronic dictionary that pronounces words being looked up and reads definitions.

## Teaching Dictionary Skills

Instruction should be functional. Nothing is quite as dull as completing dictionary worksheets. However, students will need some direct instruction in key dictionary skills. One of the best ways to teach dictionary skills is to model the use of the dictionary. When the spelling, meaning, or pronunciation of a word is questioned in class and you are unsure of the correct answer, freely admit it and model how you use the dictionary to answer questions that you have about words.

### *Deriving Correct Meanings*

The most difficult dictionary skill of all is to derive the correct meaning of the word being looked up. Acquaint students with the various sources of information about a word's meaning. For instance, in the *Thorndike Barnhart Beginning Dictionary* (Thorndike & Barnhart, 1992), the word *trombone* is shown in an illustration in addition to being defined. The word *triumphant* is defined, used in an illustrative phrase, and used in an illustrative sentence. The word *boycott* is defined and accompanied by a brief account of its origin.

Encourage the use of glossaries. Because glossaries have a limited number of words and fewer definitions, they are easier to use than dictionaries.

Some dictionary definitions do not provide enough information for the reader. For instance, if *laser* is essential to the meaning of a passage, the reader might need to consult an encyclopedia to acquire in-depth information.

Many words have several different meanings. Perplexed by the number of different meanings and unskilled in dictionary use, low-achieving readers tend to select the first meaning. Typically, they fail to look for examples of the word in use or accompanying illustrations. Model the process of choosing a definition by demonstrating how you use context to direct your choice.

Students also need multiple encounters with words so they get a feel for how these words are used. Additionally, the traditional assignment of looking up words in the dictionary and using them in sentences should probably be eliminated. In addition to being a tedious assignment, most students aren't able to use a new word in a sentence, unless it is very concrete, until they have multiple encounters with it.

Encourage students to take advantage of phonemically respelled words in periodicals, trade books, and texts. Students tend not to use aids such as this unless the teacher emphasizes them.

### *Determining the Correct Pronunciation*

For reading purposes, it isn't necessary to derive the correct pronunciation of a new word. Getting the meaning is all that's needed. One young reader thought *colonel* was pronounced /kol-uh-nul/. Since she understood that the word referred to a military officer, her comprehension didn't suffer. However, not knowing the pronunciation of the word, she was unable to recognize it when she heard it so was unable to add to her knowledge of the word when it was spoken by others. In addition, had she used it in her own speech, no one would have known what she was talking about. Learning how to derive the pronunciation of a new word is an important skill.

When teaching the pronunciation key, build on what students already know. Except for the symbol /ŋ/ used in *sing* and the /zh/ symbol for the sound heard near the end of *measure,* students will be familiar with all symbols for the consonant sounds, since they do not differ from the letters used to represent their sounds. Students will also be familiar with symbols for short vowels, since they are the same. Long vowel symbols are easy to learn since they are symbolized by a macron mark (¯). The only symbols students will have to learn are those for schwa, r-vowels, and the other vowels (those that are neither long nor short). Students also need to know that the pronunciation key may vary slightly from dictionary to dictionary.

After giving an overview of the pronunciation key, emphasize the familiar elements and model their use. Have students use the pronunciation key to construct pronunciations for short, straightforward words. Choose words from tradebooks and content area books that they are reading. Select words whose spellings don't effectively represent pronunciations: *python, quartz, gnu, queue.* As they encounter words whose pronunciations are unknown, have students use the dictionary to reconstruct pronunciations.

As students encounter words like *route* and *tomato,* which have variable pronunciations (ro͞ot, rout), (tə mā tō, tə ma tō), lead them to see that people in different parts of the country speak different dialects so that their pronunciations of certain words differ and they may use certain expressions and words in different ways. Discuss the fact that all dialects are equal, and that many words may be pronounced in more than one way. Thus /ro͞ot/ and /rout/ are equally correct. The pronunciation chosen should be the one that matches the speaker's dialect.

### *Electronic Dictionaries*

Many CD-ROM dictionaries have speech capability. Poor readers can use this feature to have the dictionary read the entry word or any words in a definition that they can't read on their own.

As noted earlier, one way of motivating students to use the dictionary is to obtain an electronic version. Electronic dictionaries are becoming more and more popular and are appearing as features of word processing programs, in CD-ROM software packages, and in handheld versions. Apart from the novelty factor, an electronic dictionary is easier to use because it locates words faster and, if the dictionary has a speech component, the student does not have to use the pronunciation key. Poor readers can use this feature to have the dictionary read any words in a definition that they can't read on their own. In addition to providing definitions, talking dictionaries can be used in any grade to help both low- and high-achieving students pronounce printed words that they are unable to decode.

### *A Functional Tool*

Knowing when to use a dictionary is just as important as knowing how to use it. When encountering a new word in their reading, students should use phonic, syllabic, and/or morphemic analysis strategies and context clues to derive the meaning and/or pronunciation of the word. If the word is not crucial to an understanding of the selection, the reader should skip it. The dictionary should only be consulted when the unknown word is essential to the meaning of the passage. Otherwise, looking up words disrupts comprehension. However, looking up problem words after reading a selection is a good idea. It is also a good idea to look up words whose meanings have been derived from context. Again, this should be done after the selection has been read. Looking up a word gives readers feedback, allows them to revise their definitions, and provides more information about the word and so is an excellent vocabulary expander and builder.

Using the dictionary also has an affective component. Many low-achieving readers fail to use the dictionary because they have negative experiences with it. Avoid asking students to use the dictionary before their reading skills are up to it or without giving adequate preparation time. Provide guidance as needed and keep dictionary use functional. Only have students use it when there is a genuine need. Avoid traditional dictionary assignments that are nonfunctional and tedious. For instance, don't ask students to look up all their new vocabulary words in the dictionary. But do ask them to use the dictionary to check the pronunciation of a new word, to check the tentative word meaning derived from context, to look up a word that is essential to the meaning of a piece they are reading, or to check the spelling of a word. And do make use of the latest technology. In short, students should use the dictionary in the same way that an expert reader and writer would.

## *Balanced Use of Strategies*

Given the complexity of the English language and the changing needs of readers as they encounter materials of increasing difficulty, there is a need for a variety of word-analysis strategies. Phonics and syllabic analysis are required for sounding out words. Morphemic analysis and dictionary usage are essential when the meanings of words are unknown. Context is useful for identifying words that the reader can't sound out and for deriving the meanings of unknown words. These strategies are often used in integrated fashion to support each other and as cross checks. In a balanced program of word analysis, students need to know which strategy to use in which situation. They also need to be able to integrate strategy use.

## *Minicase Study*

An eighth-grader, Alicia has a fifth-grade instructional level and she has a hard time keeping up with her school work. One of her difficulties is decoding multisyllabic words. Not only does Alicia have difficulty sounding out multisyllabic words, she also fails to emphasize meaning. Many of the words she sounds out are not real words. For instance, she read *tretorius* for *treacherous* and *avication* for *aviation* and *descrease* for *decrease.* Alicia's teacher was puzzled. Did Alicia have difficulty putting the words into syllables? Was limited vocabulary part of the problem? For instance, if Alicia didn't know the meanings of *aviation, treacherous,* or *decrease,* then decoding them wouldn't have done any good, unless she could have derived their meanings from context.

To explore these unanswered questions and determine why Alicia had difficulty with the words, her teacher went back over the items that Alicia had missed. She determined that some of the words missed were in Alicia's listening vocabulary, but some weren't. Also she found that when given a second chance and some support, Alicia did a little better. As a result of these additional insights, a multifaceted approach was designed. Syllabication and morphemic analysis and dictionary usage are being taught. However, they were taught within the context of the content-area reading that Alicia was required to complete for school.

Multisyllabic words are drawn from selections that Alicia will be reading soon in her regular assignments. When possible, words are chosen that fit into one of the multisyllabic patterns that Alicia has difficulty with: the *ence* pattern as in *convenience and confidence,* for instance. In addition, Alicia has been taught the pronounceable word–part and analogy strategies for identifying multisyllabic words. These strategies are integrated with context, and meaning is stressed so that the words Alicia constructs are real words and fit the sense of the sentence and passage.

Gradually, morphemic analysis and dictionary skills have been added to the program so that Alicia has strategies for coping with the many new words that appear in her content-area texts. Emphasis is placed on learning roots and affixes that appear in the content-area vocabulary that she is learning. Alicia also has learned to make better use of context clues and to use the glossary when necessary. Over time, Alicia is making gradual but encouraging progress.

## *Summary*

All too often, low-achieving readers have difficulty applying phonics knowledge to multisyllabic words and so, need explicit instruction in this area. Approaches for teaching the decoding of multisyllabic words include traditional rules and patterns combined with word building. The strategies of seeking out pronounceable word parts and using analogy/comparison-contrast to decipher multisyllabic words should also be taught.

Low-achieving readers should be taught a number of meaning-based strategies for identifying new words. These include morphemic analysis, context clues, and dictionary skills. Morphemic analysis involves the analysis of morphemes, or meaningful units of words, such as roots, prefixes, and suffixes.

Morphemic elements should be taught inductively and should build on what students know. Morphemic elements should also be grouped in some way so students can see relationships. Focus should be placed on teaching those elements that students have the greatest need to know and which are likely to transfer to new words that they will meet. Being easier, prefixes should be taught before suffixes but shouldn't be taught before students are reading on a second- or third-grade level. Roots, which are the most complex forms, should be taught last.

With instruction, low-achieving readers can double their ability to use context clues effectively. Using context is a two-stage process. In stage one, students use context and prior knowledge to construct a possible meaning. In stage two, students try out this possible meaning. If it is not satisfactory, they begin the process all over again. Major context clues include: definition, synonyms, comparison-contrast, function indicators, example, and experience.

An essential tool for low-achieving readers, the dictionary helps students cope with difficult words and build their vocabularies. It is important that low-achieving readers use a dictionary that is on the appropriate level. Electronic dictionaries should also be introduced. Using the dictionary requires three major skills: locating the word, selecting the appropriate definition, and reconstructing pronunciation. The dictionary should be presented as a functional tool to be used as needed.

## *Application Activities*

1. Plan a lesson teaching an element in morphemic analysis, context clues, or dictionary usage. If possible, teach the lesson and evaluate its effectiveness.
2. Examine three children's dictionaries. Pay particular attention to the way words are defined. Look up a set of five to ten words and compare the definitions provided in terms of accuracy, completeness, and understandability. Which of the dictionaries seems most useful for low-achieving readers? Why?
3. Examine an electronic dictionary. How does it compare with a regular dictionary? In what ways might low-achieving readers find it more useful than a regular dictionary? What difficulties might they have using it?

# Chapter 11

# Building Vocabulary

## *Using What You Know*

The previous chapter discussed syllabic, morphemic, and contextual analysis, and dictionary usage, which are four key strategies for learning new words. This chapter presents principles and techniques for teaching new words and strategies for remembering them. What are some words that you have learned recently? How did you learn these words? Have you ever taken a course in vocabulary development or embarked on a program of self-study to improve your vocabulary? What techniques did you use? How effective was the program? What might be the components of a vocabulary program for low achieving readers?

## *Anticipation Guide*

Read each of the following statements. Put a check under "Agree" or "Disagree" to show how you feel about each one. If possible, discuss your responses with classmates.

| | Agree | Disagree |
|---|---|---|
| **1.** Limited vocabulary is the major cause of poor comprehension. | ________ | ________ |
| **2.** Nearly all low-achieving readers have a less well developed vocabulary than do achieving readers. | ________ | ________ |
| **3.** Instruction in vocabulary is bound to have a positive impact on comprehension. | ________ | ________ |
| **4.** New words are best taught when there is a need to know them. | ________ | ________ |
| **5.** A certain amount of time should be set aside each day for vocabulary instruction. | ________ | ________ |

## *Low-Achieving Readers and Vocabulary*

Maria (1990) notes, "The reader's level of vocabulary is the best predictor of his or her ability to understand text, and the number of difficult words in a text is the best measure of its level of difficulty" (p. 111).

When V. Anderson (V. Anderson & R. Henne, 1993) asked sixty low-achieving readers in the sixth grade what makes reading hard, the predominant response was "the words." When she asked them if they had any problems when they read, the answer was once more, "the words." When asked to tell what good readers do, the sixth-graders noted that the good readers knew the words and read fast.

Although there is more to reading than just knowing the words, limited vocabulary is both a cause and an effect of poor achievement in reading. As the students in Anderson and Henne's (1993) study noted, reading is difficult if you don't know the words. And if you read less because you don't know the words your vocabulary will fail to grow at the optimum rate. While students learn new words from family, friends, TV and radio, class discussions, and other sources, reading is a major source of new words.

As might be expected, high-ability learners know more words than low-ability students. In one study, the highest-ability high school seniors knew four times as many words as did their lower achieving counterparts (M. K. Smith, 1941). In addition to not knowing as many words as good readers, poor readers have a more restricted knowledge of the words they do know (Shand, 1993). They may be able to supply just one meaning for a multiple-meaning word, for instance.

Socioeconomic status also has an impact on word knowledge. Children from middle-class homes knew almost twice as many words as did children from poor homes (Graves & Slater cited in Beck & McKeown, 1991).

Since most of the words that appear in primary level texts are common and concrete, this cumulative vocabulary difference doesn't begin to interfere with students' learning until about grade four. At that point, content area texts are used more heavily, and then the vocabulary starts to become more abstract and more technical (Chall, Jacobs, & Baldwin, 1990).

## *Stages of Word Learning*

Dale and O'Rourke (1971) list four stages of word knowledge:

1. *I never saw it before.*
2. *I've heard of it, but I don't know what it means.*
3. *I recognize it in context—it has something to do with . . .*
4. *I know it. (p. 3)*

Another way of looking at vocabulary knowledge is to assess the depth to which a word is known or how the student can use the word. Stahl (1986) describes three degrees of word knowledge: definitional, contextual, and generative.

Definitional knowledge means that the student can give a definition of a word. A *monitor* is "a device used to check or control." A *nomad* is "a member of a tribe who moves from place to place to get food for cattle." Contextual knowledge means that the student understands the "core **concept** the word represents and how that concept is changed in differ-

*Concept:* generalization formed by considering particular examples or specific characteristics of objects, actions, or states that share certain characteristics.

ent contexts" (Stahl, 1986, p. 663). The student would understand, that although a monitor in the lobby of an apartment building and monitor worn by a heart patient have something in common, they also have differences. Generative knowledge means that the student could use the word appropriately in speaking or writing.

Before teaching new words, you must ask: "What does the student need to know about the word?" For novice readers, it may be simply a matter of learning the graphic form of a word. The word may be one that they recognize when they hear it, but they don't know its printed form. Although the word *pneumonia* may be in students' listening vocabulary, they may not recognize its printed form. When presenting a word of this type, teach only the part that is unknown. If the students know the meaning of the word, do not waste time defining it or using it in several contexts. Emphasize, instead, the *pneu* spelling of /no͞o/, which would most likely be the unknown part of the word.

With experience, students deepen their understandings of words stored in their lexicons. Initially, the word *cat* may refer to the family's pet. In time, it encompasses other cats and eventually becomes a category label for wild as well as domestic cats.

When teaching vocabulary, it helps to think in terms of concepts. Through their life experiences, low-achieving readers may have acquired a number of concepts for which they have no labels. For instance, students have undoubtedly seen or read about hens but would be puzzled if they encountered the word *pullet*. It wouldn't be necessary to talk about the characteristics of a hen. Teaching would center around helping students remember that the word *pullet* means "young hen." This is an instance where you would be teaching a label for a familiar concept.

Ironically, there are many instances where students know the labels but not the concepts. This is especially true of abstract words like *republic* or *democracy* and technical words like *ROM* and *laser.* These are words that students may have seen or heard but whose meanings may not be clear to them. And then there are words that embody new concepts and have unfamiliar labels: *osmosis, photosynthesis, introvert.* A word like *magenta* or *pullet* can be taught in a minute or two, but a word that embodies a new concept or a new label will take considerably more time and effort.

Teaching vocabulary also involves clarifying and deepening students' understanding of known words and helping students use new words in their speaking and their writing. See Table 11-1 for a listing of states of word knowledge and recommended instruction for each stage.

## *Word Knowledge and Comprehension*

Vocabulary poses a special problem for students still learning English. Garcia (1991) found that more than 10% of the words used in a test passage were unknown to Hispanic youngsters.

Although having a rich vocabulary is important in its own right, it is often taught as a means of improving comprehension. Reviewing fifty-two vocabulary studies, Stahl and Fairbanks (1986) found that average students, if given the right kind of vocabulary instruction before reading a selection, did as well as bright students on a series of comprehension tasks. The implication for low-achieving readers is obvious. Given the right kind of instruction, they might do as well as average readers. In-

**TABLE 11-1 States of Word Knowledge**

| State | Instruction |
|---|---|
| 1. Knows word when hears it but doesn't recognize printed form. | Teach printed form. |
| 2. Knows word's oral and written form but doesn't use it. | Promote generative knowledge. Give examples of its use. Clarify word. Encourage its use in a "safe" environment. |
| 3. Knows the concept but not the label. | Teach the label and relate it to the concept. |
| 4. Has partial knowledge of the word. May have definitional but not contextual knowledge. | Develop fuller meaning of the word. Examine the word in several contexts. |
| 5. Recognizes the label but has no real conceptual knowledge of the concept: *republic*. Or the word may have a familiar every day meaning but an unknown technical meaning: *energy, motion*. | Develop the concept. |
| 6. Both the concept and the label are unknown. | Develop the concept and and the label. |

Adapted from: "Vocabulary Knowledge and Comprehension: A Comprehension-Process View of Complex Literacy Relationships," by M. R. Ruddell. In R. B. Ruddell, M. R. Ruddell, & H. Singer (Eds.), *Theoretical Models and Processes of Reading* (4th ed.) (pp. 414–417). Newark, DE: International Reading Association, 1994.

In addition, there are some words for which a student has partial knowledge. Students may know that a colonel is someone who is in the armed services, but may not realize that *colonel* designates a rank just below general. Or students may know a word but not use it because they are unsure of its meaning or pronunciation or both.

struction must go beyond simply supplying definitions for words. The instruction must be thorough and deep. Students must have contextual knowledge; definitional knowledge is not adequate. They should be given examples of the word used in context, unless the word is one that can be pictured. Showing a picture of a butte, for instance, would be more effective than using it in a sentence, although doing both would be better still. According to Beck and McKeown (1991) two other features are also essential if comprehension is to be improved: "fluency of access to word meanings and richness of semantic network connections" (p. 806).

If students are reading passages similar to the following, in which the boldfaced terms are new words, comprehension will likely suffer unless they can access the meanings of those words rapidly and accurately and use them to help construct the meaning of the passage. If they have only been given definitions of the words, chances are that in itself won't be sufficient to improve their comprehension of the selection. They will lack the kind of contextual knowledge needed to understand the words in their settings. And, because they were only introduced to the words once, they may forget them, or may require additional time to recall the words, either of which will hinder comprehension.

> *Clovis People were very successful big game hunters who first appeared in the western plains soon after the* ***glaciers*** *began to* ***retreat.*** *Some scientists think the Clovis people were the first American settlers and that they arrived sometime 15,000 years ago. Others think they were* ***descendants*** *of* ***immigrants*** *who arrived much earlier. Scientists may disagree about who the Clovis people were, but everyone agrees that they were* ***thriving*** *over wide areas of North and South America by*

*11,500 years ago. Within just a few centuries they had spread from coast to coast. Thousands of their* ***artifacts*** *have been found linking river valley to river valley from Washington State to Nova Scotia and from Alaska to the southern tip of South America. Scientists identify Clovis people by the* ***distinctive fluted*** *(grooved) spear points they made. These points are called Clovis because they were first found near Clovis, New Mexico. Clovis points have since been found all over North America and places in Central and South America. (Satler, 1993, p. 43)*

Today's explosion of knowledge is accompanied by the creation of new words. New inventions and ideas require new words.

### *Improving Comprehension*

Teaching vocabulary to improve comprehension then will require the following:

**1.** Teaching to contextual knowledge. Give the word's definition, and use it in context.

**2.** Establishing relationships. Show students or help them discover how new vocabulary words are related to each other and to words they already know. For instance, talk about ways in which *descendants* of *immigrants* might *thrive* and what kinds of *artifacts,* besides spear points, they might leave behind. Also relate the new word *thriving* to the known phrase *doing well* and the new word *descendants* to the known phrase *children of.* This type of discussion both broadens and deepens knowledge of a word so that a student is better able to make connections between new words and known words.

**3.** Providing multiple exposures. At least three exposures, and preferably more, should be provided. This promotes accessibility. Ideally, these exposures should involve active manipulations of the word—completing an analogy, giving an example, supplying an opposite, relating the word to one's own experience—so that the students must think about the words (Stahl & Fairbanks, 1986).

## *Incidental versus Systematic Instruction*

An incidental approach is one in which skills are taught when the need arises.

There are two main approaches to teaching vocabulary: incidental and systematic. In the **incidental approach,** vocabulary is taught as needed. Words likely to pose problems in a story or informational piece are taught before students read the selection. As an unknown word is encountered in class, it is discussed. The main advantage of the incidental approach is that students apply their knowledge immediately and they can see a need for learning the new words.

A systematic approach is one in which skills are taught on a regular planned basis.

In the **systematic approach,** words are taught as needed, but time is also set aside for the systematic study of vocabulary. This may be a few minutes out of each day or one period a week. The main advantage of the systematic approach is that vocabulary study is given more emphasis. If tied in with word histories, crossword puzzles, and word games, a systematic vocabulary study can create an interest in words. Beck, McKeown, and Omanson (1987) estimate that as many as 400 words a year can be learned in a systematic program. Based on their review of the literature on vocabulary instruction, Baumann and

Kameenui (1991) recommend that teachers "Provide poor readers and at-risk learners a systematic and sustained program of vocabulary instruction that teaches them more words and strategies in less time" (p. 626).

## *Principles of Vocabulary Instruction*

Whether you take a systematic or incidental approach to teaching vocabulary or a combination of the two, there are certain basic principles that form the foundation for an effective program. The first principle is to establish goals.

### *Establishing Goals*

Establish vocabulary learning goals with your students (Baumann & Kameenui, 1991). Include them in the goal setting process. Ask: "Why do you want or need to learn new words?" One goal might be to build self-confidence. Another goal might be to improve reading comprehension. Still another might be to improve written and spoken expression. Students, especially ones who are academically behind, delight in learning long words. Accustomed to doing "baby" work, learning new words gives students a sense of concrete accomplishment.

Other goals might involve inspiring students to enjoy words or teaching them how to acquire words independently. Baumann and Kameenui (1991) suggest three objectives: "(1) Teach students to learn words independently. (2) Teach students the meanings of specific words. (3) Help students to develop an appreciation for words and to experience enjoyment and satisfaction in their use" (p. 627).

### *Building on What Students Know*

With low-achieving readers, it's easy to see what they lack, to see the glass as half empty rather than half full. However, it's important to take full advantage of the knowledge students bring with them. When presenting new words, build on what students know. In presenting the word *periodical,* for instance, ask students if they or their families subscribe to magazines or newspapers. Ask them where they might go if they wanted to read old magazines. See if anyone knows in what room or section of the library magazines are kept. Note that the room is often called the Periodicals Room because that's what magazines are known as. Explain that they are called *periodicals* because each magazine covers a certain period of time. Discuss what other publications might be found in the periodicals section. Have students give an example of a periodical that they read. In developing the meaning of *jubilant,* ask students to tell what kinds of things make them very happy or jubilant. After introducing both words, have students tell how a periodical might make them jubilant.

> Carr (1985) directed students to establish personal clues for new words. Having been introduced to the words *jubilant* and *periodicals,* students noted favorite periodicals and events that made them jubilant.

### *Building a Depth and Breadth of Meaning*

Present a word in several contexts. Simply defining a word and supplying a single example of its use may lead to a false concept of the word's meaning. A *magnificent* sunrise may be translated as a bright sunrise. Hearing about a magnificent gift, a magnificent deed, and a magnificent speech should broaden the students' understanding of the word so that when they read about a magnificent statue, they understand that it is not a bright statue.

As suggested earlier, it's also important to build relationships among words. When presenting *interior,* also teach *exterior.* Have students supply a synonym for *interior* or complete an analogy that contains *interior:* inside is to interior as _______ is to exterior.

### Creating an Interest in Words

Use joke and riddle books to help students see that words can be fun. In addition to having a few laughs, students will become more aware of words, more receptive to learning new words, and will develop a deeper appreciation of words they already know. Explore the histories of words. Investigate the histories of words like *boycott, Braille, gardenia,* and *robot.* Discuss, too, how words change and note new words that have come into the language.

### Relating Words to Students' Lives

Most important of all, relate the learning of new words to students' everyday lives. As Dale and O'Rourke (1971) noted, once we are introduced to a new word, it pops up in our reading, on the TV shows that we watch, and in conversations. Encourage students to note examples of the usage of words that they have recently studied. They can write on a card the word and the context in which it was used, and share that with the class. Also have students share examples of ways in which they have used recently learned words in their writing or speaking.

### Promoting Independent Word Learning

Show students how to increase and expand their vocabularies by using the tools of word learning: context, morphemic analysis, glossary, dictionary, and thesaurus. Research suggests that when students are taught how to use the tools of word learning, they acquire vocabulary at a faster rate (Baumann & Kameenui, 1991).

## Techniques for Teaching Words

One encouraging aspect of teaching vocabulary is that all of the techniques work (Beck & McKeown, 1991). All result in increased word knowledge. However, some techniques work better than others. And some techniques are effective in some situations but not others. In choosing a technique, consider three factors:

1. What is the nature of the word? Is it abstract, concrete, common, rare? Is it a technical word? Does it have many meanings?
2. What background will students bring to this word? Will this be a word with which they are vaguely familiar? Do they have the conceptual background but lack the label? Do

they lack the conceptual background but have the label? Do they lack both the label and the conceptual background?

3. How will the students use this word? Is it essential to the meaning of a story they are about to read? Is it a high-utility word that will appear again and again in this and other selections? Do you simply expect them to recognize it when they hear it? Will they be required to use it in their writing or speaking?

## *Conceptual Teaching of Key Words*

When selecting words for instruction, choose words essential for an understanding of key concepts, words probably not known by students, and words likely to occur in future selections.

In some selections, especially lengthy content-area pieces, there may be twenty or more words that might be unfamiliar to students. This is too large a number of new words for students to learn. An upper limit of seven is more manageable, so you must make choices. Since your overall objective in teaching words prior to the reading of a selection is to improve students' comprehension, decide, first of all, what you want students to comprehend and then choose the vocabulary words that they would most need to know in order to learn those ideas. For example, as a result of reading the first four pages of *Thurgood Marshall: Fight for Justice* (Bains, 1993), you might want students to learn the following concepts:

- Thurgood Marshall was learning about the Constitution.
- Thurgood wondered why African-Americans weren't given equal rights that the Constitution said all Americans have.

Then go through the selection and choose those words that are needed for an understanding of the major concepts but which might pose problems for students. Emphasize high-utility words, words that are sure to occur in future reading. Listed below are words needed to understand the major concepts in *Thurgood Marshall: Fight for Justice.*

| | |
|---|---|
| Constitution | equal protection |
| Fourteenth Amendment | lecture |
| memorized | deny |

If the number of new words in a selection is unreasonably large, you may decide that the selection is simply too difficult. It may exceed the students' instructional level.

The concepts of denying someone that which is his due, lecturing someone who has misbehaved, and studying until one knows something by heart would be in students' background of experience but they may not be familiar with the labels for these experiences: *deny, lecture,* and *memorize.* Several of the words chosen, *Constitution, Fourteenth Amendment, equal protection,* will require building or expanding concepts.

Once the words have been chosen, you would then determine the best way to teach them. Conceptual learning needs techniques that lead students into deeper levels of processing. As Baumann and Kameenui (1991) note, learning new concepts requires developing semantic relatedness and activating prior knowledge. This involves showing how new words are related to each other and how they relate to students' backgrounds and words that they already know. When they integrate new words into their schema, readers are better prepared to use those new words to construct the meaning of a passage.

Actually, virtually all vocabulary instruction should involve some elements of semantic relatedness and prior knowledge. For example, although all children have been scolded for misdeeds, they may not have had the type of scolding that includes explaining why their actions were wrong and why they should not repeat them, a concept conveyed by the label "lecture." Unless a connection is made through discussion or some other means between the label *lecture* and the experience of being scolded, then students might not truly understand what *lecture* means. It is also important to develop the concept more fully by showing how a lecture is accompanied by an explanation of why the conduct is not appropriate and why it should not be repeated.

Since most words can have many meanings, care needs to be taken that the meanings provided for the new words match those that the words have in the selections. For instance, *lecture* can mean "a speech" or "a scolding" and *deny* can mean "to say something is not true," "to disavow," or "refuse to grant." If the students access the wrong meanings, they may misinterpret a portion of the passage.

## *Brainstorming Techniques*

**Brainstorming:** group technique used to activate thinking by encouraging participants to volunteer whatever thoughts or associations come to mind when provided with a stimulus word.

One group of approaches that activates prior knowledge and helps students organize new concepts and their labels is brainstorming. In **brainstorming,** the teacher invites students to volunteer their mental associations with a word or topic. In addition to activating students' prior knowledge, brainstorming techniques provide the teacher with an opportunity to evaluate students' background of information. For instance, the teacher may not know whether students have any knowledge of the Constitution or, if they do, how extensive or accurate that information is. Brainstorming is a good way to find out. Once the teacher has some sense of the students' understanding of the Constitution, she or he "can then clear up misconceptions and make sure that new concepts and words are related to experiences that are meaningful to those particular students" (Lipson & Wixson, 1991, p. 560).

### *List–Group–Label*

In one of its simplest forms, brainstorming can be presented through a List–Group–Label framework (Taba, 1967). The topic to be brainstormed is written on the board and students are invited to tell what the topic makes them think about. Writing *Constitution* on the board, for example, you would invite students to tell what comes to mind when they think of this word. All responses are listed, even those that don't seem to have any connection to the topic. After responses have been listed, the class—working together—categorizes the words into groups of three or more (a word may be placed in more than one group). After all items have been classified, they are given category labels. As they group the words and label them, students explain why certain words should be placed together and why their category name is appropriate. Since grouping or categorizing is a difficult task for many poor readers, you might model the process of categorizing and labeling items for one of the categories. As students become more proficient, they can take more responsibility for grouping and labeling.

As students supply responses, you evaluate the accuracy and extent of students' knowledge of the topic. As a member of the group, you may volunteer words during the brainstorming portion of the procedure. For instance, if students failed to mention *equal* or *equality,* you could insert them in the list. Lest the number of items to be grouped grow unwieldy, limit the number of brainstormed items to twenty-five or so (Tierney, Readence, & Dishner, 1995).

If you notice that the students' knowledge of the Constitution is uneven, provide them with enough of an overview of the Constitution so that they understand its basic intent, especially that it guarantees certain rights to all Americans. Since your main goal is to instruct students in essential vocabulary so that they can better understand the biography of Thurgood Marshall, you need not provide an in-depth study of the Constitution. However, if you are the reading teacher you might coordinate your lessons with those of the classroom teacher, who might undertake a study of the Constitution as part of a "Justice for All" unit. An effective way to refine students' concepts of the Constitution would be through a simulation. A sample simulation is discussed later in the chapter.

## *Graphic Organizers*

**Graphic organizer:** diagram used to show how words or ideas are related. Graphic organizers can be used to improve vocabulary knowledge and comprehension of a passage and as a preplanning device in writing.

**Graphic organizers** are semantic maps, charts, diagrams, and other visual devices that help students see and establish relationships among words. Graphic organizers seem to work especially well with students who might have difficulty seeing relationships when they are only expressed verbally.

### *Semantic Mapping*

**Semantic map:** places the main idea in the center and uses a series of lines and circles to show how subordinate ideas are related to it.

**Semantic mapping,** which is probably one of the most widely used graphic organizers and is based on the list–group–label technique, combines brainstorming and graphically organizing information. After brainstorming, categorizing, and labeling, the class arranges items graphically to show their relationships. Semantic maps are also flexible. Items can be added to them during or after reading or even during subsequent lessons. Validated by research (M. R. Ruddell, 1994), semantic maps are especially helpful to low-achieving readers who have difficulty organizing information and may have negative associations with more verbal methods of arranging data, such as outlines. The steps in semantic mapping include: announcing the topic, brainstorming, grouping and labeling, creating a map, discussing and revising the map, and extending the map. The lesson to follow describes how a fourth-grade corrective group created a map for Earth in preparation for reading *Blastoff to Earth: A Look at Geography* (Leedy, 1992).

### Semantic Mapping Lesson

*Step 1: Announcing the Topic and Inviting Brainstorming Responses*

The teacher wrote the word *Earth* on the board and invited a student to read it. Then the teacher asked the class to tell what comes to mind when they think of the word *Earth.* Students responded with the following words: *land, water, ocean, mountains, United States, rivers, South Pole.* No one mentioned the names of any specific oceans, so the teacher asked probing questions. Students volunteered *Atlantic* and *Pacific.* No one mentioned continents either, so the teacher added that word. The teacher asked the class if they knew what continents are. One student explained that they are "large pieces of land" so *large pieces of land* was added to the list. When asked to name the continents, students could only think of America. The teacher explained that America is actually divided into two continents: North America and South America. Both these terms were added to the list.

*Step 2: Grouping and Labeling Responses*

Students discussed ways of grouping the words and possible titles for word groups. A preliminary map was constructed.

*Step 3: Discussing and Revising the Map*

The class discussed the map. One student remembered that Africa is a continent, and so that was added to the map. During the discussion, concepts were clarified. The teacher noted that the continent in which the South Pole is located is Antarctica, and so the map was adjusted.

*Step 4: Using the Map*

Students used the title and cover illustration to predict what *Blastoff to Earth* might be about. Students read *Blastoff to Earth* to evaluate their predictions and find out more about Earth. The semantic map was displayed so that students could use it as a reference as they read. After students read and discussed the selection, the map was reviewed and students were invited to add additional elements. The names of the remaining oceans and continents were added as were the names of additional land forms. During subsequent sessions, as students learned more about the Earth and its major features, they added to the map and made several other changes. Learning that Europe and Asia were considered to be one continent, they added *Eurasia* to the map. The map is presented in Figure 11-1.

In addition to being a prereading vocabulary–development technique, semantic maps can also be used as a way of summarizing the content of a selection or as a prewriting activity. However, in order to be of optimum value, students should participate in the creation of maps. If teachers create maps, they are the ones who sift the information and so students don't have the opportunity to organize and process the terms. According to research by Berkowitz (1986), students performance doesn't show much improvement unless they have a hand in creating maps.

#### *Pictorial Maps*

Maps need not be verbal. They can also be visual or a combination of verbal and visual items. The words in semantic maps can be illustrated with drawings, or drawings can be used instead of words. This works especially well when working with concrete items.

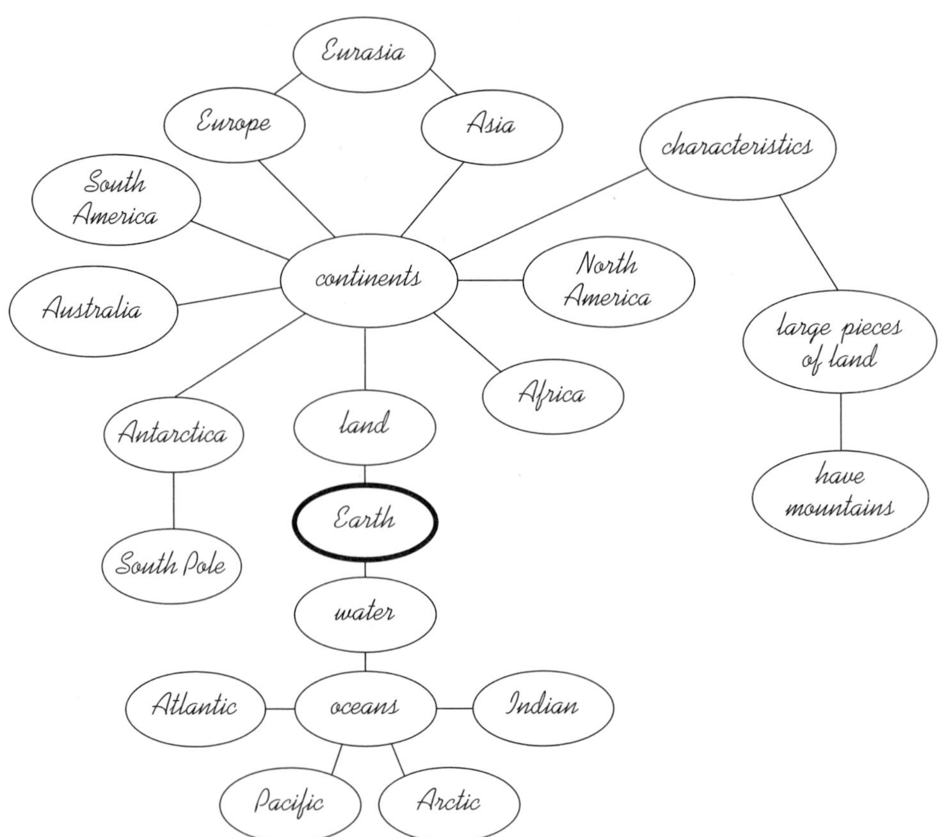


**FIGURE 11-1 Semantic Map of Earth**

> **Semantic feature analysis:** uses a grid to compare objects, people, or ideas on a number of characteristics.

### *Semantic Feature Analysis*

Like semantic mapping, **semantic feature analysis, SFA,** which involves comparing the characteristics of a series of related words, has been shown to be effective in improving both vocabulary and comprehension. The SFA has been especially effective with poor readers and students with learning disabilities (Pittelman, Heimlich, Berglund, & French, 1991). Through having students assess the main features of words, SFA activates prior knowledge, and helps students explore and organize relationships among words. Through eliciting the ways words in a category are the same or different, SFA helps students to establish relationships among words and to note shades of meaning. It fosters precision in word knowledge and usage.

Although a useful tool, SFA works best with words that have features that are either present (+) or absent (–). However, the SFA can be adapted to include a graduated scale: A = always, S = sometimes, or N = never, for instance.

### Semantic Feature Analysis Lesson

*Step 1: Choosing a Category*

Choose a topic or category. In the beginning stages, choose categories that are concrete and less complex. Tell students what the category is and ask them to give examples. In preparation for reading *Pocket Facts, Wild Animals* (Steele, 1990b), the category *mammals* is presented. Students are asked to name mammals. Prompts are provided, if necessary.

*Step 2: Creating a Grid*

Place an outline of a grid on the board or on an overhead transparency. List "mammals" in a column on the left. Encourage students to suggest features or characteristics that at least one of the mammals possesses. Not all features have to be identified at this point. Some may be added later.

*Step 3: Determining Feature Possession*

Put a plus (+) in the block if a particular mammal possesses the feature being considered or a (–) if it doesn't. The plus need not signal that the creature always possesses the feature; it can mean that it usually does. If the group is not sure whether the mammal does or does not possess a particular feature, put a question mark in the box. Discuss items, especially those about which students are uncertain.

*Step 4: Discussion of the Grid*

Discuss the grid with the class. If it is missing some words or features important to the overall concept, add them. After the grid has been completed, discuss its overall significance. Have the class note major similarities and differences among the mammals. Encourage the group to sum up the ways in which mammals are the same and the ways in which they are different. Have students read *Wild Animals* to find out more about mammals.

*Step 5: Extension*

After students have read *Wild Animals,* discuss it and extend the grid to include mammals described in the text but not listed on the grid. The class may also want to list additional features of mammals. The completed SFA grid is displayed in Figure 11-2.

### *Venn Diagram*

**Venn diagram:** uses two or more overlapping circles to compare objects, people, or ideas. The overlapped space is used to show commonalities. The other spaces are used to show differences.

The **Venn diagram,** which is a device that uses overlapping circles, fosters the comparison and contrast of semantic features. In a Venn diagram, concepts are compared and contrasted. Features shared by the concepts are placed within the overlapping circles. Characteristics peculiar to each concept are placed in the outer portions of the circles. A Venn diagram comparing and contrasting African and Asian elephants is presented in Figure 11-3. To make the comparisons more concrete, the diagram is illustrated with drawings of an African and an Asian elephant.

Although they may be used before reading, especially when students are reading a selection that compares and contrasts two items (electric-power versus gas-powered cars, crocodiles and alligators, or toads and frogs), Venn diagrams probably work better as post-reading organizers.

## *Other Vocabulary Building Devices*

Other vocabulary building devices include "possible sentences," predict-o-grams, simulations, and word sorts.

| | eat plants | eat meat, fish, or bugs | babies born live | lay eggs | have pouches | can run or jump | can swim | can fly | hibernate | attack people | live on land | live in water |
|---|---|---|---|---|---|---|---|---|---|---|---|---|
| bats | ? | + | + | – | – | – | – | + | + | – | + | – |
| bears | + | + | + | – | – | + | + | – | + | + | + | – |
| elephants | + | – | + | – | – | + | + | – | – | + | + | – |
| foxes | – | + | + | – | – | + | ? | – | – | – | + | – |
| giraffes | + | – | + | – | – | + | ? | – | – | – | + | – |
| kangaroos | + | – | + | – | + | + | ? | – | – | – | + | – |
| lions | – | + | + | – | – | + | ? | – | – | + | + | – |
| platypuses | – | – | + | + | – | + | + | – | – | – | + | – |
| seals | – | + | + | – | – | – | + | – | – | – | – | + |
| skunks | ? | + | + | – | – | + | ? | – | – | – | + | – |
| whales | + | + | + | – | – | – | + | – | – | – | – | + |

**FIGURE 11-2 Semantic Feature Analysis: Mammals**

In studies with fifth-graders, use of possible sentences resulted in improved recognition of difficult vocabulary and enhanced recall of key concepts (Stahl & Kapinus, 1991).

### *Possible Sentences*

Possible sentences, one of the simplest vocabulary building techniques, may also be one of the most effective. It taps prior knowledge, arouses students' curiosity and interest, elicits predictions, fosters discussion, and helps students detect relationships among known and unknown words. As with many of the other vocabulary techniques, the first step in the possible sentences technique is to determine the major concepts that you want students to learn, and then list the key vocabulary needed to learn those concepts (D. W. Moore & S. A. Moore, 1986; D. W. Moore, Readence, & Rickelman, 1989). List six to eight potentially difficult words (Stahl & Kapinus, 1991). Then choose the same number of words that are necessary to understand the key concepts, but which are easy.

Write the words on the board. Invite students to read them and tell what the difficult ones mean, but supply pronunciations and definitions if no one else can. Briefly discuss the words. Note that they are taken from a selection that students are about to read. Have them

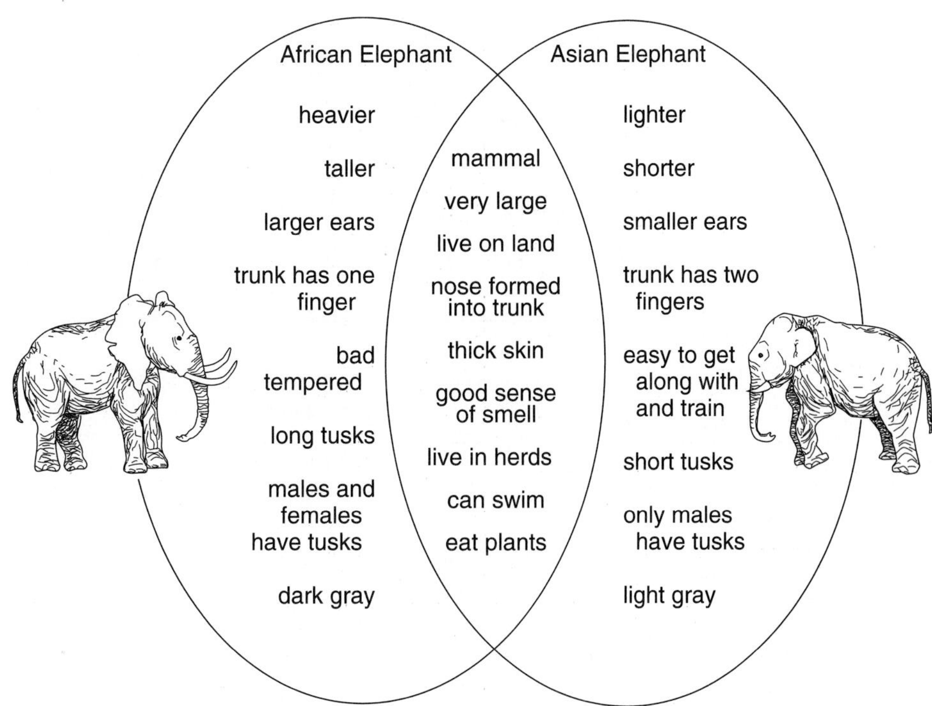


**FIGURE 11-3 Venn Diagram: Comparison of African and Asian Elephants**

predict what the selection might be about. Then challenge students to create sentences in which at least two of the words from the list will be used. The sentences should be ones that might appear in the text students are about to read. Model the creation of one such sentence, explaining as you compose the statement, why you think it might appear in the passage. Then have students create sentences. Note that words may be used in more than one sentence. Write students' sentences, including those that are not accurate, on the board. Stop after all the words have been used. Students then read the selection to see how accurate their sentences are. After students have completed their reading, discuss the accuracy of their sentences. Encourage them to use the text as a reference to clarify confusions, resolve disputes, or back up assertions. Edit or delete sentences that are inaccurate. Students may also expand sentences to include new information garnered from the selection. After discussing the sentences, encourage students to compose additional sentences using the words. This is especially important if students' sentences have not captured the key concepts in the selection. Since using new words in sentences is a difficult task, supply help as needed. Record the students' sentences on the board. Students may copy these sentences into their notebooks so that they have a record of key concepts contained in the selection. A possible sentences exercise completed by a group of sixth-grade low-achieving readers is presented in Figure 11-4. The exercise was written in preparation for reading the first chapter of *Ellis Island* (Reef, 1991), an easy-to-read book about the famous site.

| | |
|---|---|
| immigrants | ocean |
| voyage | ships |
| Ellis Island | America |
| processed | countries |
| descended | pass |
| inspection | harbor |

*Students' Sentences*

1. Immigrants from many countries came to America.
2. The immigrants made a long voyage by ship across the ocean.
3. After a ship docked, the immigrants were taken to Ellis Island.
4. Immigrants were processed at Ellis Island.
5. The immigrants had to pass an inspection at Ellis Island.
6. Many of us are descended from immigrants.

**FIGURE 11-4 Possible Sentences with Key Words**

> Predict-o-grams can also be used to reinforce the concept of story grammar, which is an analysis of the major parts of a story.

### *Predict-O-Grams*

In an intriguing device called a "predict-o-gram," the teacher has students group words that they believe will tell about characters, plot, setting, and other parts of a narrative (Blachowicz, 1986). Choosing words that are likely to be unfamiliar, as well as some known words, the teacher lists them on the board and discusses them with students. She then asks students to classify the words according to their prediction about how they will be used in the story. Will they be used to tell about setting, characters, problem, plot, or resolution? Students then predict the story.

### *Simulation*

For certain abstract terms, where deep conceptual understanding is desired, you might try a simulation. For instance, to convey the concept of the Constitution, you might form cooperative learning groups and have students pretend that they were on a spaceship heading for Mars when the ship's guidance system broke down, and they ended up on a distant planet. With no hope of ever returning to Earth, they have decided to set up a new country and to draw up a set of rules for the people in this new country. After students have completed drawing up their rules, discuss them. Lead them to see that this is what was done in 1789 in the United States. A meeting was held to set up a basic set of rules called the Constitution. Compare the rules set up by the group with the Constitution's major provisions.

> Words might be ranked to show differences in power, size, or intensity (Nagy, 1988). The following words might be ranked in terms of intensity: *cold, chilly, freezing, cool, frigid, nippy, wintry.* (Judgments will be somewhat subjective.)

### *Word Sorts*

As noted earlier, the word sort technique is a categorization device that can be used to manipulate words. It can be especially useful for grouping technical terms (Tonjes, 1991). The words are placed on slips of paper or 3 × 5 cards and the sorts can be open or closed. In a closed sort, students are given the category names. In an open sort, they must compose category names. An open sort forces students to see relationships and state what those relationships are. Listed below is a completed sort taken from *Observing the Sky* (Stott, 1991).

| **Planets** | **Constellations** | **Comets** |
|---|---|---|
| Mercury | Scorpio | Halley |
| Venus | Taurus | Hale-Bopp |
| Earth | Ursa Major | Encke |
| Mars | Ursa Minor | |
| Jupiter | Draco | |
| Saturn | | |
| Uranus | | |
| Neptune | | |
| Pluto | | |

### *Developing Vocabulary through Wide Reading*

A primary source of new words is wide reading. Unfortunately, poor readers tend to read less, which is one the reasons they are poor readers. Reading less, they acquire fewer vocabulary words. The key to fostering reading among poor readers is to provide materials that are interesting to the students and which are on their level. These materials need not be books. They can be newspapers, magazines, and how-to manuals (see Chapter 17 for specific suggestions for motivating wide reading). Books that are particularly effective for developing vocabulary are informational books and periodical articles, especially if they define words in context or provide illustrations that depict or clarify the meaning of terms. Listening to or reading along with taped books is also a good way to build vocabulary.

### *Developing Vocabulary through Reading Aloud*

The structured overview and the Frayer model are frequently used in content-area teaching to introduce vocabulary and can be found on pages 368 and 369.

A rich source of vocabulary development is reading aloud. In one study, kindergarten-age children were able to pick up some new words through a single reading that involved no discussion of the new words (Senechal & Cornell, 1993). However, discussing the words results in even greater gains. Second-graders learned three out of a possible twenty words through listening to stories. With discussion and teacher explanation, the students acquired eight of the words (Elley, 1989). Since they generally do less reading, low-achieving readers, even older ones, should be read to on a regular basis. In addition to building background, this will also build vocabulary. Although a discussion or explanation of some hard words could be a natural nonintrusive aspect of reading aloud to students, care needs to be taken that you don't detract from the students' enjoyment of being read to.

## *Techniques for Remembering Words*

A number of techniques have been described for developing a deeper understanding of words and for organizing them. Items that are well understood and well organized are easier to remember. Creating memorable images also helps students to retain words. Sometimes this happens naturally: a word that we encounter in our reading paints such a vivid picture or has such an unusual sound that it sticks out in our minds. As teachers, we can make words more vivid by dramatizing them or having students learn them through simulations, or we can create new connections by recounting a word's colorful history. Recounting the origin of *boycott* or *silhouette* should make these words more memorable.

## *Key Word Approach*

**Key word** approach: strategy in which students associate a word to be learned with a familiar key word and an image to help them remember the new word.

There are also techniques known as mnemonic devices that aid memory. One of the most carefully researched of these techniques is the **key word approach.** In the key word approach, students create an image that forges a link between the new word and its meaning. The key word is a term that serves as both a key to the meaning of the target word and also evokes an image that calls to mind the word and its meaning. If possible, the key word embodies a portion of the target word. For instance, in one study, the key word for *angler* was *angel.* The mnemonic image showed an angel sitting on a cloud fishing. Two angels on a higher cloud have the following conversation:

*Angel 1:* That ANGEL down there sure knows how to catch a lot of fish.

*Angel 2:* That's because he's an expert ANGLER (J. R. Levin et al., 1984).

The key word method works best if students create their own images. Creating a keyword and an image involves thinking about the target word and the kind of image that might be used to depict it. This process, especially the creation of an image, leads to a better understanding of the word because the student has to think of images that would appropriately portray the word. Young students and some older low-achieving readers may need help creating mnemonic images. However, involve the students as much as possible in the process. The box that follows shows how the words *beseech, benefactor,* and *veteran* might be presented through the key word approach.

### A Lesson in Teaching the Key Word Approach

*Step 1: Introducing the Approach*

Ask students if they have ever had difficulty remembering the meanings of new words. Discuss problems they have had. Also discuss methods that they use to study vocabulary. Tell them that you will be showing them a special way to learn new words. Explain to them that this method works extremely well because you create pictures in your mind to help you remember each word and its meaning.

*Step 2: Explaining the Technique*

Demonstrate the technique with a word that students are having difficulty with or need to learn. Selecting the word *peninsula,* for instance, explain that you are going to think up a key word and a picture to help you remember the word *peninsula.* Inform the class that you are going to use the word *pen* because it is the first part of *peninsula.* Then explain that you are going to create a picture in your mind that uses the

**A Lesson in Teaching the Key Word Approach** *Continued*

key word *pen* and shows the meaning of *peninsula.* You picture yourself drawing a peninsula with a pen. The peninsula has the shape of a pen. Explain that you picture a very large pen that is covered with diamonds and the map that you are working on is also very large. In fact, it covers the floor of your room. Tell students that making the picture in your mind unusual or silly will help you remember it. Then tell the class that when you see the word *peninsula,* you will think of yourself drawing a peninsula with a pen. It also helps if you put the key word and new word in a sentence that shows the meaning of the new word: I will use my pen to draw a peninsula on this map.

*Step 3: Presenting New Words*

Present the words *beseech, benefactor,* and *veteran.* Discuss the meanings of each and some possible key words and interactive images: a bee beseeching for honey; Ben, your benefactor, giving you food, a TV, a CD player, a computer, a bike, and stacks of money; your pet's vet in a parade for veterans. The vet is followed by your pet and other pets, dressed in military garb and carrying flags in their teeth or paws.

*Step 4: Guided Practice*

Provide practice in the use of the technique. For instance, you say the word *beseech* and have the class tell what the key word is and describe the interactive image. Students then tell what the word means. Also say the key word *bee* and have students supply the target word, the interactive image, and the target word's meaning. Continue until students have a firm grasp of the technique.

*Step 5: Application*

Have students apply the technique independently, if they are able to create their own key words and interactive images. From time to time, review the technique and encourage students to use it.

## *A Full Program of Vocabulary Development*

Although this chapter has taken a strong stand in favor of direct, systematic instruction in vocabulary, it is important to take full advantage of informal incidental opportunities to learn new words. Don't restrict vocabulary study to a set amount of time each day or week. Bring in new words that appear in daily newspapers or TV shows and encourage students to do the same. Often words that are probably unfamiliar to students dominate the news: *inflation, recession, crimes against humanity, famine, scientific breakthrough.* If appropriate, bring these to students' attention and discuss them, or better yet, encourage students to bring in new words that they encounter. Pay special attention to the words that students are learning in science and social studies and other content areas. Reinforce these in many contexts. Above all, create an interest in and enthusiasm for words. Play word games. Discuss puns and other verbal wordplay. Have a vocabulary bulletin board and a word of the day. Obtain a calendar that introduces new words. Discuss the etymologies of words and track new words coming into the language. Take full advantage of talking or CD-ROM dictionaries. Use a variety of teaching techniques. Most important of all, provide students with the tools for learning new words and evoke the motivation to do so.

## *Minicase Study*

As you recall from the previous chapter, Alicia is an eighth-grader reading on a fifth-grade level. Although she has good solid average intelligence, good work habits, and a supportive family, she is struggling with reading, especially in the content areas. Although Alicia is able to decode single-syllable words, she stumbles over multisyllabic words. Instruction in multisyllabic patterns and the use of analogy and pronounceable word–part strategies improved her skill in that area. However, because of a limited vocabulary, Alicia is struggling with her science and history texts, which at this level include many advanced, technical words. Alicia's score on the *Peabody Picture Vocabulary Test* and her struggle with words in her content-area texts indicate that her overall vocabulary development is lagging. For instance, in her reading she did not know the meanings of words like *haughty, sacrifices, circumference, decrease, aviation,* and *exaggeration,* words that the typical eighth-grader would know.

In addition to teaching Alicia strategies for decoding difficult words and deriving meanings of new words using context or morphemic analysis, her teacher has devised a multifaceted program for developing new vocabulary. First of all, Alicia is encouraged to read widely from self-selected magazines, newspapers, and books. Each week, she records on note cards ten new words drawn from her reading. On one side of the card, she notes the word and the context in which it appeared and what she thinks the word means. On the other side of the card, she writes the dictionary or glossary definition, thus checking her use of context. She discusses her new words with a peer partner. The two also quiz each other on the new words. In addition, Alicia is encouraged to use her new words in her speaking and writing.

Efforts are being made to build an interest in words. When the word *narcissistic* cropped up, the teacher explained the history of the word. That led to a study of words based on the names of Greek and Roman deities. When Alicia had difficulty with *transportation,* other words containing *trans* and *port* were studied.

As she has an artistic bent, Alicia was encouraged to draw diagrams and label them. For instance, when studying the parts of the brain, she copied a diagram of the brain and labeled each of the major parts. Seeing relationships among words was also stressed. When studying words from a selection, she has been encouraged to create a web, semantic feature analysis, or other graphic device to help her understand how the new words were related.

Because Alicia's poor vocabulary was interfering with her comprehension of her science and history texts, an extra effort has been made to build a conceptual understanding of key terms before Alicia reads the selection. As a result, her understanding of the content-area material has been showing an encouraging improvement.

## *Summary*

Because they don't read as much as achieving readers, problem readers don't usually have as large a store of vocabulary. This deficit grows worse as low-achieving readers progress through the grades. However, because it reflects background knowledge and speeds the reading process, vocabulary is the single-most important factor in comprehension. To foster comprehension, vocabulary instruction must be intensive. It must go beyond definitional knowledge to a contextual or conceptual status, should include multiple encounters, and should develop relationships.

Vocabulary instruction can be incidental or systematic or both. In the incidental approach, vocabulary is taught as needed. In the systematic approach, time is set aside for vocabulary instruction on a regular basis, so there is more focus on direct vocabulary development. Approximately 400 words can be thoroughly taught in a systematic program in a year's time.

Principles of teaching vocabulary include establishing goals, building on what students know, building a depth and breadth of meaning, creating an interest in words, relating words to students' lives, and promoting independent word learning. Techniques for teaching words include conceptual teaching of key words and brainstorming techniques, such as the list–group–label and semantic mapping approaches. Graphic techniques include semantic mapping, pictorial maps and webs, semantic feature analysis, and the Venn diagram. Other vocabulary teaching techniques described in the chapter are possible sentences, predict-o-grams, word sorts, and simulation. Wide reading and being read to were also discussed as ways of expanding vocabulary.

Strategies for remembering words focused on building understanding and the key word method. The key to developing vocabulary is to make the study of new words relevant and interesting.

## *Application Activities*

1. Try using a semantic map, Venn diagram, and a semantic feature analysis on some words that you're learning. Evaluate the effectiveness of each of the devices. What are the strengths of each? What are the weaknesses?

2. Compile a bibliography of books or word games that you might use with current or future students.

3. Use the key word technique to learn five new words. If possible, try out the technique with a group of students.

4. Following the recommendations made in this chapter, plan a vocabulary development lesson. If possible, teach the lesson and evaluate its effectiveness.

# Chapter 12

# Building Comprehension

## *Using What You Know*

In a sense, this chapter is the core of the text. For the most part, the previous chapters covered techniques for teaching the kinds of beginning reading and word level skills and strategies that make comprehension possible or enhance it. Three of the chapters that follow will explore ways of applying comprehension skills and strategies to the content areas, using comprehension skills to study, and using writing to improve comprehension.

This chapter presents comprehension as an active process in which the reader constructs meaning. When you are reading, what steps do you take to foster comprehension? What are some of the reasons students might have difficulty comprehending? What steps might be taken to help them?

## *Anticipation Guide*

Read each of the following statements. Put a check under "Agree" or "Disagree" to show how you feel about each one. If possible, discuss your responses with classmates.

| | Agree | Disagree |
|---|---|---|
| **1.** A lack of background knowledge is the main cause of poor comprehension. | ______ | ______ |
| **2.** How much a reader comprehends depends mainly on the kinds of comprehension strategies that she uses. | ______ | ______ |
| **3.** Most low-achieving readers should have little difficulty learning highly effective comprehension strategies. | ______ | ______ |
| **4.** The fastest way to improve comprehension is to use challenging materials. | ______ | ______ |
| **5.** Generally speaking, comprehension deficiencies are easier to remediate than are decoding difficulties. | ______ | ______ |

## *Theories of Comprehension*

Comprehension was once seen as a passive process in which the reader's main mission was to grasp the author's message. Today comprehension is seen as an active process in which the reader plays a very active role, constructing meaning based on his cultural and experiential background, purpose for reading, and the overall setting. The most widely accepted description of this view of reading is schema theory. A related view of comprehension is expressed in the mental models theory of reading.

### *Schema Theory*

The ad sitting on the kitchen table caught my eye. In a boldfaced head it was touting two books on farming. "Farm twice as effectively with half the effort!" A caption promised, "Farming made easy with these two expert guides."

The ad had been clipped by my wife, who intended to order the books. Since we don't even have a garden, much less a farm, I was puzzled by her interest in the books, until I read the rest of the ad.

What do you think the books will be about? What comes to your mind as you think about farming? My comprehension of the ad was based on my knowledge of farming. I pictured tall rows of corn, squealing pigs, bleating sheep, and a weathered barn. Even though I've never lived on a farm, I brought a fairly substantial background of knowledge to the ad. Had I grown up on a farm, I would have brought an even richer background to the ad. And that's what reading comprehension is. It isn't so much a matter of getting meaning from a selection, it's more a matter of bringing meaning to an ad, a story, or an article. Comprehension is an active constructive process which activates our schema. A **schema** is a generic concept, composed of our past experiences organized and filed away (Rumelhart, 1980). Schemata (the plural of schema) are based on our background of experience. We have schemata for persons, places, objects, and events. The richer our experiences and the better organized they are, the richer and more useful are our schemata. Comprehension depends, to a large extent, on the adequacy of our schemata.

> **Schema** (pl. schemata): abstract representation of knowledge organized and stored in memory. Schemata represent knowledge at various levels of abstraction. We can have a schema for baseball, growing tomatoes, liberty, etc.

Comprehension is a flexible process. We may read something that conflicts with our ideas and concepts, so we must be prepared to modify our schema. And sometimes we have schema but fail to activate it, or we activate the wrong schema, which is what I had done.

As I read further, I learned that the ad was about real estate farming, so I dropped my dirt farming schema and activated my schema about real estate farming. I realized that the word *farming* was being used in a figurative sense and referred to my wife's way of getting new clients. As a real estate agent, she has a farm, an area assigned to her by the broker for whom she worked. Each month she sends ads to the homeowners in her farm and occasionally she calls them. Now the ad made sense. However, had I not had indirect experience with real estate farming, I would not have had the proper schema to activate and so would have had some difficulty comprehending the ad.

## *Mental Models*

**Mental models:** images or verbal representations of elements such as characters in a story or cause–effect relationships. Comprehension consists of constructing a mental model of events as they unfold.

Although schema theory provides an appropriate explanation of what happens when the reader encounters known ideas and events, it is not as satisfactory when new ideas or events are involved (McNamara, Miller, & Bransford, 1991). In a **mental models** view of reading comprehension, readers create in their minds representations of what they have read. The reader may create an image of a character in a story or a mental representation of a house that has been described or a mental depiction of a series of steps to be followed. Schemata are still involved. Readers create representations based on their schema for people or houses, but the emphasis is on building new knowledge rather than activating old schema. In addition to images, mental models can also contain "nonperceptual information, such as goals and causal relationships" (McNamara, Miller, & Bransford, 1991).

We can remember text that we have read either by remembering the ideas contained in the text or the mental representation of the text that we created. For example, if a story mentions three cats, a black cat, a striped cat, and a gray cat, we can recall the ideas: one cat was black, one cat was striped, one cat was gray, or we can create mental models of images of the three cats. Mental models are generally easier to recall than words. Whether emphasizing a schema activation or mental models theory of reading, the role of the readers is an active one. Readers need to activate their schema as they read and to create mental models of texts.

## *Causes of Comprehension Difficulty*

Although schema deficiencies such as inadequate background and poorly developed concepts or failing to create adequate mental models can cause comprehension problems, there are numerous other factors that impede understanding. Reader factors that might cause a comprehension problem include lack of basic decoding skills, limited vocabulary, overuse of background knowledge or a lack or flexibility in considering new ideas, failure to read for meaning, and a lack of strategies or failure to use strategies appropriately (MacGinitie & MacGinitie, 1989; Manzo & Manzo, 1993; Maria, 1990). These factors, of course, interact with the task, the text, the techniques being used, and the situation. A reader may be successful with some kinds of tasks and in some environments, but not with others. As you read this chapter, you will notice several instances where poor readers did just as well as good readers when given easier books. You will also notice instances in this and other chapters where poor readers performed as well as achieving readers because they employed specific strategies, a particularly effective technique was used to instruct them, or the learning situation was improved in some other way. Although reader factors are emphasized in this chapter, the major reasons for comprehension difficulties involve inappropriate texts, teaching techniques, and instructional settings.

## Lack of Basic Decoding Skills or Fluency

If students are stumbling over a number of words or if their decoding is so slow that it is draining much of their mental energy and attention, their comprehension will suffer. When students' decoding is fluent, so that they don't have to think about decoding the words, then they can devote their full attention to comprehension. One solution is to provide instruction in basic decoding skills and/or fluency. However, the problem may lie in the choice of text. If students are having difficulty with more than 5 percent of the words, they should be given easier texts or some sort of extra assistance. Once student word recognition dips below 95 percent, comprehension starts to break down (Killgallon, 1942; Kletzien, 1991).

There is some disagreement about the percentage of word recognition required for adequate comprehension. See Baumann (1989) and Powell (1971) for a discussion.

When working with students who are still acquiring English, care needs to be taken in distinguishing between students who are having difficulty with basic decoding skills and those who mispronounce words in English because they are still learning the language. Moll et al. (cited in Garcia, Pearson, & Jiminez, 1994) found that students who were proficient readers in Spanish but were still learning English received very little instruction in comprehension when reading in English. This was due to the fact that their teachers misinterpreted their mispronunciations as signs of decoding difficulties, and so focused on word recognition skills.

## Lack of Academic Vocabulary

In their study of poor children, Chall, Jacobs, and Baldwin (1990) noted a condition known as the fourth-grade slump. In the first three grades, the students whom they studied did just as well as the more affluent children. For the most part, the words that appeared in their primary-grade reading materials and content-area books were common ones. Parents were able to give their children the help they needed. However, beginning in fourth grade, the texts grew decidedly more difficult, more abstract, and more academically oriented, often exceeding the parents' limited academic backgrounds and ability to help. The children started falling behind.

What's needed for students such as these is a planned program of vocabulary building as described in Chapter 11 coupled with extra preparation with difficult vocabulary words before a selection is read. Instruction in the use of context clues and the glossary or dictionary would also be helpful.

Students who are still learning English face a special challenge. On average, it takes about two years of experience with English before these students can converse with relative ease. However, learning academic English, the abstract decontextualized language used in classroom explanations and textbooks, takes much longer. By some estimates, it takes at least five years (Cummins, 1994). Unfortunately, because the students use conversational English with relative fluency, the teacher may not realize that academic English is a struggle for them. There are a number of techniques that can be used to support these students' emerging academic English skills and foster comprehension at the same time. These include using visuals, planning hands-on activities, and arranging for small-group discussions. In small-group discussions, students still learning English have a better chance of understanding what is being said and also of being understood. Both language and conceptual development are enhanced. It also important to affirm and build on the students' culture and native language.

## *Limited Background*

If students are relatively unfamiliar with a topic, seek out materials that provide an overview and do not assume a great deal of background information.

Having an adequate background of information is crucial for comprehension. Students who aren't sure of the difference between the Revolutionary War and the Civil War will have difficulty comprehending a biography of George Washington. Children who don't know the parts of a plant will have difficulty understanding an article on the fertilization of plants.

Like inadequate vocabulary, inadequate background is both a cause and effect of poor reading. Students who read less learn fewer new words and fewer new concepts. Having an impoverished vocabulary and background further impedes their growth in reading. Ways of building background include taking field trips, reading to children, discussing important topics, viewing filmstrips and CD-ROM programs, interacting with laser-disk programs, and reading materials on the appropriate level of challenge. Apparent inadequate background may also be a materials problem. If students are having difficulty with a full-blown biography of Eleanor Roosevelt, they would probably get more out of an easier, less fact-packed biography of the former first lady.

Before students read, spend extra time building concepts, especially those that are important to the comprehension of the main ideas in the selection to be read. Above all, encourage the reading of informational books on the appropriate level of difficulty. A technique that would be especially appropriate would be the DRA (Directed Reading Activity), which is explained later in this chapter.

## *Students Who Overuse Background*

Some students, especially those who may have weak decoding skills or whose decoding skills were slow to develop, habitually overrely on background knowledge to construct the meaning of a text. Using picture clues and the bits of the text that they are able to read accurately, they piece together the story's plot or the article's information. While this strategy may work well in the early grades when texts are simple and heavily illustrated, it leads to misinformation and misinterpretation as students encounter increasingly more complex materials. As MacGinitie and MacGinitie (1989) note, "Students who do not know many of the words in what they have been asked to read may be driven to answer questions on the basis of what they already know" (p. 38).

Some students may be able to handle the words in the selection but may simply not accept any information that conflicts with what they already know or believe (Maria & MacGinitie, 1987). They fail to modify their schema on the basis of new knowledge. This may be an attitudinal as well as an intellectual issue and is an area of major concern in science reading. Many of us entertain common sense beliefs about how the world works. The beliefs are logical but may not be scientifically accurate. Many students believe that plants get their food from the soil (Roth, 1991). Even after reading that plants produce their own food, the students, both good and poor readers, retained their erroneous belief.

Techniques that involve discussing ideas, including misconceptions, before and after reading would be especially useful with students who overuse prior knowledge or fail to modify schema in the light of new knowledge. Also, having students verify conclusions by reading passages that support their responses is a helpful technique.

### *Students Who Fail to Read for Meaning*

Some students have no purpose or goal for reading. Their assignment may be to read five pages or a chapter, which they do. But they simply plow through the material. Their goal is to complete the assignment. They give no thought to understanding the material. They may not even realize that they are failing to comprehend the material they are reading. This style of reading is a natural outgrowth of earlier reading difficulties or an overemphasis on decoding. Struggling to say the words right and seeing reading as a process of accurate pronunciation, these students fail to read for meaning or are so overwhelmed by the task of decoding that they are unable to read for meaning. Activities that engage students in the reading process would be especially helpful. Students also need instruction in comprehension strategies and strategies that require them to be aware of whether or not their comprehension is adequate.

### *Lack of Strategies or Failure to Use Strategies*

Reading is an active strategic process. A strategy is a planned, purposeful cognitive tool that can be used to direct and improve comprehension. Whereas strategic reading is characteristic of expert readers, novice and poor readers are deficient in this vital area. Novice and older unskilled readers "often focus on decoding single words, fail to adjust their reading for different texts, or purposes, and seldom look ahead or back in text in order to monitor their comprehension" (Paris, Wasik, & Turner, 1991, p. 609). Despite this rather grim assessment of problem readers, the good news is that poor comprehenders often show remarkable progress when given a program of instruction in the kinds of comprehension strategies described in the next section.

## *Comprehension Strategies*

Strategic readers are able to use four sources of knowledge in a flexible way: (1) knowledge of a variety of appropriate strategies; (2) knowledge of one's self as a learner; (3) knowledge of the demands of the reading task which makes it possible for the reader to select, use, monitor, and evaluate strategies; and (4) background or world knowledge (Palincsar, Winn, David, Synder, & Stevens, 1993). In addition, readers must be motivated to use their knowledge of strategies (Paris & Okra, 1986) and have confidence that they will work

This text has organized strategies according to the cognitive processes that they demand. There is some overlapping. For instance, all strategies should involve some degree of monitoring.

(Dole, Brown, Trathen, 1996). Garner (1994) concluded that a lack of interest in the text and a lack of confidence in strategies will diminish the students' willingness to use strategies.

There are dozens of comprehension strategies. However, they can be classified according to the cognitive operations that they incorporate: preparing, selecting and organizing, elaborating, rehearsing (studying), and monitoring. There are also affective or motivational strategies (Weinstein & Mayer, 1986).

## *Preparational Strategies*

Preparational strategies are those that a reader uses to prepare for reading. These include activating prior knowledge, previewing a selection, predicting what might happen in a story or what information a nonfiction piece will convey, and setting a goal for reading.

Before reading a selection about acid rain, the reader asks herself or himself: "What do I know about acid rain?" If there is a prereading discussion, the teacher might activate prior knowledge. Failing to activate prior knowledge, poor readers may not connect information in the text with what they already know. A good way to teach activating prior knowledge is through modeling. If you model the process, use a real-life example: a piece that you're reading. For instance, you might say, "I'm taking a class at night. And for homework I have to read about the brain. At first, I thought, 'This article is going to be really hard. I don't know anything about the brain.' But then I said to myself, 'Yes, I do. Let's see. I know the brain has two sides: the right hemisphere and the left hemisphere. I also know the brain has parts called *lobes* and billions of nerve cells called *neurons.*' "

**Purpose** for reading is the information that you seek, a question to be answered, or a prediction to be assessed. A **goal** is your objective for reading. Are you reading for pleasure, to follow a set of directions, or to prepare for a test?

Low-progress readers often lack a purpose or clear goal in reading. Discuss goals and purposes with students. Ask: "Why are you reading this? What do you hope to find out?"

### *Setting Purpose and Goal*

The **purpose** for reading might grow out of activating prior knowledge. For instance, in the example above, your activation of prior knowledge may cause you to realize that you know that the hemispheres of the brain are connected, but you aren't quite sure how they are connected. Your purpose (question to be answered) in reading might then be to find out how the hemispheres of the brain are connected. Readers also need to set a **goal** for reading. If you are reading just for your own information, your reading may be casual. If you are preparing for a test, then you would adopt a study style of reading. Your goal would be to both understand and retain what you had read. Model for students how you might set a purpose and a goal for your reading.

### *Previewing*

Previewing is a natural accompaniment of predicting. In **previewing,** the reader spends a minute or two reading the title, headings, the first paragraph or introduction, the last paragraph or summary, and scanning any illustrations, charts, graphs, or tables that accompany the piece. As readers preview, they gain an overview of the piece they are about to read. They should also activate schema, make predictions, set a purpose for reading, and create a plan for reading the piece. Should it be skimmed? Should it be read slowly and carefully? Should it be read section by section? Should it be read as a whole? A good preview can function as a framework for organizing the main ideas in a selection or as "a kind of a blueprint for constructing a mental model" (Gunning, 1996, p. 198).

### Predicting

Making predictions depends upon the students' background. Students have a more difficult time if they are reading about an unfamiliar topic because they have little basis for predicting.

A highly popular strategy, **predicting** forces an activation of prior knowledge. Using a prediction strategy, a reader makes an educated guess about the course of events in a story or the kind of information that will be contained in a nonfiction piece. We make predictions on the basis of what we know. Predictions can also determine our purpose in reading. We may read the selection to compare our predictions with what actually happens. It is important to use this strategy flexibly. Remember that poor readers sometimes fail to modify their beliefs when they read information that contradicts them. They need to be prepared to modify predictions based on information contained in the text.

## Selection/Organizational Strategies

When vocabulary is difficult in a selection, as it so often is for poor readers, they must focus on decoding and process smaller units of text, perhaps only two- or three-word segments (Kletzien, 1991). Caught up in looking at individual words and details, they may fail to grasp main ideas. Selection/organizational strategies include deriving a main idea, selecting relevant details, organizing details, summarizing, and creating graphic organizers. All of these strategies involve integrating textual information in some way. Of these, deriving the main idea of a selection is the most essential. The main idea provides the underlying pattern for organizing a passage's vital details. Being able to derive main ideas is a prerequisite for summarizing, note taking, outlining, and creating graphic organizers.

### Deriving Main Ideas

**Main idea:** what a piece of writing is all about—the gist or summary statement of the passage.

Definitions of main idea vary as do the activities designed to promote grasping the main idea (Baumann, 1986). The **main idea** can be best thought of as a summary statement that subsumes all of the details in a piece of writing. The main idea of a paragraph would include what all the ideas in a paragraph are talking about.

In essence, constructing the main idea is a classification exercise. The reader must note similarities among the details in a paragraph and then must choose the sentence that tells about all the others (if the main idea is stated) or construct a statement that includes all the details in a paragraph (if the main idea is not stated). A good way to initiate main idea instruction is to have students classify items, ideas, and whole sentences. For instance, young children could be asked to sort objects in a classroom and give those sorted objects a name. Students might sort toys or tools. Later, they can categorize words, indicating which word tells about all the others: *lions, elephants, whales, animals, dogs.* Once students have grasped the idea of categorizing, they can classify the sentences in a paragraph and tell which sentence tells about all the others. In the following paragraph, for example, students should be able to tell that the first sentence states the main idea.

> Soybeans can be eaten in many different ways. Soybean flour and oil are used to make pancakes, cookies, candy bars, soups, and many other foods. Soybean flour is used to make foods that look and taste like meat. Soybeans can also be used to make a sauce that adds flavor to foods.

After students have become adept at picking the sentence that "tells about all the others," omit the main idea sentence from the paragraph and have them generate a main idea statement. This is a far more difficult task, so provide guidance as needed. Also reinforce the concept of main idea by helping students use titles, topic sentences, headings, and subheads as clues to main ideas in a text. In a study by K. K. Taylor (1986), many students, but especially the poor readers, failed to use titles and topic sentences to derive main ideas in selections, even though both contained the main idea of the passage.

Eventually, students should derive main ideas from real paragraphs in real books. Start with brief paragraphs that have a clearly stated main idea in the first sentence. Then move into longer selections and include ones in which the main idea sentence appears in the middle or end of a paragraph. Although the main idea or topic sentence can appear anywhere in a paragraph or may even be implied, poor readers tend to select the first sentence as the topic sentence (Gold & Fleischer, 1986).

Drawing from children's books or textbooks, choose well-written paragraphs that contain topic sentences that appear in various places in the paragraph. Social studies texts might be a good source. Nearly half of the paragraphs in social studies texts contain topic sentences. However, these appear as the first sentence of the paragraph only 27 percent of the time (Baumann & Serra, 1984). As students choose topic sentences, have them verify their selections by explaining how other sentences in the paragraph support the main idea.

Apply the concept of main idea to longer pieces of writing. In a well-written science or social studies text or informational children's book, point out main ideas. Discuss the fact that just as paragraphs have main ideas, so, too, do sections of text. Show how headings often indicate the main idea of a whole section.

> Obtain books on high-interest topics that are written on the appropriate level. You might start with Pocket Facts books (Crestwood House), in which brief paragraphs are preceded by headings that signal the main idea.

***Implied Main Ideas***

Adapting the strategies used by expert readers (Afflerbach, 1990), teach students to create main ideas by implementing the following steps:

1. Use textual cues (title, heading, major illustrations, introductory sentence) to construct a tentative main idea statement.
2. As you read the passage, judge whether or not the sentences support the main idea. If not, revise the main idea statement.
3. Judge whether all or most of the sentences support the main idea. (Often, in well-written prose, passages will contain a sentence or two that is kind of an aside, a detail that may be interesting and related to the overall topic but which does not support the main idea). If most of the sentences do not support the main idea, then see what all or

most of the sentences have in common, and construct a main idea statement that tells what they are about.

Begin with brief passages and gradually introduce longer segments of text. If possible, have students apply the steps to texts that they use in their content area subjects. Also use writing to reinforce the concept of main ideas. Help students develop topic sentences into well-constructed paragraphs. You might use paragraph frames similar to the ones in Figure 12-1 to assist students. Once students have achieved a basic understanding of topic sentences, encourage them to compose and develop their own.

### *Summarizing*

Summarizing is the most effective comprehension strategy of all (Pressley, Johnson, Symons, McGoldrich, & Kurita, 1989). Summarizing is a method for both improving and checking comprehension. Because it involves selecting, organizing, and restating the main details in a passage, summarizing enhances understanding and promotes retention. It also forces a self-evaluation of comprehension. If you haven't comprehended a selection adequately, you won't be able to summarize it.

Summarizing should not be confused with retelling. In a retelling, students may tell all that they know or all that they can remember. In a summary, only the important details are retold and are related in condensed form (Maria, 1990). One of the reasons summaries are difficult to compose is that they involve two processes: selection of important details and reduction or condensation of these details (Hidi & Anderson, 1986).

***Frame 1***

Some fish have names that tell what they look like.
The glassfish ______________________________.
The pipefish ______________________________.
The parrotfish ______________________________.
These fish have names that really fit.

***Frame 2***

Computers are one of our most useful tools. Computers are used
______________________________.
Computers also ______________________________.
Computers can even ______________________________.
Now we wonder how we ever got along without computers.

***Frame 3***

My favorite day of the week is ______________________________.
For one thing, ______________________________.
For another, ______________________________.
Best of all, ______________________________.
It's too bad there aren't two ________ in every week.

**FIGURE 12-1 Paragraph Frames**

Summarizing is difficult. In addition to selecting the most important information, the summarizer must condense information by combining and synthesizing ideas.

**Teaching Summarizing.** Although summarizing demands adequate comprehension, writing a summary involves more than just understanding a passage. It also entails using specialized written language skills (K. K. Taylor, 1986). Because written summaries involve complex writing skills, instruction might be initiated with oral summaries. Although oral summaries are more exacting than retellings, retellings can provide solid preparation for summarizing. To make retellings more valuable, guide students so they emphasize essential details. Through careful questioning, help them highlight the most important information. Ask questions such as: "What was the most important thing that Marisol did? What three things happened to James?"

The strategies used to grasp main ideas can also form a basis for summarizing. Surveying a text provides an overview of the main ideas in a selection. Predicting also tends to make the reader focus on major events and ideas.

Use naturally occurring occasions to model summarizing. For instance, after explaining that you are summarizing, sum up a demonstration, lecture, or discussion. Summarize the main events in a story or the major details in a science or social studies article. As students catch onto the idea, ask them to summarize discussions, a current event, or a section from a story or article.

Some students believe that summaries should feature the most interesting or most difficult details in a selection or sentences from the selection that are richly detailed (K. K. Taylor, 1986; Winograd, 1984). Stress the fact that summaries should feature the most essential details.

### A Lesson in Writing Summaries

Once students have some familiarity with oral summaries, present a series of steps that could be helpful in composing a written summary. As adapted from Brown & Day (1983), these include:

*Step 1: Explain and Show*

Explain the importance and also provide several examples of summaries showing that they are a condensation of the major details in a selection.

*Step 2: Find Main Idea*

Show students how to use the title or headings and topic sentence to get a sense of the main idea of the selection.

*Step 3: Topic Sentence*

Show students how to choose the topic sentence or create one if the main idea is implied.

Integrating the use of strategies can be highly effective. Weisberg and Balajthy (1990) taught secondary students reading on a fifth-grade level to identify main ideas, construct graphic organizers, and write summaries.

*Step 4: Select Details*

Show students how to select essential details.

*Step 5: Paraphrase, Condense*

Show students how to paraphrase and condense essential ideas.

This involves explaining how to combine and collapse details into a more general statement. For instance, the sentence "Maria read her science chapter and answered the questions at the end, read twenty pages of the novel the class was reading, and then worked on her social studies project" could

### A Lesson in Writing Summaries *Continued*

be combined and condensed into: "Maria did her homework."

*Step 6: Compare*

Compare the summary with the original.

Ask: Does it contain all the important information? Is the information correct?

*Step 7: Check for Clarity*

Concerned more about content than expression, students might compose a summary that is complete and correct but poorly written. The student should go back over the summary, asking: "How does the summary sound? Is it clear? Is it easy to understand?"

To aid students in creating summaries, provide frames like those shown in Figure 12.2. Gradually wean the students from the frames so that they will take over full responsibility for writing summaries. Start with brief, well-constructed passages, so that the frames will be easier to complete. However, the passages that are being summarized should have meaning to the students. It might be a passage from their science or social studies text or a tradebook that is exploring a topic of interest. As they learn the how and what of summarizing, they should also be learning the why: summarizing will help them understand and remember information that is important to them in school or out-of-school activities. Summarizing passages from a section on which students will soon be tested would be an excellent activity. Students are more likely to learn and use strategies for which they can see a genuine value (Schunk & Rice, 1987).

We need fats in our diets. Fats ________________. Fats also give us __________. Fats also help ________________.

There are two kinds of fats. Solid fats can be found in __________. Solid fats are made from __________. Liquid fats are found in __________. Liquid fats are made from ________________.

Fats can saturated or unsaturated. Saturated fats are found mostly in __________. Unsaturated fats can be divided into two groups, __________ and __________. Unsaturated fats usually come from ________________. Unsaturated fats are healthier because ________________.

Source: *Fats* by R. Nottridge, 1993, Minneapolis, MN: Carolrhoda Books.

The Phoenicians worked at many different trades and occupations.

1. ________________________________________.
2. ________________________________________.
3. ________________________________________.
4. ________________________________________.

Source: *The Phoenicians*. P. Odik. Englewood Cliffs, NJ: Silver Burdett. 1989.

**FIGURE 12-2 Frames for Summaries**

**Graphic Organizers As Summaries.** Graphic organizers can also be used to summarize text. Because they don't necessitate writing a paragraph, graphic organizers are easier to create than traditional summaries. Graphic organizers also do a better job of highlighting important information and showing relationships among ideas. Graphic organizers can be written in their own right or may be used in preparation for composing a written summary. Graphic organizers that might be used to create summaries include semantic maps and Venn diagrams, which were introduced in Chapter 11. A sample semantic map summarizing a brief text on fruit is displayed in Figure 12-3. For additional examples of graphic organizers used with content-area texts, see Chapter 13.

Elaboration strategies are built on preparational and organizational strategies. Information can't be transformed, evaluated, or applied unless it has first been understood.

## *Elaboration Strategies*

Using elaboration strategies, the reader transforms, judges, applies, or adds to information from the text in some way. Through elaboration, the reader may draw an inference, create a mental image, or evaluate the material that was read. Involving a higher level of comprehension and

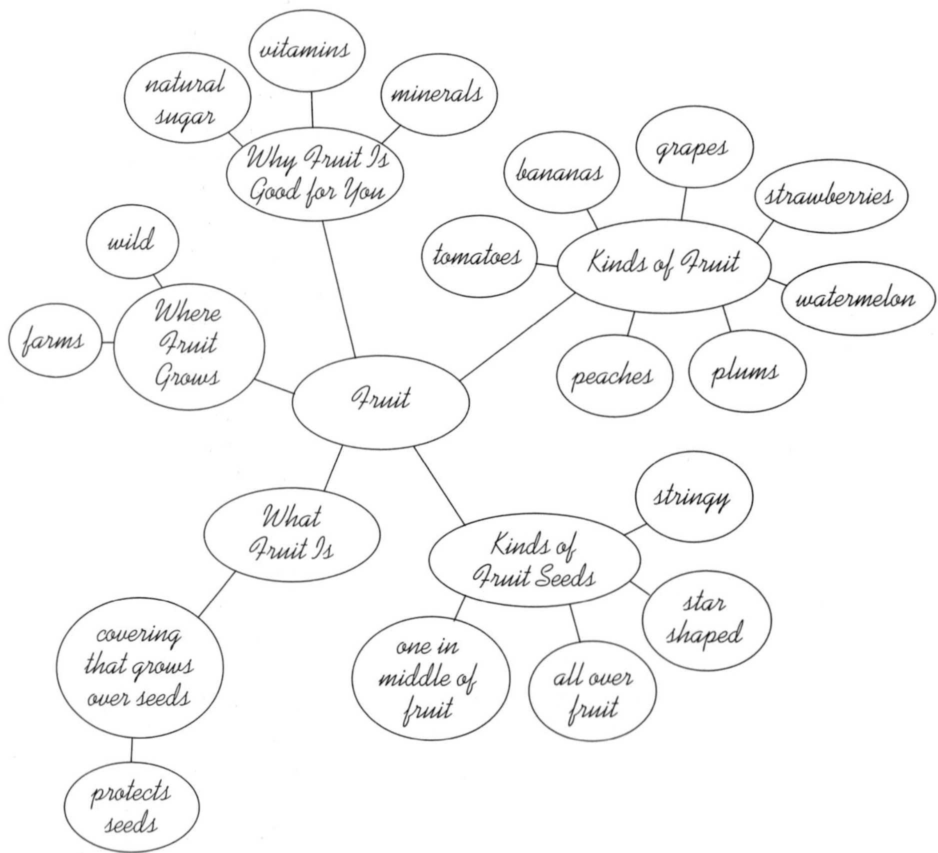


**FIGURE 12-3 Semantic Map**

Source: *We Love Fruit.* F. Robinson. Chicago, IL: Children's Press, 1992.

a deeper level of processing, elaboration typically improves comprehension by 50 percent (Linden & Wittrock, 1981).

### *Inferences*

Inferring is a main elaboration at all reading levels. Much of the information that a reader derives from text is the result of constructing inferences. If we read "the batter struck out in the ninth inning and the game is over," we infer that baseball was being played, the batter was on the losing side, and there were two outs when the batter stepped up to the plate. The author doesn't have to tell us this. **Inferences** are the details, judgments, or conclusions that readers construct as they read. Inferences are based on readers' schemata and/or information contained in the text.

As might be expected, all readers, but especially lower-achieving ones, have difficulty making inferences (National Assessment of Educational Progress, 1986; Holmes, 1987; Wilson, 1979). In her study of reading disabled sixth-graders, McCormick (1992) found that whereas low-achieving readers were able to answer 70 percent of the literal comprehension questions, they were only able to respond to 61 percent of the inferential ones.

Why do low-achieving readers have difficulty with inferential questions? Since answering inferential questions requires combining information in the text with background or prior knowledge, having an impoverished background is one possible cause. Ironically, McCormick (1992) found that overreliance on background knowledge was a major cause of erroneous responses. In these instances readers rejected or ignored text information and used personal background knowledge to respond to questions. McCormick explains, "It may be that low-achieving students have had less access to text information because of word recognition difficulties and over time have developed a pervasive strategy of simple guessing at possible responses based on knowledge already stored in their schemata" (p. 73). Other major errors included answers that were too specific or were only marginally related to the question. In the first instance, students were distracted by irrelevant information. In the second instance, they failed to consider all the information in the selection, focusing instead on one specific detail, rather than considering several details.

As Wilson (1979) explains, poor readers tend to give "intuitive" answers, responses rooted in personal knowledge rather than in the text. In a similar vein, Phillips (1988) and Kimmel and MacGinitie (1984) found that low-performing readers used a kind of perseverative strategy in which they held firmly to an erroneous response despite conflicting evidence.

Techniques designed to improve the inferencing ability of low-achieving readers would need to compensate for overreliance on prior knowledge, inadequate use of text, and lack of flexibility in reasoning about what one reads. It would also need to build students' confidence in their ability to draw inferences from text.

One approach that does an excellent job of incorporating these factors is Hansen and Pearson's (1982) prior knowledge prediction strategy. Although relatively simple to apply and teach, the strategy is powerful. After being taught the strategy, low-progress readers did just as well with inferences as did higher-achieving readers.

### Prior Knowledge Prediction Strategy Lesson

*Step 1: Creating Questions*

As with a number of successful techniques, the first step in teaching the technique is to analyze the selection to be read for two or three central ideas. For each central idea, create two questions. The first question, which is designed to activate the appropriate schema, asks students about any experiences that they may have had that would be similar to the central idea. For instance, if the central idea is: "A best friend moved away," then you would create a question similar to the following: "Have you ever lost a friend because your friend moved away or you moved away?" Then you would ask a prediction question that is related to the schema activation question and the central idea. "In the story we're about to read, Jeremy's best friend is moving away. What do you think Jeremy will do?"

*Step 2: Prereading Discussion*

In the prereading discussion, the teacher asks the schema-activation question and then the prediction question. The discussion is critical. Low-achieving readers often have difficulty activating appropriate schema. During the discussion, a student might think, "I've never had a friend move away" and so is unable to activate relevant schema. But then a student explains how he felt when his uncle and aunt moved away. He explains that they were young and had no children of their own, and had taken him many places. The discussion reminds the first youngster of how she felt when her cousin moved, so she is then able to activate the appropriate moving-away schema.

Through discussions, students reveal their thought processes and help each other to learn.

*Step 3: Silent Reading of Selection*

Students read to assess their predictions.

*Step 4: Post-reading Discussion*

The post-reading discussion is also an important part of the technique. After discussing students' predictions, ask related inference questions. All too often, questions asked of low-achieving readers are restricted to the literal level. Or the higher level questions that they are asked simply require an opinion. Inference questions should involve using both the text and prior knowledge: How did Maria feel when her friend move away?

*Step 5: Verifying Inferences*

Since low-achieving readers overrely on prior experience, it is important that they be asked to justify inferences. If a student infers that the main character in the story, Maria, is sad because her friend moved away, then the student should be asked to supply evidence from the selection that indicates Maria is sad.

#### *Importance of Modeling*

The research by McCormick (1992) suggests that low-achieving readers may have limited experience drawing inferences. It is essential that the process be explained and modeled with lots of opportunities for guided practice and application. You might also follow a "gradual release of responsibility" model (Pearson & Gallagher, 1983). Using brief passages, you draw an inference and have students find the supporting evidence. Once they have become proficient at locating evidence, switch roles. You supply the evidence and have them draw the inferences. Ultimately, students both draw the inferences and supply the evidence. Begin with short selections and gradually work into longer ones.

#### *Responsive Elaboration*

Because faulty reasoning or use of inappropriate reasoning strategies is the cause of many erroneous inferences, a technique known as responsive elaboration may help students rea-

**Responsive elaboration:** the teacher analyzes a student's answer to determine what reasoning processes the student is using and then, building on that analysis, elaborates the student's response.

son their way to credible inferences (Duffy & Roehler, 1987). As its name suggests, **responsive elaboration** is a teacher prompt or an elaboration made in response to a student's erroneous answer. Focus is on the process rather than the answer. Analyze the student's response and try to figure out how she or he arrived at that answer. Ask yourself, "What strategies or thought processes did the student use? What can I do to correct the process?" Here is an example of how a teacher used responsive elaboration to restructure an inference that was based on inadequate information.

*Student:* (making erroneous inference): Jake was a coward.

*Teacher:* What leads you to believe that Jake was cowardly?

*Student:* The story says he was so filled with fear when he saw the snake that his knees were knocking. He felt like running away even though the snake was about to bite his baby sister.

*Teacher:* Did he run away?

*Student:* Yes.

*Teacher:* What did he do before he ran?

*Student:* He picked up a big rock and threw it on the snake.

*Teacher:* What else did he do?

*Student:* He grabbed his baby sister, and then he ran.

*Teacher:* Would that have taken courage? The snake might still have been alive.

*Student:* Yes. I suppose so.

*Teacher:* All of us have fears, but we show courage when we overcome our fears.

### *QAR*

Although many low-achieving readers overrely on prior knowledge, some are textbound and respond to inferential questions with, "I can't find the answer in the book." This is especially true of younger low-achieving readers. In addition to explaining the value and purpose of inferential questions, you might try **QAR** (question–answer relationship). To show students that not all answers are in the book, QAR was created to help students locate the source of answers, whether they be literal or inferential (Raphael, 1984, 1986). QAR activities are designed to help students determine whether an answer is:

1. Right there: Answer is contained within a single sentence in the text.
2. Putting it together: It is necessary to put together information from several sentences to obtain an answer.
3. On my own: The answer is part of the student's prior knowledge.
4. Writer and me: The reader must combine personal knowledge with information from the text to construct an inference.

To introduce QAR, write a paragraph similar to the following on the board. The selection and accompanying questions are designed to demonstrate the various sources of answers.

With the sun in her eyes, the driver pulled over into the highway's slow lane and eased up on the gas. Glancing up at the large metal sign overhead, she was relieved to see that she had only two exits to go. She had started driving early in the morning, just before six A.M. Now it was nearly six P.M.

To show students where answers to questions can be found, ask questions of the following type:

- Where was the driver? (right there)
- How much farther did she have to go? (right there)
- How long had she been driving? (putting it together)
- In which direction was she heading? (writer and me)
- How do you feel after you've been in a car for a long time? (on my own)

To help students become more aware of the sources for answers to questions, have them create questions about a passage that are "right there," involve "putting it together," or are "on my own," or "writer and me."

As you discuss answers to the questions and the sources of the answers, emphasize the fact that answers aren't always directly stated. During subsequent sessions, ask varied questions: some that can be answered with information in the text and some that require using background information and the text or just background knowledge. Along with discussing answers, also identify sources of answers.

### *Imaging*

What might be some ways of enhancing low-achieving readers' comprehension of the following passage?

*Imagine it is 140 million years ago. The oceans are warm and palmlike trees grow everywhere. Dinosaurs of all shapes and sizes roam the earth. Some of the dinosaurs are no bigger than a chicken. Others are taller than a six-story building. Some have horns and spikes. Others have duck bills and bird feet. There are no people yet. It is the middle of the Mesozoic (mez-uh-ZO-ik) Era. (McMullan, 1989, pp. 6–7)*

**Imaging** is the process of creating visual, auditory, or other representations as one reads, listens, views, or thinks.

One technique would be to use imaging. In **imaging,** students create visual, auditory, or other sensory-based mental representations of characters, objects, events, or other elements in a selection. Although a neglected technique, imaging is a powerful, easy-to-teach, easy-to-learn device that students enjoy applying. Research suggests that it increases comprehension (Sadoski, 1983, 1985) and improves comprehension monitoring (Gambrell & Bales, 1986). Students who create mental images are better at understanding what they read and detecting inconsistencies while reading than those who don't.

## Imaging Lesson

*Step 1: Introducing Imaging*

> While the verbal coding system might analyze and organize information in the form of words, the imaging system generates mental images (Sadoski, Goetz, Fritz, 1993).

To introduce imaging, explain what it is and why it is a valuable comprehension strategy. Then model the process. Show how you would create images of a concrete passage.

*Step 2: Focusing*

Encourage students to relax and clear their minds of distracting thoughts. Have students close their eyes and listen to a brief, concrete passage, forming pictures in their minds as they do. Direct students to draw pictures of their images. This fixes the images so that when the class discusses them, individual students don't forget what their original images looked like (Maria, 1990). In the beginning, you might use single sentences or very brief paragraphs. Once students have begun to grasp the idea of imaging, try using longer pieces.

> When they used visualizing, low-achieving readers were better able to understand what they read and to integrate new and old information (Pressley, 1977).

*Step 3: Discussing*

Discuss students' images, but before doing so, talk over the fact that because each of us is a different person and has different experiences, each of us will create individual images. To show students how different people create different images, compare the illustrations in different versions of classic stories, or compare illustrations of similar events or scenes from several content-area texts. When discussing students' images, use probing questions to get more detail and also to focus on important ideas. As with other activities, students can get bogged down in unimportant details.

*Step 4: Guided Practice*

After students have caught onto the idea of creating images, ask them to create pictures of text in their minds as they read. Start off with brief concrete text and then move into longer pieces, including content-area texts. After students have read the passage and sketched their images, ask questions that focus on the main content. Also pose questions that help them to create fuller images. If the passage lends itself to it, ask questions that go beyond the visual. In addition to asking, "What did you see?" ask: "What did you hear? What did you feel? What did you touch? What did you smell?" If students have difficulty creating an image or have left out elements, encourage them to reread the passage and create an image of the piece, adding elements to their mental representation. One interesting activity would be to visualize the main character of a story or a setting and then compare one's mental picture with that created by the illustrator.

> Poor readers don't use imaging as much as good readers, but show significant improvement after instruction (Gambrell & Bales, 1986).

*Step 5: Review and Application*

After introducing imaging, continue to review and reinforce it. Suggest its use where it might be especially appropriate: imaging scenes, characters, or events in fiction; imaging events or scenes in history, places in geography, and processes in science. Encourage students to use drawings, even if they consist mainly of stick figures. Also encourage the creation of charts, diagrams, geographical and semantic maps, and other graphic displays to organize information that they have read. Periodically, make imaging a part of pre-reading activities, assignments, and discussions so that it becomes second-nature to students.

> Images can call forth ideas and words, and words and ideas can evoke images. For instance, we can create images for justice and democracy and other abstract concepts (Sadoski, Paivio, & Goetz, 1993).

One advantage of imaging is that it involves the students in their texts so that they are more likely to engage in deep processing. Another is that it sparks more participation in students who are typically passive. In her use of imaging, Maria (1990) reports that many of the students who were most active in discussing their images were those who normally had little to say in class. A third advantage of imaging is that it will be a new technique for many students and so should prove to be motivational.

As with any other strategy, students should learn when, where, and why to use imaging as well as how to use it. As part of your instruction, explain why imaging is a useful strategy. Also point out that it works better with some kinds of writing than with others. Consider individual differences in the use of imagery. Some students will undoubtedly find imagery difficult to use, so you may stress the use of nonvisual strategies with them.

## *Metacognitive Awareness*

Although Anna, a fifth-grader, spent thirty minutes poring over an article on the formation of rocks, she had little to show for her effort. When asked questions about the article, she was unable to respond. As she was reading, Anna wasn't really getting much meaning from the text. She didn't understand what she was reading. And she didn't realize that she didn't understand. She lacked metacognitive awareness.

All of us have difficulty with comprehension from time to time, but usually we are aware of the difficulty. We realize that our attention was diverted, and don't have the slightest idea of what we just read. Or we realize that we have gotten lost in a tangle of legalese when reading a contract. Or we don't understand the steps for installing a new piece of software. Realizing that we are not comprehending, we take corrective action: reread, get help with difficult terms, or examine a clarifying illustration. However, since they often don't realize that they are not understanding, low-achieving readers fail to take steps to repair faulty comprehension.

**Metacognitive awareness:** being conscious of one's thought processes.

**Metacognitive awareness** is the ability to think about our cognitive processes. It is knowledge about "ourselves, the tasks we face, and the strategies we employ" (Garner, 1994, p. 717). According to Paris (1991), "As children gain experience with a task such as reading, they begin to understand their own abilities, the characteristics of a text that make reading easy or difficult, and the strategies that can be employed to aid comprehension" (p. 34).

In addition to being less likely to detect a comprehension problem, low-achieving readers are also less likely to choose a corrective strategy even when they do detect a problem. While achieving readers report rereading a confusing passage, poor readers are more likely to say that they would "skip it" (Garner & Reis, 1981). The four crucial areas in metacognition are: (1) knowing oneself as a learner; (2) regulating; (3) monitoring; and (4) correcting (Baker & Brown, 1984; Garner, 1994).

### *Knowing Oneself As a Learner*

Generally a student knows what his background of knowledge is and knows himself as a reader. He may realize that he is a fast, global reader with a poor background in science. Self-knowledge, however, can be faulty. A student may believe that he knows all there is to know about snakes and so fails to read with an open mind an article that contradicts his deeply held but erroneous concepts. Or the student may believe that he is dumb and that he will not learn new material no matter how hard he tries (Paris, 1991). Beaten before he starts because of a poor self-concept, the student may not exert a wholehearted effort and may not apply the strategies that he has mastered. Helping low-achieving readers know themselves as learners often involves correcting false notions and building confidence.

### *Regulating*

Regulating means that the student exercises cognitive control over her learning. The student knows strategies and knows how, when, and where to use them. The student also knows what to read to fulfill a specific purpose. For instance, in studying for a science quiz, the student with a fast, global style will shift to a slower-paced analytic approach when she realizes that the quiz will be factual. She may choose to use a specialized study technique or simply take notes or engage in some form of self-questioning. She may focus on the textbook sections that describe areas that the teacher emphasized in class.

### *Monitoring*

**Monitoring:** mental checking of one's cognitive processes. In reading, monitoring is an awareness of whether a passage is making sense or not.

**Monitoring** means that the student evaluates her understanding. After each section, she may attempt to summarize what she has read or engage in self-testing by asking herself questions about what she has read. If a section doesn't make sense, she may reread it, look up difficult words in the glossary, refer to illustrations, or ask a friend, parent, or teacher for help. Imaging or summarizing can be another form of monitoring for meaning. If a student has difficulty creating images or summaries, it may be due to faulty comprehension.

Poor monitoring may also be related to poor comprehension strategies and the material's level of difficulty. In several experiments, inconsistencies and nonsense words were inserted in selections read by good and poor readers in the fourth grade. When low-achieving readers' understanding and recall of a passage was inadequate because the text was apparently too difficult, they noted fewer inconsistencies or nonsense words in the text (Paris & Myers, 1981). However, when the text was simplified, poor readers noted as many errors as the good readers. When the reading material is too difficult, poor readers are unable to make full use of the strategies they possess. If too many of the text's words are unknown, the poor reader may not comprehend well enough to see that there are inconsistencies.

Learning to monitor one's comprehension is partly developmental. In general, older students are better at monitoring than younger ones. The nature of monitoring also changes as students develop. Young students and low-achieving readers tend to focus on lower level elements. They are concerned about processing words and sentences, whereas older readers and more competent students are more aware of their understanding of paragraphs and larger sections of text.

### *Correcting*

Being aware of a problem in comprehension is a necessary first step in solving that problem. The second step is correcting the problem. There are a number of actions that can be undertaken to repair faulty comprehension. These include but are not limited to the following:

- *Rereading a confusing sentence or paragraph.*
- *Reading ahead to see if that clarifies the meaning of a passage.*
- *Obtaining the meaning of an unknown key word.*
- *Using illustrations as an aid.*
- *Slowing down the rate of reading.*
- *Using an encyclopedia or other reference to clarify a confusing concept.*
- *Looking back over the text to find details that one has forgotten.*
- *Asking oneself questions.*
- *Putting a confusing passage into one's own words.*
- *Relating ideas to one's own experience.*
- *Talking over the passage with a friend, a parent, or the teacher. (Taylor, Harris, & Pearson, 1988)*

***Instruction in Metacognition***

Instruction in metacognition should be ongoing and multifaceted, systematic and also on-the-spot as needed. Every strategy lesson should have a metacognitive aspect. Whenever students are taught a new strategy, they should also be taught how, when, and where to apply that strategy and what to do if the strategy doesn't work. Students, especially low-achieving readers, should be taught that reading should always make sense. Based on a review of the research, Winograd, Lipson, and Wixson (1989) constructed a plan for teaching metacognitive and other strategies.

**A Lesson in Teaching Metacognitive Strategies**

*Step 1: Describing the Strategy*

The strategy is explained in detail. The teacher provides a description and examples of the strategy so that the students know what the strategy is and how it works.

*Step 2: Explaining Why the Strategy Is Important*

Explain and model why the strategy is valuable. Low-achieving readers may not realize that even the best readers have difficulty with comprehension at times and need to be aware of whether or not their reading makes sense. Also note that checking one's reading periodically enables the reader to clear up puzzling parts and helps the reader to remember the material longer.

*Step 3: Demonstrating the Strategy*

Using modeling or another technique, show how you would use the strategy. Placing a brief selection on the board or an overhead, show how you pause at the end of a paragraph and ask: "Does this make sense?" Choose a tricky paragraph, one that you misread the first time, and show students how you stopped when the piece stopped making sense. You might also discuss the steps you would take to repair the comprehension gap.

*Step 4: Explaining When and Where to Use the Strategy*

When teaching a strategy, be sure to note when and where it is to be used. For instance, when teaching correction strategies, note when it's appropriate to

### A Lesson in Teaching Metacognitive Strategies *Continued*

reread the sentence or the paragraph. Also point out when it might be a good idea to read ahead because the next sentence or paragraph explains the word or idea with which you were having difficulty.

*Step 5: Explaining How and Why to Evaluate a Strategy*

Explain how to evaluate a strategy and why evaluation is important. For instance, explain that you need to see if rereading a sentence works, because it if doesn't you will need to use another strategy.

*Steps 6 and 7: Guided Practice and Application*

As part of instruction in metacognitive strategies, students need opportunities to try out strategies with guidance and feedback from their teachers so they can clarify misunderstandings, make necessary adjustments, and get the feel of the strategy. Be sure to affirm students' successful efforts with specific praise: "I like the way you reread that sentence when you saw that it didn't make sense" or "I like the way you used the diagram to help you understand the paragraph." They also need ample opportunity to apply the strategy to a variety of texts in a variety of situations so that the strategies become automatic, and they can see which ones work best in which situations.

Although working with low-achieving readers, do not assume that they don't have any strategies. Before beginning instruction, find out what strategies they do use and build on those, especially if you are working with older students.

Metacognitive awareness can be developed through collaborative learning. In pairs or cooperative learning groups, students, under the teacher's guidance, discuss their use of strategies and share their thinking.

#### *Use of Graphic Guides*

As an aid to strategy use, Paris, Cross, & Lipson (1984) used posters and slogans, such as "Be a reading detective" to remind students to use strategies as they read. A list of metacognitive strategies emphasized in the program include the following:

***Think Ahead***

*What is this selection about?*
*What do I already know about it?*
*What do I want to find out?*
*What is my goal?*
*How should I go about reading in order to meet my goal?*

***Think While Reading***

*What have I read about so far?*
*Do I understand it? If not, what should I do?*
*What is the author saying and what do I think about it?*

***Think Back***

*Have I learned what I wanted?*
*How can I use what I read?*
*(Alvermann, Bridge, Schmidt, Searfoss, & Winograd, 1989, p. R8)*

### *Informal Instruction*

In addition to formal instruction, take advantage of informal, on-the-spot opportunities to promote metacognitive awareness. Before students read a selection, ask them how they will read it—fast or slow? Also ask what they will do to check their understanding. If a selection has confusing or densely written sections, discuss ways in which those sections might be read. In the after-reading discussion, have students tell how they handled difficult or confusing portions of a selection. Ask questions that lead students to discuss their use of metacognitive strategies. "Were there are confusing passages in this article? How did you handle the confusing parts? What do you do when the selection stops making sense?"

From time to time, model metacognitive strategies that you use, and have students explain the metacognitive strategies that they use. To reinforce monitoring for meaning, have students use sticky notes to indicate passages that were difficult. Discuss those passages with students. Talk over strategies that they might use to understand the passages better.

## *Importance of Using Appropriate Materials*

> Poor readers' difficulty with monitoring may be caused by material that is too difficult. If they spend much time grappling with unknown words, they may become accustomed to reading "nonsense" and not develop the habit of monitoring for meaning.

Regardless of what technique is used to teach comprehension strategies, it is absolutely essential that the text be on the appropriate level of difficulty. In her study of good and poor readers in high school, Kletzien (1991) found that strategy use declined as the text grew harder. Both good and poor readers used the same strategies at the independent reading level. Overall, they used focusing on vocabulary, rereading previous text, making inferences, using prior knowledge, and, to a lesser extent, recognizing sentence and passage structure. At the instructional level the better readers demonstrated somewhat greater flexibility in the use of strategies. However, at the frustration level, poor readers "evidenced a precipitous decline in strategy usage (both in variety of strategies and in number of times strategies were used)" (Kletzien, 1991, p. 79).

At the frustration level, strategy use deteriorated to a focus on small segments of text: individual words or phrases. Complaining that there were too many hard words, some of the subjects simply gave up. Explaining the drastic change in strategy use as texts grew too difficult, Kletzien (1991) commented:

> *Because vocabulary and sentence structure were much more complex at this level, subjects had to work much harder at the lower-level tasks of word recognition and understanding of individual sentences, leaving less cognitive capacity available to understand the meaning of the passage as a whole and to integrate the content with what they already knew. Even subjects who reported using prior knowledge, appeared to have done so out of desperation. One subject, obviously overwhelmed by the difficulty of the material, reported, "I have no idea what this is talking about; I am just trying to remember anything I know about Africa." (p. 82)*

## *Beyond Strategies*

There is more to strategy use than knowing how, when, and where to use them. There is also an essential affective component. Just as you build on what students know in word recognition, you should also consider what they know when building comprehension strategies. Besides being an effective instructional strategy, this fosters students' self-esteem.

In typical discussions, there is an emphasis on the correctness of the answer. However, students can have the right answer for the wrong reason or the wrong answer for the right reason. Besides, the object of instruction is not to obtain answers, right or wrong; *the goal is to improve students' use of strategies.* When students respond correctly and the strategy or thinking process they used to obtain the response is obvious, affirm their use of the strategy: "I liked the way you used pieces of information from the story to conclude that the main character is kind." If the thinking or strategy isn't obvious, have the student explain it: "Why do you think the main character is kind?" If the student gives no response, rephrase the question or provide a probe that gives support. If the response is not fully correct, build on what the student provided. If the student responded that the main character is selfish, ask the student why she or he thinks so. (It could be a perfectly legitimate interpretation.) If the student has not considered all the evidence, encourage her or him to do so. You might say, "Let's go back to the story and take a look at the main character's actions."

If a student is unable to respond at all, even with rephrased queries, help her or him use a strategy that will lead to a response. You might say, "Let's look at what it says about the main character on p. 22." In this way, you are showing the student how to use a strategy (looking back at the text) and you are involving her in obtaining the answer. This is far better than simply supplying the answer, which leaves her no better off than she was and, in fact, may confirm or contribute to a sense of academic powerlessness.

Once the focus is shifted from task completion or getting right answers to the process of learning how to comprehend, your natural tendency will be to choose activities that foster strategy-building and independence. The question that you need to keep in mind is not: "Is the answer correct?" It should be: "How I can build on what the student knows?"

In a study involving primary and middle-grade students who were low-achieving readers, Thames & Reeves (1994) found that when cognitive instruction that built on what students know was combined with self-selection of reading materials, poor readers maintained their academic self-esteem. The academic self-esteem of the members of a control group, who were taught in traditional ways, plummeted.

> Struggling readers often focus on low level–literacy processes. Seeing reading as getting the words right, they devote their energies to pronouncing each word correctly and neglect comprehension.

## *Collaborative Strategy Instruction: An Exemplary Program*

From a teaching standpoint, the students looked virtually hopeless. The failures of a group of low-achieving sixth- through tenth-graders had left them apathetic and discouraged. All were operating at least two years below grade level. Their views of reading and writing were mechanistic, uninformed, and unenthusiastic (V. Anderson & Roit, 1993).

Taking part in an experimental program that combined strategy instruction with collaborative learning, the students made substantial progress. The key idea of the experimental program was that students have natural problem solving abilities which they use in their everyday lives but fail to apply to reading and writing tasks. In the program, reading was presented as a problem to be solved by the group. Each group consisted of five students and a teacher. Strategies were not prescribed but were decided upon by the group. As a member of the group, the teacher was an active participant who discussed and modeled strategies, but did not dictate them.

Recognizing that these students, having been in school for a number of years, have strategies for dealing with text but might not use them, the teachers built on these strategies. Based on observations of eighty students involved in the project, the researchers compiled a list of ten strategies that students used in their everyday lives, some of which included: recognizing a problem, knowing what matters, making sense, getting back on track, explaining, wrapping up experiences, and so forth; these are actually students' labels for widely used text reading strategies, such as predicting, summarizing, and monitoring. Teachers helped students adapt and refine their everyday strategies so that they could be applied to understanding text.

Having endured criticism from themselves and others, older low-achieving readers are reluctant to talk about, or even admit, their problems with reading. Using a quality termed "cognitive empathy," teachers looked for signs that a student was struggling: a quizzical look, a sigh, a discouraged expression. Teachers capitalized on these teachable moments to show empathy and to encourage students to reveal their thinking. In the following exchange, in which a group of students are having difficulty with the term *human aging,* the teacher's role as a facilitator is demonstrated.

> This is an excellent example of responsive elaboration. In response to the students' statements, the teacher leads them to use the overall sense of the passage to obtain the correct identification of "aging."

*T:* I see a confused look here. Which part is confusing you?

*S1:* The part that says, "human again."

*T:* I guess it isn't really "again." Does anyone have a strategy to figure that one out? You usually have very good ones.

*S2:* "Agging"

*T:* Do you know what "agging" means?

*S2:* To bother?

*T:* I think that if I relate this word to the title, "Growing Old," that would help me to get an idea.

*S1:* Aging.

*T:* Aging. What helped you get that?

*S1:* After you said growing old, I looked at the title and I just remembered that someone growing old is aging. (V. Anderson & Roit, 1993, p. 6)

Imitating the teacher's behavior, the students soon began to show cognitive empathy toward each other. Students began giving suggestions to each other and discussing strategies that they used.

Collaborative strategy instruction helped students become aware of the strategies they already possessed and build on that knowledge.

Throughout the project, the emphasis was placed on the processes used to understand text rather than on getting the right answers. "The learning goal—becoming a more active reader in order to understand text better—was clear and consistent" (V. Anderson & Roit, 1993, p. 28). Discussions were conversational. Instead of just asking content-specific factual questions, teachers asked and encouraged students to ask the kinds of questions that might pop up in a natural discussion of text. "What is this passage about? What is important here?" These are questions that students might well ask themselves during their reading. Although lessons might vary from day to day, and from teacher to teacher, the following box contains the steps in a typical lesson.

**Collaborative Strategy Instruction Lesson**

*Step 1: Choose a Text*

Students choose a text. Each group had a library of informational pieces that students might read.

*Step 2: Survey the Text*

Students survey the text to get an overview and look for possible problems that might hinder comprehension. At this point, students pick out vocabulary that is unfamiliar. The difficult vocabulary from the text is then discussed.

*Step 3: Predict*

Students decide what they think the text might be about and what they would like to learn from it.

*Step 4: Read in Segments*

Students read the text in segments. Problems with the text are discussed. Text is discussed in terms of purposes initially set. Students also discuss any problems they experienced comprehending the text. They talk over strategies used, which ones worked and which didn't and how they might apply what they learned about reading to other texts. During discussions, teachers might also model how they use strategies to solve reading problems. For instance, a teacher might show the group how she read to the end of a sentence to get sufficient context so that she could guess the meaning of an unfamiliar word.

Students were active participants in their learning. They selected materials to read and identified the vocabulary words they felt might be difficult. They also discussed problems they had understanding the text.

## *Questions*

Questions are a powerful tool. We can improve students' reading performance simply by using the right kinds of questions (Hansen & Pearson, 1980). Questions also serve a multitude of purposes. Questions can be used to evaluate, to highlight important information, to lead a student to a conclusion or to a higher level of thinking, to get a discussion going or to keep it going, to review content, or start a strategy lesson (Hyman, 1978). Questions also serve affective purposes. We can use questions to make a student feel part of a group, share feelings, or display her knowledge on a particular topic. Teachers can also use questions to trap a student who hasn't been paying attention. However, this is done at a price. If questions are used to embarrass or control, then they become threatening and the accepting atmosphere is corroded. Hyman (1978) recommends that the teacher handle the issue of paying attention by simply "calling for the students' attention in a straightforward way" (p. 4).

Both good and poor readers have been asked too many literal questions. About 80 percent of the questions asked in the typical reading lesson are factual (Ruddell, 1979).

Judging from research and experience, low-achieving readers have been ill served by questions. In general, they are asked lower-level questions, are given fewer prompts, and less time to respond than are achieving readers. And the teacher is more likely to call on another student "to help out" the poor reader (Allington, 1984).

## *Creating Questions*

### *For Narrative Selections*

Since questions are such an important element in instruction, especially for poor readers, questioning techniques need to be planned with care. Analyzing narrative selections, Beck, Omanson, and McKeown (1982) identified the key elements in a story and constructed a map which linked these units. The key-elements map (sometimes simply known as a story map) became a blueprint for constructing questions. The revised questions were especially helpful to the less-skilled readers. The researchers found that less-skilled readers had difficulty structuring the content of the story into a cohesive whole; however, responding to questions that focused on the story's main happenings significantly assisted less able readers in their attempts to create a mental map of the selection.

Creating a key elements map can be done informally by following these steps:

- List the theme, moral, starting point, or basic premise of the story.
- List the major events in the development of the plot. Include implied as well as stated events.
- List concepts or ideas that you feel students would need to know in order to understand the theme and other major elements in the story.

When students read stories accompanied by map-based questions, their comprehension improved by 10%.

Pre-reading questions should prepare students for the theme and major plot occurrences. There should also be questions that guide students through the selection. Post-reading questions should help students understand the basic facts of the story: "Who were the main characters? What happened?" Once students understand the basics of a selection, they can build on those basics and answer higher level questions about theme, quality of story, use of literary techniques, and so forth. For an example of a simplified key elements map and questions based on the map, see Figures 12-4 and 12-5.

| | |
|---|---|
| Theme (Moral): | You don't have to be big or strong to help someone. |
| Plot: | 1. A dove saves an ant from drowning.<br>2. A hunter is about to catch the dove.<br>3. The ant bites the man.<br>4. The dove flies free. |
| Needed Concepts or Ideas: | A dove is a bird.<br>A fable is a story that teaches a lesson. A fable usually has animals as main characters but the animals act like people. |

**FIGURE 12-4 Story Elements Map**

Source: *The Ant and the Dove.* Chicago, IL: Children's Press.

### *Before Reading*

Have you ever been in danger or trouble?
Have you ever been chased by a dog or lost?
Have you ever been sick? Have you ever fallen down and hurt yourself?
Who helped you? Have you ever helped anyone? Read *The Ant and the Dove.* Find out how the ant and the dove helped each other.

### *After Reading*

How did the dove help the ant?
How did the ant thank the dove?
What did the ant promise to do?
What question did the dove ask?
Why did the dove ask: "What could an ant do?"
How did the ant help the dove?
What lesson does the story teach?
Is this lesson true? Have you ever known of a small person helping a big person or a child helping a grown up? Do you know what kind of story this is? What kind of story teaches a lesson and has animals that act like people?

**FIGURE 12-5 Questions Based on a Story Elements Map**

### *For Informational Pieces*

The discussion questions for an informational piece would be based on the major concepts covered in the selection. The teacher would list two to four ideas that he feels are important. Pre-reading questions would be designed to activate relevant schema and build background necessary to understand the article. Questions would also be posed that would help students focus on the main concepts in the selection. Post-reading questions would help students clarify and organize concepts, and relate new information to old. Once students had a grasp of basic information, they could respond to questions that involved evaluating information and applying it.

## *Levels of Questioning*

Having had an unbalanced diet of low-level questioning, low-achieving readers need questions that involve all cognitive levels. However, this doesn't mean that literal questions should be neglected. Poor readers do show improvement when given low-level questions (Medley, 1977). They need to know what happened in the story or what the main facts in the article are. At that point, they are ready to be lifted to higher levels.

Questions can be classified in a number of ways. One way of arranging questions is according to the cognitive processes involved. Adapting Weinstein and Mayer's (1986) system, which was used to classify strategies, the following taxonomy evolves. The first level, comprehending, is drawn from Bloom's taxonomy (1957).

| | |
|---|---|
| **Comprehending** | Students understand prose on a literal level. They can recite five facts stated in a selection, name the main characters, indicate dates and places. This level also includes having students put information in their own words. |
| **Organizing** | Students select important details from the selection and construct relationships among them. This involves identifying or constructing main ideas, classifying, noting sequence, and summarizing. |
| **Elaborating** | Elaborating entails making connections between information from the text and prior knowledge and includes a wide range of activities: making inferences, creating images and analogies, and evaluating or judging. |
| **Monitoring** | Monitoring involves being aware of cognitive processes. It involves knowing whether a selection makes sense and knowing what steps might be taken to repair comprehension. |

Listed below are examples of each type of question. They are drawn from *Baseball's Best: Five True Stories* (Gutelle, 1990), an easy-to-read book that would have appeal to older readers.

**Comprehending.** Which of the five players hit the most home runs? Which has the longest hitting streak? Which one was both a good pitcher and a good batter?

**Organizing.** In what ways were the five players alike? In what ways were they different?

**Elaborating.** Which player was most generous? Why? Which player changed baseball the most? Why? Which player was the best? Why do you think so? Picture Jackie Robinson stealing his first base in the major leagues. What do you see? What do you hear?

**Monitoring.** Did you find any confusing parts? Did you run into any words that you couldn't read or whose meanings you didn't know? If so, what did you do? Can you summarize each player's main accomplishments? If you forget how many home runs Hank Aaron hit or the number of games in which Joe DiMaggio hit safely, what might you do?

## *Atmosphere*

How questions are asked is almost as important as what questions are asked. Having had negative experiences with questions, low-achieving readers need an accepting, supportive atmosphere. Instead of being oral quizzes, discussions should be genuine opportunities to build the concepts, background, and thinking skills so necessary for comprehension.

### *Wait Time*

Speaking about wait time, Hyman (1978) comments, "If the teacher does not begin to talk after each student finishes, the teacher nonverbally encourages the students to talk" (pp. 102–103).

One small but very positive change that literally takes seconds to implement is to increase wait time. Typically students are given a second or less to respond to the teacher's questions. If there is no response, the teacher repeats the question, or, most often in the case of poor readers, calls on another student. After the student responds, the teacher waits less than a second before reacting to the answer (Hyman, 1978). However, Hyman (1978), Lake (1973), and Rowe's (1969) studies have shown that when the teacher increases the wait time from one second or less to three to five seconds, the following occurs:

- Fewer no responses and I don't knows
- Longer, more thoughtful responses
- Greater number of correct answers
- Greater number of alternative responses
- More evidence of reasons for answers
- Greater confidence as indicated by a tone of assurance in the voice
- Fewer responses that conveyed a "Is this what you wanted?" tone
- Greater number of responses from the lower-achieving students

Students weren't the only ones who benefited from longer wait times. Teachers demonstrated increased adaptability, asked fewer but more varied questions, and raised their expectations for slower students (Hyman, 1978).

## *Probes and Prompts*

Questions can be used to help students focus on the topic, expand their responses, substantiate their answers, and to lift students to higher levels of thought (Taba, 1965).

While establishing an encouraging atmosphere and using wait time are essential elements in a discussion, prompts and probes are also important. At times, low-achieving readers know the information requested by higher level questions, but have difficulty formulating their responses. This could be especially true of students who are still learning English. Prompts can help them shape their answers (Hyman, 1978). For instance, to help students form concepts by grouping similar data, you might ask such questions as: "Which of these items go together? What do all of these have in common? What would you call all of these items?"

If students' answers are too brief, use an elaboration probe: "Would you please tell me more? Would you please explain." If students are offering unsubstantiated opinions, use a specific probe: "You said you didn't like the story. What was there about the story that you didn't like? You said the main character was sly. What did she do that was sly?"

Besides providing probes and prompts, the teacher may provide additional needed information which enables students to revise or create a new concept (Cairney, 1990).

If a response is unclear, you might use a restating-crystallizing probe. In this probe, you restate what you believe the student said and then ask if your restatement is correct: "You seem to be saying that Roger was the cause of the family's problems. Is that right?" The purpose of a restating-crystallizing probe is to help the speaker clarify her or his thoughts. It can also be used to keep the speaker on track if she or he has gotten off the topic. You're also telling the speaker that you are paying close attention to him and that his opinions are worth hearing (Hyman, 1978).

## *Lesson Plans That Foster Comprehension*

Questions and discussions and direct instruction in strategies designed to improve comprehension are often conducted within the framework of a lesson plan. The best known and most widely used lesson-plan formats are the directed reading activity and the directed reading–thinking activity.

### *Directed Reading Activity*

**Directed reading activity** (DRA): traditional five-step plan for conducting a reading lesson that has as its core the reading of a selection.

The **directed reading activity** (DRA) has a long history in the field of reading and incorporates the following five steps: preparation, silent reading, discussion, rereading, and follow-up or extension. Updated to incorporate recent research and practice, today's DRA focuses on activating prior knowledge, strategy instruction, and emphasizes gearing activities to the major concepts and structure of the selection to be read. The steps in the DRA, which have been modified for use with low-achieving readers, are described in the box to follow.

**A Directed Reading Activity Lesson**

The outcome of the preparing stage of the DRA is to set a purpose for reading. The purpose can be set by the teacher, by the students, or both.

*Step 1: Preparing*

In this step, you do whatever is necessary to prepare students for a successful, engrossing reading of the selection, which could be a newspaper article, a story in a basal reader, a chapter from a children's book, or an article from a magazine. As part of the preparation, introduce the selection, activate prior knowledge, build background, and develop needed vocabulary and concepts and whatever thinking skills or reading strategies that might be needed to handle the selection. In general, background-building activities should remind students of what they already know about a topic, tie new information to students' background knowledge, and focus on the important ideas in the selection to be read (Adoption Guidelines Project, 1990).

Also engender interest in the selection and set a purpose question for reading. The purpose could be

## A Directed Reading Activity Lesson *Continued*

set in cooperation with the students. If possible, students might be involved in the selection of the piece to be read. They might also be involved in choosing the difficult vocabulary to be introduced and should discuss how the story is to be read and what strategies might work best with the piece. Often alienated by past failures, poor readers need to feel involved.

### *Step 2: Silent Reading*

In general, the initial reading of a selection should be silent. The purpose of the DRA is to foster comprehension. When students read orally, they focus on pronouncing the words correctly. When students read silently, the focus is on constructing meaning. Reading silently also provides students with the opportunity to apply word identification skills. Freed from the pressure of reading aloud, students can use pronounceable word–part, analogy, context, or other word identification strategies to figure out difficult words.

During this portion of the lesson, observe students, note needs, and provide help to students. Students can read the whole selection all at once or read it in sections. After each section, there is a brief discussion. Breaking up a suspenseful narrative piece into sections could lessen students' enjoyment of the selection. However, it might be wise to read a fact-packed informational piece in segments. Students might need and welcome the additional guidance provided by discussing segments of the text. Younger readers and students with severe reading problems probably benefit from having the reading broken up into more manageable portions. Older, less-disabled readers would be better able to read selections as a whole.

### *Step 3: Discussion*

The discussion generally begins with students responding to the purpose question. If students read to find out how skyscrapers are built, the opening question would be: "How are skyscrapers built?" To help students get started, the question might be sliced (Pearson & Johnson, 1978), that is, broken into easier segments: "What is the first step in building a skyscraper? The second?" During the discussion, confusions are clarified and concepts are expanded. Ideas from the selection are organized and students relate new information in the story to information already in their background. Low-achieving readers may not see relationships among ideas and may have difficulty constructing a main idea from a series of details. Carefully crafted questions can help students organize and integrate information. You might also do some on-the-spot teaching. For instance, one student was unsure of the word *piles*. He wondered how piles of steel could be used to hold up a skyscraper. The class discussed the word as it was used in context: "Long, thick piles of steel are sunk into the land, down to a bed of hard rock. Those piles hold up the base of the building" (Stanchfield & Gunning, 1986, p. 164). They concluded that piles had a different meaning from its ordinary use as "a heap." Checking in the dictionary, they learned that it was a heavy beam driven into the ground or bed of a river.

During the discussion, be alert to students' needs. For instance, you might have noticed that they had difficulty with some of the compound words that appeared in the selection: *landfill, framework.* Perhaps, they also had problems keeping the sequence of events in mind. Mentally plan to review those areas during the rereading or follow-up portions of the lesson.

### *Step 4: Rereading*

Students reread the selection for a new purpose: to obtain information they missed during the initial reading, to clarify misconceptions, to focus in on a particular aspect of the selection, for a deeper appreciation or understanding, or a similar purpose. The rereading often offers an opportunity for a purposeful oral reading: to dramatize a portion of the selection, to read a humorous or descriptive passage, to clarify a disputed point, for instance. Although listed as a separate step, the rereading often flows into the discussion stage, when you ask a student to read the sentences in which *piles* appears or the passage that explains how the crane is taken down from the top of a skyscraper, for instance. The rereading

*Continued*

**A Directed Reading Activity Lesson** *Continued*

could also be an entirely separate step. For example, you may want to review strategies for comprehending sequence and have students apply these strategies as they reread the selection.

*Step 5: Follow-up*

The follow-up, which is an optional part of the lesson, could take many forms but should extend the main concepts or strategies stressed in the lesson or build on the lesson's content. For the skyscraper lesson, students might observe one being built and write about it, might read a book on their level about skyscrapers, or might read and discuss the poem, "Giants of the City" by Marge Blaine. Whatever the activity, it should provide opportunities for further development of reading and writing skills.

The DRA differs from the text walk. Depending as it does on illustrations, a text walk is best used with heavily illustrated books. As students grow in skill, shift to the DRA or a similar format.

### *Sample DRA*

To create a directed reading activity, first analyze the selection to be read. Note the main ideas, concepts, or principles that you wish students to learn (if the selection is fiction, you would compose a key elements map). These become the focal point for your lesson. Then list the vocabulary necessary to understand the key ideas. For instance, the major ideas in "Amazing Rescue Underground" (Shea, 1992), which is written on a second-grade level but would appeal to older students, would include the following:

- Jessica, a toddler, was trapped in an abandoned water well.
- A team of rescue workers saved Jessica.

After listing the major ideas, go back over the story and jot down the vocabulary words or concepts in the story that would need to be known in order to comprehend the major ideas in the selection. "Amazing Rescue Underground" has more than twenty words that might be potentially difficult. However, that is far too many for students to learn at one time. The list can be narrowed down to the following six:

| | | |
|---|---|---|
| abandoned well | backhoe | paramedics |
| rescue | microphone | cable |

After listing the difficult words, examine the article and determine its structure and what strategies would be needed to understand it. The piece has a dual structure. Primarily, it is sequential. It narrates and describes a series of steps taken to rescue the child. But it also has a cause–effect structure. A helpful strategy for students would be to ask: What did the rescue workers do and why? Drawings in the article also contribute to an understanding of the story. For instance, it mentions that a rathole rig was used to dig. Drawings depict a rathole rig better than any words could.

At this point, you are now ready to structure a preparatory discussion that will activate schema, build background and vocabulary, set a purpose, guide students in the use of reading and thinking strategies, and, last but not least, motivate the students to want to read the selection. Note how this is done in the sample DRA presented in the following box, keeping in mind that this selection could have been handled in a number of different ways.

## Directed Reading Activity for Amazing Rescue Underground

### *Step 1: Preparing*

> The preparational stage should only take about 10 to 15 minutes. Don't spend so much time preparing students that they don't have time to read.

Writing the title, *Amazing Rescue Underground,* on the board, ask the class what they think the story might be about. To make sure that the class knows what *rescue* means and will recognize it in print, point to it as you say it and amplify and clarify students' responses, if necessary. Direct the class to turn to the story on p. 28 and to examine the illustration. Ask, "Based on the illustration, what do you think the story will be about?" As the illustration is being discussed, point out the cover for the abandoned well in the foreground. Write *abandoned well* on the board. As students discuss the possible content of the story, point to the vocabulary, previously written on the board, and ask why each might be needed in a rescue at an abandoned well: *microphone,* a *backhoe, paramedics,* and a *cable.* Assessing the students' knowledge of each term, devote as much time to each as is needed. Having built the needed vocabulary and background and activated students' prior knowledge, set a purpose for reading. Pointing out that Jessica, the child in the purple overalls, falls in the well, ask students to read to find out what steps were taken to rescue her and why. Suggest that as students read, they use the pictures in the selection to help them understand what has happened and also to picture in their minds important scenes that are not shown.

> This is a reminder for students to use imaging as they read the story.

### *Step 2: Silent Reading*

As the students read silently, note whether they are having any difficulty. For instance, if you see that several students are trying to sound out *petroleum* and one seems stumped by *inquiries* and *ambulance,* make a note to review pronounceable word–parts and analogy strategies as applied to multisyllabic words. Also review context clues.

### *Step 3: Discussing*

Begin the discussion with the purpose question: "What steps were taken to rescue Jessica and why?" The class talks over the steps that were taken and why each was taken. Having been engrossed in the story, they have a good sense of the sequence of events. However, there may be some confusion. For instance, some students might believe that the paramedics helped with the digging. If so, ask students to locate and read passages that clarify that point. (This is a valid purpose for orally rereading passages.) Other issues are also discussed as they come up: why the second hole had to be dug, why it had to be dug by hand, how the mother helped, how Jessica must have felt, what it was like to drill the tunnel, how long it took to drill the tunnel, what petroleum jelly is and why is was used.

### *Step 4: Rereading*

During the discussion, you might note that the students had difficulty explaining why the rescue took two days. Have the class skim through the selection to find passages that tell why the rescue took so long. Help them calculate the time that it took to dig the tunnel. Also review strategies for figuring out some troublesome words: *petroleum, ambulance, inquiries.*

### *Step 5: Follow-up*

> Low progress readers are behind and so need to have their progress accelerated. Do not spend too much time on any one story. Two days should be adequate.

Building on the words, *microphone* and *paramedic,* extend students' understanding of the forms *micro* and *para.* If the class still has some questions about the rescue and they want to know what happened to Jessica since the rescue, bring in a magazine article that gives her last name. Then with the help of the media specialist, the class might locate updates on Jessica McClure. The class might also view a made-for-TV movie of the rescue and compare the TV version with the selection they have read.

## *Directed Reading–Thinking Activity*

**Directed reading–thinking activity** (DR–TA): form of the DRA in which students make predictions and read to verify their predictions.

Based on the DRA, the directed reading–thinking activity (DR–TA) places greater emphasis on student involvement. In the **DR–TA,** students predict what the selection might be about and then read to evaluate their predictions. Because they are more active participants in a DR–TA, students also shoulder greater responsibility for their learning. They must be able and willing to generate questions, know how to ignore irrelevant material in their quest to have their questions answered, suspend judgment, and read flexibly. They must also be able to modify their predictions if they encounter information that conflicts with their ideas (Stauffer, 1969). The DR–TA can be an especially effective technique for use with low-achieving readers because it involves them more directly and more personally in the reading process. Like the DRA, the DR–TA also has five steps.

### A DR–TA Lesson

#### *Step 1: Preparing*

The preparation stage of the DR–TA is less extensive than that of the DRA. Under your guidance, students discuss the title and predict what they believe the story might be about. They then examine and discuss illustrations and tell whether or not they would change their predictions. Headings and the first paragraph might also be used if the title and illustration(s) are not helpful. In order to involve all students, make sure that each one makes a prediction, or at least agrees with a prediction that someone else has made. List the predictions on the board and have students say with which one they agree. After making or choosing their predictions, students read to evaluate them.

The DR–TA requires that students bring some background knowledge to a selection. Without adequate background, students will have difficulty making predictions.

For instance, in preparation for reading the first chapter of the *Chalk Box Kid* (Bulla, 1987), you might discuss the title and have students predict what the story seems to be about. Discuss the cover illustration and encourage students to use additional information to adjust or elaborate on their predictions. Because the title and illustration provide a very limited basis for making predictions, read the initial portion of the text, down to the sentence on the second page of the story that says, "So far it was his very worst birthday." Discuss that segment of the text and have students make a final prediction as to what might happen in the first chapter. Write their predictions on the board. Make sure that everyone is involved either in making a new prediction or supporting a prediction that has already been made.

Although not typically included in a DR–TA, provision might also be made for pre-reading assistance with difficult vocabulary words and concepts. Write key vocabulary words on the board, and discuss each one. You might suggest to students that they use the words as an added basis for making their predictions.

#### *Step 2: Silent Reading*

Students read until they are able to respond to their predictions. This might occur after a page of reading or at the end of the selection. As students read, they should be prepared to revise their predictions if necessary.

#### *Step 3: Discussing*

The discussion stage of the DR–TA is very similar to that of the DRA, except that the discussion is initiated with a consideration of students' predictions. Students evaluate their predictions. If they stayed with their original predictions, they supply reasons or details to support their positions. If they revised

**A DR–TA Lesson** *Continued*

them, they tell how and why they did so. The discussion can also be expanded to encompass major elements in the selection just as was done in the DRA discussion.

*Step 4: Rereading*

Same as in the DRA.

*Step 5: Follow-up*

Same as in the DRA.

The DR–TA, with its emphasis on making, verifying, and revising predictions, is an excellent technique. However, it does not work well if students need extensive guidance or have such limited background for a selection that they have very little basis for making predictions. It does, however, provide a bridge from heavily teacher-directed procedures, such as the DRA, to strategies that the student applies independently and is an excellent device for turning passive readers into active ones.

## *Other Techniques for Building Comprehension*

**Cloze:** way of assessing comprehension by having a student fill in missing words that have been deleted from a selection.

### *Cloze Procedure*

Short for *closure,* **cloze** is a procedure in which students read selections in which words have been deleted. Generally, every fifth, seventh, or tenth word has been removed, but other patterns of deletion are possible. As they read, students attempt to restore the omitted words. Try the following cloze exercise. As you fill in the blanks, ask yourself: "What does this task require me to do? What strategies does it require me to use? What kinds of readers would benefit from this type of activity?"

A Famous Author

The only daughter of rich parents, Beatrix Potter spent most of her days by herself. There were no other _________ and boys around to _________ with. But she did ________ to draw. She spent _________ happy hours drawing pictures _________ plants and animals.

Later, _________ she was grown up, _________ sent letters to a _________ little boy. The little _________ was sick. In her _________, she told stories. One story _________ about a rabbit who _________ into trouble when he _________ into a farmer's garden. _________ little boy liked the _________. So did other boys _________ girls.

Beatrix Potter decided _________ make a book out _________ the story about the ________. Some people cautioned her _________ to. They believed she _________ only sell a few _________ and would lose a _________ of money. But Beatrix Potter _________ ahead with plans for _________ the book. As it _________ out, boys and girls _________ over the world liked _________ book. Can you guess _________ the title of Beatrix Potter's _________ is? If you said, "*The Tale of Peter Rabbit,*" _________ are right.

Beatrix Potter _________ twenty-two other books and _________ a famous children's author. _________ books were mostly about _________, kittens, and other animals. _________ the book that boys _________ girls liked best was _________ first book. Although *The Tale of Peter Rabbit* _________ been around for close _________ one-hundred years, it is _________ being read today. In fact, it is one of the best-liked children's books of all time.

Here are the words that were omitted: *girls, play, like, many, of, when, she, friend's, boy, letters, was, got, sneaked, The, story, and, to, of, rabbit, not, would, books, lot, went, publishing, turned, all, her, what, book, you, wrote, became, Her, ducks, But, and, her, has, to, still.* Check your responses. How did you do?

Because words are omitted, cloze forces us to use our background knowledge and knowledge of language to restore the missing words. Cloze also demands a close attention to meaning. You can't fill in a blank if you don't have a good grasp of what you've read. If you haven't comprehended what you've read, you have no basis for filling in the blanks. Cloze works especially well with students who overuse phonics clues, fail to use context, or fail to read for meaning.

Discussion is an essential element in the application of cloze (Jongsma, 1980). Students should justify their choices, especially if exact replacements aren't required. Explaining their responses clarifies their thinking, and it's also helpful for them to hear why others made the choices they did. Discussion also makes for a livelier lesson.

> The cloze procedure can also be used as a comprehension test or as a way of estimating the difficulty level of a text.

Although you might choose to accept reasonable substitutes in lieu of exact replacements, have students compare their finished products to the originals. Comparison of their choices with the words used by the author should be interesting and should help students see the importance of word choice. If you do make this kind of comparison, inform students that they're doing fine if their responses match those of the author half of the time. The standard for a cloze score at the instructional level is 44–57 percent. Table 12-1 presents the criteria for cloze levels.

Before students start a cloze exercise, give them some tips for completing it. They should read the whole piece first to get an overview. During their second reading of the selection, they should read to the end of each sentence or beyond before attempting to fill in the blank. Students naturally stop at the blank, but often the words beyond the blank provide essential information. Clues might even be found in the next sentence or two. After students have filled in the blanks, they should go back and see if there are any changes they wish to make.

**TABLE 12-1 Criteria for Cloze**

| Level | Percentage of Correct Replacements |
|---|---|
| Independent | > 57 |
| Instructional | 44–57 |
| Frustration | < 44 |

Tell students to ignore spelling. If students worry about spelling, they will lose their focus, and also restrict their responses only to words they can spell.

### *Constructing Cloze Exercises*

Choose material that is interesting and on the appropriate level of difficulty. Don't use material that presents a number of new concepts because this makes it extra hard to fill in the blanks. In classical cloze, which was originally used to assess the difficulty level of printed materials, selections were 250 words in length and every fifth word was omitted so there would be a total of 50 deletions. Having fewer deletions makes the task easier. Controlling deletions also simplifies the task. Content words, such as nouns and verbs, are more difficult to restore than structure words, conjunctions, prepositions, and articles. Deletions made at the middle or end of a sentence are also easier to restore than are deletions made at the beginning of a sentence (Rye, 1982). Deletions are also easier to restore if the clues to the deletion precede it rather than come after it.

The types of deletions you make depend on the strategies you wish to reinforce. Restoring deleted content words, especially nouns and verbs, requires comprehension of details. Restoring structure words involves using language cues and noting relationships. Whether using classical or adapted cloze, do not delete any proper nouns or any words from the first or last sentence.

### *Introducing Cloze*

Although many students enjoy the challenge of cloze, it needs to be introduced with care. Students, especially those who are lacking in confidence, may be upset by the task if they don't understand its nature. When introducing cloze, explain the nature of the activity and tell students what it's called and why. Students respond positively when they are treated as competent individuals capable of learning mature concepts. Also model the process of filling in the blanks in a sample cloze exercise. Emphasize the need to use language as well as content clues and to go beyond the blank when necessary. Provide guided practice.

Because cloze is a fairly difficult activity, it is not recommended, in its classical form, for students reading below a third-grade level. However, students operating on a lower level can engage in modified cloze or masking.

### *Modified Cloze*

In modified cloze, also known as mazes, students fill in the blanks by choosing one of three or more options so that cloze becomes a multiple choice activity. Modified cloze, although not as valuable as classic cloze, would be a reasonable alternative for students who have difficulty with classical cloze because of word retrieval problems or who are overly concerned with spelling.

> *Degrees of Reading Power* is a nationally used reading test that assesses comprehension through the use of a modified cloze.

### *Masking*

Masking is a form of cloze frequently used in shared-reading situations. After an initial reading of the selection, the teacher covers predictable words with masking tape and as she or he comes to the word asks students to predict what the covered word might be. After students make and discuss their predictions, the covered word is unmasked. This exercise is especially valuable for students who neglect context clues.

### *Think Alouds*

As noted in Chapter 4, think alouds can be used to obtain additional information about the processes that a student uses in comprehension or word analysis. Think alouds can also be used as an instructional technique. For instance, one way for you to demonstrate the thinking processes that go on as you make a prediction, summarize a story, use context to figure out a hard word, or engage in any number of reading or writing processes is to let students know your thought processes through thinking aloud. You simply tell what is going on in your head as you make a prediction: "Based on this heading, I predict that this section will tell about some helpful kinds of beetles."

When introducing think alouds to students, first explain what they are, how they might help comprehension, and how, when, and where they might be used. Then model a think aloud, and provide for guided and independent practice. As you model a think aloud, stress comprehension strategies that you have previously taught, such as predicting and summarizing, and metacognitive strategies, such as checking and repairing.

Still another use of think alouds is to have students apply them as they read a selection. They can think aloud with a partner, with the partners reading alternate paragraphs and telling each other what they were thinking about as they read. The listening partner can ask probing questions such as "What were you thinking about? Were there any confusing parts. Were there any hard words?" The listening partner might fill out a brief think-aloud form, which can be a vehicle for discussion between the two.

Think alouds help students become more aware of the ways in which they process text and use monitoring and other comprehension strategies. Think alouds also allow us insight into the students' thought processes and the manner in which they are applying strategies. Therefore, think alouds provide a unique opportunity for on-the-spot guidance. For instance, if a student admits to being confused by a passage and doesn't seem to know what to do about it, you can lead her or him to some possible repair strategies, asking such questions as: "What don't you understand? What is blocking your understanding? What do you need to know? What might you do to make this clear? Would rereading the sentence help? Would starting over help?"

## *Using a Variety of Teaching Techniques*

It is essential to use a variety of techniques when teaching comprehension to struggling readers. Often, it is necessary to present the same strategy in different ways. In addition, some techniques are teacher directed and might be appropriate for students who need structure. Others allow for more student involvement and are good for activating passive students and promoting independence. An overview of major teaching techniques is presented in Table 12-2. Additional teaching techniques, especially those that are used with expository texts, are discussed in the next chapter.

**TABLE 12-2 Comprehension Teaching Techniques**

| Technique | Characteristics |
|---|---|
| DRA | Provides structure and guidance. Builds background and vocabulary. Teacher directed. |
| DR–TA | Fosters previewing and setting purposes. Stresses student involvement. |
| Cloze | Fosters reading for meaning and use of context. Especially effective for students who fail to read for meaning. Should only be used with students reading at least on a third-grade level. |
| QAR | Fosters literal and inferential comprehension by having students seek appropriate sources of information. Good for younger students. |
| Think-alouds | Provides insight into thought process used during comprehension. Can be used to teach any strategy and along with other techniques. |

## *Minicase Study*

Although Jennifer was a nine-year-old third-grader and had no difficulty with decoding at grade level, her comprehension was poor (Sawyer, 1985). When asked to retell selections at second- and third-grade levels, Jennifer's responses were brief, very general, and involved simply stating the topic: "It's about bears and honey." She was unable to supply details about the selection and, when asked specific questions, based responses on her background knowledge and not from the text. For the most part, responses were only marginally related to the questions. However, at first-grade level, Jennifer produced an acceptable retelling, one that was accurate and fairly detailed. She also correctly answered nine of ten comprehension questions.

Further testing indicated that Jennifer was able to understand simple sentences but had difficulty with complex sentences, especially those that had embedded clauses as in: "It was the first time Bill went to camp." Jennifer also had difficulty integrating information across paragraphs. In addition, Jennifer experienced problems following directions, apparently because she failed to focus on key words. Jennifer was able to organize information, but she had difficulty explaining how or why she organized it. Although she was able to categorize items correctly, she was unable to supply a category name or title.

A program of remediation focused on comprehension and, in particular, the thinking skills that are an essential element in comprehension. Instruction was initiated with materials on a late first–grade to beginning second–grade level. Activities designed to foster application of prediction strategies on the sentence level included cloze exercises (President ________ freed the slaves) and complete-the-sentence exercises (Columbus sailed west because __________________.). To foster comprehension across sentences, Jennifer was also asked to complete unfinished paragraphs (The day was dark and gloomy. Hurricane warnings were in effect and the winds were howling around the house. Suddenly, sheets of rain began to blow toward the beaches. May's father rushed in through the door and said, "__________________").

To activate Jennifer's schema and to help set a purpose for reading, semantic maps or structured overviews were suggested for use with her before she read a selection. Because Jennifer spoke mainly in short, simple sentences, activities to develop oral language were also recommended (Sawyer, 1985).

## *Summary*

According to schema theory, comprehension is an active, constructive process which activates our schemata. Comprehension can go awry if we lack the necessary schema, fail to activate it, or activate the wrong schema. The mental models view complements the schema theory of comprehension. According to the mental-models point of view, readers create mental representations as they read.

Causes of poor reading comprehension are multiple and involve an interaction of reader, task, text, teaching technique, and situation. Major causes within the reader include limited vocabulary, language deficiency, deficient decoding skills, inadequate background or poorly developed schema, lack of intellectual curiosity or interest or flexibility in considering new ideas, inadequate use of thinking skills, lack of strategies, or failure to apply strategies. Overreliance on background and failure to read for meaning also cause comprehension difficulties. Although reader factors were emphasized in this chapter, teaching techniques, using appropriate texts, and the quality of the overall learning situation have a critical impact on comprehension.

One key to comprehension is the effective use of strategies. A strategy is a planned, purposeful cognitive tool that can be used to direct and improve comprehension. Strategies can be classified according to the cognitive processes they incorporate: preparing, selecting and organizing, elaborating, rehearsal (studying), and monitoring (metacognition). Preparational strategies are those that a reader uses to prepare for reading. Selecting and organizing strategies are those involved in choosing relevant information and relating two or more ideas. Elaboration strategies require integrating information from the text with information from the reader's background. Metacognitive awareness is the ability to think about cognitive processes and involves four elements: knowing oneself as a learner, regulating reading processes, checking reading processes, and correcting difficulties in comprehension.

Questions, when properly asked, can build comprehension and improve attitudes. Questions should be balanced and include items from all levels: comprehending (literal level), selecting/organizing, elaborating, and monitoring (metacognition). Creating an accepting atmosphere is important to questioning. Using wait time and prompts enhances the effectiveness of questions. When properly used, questions can be used to scaffold instruction.

The directed reading activity (DRA) is an instructional framework that incorporates the activation of schema, building of background and vocabulary, and the use of strategies and questions to build comprehension. The directed reading-thinking activity (DR–TA) is modeled on the DRA but gives the student a more active role.

Cloze, which is short for *closure,* is a procedure in which students read selections in which words have been deleted. As they read, students restore the deletions. In simplified versions, students use multiple choice items to fill in the cloze blanks (mazes) or respond to one item at a time under the teacher's guidance (masking).

Another technique for teaching comprehension is think-alouds. In think-alouds the readers describe their thought processes as they read. Think-alouds can be used by the teacher to model comprehension processes. Think-alouds, when used by students, help them to become more aware of their thinking and reading processes.

## *Application Activities*

1. Plan a lesson presenting one of the strategies described in the chapter. If possible, teach the lesson and evaluate it.

2. If you are now teaching, try using wait time and probes for a week. What changes do you notice in your students? In yourself? Ask a colleague to act as a coach and observe your performance and give you suggestions for improvement. If you are not teaching, try the technique in a small discussion group.

3. Plan a DRA or DR–TA and teach your lesson if possible. If you teach the lesson, write an evaluation of it.

4. Construct a cloze activity and try it out with a class. How did the class react?

5. Do a think aloud with a partner on a challenging informational piece or a difficult piece of fiction. What strategies is your partner using? What strategies are you using?

# Chapter 13

# Reading to Learn in the Content Areas

## Using What You Know

Although most of the skills and strategies needed to comprehend content-area texts were introduced in the previous chapter on comprehension, research shows that students often fail to transfer general skills and strategies to specific areas. A number of techniques and approaches for teaching the application of literacy skills to the content areas are discussed. What has been your experience reading in content areas? Which subject matter texts in your undergraduate or graduate courses did you find particularly difficult? What made them difficult? What strategies did you employ to improve your comprehension? What special difficulties might low-achieving readers experience as they attempt to read content-area material? What steps might you take to help low-achieving readers read content-area texts?

## Anticipation Guide

Read each of the following statements. Put a check under "Agree" or "Disagree" to show how you feel about each one. If you can, discuss your responses with classmates.

| | Agree | Disagree |
|---|---|---|
| **1.** The content area teacher is not responsible for teaching reading or study strategies to poor readers. | ______ | ______ |
| **2.** The main reason low-achieving readers have difficulty with content-area texts is because they lack general reading skills and strategies. | ______ | ______ |
| **3.** A major barrier to comprehension of content-area texts is a lack of background knowledge in that area. | ______ | ______ |

4. Content-area texts for low-achieving readers should be written on easy reading levels and should contain fewer concepts. ________ ________
5. Low-achieving readers should get most of their content-area information from lectures, discussions, experiments, and audiovisual aids, rather than from books. ________ ________

## *Content-Area Reading*

As students progress through the grades, the emphasis in reading shifts from recognizing and reconstructing to acquiring and constructing. (Herber & Herber, 1993). As students encounter science, social studies, and other content-area texts, learning to read and write gives way to reading and writing to learn.

With its technical vocabulary, greater density of ideas, increased demands on conceptual knowledge, and more complex organizational patterns, content-area reading makes new demands on students. For students with marginal skills and limited backgrounds, the demands may be overwhelming. Students whose work was satisfactory when reading simple narratives fall apart when confronted with content-area materials. Often this happens around grade four, when the shift from simple narrative and easy informational text to more complex literary selections and more technical expository prose becomes pronounced.

## *Framework for Teaching Content-Area Reading*

Teaching content-area reading consists mainly of applying and adapting techniques and approaches described in the chapter on comprehension. A convenient way to look at a content-area reading lesson is to view it within the framework of a directed reading activity. A content-area reading lesson is basically an adaptation of the directed reading activity or directed reading–thinking activity. It includes establishing key ideas, preparation for reading, guided reading, rereading, extension, and application.

To help students relate their background of experience to content-area concepts, express the concepts in such a way that students can bring their prior knowledge to bear (Herber & Herber, 1993). A key concept such as that of representative government might be expressed as: "Sometimes we let others speak for us."

### *Establishing Key Ideas*

As noted when discussing the DRA and a number of other teaching techniques, the starting point of effective instruction is to decide which key ideas or concepts you want your students to learn and then to structure questions and activities around them. Barron (1969) recommends that you analyze the selection to be read or unit to be introduced and select two to four key concepts. This will give focus to your lesson and help you to determine how to prepare students for the reading of a selection and how to guide their efforts.

## Preparation for Reading

Preparation for reading in the content area may take many forms but generally includes: activating schema and building background, expanding vocabulary, building reasoning skills and reading strategies, establishing a purpose for reading, and motivating students.

### Activating Schema/Building Background

Among the strengths students bring to the content areas are background of relevant knowledge, ability to reason, understanding of language, and ability to communicate with others (Herber & Herber, 1993).

No matter how arcane the topic, students will usually have some background knowledge to bring to it. What is important is helping students use what knowledge they have to build a bridge to the new material they are about to read. One characteristic of low-achieving readers is that even when they have relevant background knowledge, they may not realize it. An essential element in the preparation process will be helping students discover what they do know about a topic. Part of helping them discover what they know is to create questions that tap into their prior knowledge. For instance, when developing the concept of representative government, you might relate this to how a class votes for a representative for the school's student council. Building on this concrete experience, lead students into a discussion about how the colonies were governed by Great Britain and had no representatives to speak for them.

### Expanding Vocabulary

Once you have established the key ideas that you wish to emphasize, choose the vocabulary words that you feel students might have difficulty with but which are essential for an understanding of the key ideas. A selection may have twenty to twenty-five or more words that you feel might be difficult for your students. Learning all those words would be overwhelming. By concentrating on those words that are most essential for an understanding of the key ideas, you limit the number of words that need to be introduced. When introducing new words, keep the number to six or seven.

### Building Reasoning Skills/Strategies

When analyzing the selection, note the reasoning skills or strategies required to read it. If it's a fiction piece, it may demand making inferences. A social studies selection may require drawing a conclusion or making an evaluation. A description of a science process may entail imaging. Also note the structure of the piece. Readers may be able to use the structure to help them organize the information. For an article on air pollution, they may be able to use the structure to organize the information into a series of causes and effects. For a piece on regions of the United States, they may be able to organize the information in a comparison/contrast format.

### Establishing Purpose/Motivating Students

Decide what you want students to learn, and convey that information to students. This will give focus to your lesson.

A purpose for reading should also be set. This purpose might involve questions that the students have about a topic. The students should also be motivated to read. Getting them involved in setting purposes, arousing their curiosity about intriguing topics, and helping them to relate topics to their lives generate interest in reading.

### *Guided Reading*

The first reading should be silent and might be guided by questions, as in the directed reading lesson or by a prediction, as in the directed reading–thinking activity. Or you might use a study guide, an anticipation guide, or self-constructed questions as used in a KWL approach. These procedures are explained later in the chapter.

### *Discussion*

The discussion of material read might be similar to that conducted in a DRA, or it might be part of a lecture on the topics covered in the text. Discussions might also take place in cooperative groups as students reflect on what they've read. Students still learning English may do better in a small discussion group. They are more likely to participate and will probably find that language is less of a barrier in a small group. These students may also benefit from the opportunity to use their home language to discuss new concepts. As Barba (1995) notes, "New knowledge can be integrated with existing knowledge only when existing knowledge (which may have been constructed in the student's native language) is restructured and students elaborate on what they already know" (p. 15).

### *Rereading*

In the content areas, a rereading would tend to expand on, clarify, or organize information rather than focus on reinforcing reading skills and strategies.

### *Extension/Application*

Extension/application activities might take the form of additional reading about the topic, conducting a survey, performing an experiment, or writing an essay or report. It often involves putting the new information to use in some way.

## *Text Structure*

Fostering comprehension in the content areas may also entail building an awareness of text structure. To get the most out of their reading, students need to be able to recognize and make use of narrative and expository text structures. Knowledge of text structure can also help them improve their writing skills.

## *Narrative Text Structure*

What comes to mind as you read or hear the following passage?

> *One fine afternoon Anansi the Spider was walking by the river when he saw his friend Turtle coming toward him carrying a large fish. Anansi loved to eat fish, though he was much too lazy to catch them himself. (Kimmel, 1992)*

Being familiar with stories, chances are you expect to hear a tale in which Anansi and Turtle are the main characters. You expect the tale to have a problem, which after a series of

**Story schema:** reader's concept of a story. Includes setting, problem, goal, characters, major episodes or plot, and resolution.

events, will be resolved in some way. In other words you have a schema for stories, a cognitive framework that tells you stories have characters, a setting, a problem, major events, and a resolution of the problem. If your sense of story—your **story schema**—is well developed, you may also know that stories might also have a theme or moral or may be used to explain the origin of some phenomenon of nature.

By kindergarten, most students have a basic sense of story elements, although they would not be able to name or explain them. Story schema is important for comprehension. As Harris and Sipay (1990) explain, "Children use their story schemata as a framework for comprehending a story by setting up expectations for certain contents occurring in a particular sequence" (p. 566). Unfortunately, low-achieving readers may have a poorly developed sense of story. When discussing stories they have read, low-achieving readers have more difficulty with transition words and other devices used to tie story elements together. When retelling stories, they tend to omit important information about the setting, characters, and the ending and may have difficulty with the sequence (Garnett, 1986).

The best way to develop a sense of story is to read to students. After hearing many stories, they naturally set up a series of expectations about what takes place in a story. As you discuss stories, you might also highlight the most important elements in a story, asking questions such as:

Where did the story take place?
Who were the most important characters in the story?
What did Anansi plan to do?
How did Turtle trick Anansi?
Why didn't Warthog believe Anansi?
What did Anansi learn?
What lesson do you think the story teaches?

Questions should be geared to the key elements of the story. These help students form a solid sense of story. One way to make sure questions are keyed to the major elements in a story is to create a key elements map (Beck, Omanson, & McKeown, 1982). The creation of a key elements map is described in Chapter 12. Student versions of key elements maps, which are also known as "***story maps,***" can be used to enhance low-achieving readers' comprehension (Cunningham & Foster, 1978; Fitzgerald & Spiegel, 1983). A sample student story map is presented in Figure 13-1.

**Story map:** graphic display showing the major elements in a story. Often the focus is on the plot.

A story map may also be presented as a web. Story webs are similar to semantic maps but are generally simpler. They typically show just the main ideas and supporting details. Webs can be used to show the traits of the main character, a sequence of events, the plot of the story, the setting, or any other element that you wish to depict.

Writing also helps develop a sense of story. Students might begin by imitating a simple, predictable pattern, such as the one in *Millions of Cats* (Gag, 1928). In time, they can try more complex patterns. As students develop a sense of story, they can also take a deeper look at theme, more complex plots, and more realistic characterization.

| | |
|---|---|
| Setting: | *By the river* |
| Characters: | *Anansi*<br>*Turtle*<br>*Warthog* |
| Problem: | *Anansi wanted a fish.* |
| Main Happenings in Story: | *Anansi asked Turtle to teach him to fish.*<br>*Anansi made a net.*<br>*Anansi put the net in the river.*<br>*Anansi caught a fish and cooked it.*<br>*Turtle ate the fish.*<br>*Anansi asked Warthog for justice.*<br>*Warthog did not believe Anansi.* |
| Outcome: | *Spiders learned how to weave nets.* |

**FIGURE 13-1 Story Map**

**Story grammar:** shows how the major parts of a story are interrelated. A story grammar might contain the following: setting, problem, goal, characters, major episodes, and resolution.

***Other Techniques for Developing a Sense of Story***

Techniques that actually involve the use of **story grammar** to predict and build comprehension are the probable passages, predict-o-gram, and story impressions techniques. Probable passages is similar to possible sentences and predict-o-gram, which were discussed in Chapter 11. In probable passages, students use their inferential skills to predict which vocabulary words tell about which story grammar category: setting, characters, problem, resolution, or ending. Once they have placed vocabulary words in story grammar categories, students predict what the story might be about. This can be done orally, or students might create a written probable passage that summarizes the story. In addition to fostering a sense of story grammar, comprehension and vocabulary knowledge, probable passages also promotes summarizing skills.

Story impressions also uses vocabulary from the story to activate students' story schema. Designed specifically for corrective readers, story impressions has been shown to be an effective technique for fostering improved comprehension (McGinley & Denner, 1987).

In story impressions, students use a series of words and phrases from a selection to reconstruct the story. Words and phrases that offer useful clues are chosen. Although students are encouraged to structure a story that is as close as possible to the actual story, faithfulness to the original tale is not the essential factor in students' achievement. The ability to use the clues to construct a logical tale is the main factor in improved comprehension. To present story impressions, try the following steps.

### A Lesson in Developing Story Impressions

*Step 1: Developing a Set of Story Impressions*

First, read the whole story. Then reread it and select words that highlight characters, setting, and key elements of the plot. Whenever possible, use the exact words from the story. Use single words, or phrases limited to three words. Choose ten to fifteen clues and arrange them in order. Use arrows to show that one element leads to another.

*Step 2: Explaining Story Impressions*

Explain the purpose of story impressions and how it works. Have the title of the story read and tell students that clues from the story are listed on the board. Explain that they will be using the clues to create a story and then they will read the actual story to compare what they have written to what the author has created.

*Step 3: Reading the Clues*

Read the clues with students. Discuss any words that might be unfamiliar. Encourage students to think about the kind of story that might be created based on the words listed.

*Step 4: Creating a Story Impression*

After discussing the clues, you and the class create a story impression based on the clues. Students may add words and phrases not presented. Focus on creating a story that is interesting and logical. After the story has been composed and written on the board, discuss it, and encourage students to evaluate it and make revisions if needed.

*Step 5: Reading of Author's Story*

Direct students to read the author's story and compare their version with the author's story.

*Step 6: Discussing the Story*

Discuss the author's story. Compare the author's and students' versions. As students become proficient in this technique, they might create and discuss story impressions in small cooperative learning groups. Story impressions can also be used as part of the writing program (McGinley & Denner, 1987). They provide excellent practice in constructing narrative pieces.

A list of story impression clues based on Poe's "A Tell-Tale Heart" and a low-achieving reader's construction of a story based on the clues is presented in Figure 13-2.

## *Expository Text Structures*

What makes the following paragraph easy or hard to read?

We organize information from our reading according to the structure of the ideas in a selection. The main idea is at the top of the structure. Supporting details are organized around the main idea.

*Skin has four important jobs. One, it keeps harmful bacteria out of your body. Two, it keeps the water in your body from drying up. The outer layer of skin is waterproof. And oil glands in the skin produce oils that keep the skin moist. Three, skin regulates the temperature of your body. Layers of fat in the skin help to keep you warm. Sweat glands in the skin let the body give off moisture through the skin. This helps you cool off. Four, skin is the sense organ of touch. (Bledsoe, 1990, p. 185)*

The paragraph, which was taken from *Fearon's Biology,* a text for below level readers, is well structured. It has a main idea, announced in the first sentence, following by a listing of four details. By using the structure of that paragraph, the student can better understand

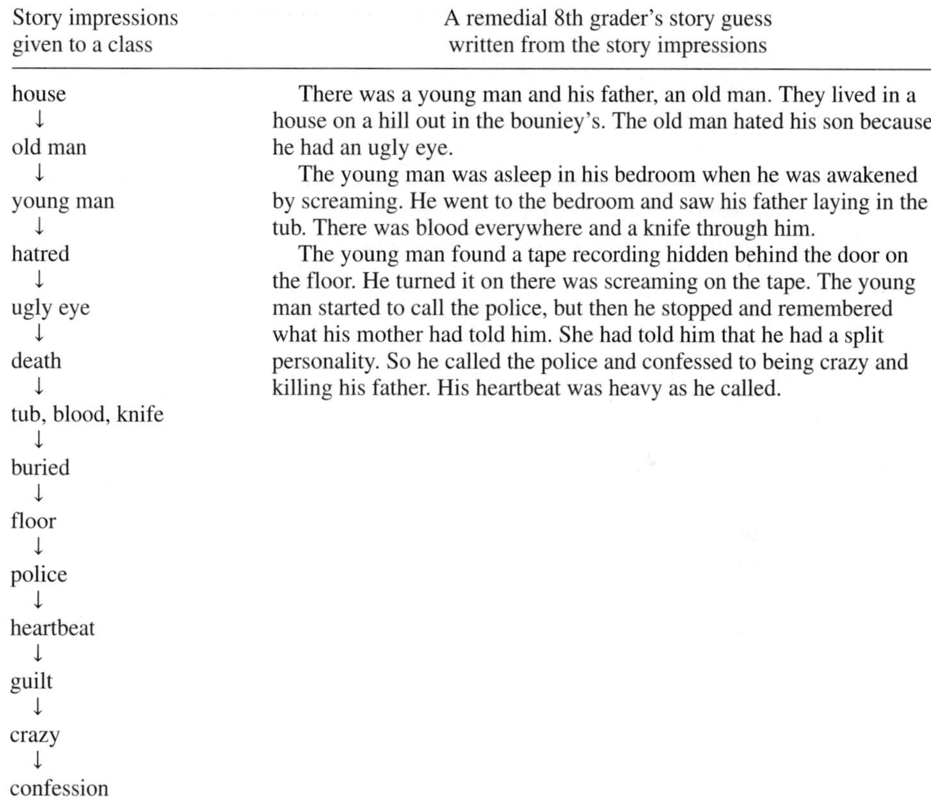

| Story impressions given to a class | A remedial 8th grader's story guess written from the story impressions |
|---|---|
| house<br>↓<br>old man<br>↓<br>young man<br>↓<br>hatred<br>↓<br>ugly eye<br>↓<br>death<br>↓<br>tub, blood, knife<br>↓<br>buried<br>↓<br>floor<br>↓<br>police<br>↓<br>heartbeat<br>↓<br>guilt<br>↓<br>crazy<br>↓<br>confession | There was a young man and his father, an old man. They lived in a house on a hill out in the bouniey's. The old man hated his son because he had an ugly eye.<br>The young man was asleep in his bedroom when he was awakened by screaming. He went to the bedroom and saw his father laying in the tub. There was blood everywhere and a knife through him.<br>The young man found a tape recording hidden behind the door on the floor. He turned it on there was screaming on the tape. The young man started to call the police, but then he stopped and remembered what his mother had told him. She had told him that he had a split personality. So he called the police and confessed to being crazy and killing his father. His heartbeat was heavy as he called. |

**FIGURE 13-2 Story Impressions (Prereading) Activity Based on Poe's "The Tell-Tale Heart"**

From "Story Impressions: A Prereading/Writing Activity" by William J. McGinley & Peter R. Denner. *Journal of Reading, 31,* (1987), 248–253. 

its content. In fact, the structure provides a map of the information presented in the paragraph. Using that map should improve the encoding of the information. Students will know that they will be looking for four items as they read the paragraph. The structure also helps the readers organize the information: one main idea and four details. Knowing the structure, the student would be better able to take notes, create a semantic map, or outline the paragraph.

Typically, young and low-achieving readers fail to use text structure as a reading strategy. For younger readers, this may be due, in part, to a lack of experience with expository text. For older low-achieving readers, it may reflect a lack of knowledge about text structure strategy or simply failure to use this strategy. Using the text structure strategy, good readers seek the author's main idea and then relate the details to that main idea. The students then create a mental representation of the text which reflects the text structure (problem–solution, cause–effects, for instance). When recalling the text, they retrieve the major idea first and then the details. Poor comprehenders, on the other hand, do not organize information and simply encode a passage as a list of unrelated items. As B. Meyer, Brandt, and Bluth (1980) comment: “The reader has no focus and simply tries to remember something from the text” (p. 80). The result is a “list-like collection of descriptions about the passage topic with no attempt to interrelate them” (p. 80).

Awareness of expository patterns apparently develops after narrative ones. For many students, a working awareness of expository text structures may not develop until about third grade. A likely order of development would follow this sequence: time sequence, enumeration/description, explanation/process, comparison/contrast, problem/solution, and cause/effect.

***Types of Expository Text Structure***

Expository texts are organized in a variety of ways. Major types of organization are listed below:

**Time Sequence.** This structure is a listing, but time order is indicated. Signal words include: *after, at last, before, finally, later, long ago, then, today, tomorrow, yesterday,* and the names of specific days, times, and dates. Time sequence is frequently found in fiction and in history texts.

> *Ferdinand Magellan, A Portuguese captain, was commissioned to sail in search of the Far East in 1519. He sailed across the Atlantic Ocean and reached the coast of South America. His ships then journeyed southward, finally reaching the tip of South America where he found a waterway that became known as the Strait of Magellan. Its stormy, rough waters led from the Atlantic to the Pacific Oceans. Magellan had at last found the magic water route around the new world. (King & Napp, 1989, p. 10)*

**Enumeration/Description.** This structure also may present details in a simple list, provide a series of descriptive details, or give a series of examples. No cause–effect, time, or other relationships are used. May be cued by words, such as the following: *for example, one, two,* and other number words. Enumeration/description is frequently found in fiction and social studies but may also be found in science.

> *The coral snake lives in the southern United States. It usually lives in a damp, cool spot under fallen leaves, and looks for lizards or other snakes to eat. (Scott, 1993, p. 23)*

> Knowledge of text structure can be used to organize in one’s mind information that one has read and can also be used to structure information that one is writing.

**Explanation/Process.** This structure explains how something works or is done, such as, how a laser disk player works, how plants make food, how a president is elected, how rocks are formed, or how we hear. Explanation/process passages dominate scientific writing.

> *In conduction, heat is moved along by molecules bumping into one another. Suppose you put a spoon in a cup of hot coffee.*

*The top of the spoon doesn't touch the coffee at all. Yet it will soon be hot. This is because of conduction. The coffee heats the bottom of the spoon. The hot molecules on the bottom of the spoon bump into other spoon molecules. This warms them up. In turn, these molecules warm up the next ones up the spoon. The heat moves right on up to the tip of the spoon. (Bledsoe, 1994, p. 199)*

**Comparison/Contrast.** Focusing on similarities and/or differences, this structure has cue words such as: *although, but, however, similar, different, on the one hand, on the other hand.* Comparison/contrast structures are frequently found in social studies texts but are also found in science writing.

*Rabbits are much like rodents. There are two big differences. Rabbits have four cutting teeth while rodents have only two. Also rabbits have very strong back legs. These make rabbits very good hoppers and leapers. (Bledsoe, 1988, p. 165)*

**Problem/Solution.** In this type of structure, a problem is presented and then its solution specified.

*Kids in the U.S. throw away more than four billion little drink boxes a year. Drink boxes can sit for 300 to 400 years in a landfill. As an answer to this problem some cities and school systems have drink-box recycling programs. If there isn't a drink-box recycling program in your area, ask your student council to start one. Better yet, try filling a thermos or sports bottle with juice instead of buying drink boxes—and urge your friends to do the same. (Lowery & Lorbiecki, 1993, p. 17)*

**Cause/Effect.** A cause is described, and then its effects presented in this structure. In a variation, the effect or effects are presented and then the causes are given.

*Fishing, hunting, and trapping are one cause of animal extinction. Another cause is the clearing away of plant life. Animals that lived in these places die because their homes have been destroyed. (Bledsoe, 1988, p. 247)*

> Newspaper articles often follow a journalist structure (Simonsen, 1996). The main idea of the article is highlighted in the first paragraph, and the details follow in the remaining paragraphs.

Although a piece of writing may have a predominant structure, most combine two or more organizational patterns. The following piece is composed primarily of a comparison/contrast pattern that compares plant and animal cells, but the pattern flows naturally into an enumeration/description pattern as cell walls are described and the function of chloroplasts is explained.

*Plant and animals cells have a few important differences. First, plant cells have cell walls. The cell wall is outside the membrane. It is harder and stronger than the membrane.*

*Plant cells usually have bigger vacuoles than animal cells. This is because plant cells must store a lot of water. Often, however, animals cells have more vacuoles than plant cells.*

*The most important difference is that plant cells have something called chloroplasts. Chloroplasts store a green coloring. This green coloring traps sunlight. Plants use the trapped sunlight to make their food. (Bledsoe, 1994, p. 43)*

Well-organized text is easier to process. It is also easier to understand and is generally remembered longer. We tend to remember text in the way it was organized. We are likely to recall the events in a time-sequence passage in the order in which they occurred, for instance.

Older students and better readers are more aware of organizational patterns and make more effective use of them. However, text structure can be taught to poor readers and has resulted, in some studies, in both improved comprehension and improved writing (Gordon, 1990). Instruction seems to be most effective when both reading and writing are involved (Horowitz, 1985).

## *Teaching Text Patterns*

To teach text structures, start with the easiest pattern. For younger children, the time sequence pattern seems easiest (Englert & Hiebert, 1984). For older students, the comparison-contrast pattern seems to be the best choice for initial instruction (Meyer & Rice, 1984).

To teach a time-sequence pattern, begin with everyday activities. Compose a list of the day's activities, or, in an experience story, recount a recent trip. Include and emphasize time signal words: *next, after, soon.* Next, read a brief well-structured selection with the class. Using a think-aloud procedure, show how you would use cue words and the sense of the selection to determine the structure of the passage and, in turn, use the structure to improve comprehension (Gordon, 1990).

Discussing the time-sequence passage about Magellan, you might say, "The first sentence tells me that Magellan started out in 1519. This paragraph looks like it will have a time sequence order. Yes, here it says he sailed across the Atlantic and then went southward. This is definitely a time-sequence passage. As I read this passage, I'll try to keep the events in order."

"You can tell a time-sequence passage by the way the events happen one right after another and also because there are words that signal time order. Dates such as *1519* signal time order. Can you find other words that signal time order?" The class would discuss the role that *then, finally,* and *at last* play in cueing time order.

Under your guidance, have students read brief, well-structured time-order passages. Help them pose questions that take advantage of the structure of the passage. When discussing the selection, ask a question that incorporates time structure. For instance, for the Magellan passage, you might ask students to trace in order the main parts of Magellan's journey around the world. Asking how many ships or men took part in the journey are valid questions but don't take advantage of the structure of the passage, which is what you are emphasizing.

Have students compose graphic organizers which show the structure of the piece. For time-sequence passages, you might use a time-line or a series of boxes as in Figure 13-3 that show time order. For explanation/process show the steps in the explanation or process in a series of boxes. For comparison/contrast, you might use a Venn diagram (see p. 301). For enumeration/description, you might use a semantic map or web (see p. 298).

To reinforce the use of signal words, cut up a passage that incorporates cue words and have students reassemble it as in the exercise below. Select a passage similar to the following in which putting the passage back together again would be difficult without cue words.

> Have you ever wondered how dolphins are trained?
> Next, the dolphin is taught to look at the trainer.
> At last, the dolphin is taught to do easy tricks like taking a bow.
> First of all, a dolphin has to be trained to eat dead fish because in the wild, dolphins only eat live fish.

Have students compose time-order pieces. You may want to have them use well-structured passages as models or supply frames as in Figure 13-4. Starting with simplified sequence patterns, Cudd and Roberts (1989) report using frames as early as the second half of first grade.

If you do use frames, gradually phase them out so students are creating their own pieces. Also encourage the use of signal words; but as students grow in writing skill, lead them to see that the overuse of signal words can produce prose that is wooden. After students have a fairly good grasp of one pattern, introduce another. (For more information on using text structures in writing, see Chapter 15.)

Encourage students to use their knowledge of patterns in their studying as well as in their reading and writing. For instance, when taking notes, students should take advantage of the text pattern so that major historical events are listed in order and effects are listed under causes or vice versa.

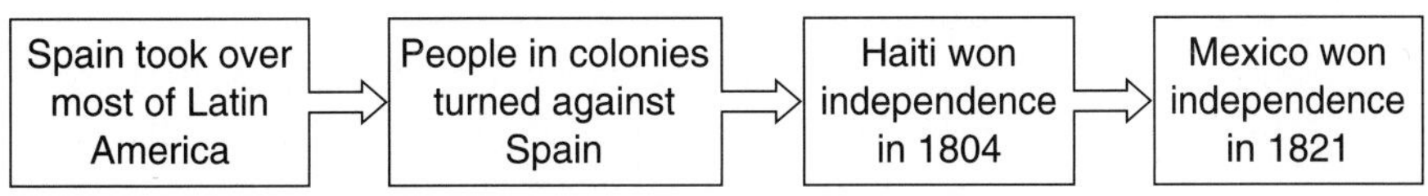


**FIGURE 13-3 Sequence Chart**

____________________ is easy. First, you ____________________.
The next step is to ______________________________________.
Then you ____________________________________________.
Finally, you _________________________________________.
Just four simple steps, and you're finished.

**FIGURE 13-4 Frame for an Explanation/Process Sequence Paragraph**

**Structural organizer:** helps students take advantage of the organization of a selection in order to enhance comprehension and retention.

### *Using the Structural Organizer*

The structural organizer can be a powerful technique for guiding students in the use of text organization as a reading strategy. In one study, ninth-graders who used a structural organizer recalled 77 percent more than did those who read as they usually did (Slater, Graves, & Piche, 185). A structural organizer is a study or reading guide in which the organization of the text is briefly explained and a partially completed outline or other organizer is supplied. The reader is told how and why to finish the outline. Figure 13-5 shows a structural organizer.

**_Chapter 15: How We Use the Land_**

In this chapter, which talks about using land, William Lefkowitz, the author, uses two types of writing patterns: main idea and details and cause and effect. Read the section to answer these questions:

Why is there a limited amount of usable land? (p. 175, par. 1)

*Causes for Limited Amount of Usable Land*

1. ______________________
2. ______________________
3. ______________________
4. ______________________
5. ______________________

What are the seven major uses of land in the United States? (pp. 176–177)

*Seven Major Uses of Land*

1. ______________________
2. ______________________
3. ______________________
4. ______________________
5. ______________________
6. ______________________
7. ______________________

What are the three causes of shrinking farmland in the United States? (pp. 180–181)

*Three Causes of Shrinking Farmland*

1. ______________________
2. ______________________
3. ______________________

**FIGURE 13-5 Sample Structural Organizer**

Exercise based on *Fearon's United States Geography* by W. Lefkowitz, 1990. Belmont, CA: Fearon Education.

## Instructional Techniques for Fostering Content-Area Comprehension

There are numerous techniques for fostering comprehension in general reading and in the content areas. It's important to have a variety of techniques as this sparks interest. Some techniques are especially effective in building background, whereas others can be effective in activating schema, creating interest or organizing information. Some are teacher directed; others are more student centered. The well-prepared reading teacher has knowledge of a variety of techniques, but, more importantly, knows which techniques work best in which situations. As you read about each technique, think of its advantages and disadvantages and the situations in which it might work best. Techniques have been grouped according to when they would most likely be used: before, during, or after reading.

### Before-Reading Techniques

The purpose of before-reading teaching techniques is to help students get an overview of the selection to be read, to activate prior knowledge, build background knowledge and vocabulary, set goals, and establish strategies for reading and reasoning. Before-reading techniques feature the anticipation guide, PReP, structured overview, and Frayer model. In the previous chapter, the directed reading activity and directed reading–thinking activity were presented as devices to prepare students to read. The initial portions of these techniques may also be used to prepare students for reading a content-area selection.

Anticipation guides have the potential to spark a lively discussion and interest in the topic. This activates prior knowledge and fosters motivation for active reading.

#### *Anticipation Guide*

At this point, you should be fairly familiar with the anticipation guide. It has appeared at the beginning of each chapter. An anticipation guide consists of a list of three to six controversial or debatable statements. Students respond to the statements by indicating whether they agree or disagree with them.

Anticipation guides force students to think about a subject before they read about it. While activating their prior knowledge, it may also bring to the fore erroneous concepts that they have about a topic. Low-achieving readers tend to hold onto beliefs even when these are contradicted in print (Lipson, 1984; Maria & MacGinitie, 1987). Anticipation guides, by bringing forth erroneous beliefs, make these easier to deal with. Here are the steps for creating and using an anticipation guide (Head & Readence, 1986).

**Steps for Introducing an Anticipation Guide**

*Step 1: Identifying Major Concepts*

Note two or three major ideas that you wish students to learn.

*Step 2: Determining Students' Background*

Considering students' general store of knowledge and beliefs and content of the selection to be read,

*Continued*

### Steps for Introducing an Anticipation Guide *Continued*

what misunderstandings might they have about the topic? Jot these down.

*Step 3: Creating the Guide*

Write three to six statements that encompass key concepts. Compose statements that tap areas in which students have misconceptions or doubts. Do not compose statements about areas in which students have no knowledge because they won't be able to say whether they agree or disagree. The best kinds of statements are those for which the students have enough information so they can respond, but not so much that they won't be acquiring new information as they read. Be careful not to write statements that are really true-false items and which don't require students to assess their knowledge, beliefs, and opinions (Head & Readence, 1986).

*Step 4: Introducing the Guide*

Explain the guide. It may be placed on the board or on sheets. Read the directions and the statements orally and ask students to respond to each statement by checking "Agree" or "Disagree." Students may work independently or in small groups. Small groups may be more effective in getting students to consider their ideas on the topic, including misconceptions.

*Step 5: Discussing Responses*

Discuss each statement. You might have students raise their hands to indicate if they agreed or disagreed. Have students explain their reasons. Try to elicit at least one agree and one disagree statement for each item so students are better able to evaluate both sides of an issue. The discussion should help students open their minds as they consider their beliefs in relationship to the beliefs of others. The discussion should also motivate students to want to read so they can evaluate their beliefs.

*Step 6: Reading of Text*

Restate the gist of students' responses. Then have them read the selection to evaluate their answers.

*Step 7: Discussing Text*

Students can discuss the text and their responses to the original statements once more, this time in the light of having read the selection. They can talk over how reading the text had an impact on their original responses.

#### *Extended Anticipation Guide*

The extended guide adds a second part in which readers indicate whether or not they have found support in the text for their responses (Duffelmeyer, Baum, & Meekly, 1987). If they have not found support, they rewrite in their own words information from the text which conflicts with their beliefs. Because the extended anticipation guide requires the student to paraphrase information that conflicts with a misconception, it should be more effective in motivating students to revise erroneous information.

#### *PReP*

When teaching low-achieving readers, it's important to have a sense of their backgrounds. Oftentimes, their background knowledge has gaps in it. You are surprised to learn that they know almost nothing about the Vietnam War or lasers. At other times, they know more than you think they do. Maria (1990) was surprised to discover that the low-achieving students with whom she was working with had some knowledge of knights.

A technique that combines assessment and instruction in background knowledge and which helps students activate and use prior knowledge is the Pre-Reading Plan (PReP).

Through PReP, students activate prior knowledge, learn from each other, and anticipate the content of the text they are about to read. Meanwhile, the teacher finds out what the students know about the topic.

PReP is a three-step testing–teaching procedure that helps the teacher determine what students know about a particular topic, how that information might be organized, and what kind of language the students use to describe or explain that knowledge. The teacher can then assess how much background and vocabulary might need to be developed before the students would be able to understand the text (Langer, 1981). The box to follow shows the three steps in applying PReP.

### Steps in the Application of PReP

*Step 1: Initial Associates with the Concept*

As a prompt, use a key word, phrase, or illustration from the text to be read, such as, "Tell me anything that comes to mind when you hear the words *Supreme Court.*" Students' responses are listed on the board.

*Step 2: Reflections on Initial Associations*

In order to assess students' associations with the key word or phrase, point to each student's response and asks a question about it. If one of the responses is the word *laws,* for instance, you might ask, "What makes you think of *laws*?"

*Step 3: Reformulation of Knowledge*

To give students a chance to express associations that have been modified by the discussion, you might ask: "Based on what we have talked about, do you have any new ideas about the Supreme Court?"

The extent and depth of students' prior knowledge is reflected in their level of response during PReP. Responses can be classified as falling into one of three categories based on the criteria noted in Figure 13-6.

During the PReP discussion, build concepts. Talk about what kind of judges are on the Supreme Court. You might also lead students to see that the Supreme Court plays an important role in the government. Depending on the types of responses, students may need no instruction, a little, or a lot. Through building on what students know and using their concepts and language, you will be better able to give them the kind of preparation they need for reading a piece.

| Level of Knowledge | Associations |
|---|---|
| Little | Words that sound like the key word.<br>Firsthand experiences that may not be relevant.<br>"Supreme Court—heard about them on TV." |
| Some | Provides examples, attributes, or defining characteristics of target word.<br>"Supreme Court—judges" |
| Much | Superordinate concepts, definitions, analogies, or linking of concepts.<br>"Supreme Court—Judicial branch of government" |

**FIGURE 13-6 Levels of Prior Knowledge**

***Structured Overview***

In order to study how students read content materials, Barron (1979) took on the role of a student in a high school biology class, a subject in which he had little background. Overwhelmed by a long list of unfamiliar technical terms, he wondered how he would cope with all the new words. The solution was not long in coming.

> *Later that evening, as I attempted to read the chapters associated with the unit, a simple fact began to dawn on me.* All the vocabulary words were related in some way. *I started to arrange the words in a diagram to depict relationships, occasionally adding terms from the two preceding units. Gradually, much of the content with which I had been struggling became clear. (pp. 172–173)*

Out of this experience was born the structured overview. A structured overview builds on what students already know. It shows how new words in a selection that students are about to read or a unit that they are about to study are related to words that are familiar to them. For instance, students can better understand the word *mollusks* when they realize that it includes *clams, snails, scallops, oysters,* and *octopuses.* The original structured overview was very much teacher directed and followed a series of six steps as outlined in the following box.

### A Lesson in Teaching a Structured Overview

> Selecting key concepts helps you decide what's important and provides a rationale for selecting the words that you wish to present.

*Step 1: Selecting Key Concepts*

Read over the selection or unit to be read and select two to four concepts or ideas that you wish to emphasize. In introducing a unit on mollusks, the teacher decided that she wanted to stress the following ideas (lesson is drawn from an easy-to-read science text by Gottlieb, 1991).

- Mollusks are soft-bodied invertebrates and fall into one of three main groups.
- Snails are mollusks that have one valve.
- Clams and oysters have two valves.
- Octopuses, squid, and cuttlefish have no valves.

*Step 2: Selecting Related Vocabulary*

Analyze the vocabulary in the selection and choose words that you feel would be needed to understand the key ideas.

| | | |
|---|---|---|
| cuttlefish | squid | clam |
| mollusk | coquinas | scallops |
| invertebrate | shell | oysters |
| univalve | snail | tentacles |
| valveless | gills | bivalve |

*Step 3: Arranging Words*

Arrange the words so that you show relationships.

*Step 4: Inserting Known Words*

Add words that the students already know so that they can relate new words to known words.

*Step 5: Checking the Overview*

Look over the overview. Are relationships clearly shown? Is the overview easy to understand? A completed overview is shown in Figure 13-7.

*Step 6: Introducing the Overview*

Place the overview on an overhead projector, chart paper, or on the board. Point to the word *mollusks* and tell students that they will be reading about mollusks. Ask them what they can tell about mollusks by examining the overview. Discuss the fact that mollusks are invertebrates and so have no backbone. Talk over the three main kinds of mollusks and examples of each. Clarify any concepts that seem confusing. Make any changes to the overview that seem necessary.

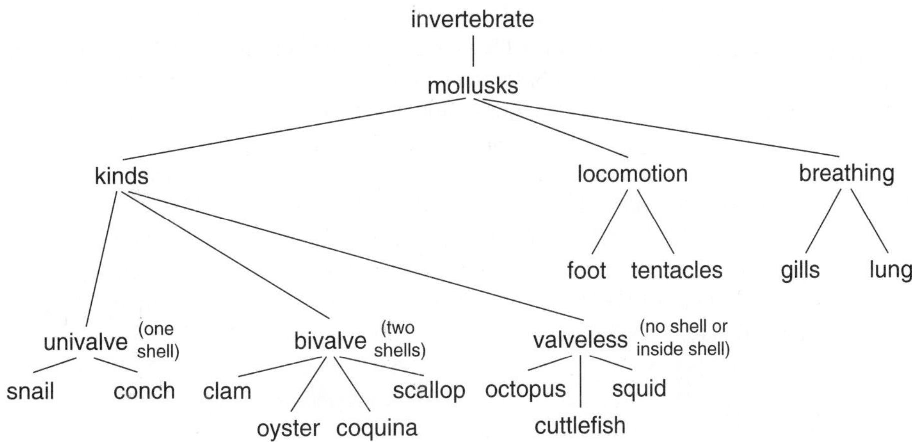


**FIGURE 13-7 Structured Overview**

Keep the overview in a prominent place so that as students read about mollusks, they can refer to the overview. As students learn more about mollusks, encourage them to add to the overview. You may want to add sections that contain key words that refer to movement, obtaining oxygen, obtaining food, or other vital activities.

**Revised Structured Overview.** The original structured overview is teacher directed and works well when students have little background to bring to a topic. In the revised structured overview, students are more actively involved. Barron (1979) found that when students played a role in constructing an overview, they learned more. He also found that the revised structured overview worked well when it was used to organize information after the students had read the target sections.

The revised overview begins with brainstorming (Estes & Vaughn, 1985). Place the key concept on the board and discuss it. A concept such as *mollusks* would probably not work well for a pre-reading structured overview because students might have little background to bring to the concept. However, you might use a more familiar concept like *clam* or *octopus* or *snail.* As the students respond, probe and supply prompts, asking such questions as: "What sea animals are like clams? What are some land animals, besides turtles, that have shells?"

After listing on the board what students know, you might add some of your own items, especially if key concepts were omitted. You and the class would then group items that go together and devise a title or category name for them. The items would then be arranged in a structured overview. Again, at this point, you should feel free to add important concepts or vocabulary that have not been mentioned. You should also review the overview and tie it in with the students' purpose for reading the selection. The students might use the overview to predict what the selection will be about. Students might add to the overview after they have read the selection.

The Frayer Model works best with high-level complex concepts that have a hierarchical organization.

### *Frayer Model of Conceptual Development*

Because they are small, crawl on the ground, and have a somewhat similar appearance, spiders, insects, mites, and ticks are often lumped together. Even students who know that spiders aren't insects are surprised to learn that neither are ticks or mites. A procedure that has been successfully used to teach concepts to low-achieving readers in both social studies and science is the Frayer model of conceptual development (Peters, 1979).

A carefully thought-out, systematic procedure, the Frayer model develops concepts through discovering relevant attributes, considering irrelevant attributes, and noting examples and nonexamples. The concept is also placed within a hierarchy so the students see superordinate, coordinate, and subordinate categories. This allows students to see how the concept fits in within an overall conceptual scheme. Seeing all these relationships, students learn concepts better because they have more semantic cues. Here is how the concept of *insects* might be taught.

#### The Frayer Model Lesson

*Step 1: Brainstorming the Concept*

In order to involve students and find out what they know about the topic, write the topic word on the board and ask students to tell what comes to mind when they hear the word *insect.* List students' responses on the board.

*Step 2: Discussing Examples of the Concept*

From the information listed on the board, note examples of insects. If there are few examples, list additional ones.

*Step 3: Discussing Relevant Characteristics*

Talk over what insects have in common, i.e., six legs, three body parts.

Through seeing superordinate, coordinate, and subordinate categories, students can better grasp how key concepts are interrelated.

*Step 4: Arranging Concepts in a Hierarchy*

Show where insects fall in the hierarchy. Show superordinate categories. Insects are arthropods. Arthropods are invertebrates. Invertebrates are animals. Then show coordinate categories. Insects belong in the same group of arthropods as do crustaceans, arachnids, chilopods, and diplopods. Discuss subordinate categories: coleoptera (beetles), lepidoptera (butterflies and moths), hymenoptera (ants, bees, wasps), diptera (flies).

*Step 5: Discussing Common Characteristics*

Help students decide what the relevant characteristics of an insect are, i.e., three pairs of legs, three body parts.

*Step 6: Discussing Irrelevant Characteristics*

Discuss irrelevant characteristics of insects: color, size, whether they have eyes, climate in which they are found.

*Step 7: Discussing Nonexamples*

Discuss why a spider, a scorpion, a tick, a mite, or a centipede would not be an insect.

*Step 8: Testing the Concept*

Provide the students with examples and nonexamples of creatures and have them tell whether they are insects or not and explain their responses. An example of Frayer's model is shown in Figure 13-8.

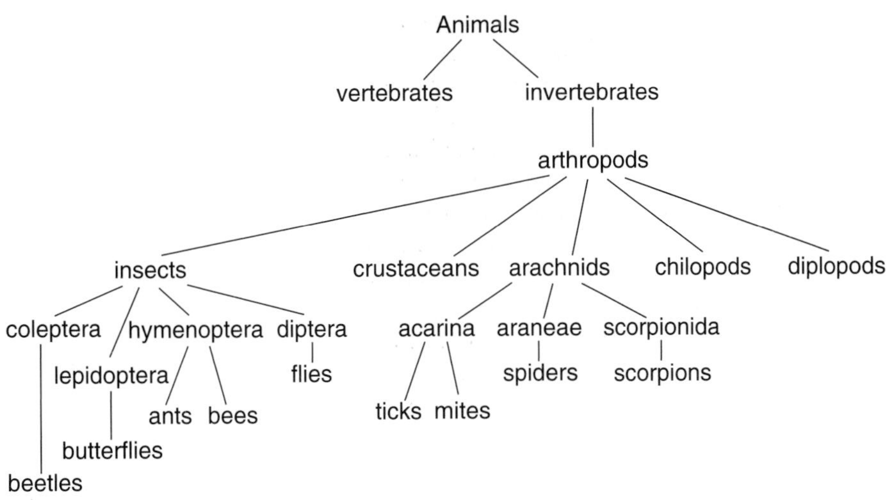


**FIGURE 13-8 Frayer Model**

## *During-Reading Techniques*

As students read content area texts, they hone in on critical information, information that answers the purpose question that was established for their reading. Students distinguish between relevant and irrelevant information or important and unimportant details. They organize information, using main ideas that they have recognized as they read or constructed. They make inferences about causes; visualize settings, characters, and processes; generate questions; summarize; predict; integrate new information with old; and modify schema if necessary. They also make use of heads and subheads, charts, photos, drawings, other graphical features, and the overall organization and layout of the chapter or section being read. In addition, they monitor for meaning and use correction strategies, such as rereading, as necessary.

In general, adept readers use many of the strategies highlighted in the previous chapter. In addition, they employ a strategy introduced earlier in this chapter: using chapter organization and text structure to enhance comprehension. The techniques that promote the use of during-reading strategies include frame questions, study guides, glosses, and think-alouds.

One key to learning the content of a subject matter is to know the questions to ask. The questions help determine what information is most important and how that information is organized.

### *Frame Questions*

In a sense, each content area attempts to answer a series of questions. Much of science is devoted to asking questions about mechanisms, processes, systems, and theories. For instance, the following questions are regularly asked about major systems of the body: What are the parts of the system? Where is the system located? How does the system work? What is the system's function? What are some signs that the

**Frames:** categories of information that reflect the structure of content-area text (Armbruster & T. Anderson, 1981). A history frame, reflecting the content area's concern with causes and effects, may detail the causes of the Revolutionary War.

system is not functioning properly? In geography, frequently asked questions include: Where is it? What are its major physical characteristics? How was it formed? How is it changing? History is concerned with questions of time and causes and effects. **Frames** are visual representations of the answers to implied or explicit content-area questions (Armbruster & T. Anderson, 1981). Frames reflect the structure of the content area. For instance, a history frame, reflecting the content area's concern with causes and effects, may detail the major causes of the Revolutionary War. One way to take advantage of the frame organization is to construct a frame matrix.

Frame matrices work best as a study guide and are effective when comparisons are being made or when the focus is on key categories of information.

### *Frame Matrix*

As its name suggests, the **frame matrix** has two major aspects: a frame, which highlights essential categories of information—such as location, area, population, climate—and the matrix which allows the comparison of two or more elements in terms of the frames or categories (see Figure 13-9).

To construct a frame matrix, seek out the important categories of information for a topic. Then note how each category might be subdivided. If you are familiar with a topic, you might set up a tentative frame and then verify it by checking the text that students are about to read (Armbruster, 1991). You might also check the topic in an encyclopedia. Encyclopedias often organize their articles around major topics or questions.

*Countries of North America*

| | Canada | Mexico | United States |
|---|---|---|---|
| Location | Northern North America | Southern North America | Central North America |
| Area | 3,851,809 sq miles (9,976,186 sq km) | 761,600 sq miles (1,972,547 sq km) | 3,536,341 sq miles (9,159,123 sq km) |
| Population | 29 million | 92 million | 260 million |
| Climate | Temperate-Cold | Warm | Varies |
| Income per person | $19,600 | $3,600 | $20,817 |

**FIGURE 13-9 Frame Matrix**

Possible frame questions for a chapter or book on weather disasters might include: What is it? What are its main characteristics? What causes it? What damage does it do? How is it forecast? What are the signs of it? How can you protect yourself against it? What are some of the most notorious ones?

In a study of states, possible frame questions might include: What is its name? Where is it? How big is it? How many people does it have? What is the average income of its people? What are its main industries? What are its natural resources? What is its capital?

A frame matrix helps students see relationships. Students can see at a glance what entities are being compared and what the major categories of information are. Making comparisons is facilitated because categories being compared are lined up side by side. The matrix also makes it obvious when information is missing (Heiman & Slomianko, 1986).

**Study guide:** written set of questions or other activities designed to assist students in their reading of a segment of content-area text.

### *Study Guides*

Coming in many shapes and sizes, *study guides* may take a variety of forms and serve a number of purposes. One recent text discusses nearly 20 varieties of study guides (K. Wood, Lapp, & Flood, 1992). Study guides lead students through the reading and thinking processes necessary to acquire the key concepts in the text (Maxworthy, 1993).

**Content Guides.** One of the simplest guides is the content guide. Low-achieving readers often find a fact-packed content area text to be overwhelming. Through questions, statements, matching items, sentence completion exercises, and the completion of graphic organizers, a content guide leads students to the significant content in the chapter. As an additional aid, the pages on which the essential information is located are generally noted.

Originally designed to provide guidance as secondary students read their content-area texts, study guides can be particularly effective when used with low-achieving readers.

**Pattern Guides.** Pattern guides make use of the structure of text. Noting the pattern of a piece of writing (time-sequence, cause–effect, problem–solution) enhances comprehension because it gives the reader a plan to follow. In most pieces of extended writing, however, the author uses several patterns. In the section covered by the Pattern Guide in Figure 13-10, the author used both a problem–solution and cause–effect pattern.

### *Glossing*

**Glossing** is a promising technique for helping low-achieving readers cope with the complexities of content-area texts. The normal interaction or transaction in reading is between reader and author. Glossing places the teacher in the interaction as an expert adviser (Stewart & Cross, 1991).

**Gloss:** form of study guide in which segments of the text are clarified through notes usually placed in the margin.

A **gloss,** which is similar to a study guide, is a series of notes or suggestions designed to improve a student's reading of a passage. The notes and suggestions are written on a sheet of paper lined up with the text as in Figure 13-11. The gloss may contain definitions of difficult terms, an explanation of a difficult concept, a paraphrase of a confusing sentence, a suggestion to tap prior knowledge, or a suggestion that

*Read Chapter 32: Living in Communities, pp. 229–234*

Problems:

What was Borneo's main problem?

______________________________

______________________________

______________________________

What was the second problem?

______________________________

______________________________

______________________________

Solutions:

How was the first problem solved?

______________________________

______________________________

______________________________

How was the problem solved?

______________________________

______________________________

______________________________

*Cause and Effects*

What were the unwanted effects of using chemicals? Fill in the boxes to show what happened when chemicals were used.

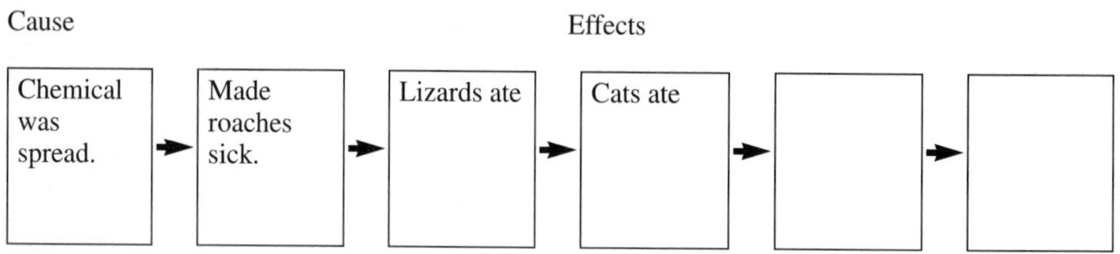


**FIGURE 13-10 Pattern Guide**

Source: *Biology, The Kingdom of Life.* Bledsoe, L. J. Castro Valley, CA: Quercus, 1988.

would in some other way enhance comprehension or metacognition. The notations in the gloss might consist of a statement, a question, a brief paragraph, or even a fill-in-the-blank or complete-the-statement activity.

Various kinds of questions might be included: those that help the student tap prior knowledge or integrate new information with old, those that help the student set a purpose for reading, those that help a student use an essential comprehension or word recognition strategy, those that help a reader check her or his understanding of the text (Richgels & Hansen, 1984).

Designed to integrate content and process, glosses typically include activities that focus on both. A gloss may also be designed to focus on a particular area, such as difficult vocabulary or a particular strategy, such as using the organization of the passage. The gloss might also be used to make a text more readable. All too often, there is a gap between the reading ability of the low-achieving readers and the difficulty level of the text. Steps that might be taken in a gloss to make the text more accessible, include the following:

- Give the reader an easy-to-read overview of the text.
- Highlight the most important information.
- Paraphrase in more understandable language essential segments that would be too difficult for students to read on their own.

*Read "Proclamation of 1763" in Our Nation's History, pp. 64–65. As you read, use this gloss. A proclamation (prok-luh-MAY-shun) is a government order. Remember that the Treaty of Paris gave England all French land east of the Mississippi, except for New Orleans. England also got Florida from Spain.*

# A New Nation Begins to Grow

PART 1

## Proclamation of 1763

*This is the main idea of the whole section. As you read, ask yourself: "What problems developed?"*

British control of America was firmly established with the Treaty of Paris. New problems soon developed, however. The first problem was caused by an *incident* that took place in the spring of 1763. Great numbers of colonists settled in the Ohio Valley, west of the Appalachian Mountains. An Ottawa Indian chief, Pontiac, knew that Indian land was in danger of being lost to the English settlers. Chief Pontiac organized several Indian *tribes* and attacked colonial settlements with some success.

This concerned King George III. He became the English ruler in 1760. He was encouraged to sign the Proclamation of 1763. This policy would help to avoid conflicts with the Indians. Under this act, all settlers west of the Appalachians were to leave the Ohio Valley and return to the established colonies. This land was only for the Indians.

*Conflicts are fights or disagreements.*

*Why were the colonists against the new law?*

The colonists were strongly opposed to this new British law. Colonists had fought, and many had died, in the long French and Indian War. Now the Crown of England was saying that no one could go west. According to the king, this proclamation was passed to protect the colonists from any further Indian attacks. Many colonists felt that the Proclamation was unfair and that its real purpose was to quiet the Indians. They also felt that, if necessary, they could fight their own battles with the Indians. These frontier settlers were well aware of the risks and were

*George III became ruler of England in 1760.*

**FIGURE 13-11 Gloss**

*From: Our Nation's History,* pp. 64–65 by John Napp and Wayne King © 1992, 1989 American Guidance Service Inc., 4201 Woodland Road, Circle Pines, MN 55014. 

- Give the meanings of essential vocabulary.
- Gloss photos, drawings, and charts, and other graphic pieces of information. Even if the text is virtually indecipherable for students, they can learn from the diagrams and other illustrations and from the gloss that you provide.
- Provide an easy-to-read summary of the most important information.

**Creating a Gloss**

If a text is far too difficult, create a gloss that directs students to portions that they can comprehend: illustrations and captions, for instance. Through discussions or summaries of the text, present key ideas not explained by illustrations and captions.

*Step 1: Examine the Text*

Decide which two or three concepts you would like students to learn. Note the difficult vocabulary that would be needed to understand the key concepts. Note also the organization of the passage and the main strategies that might be used to understand the passage, such as inferring, summarizing, evaluating, imaging.

*Step 2: Write the Gloss*

Keeping in mind the student's prior knowledge and command of strategies, decide which elements you would like to emphasize, and write a gloss accordingly. Focus on a few elements. Limit your gloss to one or two items per page. Students find it difficult and tiresome to cope with too many items (Stewart, 1993). This also makes it less burdensome for you.

Study guides, including glosses, can act as "personal tutors" (Wood, Lapp, & Flood, 1992, p. 75).

*Step 3: Consider and Refine*

Line up a sheet of paper with the text and print your gloss next to the target text. If this is a duplicated sheet, write your gloss directly in the margin and photocopy. As you write your gloss, imagine that you are with your students as they are studying. Think of the questions they might have about the material, the words they might stumble over, and the elements they might find confusing. Imagine, too, what you might say that would help them to read purposefully and strategically, monitoring for meaning as they progress through the passages. Let the answers to those questions, guide your construction of a gloss. A sample gloss is presented in Figure 13-11.

## *After-Reading Techniques*

After reading content-area material, students should engage in some activity that will help them integrate the information they have just read with what they already know. Students should also evaluate new information and apply it in some way, if possible. The directed reading and directed reading–thinking lessons, which were presented in the previous chapter, include provision for after-reading activities. Other techniques that incorporate after-reading techniques are reflection, graphic post-organizers, and extending and applying.

Allow students still acquiring English to discuss new concepts in a small discussion group in their own language. This will allow them to use their old knowledge to help them understand new knowledge.

### *Reflection*

Comprehending content-area text isn't sufficient. Readers must integrate it with their own knowledge and retain it. One of the best ways to accomplish this dual goal is to reflect upon one's reading. As Estes and Vaughn (1985) state:

> *The opportunity to reflect and react to what one has read solidifies learning. The purpose of reflective reaction is to allow readers to examine relationships between what they know and what they have read. People remember what they can relate; people comprehend what they can*

> *integrate into their cognitive structure. Students need to understand that reading comprehension, if by that we mean understanding what is read, does not stop with the end of the act of reading. It continues as understandings are deepened in reflection. (p. 177)*

Although reflective reaction can take place within a whole class discussion, it works better in a small group setting. Students have more opportunity and are more willing to talk when there are just a few of them. Students need a topic or series of questions upon which to focus. If students have completed a study, anticipation, or other guide, then that can become the basis of their discussion.

Cooperative learning of the type involved in reflective reaction has many benefits. It "multiplies opportunities for students to receive explanations on matters that have caused them problems" (Herber & Herber, 1993, p. 110). In addition to providing students the opportunity to learn from each other, it encourages them to clarify and expand their thinking as they explain their responses. As mentioned previously, small discussion groups are especially helpful for students who are still learning English.

### *Graphic Post-Organizer*

If a structured overview was presented as a pre-reading activity, it can also be used as a graphic post-organizer. All that needs to be done is to replace some of the terms with blanks. After having read the selection, the students can then fill in the blanks.

Once students grasp the concept of structured overviews or graphic post-organizers, they can construct their own. Students are given index cards containing key words from the selection read (or they can copy the words from the board). They are also given blank cards so they can add their own words. Meeting in small groups, students arrange the words to form a graphic post-organizer.

Students discuss items as they decide how to place them. The teacher circulates and gives guidance as needed. After the groups have completed their post-organizers, the class as a whole then constructs one organizer. The key element in this procedure is to encourage students to discuss why elements are arranged in a certain way. Not surprisingly, it is apparent that the more students are involved the more they learn. Post-organizers, with student involvement, result in more learning than do teacher-directed structured overviews (D. Moore & Readence, 1984).

### *Extending and Applying*

Students can extend and apply content-area reading in a variety of ways. They can read trade books or periodicals that elaborate on and extend information presented in the text. They can conduct experiments, surveys, and observations. They can seek information from nonprint sources: interviews and audiovisual materials. They can keep a journal of observations, write letters to the editor, create posters or ads, write plays, or compose reports. Students can also apply what they have learned to their own lives. As an application of information learned in health units, for instance, they can change their diets and get more sleep and exercise. After an ecology unit, they can take steps to increase recycling and decrease waste.

## *KWL Plus: A Before-, During-, and After-Reading Technique*

Widely used, KWL Plus (What We *K*now, What We *W*ant to Find Out, What We *L*earned, What We Still Want to Know), incorporates before-, during-, and after-reading strategies. KWL grew out of teachers' search for a more effective instructional approach. In this instance, Ogle (1989) and her colleagues were seeking a way to "build active personal reading of expository text" (p. 206). The teachers wanted an approach that involved all students, including the one-third who were typically passive. The technique would be one that stresses activating prior knowledge, would help counter erroneous concepts, and would help students relate new information to their background of knowledge.

### *Group Brainstorming*

KWL provides students the opportunity to learn from each other and also gives the teacher insights into the students' level of knowledge about a topic.

KWL begins with brainstorming a topic. In preparation for reading an article about the Pacific Ocean, you might write the word *ocean* on the board and have students tell what they know about oceans. You then write words and phrases volunteered by students. Conflicting information may be offered. If so, this can be posed as a question to be answered. For instance, if students disagree about the number of oceans, one of the items under "What we want to find out" would be, "How may oceans are there?"

### *Individual Brainstorming*

After the group brainstorms, students individually list on their KWL Plus sheets what they know about the topic. (The KWL Plus forms contain four columns: What We Know, What We Want to Find Out, What We Learned, What We Still Want to Know, and a space for noting categories of information that are expected to be addressed in the text that will be read. A sample KWL Plus sheet is shown in Figure 13-12.) The group brainstorming helps students activate their background knowledge and so aids them in assessing what they know about the topic. Because you have listed the group's ideas on the board, spelling should not be a barrier for students who have difficulty in this area.

### *Categorizing*

After completing their lists, students are asked to categorize what they know. They can use a single letter or abbreviation to indicate categories: *l*—location of ocean, *s*—size of oceans, *c*—creatures who live in the ocean, and so forth. If students are unfamiliar with categorizing, discuss which of the ideas that have been listed on the board should be grouped together and what their group names might be. You might also model the process of categorizing and constructing category names.

If you wish to simplify KWL, both categorizing and anticipating may be omitted. Although they are recommended by Ogle (1989), most teachers don't use them.

### *Anticipating*

As an optional step, after completing the classification activity, students anticipate the categories of information that might be presented in the article they are about to read. Ask students to tell what topics the author will probably cover in the article, asking, "If you were the author, what would you tell about the oceans? What main topics would you write

Name ______________________ Date __________

Topic ______________________

| What we know | What we want to find out | What we learned | What we still want to learn |
|---|---|---|---|
| H Dolphins live in the sea. | Are dolphins fish? | Dolphins are mammals. Have to breathe air. Give milk to babies. Are warm blooded. | |
| C Dolphins can swim fast. | Do dolphins have enemies? | Orca whales and sharks. | |
| C Dolphins are smart. | How do dolphins protect themselves? | Swim away from danger. Bulls make circle and bump enemies. | Are dolphins found in all oceans? |
| F Dolphins eat fish. | How do dolphins find food? | Use clicking sounds that bounce off sea animals and come back to them. | Are there different kinds of dolphins? |
| C Dolphins can be taught to do tricks. | How are dolphins trained to do tricks? | No answer | How are dolphins trained to do tricks? |

Categories of Information

Where Dolphins Live
What They Eat
How They Look
What Their Main Characteristics Are
How They Care for Their Young
What Their Living Habits Are
How They Get Food

**FIGURE 13-12 KWL Plus Sample**

From *Dolphin* by Morris, R. A. (1975). New York: Harper.

about?" Anticipating categories should help students organize information as they read. On their sheets, students record the categories that they believe the author will probably address.

### *Questioning*

The final activity in the prereading stage involves posing questions. Students tell what they want to find out. As in the brainstorming portion of the lesson, this is both a group and an individual endeavor. Throughout the lesson, note areas of partial, conflicting, and missing information; through discussion, help students consider these areas and, later, pose questions about them. After asking the class to tell what they want to find out, list their questions on the board. If the questions don't cover the essentials, probe in order to lead students to create additional questions. Ogle cautions that the text should not be read until "some real questions to guide the reading, have emerged from the group" (1989, p. 214). On their KWL sheets, students list the questions that are most important to them. If they wish, students can simply copy the group's questions. However, with experience, students tend to personalize their list of questions.

As students note the answers to their questions, they might also list information that they weren't looking for but which is valuable and interesting.

### *Reading*

Students read the selection to have their questions answered. New information is written in abbreviated form under the "What we learned" column. If questions are not answered or if new questions arise, these can be noted in a fourth column, "What we still want to know."

### *After Reading*

After students have completed their reading, the article is discussed. Students talk over what they learned. Information is elaborated and clarified. Comparing what students said they knew and what they learned provides an opportunity to correct misconceptions, if they still exist. Information students learned is written on the board. This models notetaking and gives students a chance to revise their notes. Students also discuss questions that they still have about the topic.

If the information is important, students might also create a semantic map graphically depicting major details, or they might prepare an information map, which uses frame questions and is described in Chapter 14. If the class wishes, they might also pursue any unanswered questions or new ones that may have cropped up. As part of their discussion, they can talk over possible sources of information for their unanswered questions.

**Sample KWL Plus Lesson**

*Before Reading*

*Step 1: Brainstorming*

In preparation for reading *Dolphin* (R. Morris, 1975), a mature appearing paperback written on a second-grade level, encourage students to brainstorm the topic of dolphins. Writing the word *dolphins* on the board, ask, "What do you know about dolphins?" Students' responses are listed on the chalkboard. If one student says that dolphins are fish and another says they are not, ask each student to explain her or his reasoning. The class might decide to make the classification of dolphins one of the things that they want to find out. After the group brainstorms, students write down in the first column what they know about dolphins.

**Sample KWL Plus Lesson** *Continued*

*Step 2: Categorizing*

Information is categorized and students discuss the kinds of topics the book might present: They might decide that the book will tell where dolphins live, what they eat, how they look, what their main characteristics are, how they care for their young, what their living habits are, how they get food.

*Step 3: Discussing What You Want to Find Out*

Students then discuss what they want to find out. They might want to find out whether dolphins are fish, how they get food, whether they have enemies, how they protect themselves, how they learn to do tricks, and how smart they are. The class's questions are listed on the chalkboard or a large sheet of paper. Students list their individual questions on their sheets.

*Step 4: During Reading*

The class reads and notes what they found out and what they still want to learn. They see that the author gives information about the birth and care of a young dolphin, which was not an area in which they were seeking information.

The class might also construct a semantic map highlighting information that they acquired about dolphins.

*Step 5: After Reading*

Students discussed what they learned. If there is still a bit of confusion about whether the dolphin is a fish or a mammal, the section of the text dealing with that is reread. To further clarify the matter, you might discuss with the class the characteristics of mammals. Students might note questions that weren't answered: How smart are dolphins? How are they trained? The class may also have wanted to know whether dolphins were found in all oceans and how many different kinds of dolphins there are. The class discusses where that information might be found.

## *Outstanding Collaborative Approaches*

Working collaboratively with the teacher and other students has proved to be a powerful technique for improving the comprehension of low-achieving readers. Two of the most carefully documented and highly effective of the collaborative techniques are ReQuest and reciprocal teaching. ReQuest, which is easier to implement, can be used along with or as a stepping stone to reciprocal teaching.

### *ReQuest*

ReQuest was designed so that teacher and student would discuss one sentence at a time; however, some users have analyzed whole paragraphs as a unit rather than single sentences.

Although he had excellent word recognition skills, William's comprehension was just about nil. Even when the task was reduced to reading short, easy paragraphs, William's comprehension barely improved. At that point, William's teacher decided to try ReQuest (Manzo, 1969; Manzo & Manzo, 1993). ReQuest is a rock-bottom technique that approaches comprehension at the sentence level but which activates even the most passive student.

ReQuest requires both teachers and students to construct questions and answers about single sentences. The teacher is the master craftsperson, the student, an apprentice. In the procedure, the teacher models both asking and answering questions. Although initially designed to be a corrective one-on-one technique, ReQuest may be adapted for group use.

**Introducing ReQuest**

*Step 1: Prepare to Read*

You and the student read the title and first sentence of the paragraph of a selection. You may also look at any illustrations or other graphic elements that might be a part of the introduction.

*Step 2: Explain*

Explain to the student that she may ask as many questions about the first sentence, title, and illustrations as she can. The student is told to ask the kinds of questions that a teacher might ask.

*Step 3: Set a Purpose for Reading*

The student asks questions, and you answer them. Then you ask questions about the first sentence, title, and illustrations. The objective of your questions is to model questioning behavior, to orient the student to the material, and to provide background for setting a purpose for reading.

*Step 4: Continue Questioning*

Questioning proceeds as in Step 3. First, the student asks questions. Then you do. As the two of you move through the paragraph, you ask questions that involve putting together information from several sentences. ReQuest continues until a purpose for reading is established but lasts no longer than ten minutes. The concluding question is: What do you think the rest of the selection will be about?

*Step 5: Student Continues Reading*

The student reads the rest of the selection silently for the purpose or prediction that has been established. The student is encouraged to read flexibly and to adjust purpose for reading, if necessary.

*Step 6: Discuss the Selection*

The ReQuest procedure can be used with any subject, in any grade, but seems to work best with informational text. However, Maria (1990) reports using ReQuest successfully with narrative material. ReQuest has also been used with students in such a way that the paragraph rather than the sentence is used as the basis for analysis.

"The greatest strength of ReQuest seems to be in that it gets students to overcome some of the subtle liabilities that tend to inhibit questioning—such as having to admit ignorance, and not knowing how to frame questions, and simply not realizing what it is that they don't know" (Manzo & Manzo, 1993, p. 317).

ReQuest has been used in group situations, with students taking turns asking and answering questions. ReQuest has also been used with kindergartners who have constructed and answered questions about pictures.

However ReQuest is used, Manzo and Manzo (1993) caution that teachers should model higher-level questioning. Students tend to construct the same kinds of questions that have been asked in their classes. Unfortunately, many of these are on a low level. Manzo suggests that the teacher do two things to improve the level of questioning: "(1) Try to ask the types of questions that you would hope someone might ask you; and (2) try to ask questions that reflect the highest objectives of your teaching as well as more literal or reconstructive ones" (p. 317).

## Reciprocal Teaching

In a sense, reciprocal teaching is both an expansion and extension of the ReQuest procedure. Designed for use with small groups, reciprocal teaching also involves students as active participants and, like ReQuest, uses a teacher–apprentice model. Incorporating four powerful comprehension strategies—questioning, summarizing, predicting, and

**Reciprocal teaching:** fosters the development of key strategies—predicting, questioning, summarizing, and monitoring within a teacher-guided cooperative learning framework.

clarifying—**reciprocal teaching** has had a great deal of success with corrective readers of various levels (Palincsar & Brown, 1986). Because it is a complex technique, it is recommended that it be used for at least twenty days.

Although reciprocal teaching is an outstanding example of cooperative learning, the teacher is very much an active participant. A key element in reciprocal teaching is scaffolding in which the teacher supports the learners much as a master craftsperson would support apprentices. The student apprentices take on greater responsibility as they acquire increased expertise.

One of the most valuable comprehension strategies is for the reader to create questions and read to answer the self-created questions.

The focus of the lesson is a brief text. At first, the teacher conducts the lesson. Later, a student is appointed to be a teacher. The student-teacher makes a prediction based on the title and illustration, or the beginning of the selection being read. (If the class has read a segment of the selection, then the prediction is based on what has been read.) A segment is then read silently by the group. After the segment has been read, the student-teacher generates and poses one or more questions, summarizes what has been read, and, at the end of the discussion, makes a prediction about the upcoming segment. At that point, a new student-teacher is appointed.

At any time during the discussion, students can ask for clarification if there is a word they don't know or if any other aspect of the story is puzzling. Poor comprehenders typically fail to realize that they don't understand what they are reading. Clarifying is a way to show them how to monitor for meaning and to take steps to repair faulty comprehension.

### *Introducing Reciprocal Teaching*

The purpose of reciprocal teaching is explained and students are taught how, when, where, and why to use each of the four strategies: predicting, questioning, summarizing, and clarifying. One of the strengths of the procedure is that strategies are modeled and monitored in the context of actual reading. Because the students are actively involved in both their roles as students and student-teachers, the teacher is able to evaluate progress and provide needed feedback, always in the context of actively reading and discussing text. Through interaction with the teacher and interaction with peers, students' competence is lifted, via scaffolding, to higher and higher levels.

In the beginning the teacher's efforts are very direct as she or he explains and models strategies. Later, as students become increasingly more expert in the use of strategies, the teacher operates as a coach, makes corrections and adjustments, provides useful suggestions, and urges students onward.

At first, the teacher may have to create summaries, predictions, and questions for students to imitate. Gradually students generate questions, predictions, and summaries.

### *Stages of Dialog*

In tryouts students' progress in reciprocal teaching was dramatic but not immediate. Although the teacher modeled the strategies, initially some students had great difficulty assuming the role of teacher. As the teacher continued modeling and coaching, use of strategies improved until questions and summaries became more like those of the teacher's. Students began putting them in their own words rather than simply lifting whole phrases from the text. Questions and summaries also began to encompass larger segments of text.

Much of the progress was due to the manner in which the teacher geared instruction to the needs of the individual learner. A key factor in reciprocal teaching is the gradual handover of the control of the strategies from the teacher to the student, a handover that is governed by the student's rate of development. Direct instruction, plenty of practice, and gradual release of responsibility are at the heart of the success of reciprocal teaching. (Brown & Palincsar, 1985). Note in the sample dialog in Figure 13-13 how the teacher worked with a small group of low-achieving readers. Student A is the leader for this segment. The teacher is T.

**Exemplary Teaching: Project Success**

An intervention program for students in grades three through six known as Project Success incorporates an adapted form of reciprocal teaching (Cooper, 1996). Designed for students whose main difficulty is comprehension, Project Success also features an emphasis on the reading of high interest informational text on the appropriate level of difficulty, use of graphic organizers, and reflection. A typical forty-minute class includes rereading or discussing familiar books (five minutes); reviewing a strategy or the previous day's graphic organizer (five minutes), and preparing for reading by conducting a quick text walk-through similar to the story introduction in Reading Recovery or a preview or construction of the initial portion of a KWL chart (ten minutes). Reading of text (fifteen minutes) is followed by the completion of a graphic organizer or KWL chart and discussion of the selection using reciprocal teaching (five minutes). A flexible program, Project Success can be taught by the classroom teacher or by a specialist working in the classroom or resource room. Students who have the greatest need are selected for Project Success. However, groups are limited to no more than six.

Assessment is ongoing. Student progress is monitored through periodic retellings, running records, IRIs, on-going observation, and student self-evaluation. Students are released from the program when they are able to successfully read two or three pages from the text being used in the classroom. Tested in several sites, the program has met with encouraging success.

## *Content Knowledge*

Throughout this text the emphasis has been on the processes of reading and writing, especially the teaching techniques and strategies used in learning text. However, process and content must be integrated. Content shapes the techniques and strategies that we and our students use. It's difficult to make inferences in areas in which we have limited knowledge. Noting main ideas is easier when we are acquainted with a subject and have a sense of what the subject's major and minor issues are. The process is somewhat circular. The more students know, the more they are prepared to learn. The more they know, the better they can apply strategies. The better they apply strategies, the more they learn. Use of strategies increases knowledge, which fosters more effective use of strategies.

### *Can Snakes Sting with Their Tongues?*

No—snakes' tongues are completely harmless. They're used for feeling things and for sharpening the snakes' sense of smell. Although snakes can smell in the usual way, the tongue flickering in the air picks up tiny particles of matter. These particles are deposited in two tiny cavities at the base of the nostrils to increase the snakes' ability to smell.

1. A: Do snakes' tongues sting?
2. K: Sometimes.
3. A: Correct.
   This paragraph is about do snakes sting with their tongue, and different ways that the tongue is for and the senses of smell.
4. T: Are there any questions?
5. C: Snakes' tongues don't sting.
6. T: Beautiful! I thought, boy, I must have been doing some fast reading there because I missed that point. A, could you ask your question again?
7. A: Do snakes' tongues really sting?
8. T: Now, A, since you have asked the question, can you find in that paragraph where the question is answered?
9. A: No, snakes' tongues are completely harmless.
10. T: So we'll try it again. Can you generate another question that you think a teacher might ask?
11. A: What are the tongues used for?
12. T: Good!
13. L: The sense of smell.
14. T: Is that correct? A, do you disagree? Yes.
15. A: That answer was right, but there are other things that the tongue can do.
16. L: But she only said tell one, she didn't say tell all of them.
17. T: O.K.
18. B: It is used to pick up tiny particles.
19. T: O.K. I think that this is an important point. You have the basic concept which is correct, O.K., but what the question really is saying is, is it used for smell? O.K.?
20. B: They are used for feeling things for sharpening snakes' sense of smell.
21. T: O.K. They are used for sharpening the snakes' sense of smell. Are they used for smelling? That's the point we aren't clear on.
22. L: In my answer I said it is for the sense of smell.
23. T: This is fine; this is what the technique is all about. What it means is not that you are right or wrong or good or bad. What it says is that we have just read something and have had a disagreement about what it says. We need to work it out.
24. A: My prediction is that they will now talk about the different things about snakes. Where they live, and what they eat and stuff like that.

**FIGURE 13-13 Sample Reciprocal Teaching Dialog**

From: Brown & Palincsar, (1985), *Reciprocal Teaching of Comprehension Strategies: A Natural History of One Program for Enhancing Learning* (Table 5). (Tech. Report No. 334). Champaign, IL: University of Illinois.

## *Teaching Essential Concepts*

The traditional approach to teaching content area subjects is to attempt a broad coverage of a wide array of topics. A better approach, especially when instructing low-achieving readers, would be to focus on the most essential topics and cover these in depth, an approach recommended by the American Association for the Advancement of Science (Rutherford & Ahlgren, 1990). Schumm, Vaughn, and Leavell (1994) recommend using a planning pyramid, with the base representing topics that all students should learn; the middle portion, what most should learn; and the apex, what a few will learn. This doesn't mean that low-achieving readers will be limited to learning the most basic topics. Students should not be denied access to advanced concepts on the basis of reading ability. The amount a student learns beyond basic concepts should be dependent upon background, interest, motivation, and resources available.

## Textbooks in the Content Areas

> The readability of more than 3,000 content-area texts can be found in Touchstone Applied Science Associate's *Readability of Textbooks* (1996) and *Readability of Textbooks in a Series* (1994).

The amount students learn is also dependent on the quality and appropriateness of their textbooks. All too often texts in the content areas are too difficult for low progress readers. An elementary school science text may introduce 200 to 400 new terms or more (L. Meyer, 1991). The vocabulary load is even heavier at higher levels. Some high school chemistry texts contain as many as 3,000 technical terms (Holliday, 1991). Social studies texts may also be too difficult, and many are written on a level that is above the grade level for which they were intended. According to a study by Chall and Conard (1991), the average fourth-grade social studies textbook is written on a fifth- or sixth-grade level of readability. In a study of ten eighth-grade history books, Kinder, Bursuck, and Epstein (1992) found that all ten were written at least one year above grade level, with the average readability level being 10.9.

If the regular text is simply far too difficult for students, consider obtaining a text that is written on a simpler level. A list of some easy-to-read science and math texts is presented in Table 13-1. A list of some easy-to-read social studies books is presented in Table 13-2. You might also use easy-to-read trade books that cover the topics you wish to explore (see Appendix B). Because easy-to-read texts may be less detailed than the regular texts, you might want to supplement the information contained in the text with discussions, use of audiovisual aids, and other activities. For students with severe reading problems, consider using taped versions of the text. Students who are unable to read their texts because of a documented reading disability may qualify for books taped for the blind. Talking Books, a service sponsored by the National Library Service for the Blind and Physically Handicapped (Library of Congress, Washington, DC 20542), provides for individuals who are blind, who have physical disabilities, or who have organic reading disabilities, taped versions of periodicals and popular books, including children's titles. Recording for the Blind and Dyslexic (20 Roszel Road, Princeton, NJ 08540), a private organization, provides taped versions of school textbooks for students with reading problems.

### Adapting Texts

Another possibility is to adapt the textbook, a procedure that may result in significant gains for low-achieving readers (Lovitt, Rudsit, Jenkins, Pious, & Benedatti, 1986). Adapting an entire text would be a monumental undertaking. Choose only those chapters that contain the most essential concepts and focus on the most important information in the chapter. Adapting a text to make it easier is more than just substituting easy words for hard words or short sentences for long ones. One reason informational texts are so difficult is because they try

**TABLE 13-1 Easy Science and Math Texts**

| Text | Publisher | Reading Level |
|---|---|---|
| *Science Texts* | | |
| Basic Biology 2nd Ed. | Globe Fearon | 3.8 |
| Basic Health 2nd Ed. | American Guidance | 3.6 |
| Biology, Kingdoms of Life | Globe Fearon | 2.2 |
| Earth Science | American Guidance | 3.6 |
| Fearon's Biology, 2nd Ed. | Globe Fearon | 4 |
| Fearon's General Science, 2nd Ed. | Globe Fearon | 4 |
| Fearon's Health, 2nd Ed. | Globe Fearon | 4 |
| General Science | American Guidance | 3.8 |
| General Science Program | Globe Fearon | 2.5 |
| Health for Our Times | Booklab | 5 |
| Magic of Animal Science | American Guidance | 4.2 |
| Matter, Motion, and Machines | American Guidance | 3.6 |
| Mysteries of Plant Life | American Guidance | 3.9 |
| Physical Science | American Guidance | 2.6 |
| Science of Living Things | Globe Fearon | 3.5 |
| Science Today | Steck Vaughn | 1–4 |
| Wonders of Science | Steck Vaughn | 2–3 |
| *Math Texts* | | |
| Basic Mathematics Skills, 2nd Ed. | American Guidance | 3.5 |
| Essential Math Skills | Phoenix | 5.6 |
| Fearon's Basic Mathematics | Globe Fearon | 4 |
| Life Skills Mathematics, 2nd Ed. | American Guidance | 3.9 |
| Math for Business | American Guidance | 4.4 |
| Mathematics, 2nd Ed. | Globe Fearon | 4 |
| Mathematics for Consumers, 2nd Ed. | American Guidance | 3.3 |

**TABLE 13-2 Easy-to-Read Social Studies Texts**

| Text | Publication | Reading Level |
|---|---|---|
| America's Story | Steck Vaughn | 2–3 |
| Experiencing World History | American Guidance | 3.8 |
| Exploring American History | American Guidance | 3.9 |
| Fearon's United States Geography | Globe Fearon | 4 |
| Fearon's United States History | Globe Fearon | 4 |
| Fearon's World Geography and Cultures | Globe Fearon | 4 |
| Fearon's World History | Globe Fearon | 4 |
| Geography of the United States | American Guidance | |
| History of the United States | Booklab | 4 |
| Our Nation's History | American Guidance | 3.8 |
| Quercus World History | Globe Fearon | 2.4 |
| Steck Vaughn Social Studies | Steck Vaughn | A–1, B–2, C–2, D–3, E–3, F–4 |
| Survey of World Cultures | American Guidance | 4.0 |
| United States Government, 2nd Ed. | American Guidance | 4.0 |
| World Geography and You | Steck Vaughn | 2–3 |
| World History and You | Steck Vaughn | 4 |

to cover too much and end up being a dense recitation of facts. One way of making a text easier would be to expand on key concepts and omit or eliminate nonessential details.

Here are some suggestions for adapting text:

- Signal main ideas. Use headings and topic sentences to announce key concepts. Also provide a brief preview, perhaps in the form of a graphic organizer, and a concise summary.
- Develop fully key concepts. Do not introduce extraneous details, even though they may be interesting.
- Use signal words to foster cohesiveness. Use lots of *buts, ands, on-the-other-hands,* and other words that help show relationships among ideas.
- Use straightforward language patterns. Avoid passives and long, involved sentences.
- Use fewer pronouns than you normally would. That way students won't become confused wondering what the pronoun's antecedent is.
- Use concrete language and give lots of examples.

The teacher of low-achieving readers needs to increase their access to information by making their texts more accessible and by providing sources of information that don't require reading.

***Directed Listening–Thinking Activity***

Another option for handling a text that is too difficult is to use the format of a Directed Listening–Thinking Activity to read it to students (Gillet & Temple, 1994). Similar in structure to the Directed Reading–Thinking Activity, except that students listen instead of read (Stauffer, 1969), the Directed Listening–Thinking Activity is presented in the following box.

**Steps in the Directed Listening–Thinking Activity**

*Step 1: Making Predictions*

Under your guidance the students survey and discuss the title, headings, and illustrations of the chapter or section to be read. You read the titles and headings to students. Based on the survey and discussion, students predict what the content of the selection might be. Predictions are written on the board.

*Step 2: Listening to the Section*

As you read, the students listen. Stop periodically to involve students in modifying predictions, summarizing text, asking questions about the text, evaluating what is being read, relating new information to old information, noting hard words and key terms, and using diagrams, charts, graphs, and other illustrative materials. During your oral reading, you can model the use of effective strategies and gradually lead students to use those same strategies as they listen so they learn how to summarize, question, and monitor for meaning.

*Step 3: Discussion*

Students discuss the selection in light of their predictions. Discuss how the content differed from students' predictions. Provide needed elaborations and explanations and clarify confusing concepts. Note how the information relates to the students' background of knowledge and how they might apply information in the text. After the selection has been discussed, you might guide students as they dictate a summary of the material presented. Write their dictated summary on the board and review it with them. It can be copied by students into their notebooks or you can duplicate it so that students have material to read and study on their own. A dictated summary is found in Figure 13-14.

***How Plants Make Food***

Green plants make their own food. They use sunlight to do this. The light causes a gas called carbon dioxide to combine with water. When water and carbon dioxide combine, they form sugar. The plants use this sugar to grow and stay well. Using light to make food is called photosynthesis (FOH•tuh•sin•thuh•sis).

By making food, plants help us to breathe. When water and carbon dioxide combine, oxygen is made. We need oxygen to breathe. Without plants, we would have no air to breathe. Plants keep us alive.

**FIGURE 13-14 Student Dictated Summary of a Content-Area Selection**

> If audiovisual materials and easy trade books are available and there are varied opportunities for observation and hands-on experiences, the poor reader will have greater access to content-area information.

### *Hands-On Approach*

If the science textbook is simply too difficult for low-achieving readers to handle, even with the use of glosses, study guides, graphic organizers, or adaptations, and there are no easier versions available and taped texts or DL–TA is not a feasible option, then you might try an inquiry-concept-information approach (Esler & Esler, 1989). In this approach, the focus is on process and experimentation. In the typical science text, the student reads about a concept and then performs an experiment. In an inquiry-concept-information approach, the experiment comes first and is used to introduce concepts and important information.

Students observe the experiment and then discuss the science concepts and related information illustrated by the experiment. Vocabulary for these science concepts would be introduced at this time. Vocabulary and concepts would be easier to learn because they would be based on students' hands-on experiences. The teacher might lead the students to compose a written summary of the unit's major concepts. This summary, which could include illustrations, might be used instead of the text or as an introduction to the text. Being familiar with the major concepts covered and related technical vocabulary, students would be in a better position to handle the text.

In a comparison of elementary science teaching in two school districts, Mastropieri and Scruggs (1994) found that students who were deficient in reading and writing skills performed better with an activities-oriented rather than a book-based program and encountered fewer hindrances to learning. More importantly, they apparently received a better grounding in science.

## *Teaching Literature*

When teaching literature to low-achieving readers, a key question is: What works shall be introduced? Often, as students move up through the grades, there is an expectation that certain literary works will be introduced. In fifth grade, this might be *And Now Miguel.* In seventh grade, it might be *Treasure Island.* In twelfth grade, *The Great Gatsby* might be assigned. In some instances, the class may have an anthology that consists primarily of selections written on grade level or above. Because of their reading problems, low-achieving readers may have difficulty reading some literary selections. The issue is one of providing students with quality literature that they can understand and appreciate. There are several ways of accomplishing this goal.

Choose selections that students can read. Not all pieces of literature are equally difficult. In American literature, for instance, Hemingway is easier to read and understand than Faulkner. A number of the classics are surprisingly easy to read. Table 13-3 provides estimated readabilities of a number of well known works. The readability scores only factor in sentence complexity and difficulty of vocabulary. Background of experience, conceptual development, and emotional maturity are essential elements in understanding a piece of literature and would need to be considered along with readability estimates.

Other measure that can be taken to make literary works accessible to low-achieving readers include the following:

- Provide extra support. If the selection is challenging but not overwhelming, build background and vocabulary, provide glosses or other study guides, and read difficult portions to the students.
- Use audiovisual aids. Use filmstrips, taped recordings, videocassettes or CD-ROM versions of the works. If students simply can't handle the reading, read the piece to them or obtain taped versions of the work. Many of the classics are available on audio tape (see Table 13-4). Students might read along as they listen to a taped reading of the text. Even though students won't have to decode the words, they will still need assistance with comprehension and appreciation, so working with vocabulary, concepts, background, and aesthetic elements will be essential.
- Use abridged or adapted versions. Abridged versions are simply shortened versions. The author's language has not been simplified. Literacy Volunteers of New York has abridged and added explanatory notes to a wide variety of contemporary literature and popular pieces that include Robert Fulghum's essays in *It Was on Fire When I Lay*

**TABLE 13-3 Sampling of Easy-to-Read, High-Quality Books**

| Book | Reading Level |
|---|---|
| Fritz, J. (1958). *Cabin Faced West.* New York: Coward-McCann. | 4–5 |
| George, J. (1959). *My Side of the Mountain.* New York: Scholastic. | 4 |
| Goodall, J. (1988). *My Life with the Chimpanzees.* New York: Simon & Schuster. | 5–6 |
| Hamilton, V. (1985). *The People Could Fly: American Black Folktales.* New York: Knopf. | 3–4 |
| Hamilton, V. (1967). *Zeeley.* New York: Macmillan. | 4–5 |
| Hemingway, E. (1952). *Old Man and the Sea.* New York: Scribner. | 4–5 |
| Kumgold, J. (1953). *And Now Miguel.* New York: Harper. | 4 |
| Lowry, L. (1989). *Number the Stars.* Boston: Houghton Mifflin. | 5–6 |
| Mowat, F. (1961). *Owls in the Family.* Boston: Little, Brown. | 5–6 |
| O'Dell, S. (1986). *Streams to the River, River to the Sea.* Boston: Houghton Mifflin. | 3 |
| Paterson, K. (1977). *Bridge to Terabitha.* New York: Avon. | 4 |
| Saroyan, W. (1943). *Human Comedy.* New York: Harcourt, Brace, Jovanovich. | 4–5 |
| Steinbeck, J. (1939). *Grapes of Wrath.* New York: Bantam. | 5–6 |
| Uchida, Y. (1978). *Journey Home.* New York: Atheneum. | 5 |
| Voight, C. (1982). *Dicey's Song.* New York: Fawcett. | 5 |
| Yepp, L. (1977). *Child of the Owl.* New York: Harper. | 5 |

**TABLE 13-4 Adapted and Abridged Classics**

| Adapted Text(s) | Publisher | Description |
|---|---|---|
| Globe's Adapted Classics | Globe Fearon | Classics from American and English literature. Reading levels: 3–4 to 7–8 |
| Lake Illustrated Classics | Lake | British and American classics are presented in illustrated strips. Reading level: 4 |
| Longman Classics | Longman | Classics in British and American literature. Reading levels: 3–6 |
| Pacemaker Classics | Globe Fearon | Classics from English and American literature. Audiotapes are available. Reading levels: 3–4 |
| Phoenix Everyreaders | Phoenix | Presents classics from American and British literature. Reading level: 4 |

Abridged versions work well for some authors. Being paid by length, Dickens tended to use more words than necessary. *David Copperfield* and *Tale of Two Cities* can be acceptably abridged.

*Down on It* (1992), Larry McMurty's *Lonesome Dove* (1992), Jane Goodall's *In the Shadow of Man* (1992), Alice Walker's *The Temple of My Familiar* (1992), and excerpts from classic American plays. The texts also provide brief overviews of the pieces to be read, suggestions for reading them, and a biography of the author. Just 64 pages in length, these paperbacks have a mature, appealing format. Although designed for adult new readers, some, if selected with care, could be used with secondary school students.

Adaptations of literary works are more controversial than abridgements because adaptations involve changing and possibly distorting the author's words. If the issue is one of having students read an altered version of the original versus not reading it at all because it is too difficult you may decide to use the adaptation. Selected sources of adapted and abridged classics are presented in Table 13-4.

The reader's stance is on a continuum from *efferent* to *aesthetic*. Reading directions to assemble a bicycle would be efferent. Reading a poem about death could be highly aesthetic if it evoked strong emotion.

***Personal Response***

Reading literature, of course, is much more than just understanding the words or the ideas. For instance, a class that reads a genuinely humorous story, such as O'Henry's "Ransom of Red Chief," and doesn't laugh didn't understand the story, even though they may be able to give you a detailed account of the plot. As noted earlier, Rosenblatt (1994) explains that there are two types of reading: efferent and aesthetic. In efferent reading the focus is on reading for details or information: "attention is centered predominantly on what is to be extracted and retained after the reading event" (p. 1066). Aesthetic reading involves an emotional or aesthetic response.

When literature is read, the emphasis should be on an aesthetic reading, on evoking a personal response from the reader. Eliciting a genuine reader response involves setting up situations in which students feel encouraged to respond freely to literature. First of all, selections should be chosen that lend themselves to reader response. Second, activities and questions should be geared to a personal response. Questions that encourage readers to relate some aspect of the selection to their own lives are especially helpful. In discussions of the piece, emphasis should be on personal response and interpretation. Small group discussions work especially well because students are more likely to share honestly and openly in such a setting.

### *Self-Selection*

One element that fosters response is reader selection. If possible, readers should have a choice in at least some of the pieces they read. This need not be a fully open choice. You might have them choose which of three novels they would rather read, for instance. Students become more involved when they are part of the selection process.

### *Readers' Theater*

Students learn more by doing than they do by simply observing or discussing. Since no stage or props are required and the script doesn't have to be memorized, readers' theater is easy to implement and highly effective in enhancing comprehension and motivation. In **readers' theater,** participants dramatize poems, short stories, or even excerpts from historical biographies. Ready-made scripts can be used, or participants can prepare their own. Readers' theater can be used at any level from primary grades through college. Readers' theater works especially well with low-achieving readers because it provides them with the opportunity to reread a text several times so that they become thoroughly familiar with it. It also gives them an in-depth look at a selection.

**Readers' Theater:** dramatization of a story, play, poem, or other piece by having it read aloud by one or more persons. Generally, the piece is transformed into a script before being read.

Readers' theater begins with a careful reading and discussion of the selection and is followed by the preparation of a script and its performance. The following box highlights the steps involved in readers' theater.

#### Readers' Theater Performance

Although no stage or props are required in readers' theater, participants might sit on stools. Pantomiming and gestures are used when appropriate, but should be used sparingly.

*Step 1: Reading the Selection*

The selection is read and discussed. Prereading preparation includes activating schema, building background and vocabulary, considering strategies to be used during the reading, and setting a purpose for reading.

*Step 2: Preparing the Script*

After the selection has been discussed in much the same way as it would be in a directed reading activity, students who will reenact the piece reread the play and discuss the characters and may create a character map (Hoffman, 1993). The teacher can let students decide who will take which parts, or assign parts himself. If the group includes adept and low-achieving readers, the teacher might choose parts for the low-achieving reader that involve less reading and are easier to read.

There are a number of ready-made scripts for readers' theater. A series of scripts, *Spotlight on Readers' Theater,* is available from Phoenix Learning Resources.

The script may be written by the teacher or the group. Group writing is preferable, but guidance might be required. The group discusses how they

**Readers' Theater Performance** *Continued*

want to rewrite the script. Dialog from the selection should remain intact. Narrative segments from the selection might be summarized, especially if they are lengthy. Or they may be translated into dialog. Additional narration may need to be composed for the sake of clarity.

Students can highlight their dialog with markers. Narrations can be underlined. Narrator's lines can be added as needed to introduce scenes, provide transitions, or summarize events (Hoffman, 1993).

*Step 3: Interpreting the Script*

Once the script has been prepared, students discuss how they will portray each character: what facial expressions they will use, what gestures they will employ, and how they will use their voices to convey emotions (Tompkins & Hoskisson, 1991).

*Step 4: Practicing*

Students practice reading their scripts. At the end of each reading, they discuss things that each did well and what might be done to improve the performance or the script.

*Step 5: Performing*

The script is performed for the class.

Pieces that work best for readers' theater are those that have a great deal of dialog and a minimum of narration. Stories or even chapter books and novels can be portrayed through readers' theater. For long works, it might be best to portray excerpts of key portions of the text.

## *Theme Units*

**Theme unit:** organization of instruction around a particular topic or idea.

**Theme units** that involve the content areas are especially useful for low-achieving readers. It allows them to build upon and extend the background and vocabulary they have on a particular theme. Since they will be seeing a core of vocabulary words over and over, it gives them the repetition of words that many so desperately need. It also helps students to make connections and to elaborate on their learning.

Possible themes are endless but should be built on students' interests. Theme units might involve a single content area or may include two or more. For young children, pets or dinosaurs might be an appropriate theme. For older students, an appropriate theme might be endangered wildlife, machines, ecology, inventors, or other outstanding people (see Exemplary Teaching example below).

**Exemplary Teaching: Motivating Learning**

Having failed with books and paper and pencil tasks, low-achieving readers appreciate hands-on experiences. Taking advantage of the opportunities offered by her seaside home, one literacy specialist enlivened a sea creatures unit by bringing in specimens from Long Island Sound. The youngster who normally couldn't think of a word to write had no difficulty recording his observations of the live crab that his teacher brought in. As he examined the crab, he had lots of questions, the main one being, "Will the

*Continued*

**Exemplary Teaching: Motivating Learning** *Continued*

crab pinch me with its claws?" Questions led to the reading of a nonfiction book on sea creatures. Since that book didn't answer all of the youngster's questions, other texts were consulted.

When the teacher brought in a lobster, the youngster wanted to know how a lobster was different from a crab. At the teacher's suggestion, the youngster recorded his observations. With the help of his teacher, a chart was constructed comparing the two creatures. Again, books on sea creatures were consulted to supply information not yielded by observation. As the weeks passed, the chart grew as did the student's knowledge of sea creatures and his ability to read for information, take notes, create charts, and summarize information. Poems and fiction books related to the theme were also read and sea songs were read and sung.

## *Minicase Study*

Although Josh's word recognition was adequate, his comprehension was extremely poor, especially when he was required to read informational texts. As a result of his woefully inadequate comprehension, Josh, a sixth grader, was failing science. IRI results confirmed Josh's poor comprehension. Although word recognition was adequate up through sixth grade, Josh's comprehension was poor at every level from the third grade up.

Using a think aloud, the reading specialist determined that Josh's goal in reading was to complete the assignment. He wasn't seeking meaning from his reading. A very passive reader, he had few strategies and simply plunged into his text without previewing, activating schema, or setting a specific purpose. Once he started reading, Josh did not monitor to see if the text made sense. Nor did he stop at key points in the chapter or at the end to summarize what he had read. When queried, Josh was unable to answer a single question about the section on rocks that he had read as part of a think-aloud. The reading specialist also noted that the text was a bit too difficult for Josh. Because Josh's comprehension was so poor, the reading specialist tried ReQuest with him. Intrigued by the idea of creating questions for the teacher, Josh's comprehension improved while he was working directly with the teacher but deteriorated when he read on his own. Focusing on short segments, the teacher adapted the procedure so that it included the whole text. As Josh's comprehension improved, the teacher began gradually increasing the length of the selections and decreasing the amount of direct guidance. The teacher also began introducing previewing, predicting, self-questioning, and other strategies.

Because the science text was too difficult for Josh, easy-to-read trade books that explored the same concepts as the science texts were used. The teacher also provided lots of opportunities for Josh to engage in hands-on activities and use audiovisual aids to build background. As Josh became a more active and a more strategic reader, his grasp of content-area material improved.

## *Summary*

With its technical vocabulary, greater density of ideas, increased demands on conceptual knowledge, and more complex organizational patterns, content-area reading can be overwhelming for students who have marginal reading skills. In addition to being overstuffed with facts, many content-area texts are written on a level beyond the grade for which they were intended. Teachers of below-level readers can seek easier texts, use trade books written on the appropriate level of difficulty, provide additional assistance with the text, use glosses, use taped versions of the text, make greater use of sources of information that don't require reading, and use hands-on activities. Texts can also be adapted, but this is time-consuming.

Teaching students how to use text structures fosters comprehension. Other instructional techniques that can be employed to foster comprehension in the content areas can be categorized as those that are used before, during, or after reading. Before-reading techniques feature the anticipation guide, PReP, structured overview, and Frayer model. During-reading techniques feature frame questions and study guides, including glosses. After-reading techniques include reflecting, graphic post-organizers, applying, and extending. KWL is an approach that encompasses before-, during-, and after-reading techniques. Two collaborative techniques that incorporate several highly successful comprehension strategies are ReQuest and reciprocal teaching.

Dealing as it does with material that is predominantly narrative, literature books are somewhat easier to comprehend than are social studies or science texts. In addition, teachers of low-achieving readers have a wider range, in terms of difficulty level, of literature texts from which to choose. For low-achieving readers, the teachers may choose texts that are of high quality but which are less demanding to read.

Theme units are especially helpful for low-achieving readers because they produce an in-depth experience with core concepts and vocabulary, and help students integrate their learning.

## *Application Activities*

1. Examine several content area texts designed for the grade level in which you are interested. Based on your analysis of the texts, what background knowledge, skills, and strategies would be needed to read the texts?

2. Examine texts written for low-achieving readers. Analyze the texts. What makes them easy to read? What are the major disadvantages and advantages of using easy-to-read texts.

3. Obtain five easy-to-read trade books that might be used to teach major concepts in one of the content areas. If you are teaching, select trade books that fit in with your curriculum. Try them out with students. What are the advantages and disadvantages of using trade books to teach content-area concepts?

4. Construct a KWL Plus lesson and teach it, if possible. If you can't teach it, try using it with this or another text.

5. Construct a study guide or a gloss. If possible, introduce it and arrange for a group of students to use it.

# Chapter 14

# Building Study Strategies

## *Using What You Know*

Although being able to study effectively demands adequate comprehension, adequate comprehension does not automatically translate into the ability to study. Studying requires the ability to retain information and organize it in such a way that it can be communicated through an essay, an objective test or some other form of assessment. This chapter looks at the basic principles that underlie studying. It also explores a number of strategies for studying and retaining information.

How do you go about studying? What strategies do you use? Are you an organized, disciplined learner, or do you have some problems in this area? How would you go about teaching low achieving readers and writers to study?

## *Anticipation Guide*

Read each of the following statements. Put a check under "Agree" or "Disagree" to show how you feel about each one. If possible, discuss your responses with classmates.

| | Agree | Disagree |
|---|---|---|
| **1.** An effective study strategy is to read the material over and over until you know it. | ________ | ________ |
| **2.** The biggest obstacle to effective studying is a lack of discipline. | ________ | ________ |
| **3.** Objective tests are easier to study for than essay tests. | ________ | ________ |
| **4.** Study skills are neglected at all levels of schooling. | ________ | ________ |
| **5.** For most older low-achieving readers, study skills are usually a top priority. | ________ | ________ |

## Reading to Learn and Remember

The first step in teaching students how to study is to find out where they are. To experience the process of studying, read the following selection as though you were preparing to take a quiz tomorrow.

### Where Does Color Come From?

*Color is determined by the wave length of light. Visible light is made up of several different wavelengths. These different wave lengths make bands of colors. Red, orange, yellow, green, blue, indigo, and violet are the seven colors in visible light.*

*These are the same colors you see in a rainbow. Rainbows are caused by sunlight passing through drops of water. The drops of water refract the white light. Different colors of light bend different amounts, so they separate into a band of seven different colors. This band is called a* **spectrum.** *It is made up of red, orange, yellow, green, blue, indigo, and violet. All these colors together produce white light.*

*You can create a spectrum yourself by letting sunlight shine through a prism. A* **prism** *is a triangular-shaped object made of clear glass. (Bledsoe, 1994, p. 205)*

## Requirements for Successful Studying

Successful studying requires metacognition in addition to a command of useful study strategies. Students must know how and when to use strategies.

As an expert reader, you probably used a number of strategies for comprehending and retaining the material. For instance, you may have used the acronym, ROY G. BIV to help you remember the names of the colors of the spectrum. You probably were also able to gauge when you had studied enough. You may have given yourself a self-test to see how you were doing. You might also have sought a quiet place to study, or at least you put distracting thoughts our of your mind. You probably wondered what kind of a quiz you would be given because you know different types of quizzes require different types of studying. Now put yourself in your students' or prospective students' shoes. How might they go about studying difficult informational text? How effective might their studying be?

Knowing how to study is a complex task, which is both cognitive and affective. As Kletzien and Bednar (1988) note, students need to take control of their studying. This, in turn, involves four variables: knowing oneself, setting goals, assessing tasks, and employing strategies.

- Students must know their personal strengths and weaknesses as learners.
- They must be able to set reasonable goals and keep these in mind.
- They must be able to size up learning tasks, knowing what may make them easy or difficult.
- They must know appropriate strategies to apply to reach their goals.

In addition, students must have performance awareness (Wade & Reynolds, 1989). They must be able to evaluate their performance when they study so they have a sense of whether or not they know the material sufficiently to complete the upcoming test successfully. Otherwise, they don't know whether to continue studying or not.

### *Know Oneself As a Learner*

Low-achieving readers often have a poor opinion of themselves as learners. Having failed in the past, they may see themselves as not being able to study adequately. They may even have given up trying to experience success in their school work. Too often, students attribute a lack of success to a lack of ability. If failure is attributed to lack of ability, students have little recourse but to give up trying. They lack a sense of self-efficacy. The students need to see a connection between success and hard work and a link between high achievement and working smart. The assessment task also has to be moderated so that it allows for a successful performance. If tests are so hard that low-progress readers have little chance of passing them, they will soon give up trying.

> When giving an assignment, purposes should also be made clear: to learn about the two major types of trees, deciduous and evergreens, for instance.

### *Goals*

All too often the student's only goal is to complete the assignment. The focus should be on learning rather than on task completion. Students need a goal for reading: to read for enjoyment, to learn how to perform a task, or to learn and remember material for a test. The goal will help determine the nature of the task.

### *The Task*

The task includes the type of material to be read, its difficulty, and its length. The goal also has a bearing on the task. Reading *Catcher in the Rye* for pleasure is a much different task from reading it for a test. Reading directions so that one can plant a tree requires a different kind of reading than reading about trees in order to pass an objective test.

### *The Strategies*

> Analyze the study demands that are made of students by you and other teachers in your school. Also consider tasks, such as taking phone messages, that students engage in outside of school.

Once students have a clear idea of their learning goal (what they hope to be able to do), their purpose for reading (questions to be answered), and the task, they are in a better position to determine strategies for completing the reading. Strategies should include those that help the student prepare for the reading (surveying, predicting), those that foster comprehension during reading (summarizing, inferring), and those that aid retention (taking and studying notes, creating and studying graphic organizers).

There are a number of popular strategies for studying textbooks. These include but are not limited to underlining, outlining, taking notes and completing study guides or graphic organizers, and the venerable SQ3R. By and large, these strategies are successful. However, their success depends on the four variables mentioned earlier: self-knowledge, goals, task, and strategies. The readers' prior knowledge, reading ability, and motivation will also have an effect on the success of the strategy as will the content difficulty and organization of the text. To successfully apply a study strategy, it is essential that the student know the strategy and that there be a match between the strategy and the task (Caverly & Orlando, 1991).

## *Aids to Studying*

Successful studying has more requirements than simply comprehending because it bears the extra burden of retrieval. If you can't remember information, it doesn't matter whether you understood it or not when you first read it. However, as a practical matter, understanding is a key component of information retrieval. Material that is well understood is easier to understand. As Memory and Moore (1992) note, there are three time-honored aids to studying: principles, organization, and association.

### *Principles*

**Principles:** generalizations or rules that underlie events, concepts, or processes.

The best way to promote both comprehension and retrieval of information is by teaching **principles.** If students understand the principles behind certain actions, events, or processes, they are better able to understand new information and to retrieve it later on. For instance, readers who understand the principle of supply and demand will be better able to understand why prices fell during the Great Depression. They would also be better able to understand how the loss of jobs caused a drop in demand, and the drop in demand, in turn, caused even more jobs to be lost.

In human biology, students are faced with learning that arteries are thick and elastic and carry oxygen-rich blood away from the heart, but veins are thin and less elastic and carry blood laden with carbon dioxide to the heart. The difference between veins and arteries seems arbitrary and so is difficult to remember (Bransford, 1994). However, if a principle is invoked or an explanation supplied, then the information becomes more meaningful and easier to remember.

If the reader is told that arteries are thicker and more elastic because blood is pumped through the arteries in forceful spurts and therefore arteries must be elastic so that they can expand and contract as they push the blood forward, readers are better able to remember which is thicker and more elastic, a vein or an artery. The readers are able to use a principle to help them remember whether a vein or an artery is more elastic and thicker, rather than relying on sheer memory or some mnemonic device.

The moral is clear. Make learning as meaningful as possible. If the selection provides a principle, the teacher should make sure that it is emphasized. If the underlying principle has not been stated, then help students discover it. Bransford (1994) discusses a content-area selection that describes various types of shelters that Native Americans constructed but doesn't explain why some were permanent, while others were easily disassembled, and some had slanted roofs and others did not. Again, the information would be arbitrary until the teacher helped the students discover the principles behind the construction of the dwellings: living habits, climate, and availability of materials.

If neither the teacher nor the text makes the material meaningful, then the student needs to seek underlying principles. One of the study strategies that students need to be taught is how to make information meaningful.

One way of helping students retain principles is to have them apply them (Memory & Moore, 1992). For instance, after understanding why dwellings are built in different ways, you might ask students to survey the construction of homes in their area and discuss why they were built that way. You might ask such questions as: "Why do homes in cold areas have sharply pitched roofs? Why are homes in warm places painted in light colors?" In order to build knowledge of principles, you need to ask a lot of why questions, after, of course, basic facts have been established.

### *Organization*

**Organization:** manner in which ideas, events, processes, or other items are related.

The second-best comprehension and memory aid is **organization.** If students see the organization of a passage: main idea–details, cause–effect, and comparison–contrast, they are better able to see major ideas and cluster or chunk information. By grouping the following animals into categories: dogs, horses, cows, and cats, you will find that you can learn them faster and recall them more easily than if you just tried to memorize them as listed.

| | | | |
|---|---|---|---|
| Collie | Manx | Siamese | Morgan |
| Holstein | Bulldog | Jersey | Pomeranian |
| Calico | Clydesdale | Beagle | Guernsey |
| Ayrshire | Tabby | Brown-Swiss | Bloodhound |
| Palomino | Arabian | Appaloosa | Persian |

Questions and graphic organizers that mirror the organization of the selection help students cluster information. Previewing helps students detect the organization of a selection. The headings, for instance, may provide an outline of the chapter (Memory & Moore, 1992). Certain study techniques, such as outlining, also help students detect the organization of a piece.

### *Association*

**Association:** link between ideas, processes, events, or other items.

Although principles and organization are powerful study aids and should be used if at all possible, simple **associations** can also be helpful, especially if the material to be learned is arbitrary. Memory devices have been successful throughout the ages to help learners better remember facts, terms, and similar types of information. Study strategies that foster organization and association are presented next.

## *Organizational Study Strategies*

There are a number of study strategies that help students organize information. In these strategies, some form of noting and recording major ideas is advocated. The organizational strategies explored include SQ3R and notetaking.

**SQ3R:** five-step study technique: survey, question, read, recite, review.

## *SQ3R*

The oldest and the most widely advocated system for learning from text is **SQ3R,** which stands for Survey, Question, Read, Recite, Review. Devised by Francis Robinson (1970) in the 1940s and updated over the years, SQ3R is based on sound psychological principles of learning, with the five steps to be implemented as follows:

### Steps in SQ3R

*Step 1: Survey*

Survey the chapter to obtain an overview of what you are about to read and to see what you already know about the topic. Read the title, introductory paragraph or overview, headings, and subheads, and summary. Predict what the section is about. Activate prior knowledge. Ask yourself: "What do I know about this topic?"

Activating prior knowledge has been added to SQ3R to update it (Vacca & Vacca, 1986).

*Step 2: Question*

Turn each heading into a question. The heading "Fruits Protect Seeds" is transformed into the question, "How do fruits protect seeds?" If you are taking notes, you might jot the question down.

*Step 3: Read*

Read the section to answer the question that you posed. Reading to answer a question keeps your focus active and purposeful.

*Step 4: Recite*

When you come to the end of a section, recite. See if you can answer the question that you posed: "How do fruits protect seeds?" This section is metacognitive. It forces you to check your comprehension. If you can't answer the question, go back over the section and find the needed information. Recitation may be oral or written. A written recitation can later be used as notes for study. Use two-column notes, putting the question in the left and the answer in the right. If you record your responses, make sure they are very brief so the procedure doesn't become time-consuming and tiresome. Also refrain from taking notes until you have read the entire section.

*Step 5: Review*

After the entire assignment has been completed, review what you have read. This will help you see the overall significance of what you have read, organize information, and integrate new information with prior knowledge. In addition to deepening your understanding of the material, it will help you remember it. Some authors suggest inserting a sixth step, an *R* for reflection. After reading, you might think over what you have read (Pauk, 1984).

When teaching SQ3R, encourage students to personalize its application so it fits their needs. Some students may want to recite by writing, while others may prefer to recite orally.

When properly taught and applied, SQ3R has been shown to be an effective study technique. However, it does take low-achieving readers longer to learn to use the technique (Caverly & Orlando, 1991) and it should be taught early, before students have a chance to pick up ineffective study habits (Early & Sawyer, 1984).

When teaching SQ3R, build on what students already know about reading and studying. Chances are they are already being taught to survey and generate questions and read to answer those questions. Also begin with easy, well-structured content materials. Although you can teach SQ3R in a few sessions, learning to apply the technique might take months.

You might have conferences with students periodically to discuss their application of SQ3R. At that time you might go over their SQ3R notes. Since studying is idiosyncratic, allow individual adaptations of SQ3R.

A key factor in the success of any study technique that students use is attitudinal. Using SQ3R or another study system requires hard work and active involvement. Passively reading and even rereading material is easier (Askov, 1991). Students need to see that the extra effort is paying off in their learning more material and earning higher grades. You also need to help students streamline the technique so there is no wasted effort.

## *Notetaking Skills*

Notetaking promotes selective attention. Through taking notes, students are more likely to focus on main ideas.

Notetaking is a complex skill that involves comprehending, organizing, and recording essential information. As students move up in the grades, notetaking becomes increasingly vital. Notetaking is a difficult endeavor for all students but is especially troublesome for poor readers. When introducing notetaking, discuss ways in which students take notes in their everyday lives. Although students may not have taken formal notes for academic purposes, they have probably taken telephone messages, which are forms of notetaking, or they may have jotted down a set of directions for going to an unfamiliar place or for playing a new game. In school, writing down homework assignments, recording the outcomes of a meeting of a cooperative learning group, listing possible topic ideas, and keeping a writer's journal or learning log are also forms of notetaking. Learning strategies are easier to implement when students realize that they are extensions of activities that they already perform.

Discuss the benefits of taking notes. Lead students to see that notetaking, in addition to being a way of recording ideas so they won't be forgotten, improves understanding because it helps them select the most important ideas and organize them. Also lead them to see that notetaking helps us remember ideas, because if we understand and organize ideas we will remember them longer.

### *Structured Notetaking*

One good way to motivate notetaking, especially among low-achieving readers, is to initiate instruction using graphic organizers to take notes from brief, well-organized segments of text. The choice of graphic organizers would be determined by the text organization. A descriptive paragraph might be depicted by a spider web, with the main idea in the center, and the supporting details shooting out from the center.

Another structured way to present notetaking is through the use of two columns. The first column would contain main ideas in question or statement form, the second column, the supporting details. In the beginning, you might want to use structured formats with highly organized text. Some highly structured two column formats include: main idea/detail, cause/effect, opinion/proof, conclusion/proof, or problem/solution. Samples of these are shown in Figure 14-1. Steps for taking two-column notes from text are listed below.

### A Lesson in Taking Notes from Text

The most basic and least beneficial form of notetaking is simply copying from the text. More elaborated forms include: putting the text ideas into one's own words, showing hierarchical and other relationships, and including one's own ideas.

Using a well-organized piece of text, preferably one that contains headings and subheads and is drawn from material that they are required to study, show students how you would take notes.

*Step 1: Preview*

Preview the material to get an overview of the selection, make predictions based on the overview, and activate prior knowledge. This process could be turned into a series of questions.

> What is this all about? (preview)
> What do I know about this? (prior knowledge)
> Why am I reading this? What do I want to find out? (overall purpose)

Some students underline or highlight information with a marker. Students should mark only essential information and should also use some sort of system to show a hierarchy of information.

*Step 2: Model Use of the First Column*

Based on the preview, show students how you jot down questions in the left column that you think will be answered by the text. If there are headings, show how you can turn each heading into a question just as was done with SQ3R. Show how you would turn the first heading into a question and then read to answer that question. (At times headings are misleading. The section encompassed by the heading might not explore the topic suggested by the heading, or it may contain additional information. Or it may cover a different topic from the one suggested by the heading. In those situations, the reader must create questions that reflect the text. In the initial stages of instruction, use text that has headings that accurately announce the main idea of the section.)

*Step 3: Explain*

Explain that as you read the section, you keep your question in mind, but read flexibly and are prepared to change the question mentally, if necessary.

*Step 4: Model Use of the Second Column*

Show how you write down your notes in the second column as in Figure 14-2, which shows a question and answer format for taking notes from text. Explain how at first you try to answer the question without looking back at the text just as you did with SQ3R. After answering the question by jotting down notes, you check to see if you have all the important information. If not, you add missing details. You explain that only the important information that answers the questions should be included. This should be written in telegraphic form, with abbreviations used to save time.

Because notetaking is a complex activity, begin with easier tasks. Start with text that is highly organized and with notetaking formats that are highly structured. Also limit the notetaking to brief selections.

## *Lecture Notes*

Taking notes from lectures is more difficult than taking notes from reading. The statements made in a lecture are transitory, and the organization of the information is not highlighted visually as it would be in an informational text containing heads and subheads. Since there are significant differences between the two activities, students need instruction in both.

| Main Ideas | Details |
|---|---|
| *Lightning comes in many shapes* | *Streak—one or more lines*<br>*Forked—has branches*<br>*Sheet—huge light*<br>*Heat—red flash*<br>*Ribbons—waves like ribbons*<br>*Beads—looks like a string of beads*<br>*Ball—seen in homes and airplanes* |

| Problem | Solution |
|---|---|
| *Many countries do not have enough food* | *Use more land for farming*<br>*Use better ways of farming*<br>*Kill crop-eating insects*<br>*Share with countries that need food* |

| Opinion | Proof |
|---|---|
| *Benjamin Banneker had many talents* | *Made wooden clock*<br>*Made discoveries about bees and locusts*<br>*Made discoveries about tides and eclipses*<br>*Spoke out for freedom, equal rights, and peace* |

**FIGURE 14-1 Structured Formats for Notetaking**

*Chapter 3: Earth's Resources*

| | |
|---|---|
| *What are resources?* | *things people use to meet their needs* |
| *What are Earth's resources?* | *food, water, air, fuel, materials* |
| *What are renewable resources?* | *air, water, animals, plants—will be more and more of these* |
| *What are nonrenewable resources?* | *oil, coal, gas, metals—once these are used up, there will be no more* |
| *How are coal, oil, and natural gas used?* | *main sources of energy* |

**FIGURE 14-2 Question and Answer Notes from Text**

### *Assisted Notetaking*

Effective notetaking of orally presented information depends on active listening. Students should have a purpose for taking notes, should have an overview of the topic, and should be attempting to select main ideas and major supporting details. Ease students into notetaking by arranging for them to take notes in interviews or other question-and-answer situations. Questions provide an excellent framework for taking notes. Students might take notes on questions asked of a guest speaker or a person being interviewed for a report. Taking notes could be part of role playing, as students pretend to be reporters and take notes as they get information about an important story.

To provide practice for taking notes on classroom presentations, present short, well-organized lectures and give students a partial outline of the lecture. For instance, you might provide the major topics of the lecture and two of the three subtopics for each and have them add the missing subtopics.

> If students are having difficulty taking notes, ask to see samples and analyze their performance. Note where they are having difficulty and provide help accordingly (Heiman & Slomianko, 1986).

Using cueing techniques is also helpful. Tell students the main idea of the lecture. You might even write it on the board. Also use signal words to indicate the number of details. "There are three main kinds of rocks. There are six kinds of nutrients. Here are the four main effects of that law." Highlight important terminology and write it on the board. Also summarize your lectures and pause occasionally to give students time to catch up. Over time, have students take increased responsibility for taking notes. Requiring as it does the ability to distinguish important from unimportant information, independent notetaking should not be undertaken by students who are unable to identify main ideas (Santa, Abrams, & Santa, 1979). If students are unable to distinguish important from unimportant details, "they will tend to take verbatim notes of irrelevant concepts" (Caverly & Orlando, 1991, p. 121).

> Students should reflect on the information in their notes. They ask: "How does this information fit in with what I already know? How might I use this information?"

### *The Cornell Notetaking System*

Originated nearly a half century ago at Cornell University by Walter Pauk, (1989), the Cornell notetaking system features taking two- or three-column notes. The student records notes in the second column of a sheet of paper that has been divided into two columns. The column on the left is 2½ inches wide. The second column is six inches in width. Notes are taken in telegraphic style in the larger column. As soon as possible after taking notes, students should add missing information, clarify confused information, and rewrite portions that might be unclear. Once that has been done, the student rereads the notes, runs through the lecture in her or his mind, and reduces each major idea to key words or phrases, which are written in the lefthand 2½-inch column. The key words or phrases become cues to ideas and details in the wide column. As an alternative to reducing notes to key words, the student may elect to create questions that encompass major ideas in the notes. Using a blank sheet of paper, the pupil covers up the notes and uses the key words or questions to quiz herself or himself on the material.

A third column of notes might also be used when students are combining lecture and text notes (Pauk, 1989). The notetaking page is set up with a 2½-inch column and two 3-inch columns. Lecture notes are recorded in the center. Question or cue words are written in the left-hand column. Notes from the text are written in the third column. The notes from

> The advantage of three-column notes is that they foster the integration of lecture and text notes. As an alternative, the third column can be used to highlight vocabulary or questions one has about the material.

the lecture and the text are aligned with the question or cue words in the first column. There is another way to use the third column: Instead of using it to combine lecture or text notes, the third column can be used to define key terms or raise questions, as in Figure 14-3.

## Other Forms of Notetaking

> Information maps provide an excellent technique for reviewing notes in preparation for an end-of-unit, end-of-semester, or end-of-year test.

Graphic organizers and techniques such as KWL Plus and frame matrix, which were covered in a previous chapter, and information map and outlining are notetaking activities. The checklist in Figure 14-4 lists the objectives that students should meet when taking notes, regardless of the notetaking style they choose.

### Information Map

An information map is similar to a frame matrix. As you will recall, the frame matrix has two major aspects: a frame—which highlights essen-

*Nov. 7 Geography*

| | | |
|---|---|---|
| | *Earth's Nonrenewable Resources* | *Nonrenewable—once it's gone, it's gone* |
| *What are earth's nonrenewable resources?* | *Oil, coal, metals* | *Resources—things we can use* |
| *What is oil made from?* | *Oil made from tiny sea plants and animals that sank to ocean floor* | |
| *How was oil created?* | *Tiny plants and animals were buried under sediment. Sediment pressed dead matter into oil.* | *sediment—small bits of matter that fall to bottom of body of water or liquid.* |
| *How is oil gotten from the ground?* | *Crude oil is drilled from ground.* | *Crude oil is thick & black. Has to be refined before can be used.* |
| *How is oil used?* | *Oil makes heating oil, motor oil, gas, plastic, etc.* | *What other products are made from oil?* |

**FIGURE 14-3 Three-Column Notes**

| Name ______________________ | | Date______________ | |
|---|---|---|---|
| 1. Does the student select main ideas? | seldom | sometimes | usually |
| 2. Does the student select supporting details? | seldom | sometimes | usually |
| 3. Has the student captured most of the main ideas and details? | seldom | sometimes | usually |
| 4. Is the information organized? | seldom | sometimes | usually |
| 5. Is the student able to generate questions? | seldom | sometimes | usually |
| 6. Is the information consolidated? | seldom | sometimes | usually |
| 7. Has the student used abbreviations? | seldom | sometimes | usually |
| 8. Are the notes legible? | seldom | sometimes | usually |
| 9. Does the student take adequate notes from lectures? | seldom | sometimes | usually |
| 10. Does the student take adequate notes from reading materials? | seldom | sometimes | usually |

**FIGURE 14-4 Notetaking Checklist**

tial categories of information such as location, area, population, climate—and the matrix, which allows the comparison of two or more elements in terms of the frames or categories (see Figure 13-9 on p. 370). The frame matrix is especially useful when comparisons and contrasts are being made. The key difference between a frame matrix and an information map is that the categories on the left (the frame items) are translated into questions, which makes them easier for students to handle and also makes it more useful as a study guide. Students can self-test themselves by covering the answers in the cell matrices and asking the questions on the left. After reciting the answers to themselves, they can then check their responses, reviewing any problem items as they do so. Information maps don't have to be restricted to major questions; they can be used anytime there are a series of questions that can be asked about two or more topics. They are especially helpful for comparing and contrasting details. Information maps can be constructed for a limited topic, such as comparing the body's sense organs, or they could be constructed for topics studied over a full unit or semester (Heiman & Slomianko, 1986). For instance, an information map could be constructed comparing all the countries in South America, the major systems in the body, or mammals. An extended information map might be completed over a period of months and cover a portion of a wall.

Questions in an information map should follow two criteria. All questions should apply to all of the categories. And questions should not be of the type that could be answered with a "yes" or a "no" (Heiman & Slomianko, 1986).

In addition to being used to study important information for a test, information maps can also be used as a basis for writing, especially when the pieces being written involve making comparisons. A sample information map is presented in Figure 14-5.

## *Associational Strategies*

How many days are there in May or September? Most of us, when asked that question, resort to the rhyme "Thirty days hath September, April, June, and November." We can't use understanding because there is no particular principle for determining that, except for February, some months have thirty days and some thirty-one. Rather than resorting to brute

| | water | minerals | vitamins | proteins | carbo-hydrates | fats |
|---|---|---|---|---|---|---|
| What is this nutrient? | liquid made up of 2 parts hydrogen, 1 part water | nonliving substances —zinc, iron, potassium, calcium, sodium | living molecules | large, heavy molecules | sugars and starches made by plants | oily substance found in animals and some plants |
| How does it help the body? | cleans body, keeps body cool, helps cells do their work | strengthens muscles, bones, teeth; helps nerves, muscles, and cells work | helps skin, hair, muscles, heart, blood, nerves, teeth, bones, eyesight, growth, breathing, preventing illness | build muscle, help body move, carry materials in circulatory system | is source of energy and fiber, cleans digestive system | is source of fuel, energy |
| Where can it be found? | water, juices, milk | most foods | most foods | meat, fish, eggs, dairy products, grains, beans, nuts | sugar, grains, cereals, beans, fruits, vegetables | butter, margarine, cooking oil, fried foods, nuts, beef, pork |

**FIGURE 14-5 Sample Information Map: Nutrients**

**Mnemonics:** strategies such as rhymes and acronyms that rely on creating artificial rather than meaningful associations.

memory, we use a **mnemonic.** Levin (1993) states that a mnemonic strategy "involves a transformation of otherwise difficult-to-remember material into something more memorable" (p. 236).

Most of the association devices explored in this section incorporate mnemonic devices. Mnemonic devices have a long history. Many of the traditional nursery and other rhymes are mnemonic devices designed to help school children in bygone years memorize important facts.

### *Acronyms*

**Acronym:** word formed from the first letters in a series of words as in Zip (Zone Improvement Program) Code.

In an **acronym,** each letter stands for a word. A word is made up of the first letter of each of the words to be memorized. The best known example is probably HOMES for the names of the Great Lakes: Huron, Ontario, Michigan, Erie, and Superior. In recalling the names of the Great Lakes, the students uses HOMES as a mnemonic aid so that the letter *h* reminds them that the name of one of the Great Lakes begins with an *h,* the letter *o* reminds them that the name of another of the Great Lakes begins with an *o,* and so on. Another well-known acronym is ROY G. BIV to help retrieve the colors of the spectrum: Red, Orange, Yellow, Green, Blue, Indigo, and Violet.

### *Rhymes*

The key word strategy which was presented earlier as a device for learning the meanings of new words is an example of a mnemonic or associative strategy.

Rhymes are another mnemonic device that have been used for hundreds of years to aid students' memories. Because the associations between the pieces of information to be learned are arbitrary and no meaningful connections can be constructed, rhymes are used to assist memory. Two of the best-known rhymes include the one indicating how many days each month has, and the one used to help with the spelling of words containing adjacent *i* and *e:*

Thirty days hath September,
April, June, and November.
February hath twenty-eight alone,
And all the rest have thirty-one.

Use *i* before *e* except after *c.*
Or when sounded as *a*
As in neighbor and weigh.

### *Acrostics*

**Acrostic:** sentence or rhyme or series of words in which the first letter in each word stands for a word or spells out a word.

An **acrostic** is a sentence or rhyme in which the first letter of each word stands for the first letter in a series of words to be memorized. For instance, the sentence, "My Very Educational Mother Just Served Us Nine Pizzas" could be used to help recall the names of the planets: Mercury, Venus, Earth, Mars, Jupiter, Saturn, Uranus, Neptune, Pluto" (Richardson & Morgan, 1997, p. 322).

## *Study Habits*

Poor or ineffective study habits are a major cause of failure. A large proportion of students have inefficient study habits. When students are asked how they would study a section of expository text in order to recall as much as they could, most typically respond that they would simply reread the material or just concentrate. Some will admit to having no strategy for remembering the material. A first step in helping students who have become discouraged or have given up, is to show them that they *can* learn. In a number of studies cited in earlier chapters, low-achieving readers achieve higher grades when they are taught effective strategies.

To determine how best to break the cycle of failure, survey students. Find out how they study for tests. Find out which subjects or which kinds of tests are most troublesome and plan a program of intervention. Enlist the aid of the subject matter teacher.

When it comes to studying, low-achieving readers aren't the only ones that need help. Many of the best readers perform significantly below potential because of poor study habits. If possible, extend assistance to all who need it.

## *Metacognitive Aspects of Studying*

Students may not be aware of how much studying is required in order to learn a list of new words or several concepts thoroughly. They may need to learn a criterion for adequate performance.

As with other areas of literacy, the metacognitive aspects of studying are often the most essential. Help students become aware of the kinds of tests that they will be taking so they can choose appropriate study strategies. Memorizing dates and important facts should help on an objective test but would be of less value on an essay test.

Students also need to know what to study: all of the chapters covered? Selected portions of the chapters, handouts, notes? They also need to know whether the test is cumulative. Will it cover all the information from the beginning of the term or just the information for the last unit or since the last major test?

### *Using Self-Knowledge*

In addition to knowing what to study, students need to know how, when, where, and how long to study. Knowing oneself as a learner, a student should know the best time to study. Some might do better studying early in the morning. Others are at their best at night. Some prefer an informal environment; others do their best work at a desk. Some students need lots of structure. Others like to have choices about when and where and how they study (Carbo, Dunn, & Dunn 1986). Help students become aware of the conditions under which they study best. These should be conditions that are comfortable but which also result in improved performance. After students get high grades on a test, you night discuss with them how they went about studying for that particular test.

### *Overcoming Obstacles to Studying*

Teachers should also help students discover impediments to study: (1) lack of self-discipline, (2) lack of time, (3) boredom, (4) lack of perseverance, (5) distractibility. Work out with students ways of overcoming these obstacles.

**Lack of Discipline.** Set a routine. Study at the same time and same place. The place should be free of distractions, although if the student works better with background music, that should not be considered a "distraction." Break large tasks into smaller, more manageable ones. Instead of tackling a whole chapter, break it up into three-page or five-page sections. Start with the easiest and most enjoyable task to build a sense of accomplishment. Use rewards such as a ten-minute break for every fifty minutes of studying. Or you might encourage students to keep a chart showing number of minutes spent studying each night. At the end of each week, give the students checks or stars for completing their charts. The best motivator is success. If students do well after studying, they have an incentive for studying harder. Counseling may be in order for students who can't seem to make themselves study.

**Lack of Time.** Have students chart how they spend their time during a typical day. Analyzing time spent, determine when might be the best time to study. Also select a place to study. If students live in crowded apartments, they might decide to study in school or at the local library or study early in the morning while everyone else is still in bed.

**Boredom.** Show students how to set goals and become an active learner. Use self-testing to challenge oneself. Tackle boring tasks in short but concentrated segments.

**Lack of Perseverance.** Begin with short periods of study, perhaps just ten minutes. Gradually build up to longer periods. Also use self-rewards. Try beginning with the easiest or most interesting task.

**Distractibility.** Getting rid of all distractions, use self-talk: "I will read three pages. I will concentrate on my reading. I will ask myself questions about what I have read. If I can answer the questions, I will reward myself and take a break." Stress with these students that brief periods of focused study are better than long periods interrupted by internal and external distractions.

***Planning and Evaluating Study Habits***

Help students devise individual study plans. These plans might include when and where the students plan to study. Plans should be long-term and short-term. If students have long-term projects, they might indicate how they plan to complete those projects. In the beginning, students might evaluate their study sessions by using a form such as the Study Log shown in Figure 14-6, reflections which they have written in a learning log, or through discussions. The evaluation should include what study tasks the students undertook, what study strategies they used, and approximately how much time they spent on each task. They should also report any problems they had and assess the effectiveness of their study efforts. This will help students gain a greater awareness of what it means to be an effective learner. Students will also be able to see which strategies work best and how much time tasks take.

Name ______________________

| Study Task | Date, Time, and Place of Studying | Time Spent Studying | Study Method Used (Outline, SQ3R, etc.) | Questions, Difficulties, Comments | Results (Test Grades, Quizzes, Class Discussion) |
|---|---|---|---|---|---|
| *Read chapter about kinds of rocks* | *1–6 7–8:10* | *1 hr, 10 min* | *Inf. Map* | *Many hard words* | *Quiz—90* |
| *Read chapter on WWI.* | *1–6 8:30–9* | *30 min* | *SQ3R & Review notes* | *Many names & dates* | |
| *Study for test on WWI* | *1–7 7–7:50* | *50 min* | | | *Test—C Knew causes of war but not names & dates* |

**FIGURE 14-6 Study Log**

## *Preparing for Tests*

Knowing how to take a test is a functional lifeskill for students. Fairly or unfairly, their grades and futures will be determined, in part, by their skill in taking tests. The first step in preparing for a test is to know what kind of test will be given. Each type of test has its own special requirements. An essay test demands knowledge of major themes and main ideas. A fill-in-the-blanks or short-answer test puts a premium on being able to store away and recall names, dates, definitions, and events. A multiple choice test is also concerned with details. Although it relies less on memory, it may involve making fine discriminations so it may make more demands on understanding.

The best time to start preparing for a test is the first day of class. Grasping material from the start is essential as is organizing it and reviewing it from time to time. Using two-column or three-column notes, creating information maps, and other organizers are good ways to prepare for a test. Spaced review is also generally better than massed review, especially when facts or processes are being studied. Spaced review means that students space out their studying over a period of days and weeks. In massed review, students study for lengthy periods of time. Cramming is a form of massed review.

Students should also study the material in the same way that they will be expected to demonstrate their knowledge of it. If they will be asked to identify the parts of a frog in a lab practicum, then they should practice doing just that. Or if they will be asked to write essay questions, they should create skeletal answers to possible essay questions.

## *Alternate Testing*

The aim of essay and other tests is to obtain a fair and accurate assessment of how much the students have learned. If students' writing skills are so deficient that their written responses will fail to demonstrate how much they've learned, alternate methods of assessment, such as oral exams or untimed tests, should be explored (Alley & Deshler, 1979). Or, after taking a written test, students who have serious difficulty composing written responses, might be given the opportunity to expand on their responses orally. Students who are still learning English might also be more fairly assessed if given an alternate form of testing or more time.

## *Test Anxiety*

Low-achieving readers often suffer from a double burden when faced with tests. In addition to being less capable readers and writers, they are also more likely to suffer from **test anxiety.** Unfortunately, test anxiety may set in as early as grade three and afflict one student out of every five (Gaudrey & Spielberger, 1971). While it is normal to experience butterflies on the day of a major test, some students are so stressed by tests that their scores are lower than they should be. After the exam has been turned in, the test-anxious student may report a rush of recall (Wark & Flippo, 1991). Test anxiety can be reduced in a variety of ways. Instruction in test-taking skills helps. However, instruction in study skills only helps if it is combined with some method of stress reduction or alleviation of worry. Test-anxious students also do better if they don't perceive the test as being overly difficult and if difficult items are preceded by easy ones (Hembree, 1988).

**Test anxiety:** state of intense apprehension resulting from anticipation of taking a test. Physical symptoms may be present, and the individual's mental functioning may be disrupted.

A program designed to alleviate test anxiety should include the following elements:

- Instruction in comprehension and study skills.
- Instruction in test-taking skills.
- Instruction and counseling that builds self-esteem and helps students handle stressful situations such as taking tests.
- Instruction in cognitive self-talk. Students are taught to resist negative thoughts with positive self-assertions that encourage them to take a deep breath and relax, take their time on the test and do their best, and use specific test-taking strategies, such as doing the easy items first and then working on the difficult ones. (Wark & Flippo, 1991)

Of course, the best way to handle test anxiety is to see that it never starts (Hembree, 1988). A learned behavior, test anxiety doesn't gain a foothold until the end of the primary grades. A secure, noncompetitive environment where students are working on their level and made to feel good about themselves as learners should help reduce the number of students afflicted.

Test anxiety is linked to fears of negative evaluation, a dislike of tests, and inadequate study skills. Students with high test anxiety have lowered self-esteem and feel less in control of outside events.

## *Reading Rate*

An excellent reader, Barbara sailed through novels at a rapid rate. Unfortunately, as she moved up through the grades, her marks in the content areas fell. Attempting to speed through difficult science and social studies texts the way she zipped through novels, she understood and retained very little of what she read. On the other hand, Marcella plodded through novels and newspaper articles at the same slow rate that she read her fact-packed social studies or science text.

**Rate of reading:** number of words per minute at which a person reads. Rate of reading is a complex issue, since reading rate varies with goal, purpose, and type of material.

Both students have a problem. They aren't adjusting their **rate of reading** to the demands of the task. A third student, Jesse, reads everything too slowly. A senior in high school, he reads approximately 85 words a minute. Reading so slowly, he finds it next to impossible to keep up with the heavy reading demands of his academic courses.

## *Adjusting Reading Rate*

Students like Barbara, Marcella, and Jesse need to adjust their rate of reading to fit their purpose. Again, this is part of knowing oneself as a learner, understanding one's purpose for reading, and sizing up the learning task. According to Carver's (1990) extensive review of the research, there are five processes of reading. From slowest and most intensive, these are memorizing, learning, normal reading, skimming, and scanning. Unless the material is especially difficult or offers decoding problems, students' normal rate of reading is governed by their rate of thinking. For high school students, the average reading speed is 250 WPM. (See Table 4.3 on p. 83 for average reading rates for elementary school students.)

Rate of reading increases almost automatically as students become more strategic readers. If students preview, have a purpose for reading, and develop a more extensive reading vocabulary, their reading rate, in most instances, automatically increases. Students who are passive readers, easily distracted, with no purpose for reading other than getting to the end, will naturally read more slowly. Excessive oral reading, an overconcern for correctness, and an obsession with details will also slow down students' reading speed. Student's rate of reading may be slowed if they spend all or most of their time reading study-type or difficult materials. Students need to encounter a certain amount of easy reading to achieve or maintain their normal reading rate (Carver, 1990).

In an earlier chapter, it was noted that some students were slower at retrieving words, letters, and digits. It is possible that this slowness in processing may show up in later years as slow reading. According to Denckla and Rudel (1976), some students may read at a slower rate because their neural pathways are less efficient, which causes alternate pathways to be used as compensatory mechanisms. It's a little like taking back roads rather than a superhighway. It takes information longer to get there, but it gets there nonetheless. However, as Richek, List, and Lerner (1989) note, "even slow-tempoed individuals may profit by learning more efficient reading habits" (p. 269). If after adequate instruction and ample practice, students fail to make satisfactory progress, and it is obvious that the students have a slow tempo, you might work out strategies, including using nonprint sources of information, to help them compensate for this slowness (Roswell & Chall, 1994). For instance, they will need to plan adequate time for their reading, and they also need to focus on obtaining the most essential information. They should also be helped to understand why they read at a slower rate. Explain, too, that slowness in reading does not reflect on their ability to learn. Help them to understand that they can get get as much out of their reading as the speediest readers. It will just take them a little longer.

## *Increasing Reading Rate*

An excessively slow rate of reading could be a sign of an underlying difficulty. The text may be too difficult, or the student may be reading word for word.

Reading rate doesn't become a matter of concern until about grade eight or nine, when students begin to encounter increased demands to read novels and lengthy text books. Reading rate may be increased in a number of ways:

- Make sure students are reading materials on their proper level. To increase speed, try giving them easy materials.
- Teach students to use appropriate preparational and other strategies.
- Adequately prepare students before they begin reading.
- Build vocabulary so students don't stumble over difficult words.
- Foster purposeful, active reading.
- Eliminate unnecessary oral reading and questions that involve trivial details. These slow down reading.
- Build students' confidence in their reading.
- Check out excessively slow reading. See if you can determine its roots and then plan a program based on your findings.

Although tried in the past, eye movement exercises seem to have little value. Neither does telling students to skip unimportant words or to eliminate inner speech. Research suggests that we process just about every word as we read and that inner speech is a necessary part of reading. As Carver (1990) explains, silent speech is an aid to short-term memory.

## *Skimming and Scanning*

**Skimming:** reading at a rapid rate in order to obtain an overview or the gist of a passage.

In **skimming** students read rapidly to get an overview of the information in a piece of text. Readers skim when they just want to get the gist of a piece and aren't concerned about the details. A reader might skim an article to see if it has needed information. Inundated with information, we need, more than ever, to be adept at skimming so that we don't waste time poring over information that has little value to us.

Low-achieving readers tend to read everything at a slow rate. Introduce skimming to them when the task demands it: when they are reading an article to see if it contains useful information, or when they have limited time but need to get the gist of an article or chapter. You might model skimming by showing them how you rapidly go through notices and junk mail. Show how you toss away some pieces as soon as you see they don't apply to you, but others you read with care because they are important to you.

**Scanning:** reading at a rapid rate in order to obtain specific bits of information such as a name or a date.

**Scanning** is the fastest of the reading processes and involves going through material very rapidly to find a very specific piece of information: a telephone number, a name, a date, a fact. Again, teach this skill as the need arises. When checking on a fact in an article or story that students have just read, show students how you would scan the text until you found the information.

## A Balanced Program

As student progress through the grades, studying takes on more importance. Some students who were adequate readers in the lower graders experience difficulty because they have not acquired adequate study strategies. A balanced program should instruct students in the kinds of strategies they need to cope effectively with the demands made inside and outside of school. In addition to knowing how to use key strategies, students also need to know which strategies work best in particular situations.

## Minicase Study

Noting her low grades, Carmen's teacher discussed her performance with her and arranged for Carmen to obtain specialized help from the reading teacher. Through an informal interview and by using a think-aloud as Carmen demonstrated how she studied for quizzes, the reading teacher determined that Carmen was not studying efficiently or effectively. She had virtually no study skills and no specific goal, except to obtain passing grades.

The first thing the specialist did was to help Carmen set specific learning goals for each reading assignment. She also helped Carmen set up a study schedule and determine the best time and place to study.

Noting that Carmen seemed to lack confidence and didn't give herself credit for what she did know, the specialist used KWL Plus with her. Discussing what she knew and deciding what she wanted to learn helped Carmen personalize her learning. As Carmen's comprehension and sense of personal involvement grew, the specialist introduced SQ3R. Emphasis was placed on preparing for the types of questions that the teacher typically asked in classroom recitations and written tests.

Carmen was also instructed in the use of text structure to help her comprehend and organize key ideas in science and social studies, the two areas in which she was having most difficulty. As Carmen progressed, the reading teacher helped her construct information maps based on her SQ3R notes. The reading teacher also showed Carmen how to use the information maps to prepare for quizzes and tests.

Carmen's grades gradually improved. As Carmen began to see rewards for studying, she put more effort into her work, and by year's end she was passing all subjects.

## *Summary*

In order to study effectively, students must know themselves as learners. They must be able to size up a learning task, set reasonable goals, and have a solid grasp of effective study strategies.

There are three approaches to studying: principles (understanding), organization, and association. The most widely used study strategy is SQ3R: survey, question, read, recite, review, to which a sixth step, reflect, is sometimes added. SQ3R is an organizational strategy. Other organizational study strategies include various forms of notetaking, and information maps.

Because notetaking is a complex activity, novice note takers might take notes in the form of semantic maps or webs before adopting a two-column or three-column style. Instruction in taking notes from text should precede instruction in taking notes from lectures, which is a more difficult task.

Associational memory devices include mnemonic approaches: rhymes, acronyms, and acrostics.

Poor study habits are a major cause of academic failure. Assessing students' study strategies and habits, building students' knowledge of self as a learner, instructing, coaching, and counseling are techniques that can help to improve students' study habits. However, ultimately students must take responsibility for their own learning.

Motivation to study stems, in part, from seeing that one's studying pays off in the form of higher grades. Knowing how to take tests is a functional lifeskill for students. Students need to know that a study plan for an objective test will be different from a study plan for an essay test. Reducing test anxiety should be a component of test preparation instruction.

Disabled and achieving readers are often hindered by an excessively slow rate of speed. An important element in reading efficiently is adjusting rate of reading to purpose for reading.

## *Application Activities*

1. Try out SQ3R with some material that you wish to learn. Use it for at least five sessions. Assess its effectiveness. What are its advantages? What are its disadvantages?
2. Try out an information map. What are its advantages? What are its disadvantages?
3. Use the acronym, acrostic, or rhyme strategies to learn facts. Do they seem to be useful techniques? Do you think they would be helpful for low-achieving readers? Why or why not?
4. Teach one of the study strategies covered in this chapter to a disabled reader or a group of low-achieving readers. Assess the effectiveness of the lesson.

# Chapter 15

# Building Writing Strategies

## *Using What You Know*

Beset by difficulties in organizing their ideas and frequently handicapped by poor spelling and illegible handwriting, low-achieving readers find writing even more difficult than reading. The process approach, with its emphasis on the message as opposed to the mechanics, is a powerful tool for teaching disabled writers and will be emphasized in this chapter. Focus will also be placed on presenting strategies that have proved to be effective with low-achieving readers and writers.

How do you feel about writing? What kinds of writing do you find relatively easy? What kinds do you find difficult? What strategies or routines do you use to help you write? How would you go about helping low-achieving writers?

## *Anticipation Guide*

Read each of the following statements. Put a check under "Agree" or "Disagree" to show how you feel about each one. If possible, discuss your responses with classmates.

| | Agree | Disagree |
|---|---|---|
| **1.** Good writers are born, not made. | ______ | ______ |
| **2.** If you can say it, you can write it. | ______ | ______ |
| **3.** The more planning you do beforehand, the better the writing. | ______ | ______ |
| **4.** The hardest part of writing is revising. | ______ | ______ |
| **5.** The major problem most young students have with writing is spelling. | ______ | ______ |

## *The Writing Process*

Writing is both more complex and more abstract than talk. When people talk to each other, they are aided by cues to start, to stop, to continue, to clarify, or to elaborate. When composing, writers are on their own (Bereiter and Scardamalia, 1982).

An effective way to help novice and underachieving writers develop needed skills is by teaching writing through a process approach, one that grows out of oral language but which gradually develops into a more complex language system. As with developing reading skills, the emphasis is on building on what students know. And that means digging deeply. When working with problem writers, it's easy to be stopped cold by surface features and go no further. You need to look beyond awkward wording, dysgraphic handwriting, bizarre spellings, random use of capital letters, and look into the message the students are attempting to convey and the processes they are using. The process approach to writing emphasizes composing and revising and puts mechanics in perspective so that they don't become the be-all and the end-all of writing instruction.

**Writing process:** model of teaching writing that views writing as being composed of planning, composing, revising, editing, and publishing.

The five elements in the **writing process** are prewriting—which includes all that is done in preparation for writing—composing, revising, editing, and publishing. Although these elements are listed separately, they operate in circular or recursive fashion. Before I write, I plan and prepare, but actually I'm composing in my head as I plan, and as I write I might revise and even edit and also plan what comes next. I might do much of my planning after I've started writing. I may not even know what I'm going to write until I've actually written it. Fiction writers report being motivated to write so they can see how the story comes out. With this type of writing, characters often take on a life of their own.

### *Prewriting*

**Prewriting:** part of the writing process that includes all the things that a writer does before composing, including selecting a topic and planning.

**Prewriting** consists of all those things that a writer does to prepare for writing. It could take ten minutes, or it could be an idea that someone's been mulling over for ten years. The core of prewriting is topic selection. If students are going to invest time and energy and put themselves into their writing, they must have a sense of personal involvement in their writing. The best topics are those that students select for themselves because they have a personal interest in them and about which they know a great deal or want to explore.

#### *Modeling Topic Selection*

Since underachieving writers may have limited experience selecting topics, model the process for them. For instance, if the students are writing about famous Americans as part of a biography unit, list some of the people you might want to write about. List four or five names on the board and think aloud your reasons for your choices as in the following example:

Martin Luther King
Sally Ride
Roberto Clemente
Thomas Edison

Give an honest appraisal of which one you would like to write about. You might give the pros and cons of each topic, saying, "I know Martin Luther King worked hard for justice and equal rights and Sally Ride was the first women astronaut and Roberto Clemente was an outstanding baseball player and tried to help poor people, but I'm most interested in Thomas Edison. He went on to become one of the most famous inventors of all time, but I heard that he had trouble with school. I'd like to find out more about his growing up days and write about that."

Lacking confidence in underachieving writers, teachers often supply them with topics and wonder why their finished products are brief and devoid of creativity.

Sources of topics are endless. Students can write about their everyday lives: what they've seen, heard, or read about in class or outside of school. This might be a class trip, an interesting project, being the new boy or girl in class, the school principal, a guest speaker, a piece of information in a science or social studies book, or an article in *Sports Illustrated for Kids.*

Notebooks provide their owners with the opportunity to collect ideas and information over a period of time before setting out to write. Choosing a topic becomes a matter of selecting ideas that have had time to ripen.

Research is another possibility. Students can explore topics about which they have limited knowledge but which interest them: they can explore and write about how to take care of a new puppy, how to grow tomatoes, or how CD-ROM works. They can find out more about sharks, deserts, or the stars. They can write to their favorite basketball player or singing star. They can interview their grandparents to find out about life in the 1950s or talk to a dietitian about eating the right kinds of foods. You might also encourage students to talk to family members and friends about possible topics and also to keep a notebook or file of possible subjects. The writer's notebooks are a place to generate ideas, explore topics, or jot down observations (Calkins & Harwayne, 1991).

A good way to introduce the concept of a writer's notebook is to read excerpts from yours or those of past students who have given you their permission to do so. Also discuss the kinds of things that students might record in their notebooks: an unexpected snowfall, making a new friend, wondering what the new neighbors will be like, observations of a bird building its nest, playing a game of basketball, a reaction to a frightening story or TV show, or simply recording an interesting word or phrase encountered in reading or conversation.

**Freewriting:** technique of writing spontaneously, without taking the time to plan or reflect on, or shape, one's writing.

Another way of generating writing ideas is to try freewriting or guided freewriting. In **freewriting,** students write for a specified period of time, usually about ten minutes. They can write on any topic, and they should write as rapidly as they can without stopping. The basic idea of freewriting is to break up the logjam of ideas and let the ideas flow. Freewriting also promotes fluency by demonstrating to students how much they can get down on paper when they are not concerned about organizing their thoughts or worrying about the mechanics of writing.

If students find freewriting too open ended, they might try guided freewriting. In guided freewriting, you supply students with a word and they take it from there. They jot down whatever associations the word elicits. Almost any word will do: *Saturday, money, pizza, mud, cats, mornings, TV, noise.* After freewriting or guided freewriting, students might find an idea or feeling that they wish to expand into a full-length piece.

If students are really stuck for a topic, you might suggest some surefire generic topics. For instance, play the song, "My Favorite Things" or read the book *Honey, I Love* (Greenfield, 1978) and talk over your favorite things or the things that you love. Then have students make a list of their favorite things and develop it into an autobiographical piece.

Reading is also a rich source of topic ideas. A brief article about bird watching or seeing eye dogs may motivate students to explore this topic and report on their findings. In their notebooks, students might also record favorite passages, realistic characters, unusual settings, imaginative phrases, and humorous or wise expressions that might become the basis for future writing.

### *Planning*

Drawing can be a rehearsal for writing. Moore and Caldwell (1991) devised a program in which students drew story boards showing characters, setting, story events, and main ideas before composing their pieces.

After a topic has been selected, students gather and organize information. This is a crucial step for underachieving writers. Their compositions are typically very brief, suggesting that they lack adequate content knowledge or they were unable to make use of the knowledge they do have (Graham & Harris, 1993). They may not realize how much information they have on a topic or may have difficulty organizing it and putting it in written form. To help students make use of information that they already possess, drawing and brainstorming are effective techniques. Drawing helps younger students encapsulate their ideas. When they write in response to a drawing that they have created, the drawing provides them a stable prompt for suggesting what details they might develop. Tapping as it does another dimension, drawing also helps students retrieve details that they may not have thought of. After J. L. Olson (1987) encouraged her students to draw illustrations of their subjects before writing about them, the detail in their written pieces increased markedly. An essential element in the procedure was discussion. Olson discussed students' drawings with them before they began writing. This helped them translate into words details recorded in their drawings.

### *Brainstorming*

An effective technique for helping students access details is to have them brainstorm the topic. The stimulus for brainstorming can be the topic or a single word. Model the process, emphasizing that in brainstorming you come up with as many ideas as you can think of. Students are then encouraged to brainstorm. Urge them to listen to ideas expressed by others because that may help them think of other ideas.

### *Rehearsal*

A valuable planning technique is to provide students with time to mull over their topics. Before they begin composing, professional writers may have rehearsed the piece they are about to write for days or weeks or even years. When they sit down at their desks, they are ready to write. They have already shaped the piece in their minds. Encourage students to **rehearse** topics. Try giving them previews of writing assignments a day or so ahead of time, so that they have time to think over possible topics and how they might develop them.

**Writing rehearsal:** practice of mentally composing a piece before actually writing it down.

### *Audience*

An important part of planning is considering the audience. Novice writers have a difficult time adjusting their writing for an outside reader. Being egocentric, they believe that if they can understand it, so can anyone who happens to read it. To help build audience awareness, discuss the concept of audience before students start writing. Ask such questions as: "For whom are you writing? Who will read your piece? What will you need to tell your readers so they will understand your piece?"

In the past much of the writing that students did in school was for the teacher. Students wrote to complete an assignment or to be evaluated. This limited the range of the student's writing. In today's schools, students write real pieces for a variety of audiences.

## *Composing*

Hindered by poor spelling ability, labored handwriting, and a negative association with writing, disabled writers may scrawl a sentence or two before calling it quits. The first order of business when working with low-progress writers is to emphasize content over mechanics. Stress with these students that the important thing in a first draft is to get one's thoughts down as quickly as possible and not to worry about spelling, punctuation, capitalization, handwriting, or the appearance of the paper. Tell students to spell as best they can. You might show them examples of first drafts in which the author may have used one or two letters to represent whole words or used invented spelling (see Chapters 5 and 7 for more information on invented spelling). Explain that there will be plenty of time to check spelling, punctuation, and capitalization, but that will come later.

**Composing:** act of writing. The focus should be on getting one's thoughts down rather than creating a finished, error-free piece on the first attempt.

Model the **composing** process for students and show them some rough drafts that you have written in which wholesale changes have been made. If students need more convincing, invite reporters from the local newspaper or other professional writers to talk to the class about how they write their first drafts. If labored handwriting is a serious problem, you might try having students dictate their pieces or use a word processor if they have adequate keyboarding skills.

As students compose, they may reach a point where they can't seem to continue. Encourage them to seek additional information, or they may have a conference with a peer, with you, or with a writing group. These conferences serve some of the same functions in eliciting more writing that speaker–listener interactions in conversations do. They help elicit output. It's also a good idea, as students write, to circulate around the room, providing support for students or brief miniconferences that help them access additional information. If students are still stuck, they might consider putting the piece aside and coming back to it or trying another topic.

### *Writing Conferences*

**Writing conferences:** meetings between student and teacher or student and peer editor for the purpose of discussing the student's writing.

The ultimate purpose of **writing conferences** is to help students discover that they have something to say (Murray, 1989). Through careful questioning and responding, the teacher affirms the students' efforts. Through the conference, students discover and clarify what they plan to do with their pieces and explore processes that might be used to attain their goals.

The key to the conference is listening (Graves, 1983). You must listen intensely, with an absolutely open mind, for it is in the conference that the student reveals the processes

Graves (1983) comments: "Listening is hard work . . . It isn't easy to put aside personal preferences, anxieties about helping more children, or the glaring, mechanical errors that stare from the page. I mumble to myself, 'Shut up, listen, and learn!' " (p. 100).

that he is using in his writing, the struggles that he is having, and personal perceptions that may be hindering his progress. The student who mumbles that no one will want to read his piece may be revealing a deep negative attitude about his writing, an attitude that may be inhibiting the flow of creative energy and free expression. Another student may reveal through a look of chagrin that she is ashamed of her poor handwriting or rudimentary spelling.

Conference questions help students become aware of the processes they are using so they can exert greater control over them. After students have solved a writing problem or finished a piece, you might ask questions that lead them to reflect and comment on the processes they have used: "Your new ending is more interesting. How did you go about writing it?" (Graves, 1983).

Conference questions are of three general types: opening, following, and process (Graves, 1983). Opening questions are ice-breakers designed to start the flow of the conference. These are open-ended, non-threatening inquiries: "How is it going? What are you writing about? Where are you now in your piece?" Following questions are designed to maintain the flow. Often, they are simply restatements or summaries, in question form, of what the student has told you: " You're having difficulty getting started?" or "Your team lost the championship game and you feel you're to blame?" or "You like your new school but miss your old friends?" As their name suggests, process questions focus on the writing process itself. Process questions might be of a general nature: "What do you think you'll do next? What do you want to do with this piece? Where will you start? What part do you like best? Is there a part you aren't happy with?" Or the questions can be more specific: "What happened after this? Can you explain this? As a reader, I'd like to know more about this. What can you do to make your beginning stronger? Can you think of a different way to say this?" (Turbill, 1982).

## *Revising*

**Revising:** procedure in the writing process in which the writer reviews what has been written and makes changes in content and expression.

Real **revising** means taking a fresh look at what you've written and asking yourself such basic questions as: "What am I trying to say here? Have I said what I want to say? Have I said all that I want to say? Is my writing clear? Is it as fresh and vivid as I can make it? Does it sound right? Does it feel right? Do all the parts fit?" Over time and with experience and feedback, students will develop an ear for their prose. An inner voice will tell them that something is amiss, that the piece doesn't sound or feel right.

There's a saying among writers that, "There's no such thing as bad writing; there's only bad revising." Most writers revise and revise and revise some more.

To help students gain a sense of what it means to revise, model the process. Show them how you add or delete details, rewrite sentences, move elements around, change words. However, focus on those aspects of revising that your students can handle. In the past, students were reluctant to revise because it meant recopying the entire piece. Demonstrate to students shortcuts they can take. Show them how they can use copy editing marks: arrows to move elements, carets to add. They can cross out items or even manually cut and move elements. If possible, demonstrate how a word processor might be used in the revision process. One of the advantages of using word processors is that the mechanics of revising are made so much simpler.

As students look over their rough drafts, encourage them to see if they have any questions about what they wrote. Have them put themselves in the readers' place and ask: "Would the readers understand what I'm trying to say? Have I told the readers enough? Would the readers want to know more?" Often, the major problem with disabled writers' pieces is that they haven't told enough. They have supplied a few barebone facts without elaborating.

When modeling the revising process, focus in on key items that the class as a whole seems to need. For instance, if students aren't including enough details in their pieces, then demonstrate adding information. Also alert students to the fact that revisions can sometimes be less effective and less clearly written than the original. Encourage students to reread their piece after they've revised it to make sure the revised version sounds better than the original.

### *Distancing*

Professional writers wait a day or even longer before revising. This puts emotional **distance** between them and the piece, so they can look at it more objectively. Advise students to put their pieces away for a day and then take another look at them. As students revise their pieces, encourage them to play the role of the reader and read the piece, not as the writer would read it, but as the prospective reader would. Reading the piece aloud also helps. And, of course, students should seek reaction to their piece from a writing partner, peer-editing group, or the teacher. Although writers should thoughtfully consider all suggestions, they should have a sense of ownership of the piece. They should feel free to accept or reject suggestions. The quality of the piece is the writer's responsibility.

> **Distancing:** process of allowing time to pass between the writing of a piece and looking at it to assess its merit or need for revision. Distancing fosters increased objectivity.

## *Editing*

> **Editing:** process of making corrections in a written piece. Often there is a focus on mechanical errors rather than on making changes in content.

Up until this point, the focus has been on the content of the piece. Emphasis was rightfully placed on composing rather than on the mechanics of writing. In this final step, students edit their pieces for mechanical errors. Normally, in the **editing** process all errors are corrected. Since disabled writers tend to make an excessive number of errors, you may choose to focus on just one or two areas of concern. However, if pieces are to be published, then you may want to have all errors corrected.

As with the other conventions in writing, capitalization, punctuation, and usage should be taught directly and related to the writing that students are doing. To decide which elements to teach, examine students' first drafts to see what is needed. Focus on one element, capitalization of proper names, or question marks, for instance.

### *Editing Strategies*

Once you have analyzed students' errors, discuss with them the kinds of mistakes they make. Keeping in mind any error patterns that you note, teach them strategies for minimizing errors and detecting those that do crop up. If students mix up the order of the letters in words, have them slowly and carefully read the piece exactly as it is written so that "turly," would be read as *turly* and the student would note that the word was misspelled. If students omit endings, have them check the endings of words. If students omit syllables, have them pronounce each syllable in any multisyllabic words they have written. Also students might circle any words that they feel might be misspelled.

### *Skills Lessons*

While group skills lessons should be taught on a regular basis, also provide instruction as needed on an informal basis. Whether taught as part of whole-group direct instruction or a repair-it-on-the-spot basis, skill instruction works best if it is taught when needed. As students edit, it is helpful if they have a checklist to help them. Checklists can be generic, or they can be individualized and geared to the needs of specific students. A sample editing checklist is presented in Figure 15-1.

For older students, you might provide them with a mnemonic strategy for editing, such as SCOPE:

*S* - Spelling: Is the spelling correct?
*C* - Capitalization: Are the first words of sentences, proper names, and proper nouns capitalized?
*O* - Order of Words: Are the words in the right order?
*P* - Punctuation: Does each sentence end with a period, question mark, or exclamation mark? Are commas and apostrophes placed where needed?
*E* - Express Complete Thought: Is each sentence complete? Does each sentence have a subject and a predicate? (Bos & Vaughn, 1994)

## *Publishing*

Writing real pieces for real people is an essential element in the writing process. Instead of writing textbook-prescribed bread-and-butter notes to aunts and uncles who don't exist, students should be writing real thank you notes, composing real letters to real friends who have moved away and so forth. Also, students should be writing stories and articles that will be discussed in a writing group, shared with a partner, placed on the bulletin board, put in the class or school newspaper, or published in a collection of school writings to be put in

1. Is the piece clear?
2. Are the sentences complete?
3. Does each sentence end with a period, question mark, or exclamation point?
4. Is the first word of each sentence capitalized?
5. Are the names of people (George, Uncle Fred) and places (New York, U.S., Main Street) capitalized?
6. Are all the words spelled correctly?

**FIGURE 15-1 Editing Checklist**

the class or school library. Writing for a variety of audiences causes students to grapple with the problems of making themselves understood to people having varied backgrounds. There is some evidence that writing for a real audience changes the nature of students' writing. For instance, several studies of poor writers in the intermediate and secondary grades found that these students expressed themselves effectively when writing on their own to peers or family members. Ironically, many of these same students had been judged to be poor writers on the basis of performance on school-related writing tasks (Dyson & Freedman, 1991).

**Publishing:** part of the writing process in which students share their writing in some way. The piece could be printed in a booklet or newspaper, or it could be read or dramatized.

Developing as a writer requires getting a response to one's writing. One of the advantages of **publishing,** or showing one's writing, is that it invites feedback. Without feedback, the writer has no way of gauging whether or not her or his work was understood and enjoyed by the audience. Response from others also helps students learn to see their writing as others see it, which builds a sense of audience. Through audience reaction writers can see which parts of their pieces are most effective and which parts may need clarifying or elaborating. Disabled as well as average writers need opportunities to both receive and supply response.

## *Writing Programs for Low-Achieving Readers and Writers*

Although the research on the writing of low-achieving readers sometimes paints a picture of students who have little knowledge of the writing process (Englert et al., 1988), intervention research by a number of experts portrays a very hopeful scene. In one study, neutral examiners assessed pieces written by achieving and low-achieving readers and couldn't tell which were which. Incredibly, the pieces written by the low-achieving readers had the same high quality as those written by the achieving readers. What wrought this magic? A carefully conceived program known as Cognitive Strategy Instruction in Writing (CSIW) that makes generous use of scaffolding (Dixon, Carnine, & Kameenui, 1994).

### *Cognitive Strategy Instruction in Writing*

Cognitive Strategy Instruction in Writing focuses on using text structures to improve writing and features "conspicuous strategies." Through modeling and think alouds, the teacher demonstrates and makes visible the writing process and the strategies used in her or his own writing (Dixon, Carnine, & Kameenui, 1994; Raphael & Englert, 1990). Using modeling, coaching, discussion, and other techniques, the teacher focuses on the following features of process writing: topic selection, purpose (the kinds of questions the text might be expected to answer), identification of audience, brainstorming, use of text structure, grouping ideas, using key or signal words, revising, editing, and publishing. The instructional program was broken down into four phases: text analysis, modeling the writing process, guiding students, and providing opportunities for independent writing (Raphael & Englert, 1990).

A key feature in Cognitive Strategy Instruction in writing is the use of Think Sheets. A lesson explaining how Think Sheets are used is presented on the following page.

## Teaching CSIW

### *Step 1: Analyzing the Text*

Since low-achieving readers show little awareness of text structure, either in their reading or their writing, examining text structures is emphasized. Samples from basals, trade books, periodicals, or content-area texts could be used to illustrate a particular structure. It's also a good idea to use examples written by students, perhaps from previous years. As you analyze the text, which can be written on the board or chart or on an overhead, point out and discuss the following:

- the topic of the text
- its purpose
- the kinds of questions that the reader might expect the text to answer
- audience
- the text structure itself
- signal words that might be used in the text structure

You might also note some areas in which the piece might be improved. Perhaps, there is a part that isn't clear or a step may have been omitted from a process. Or signal words might be used to improve the comprehensibility of the piece.

### *Step 2: Modeling the Writing Process*

After analyzing and discussing the text, demonstrate the composing of an informational piece by writing one yourself. If a new game is to be introduced to the class, you might write a how-to-piece explaining how the game is to be played. As you go through the process, think aloud, so the class can see how you plan and compose a piece. Make explicit your sense of audience, your purpose for writing, strategies that you might use to help your planning, such as listing the steps in a process and indicating needed materials. Also talk about the text structure that you plan to use, why you are using that structure, and what might be some signal words that could be used to "glue" the structure together. Later, after a discussion with students, model the revising and editing processes.

### *Step 3: Introducing Think Sheets*

**Think sheets:** scaffolds which prompt students to use writing strategies that they have been recently taught. Gradually, think sheets are phased out as students take fuller responsibility for their writing.

As you model the process, introduce the concept of **Think Sheets.** These are prompts that help students plan, organize, revise, and edit their pieces. Each type of writing or text structure should have its own Think Sheet. Although sample Think Sheets are presented here, it should be emphasized that Think Sheets can take a variety of forms and should be tailored to meet the needs of your students.

Think Sheets might provide prompts for the following (Dixon et al., 1994):

- Who is my audience?
- What is my goal?
- What do I know about this topic?
- What can I tell the readers at the beginning to get them interested?
- What do I need to tell my audience so they will understand what I am trying to say?
- How can I group my ideas? (steps in a process, similarities or differences in a comparison/contrast piece, reasons in a persuasive piece, solution to a problem, causes of a problem, etc).
- What signal words might I use? (*first, then, because, and, but, however, moreover,* etc.).
- What might be a good ending sentence? (sum up, leave with a thought or question).

Depending on how much help students need, separate Think Sheets might be used for each major phase of the writing project. The Think Sheet in Figure 15-2 provides an example of prompts that a student might use to plan a piece. After completing a Plan Think Sheet, the student might then work on an Organize Think Sheet (Figure 15.3), which answers such questions as: What is being explained? What materials etc. are needed? What are the steps?

Author's Name ____________________________ Date ________________

Topic: ____________________________________

**Who: Who am I writing for?**

________________________________________________________________

________________________________________________________________

**What: What do I want to tell my readers?**

________________________________________________________________

________________________________________________________________

________________________________________________________________

________________________________________________________________

**How: How can I organize my ideas?**

_______ Explanation _______ Problem/Solution

_______ Comparison/Contrast _______ Other

_______ Main Idea/Details

**FIGURE 15-2 Plan Think Sheet**

Adapted from: *Cognitive Strategy Instruction in Writing Project.* C. S. Englert, T. E. Raphael, L. M. Anderson. East Lansing, MI: Institute for Research on Teaching, 1989.

Author's Name ____________________________ Date ________________

**What is being explained?** ____________________________________________

________________________________________________________________

**What materials are needed?** __________________________________________

________________________________________________________________

**What are the steps?**

First, ____________________________________________________________.

Next, ____________________________________________________________.

Third, ____________________________________________________________.

Then, ____________________________________________________________.

Finally, ___________________________________________________________.

**FIGURE 15-3 Organize Think Sheet (Explanation)**

Adapted from: *Cognitive Strategy Instruction in Writing Project.* C. S. Englert, T. E. Raphael, L. M. Anderson. East Lansing, MI: Institute for Research on Teaching, 1989.

Once both the Plan and Organize Think Sheets have been completed and discussed, students write their rough drafts. When students write their rough drafts, they write them on colored paper. This is a reminder that they are writing an initial draft, one that must be revised before being copied onto white paper.

***Revision Think Sheets***

When students first wrote information pieces using CSIW, their topics tended to deal with everyday activities. In time, they used their newly acquired writing skills to compose subject-matter pieces.

The last two major think sheets are the Self-Editing and Revision Think Sheets. Self-Editing Think Sheets are filled out by students before they submit their pieces for peer editing. After having conferences with peer editors, students use the Revision Think Sheet to complete a plan for revising the piece. The Self-Editing Think Sheets have three concerns (see Figure 15-4). After asking writers to tell what they like best, the Self-Editing Think Sheet requests that writers reexamine their pieces and note any parts that they might want to change. Writers are then asked to list any questions that they have for their editors.

The Revision Think Sheets ask students to note their plans for revision because the researchers found that, unless they make specific plans, students tend to simply recopy their papers, making only a few surface revisions, despite having gone through self-editing and peer-editing procedures (Raphael, Englert, & Kirschner, 1989). When carefully monitored and guided, peer editing also provided students with a sharpened sense of audience, which in turn may lead to more substantive revisions. When a peer editor states that he would like to know more about a topic and that a part of a piece is not clear, then the writer is more likely to add information and clarify. A Revision Think Sheet is shown in Figure 15-5.

***Guiding Students***

After writing three pieces with decreasing amounts of assistance, students are asked to write a final piece on their own.

Students write several pieces under your guidance. Students are asked to use the text structure being studied but are free to write on any topic that makes use of that structure. The first paper may be composed by a group. The second paper can be written by individual students, but the students receive extensive teacher and peer support. A third paper is also written by individual students, but the students take increased responsibility for their work. However, peer or teacher support is provided as needed (Dixon et al., 1994). Gradually students learn to write pieces that incorporate two or more text structures.

In using CSIW, it should be kept in mind that the heart of the program is the modeling and careful guidance that the teacher provides and the guided sharing in which the students engage. The think sheets are simply helpful scaffolds that prompt students to use strategies that they might not have been able to apply without some guidance or which they may have overlooked. In time, students should be helped to incorporate the strategies prompted by the think sheets so that they are able to use the strategies on their own, without the reminders provided by the think sheets.

## *Harris and Graham's Strategy Instruction*

Strategy instruction is also the centerpiece of a writing program for disabled writers devised by Harris and Graham (1992). However, the Harris-Graham program is broader than CSIW.

Author's Name ____________________________ Date ________________

1. After rereading my paper, what do I like best?

_____________________________________________

_____________________________________________

2. Did I tell what was being explained?

_____________________________________________

_____________________________________________

3. Did I tell what materials were needed?

_____________________________________________

_____________________________________________

4. Did I write down all the steps?

_____________________________________________

_____________________________________________

5. Is each step clearly explained?

_____________________________________________

_____________________________________________

6. Did I use signal words?

_____________________________________________

_____________________________________________

7. What parts do I want to change?

_____________________________________________

_____________________________________________

8. What questions do I have for my editor?

_____________________________________________

_____________________________________________

**FIGURE 15-4 Self-Edit Think Sheet (Explanation)**

Adapted from: *Cognitive Strategy Instruction in Writing Project.* C. S. Englert, T. E. Raphael, L. M. Anderson. East Lansing, MI: Institute for Research on Teaching, 1989.

Whereas CSIW focused on text structure, the Harris-Graham program includes a wide range of strategies and emphasizes the setting of goals. A goal could involve any aspect of writing from content to overall organization to mechanics. A student's goal could be to increase the length of her writing, include more suspense in a story, use questions for opening sentences, use more picturesque language, spell every work correctly, or use complex sentences 25 percent of the time, and so forth (Harris & Graham, 1992). Setting goals might be done on the basis of observing the students at work, discussing the students' past work, or asking the students to tell what aspect of writing they would most like to improve. Listed in the following box are suggested steps for strategy instruction as adapted from Harris and Graham (1992).

**Suggestions from My Editor**

What suggestions has your editor given you?

1. ____________________
2. ____________________
3. ____________________
4. ____________________
5. ____________________
6. ____________________

Decide on the suggestions you want to use. Put an X next to all the suggestions you would like to use in revising your paper.

**My Ideas for Revising My Paper**

Now decide on any other changes that you might like to make. Ask yourself:

Is there any way I can make my paper more interesting?

____________________

____________________

Is there any way I can make the paper clearer or easier to understand?

____________________

____________________

**Returning to Your Draft**

On your draft, make all the changes you think will make your paper better. Use ideas from the list above, from your self-edit think sheet, and any other ideas you have for your paper. When you are ready, you can write your final copy.

**FIGURE 15-5 Revision Think Sheet**

Adapted from: *Cognitive Strategy Instruction in Writing Project.* C. S. Englert, T. E. Raphael, L. M. Anderson. East Lansing, MI: Institute for Research on Teaching, 1989.

## A Lesson in Teaching Writing Strategies

> Strategy instruction is tied to students' goals. Once students have formulated a goal for their writing, they are taught a strategy that helps them to reach that goal.

### *Step 1: Introducing Strategies and Setting Goals*

Help students set individual or group goals. Once goals have been decided, explain what strategy instruction is. Explain that almost any operation that improves writing can be taught as a strategy. Discuss with students the strategies you use when you write. In collaboration with the students, you decide which strategy might be introduced to help them reach their goals. For instance, if the students have difficulty generating content and if their goal is to write more elaborated pieces, brainstorming might be chosen as a strategy to be presented.

*Continued*

**A Lesson in Teaching Writing Strategies** *Continued*

*Stage 2: Preskill Development*

Students are taught any skills needed to understand and apply the strategy about to be taught. For instance, if students are going to be taught how to use paragraph patterns to organize their writing, they would first need to be taught how paragraphs are organized.

*Stage 3: Discussion of the Strategy*

Explain the strategy, its steps, its value, and when and where it might be used. A very basic strategy that you might teach students is how to develop a paragraph using examples. You might have students examine pieces of writing in which examples are used to develop a topic. Discuss the paragraphs and the value of using examples to writing convincing pieces. Discuss when and where examples might be used. Have students tell how they might use the strategy in their writing.

*Stage 4: Modeling the Strategy*

Model the strategy using any prompts, charts, mnemonics, or other aids that students might find helpful. For instance, you might write a piece telling why you think your cat is smart. Model the process of writing the piece. Note the steps that you use in writing your piece:

*S*tate the topic.
*W*rite examples to prove the topic sentence.
*E*xplain each example,
*A*dd an interesting ending.
*T*ake a look at the piece to see if you have used convincing examples.

*Step 5: Providing Scaffolding*

Use think sheets, mnemonics, visual displays, or other devices to prompt students so that they follow all the steps. As incorporated into Stage 4, the mnemonic prompt for using examples is SWEAT. "With a little SWEAT, you can write an interesting piece." Using the mnemonic, students memorize the steps in the strategy.

*Stage 6: Collaborative Practice*

Students try out the strategy. During conferences, emphasize the strategy that has just been taught. Provide feedback and guidance. Feedback should be specific, "I like the way you used SWEAT to help you put three exciting examples in your piece."

Review sessions are essential. These remind students of the steps in a strategy and provide opportunities for fine-tuning and adapting strategy use.

*Stage 7: Application*

Students apply the strategy on their own. However, review sessions are held to refine strategy use and to foster transfer.

## *CRISS Writing Strategies*

Using writing as a means of learning is emphasized in CRISS (*CR*eating *I*ndependence through *S*tudent-owned *S*trategies), an exemplary program designed to help students learn content area materials. Highly successful with low achieving readers and writers, the writing component of CRISS stresses direct instruction and plenty of support for the learners. One form of support is the use of a series of highly structured writing formats including framed paragraphs, opinion/proof paragraphs, and RAFT, a procedure that focuses on four major aspects of writing (Santa, Havens, & Maycumber, 1996). CRISS writing strategies can be taught within the framework of the Lesson in Teaching Writing Strategies that was explained earlier in this section.

### *Framed Paragraphs*

Framed paragraphs should be presented in such a way that, over time, they require more and more input from students until, ultimately, students don't need to use them anymore.

The most highly structured form of writing is the framed paragraph. Framed paragraphs provide the main idea of the piece, indicate how many details the piece will contain, supply transition words, and may even provide a conclusion. While providing a maximum of support, framed paragraphs show students ways of organizing their ideas. A sample frame paragraph is shown in Figure 15-6. Also refer to the Exemplary Teaching Lesson to see how one teacher made use of her version of framed paragraphs.

### Exemplary Teaching: Building on Interests

Discouraged by years of perceived failure, Jason, a seventh-grader, decreed that he would no longer write. No more essays or book reports. Not even journal entries. He couldn't write, and that was that. Capitalizing on Jason's interest in baseball, his corrective specialist, Carigan-Belleville (1989) asked him how his team had done on the previous Saturday. After discussing the game with him, she asked if he would give her three reasons why his team deserved to win. After Jason did so, she suggested that he put that in writing, using the following format:

Question: Who won Saturday's baseball game?

Five-sentence paragraph:

1. Topic sentence (answer to the question)
2. Reason #1
3. Reason #2
4. Reason #3
5. Conclusion (restate topic sentence in different words) (pp. 57–58)

Although the format might have hindered the free expression or creativity of some young writers, it was just what Jason needed. Using clear cues and a highly structured format, Jason was able to write a paragraph successfully.

Later, Jason started using story starters such as "If I had more money . . ." Jason also began writing in his journal. In addition, Carigan-Belleville arranged for Jason to dictate his stories into a tape recorder, using the taped versions as a kind of rehearsal for the written pieces. Jason's willingness and ability to write improved significantly. As a side benefit, Jason also became more interested in reading.

Starting a Coin Collection

If you want to start a coin collection follow these steps.

First, ______________________________.

Next, ______________________________.

Then ______________________________.

Finally, ______________________________.

Once you've followed these steps, you'll have a hobby that you can enjoy for many years to come.

**FIGURE 15-6 Frame Paragraph**

The opinion/proof format can be used with other kinds of writing: cause/effect, problem/solution, main idea/details.

### *Opinion/Proof*

If students seem to need extra support for their writing, you might have them try an opinion/proof piece. The opinion/proof is a basic type of writing in which students back up an opinion with evidence or reasons. Opinion/proof pieces can be used in connection with informational text or as the basis for developing a piece on any topic.

To structure an opinion/proof piece, the student divides a sheet of paper in two. The opinion is placed in the left-hand column. The proof is placed to the right. Once the opinion has been stated and the proof written down, the student can then develop his piece. As students write their pieces, they should be encouraged to elaborate so that the piece they write isn't just a restatement of the outline. They also need to compose a conclusion. A sample opinion/proof piece is shown in Figure 15-7.

### *RAFT*

**RAFT:** structured approach to writing that helps students focus on four key elements: **R**ole of the writer, **A**udience, **F**ormat, and **T**opic.

When writing essays for content area subjects, students often turn in pieces that lack clarity and depth, two flaws that are occasioned by an assignment that is too general and too vague (Santa, 1988). **RAFT** is an approach that sharpens the writing by helping the student focus on four elements: *r*ole of the writer, *a*udience, *f*ormat, and *t*opic. RAFT pieces can be written from the student's viewpoint, but quite often they are not.

**R** Role of the writer. The writer can be an historical figure, a scientist, president, rock star, lawyer, police chief, or even an animal or inanimate object.

**A** Audience. Typically students write for the teacher, so that their pieces tend to be bland. The audience could be a judge, a legislator, future generations, the people of the world, an historical figure, a sports star, parents, or whomever else the writer might want to address.

**F** Format. The piece could be a letter to the editor, an essay, a news story, a TV script, a diary entry, a speech, a memo, or whatever format seems appropriate.

**T** Topic. The statement of the topic is accompanied by a strong verb so that it is an expression of the writer's purpose: **demand** a refund for a faulty product, **persuade** a radio station to let the town's teens have an hour show each week, **convince** an investor to back your new invention.

To introduce RAFT, explain its purpose and components and model writing a RAFT piece. Once students understand RAFT, brainstorm possible topics. The topics might fall under a general theme. For instance, if you are studying immigration, have students suggest possible RAFT pieces: a ship owner composing an ad persuading Italian peasants to sail to America, an Irish teen describing in a letter to his parents his or her first few days in Boston, an editorial writer hailing the newcomers.

In time, students should create their own RAFT topics. They should also go through all the stages in the writing process, including revising, editing, and publishing as well as preplanning and composing. Refer to the Minicase at the end of the chapter to see how RAFT was used to help an extremely reluctant writer.

| Opinion | Proof |
|---|---|
| Basketball is the best sport. | Basketball has a lot of action.<br>Basketball can be played just about anywhere.<br>Basketball can be played inside or outside.<br>You don't need a lot of equipment to play basketball.<br>You don't need a lot of people to play basketball.<br>Anyone can play basketball. |

In my opinion basketball is number one. Basketball has lots of action. There's no standing around like there is in baseball. You can also play it just about anywhere. You don't need a huge field. All you need is a hoop. And you don't need a lot of fancy equipment. All you need is a ball. And you don't need to get together a crowd of people before you can play. You can play with any number from two to ten. You can even shoot some hoops on your own. You can't beat basketball. It's the champion of sports.

**FIGURE 15-7 Opinion/Proof Paragraph**

## *Collaborative Strategy Approach*

Less structured and more student-centered than the three previously presented systems, the collaborative strategy approach combined instruction in writing strategies and text models. Students' writing was related to their reading. After completing a selection, students would note the kinds of information covered in the text and the text's structure. Students would then decide how they might use the kinds of structure and information presented in the text in their own writing. For instance, if the author used a problem–solution organization in a selection the students had read, the students would talk over problems they have and possible solutions. Using the selection they had read as a model, they would then compose a problem–solution piece (V. Anderson and Henne, 1993).

At the beginning of the Collaborative Strategy Instruction study, students were reluctant to write. At the end of the four-month period, the students were writing four to six double-spaced, typed pages (V. Anderson and Henne, 1993).

A key element in the approach was the use of a teaching segment known as writer's craft. From a selection that had just been read, students would examine, discuss, and use a stylistic device. Stylistic devices included writing interesting topic sentences; paragraphing; elaborating by supplying causes, effects, reasons, examples, or descriptions; using a vivid vocabulary; developing character using dialogue; using signal words to indicate time-order or other relationships; and using any of a variety of other stylistic devices.

Writer's craft consists of strategies and so can be taught within the framework of the Lesson in Teaching Writing Strategies explained earlier in this section.

## *Why the Programs Work*

Although the four programs for low-achieving readers and writers vary in the way they are organized and implemented, they have several essential procedures in common. All four incorporate direct instruction and emphasize strategies and writing process. All four provide additional support in the form of frame paragraphs, planning sheets, mnemonic reminders, or collaborative instruction and discussion.

All four of the programs also met with encouraging success. This success presents a clear message. When low-achieving readers and writers are provided with a carefully planned, thoroughly implemented, supportive program of writing instruction, they improve, sometimes dramatically. Students respond positively to techniques or strategies that make it easier for them to apply their skills.

## *Motivating Reluctant Writers*

Understandably, low-achieving readers and writers frequently are extremely reluctant to write. If they do write, often it's just a sentence or two composed entirely of words that they can spell. Three kinds of writing that are especially effective for helping students overcome their reluctance are freewriting—which was explained in the beginning of the chapter—written conversation, and journal writing.

### *Written Conversation*

**Written conversation:** writing improvement technique in which a teacher and student talk to each other on paper. Instead of speaking words to each other, they write them.

An effective technique for promoting fluency is arranging for the student to talk to someone on paper. A **written conversation** is generally between the teacher and the student. You and student sit side by side. You might initiate the conversation by posing a written question that helps the student describe an event or idea: "How is your basketball team doing this year?" After the student reads your question, she or he responds in writing. You reply with another written question and the student answers it with a written response. Sitting at a round table, you might carry on a written conversation with a small group of students. While one student responds to your written query, you can write a note to a second student. As students grow in proficiency, they can converse in writing with each other. The activity could also be extended into writing letters or leaving computer messages (Rhodes & Dudley-Marling, 1988).

Written conversations work well with problem writers because you gear your writing to each student's level of reading and writing proficiency and also take into consideration each student's interests. In addition, through modeling good writing, you provide scaffolding so students can move up to higher levels of writing performance. Written conversations are also non-threatening. Although a written conversation can be as brief as a single sentence, output generally increases as a result of using this device. Written conversations also have a positive effect on reading (Rhodes & Dudley-Marling, 1988).

### *Journal Writing*

**Journal:** daily record of events, thoughts, ideas, or feelings.

**Journal** writing allows students to respond to their world in a personal way. In their journals, they can react to something they've learned in school, discuss an exciting TV show or a Little League game in which they played a key role, or describe the acquisition of a new pet. Through journal writing or the use of writer's notebooks discussed earlier in the chapter, students can explore topics and techniques. It helps them discover that the events in their lives are worth writing about. Journal writing promotes fluency and exploration. Because journal writing is personal, it should not be subject to revision or correction. Focus should be on the message, not the mechanics.

### *Forms of Journals*

Journal writing can serve a number of purposes and take a variety of forms from personal diary to a semi-structured learning log. A personal journal is one in which students keep a record of events in their lives and their reaction to them. It is important to have a clear understanding about the privacy of journals. In some situations, no one reads the journal except the writer. In others, the student marks those entries that are private and those that the teacher may read. And in still other situations, all entries are open to the teacher.

**Dialog journals:** written exchanges in which students share thoughts with teachers or peers and are frequently used as a way of responding to and discussing literature.

**Dialog journals** are a two-way communication between teacher and student. The student writes and the teacher responds. Although dialog journal entries tend to center on school matters and academic issues, they may also include descriptions of trips the student is taking, plans that she or he has for the future, and other topics.

Journal entries can become humdrum. Like every other human endeavor, you and the students get out of journal writing what you put into it. Model journal writing for students. Keep a journal yourself and share it with students. Discuss possible topics for journal writing or areas that might be explored. Read excerpts from children's books in which a diary or journal plays a prominent role. Some possibilities are listed below:

Anderson, J. (1987). *Joshua's Westward Journey.* New York: Morrow.
Brisson, P. (1990). *Kate Heads West.* New York: Doubleday.
Cleary, B. (1983). *Dear Mr. Henshaw.* New York: Morrow.
Cleary, B. (1991). *Strider.* New York: Morrow.
McPhail, D. (1992). *Farm Boy's Year.* New York: Atheneum.

### *Reading Response Journals*

Journals are also used for specific purposes. One specific use is to provide a forum in which students can respond to their reading. Through writing students explore their reading. Writing provides both the time and the solitude that can lead to a deeper reflection on the impact of a selection. To initiate a **reading response journal,** model the process and provide students with some sample questions that might touch off a response. For younger students and students with severe reading problems, you might want to start off with a single question: "What did you like best about the story?" or "What did you like the least?" After students get used to responding, encourage them to ask questions of their own: "What questions, if any, do you have about the story?" Gradually add other questions: "Was there anything about the story that surprised you? Would you recommend this book to a friend? Why or why not? What do you think will happen next? What do you think the main character should do?"

**Reading response journal:** form of dialog journal in which readers reflect on their reading and compose a written response.

**Learning log:** written account of a student's learning recorded by the student.

### *Learning Logs*

Similar to reading journals, **learning logs** are designed to help students respond to and reflect on their learning. The writing is in response to questions or situations posed by the teacher. The writing should only take about ten minutes. It is not to be corrected, but it should count (Atwell, 1990).

To foster a more reflective response from students reading informational text, have them use a KWL format in their learning logs. For **K,** they can survey the chapter's headings and tell what they know about the topic; for **W,** they tell what they would like to know; for **L,** what they learned and still had questions about (Cantrell, 1997).

Learning logs are academic. Although students can respond personally to what they are learning, learning logs are not a forum for discussing personal problems. Learning logs can fulfill some of the functions of KWL Plus (see Chapter 13 for a description of KWL Plus). Students might record what they know, what questions they have, what they want to know, and what they have learned. Students can tell what their new learning means to them and how they might use it. Learning logs might also incorporate scientific observations, results of experiments, a description of how math problems were solved, results of interviews, plans for a report, answers to questions posed by you, or responses to questions that the class brainstormed. Logs are most often written as narrative entries but can include drawings, charts, graphs, geographical maps, time lines, semantic maps, or frames. The following list contains a sampling of possible prompts for the writing of learning log entries. For a more complete list, see Atwell (1990).

- How do you think geography affected the lifestyles of the different Indian groups? List as many ways as you can think of.
- List as many habitats as you can.
- If you could change one thing about our community, what would it be?
- Brainstorm a list of words that have to do with deserts.
- List the names of the explorers we've read about so far. Which is your favorite? Why?
- Draw a simple map with a key.
- If you could stand on the ocean floor, what do you think you would see? (Atwell, 1990, Appendix B).

## *Spelling*

To individualize spelling instruction, have students work with a partner on seven or eight high-frequency words each week.

Spelling can be a twofold problem. If a student is spending an excessive amount of time trying to figure out how to spell words, then there is less cognitive energy left for composing the piece. Poor spelling may inhibit the writer in another way. Ashamed of poor spelling, the writer might not look beyond the spelling to the story she or he is trying to tell. What is needed is a three-pronged approach. In addition to providing systematic instruction in spelling and extra support, focus on the content of the writing so that the student doesn't let spelling restrict her writing or, worse yet, begin to equate poor spelling with poor writing.

## Teaching Spelling

A program for teaching spelling should be individualized, since students' abilities in spelling vary greatly. The program should be based on the student's current level of functioning in spelling and an analysis of the kinds of errors made. To find a student's current level of spelling ability, administer a Spelling Inventory from the *Classroom Reading Inventory* (Silvaroli, 1994), the Gentry Spelling Grade Level Placement Test (Gentry, 1997), or another source. The student's instructional level is the highest level at which at least 50 percent of the words are spelled correctly. However, the student's level of spelling only tells part of the story. Also analyze the types of errors students made to get a sense of the kinds of processes the students are using to spell words. Note, too, the stage of spelling in which the student is operating. As discussed in Chapter 5, Research conducted by Henderson (1990) and his colleagues (Templeton & Bear, 1992) indicates that students' spelling develops in stages. By knowing what stage a student is in, the teacher can build on that knowledge and teach spelling more effectively. The Elementary Spelling Inventory, which can be found on pp. 121–123, can be used to estimate students' spelling stage.

Other routes to learning to spell include *rules* (drop final *e* before adding *ing*, as in *riding*), and *analogy* (a word whose spelling is unknown may be spelled by analogy with a known word (*grew* is spelled by analogy with *new*) (McAlexander, Dobie, & Gregg, 1992).

### *Spelling Routes*

Spelling can be accessed in two major ways, through an auditory or visual route (McAlexander, Dobie, & Gregg, 1992). Using the auditory route involves translating sounds into letters: /w/, /i/, /n/ is spelled w + i + n. Using the visual route the writer is guided by the appearance of the word so that *night* is spelled n + ight. Expert spellers are apparently better able to make use of the visual route to spelling. Although they may also use other routes and use a variety of strategies for spelling words, they have a highly developed ability to visualize the spelling of a word. Poor spellers, on the other hand, tend to use an auditory route, spelling words the way they sound (Gentry & Gillet, 1993). As a result, poor spellers often misspell very basic words, such as *before, like, green,* have difficulty spotting misspellings in their written work, and have difficulty retrieving the correct spellings of words they have studied and were able to spell correctly on spelling tests (Gentry & Gillet, 1993).

Low-achieving writers misspell a large proportion of words. What's more, their spellings might be so far off the mark as to be unreadable (McAlexander, Dobie & Gregg, 1992). Although the spelling of most low-achieving spellers is phonemic, guided more by sound than sight, some poor spellers apparently overuse the visual route. When analyzing spelling errors, ask the following questions:

- Does the student seem to be using mainly an auditory or a visual route?
- Is the student applying spelling rules?
- Is the student misspelling high-frequency words?
- Are some apparent misspellings due to faulty handwriting?
- Is the student making careless errors? (Bos & Vaughn, 1994).

It's also a good idea to note what kinds of strategies students use to help them spell words correctly. Do they attempt to visualize it? Do they try to go through it sound by sound? Does writing it out seem to help them? See, too, if they attempt to correct misspelled words in their written pieces. If they do, what strategies do they use? This information can be obtained through observation and through interviews with the students.

Spelling should be taught as part of a total language arts program. The approach to teaching spelling should be conceptual. Students need to see phonemic and morphemic relationships among words. As Hodges (1991) comments:

> *Providing for spelling instruction as though the ability to spell is only a product of memorizing specific words fails to acknowledge that, like the acquisition of other language behavior, much of what is learned about spelling is gained by noticing recurring patterns encountered in functional settings and trying out and revising hypotheses about these patterns in other writing situations. (p. 781)*

Wide reading is important to spelling because it introduces students to a variety of words in a variety of contexts, which provides a basis for establishing relationships among words (Zutell, 1979). Extensive writing is important because it provides varied opportunities for applying spelling skills, including proofreading. However, neither wide reading nor wide writing will automatically produce good spelling. Systematic instruction is also required (Hammond, 1995).

Words chosen for spelling instruction should be those that students need in their writing. If students are about to write about football, the spelling words might include: *football, sports, kickoff, score, quarterback, half-time,* and similar words. High-frequency words should also be presented. In order to help students see patterns in words, it would also be helpful to present high frequency patterns (a listing of patterns can be found in Table 9-8 on pp. 231–233).

When introducing new words to poor spellers, use active teaching procedures, such as the test-study-test method. In this method, students take a pre-test, study the words they missed, and then take a retest. It is also important to teach students a strategy for studying words. A popular strategy, which emphasizes seeing the word in the mind's eye, is the Fitzgerald Method (Fitzgerald, 1951).

1. Look at the word carefully.
2. Say the word to yourself.
3. Close your eyes and picture the word.
4. Cover up the word and write it.
5. Check the spelling.
6. If the word is misspelled, repeat steps 1–5.

If students' spelling programs are individualized, you may want to have them work in pairs or small groups. As part of their group activity, they can test each other. Short periods of practice, no more than ten or fifteen minutes, work best. As part of the spelling program, teach rules, but only teach those rules that are easy to apply and which cover a large number of words. Highly useful rules include the following:

- Drop final *e* when adding *ing*: *riding*
- Double the final consonant when adding an ending beginning with a vowel: *planning.*

### *Sorting*

A valuable activity for fostering a conceptual understanding of spelling is word sorting, especially if the sorting is geared to the students' level of spelling development. If students are in the letter–name stage and are having difficulty deciding whether words that begin with an /s/ sound are spelled with a *c* or an *s,* then they might engage in sorting activities in which they categorize words according to whether they begin with an /s/ sound, regardless of spelling and then sort /s/ words according to their spelling. Instead of memorizing rules about the use of *c* and *s* to spell /s/, students form their own generalizations.

In the within word–pattern stage, students can, through sorting, form generalizations about the use of final *e* and digraphs to spell long-vowel sounds. In the syllable juncture stage, students might, through sorting, form a generalization about when to double the final consonant when adding *ing* or *ed.* In the derivational constancy stage, students might discover when to use the prefixes *im, in, ir,* and *un.* As they group words and construct understandings that they wouldn't have developed if they had just been looking at words individually, students develop a deeper understanding of the spelling system, and, in the process, become better decoders as well as better spellers.

In addition to conceptual understanding, all students, but especially poor spellers, need lots of practice. Often students will spell a word correctly on a test but misspell it when writing a letter or story. This may indicate a lack of fluency. The student may not have had enough practice with the word (Trathen, 1995). Moreover, some words just seem to be especially troublesome. Students might keep an alphabetical list of troublesome words in a small spelling notebook for handy reference (Roswell & Chall, 1994).

### *Electronic Aides*

Students should be shown how to use the spell checkers incorporated into most of today's word processing programs. Hand-held electronic spelling aids such as *Spelling Ace* (Franklin) and *Elementary Spelling Ace* (Franklin) might also be introduced. When users type in misspelled words, these devices use data about typical patterns of phonetic misspellings to help the learner locate the correct spelling of the misspelled word. They also feature spelling games and have the capacity to store words for later review.

## *Handwriting*

> Previously, students were taught letter formation and then taught to write. Today, students are urged to write as best they can. As they experience what writing is and have a need to form letters, then letter formation is introduced.

In forming a manuscript *y,* Benjamin starts from the bottom and moves his pencil upward. After completing the longer line, he then completes the letter by starting the second stroke at about the midpoint of the first stroke. As with the first line, the second line is made from bottom to top. Although recognizable, Benjamin's *y* is poorly formed. In general, Benjamin's handwriting is marked by poorly formed letters, poor spacing, uneven lines, and a number of mirror image letters. Benjamin also has a serious reading problem. Because of difficulty learning letter–sound relationships and whole words, eight-year-old Benjamin is operating on a beginning reading level, despite having average intelligence.

Because writing makes heavy demands on memory, discrimination, perception, and fine motor skills—areas in which low-achieving readers are often weak—reading problems are frequently accompanied by deficiencies in handwriting. Because instructional time is limited and handwriting seems a less vital skill than reading, handwriting instruction may be condensed or neglected. However, if taught as a functional part of the overall language arts program, handwriting could reinforce a number of skills necessary for reading. For instance, Benjamin has a poor sense of directionality, frequently reverses letters, and, on occasion, forgets what a letter looks like. Good handwriting instruction would help Benjamin proceed in consistent fashion from left to right and top to bottom. A focus on proper letter formation would also help him to commit to memory the shapes of letters. This should help alleviate mirror images of letters and help him to remember letter forms. If tied in with phonics instruction and composing activities, handwriting can be used to reinforce and extend writing and reading instruction. Last but not least, legible handwriting can build self-esteem. Although students' reading difficulty may go undetected, handwriting is on display for teachers, parents, and peers to see. Legible handwriting can be a source of pride. And as a practical matter, students are often judged, rightly or wrongly, on the quality of their handwriting. All other things being equal, neatly written papers receive higher grades than barely legible ones. See Chapter 5 for suggestions for assessing writing.

Letter formation is taught as a means for improving the appearance and legibility of writing. The focus remains on the quality of the ideas and their expression.

## *Minicase Study*

One student in George Rusnak's class had had such bad experiences with writing that when asked to write, he responded, "Fail me if you want, I won't write!" Wisely, Rusnak decided to take two important steps: find out why the student's attitude toward writing was so negative and provide a structure that would help the student feel that he could be successful.

Rusnak started off the writing unit by asking: "What are your experiences with writing?" As students related their experiences with writing, most of which were negative, Rusnak talked over some of the bad experiences he had had when he was a student and how he coped with them.

Rusnak then introduced RAFT to support the students' attempts to write. To get students started, Rusnak provided them with an intriguing writing activity.

**Role** - worm in an apple
**Audience** - farmer
**Format** - persuasive letter
**Topic** - explaining to farmer why he shouldn't take the worm's apple

This lighthearted assignment was followed by one in which students took the role of an historical character and was related to the students' study of history. The piece had to be factual but affective. The student's personal involvement had to be evident. Supported and motivated through three drafts, the youngster who would rather fail than write transformed a 72-word empty letter into a 423-word superbly written piece. A writer was reborn (Rusnak, 1994).

## *Summary*

The five elements in writing process are prewriting, composing, revising, editing, and publishing. Prewriting includes topic selection and planning. An important component of the planning process is considering one's audience. Composing is the creation of the written piece. When composing, students should focus on the message rather than the mechanics. Rehearsing what one plans to write can aid the composing process. Revising is an essential but often neglected part of the writing process. True revising involves taking a fresh look at what one has written and making substantive changes, if necessary. Editing involves checking and correcting mechanical errors. Publishing is an important element in writing because it provides the student with a genuine purpose for writing and helps the student gain a sense of audience. Although presented separately, the elements in the writing process overlap and several may occur simultaneously.

Instruction in writing is carried out through modeling, formal and informal lessons, and conferences. A major purpose of writing conferences is to help students discover that they have something to say.

Four exemplary writing programs for low-achieving readers and writers include: CSIW (Cognitive Strategy Instruction Writing), Collaborative Strategy Instruction, Harris-Graham's program, and CRISS writing. Although the details of implementation vary, the programs all provide direct instruction in the use of strategies and support in the form of planning sheets, mnemonics, frames for writing, and/or discussion.

Journals, logs, and writer's notebooks provide opportunities for disabled writers to apply their skills in a personal way. Freewriting and conversational writing also promote fluency in written expression. All four—journals, logs, freewriting, and conversational writing—can be sources for topic ideas.

Although the focus in writing is on the message, mechanics are also important. Spelling instruction should be individualized, since students' achievement in spelling varies considerably. In addition, disabled writers need both formal and informal instruction in the mechanics of writing, with emphasis on those elements for which a need is demonstrated. Low-achieving readers and writers may also need special help with handwriting.

## *Application Activities*

1. Observe a writing class or workshop in action. Note the organization of the class and the major activities in which the students are engaged. What do you like best about the class? How might it be improved?

2. Design a planning sheet similar to those created in CSIW, or plan a strategy lesson similar to those described by Harris and Graham. If possible, present the planning sheet or strategy and evaluate its effectiveness.

3. Use RAFT, opinion/proof, or another structured writing device to write a piece. Evaluate the effectiveness of the device. How might these structured devices help low-achieving writers? How might they be inhibited by them?

4. Design a rubric for scoring a piece of writing that your students have written or will write. Try out the rubric. Revise it in the light of any shortcomings that you note. Also select from your students' writing anchor pieces that illustrate each of the rubric's categories.

# Chapter 16

# Severe Problem Cases, Students Acquiring English, and Older Students

## *Using What You Know*

Most low-achieving readers will learn to read if taught by the methods described in previous chapters. However, about one low-achieving reader out of one hundred has such a severe difficulty learning to read words that she or he may need to be taught through special word learning techniques. Two of the best known word-learning techniques are the VAKT (Visual, Auditory, Kinesthetic, Tactile) and Orton–Gillingham approaches, both of which involve tracing or writing words. Word Building, an approach described in Chapter 9, has also been used successfully with students who have severe reading problems.

Both VAKT and the Orton–Gillingham approaches have been in use for a number of years. Because they are tedious for both student and teacher, they are also somewhat controversial. However, because both techniques have been used successfully with students with the most serious reading problems, it is important that you have an understanding of them. You may have students with whom you wish to try the techniques because everything else you have attempted has failed. Even if you decide not to use the techniques, you should be aware of them since they are in fairly widespread use. If, for instance, you are a classroom teacher, and the LD teacher is using the Orton–Gillingham approach with one of your students, you can better support the program if you know something about it. In addition, many of the "new" corrective techniques are built on either VAKT or Orton–Gillingham. Portions of Reading Recovery, for instance, are based on VAKT (Clay, 1993b), and there are dozens of techniques based on Orton–Gillingham. You are in a better position to assess a new technique if you understand the principles on which it is based.

Teens and adults who have reading and writing problems often bring with them a long history of failure and may have a can't-do attitude. It is important that they see themselves as competent learners and adopt a can-do outlook. Students who are still acquiring English and are struggling with reading and writing face the dual task of learning a new language and overcoming reading and writing difficulties.

What is your experience with students who have severe reading problems? Have you ever taught or known students who couldn't seem to learn new words no matter how carefully they were taught? Have you worked with older problem readers or students whose struggle to learn to read and write is compounded by their struggle to master a new language?

## Anticipation Guide

Read each of the following statements. Put a check under "Agree" or "Disagree" to show how you feel about each one. If possible, discuss your responses with classmates.

| | Agree | Disagree |
|---|---|---|
| **1.** If properly taught, all students can learn to read. | ________ | ________ |
| **2.** Word-learning techniques that use tracing are successful because they establish additional connections in memory. | ________ | ________ |
| **3.** Generally speaking, learning words sound-by-sound or part-by-part is a better approach for low-achieving readers than learning them as wholes. | ________ | ________ |
| **4.** The older a low-achieving reader is the harder she or he is to teach. | ________ | ________ |
| **5.** If possible, students who are still acquiring English should be taught to read in their native language. | ________ | ________ |

## The Need for Specialized Techniques

A small percentage of low-achieving readers, approximately one reader out of one hundred (McCormick, 1994), seem to have such extreme difficulty learning printed words or letter–sound relationships that they may need to be taught through specialized programs. One such student is Martha.

Although she had high average intelligence, eight-year-old Martha was making very little progress in reading. Because Martha was experiencing difficulty learning to read new words, she was referred to a nearby university reading clinic. Despite intensive one-to-one instruction, she made very limited gains. Martha seemed to forget the high-frequency words she was taught soon after they were introduced. After a year of supplementary instruction, Martha was only reading on a primer level. She was able to read only nine out of twenty first-grade high-frequency words on an informal reading inventory word lists test.

## *VAKT Tracing Technique*

The struggle to learn to read was taking its toll on Martha. A vivacious youngster on the playground, she was quiet and subdued during her reading lessons. She seemed discouraged and was putting forth less and less effort. Feeling somewhat desperate, her teacher decided to try a technique that she had recently learned in her corrective reading methods class: the VAKT (Visual-Auditory-Kinesthetic-Tactile) tracing technique (Johnson, 1966). **VAKT** is an adaptation of the **Fernald** tracing technique (Fernald, 1943), which is estimated to be the most widely used approach for teaching corrective reading (Tierney, Readence, & Dishner, 1995). VAKT is a language–experience approach. As students attempt to write letters to relatives, summarize selections that have been read to them, describe experiences they have had, label diagrams or make written observations about scientific experiments, they learn the words they don't know by seeing, saying, hearing, and tracing them (VAKT) or, in later stages, by seeing, hearing, and saying them (VAK). Although most words are learned in a writing context, some words from reading selections may also be learned through VAKT or VAK.

Both the **Fernald** and **VAKT** techniques use visual, auditory, kinesthetic (sense of movement), and tactile senses to help the student concentrate on the words and to compensate for weak modalities.

Long touted by experts in the field of reading difficulties (Clark, 1988; Clay, 1993b; Fernald, 1943; Johnson, 1966; Johnson & Kress, 1966; Manzo & Manzo, 1993; Roswell & Chall, 1994), the tracing technique worked as promised. Revived by her initial success and the support of her sensitive teacher, Martha was soon learning new words with enthusiasm. Within just four weeks, she learned to read more than fifty words, which was nearly as many words as she learned in two full years of schooling.

An essential element in Martha's success was the enthusiasm of her teacher, who made learning interesting and fulfilling and affirmed Martha's successes.

A technique of last resort, VAKT is recommended only for students who have serious word learning problems. While most students have no difficulty learning to read by seeing and hearing, a small percentage of the population has such a serious difficulty learning to associate printed symbols with the words they represent that they need special methods that use kinesthetic (sense of movement) and tactile (sense of touch) as well as visual and auditory stimulation. In her guidebook on Reading Recovery for teachers, Clay (1993b) advises using a tracing approach with students who aren't learning words by visually analyzing them or by reconstructing them with magnetic letters. "If visual analysis and word reconstruction do not produce good results, introduce tracing and add the feel of the movements to the child's sources of information" (p. 56). Being a method quite different from those typically used, VAKT can offer students a sense a getting off to a fresh start. It has the potential of removing "the overlays of encountering materials and techniques that have caused failures in the past" (Lipson & Wixon, 1991, p. 527).

### *Signs of Need*

The major sign that VAKT is needed is the failure to learn or remember printed symbols despite adequate ability and opportunity. A candidate for VAKT stands out because he is very slow at learning printed words and, even after apparently learning them, soon forgets them.

Jonathan, when tested at age twelve, knew fewer than half the words on a primer list. Awilda had to trace the word *where* twenty-five times before learning it, but was unable to recognize it when she encountered it in a story minutes later. There may also be signs of stress associated with reading. Obviously distressed when her teacher handed her a book, one gifted student who had a serious word learning problem blurted out, "Excuse me! We're not going to read, are we?"

## *Prerequisites for VAKT*

Although designed for students who have the severest reading problems, VAKT does have a number of prerequisites (Johnson & Kress, 1966). The child must be able to hear, see, say, and trace the words. A child with a profound hearing loss would not be able to use the technique. In addition, the learner would need enough phonological awareness so that she or he could detect separate syllables in a word. Since the technique also involves tracing and writing letters, the child should also know how to form most of the letters of the alphabet.

## *Introductory Stage of VAKT*

VAKT works, in part, because both the teacher and learner believe in it (Johnson & Kress, 1966). The purpose of the introductory stage is to show the student how the technique works and, more importantly, to convince the student that by using it, she or he can learn to read words.

In introducing the technique, you will need the following equipment:

> The purpose of the introductory stage of VAKT is to acquaint the student with procedures for using the technique and to demonstrate that this technique will enable them to learn.

- a dictionary
- a large black crayon
- a number of strips of 4″ × 12″ paper
- a stapler
- a recording sheet

### *Establishing Rapport*

As you establish rapport, find out whether the student is left-handed or right-handed. Both teacher and student should be seated side by side, and the student should be able to observe the teacher as she or he traces new words. A right-handed teacher working with a right-handed learner would sit to the student's right. You should also determine whether the student uses cursive or manuscript handwriting. Although Fernald (1943) and Johnson and Kress (1966) recommend cursive because there is smoother flow and better sense of the wholeness of words written in cursive, manuscript is preferred by some because it matches the print that students will read.

Once you have established rapport with the learner, explain the technique. Tell the student that she will be using a new way to learn to read and spell words, one that a lot of bright students just like herself have used. Invite the student to suggest a word that she would like to learn. Tell the student that it can be a long word or a difficult word, any word that she would like to learn. One student requested that he be taught how to spell his last name. Up until that time, he had been using an initial to signify his surname. The student was ten years old.

### *Using the Dictionary*

Except for proper names, all new words are looked up in the dictionary. This ensures that accurate syllabic division is obtained and familiarizes the student with the dictionary. Involve the student in the task by asking the student what letter the word begins with and where it might be found in the dictionary. The student might also be asked to turn to the section in the dictionary where the word might be found. If looking up the word *tiny,* the student would locate the *t*'s and not the word *tiny* itself, since this would involve knowing how to spell the word and would also be too time-consuming.

Before looking up the word, ask the student how many parts (syllables) it has. Then look up the word and tell the student whether she or he is right or wrong. Alerting the student to watch carefully, you say the word and write it in blackboard-size script on a strip of 4″ × 12″ paper placed horizontally. Say each syllable as you initiate the writing of the syllable. If using cursive, cross *t*'s and dot *i*'s from left to right and then say the whole word once more. Also underline the separate syllables (as in Figure 16-1) if the word is multisyllabic. With your index and ring fingers, trace the word. Continue demonstrating the tracing technique until the student feels that she can do it.

### *Student Tracing*

The student traces the word until she feels she can write it from memory. Tracing should be conscientious and accurate. Unless the student is totally involved in the process, it will not work. Do not allow any inaccurate tracings. Inaccurate tracing includes faulty tracing of the individual letters. For reference, have a cursive or manuscript chart available. If the student begins to trace a manuscript *b* by going around and up, stop the student and show her how to trace it. The tracing should be accompanied by an explanation, "When I trace *b,* I start at the top, come straight down, and then go up and around." In addition to seeing that tracings are accurate, make sure that the student

- says the whole word
- says a syllable as she or he begins to trace the syllable
- dots *i*'s and crosses *t*'s after tracing the whole word (If the student is using manuscript writing, the *i*'s are dotted and the *t*'s crossed as they are formed.)
- says the whole word again

> Martha had to trace the word *dinosaur,* one of her introductory words, 25 times before she was able to write it correctly. However, as time went on, she required fewer tracings to learn words.

If the student skips a step or fails to follow the procedure exactly, stop her immediately. A major aim of VAKT is to establish correct habits, so you want to avoid reinforcing erroneous responses. The student may ask for a demonstration if her tracing procedures are not accurate, or may undertake additional tracings. Or you may suggest additional tracings or demonstrations, if you feel these are needed.

Manuscript | Cursive

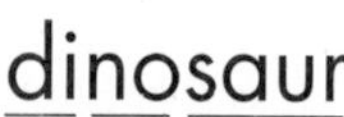


*dinosaur*

**FIGURE 16-1 Model Word Prepared by Teacher**

*Writing from Memory*

Once the student feels that she knows the word, she writes it twice from memory. With the teacher's copy being turned over, the student writes the word in normal-size script across the top of a second strip of 4″ × 12″ paper positioned vertically. The student compares her or his copy with the model copy. If correct, the student covers her writing with a third sheet of 4″ × 12″ paper and writes the target word once more. If the word is again written correctly, the student copy is dated and stapled to the teacher copy. It is then filed in a box that has alphabetic dividers. If the student has difficulty, she may be asked to trace the word again.

When tracing words, Martha tended to say them sound by sound: /m/-/y/-/s/-/e/-/l/-/f/. However, in VAKT, words are pronounced syllable by syllable: /my/-/self/.

*Keeping Records*

Records should be kept of words learned and number of demonstrations and tracings. (The symbols used to record the student's performance are presented in Figure 16-2.) These records provide an ongoing means for monitoring progress and can also be used as a basis for deciding when to move into another stage. The record displayed in Figure 16-3 shows that the word was presented in the introductory stage and indicates that the teacher demonstrated the tracing five times. The student traced the word correctly seven times in succession, then traced the word incorrectly twice in a row, but finally traced the word correctly twice in a row.

Students remain in the introductory stage until they have mastered the tracing procedures. Some students may enter Stage 1 after tracing just one or two words. Others may need additional experience and should not be rushed.

## Subsequent Stages of VAKT

**Stage 1**

In terms of tracing procedures, Stage 1 is identical to the introductory stage. The major difference is in the source of the words to be learned. Words learned in the introductory stage are chosen by the student. Words to be learned in Stage 1 are those the student needs to know for her writing.

*d* demonstration tracing

| accurate tracing

↾ partial tracing—Student was stopped because of faulty procedures.

✓ correct writing of word from memory

✓^ incorrect writing of word from memory

**FIGURE 16-2 VAKT Symbols**

*dinosaur (I)* *d d d d d* | | | | | | | ↾ ↾ | |

**FIGURE 16-3 VAKT Record**

VAKT is the word-learning component of a language-experience approach. The student may be composing a letter, a set of instructions, a shopping list, an account of a trip she has taken, or a summary of an experiment. After the experience has been discussed and organized, the student dictates what she plans to write. You record the student's dictation. After the story has been recorded, you then dictate it back to the student. Any words that the student is unable to write are presented, traced, and written from memory just as in the steps of the introductory stage.

As used in VAKT, the language experience approach has an added step. After being scribed by the teacher and read by the teacher and student, the teacher dictates to the student, who then scribes the story.

Here is how Martha, the student taught at a university literacy center, was helped as she composed an experience story. Martha told about going swimming in a pool, which the teacher wrote down and then read back to her.

> When I go swimming, I walk in the water first. Then I swim under the water. I hold my breath and get the diving sticks from my mom. Sometimes I get the sticks at nine feet. I like to do this because it is fun.

Now that the story was composed, Martha began the physical writing of it. Following the teacher's oral reading of the first sentence, Martha was able to write the first three words "When I go," but asked for help with *swimming.*

*Teacher:* "How many syllables do you hear in *swimming*?"

*Martha:* (after some hesitation) "Two?"

*Teacher:* "We'll check and see. Do you know where in the dictionary it might be?"

*Martha:* "In the middle."

*Teacher:* "Open to it."

After opening to *s,* Martha handed the dictionary to the teacher, who located the word and reported: "Here it is. You were right. *Swimming* has two syllables. Watch me while I write it for you."

Because it is based on student-dictated stories, VAKT can be used with disabled readers of all ages, including adults.

After some demonstrations and several practice tracings, Martha was able to write the word correctly twice. Although Martha was able to write a few words such as *I, go, when, the, my, get, at, to,* and *do,* she needed to trace most of the words in the story.

At the end of each session, words that had been learned by tracing were underlined. After the session, the selection was typed so Martha would have the opportunity to see it in print. Newly learned words—those that had been underlined—were typed in list form. On the following day, Martha read the words that had been put in list form and the portion of the experience story that had been typed. Words that Martha forgot were practiced once more. When Martha missed a previously learned word, she retrieved it from the file—which provided incidental practice with initial consonants and alphabetical order—traced it and again rewrote it twice from memory. The additional spelling attempts were dated and stapled to the original attempts.

When the student reads the previous day's words typed in list form, the student's performance is noted just as on the word lists test of an informal reading inventory. Performance is recorded on a photocopy. If the student can't read the words in isolation, she or he is given the opportunity to read them in the context of the experience story. A sample experience story with words underlined is shown in Figure 16-4.

My Puppy

My new puppy is small now. He is just nine weeks old. He eats a lot of food, and my dad says he will grow fast. My puppy is a St. Bernard. When he is all grown up, he will be the biggest dog in the neighborhood.

**FIGURE 16-4 Sample VAKT Story**

In addition to tracing and using new words in stories, numerous opportunities should be provided for the student to read newly learned words in other contexts. These contexts might include rhymes, poems, songs, recipes, and similar pieces. Target words should be mixed with known words so that the student is almost sure to be successful (Johnson & Kress, 1966).

## *Moving from One Stage to Another*

As students gain skills and learn words with greater ease, they move to more advanced stages. Signs that students are ready to move to a more advanced stage include fewer repetitions and less reliance on the word-learning technique that is characteristic of that level. Signs that a student in Stage 1 is ready to move into Stage 2 include: needing fewer tracings before learning a word and learning an increasing number of words with no tracing at all. The student would be demonstrating the ability to learn words by looking, saying, and hearing rather than by looking, saying, hearing, and tracing. If students in Stage 1 say they can learn a word without tracing it, give them the opportunity to do so. Have them simply look at the word and say it. As they near the completion of Stage 1, students may use VAKT with some words and VAK with others. The transition from Stage 1 to Stage 2 is made when students can learn all their new words without the use of tracing.

### *Stage 2:*

Stages 1 and 2 are the same, except that in Stage 2 the student is not required to trace. Since there is no tracing in Stage 2, 4″ × 6″ cards may be used instead of sheets of 4″ × 12″ paper. Instead of tracing the word, the student studies it from the card.

**Steps in Stage 2**

*Step 1: Identify*

The word to be learned is identified. The student asks for the word or makes an error as she or he attempts to write it.

*Step 2: Analyze the Word*

You ask how many parts or syllables the word has. The student checks the word file to see if the word is there. If not, you and the student find it in the dictionary. Note how many syllables the word has and inform the student.

*Step 3: Review the Word*

If the word is in the file box, review the word. If the word is not in the file box, say the word, say each syllable as you write each syllable, and, after having written each syllable, say the word as a whole. Syllables are underlined.

*Step 4: Say the Word*

The student studies the word by saying it as a whole, saying each syllable, and saying it as a whole once more.

*Step 5: Spell the Word*

Student attempts to spell the word correctly twice on a second card, which is held vertically.

*Step 6: Use the Word*

Student writes the word in the story.

### *Stage 3*

In Stage 3, the student uses the dictionary as a model rather than the teacher-written copy. If the word is not in the file box, the student, with teacher's help, if necessary, locates the word in the dictionary and checks syllabication. The student studies the word from the dictionary, saying it as a whole, in syllables, and then as a whole. When the student feels that she or he has mastered the word, the student writes it twice on a 4″ × 6″ card held vertically. If new, the word is then written on the front of the card held horizontally and is filed. The word is then written in the story. Stage 3 is discontinued when the student no longer seems to need it.

## *Need for a Total Approach*

VAKT is just one part of a total program for students who have severe reading problems. While the focus of the explanation of VAKT has been on mechanical procedures, the approach includes providing opportunities for investigating topics of interest, composing experience stories, reading children's books, participating in discussion groups, and doing all the things that might be done in an exemplary classroom.

VAKT should also be combined with a systematic word-analysis program such as Word Building. Initial patterns to be taught might be those that the student needs in her or his writing. For instance, noting the word *might* and *night* in a story, the teacher might initiate a study of the *-ight* pattern. Johnson (1966) cautions that VAKT and VAK are not substitutes for the development of word-analysis skills. However, the sight words learned In VAKT may become the basis for teaching phonics and other word-recognition skills.

Along with VAKT, Martha used Word Building, read a variety of children's books, and composed stories using invented spelling.

Loudon and Arthur (1940), Pickary (1949), and Bartlet and Shapiro (1956) report successful use of VAKT. Meyer (1978) cites 16 additional sources of support for it.

As with any technique, the heart of VAKT is in the quality of the teaching. VAKT works best when the teacher carefully observes the student's learning strategies and builds on what he knows. If the student is using initial consonants, for instance, build on that strength. When that student is hesitant about writing a word, ask him to tell how he thinks it might begin. Also have the student use his knowledge of initial consonants to help locate words being looked up in the dictionary.

The overall program should be both systematic and incidental. Using Word Building or another phonics program, gradually introduce needed word analysis elements. However, also take advantage of opportunities that arise naturally. For instance, if the student dictates a story about a time when she and some friends had to start rowing to shore when the motor on their boat conked out but they got a tow from a passing Coast Guard boat, then do a spontaneous study of the *ow* and *oa* spellings of long *o*.

Multisensory processing results in multiple memory traces with the kinesthetic and tactile modalities reinforcing visual and auditory pathways (Hulme, 1981). VAKT also strengthens phonemic awareness.

## *Why Is VAKT Effective?*

In addition to establishing a kinesthetic and tactile link and focusing attention, VAKT provides structure and support, builds on what the student knows, instills confidence, and has high expectations for the student. The technique removes the association of failure by providing students with a method that they had never seen before. It is also firmly grounded in language development and the students' interests. Although written more than half a century ago, Fernald's 1943 text reads like a description of a whole language program for struggling readers.

## *Orton–Gillingham Approach*

A second kinesthetic-tactile technique is the one that grew out of the experimental work of Dr. Samuel Orton (1937). On the basis of many years of work with low-achieving readers, Orton concluded that there was a group of children who exhibited a tendency to reversals and "a failure to recognize words after repeated encounters" (p. 9). He ascribed their deficiency to *mixed dominance,* a failure of one hemisphere of the brain to establish dominance. As a result of these findings, Orton constructed a teaching method that relied heavily on sound-by-sound phonics and used kinesthetic-tactile stimulation. Movement helped to eradicate the confusion between letters, and most low-achieving readers did not seem to have any major difficulties in kinesthetic function. The use of movement also tended to maintain consistent left-to-right progression.

Orton recommended a teaching method that relied heavily on sound by sound phonics and used kinesthetic-tactile stimulation because movement helped to eradicate the confusion between letters.

**Orton–Gillingham:** specialized word learning technique that uses intensive synthetic phonics reinforced by tracing.

Based on Orton's theory, Anna Gillingham and Bessie Stillman created an approach to teaching problem readers known as the **Orton–Gillingham Approach.** A no-nonsense, highly structured skill-and-drill synthetic phonics technique, the Orton–Gillingham approach presents the isolated sounds of letters and then builds these individual sounds into words "like bricks into a wall" (Gillingham & Stillman, 1960, 1983, p. 40). Phonic elements are presented through a series of cards: white for consonants and salmon for vowels. The order of introduction is carefully structured. Each student has a set of cards and is drilled on them daily. Instruction is based on three associations: letter form and sound, sound of the letter and its name, sound of the letter and its written form.

In a typical drill, the teacher shows the letter, and the student supplies its sound. The teacher says a sound, and the student names the letter. The teacher says a sound, and the student writes the letter that represents that sound. After the sounds of the letters *a, b, f, h, i, j, k, m, p, t* have been taught, they are blended together to make words: *bat, hat, jab, it.* To avoid distorting consonant sounds, the student is encouraged to pronounce the first two sounds together /ba/ and then add the final sound /t/.

Ahead of their time, Gillingham and Stillman (1960, 1983) recommended a kind of invented spelling in which students are encouraged to write "with freedom quite regardless of spelling usages" (p. 147).

After learning to read a few words, spelling is initiated. The teacher says the word. The student repeats it, names its letters: *m a n,* writes each letter as he says it: *m a n,* and then reads the word: *man.*

Later on, this spelling technique will be used to teach nonphonetic or sight words. As in the VAKT technique, students use their kinesthetic and tactile senses. They say and write the words. However, there is a crucial difference. As you will recall, in the VAKT technique, the student says each word or syllable as a whole as she or he traces it. In the Orton–Gillingham, the student says the letter name as she or he writes the letter so that the association is between the name of the letter and its form. This is done, according to Gillingham and Stillman (1960, 1983), because words like *laugh* do not lend themselves to being pronounced letter sound by letter sound. One of the problems inherent in a letter-by-letter or sound-by-sound approach is that it fails to take advantage of the regularities that can be found in an approach that uses patterns.

After students accumulate enough words, they read sentences and stories composed of the words they have learned. Sentences and stories are read silently first and then orally. Students also learn a number of phonics rules.

Multisyllabic words are taught through presenting isolated syllables such as *sip, dit, em.* After learning a group of high-frequency syllables, students combine them into whole words.

## *Place of Writing*

Copying words is encouraged as is writing from dictation. As students copy words, they engage in S.O.S. (Simultaneous Oral Spelling or naming of the letters). As students write the letters, they name them. Copying, according to Gillingham and Stillman, helps students with their spelling and may lengthen their span of visual recall. Writing from dictation aids in lengthening their auditory span. Only sentences that contain words that the student knows how to spell are dictated.

Until students have grasped basic phonics, they are not supposed to do any reading outside of that assigned by their corrective teacher. As Gillingham and Stillman explain:

> *Since the core of this alphabetic approach is to establish the concept of words as built out of phonetic units, the first essential of our technique is to break down the pupils' attitude towards words as ideograms-to-be-remembered-as-wholes and to eliminate all guessing. To attain this end it is necessary to arrange for the corrective pupil to do no reading or spelling except with the remedial teacher. (p. 42)*

> Bradley and Bryant (1985) found that the Orton technique of S.O.S. (simultaneous oral spelling) was twice as effective as other techniques that they tried.

The above recommendation to prohibit reading runs directly counter to current theory and practice. So, too, does the suggestion that guessing should be eliminated. Today students are encouraged to make intelligent guesses when they encounter unknown words so that they don't get bogged down in excessive decoding but use all available word-analysis skills including context. Although apparently in widespread use, the Orton–Gillingham approach, in order to embody current research and practice, would need to be modified in the following ways:

- Start where the student is. Pretest the student with an IRI or similar instrument and begin instruction at the point where the student has difficulty.
- Instead of forbidding wide reading, encourage it. Students do learn to read by reading. However, make sure that students are given books on the appropriate level.
- Orton–Gillingham advocates skill and drill on isolated phonics exercises. Phonics instruction should be functional and contextual. Skills taught should be those that

are needed, and are best taught when students are about to apply them in reading or writing.

- The Orton–Gillingham technique requires learning a series of phonics generalizations. Eliminate or simplify the teaching of rules, except for the ones suggested in Chapter 9. Students make very limited use of rules when attacking unfamiliar words (Gunning, 1988b).

## *Other Orton-Based Approaches*

Designed as a preventive program for children at risk for reading or writing difficulties, the Slingerland program has adapted Orton-Gillingham techniques for whole-class use (Slingerland, 1971).

A number of synthetic phonics approaches have been built on the principles espoused by Orton. One of the best known is *Recipe for Reading.* Using a spelling approach to learning words, *Recipe for Reading* (Traub & Bloom, 1975) presents the names and, later, the sounds of the letters *c, g, d, l, m, h, t, a,* and *o.* After learning the names and sounds of these letters, students learn to spell words composed of these letters. After learning to spell the words, students read them on flash cards. After a stack of words has been mastered, students write dictated phrases and sentences containing the words. This is followed by the reading of storybooks containing words previously taught. The 220 Dolch sight (high-frequency) words are also introduced. A typical lesson starts with a phonics drill and is followed by work on sentence dictation and the reading of storybooks. The session ends with the playing of phonics games.

## *Adapted Word Building*

If students have difficulty with Word Building, assess their phonemic awareness. Inadequate phonemic awareness can make learning phonics more difficult.

An adapted form of Word Building has been used with encouraging success with severely disabled readers and is highly recommended. As described in Chapter 9, Word Building focuses on the learning of patterns, so that students learn the *-at* (*cat*) pattern or the *-oat* (*boat*) patterns as a unit. For most students, this is an efficient, effective way to learn phonics. However, if students are having difficulty learning patterns, adapt the technique so that they learn individual letter sounds. When presenting the *-at* pattern, for instance, point out the separate sounds in *at*: /a/ + /t/. If students have difficulty using pronounceable word parts—if they can't pronounce the *ap* in *map,* for instance—then see if they are able to process the word sound by sound. In other words, if the student is struggling, make whatever adjustments are necessary. Although decoding a word sound by sound distorts speech sounds and is burdensome, it may be a necessary procedure for some students.

In most cases the use of a sound-by-sound approach will be temporary. As students become proficient recognizing individual sounds in words or patterns, they will grow in their ability to perceive larger elements in words. Eventually you should be able to present new elements through patterns, and students will be able to decode unfamiliar words by using pronounceable word parts.

If you adapt Word Building, Benchmark, or another word learning system and students are still struggling, use VAKT along with the phonics system. A major drawback of using VAKT is that it is so time-consuming. If time is an issue, shorten VAKT by adapting the writing portion. Instead of having the student dictate a paragraph, help her or him construct an oral sentence as is done in Reading Recovery (see Chapter 7). So that the tracing portion of the approach will reinforce the pattern being taught in Word Building, encourage the student to dictate a sentence using one or more of the pattern words. After studying the *-et* pattern, a student might dictate a sentence similar to the following: "I took my pet to the vet."

After the student has dictated the sentence, dictate it back to him and have the student write it just as in the VAKT approach. Words with which the student has difficulty should be traced. At the conclusion of the session, copy the sentence onto a strip of tagboard as in *Reading Recovery.* It can then be cut up and taken home to be read for practice. The segmented sentence should be reassembled and read the next day. Here is how a sample lesson using adapted Word Building might be taught.

### Sample Adapted Word Building Lesson

> VAKT should only be added to Word Building if the student is having difficulty learning words taught through a Word Building approach. If Word Building with adapted VAKT is not successful, try classical VAKT.

*Step 1: Presentation of Pattern*

Present pattern. (See detailed lessons in Chapter 9).

*Step 2: Creation of Pattern Sentence*

Have student create a sentence using one or more pattern words and dictate that sentence to you.

*Step 3: Writing of Sentence by Student*

Dictate the sentence to the student and have the student write it. Have the student trace any words that are difficult.

*Step 4: Tracing of Words (Stage 1)*

The student says the whole word, traces and says each syllable, and then says the whole word. The student would continue tracing the word until he felt he could write it from memory.

*Step 5: Writing the Word from Memory*

Turning the tracing copy over, the student on a strip of 4″ by 12″ paper placed vertically says the whole word, says each syllable as he writes each syllable, and then says the whole word. The student checks the spelling of the word, covers the word that he has just written, and writes the word a second time and once again checks it for accuracy. The correctly written words are dated, stapled to the tracing copy, and filed alphabetically.

*Step 6: Writing the Word in the Sentence*

The student writes the new word in the sentence and reads it. As in VAKT, keep a record of demonstrations and tracings and words learned each time. The sentence can be written on tagboard and cut up for practice reading at home.

*Step 7: Application of Word Patterns*

Word patterns taught should be applied. A list of easy trade books that might be used for the application phase are presented in Table 9-7 on p. 228. Crossword puzzles, riddles, jokes, signs, and ads can also be used to reinforce the pattern.

Classical VAKT is designed to help students learn a basic store of words that they can read immediately. Phonics skills would also need to be taught. The adapted version of VAKT recommended for use with Word Building is designed to reinforce patterns being taught. The reason sentences are written, rather than whole stories, as in VAKT, is to simplify the approach and make it easier to use and less time-consuming. However, if possible, VAKT should be used as described earlier in the chapter.

## *A Total Program*

The special word learning techniques discussed in this chapter are just one part of a total program for low-achieving readers. Writing and wide reading and content area learning should also be a part of the low-achieving reader's program. An integrated program which builds on the student's strengths would be ideal. Since students are more than likely well aware of their difficulties with reading and writing, attempts should be made to recognize and foster abilities that they have in athletics, the arts, or other areas. Although specialized word learning techniques require one-on-one instruction, low-achieving readers can be part of a group or the whole class for other learning activities.

## *Working with Older Problem Readers: Teens and Adults*

Although this text stresses prevention and early intervention, it is never too late to teach someone to read and write. Having endured a childhood that was long on sharecropping but short on schooling, Ruby S. Williams was virtually illiterate as she grew into an adulthood that included working as a domestic and raising fourteen children (Sack, 1995). At the age of eighty-four, motivated by a desire to read the Bible, she enrolled in a program that provided her with a tutor. Working several nights a week with a tutor for a period of a year, she reached her goal.

### *Assessing Older Learners*

> Since older problem readers generally are very sensitive about their difficulty, it is important that assessment and instruction sessions be nonthreatening and positive.

Having had negative experiences with tests in the past, older students generally abhor tests. Assessment should be as informal and as limited as possible and might consist primarily of the administration of an informal reading inventory. If administering an informal reading inventory, use one such as the *Classroom Reading Inventory* (Silvaroli, 1994), or the *Bader Reading and Language Inventory* (Bader, 1994), both of which have forms designed for older students. An inventory such as the *Reading Evaluation Adult Diagnosis* (Colvin & Root, 1982), which was designed specifically for adults, might also be used. Or you might construct an inventory using the kinds of materials that the learner might be expected to meet: a shopping list, a menu, a set of directions, selections that gradually increase in difficulty from a series of work manuals. Using this type of material will be far less threatening.

As you work with older problem readers, explain the purpose of any assessment device that you administer. Also inform them of the results in a positive, constructive way. Highlight strengths and any steps that might be taken to help them with their difficulty. Most important of all, focus on the older student's strengths. Build on the older learner's background of experience and any special skills that she or he may have developed.

## *Programs for Older Problem Readers*

In general, the principles and procedures for teaching older problem readers are the same as those for teaching younger problem readers. However, it is doubly important that instruction should be tied into the learner's goals. Find out from the student why she or he wishes to improve in reading and writing. For Mrs. Williams, it was the desire to read the Bible. For others it might be the desire to read to their children or to obtain a better job. For older students in school, it might be the desire to pass or graduate. Or they may want to learn how to read the manual that prepares them for the state driver's license test. Students might bring to class the actual materials that they want to read: a newspaper article, letter from a friend, a form from school or work, or a text from a content area class. And you might help them with any literacy tasks that they wish to master: filling out a job application or writing a thank you note.

Since older problem readers have probably been given an overdose of skill and drill material, start with an approach that is holistic and use materials that reflect real life: signs, labels, menus, newspapers, magazines, novels, or stories on the appropriate level. Do not use children's picture books, easy readers from a basal series, or other materials that are demeaning to students. Trade books that might be used with older problem readers are listed in Appendix B. As you can see, there are lots of materials on second-grade level and up. However, there are few materials written below a second-grade level that would be suitable for older learners. If you are working with older beginning readers, you might want to try a language-experience approach.

> If students are on a beginning reading level, you might build a sight vocabulary or initial decoding skills by using easy functional level materials, such as signs or food labels (Roswell & Chall, 1994).

Since language-experience stories are based on the reader's experiences, they match the reader's maturity level and should also be of interest to the learner. Topics chosen should reflect the needs and interests of the learner. They can be autobiographical or might be related to a hobby, the learner's work, or an interest that the learner wishes to explore.

Middle school and high school problem readers may have difficulty with their high school texts. If possible, obtain easy-to-read texts. Another possibility is to use the Directed Listening–Thinking Activity with their texts as explained in Chapter 13. The DL–TA has been used with good success by older students who have serious reading problems (Gillet & Temple, 1994). As noted in Chapter 13, most textbooks have been taped and are available free-of-charge from *Reading for the Blind and Dyslexic* for those students who have a documented difficulty with reading. Variable speed tape recorders are available for purchase from this same source.

## *Commercial Materials*

Commercial programs for older problem readers come in a variety of shapes and sizes. A sampling of reading programs that might be used with middle school and high school students is presented in Table 16-1. Programs designed for adults are listed in Table 16-2. The most popular adult reading program is *Reading for Today* (Steck-Vaughn), which ranges from prereading through sixth grade and contains a writing strand.

**TABLE 16-1 Literacy Programs for Secondary School Students**

| Title | Publisher | Interest Level | Reading Level | Overview |
|---|---|---|---|---|
| Contemporary Reader | Jamestown | 7–12 | 2.5–5 | Features informational selections and comprehension exercises. |
| Developing Reading Strategies | Steck-Vaughn | 5–12 | 2.5–6 | Presents interesting selections and comprehension strategies. |
| Five-Star Stories | Jamestown | 7–12 | 4–8 | Each book features heroes, disasters, or other high-interest topic and comprehension exercises. |
| Focus on Reading | SRA | 7–12 | 2.5–6.0 | Fictional and informational selections, some by well-known writers. Comprehension and vocabulary exercises. |
| Great Series | Steck-Vaughn | 6–12 | 2–4 | Each text features great escapes or great rescues or other events. Comprehension and vocabulary exercises. |
| New Directions in Reading | Houghton Mifflin | 5–12 | 2–7 | Anthologies of fiction, nonfiction, real world reading, and poetry. Skills books with exercises on comprehension, vocabulary, and word analysis. Writing component at upper levels. |
| Spotlight | Steck-Vaughn | 4–8 | 2–4 | Articles on celebrities. Comprehension and vocabulary exercises. |

**TABLE 16-2 Literacy Programs for Adults**

| Name of Program | Publisher | Levels | Overview |
|---|---|---|---|
| Challenger | New Readers Press | 1–8 | Focuses on building reading vocabulary and comprehension. Book 1 provides a compressed overview of basic decoding. Also has a writing series. |
| Directions | Steck-Vaughn | 2–6 | Four-book series builds comprehension and vocabulary. |
| Laubach Way to Reading | New Readers Press | 1–4 | Uses a strong phonics approach and a variety of materials. |
| Reading for Today | Steck-Vaughn | 1–6 | Features fiction, informational pieces, and life coping skills for adults. Includes decoding, comprehension, and writing. |
| Whole Language for Adults | New Readers Press | 1–6 | Provides teacher's guides and libraries of easy-to-read adult books. |

## Working with Bilingual Learners

Currently, there are more than two million elementary and secondary school students who are still acquiring English (SAE). (Spangenberg-Urbschat & Pritchard, 1994). Some of these students come to school speaking no English at all. Others have varying degrees of proficiency in English. The largest segment of SAE youngsters speak Spanish as their home language. As a group, Latino students read significantly below average and have a higher dropout rate (Williams, Reese, Campbell, Mazzelo, & Phillips, 1995). Techniques recommended throughout this text should be effective when working with SAE youngsters. However, special provision must be made for language and cultural variations. A program for SAE students should emphasize the building of English language skills, especially **academic language.**

**Academic language:** words used to label key concepts in the content areas and also abstract words commonly used in instruction.

As students acquire English, they first learn everyday conversational skills. Conversational English is contextualized and supported by such nonverbal aids as gestures, pointing to objects as you talk about them, and pantomiming. On average, it takes about two years for students to become relatively proficient in everyday English. However, being decontextualized and more abstract, the language of school in which procedures and concepts are explained, may take five or more years to acquire (Cummins, 1994). When teaching SAE youngsters, make sure that they understand the language of instruction. Depending upon the level and topic being covered, carefully explain such terms as *sounds, letters, beginning, ending, consonant, vowel, title, author, illustrations, setting, characters, main idea, conclusion, planning, revising, editing* and use them consistently. Interchanging the terms *artist* and *illustrator,* for instance, could be confusing. Avoid figurative language and idioms: *beat around the bush, after my own heart, turn over a new leaf* (Gersten & Jiminez, 1994). Use demonstrations, illustrations, or real objects whenever possible. When introducing the correspondence b = /b/, for instance, show a button, ball, and bag or pictures of these objects as you talk about words that begin with /b/.

When working with SAE students, stress content rather than form. When acquiring a language, content is learned first and then is followed by form. Olivares (1993) suggests:

> *When asking students to answer questions or give explanations orally, teachers should attend to what students are saying rather than to how they are saying it. Interrupting the message to correct a language error will discourage students from participating and remove the focus from how well they are mastering the content. (p. 44)*

### Selecting Materials

Just as when selecting texts for native speakers of English, choose books and other materials that are on the SAE students' reading and interest levels. However, also seek books that have illustrations that support the text and use straightforward predictable language. Avoid texts that cover topics, such as Halloween or baseball, for which SAE students might have limited background, unless, of course, you develop necessary background beforehand. If carefully chosen, materials can foster language development (Allen, 1994). For instance, books with repetitive patterns such as *Brown Bear, Brown Bear, What Do You See?* (Martin, 1983) can provide practice with two basic sentence patterns: the question and the statement. SAE students could model a discussion or a piece of writing on the patterns found in *Brown Bear.*

Some SAE youngsters have essential concepts that they are unable to express in English because they lack the English words that label these concepts. For instance, on the beginning reading level, counting books and books that name colors could help SAE youngsters learn the names of numbers or colors in English. There are also concept books that provide the names of farm animals (*Big Red Barn,* Brown, 1989), farm implements (*Tractor,* Brown, 1995), vegetables (*Growing Vegetable Soup,* Ehlert, 1987), tools (*Tools,* Morris, 1992) and many other items.

Reading real world materials, such as signs, menus, advertisements, announcements, phone books, and job applications should be an integral part of the program. The youngest students need to know how to decipher common signs such as *in, out, open, up, down, closed, men, women, exit, emergency exit, office, nurse.* Older students need to know how to read and fill out job applications.

If possible, use materials that reflect the students' culture. A number of books are written primarily in English but include some Spanish expressions. One simply written picture book, *Subway Sparrow* (Torres, 1993), which tells about a bird trapped on a subway car, includes text in English, Spanish, and Polish, thus providing an excellent opportunity for interaction among youngsters from three linguistic communities. If students can read in another language, they should be urged to continue reading materials in that language. For a listing of materials in other languages, consult the index in *The Elementary School Collection* (Homa, 1996). Look under *Bilingual materials* and also the particular language in which you are interested.

## *Sheltered English*

**Sheltered English:** the practice of teaching subject matter content in English to SAE students who have learned conversational English but not academic language.

Because of the integration of language arts, reading, writing, listening, and speaking reinforce each other. Increasingly, reading and writing are used to build oral language skills among SAE students. Instead of using isolated drills on syntax and vocabulary and contrived conversations, SAE students now develop English speaking skills by reading quality literature or content area materials and discussing it and writing about it. Known as **sheltered English,** bilingual immersion, or cognitive academic language learning, the approach blends content and language development (Gersten & Jiminez, 1994). A major advantage of integrating second language acquisition and content exploration is that it fosters the development of both everyday and academic language as well as higher level thinking skills.

## *Language Experience*

Along with children's books, texts, and real world materials, you might also use language-experience stories. Language-experience stories are especially effective because they incorporate the students' language and experiential background. When creating language experience stories, students should be allowed to use both English and their home language in the story just as they might do in their speech.

## *Adapting Instruction*

> Krashen (1996) recommends voluntary reading of easy books to build vocabulary and the ability to handle complex grammatical constructions. Krashen and Cho (1995) cite the case of Karen, an adult SAE student, who as a result of reading an easy series of books gained five years in reading ability, going from a second- to a seventh-grade level.

If at all possible, SAE students who are experiencing difficulty with literacy should be taught to read and write in their first language. Learning to read and write in one's native language is far easier and the skill of reading and writing in one language transfers to other languages (Fillmore & Valdez, 1986). Learning to read in a second language, of course, makes greater demands on a student. In addition to learning decoding and comprehension skills and strategies, students must also deal with unfamiliar words and sentence structures (Chamot & O'Malley, 1994). Before presenting a selection, you may want to analyze the text for sources of possible difficulty and confusion. Some possible problem areas include:

- Syntax. Does the selection contain sentence structures such as passives or contractions with which the student might have difficulty?
- Semantics. Does the selection use terms, figures of speech, or idiomatic expressions that might pose problems for the SAE reader?
- Culture. Are there cultural items such as might appear in a story about foods or sports that might be unfamiliar to the SAE reader.

> Krashen (1996) advocates comprehensible input for developing English. This includes learning language in classes, in informal conversations, through voluntary reading, and through sheltered English.

To foster both reading and oral language skills, allow lots of time to discuss stories. Also establish an accepting atmosphere and use prompts. Students may have ideas that they wish to contribute but may have difficulty formulating them. Also paraphrase responses and encourage students to expand upon them (Gersten & Jimenez, 1994). For instance, if a student answers, "Because he was afraid" to the question, "Why did the little boy hide?" You might rephrase that as, "Yes, the little boy hid because he was afraid." To expand the response, you might ask such questions as: "Where did the little boy hide? What was he afraid of? What are some things that make you afraid?"

Sometimes teachers misinterpret students' lack of fluency in English as reflecting a low level of knowledge or ability. It is important that literacy programs for SAE students foster higher order cognitive processes, lead to higher levels of student involvement, and enable students to engage in extended discourse (Gersten & Jiminez, 1994).

## *Minicase Study*

When he was accepted for instruction at the Fernald School (a special school for students with severe reading problems) of the University of California at Los Angeles, fourteen-year-old John was described as being "defeated, troubled, and angry" (Berres & Eyer,

1970). A behavior problem since kindergarten, John howled like a wolf and rolled on the floor when asked to sit in the back of the room because of distracting behavior.

Despite having average intelligence, John was reading on a first-grade level. Not surprisingly, he avoided academic tasks, and when the teacher offered him a book he "broke out into a cold sweat" (p. 34).

The first order of business was to deal with John's perception of himself. John had to learn to see himself as a capable student and act like a learner. Because John was hyperactive, he was given tasks of brief duration, was allowed to choose activities, and was encouraged to run around the school track or spar with a punching bag whenever his excess energy seemed too much to handle.

Instruction capitalized on John's main interest. He wanted to be a plumber and often helped his father, who was a plumber. Plumbing supply catalogs, invoices, and sales slips were used to foster John's literacy skills.

Because of John's severe word learning difficulty, the Fernald (VAKT) tracing technique was used with him. This was tied into his interest in plumbing. The first word that John learned was *tools.* He planned to use the word to fill out an order blank.

Because of the novelty of the Fernald technique and because it was helping him learn words that he wanted to write, John responded favorably to the approach. John remained in Stage 1 for seven months. During that period he built up enough of a reading vocabulary so that he was able to begin reading easy books. John enjoyed high-interest, low-readability books because they didn't seem "babyish."

In John's second year, he expressed a desire to read Edgar Allan Poe's tales of horror. Given extra help by the teacher, John did surprisingly well with a collection of Poe's stories. As John experienced success, his inappropriate behavior faded away. After three years at the Fernald School, John was reading at an eighth grade level. He had gained the literacy skills and confidence he needed to attend high school.

## *Summary*

About one student out of a hundred has a serious word learning problem and may need to be taught through specialized word learning techniques. Two of the best-known and most widely used word learning techniques are VAKT (Fernald) and the Orton–Gilligham.

VAKT, which is based on the Fernald tracing technique, advocates using the visual, auditory, kinesthetic, and tactile senses to learn words. Using these four senses may forge connections, which help the student remember new words. VAKT also fosters fuller attention and concentration and builds confidence.

The Orton–Gillingham approach is a highly structured intensive phonics methods that makes use of a form of tracing known as S.O.S. (simultaneous oral spelling) in which students name the letters as they write words.

Specialized word learning techniques should be presented within the context of a total program. Wide reading of appropriate level texts and writing are highly recommended. Word Building, adapted if necessary, might also be used with students who have serious word learning problems.

Having a history of failure, older poor readers and writers may feel too discouraged to try. Help them see that they are competent learners. Build on their strengths and construct a program that addresses their needs but uses appropriate materials and ties in with their personal goals.

Problem readers and writers who are still acquiring English face the double burden of acquiring a second language and overcoming their literacy difficulties. If possible, they should be taught to read and write in their native language. Acquisition of reading and writing in English is far easier if the students can read and write in their own language. Oral language and reading and writing skills are best acquired in the context of learning content. The language experience approach and cooperative learning are especially appropriate for students who are still acquiring English.

## *Application Activities*

1. Read Fernald's (1943) classic text *Remedial Techniques in Basic School Subjects* (New York: Macmillan) or the annotated version published by Pro-Ed (Idol, 1988). What kinds of suggestions did Fernald make that are still valid today?

2. If possible, observe the use of Fernald (VAKT), the Orton–Gillingham, or a program based on the Orton–Gillingham. How did the student respond to the program? What are the strengths of the program? What might be its weaknesses?

3. With a partner, try out the tracing component of VAKT. Follow the steps exactly and make sure you have the proper equipment: a dictionary, stapler, large black crayon, slips of 4″ by 12″ paper.

4. Try out Word Building in its adapted form, if necessary, with a student who has a serious word learning problem. How does the student respond to the techniques? What are the strengths and weaknesses of the program?

*Chapter* **17**

# *Materials, Voluntary Reading, and Technology*

## *Using What You Know*

All too often low-achieving readers end up with materials that are too difficult for them. This chapter explores ways of making sure that low-achieving readers are provided with appropriate materials. This chapter also discusses the importance of voluntary reading, an essential ingredient in a program of intervention or remediation. Finally, this chapter explores the role of technology. Technology can be motivational for students, and it can help them compensate for some of their learning difficulties.

To put yourself in the low-achieving reader's place, picture a time when you were required to read a text or article that was too difficult. How did you feel? How did you cope with the situation? On the other side of the coin, think about some tasks that are difficult but which the computer or other technological devices have made easier. Also think about the contribution that voluntary reading has made to your reading and intellectual development. When you were in elementary and secondary school, how much time did you spend reading on your own? What did you learn through voluntary reading?

## *Anticipation Guide*

Read each of the following statements. Put a check under "Agree" or "Disagree" to show how you feel about each one. If possible, discuss your responses with classmates.

| | Agree | Disagree |
|---|---|---|
| **1.** Students make the most progress when their reading material is on the easy side. | ________ | ________ |
| **2.** Low-achieving readers should read regular texts and not watered-down versions. | ________ | ________ |

**3.** The most neglected aspect of most corrective reading programs is voluntary reading. ________ ________

**4.** Low-achieving readers benefit more from technology than do average or gifted learners. ________ ________

**5.** Using a spelling or grammar checker deprives students of the opportunity to learn basic skills. ________ ________

## *Making the Match*

What is the first step in teaching reading, especially when working with underachieving readers? To Edward Fry, a member of the Reading Hall of Fame, step one is making the match (Fry, 1977a).

> *Before you begin teaching reading to a child, or a whole class for that matter, you must assess reading abilities in order to provide reading material at the proper level of difficulty. This is important, for a mismatch in reading material can result in disinterested readers. Material that is too difficult is frustrating and breeds failure, which in turn often causes a dislike of reading. (p. 5)*

Marie Clay (1993b), one of the creators of Reading Recovery, insists that students be given materials that are on the appropriate level of difficulty. Emphasis in Reading Recovery is on teaching students to use a balance of strategies, which include context and phonics, to read unfamiliar words. However, if too many words are unknown, students are unable to use context because they aren't able to derive enough meaning from the passage. Unable to use context, they may overrely on phonics or picture clues.

Comprehension also suffers when the material is too difficult. When high school students reading below their grade level were given material on their instructional level, they used a variety of strategies. However, when these same below-level readers were given material on their frustration level, use of comprehension strategies plummeted, and a number of students simply gave up (Kletzien, 1991). Research by Berliner (1981) and Gambrell, Wilson, and Gantt (1981) suggests that students make the most progress when reading materials in which no more than 2 to 5 percent of the words are unknown.

> In one study, students paid attention only 20 percent of the time when given a difficult text. When an easier text was substituted, attention more than doubled to 50 percent (R. Anderson, 1990).

The first step in making the match involves finding out what level of material the student is able to read. This can be done by administering an individual or group reading inventory as was explained in Chapter 4. It's also helpful to obtain information about the reader's background of knowledge in terms of the book about to be read (Chall & Dale, 1995). An easy book on ice hockey could be difficult if the student knows nothing about the sport. The second step in making the match is finding material on the appropriate level of difficulty and the appropriate level of maturity. This is not an easy task. By and large, most books are written for children of average or above-average reading level. Finding appropriate books for older low-achieving readers can be challenging. However, if you know what to look for and where to look, the task is manageable.

## *Readability: The Other Half of the Match*

Publishers of school materials generally provide reading levels for their texts. Using a formula, they estimate that the material is at a third-, fifth-, or eighth-grade level, which means that the average third-, fifth-, or eighth-grader should be able to read it. Some publishers of children's books also supply **readability** levels. A readability level may appear on the spine, the title page, or back cover. There are also several references that supply readability information on books. *The Elementary School Library Collection* (Homa, 1996) provides readability estimates for more than 8,000 books that have been recommended for use by elementary school students.

**Readability:** ease with which a book or other piece of written material can be understood.

### *Sources of High-Interest/Low-Readability Materials*

One of the problems of promoting free reading among low-achieving readers is finding books that are on a suitable level of maturity but easy enough for them to read. Fortunately, there are several annotated bibliographies of high/interest, low/readability books. These are listed below.

- *High/Low Handbook* (3rd. ed.). LiBretto, E. L. New York: Bowker, 1990.

  Reviews and provides readability estimates for 312 high-interest, low-readability books appropriate for secondary and upper elementary school students reading on a fourth-grade level or below. Also annotates one hundred books for reluctant readers. Reluctant readers are defined as those who have a mild reading difficulty.
- *High Interest–Easy Reading. A Booklist for Junior and Senior High School Students* (6th ed.). McBride, W. G. Urbana, IL: National Council of Teachers of English, 1990.

  Lists hundreds of books chosen for their potential appeal to reluctant readers. Books that have an elementary format or seem too complex are not listed. Readability levels are not supplied.
- *The Best: High/Low Books for Reluctant Readers.* Pilla, M. L. Englewood, CO: Libraries Unlimited, 1990.

  Annotates and estimates the readabilities of 374 books for low-achieving readers in grades three through twelve.
- *Easy Reading: Book Series and Periodicals for Less Able Readers* (2nd. ed.). Ryer, R. J., Graves, B. B., & Graves, M. F. Newark, DE: International Reading Association, 1989.

  Presents several dozen book series that might be used with low-achieving readers in grades four through twelve. Also describes a number of high/low periodicals.

**Readability formulas** predict the ease of reading of a particular piece of writing based on the objective assessment of such factors as the sentence length and familiarity of vocabulary.

### *Using a Readability Formula*

If no readability level is indicated for a book that you wish to use, you might estimate readability through the use of a **readability formula** or rating scale. Modern day readability formulas grew out of a concern expressed by science teachers that their texts contained too many technical terms (Chall, 1988). Dozens of factors were implicated as being possible sources of reading difficulty, but in the end the two factors that most efficiently predict the difficulty of a text turned out to be vocabulary and sentence length. Generally speaking, the greater the number of unfamiliar words, then the more abstract the ideas (Chall, 1988). All other things being equal, longer sentences are harder to understand and, as average sentence length increases, the complexity of the passage also increases. Four of the most popular readability formulas are described below.

Aspects noted on the New Dale-Chall worksheets are prior knowledge expected of the reader, vocabulary and concepts used in the text, overall organization, and use of headings and other features that affect the ease of reading the text.

**New Dale–Chall.** The most up-to-date and one of the most carefully validated of the readability formulas is the New Dale–Chall Readability Formula (Chall & Dale, 1995). The New Dale–Chall can be used to estimate the difficulty level of material from grade one through grade sixteen, but is most valid for materials in the grade three to twelve range. The New Dale–Chall's estimate of difficulty is based on average sentence length and number of words not found on the Revised Dale List. The Revised Dale List is a compilation of 3,000 words known by most fourth graders. Recognizing that interest and background knowledge are important factors in readability, the New Dale–Chall features two worksheets, one for assessing reading characteristics, including probable interest of the reader in the topic to be read, and a second worksheet that assesses cognitive-structural aspects of the text.

**Fry Readability Graph.** Easy to use and extending from grades one through seventeen, the Fry Readability Graph is the most popular of the formulas. The Fry Graph bases its estimate on two factors: sentence length and number of syllables in a word. Number of syllables in a word is a measure of vocabulary difficulty. In general, the more syllables a word has, the harder it tends to be. A syllable count is used because it is faster to count syllables than it is to look up words on a list. The Fry Readability Graph (Fry, 1977b) is presented in Figure 17-1.

A distinct advantage of the Flesch-Kincaid is that it is bundled into Microsoft Word and other popular word processing programs.

**Flesch-Kincaid.** A revision of the Flesch formula that yields grade levels, the Flesch-Kincaid's readability estimate is based on the number of syllables in a word and average sentence length (Kincaid, Fishburne, Rogers, & Chissom, 1975). It also correlates rather closely with the Fry Graph (Fusaro, 1988).

Computer software that can be used to apply the DRP formula is available from Touchstone Associates.

**Degrees of Reading Power.** The most complex of the formulas, the DRP measures sentence length, number of words not on the Dale List, and average number of letters per word (Touchstone Applied Science Associates, 1996b). Most readability formulas report their estimates in grade equivalent scores: 3.4, 2.7. However, the Degrees of Reading Power reports its levels in DRP Units. Table 17-1 translates DRP units into grade equivalent scores. These translations are approximations.

### *Advantages of the DRP System*

What sets the DRP apart from other readability measures is that it makes the whole match. Touchstone Associates produces the Degrees of Reading Power tests, which use a modified cloze format and which consists of a series of paragraphs that gradually increase in

This is a readability formula intended to help you determine the approximate difficulty or readability level of most written material.

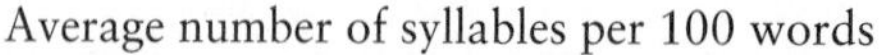

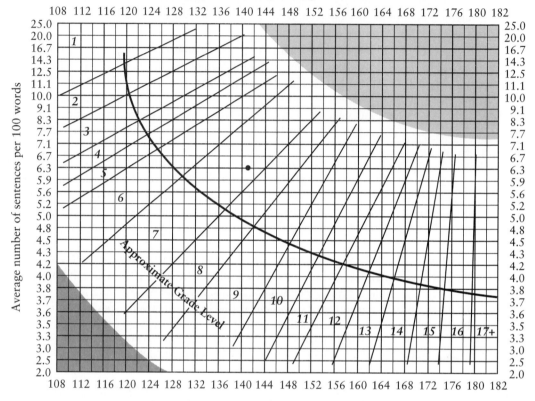


Directions: Randomly select 3 one hundred word passages from a book or an article. Plot average number of syllables and average number of sentences per 100 words on graph to determine the grade level of the material. Choose more passages per book if great variability is observed and conclude that the book has uneven readability. Few books will fall in gray area but when they do grade level scores are invalid.

Count proper nouns, numerals and initializations as words. Count a syllable for each symbol. For example, "1945" is 1 word and 4 syllables and "IRA" is 1 word and 3 syllables.

Example:

| | Syllables | Sentences |
|---|---|---|
| 1st Hundred Words | 124 | 6.6 |
| 2nd Hundred Words | 141 | 5.5 |
| 3rd Hundred Words | 158 | 6.8 |
| Average | 141 | 6.3 |

Readability 7th Grade (see dot plotted on graph)

**FIGURE 17-1 Fry Readability Graph**

Source: Edward Fry, Rutgers University Reading Center, New Brunswick, N.J. 08904. For further information and validity data see the *Journal of Reading* December, 1977.

**TABLE 17-1 Approximate Grade Equivalents of DRP Scores**

| Grade Equivalent | DRP Score |
|---|---|
| PP | 34–36 |
| P | 37–39 |
| 1 | 40–43 |
| 2 | 44–47 |
| 3 | 48–49 |
| 4 | 50–51 |
| 5 | 52–53 |
| 6 | 54–55 |
| 7 | 56–57 |
| 8 | 58–59 |

difficulty. Each passage has five blanks which the student fills in by choosing one of five possible responses. The tests function as a group reading inventory whose primary purpose is to estimate the level at which the student can read with 75 percent comprehension. Levels are reported in DRP units so that they match up with the DRP readability scores. For instance, if a child scored a 39, which translates approximately into a beginning second-grade level, books such as *Mouse Soup,* with a readability score of 38, or *Nate the Great* with a DRP score of 40, or *Halloween with Morris and Boris,* with a DRP score of 40, would be on the student's instructional level. Compilations of readability levels expressed in DRP units for textbooks and children's and young adult books can be found in the following TASA publications:

- *Readability of Textbooks (10th Edition).* Readability calculations for more than 3,000 textbooks published between 1979 and 1996.
- *Readability of Textbooks in Series, (9th Edition).* Readability calculations for more than 2,000 textbook series published between 1975 and 1994.
- *Readability of Literature and Popular Titles (Volume 1).* Readability calculations for more than 1,600 children's books.
- *Readability of Literature and Popular Titles (Volume 2).* Readability calculations for more than 1,200 children's books.
- *Readability of Literature and Popular Titles (Volume 3).* Readability calculations for more than 1,000 children's books.

A listing of the contents of *Readability of Literature and Popular Titles* (Volumes 1, 2, 3) is contained on DRP Book Link (Touchstone Applied Science Associates, 1996a). In addition to giving readability levels of more than 5,000 books, the software provides a brief annotation of each title. A flexible, highly useful program, the database can be accessed by author, title, readability level, age level, topic, book type (fiction/nonfiction), or any combination of these items. For instance, you could request a listing of easy-to-read classics on the high school level. Lists can be printed out so that you can provide recommended lists to students.

The Lexile Framework (MetaMetrics, 3501-B Tri-Center Blvd., Durham, NC 27713) is somewhat similar to the DRP system. The Lexile Framework can be used to assess both the reading ability of students and the readability of texts. The system also has an extensive listing of books leveled according to Lexile score. Using the Reading Pathfinder, teachers can generate a list of books to match students' reading ability. Reading ability can be determined by administering a Lexile inventory or Lexile test of comprehension, or by translating scores obtained on standardized tests of reading into Lexile units.

***Subjective Factors***

Except for the New Dale–Chall, readability formulas only measure difficulty of vocabulary and length of sentences. There are, of course, other factors that should be considered when choosing books for a child. Some of these include use of graphics, page layout, clarity of writing style, abstractness, and density of concepts. These are factors that don't lend themselves to measurement by a formula. A Readability Checklist that includes both subjective factors, such as prior knowledge and reader interest, and objective factors such as sentence length and vocabulary load is presented in Table 17-2. Assessing both subjective and objective factors should provide you with the optimum information for judging the suitability of a text, and enable you to make appropriate matches.

Making the match between the reader and the book requires teacher judgment. The teacher evaluates a text in terms of students' background of knowledge, interests, and purpose for reading.

## *Holistic Estimate of Readability*

An alternative to using formulas is to judge the material holistically by comparing it with a series of model passages written on a range of difficulty levels. The rater decides which passage the material is most like. If it is most like the third grade passage, then it is estimated to be on a third-grade level of difficulty. The most carefully developed of these instruments is the *Qualitative Assessment of Texts* (Chall, Bissex, Conard, & Harris-Sharples, 1996). Based on research that indicates that different types of texts require different kinds of background and different types of strategies, the *Qualitative Assessment of Texts* has six scales: one for popular fiction, one for literature, one for biographical and narrative history, one for expository history, one for the biological sciences, and one for the physical sciences. Most of the scales contain nine levels and range in difficulty from grade one through college. To estimate the difficulty level of a text, the user chooses the scale that is most appropriate and then selects 100-word samples and compares them with the scaled passages.

The *Qualitative Assessment of Texts* (Chall, Bissex, Conard, & Harris-Sharples, 1996) helps you take a look at key elements in a text and plan activities that help students better understand the text.

## *Leveling Books*

Although traditional formulas provide reasonably accurate estimates of the difficulty levels of most reading materials, they don't work at the beginning levels. Formulas don't consider such factors as usefulness of illustrations and number of lines per page, which are major determinants of the difficulty level of beginning materials. Formulas do indicate with reasonable accuracy that materials are on a first grade level. However, first grade reading encompasses a wide range of material that includes counting or color books that have just one or two easy words per page as well as books such as the Frog and Toad or Henry and Mudge series that contain brief chapters and may contain a thousand words or more. To

**TABLE 17-2 Subjective Readability Index**

| Text Factors | | | | | |
|---|---|---|---|---|---|
| *Content* | low | | | | high |
| Familiarity of Concepts | 1 | 2 | 3 | 4 | 5 |
| Concreteness of Concepts | 1 | 2 | 3 | 4 | 5 |
| *Style* | | | | | |
| Clarity of Writing | 1 | 2 | 3 | 4 | 5 |
| Elaboration of Key Concepts | 1 | 2 | 3 | 4 | 5 |
| Ease of Vocabulary | 1 | 2 | 3 | 4 | 5 |
| Simplicity of Sentences | 1 | 2 | 3 | 4 | 5 |
| Use of Anecdotes | 1 | 2 | 3 | 4 | 5 |
| Relates Text to Pupils' Background | 1 | 2 | 3 | 4 | 5 |
| *Organization* | | | | | |
| Use of Heads, Subheads | 1 | 2 | 3 | 4 | 5 |
| Focus on Major Ideas | 1 | 2 | 3 | 4 | 5 |
| Logical Flow of Ideas | 1 | 2 | 3 | 4 | 5 |
| Exclusion of Irrelevant Material | 1 | 2 | 3 | 4 | 5 |
| *Features That Enhance Comprehension* | | | | | |
| Chapter Overview | 1 | 2 | 3 | 4 | 5 |
| Summary | 1 | 2 | 3 | 4 | 5 |
| Questions | 1 | 2 | 3 | 4 | 5 |
| Graphics | 1 | 2 | 3 | 4 | 5 |
| Phonemic Respellings | 1 | 2 | 3 | 4 | 5 |
| Definitions Provided in Text | 1 | 2 | 3 | 4 | 5 |
| Glossary | 1 | 2 | 3 | 4 | 5 |
| Total<br>(The higher the total, the easier the text.) | | | | | |

| Reader Factors | | | | | |
|---|---|---|---|---|---|
| | low | | | | high |
| Background of Knowledge | 1 | 2 | 3 | 4 | 5 |
| Vocabulary | 1 | 2 | 3 | 4 | 5 |
| Overall Reading Ability | 1 | 2 | 3 | 4 | 5 |
| Interest | 1 | 2 | 3 | 4 | 5 |
| Motivation | 1 | 2 | 3 | 4 | 5 |
| Study/Work Habits | 1 | 2 | 3 | 4 | 5 |
| Total<br>(The higher the number, the better the reader.) | | | | | |

make fine discriminations among the range of first grade books, teachers in New Zealand created a readability system that assigns levels to books according to a number of subjective factors including content, length, format, and complexity of language and story structure. These characteristics were used to grade books in the Ready to Read series, a set of books used to teach beginning reading in New Zealand. Once classified, books in the Ready to Read series were used as a benchmark to indicate the reading level of children's books. A listing of the levels of more than 600 children's books on the primary level can be found in *Books for Ready to Read Classrooms* (Learning Media, 1994).

Building on the Ready to Read system, B. Weaver (1992) created a scheme for placing books into nine levels, ranging in difficulty level from grades one through three. Available, free of charge, is a classification of hundreds of children's books according to the Weaver system. These are found in the latest copy of the Storyhouse catalog. Fountas and Pinnell (1996) have also compiled a list of leveled books for students in grades one through three. Also adapting New Zealand's *Ready to Read* system, Reading Recovery has classified hundreds of children's books into twenty levels, which range from a very beginning or picture-reading level to early second grade. A partial listing of leveled books can be found in Chapter Six of *Bridges to Literacy: Learning from Reading Recovery* (Deford, Lyons, & Pinnell, 1991). Using qualitative factors identified in the New Zealand, Reading Recovery, and Weaver systems plus the quantitative factor of vocabulary difficulty, the Primary Readability Index (Gunning, 1998) places beginning reading books into eight levels of difficulty ranging from highly predicatable books that can be read just by using illustrations to brief chapter books designed for beginning second graders.

### *Sources of Beginning Reading Books*

- *Best Books for Beginning Readers.* Gunning, T. (1998). (Boston: Allyn & Bacon).

  A compilation of more than 1,000 beginning reading children's books annotated and arranged in comparative order of difficulty.
- *The Blue Pages, Resources for Teachers from Invitations, Changing as Teachers and Learners K–12.* Routman, R. (Portsmouth, NH: Heinmann).

  Provides an extended annotated listing of books for readers at all levels.
- *Beyond Picture Books: A Guide to First Readers* (2nd ed.). Bartstow, B., & Riggle, J. (New York: Bowker, 1995).

  Annotates and provides an estimate of the difficulty level of 2,495 titles deemed to be suitable for novice readers. Also provides a list of 200 first readers judged to be outstanding.
- *Books for Children to Read Alone: A Guide for Parents and Librarians.* Wilson, G., & Moss, J. (New York: Bowker, 1988).

  Annotates more than 300 books ranging from beginning reading through the third-grade level that novice readers can read independently.
- *The Elementary School Library Collection: A Guide to Books and Other Media, Twentieth Edition.* Homa, L. L. (Portsmouth, NH: 1996).

  Lists several hundred books that might be read independently by beginning readers. The books have been classified, according to the Spache formula, as being on a 1–1, 1–2, 2–1, or 2–2 level.
- *Guided Reading.* Fountas, I. C. & Pinnell, G. S. (Portsmouth, NH: Heinemann, 1996).

  Lists titles of more than 3,500 books for students in grades one to three.

## Voluntary Reading

Even slight increases in time spent reading lead to gains (R. C. Anderson, 1996). Students show significant gains when they engage in as little as 10 minutes of free reading a day (Fielding, Wilson, & Anderson, 1986).

Although this text features dozens of techniques designed to help low-achieving readers and writers move up the literacy ladder, the key to success to any reading improvement program lies in fostering voluntary reading. As Frank Smith (1988) explained, "We learn to read by reading . . ." Unfortunately low-achieving readers, since they start out having difficulty with reading, read less. Reading less, they fall further behind. In first grade, good readers have been observed reading three times as much as poor readers (Allington, 1983). Stanovich (1986) calls this the "Matthew effect," which is essentially the poor getting poorer and the rich getting richer. "The very children who are reading well and who have good vocabularies will read more, learn more word meanings, and hence read even better" (p. 381). By the middle grades, the difference in the time spent reading between the best and the poorest readers might be tenfold.

### Determining Interests

The first part of the chapter was devoted to a discussion on how to obtain materials on the appropriate level of difficulty for low-achieving readers. Of course, locating books on the appropriate level of difficulty is only part of the equation. You also need to determine students' interests so you can supply material that they can read and also want to read. One way of doing this might be to involve students in the selection of books. Distribute publishers' catalogs and have them check off titles of books that they feel they might like to read. Also discuss with students what their interests are. Note who likes sports, who likes animals, who is interested in cars, who is fascinated by dinosaurs.

### Building a Classroom Library

Include in your collection books containing jokes, riddles, puns, and songs. Also feature heavily illustrated books. Reluctant readers can start on these fast reads and move up to more substantive works.

No matter how fine a library your school has, it is important that you also have books close at hand. Students are far more likely to borrow books if they are readily available. The classroom library should be as extensive and diverse as you can make it. Because they are inexpensive and have a mature look, paperbacks are recommended, especially for older students. However, also include hardcover books. Include, too, young people's magazines and newspapers. *Sports Illustrated for Kids,* which is written on a fifth-grade level, is highly popular with young people who like sports. Even if the text is a little difficult, they can get help from the photos in this generously illustrated periodical. Be sure to feature *Know Your World Extra, Scholastic Action,* and other periodicals designed for low-achieving readers. A listing of easy-to-read periodicals is presented in Table 17-3. For an extensive listing of young people's magazines, see *Magazines for Kids and Teens* (Stoll, 1997).

#### Setting Up a Reading Area

Books should be set up in an appealing display just as they are in school and town libraries and bookstores. Covers, on at least some of the books, should be facing out. You might be

**TABLE 17-3 High-Interest, Low-Readability Periodicals**

*Action.* New York: Scholastic.
Reading levels 4–5. Interest levels Grades 7–12. Twice monthly.
*Know World Extra.* Middletown, CT: Field Publications.
Reading levels 3–4. Interest levels Grade 5 through high school. Twice monthly.
*News for You.* Syracuse, NY: New Reader's Press.
Reading levels 4–6. Interest levels secondary and adult. Weekly.

able to obtain revolving racks from distributors or publishers. Also make sure the reading area is inviting and attractive. A rug helps, as do comfortable chairs.

To maintain interest in the library corner, change the display periodically and add new titles. Use posters to feature new arrivals. Set up displays that tie in with events that are of interest to students: baseball books at World Series time, scary stories at Halloween, books about summer fun or summer jobs just before the end of the school year. For your low-achieving readers, have available a large number of books that are easy to read.

### *Establishing a Community of Readers*

In addition to creating a physical environment that fosters wide reading, also build a sense that the class is composed of a community of readers. Help students see the many roles that reading can fulfill: provide enjoyment, escape, or aesthetic pleasure; raise interesting questions; help solve problems; foster personal growth; open up new horizons; stimulate the mind and imagination. All too often students see only that reading fulfills a *school* role: it provides them with practice and helps them answer questions that the teacher asks. They may not see how reading might function in other essential areas of their lives.

> Although series books may be lacking in literary quality, they maintain a common core of characters and setting and become progressively easier to read.

Much of building a community of readers is helping students make reading an integral part of their lives. Show students how reading functions in your life. Share with them excerpts from a book of poetry or biography that you are reading. Explain how a book helped you to repair your car, understand how the class computer works, or learn new ways to teach. Then help students see how reading might function in their lives. Knowing that a student is a basketball fan, you might recommend a biography of an upcoming star. If a student has just gotten a puppy as a pet, suggest a book on raising puppies. If the class is studying Lincoln, you might recommend *Abe Lincoln's Hat* (Brenner, 1994), which is written on an easy third-grade level. If a group is interested in dinosaurs, suggest *Dinosaur Babies* (Penner, 1991) or *Dinosaur Time* (Parish, 1974), both of which are written on a first-grade level, or the slightly harder *Dinosaur Days* (Milton, 1985). For poetry lovers, recommend *Surprises* (Hopkins, 1984) or *More Surprises* (Hopkins, 1987) or Karla Kuskin's (1991) *Soap Soup and Other Verses,* all of which are on a first- to second-grade reading level. Poetry books are good choices for low-achieving readers because they usually contain a number of works that are surprisingly easy to read. Don't limit recommendations to books only. Mention interesting articles from *Scholastic Action* or *Know Your World Extra* or *Sports Illustrated for Kids.*

Discuss books with students. Talk about the books in the same way that you would if you were discussing a book with friends. Tell them what you are reading and ask them what they are reading. Read the books that they enjoy so that you can make recommendations and discuss books with them. In addition to incidental discussions, hold scheduled sharings.

Read aloud to students, even older ones, on a regular basis. Also set aside time during the day for free reading, in which students may elect to read anything they wish. As part of the community of readers, the teacher also reads, thereby modeling reading behavior and signaling that reading is an important activity. Amount of time devoted to free reading can vary. For younger students, it may be as little as ten minutes. Older students might read for up to thirty minutes. Although originally conceived as a period when students read silently to themselves (McCracken, 1971), some teachers encourage students to read in pairs or small groups and to discuss their reading. Students read more when they have a chance to share their reading (Manning & Manning, 1984; Wilson, 1992).

### *Choosing Books*

If they haven't had much experience with voluntary reading, low-achieving readers will need some guidance in choosing books. They may even lack adequate criteria for selecting books. Since they may have been given books to read that are too difficult, they may not realize that by selecting the right books, they can actually read with understanding. Because of peer pressure, they may choose books that their friends are reading, even those that may be far too difficult for them. A second-grader reading on an early first-grade level may want to read chapter books because that is what her friends are reading, even though such books would be well beyond her. Students may also reject books on their level as being too babyish. To solve this dual problem, Fielding (1996) recommends that teachers find ways to help students "read some of the books that they want to read and then find ways to make them want to read some of the books that they can read" (p. 46). Although, by and large, students should read books on the appropriate level, they should be allowed to attempt difficult books from time to time. There are a number of steps that can be taken to make difficult books more accessible. You can walk the student through a book, pointing out difficult words and concepts, before she or he reads it. You can also read difficult parts of the book with the student or do a shared or assisted reading. In an **assisted reading,** you read the difficult parts and the student reads the easy parts. A poor reader may also elect to read along with a more adept reader in a partner reading (Fielding & Roller, 1992). In a partner reading, the more adept reader reads the difficult portion and the less able reader chimes in when she or he is able to.

See Chapter 7 for a step-by-step discussion of the text-walk technique which can be adapted and used to help students cope with a difficult book.

**Assisted reading:** procedure that provides supports such as reading difficult parts of a text so students can read texts that they couldn't read on their own.

You might also read a portion of the book to the students and let them take it from there. Sometimes you can use an easier book to build needed background for a more difficult book on the same topic. For instance, *Hungry, Hungry Sharks* (Cole, 1986), which is written on an easy second-grade level, could be preparation for reading a more difficult text on sharks. Or you might obtain taped versions of books and let students read along.

When selecting books for the classroom library, be sure to have books on a wide range of difficulty, one that encompasses all the abilities in your class. For struggling readers, seek out books and other materials that are easy and interesting and which look mature. Low-achieving readers are quick to reject books that appear to be immature. Also let students see you reading easy books. Emphasize the appeal of the book rather than its low-readability level.

### *Teaching Book Selection*

From time to time, discuss book selection. During sharing time, students might share their experiences selecting books that seemed especially enjoyable or informative.

Discuss and provide instruction for book selection. Model the process. Show how you might look at the cover, read the blurb on the dust jacket, and leaf through the book to see if it looks interesting. Show how you might check out a page or two "to see how the book reads." Explain that you want to see if the book is written in an interesting way and you also want to make sure that the book is not too hard. At this point you might want to develop a list of criteria for choosing a book. A sample set of criteria is listed in Table 17-4.

## *Initiating Voluntary Reading*

You might want to start off with brief periods of free reading and gradually extend the sessions. You will need to establish ground rules for how books are selected and what kinds of materials are appropriate. If possible, have students select books before the session begins or allow selections to be made during the first five minutes. Otherwise, the time for reading will be eaten up. You might also suggest that students choose two books, so, if they don't like one, they can read the other.

### *Additional Suggestions for Promoting Voluntary Reading*

Find out which authors students like and recommend additional books by that author. If students have read one book by Betsy Byars and enjoyed it, chances are they'll enjoy other books written by her. This is doubly true of series books. Some preteens apparently can't get enough of the Baby-Sitters Club books or the Goosebumps series. Richek and McTague (1988) found that third-graders in a *Chapter I* class enjoyed reading Curious George books and showed improvement in both reading and writing when encouraged to read them. Also provide book discussion sessions. This gives students a chance to talk over their reading and it also informs other students about books that they might like to read. Students are more likely to act on peer recommendations than they are on those made by teachers, parents, or librarians (Gallo, 1985). Other ways to promote voluntary reading are listed below:

- If eligible, participate in RIF (Reading is Fundamental).
- Have students keep a record of books read.
- Selecting books is often a problem for low-achieving readers. Use book selection software such as BookLink, which was mentioned earlier in this chapter.
- Students who are turned off by conventional books might respond favorably to CD-ROM books, many of which feature animation, film clips, background music, sound effects. With CD-ROM books, students have the option of having the whole text or words that they highlight read to them.

**TABLE 17-4 Choosing a Book**

| |
|---|
| Is the book interesting? |
| Do I know all or most of the words on the page? |
| Can I read it smoothly? |
| Is it short enough, or is it too long? |
| Would I say this book is too easy, just right, or too hard? |

- Provide a preview of coming attractions. Read a few jokes from a joke book, a few riddles from a riddle book, or just enough of a mystery or adventure book so that the reader is left wondering what will happen next.
- Display activity books and accompany the books with the implements needed to conduct the activity. A book on magnets would be accompanied by magnets, a book on microscopes would be accompanied by a microscope, a book on plants would be accompanied by a pot of soil and seeds, etc.
- Arrange for older low-achieving readers to read to younger students. Have them select the books they will read. Also help them practice reading the book aloud.
- Encourage students to join book clubs, if this is not a financial hardship for anyone. Also have a swapping rack where students can trade books anytime they want by simply substituting any book that they bring in for the one they take.
- Encourage students to review books and make recommendations. One children's library in Connecticut puts a silver seal on books that its readers recommend. Post a listing of recommended books.
- Use excerpts from anthologies as motivators. Many selections in basals and secondary anthologies are excerpts. If students have particularly enjoyed a selection, give them the title of the whole work. Better yet, obtain a copy of the work. Before recommending the whole work, check it over to make sure it is suitable for students. The version in the anthology may have been adapted to make it easier. You might also recommend and obtain other books by authors featured in an anthology. Students who have enjoyed an anthology selection by Eve Bunting might want to try some other pieces that she has written.
- Hold a book fair. The book fair can be sponsored by the school, by a local book store, or a shopping mall.
- Obtain books and audiotapes to accompany them. This gives students the opportunity to become acquainted with books that might be too much of a struggle for them to read on their own.
- You might try giving students credit for their reading. Using a computer program known as Accelerated Reading, students in one middle school choose from a list of 750 books that range in difficulty from fourth grade through adult (Tofig, 1994). After reading the book, students take a brief test on the computer and are given points for their reading. Points earned depend on the nature of the book—longer books are awarded more credits—and the percentage of items answered correctly on the book quiz. Total points earned becomes a part of the students' grade. Challenged by the project, students read an average of ten books.

Accelerated Reading has a variety of programs, including several designed for below-level readers. Contact P.O. Box 95, Port Edwards, WI 54469, 800-338-4204.

## *Technology for the Reading/Writing Program*

Technology plays a dual role for low-achieving readers and writers. Through computers, videocassettes, and videodiscs, traditional topics can be presented in new and more interesting ways. Through computer simulations, students can be more deeply involved in their learning. As both hardware and software become more sophisticated, the amount of interaction between student and material can be increased. In addition, with some programs, students are able to obtain help with background information and vocabulary, receive additional instructions, have segments read aloud or branch into an easier portion.

## *Computers as Literacy Tools*

Increasingly, computers are becoming literacy tools. They can help with the organization, composition, analysis, and dissemination of information. Through adaptive technology, computers can be used to compensate for difficulties in reading and writing. Talking programs, such as *Dr. Peet's Talk/Writer* (Hartley) and *Special Writer Coach* (Tom Snyder) are especially helpful for students who have difficulty reading or writing. Hearing their piece read back to them, they will be more likely to note awkward expressions, missing *-ing* and *-ed* endings, and omitted words. Even the best writers read over glaring errors, but would probably recognize them if they heard them read aloud.

Word processing programs also help disabled writers with several production problems. Handwriting is no longer an issue, and the spell checker can be of invaluable assistance to students who have serious spelling problems. It is especially helpful for those students who fail to detect misspellings even when they search for them. Students will still need spelling skills, however. They'll need to recognize whether or not they have chosen the correct spelling for homophones like *there, their,* and *they're.* They'll also be required to select the correct spelling when offered several choices. Because making changes doesn't require a total rewrite, word processing programs lend themselves to revising and editing.

### *Computerized Writing Aids*

There are a number of word processing programs that aid in the writing process by supplying structure or prompts or both. The *Semantic Mapper* (Teacher Support Software) helps students brainstorm and organize their thoughts. *Bankstreet Prewriter* (Scholastic), *Prewrite* (Mindscape), and *Quill* (D.C. Heath) also have planning components. *FrEd Writer II, Bank Street Writer III* (Scholastic), and *Magic Slate II* (Sunburst), allow the teacher to supply customized prompts. The revising process is fostered by software such as *Writer's Helper* (Conduit), *Ghost Writer* (MECC), *Process Writer* (Scholastic), and *Grammatik Mac* (Reference Software). For instance, *Ghost Writer* aids editing by removing portions of the sentence and highlighting certain features, such as punctuation, thereby, making it easier for the student to focus on one element.

> Although far from perfect, the grammar checkers in word processing programs can help students discover errors.

**Exemplary Teaching: Using Technology**

Although he was in the fifth grade, Andrew's writing was painfully slow. Words were printed in mixed upper and lowercase letters, with many words misspelled. Because the physical art of writing was so difficult for him, Andrew wrote as little as possible, often no more than a sentence or two. Wisely, Andrew's teacher, Cora Lee Five, persuaded him to use the word processor. Even though he had not had any instruction in keyboarding, using the computer was faster for Andrew than printing. Andrew also found that it was easier to make corrections on the computer. Relieved of the painstaking task of printing his pieces by hand, Andrew gradually increased the length and quality of his compositions (Five, 1992). What is a helpful tool for most people is a virtual necessity for students like Andrew.

## *Telecomputing*

Using telecomputing also does wonders for the self-esteem of problem learners. Using high-tech tools can provide a first-class boost to youngsters who often feel like second-class learners.

One of the capabilities of the computer is that it can transport students beyond the classroom. With the proper connections and software, students can exchange e-mail with other students—including students in other countries—join groups in other schools to explore topics, work on projects, tap into data bases of information, or even communicate with the President of the United States at president@whitehouse.gov.

Rapidly becoming an essential communication tool, telecomputing is highly motivational for both students and teachers (Peha, 1995). In addition, telecomputing prods students into putting more effort into their writing. Students take more care with their writing when they are communicating with a pen pal or source of information. Students are also more collaborative as they work on projects with classmates or students in distant places.

Just as with any other set of activities or materials, technology should be integrated into your curriculum. You need to ask such questions as: How can technology foster improved reading and writing? How might students use these tools to become better readers and writers?

Through the Internet, students can obtain virtually unlimited informational resources; communicate with individuals throughout the world by e-mail, newsgroups, video, and voice; and share their own artifacts of learning with others" (Ryder & Graves, 1996–97).

Or course, caution must be taken when using a vast source of information, such as the Internet. Some of the information on the Internet is not appropriate for students, and, unfortunately, there are individuals using the Internet who might pose a danger to young people. Most experts suggest constructing a code of conduct with students and parents and using services that are children-friendly and have built-in safeguards against inappropriate material or contacts (Peha, 1995; Frazier, 1995).

## *Videos*

Videos can be used to motivate and prepare students for reading. Having seen a dramatization of the story, students may then wish to read the book from which the story was taken. Having viewed the video, students are better prepared to understand the text. Videos can also be used to complement a reading. If the video has been well done, viewing it can extend the students' pleasure and understanding.

Videos can be used to build background for difficult words or concepts or even substitute for reading a difficult selection. If a classic tale is too difficult for students to read on their own, then they can at least have the experience of seeing it on video. Informational videos, of course, make excellent background builders, especially when accompanied by preparation, discussion, and follow-up activities.

**Adapted technology:** use of devices to assist people who have a physical disability or learning problem to perform tasks that would otherwise be difficult or impossible.

## *Adaptive Technology*

**Adaptive technology** has the power to help students cope more effectively with their reading and writing difficulties. For students who have serious spelling problems, word prediction software can be a lifesaver. As soon as a character is typed, the software lists a series of words that start with that letter and could fit the context of the piece. The student can then choose rather than type the word that he intended to use, thus eliminating the need to spell the word. Because it reduces keystrokes, the software can also be used by people who have physical disabilities.

One of the latest developments in adaptive technology is the appearance of voice activated computers. Using a voice recognition device, the computer responds to speech so that the student does not have to type in a story. Here's how a voice recognition word processing program known as *Dragon Dictate* (Dragon Systems) works.

The writer says a word. The word that the computer "thinks" the writer has spoken is highlighted on the screen. Other possibilities are listed beneath it. If the computer is correct, the speaker-writer simply continues. If the computer is wrong, the speaker-writer tells the computer which word it should be. Words can also be added by vocally spelling them out or typing them in. Commands can also be spoken rather than typed. The program can be used by students whose ability to spell is very limited and by students who are physically unable to type.

For students who have serious reading problems, reading systems are available. These typically consist of a scanner, optical character reading software, a word processing program, and a speech synthesizer. The text that the student wishes to read is scanned into the word processing program. Once scanned in and analyzed by optical character reading software, it is read aloud by the computer's voice synthesizer. Anything that can be scanned in can be read. The reader will have to supply the occasional word that the scanner's software is unable to pronounce or which it mispronounces.

Additional information about adaptive technology and software is available from the following sources:

Apple Computer
20525 Marianai Avenue
Cupertino, CA 95014

IBM
4111 Northside Parkway
Atlanta, GA 30327

A sampling of adaptive software and technology devices is presented in Table 17-5. Although the software is generally relatively inexpensive, the hardware can be costly. However, grants from private groups and local, state, and federal government agencies are available to offset these costs.

## *Minicase Study*

Bright and articulate and with an excellent background of information, Troy, a third-grader, was surprisingly quiet at school. A slow-progress reader, Roy was struggling with end-of-first-grade books while his buddies had advanced to lengthy chapter books. Embarrassed by his lack of success in reading, Troy withdrew into himself.

Referred to a university reading center, Troy made limited progress. Because of his past painful experiences with reading and writing, he resisted attempts to teach him. Much of the instructional time was spent trying to keep Troy on task. He had mastered the art of sidetracking lessons into discussions that were interesting but not pertinent. He also chal-

**TABLE 17-5 Adaptive Hardware and Software**

| Program | Publisher | Format |
|---|---|---|
| Word Prediction Software | | |
| *Predict It* | Don Johnston | Apple 11GS |
| *Word Writer* | McIntyre Computer Systems | Mac |
| *Telepathic* | Prentke Romach Co. | Mac |
| Talking Software | | |
| *Kid Works II* | Davidson | PC |
| *Dr. Peet's Talk/Writer* | Hartley | Mac, PC |
| *Special Writer Coach* | Tom Snyder | Mac, PC |
| *Talking Keys* | Brady Graham | Mac |
| *Write: Outloud* | Don Johnston | Mac |
| Reading System (scans and reads text) | | |
| *Arkenstone Reader II* | Arkenstone, Inc. | PC |
| *Omni 3000* | Kurzweil Educational Systems | PC |
| Speech Recognition | | |
| *Dragon Dictate* | Dragon Systems, Inc. | Mac, PC |

lenged activities with comments such as: "Why do I have to read that book" or "I don't want to write." Often he succeeded in manipulating the instructor into a battle of wills.

Noting Troy's limited progress, provision was made for building on Troy's interest and giving him choices. The teacher offered him a choice of three or four books, encouraged him to select writing topics, and let him choose the order of activities. Troy became more cooperative but was still highly distractible. Reading had no intrinsic value for Troy. While Troy enjoyed being read to, he resisted attempts to entice him to read on his own.

Because of Troy's reluctance to read, his instructor read books to him. When she came to a particularly easy portion, she would persuade Troy to read a page or two. After each session, Troy's teacher invited him to take home one of the books that had been used in the session or a book from the center's fairly extensive library. Troy emphatically turned down all invitations.

During one session, his teacher introduced Troy to *Fox Be Nimble* (Marshall, 1990). Because the book was longer than the ones they had been working in, the teacher share read the first chapter. Troy was intrigued by Fox's antics and also liked the idea that it had chapters. He asked if he could take the book home. At home Troy read and reread the entire book. He also took it into school so that he and his friends could act out the parts of Fox and the other characters. Troy even volunteered to read segments from *Fox Be Nimble* to the whole class, something he had never done before.

Although reading was still somewhat of a struggle, Troy was motivated to use dormant strategies and to acquire new ones. He now had a reason for reading. Reading had become satisfying and enjoyable.

Capitalizing on Troy's interest in Fox, his teacher brought in other books in the Fox series. Troy read each one, and some he read twice. By this time, Troy was regularly requesting permission to take the Fox books home. In time he also began reading books by other authors. Through sustained reading of interesting texts, Troy's fluency improved. More importantly, so did his confidence and his desire to read.

## Summary

One of the most important instructional decisions that a teacher makes is matching the reader with appropriate materials. Subjective assessment should be used along with objective formulas to obtain the most valid assessment of the difficulty level of texts. In assessing difficulty level, reader's background and interests and a variety of text features need to be considered. Most educational publishers use formulas to assess the difficulty level of their materials. A number of sources provide information on the readability of trade books.

Because of a lack of skill or a dislike of reading, poor readers read less and so, fall further behind. Breaking that cycle is an essential component of an effective reading program. If low-achieving readers do not read voluntarily, they have little chance of making satisfactory progress. Key components of a voluntary reading program include obtaining easy-to-read materials that match students' interests, making students feel like readers, and stressing the value of voluntary reading.

Technology can assist low-achieving readers by providing them with materials that are interesting, instructive, and interactive. Technological tools and adaptive technology can help students compensate for learning difficulties. Technological advances that are becoming increasingly popular are CD-ROM and videodiscs.

## Application Activities

1. Use the Fry Graph or another readability assessment measure to estimate the readability level of the content-area text or a trade book that your class is reading or might read. How does your assessment compare with that supplied by the publisher?
2. Using one of the resources listed in the chapter, locate five high-interest, low-readability books. What makes them easy? With whom might you use them?
3. Visit a class or lab in which students are using telecomputing, simulation software, or other high-tech devices. What do you see as the main value of this technology? What are some of its drawbacks? If possible, try out software or other technological device with a small group of students. Note their response.
4. Plan a motivational campaign to promote voluntary reading. If possible, institute the campaign and evaluate its effectiveness.

# Chapter 18

# Organization of Early Intervention and Corrective Programs

## Using What You Know

Corrective instruction is changing. From an isolated skills emphasis in a resource room, instruction is becoming more holistic and more collaborative. There is greater coordination between the corrective specialist and the classroom teacher and, increasingly, corrective instruction is taking place in the classroom. In addition, corrective programs typically include writing as well as reading.

With what corrective reading or writing programs are you familiar? What are the components of the program? How effective is the program? What do you think should be the components of an exemplary corrective program?

## Anticipation Guide

Read each of the following statements. Put a check under "Agree" or "Disagree" to show how you feel about each one. If possible, discuss your responses with classmates.

| | Agree | Disagree |
|---|---|---|
| **1.** Corrective instruction has been proven to be effective. | ______ | ______ |
| **2.** Except for the most severe cases, the classroom teacher should have major responsibility for the instruction of her or his pupils. | ______ | ______ |
| **3.** Small-group corrective instruction is more practical than one-on-one teaching. | ______ | ______ |

4. Students in the earliest grades should be given the highest priority for corrective instruction. ________ ________
5. Although whole language approaches might work well with achieving students, corrective students need a skills approach. ________ ________

## *The Changing Face of Remediation*

In the past, remediation of reading and writing difficulties was approached as a separate strand of the literacy program. Not infrequently, the specialist deliberately planned a program that was different from the one taught by the classroom teacher. All too often, the specialist didn't even know what the classroom teacher was doing and vice versa. Further intensifying the isolation of the literacy specialist and the program was the way remediation was conducted. Typically, the student was removed from the classroom and taught in a resource room, clinic, or reading center. Classroom teachers were frustrated by having their neediest pupils miss essential lessons.

> **Inclusion:** policy of educating all students, including those with special needs, within the regular classroom. With *partial inclusion,* students may be included for some classes but not others.

Today corrective programs are becoming more holistic and are being integrated into the total school program. Because today's corrective strand stresses strategy instruction, **inclusion,** collaboration, and the principle that students learn to read and write by reading and writing, it is easier to blend remediation into the overall program. Pull-out remediation is being supplanted by arrangements that give corrective students added or adjusted reading and writing instruction within the classroom or supply them with additional easy children's books to provide the extra practice that they need. Activities such as shared reading, collaborative teaching, accommodating individual differences by making modifications, and cooperative learning have reduced the need to isolate slower moving pupils. In some holistic classes in which pupils of all abilities are integrated, outsiders can't tell the achieving children from those who have special needs.

This doesn't mean that some students won't need specialized help. Although most reading and writing problems can be remediated through careful instruction, extra review and practice, modifications, and supplementary inclass instruction, there is a small percentage of students who may need specialized help and techniques. Often this can be provided by having the specialist work with these students within the classroom. On occasion, it may mean removing the student from the classroom for intensive one-on-one instruction as in the preventive program Reading Recovery (see Chapter 7).

### *A Better Classroom Program*

Actually, the best way to attack the problem of reading and writing deficiency is to create a highly effective program for the whole school. This will minimize the number of students who need extra help. And it will also build the skills of the students who have been remediated.

> Allington (1994) stresses the need for enhancement of classroom instruction. "The primary role of special program funds and personnel would be to enhance the quality of classroom literacy instruction available to children finding learning to read and write difficult" (p. 25).

If students are placed in a special program, that program should be coordinated with the classroom program. The corrective teacher may use intensive phonics, the VAKT (Fernald), or some other specialized technique. Through discussions and careful planning, the specialist and classroom teacher can create programs that are mutually supportive. For instance, classroom teachers may schedule extra reading of books that contain short vowels because that is being taught in the corrective program. On the other hand, if the classroom teacher is presenting short vowels, the corrective teacher may provide complementary instruction, perhaps through Word Building. Both should agree, too, on which strategies the child will use to attack new words. They may decide to have the child seek out pronounceable word parts and reconstruct the word by building on those or use an analogy strategy. Or they may decide to have the child analyze the word letter by letter or holistically through context and sounding out the initial consonant. As Pikulski (1994) observes:

> *Students' total program of reading instruction should be considered when planning a program for early intervention. Tutoring and extra time pull-out programs certainly can be effective; however, for maximum impact, early intervention programs should try to insure that students are receiving excellent and coordinated instruction both in their classrooms and in the special intervention programs. (p. 38)*

## *Collaboration*

> **Collaboration** entails having classroom teachers and resource personnel work together. Collaboration may be between the teacher and the specialist, and also between specialists from different disciplines.

Collaboration is the key to providing the best possible program for low-achieving readers and writers. In a **collaboration,** the reading specialist works with the student's teacher(s), other specialists and administrators, parents, and the student to plan, implement, and monitor a program. Collaboration is especially important in reading and writing instruction. The classroom teacher should be involved in every phase of the program from assessment through instruction. During assessment it is essential to obtain information about the student from the teacher. The teacher can shed light on the students' work habits, ability to get along with others, and strengths and weaknesses in a variety of academic areas, not just reading and writing. Specialists working with the classroom teacher should decide on the best program for the student.

Setting is another important consideration. The current emphasis is on inclusionary programs in which the student is taught within the classroom. This can be quite economical in terms of time, if the specialist is working with several students from the teacher's room. One of the results of scheduling should be that students get more instructional time in reading and writing. Ironically, in many pullout programs, low-achieving readers left their classrooms for corrective instruction during reading time, thus depriving them of in-class reading instruction.

## *Professionals Working Together*

When given the opportunity to create their own corrective programs, teachers and corrective specialists, working together, created a variety of patterns of organization, including team teaching, cooperative grouping, in-class corrective programs, and combined pull-out and in-class programs (Gelzheiser & Meyers, 1990).

In some designs, corrective students spent part of their time in the resource room and part in the classroom. When the corrective teacher worked within the classroom, she assisted the classroom teacher or provided one-on-one or small-group instruction to corrective students who needed extra help. In a design that made very efficient use of time, the classroom teacher worked with the achieving readers, while the specialist taught the corrective group. Normally the corrective group would have been engaged in seatwork at that time.

At the Academy School, a public school in Connecticut, teachers take a team approach to inclusion. The specialist, who has had additional training in strategy instruction, might introduce a new strategy to the class. The classroom teacher follows up by discussing with the class how they might apply the strategy. As the students apply the strategy, both teachers provide assistance to individual students and to small groups. The specialist pays particular attention to students who have special needs but also provides help to other students. Lessons are so well coordinated and seamless that the outside observer wouldn't know which teacher was the specialist and which was the classroom teacher nor which students were ones with special needs.

> The role of the language arts specialist is changing from a corrective teacher whose mission is to work with students with severe reading problems, to a consultant involved with all aspects of the language arts program.

One benefit of the team approach is that the teachers learn from each other. The classroom teacher learns about new strategies and ways of assisting low-achieving readers and writers. The specialist learns about the curriculum and how to teach strategies in such a way that they can be used to foster learning in content areas. Instead of pulling low-achieving readers and writers out for isolated instruction, the specialist is teaching them within the context of the total classroom. The specialist's students benefit because they learn strategies that they need to survive academically. The achieving readers and writers also learn the strategies. Although the achieving readers and writers might not need the strategies for academic survival, they find them to be useful. Everyone benefits.

Although there was some concern that in-class corrective instruction might cause some students receiving help to react unfavorably, the problem readers in a study conducted by Gelzheiser and Meyers (1990) preferred in-class instruction. They appreciated getting extra help, and they also were pleased that they could remain with their peers. As a matter of fact, the corrective teachers generally supplied help to whoever needed it, whether the student was classified as being corrective or not. Being given extra help came to be seen as a normal routine, rather than a service required by a few low achievers. In addition, organizational patterns like cooperative learning, literature circles, reading and writing workshops, and conferences lend themselves to in-class corrective assistance because specialists can work in those frameworks effectively but unobtrusively.

Additional staffing also led to greater individualization. With another professional in the room, there was more opportunity for students to receive one-on-one or small group instruction.

One benefit of collaboration was a reduction in seatwork. Gelzheiser and Meyers (1990) observed, "Use of a pull-in program allowed low-achieving students to spend their entire reading period receiving instruction and eliminated seatwork" (p. 424).

There are, of course, some drawbacks to in-class corrective instruction. More planning time is required. It is essential that the classroom teacher and the specialist plan together on a regular basis. In addition, there can be a lack of flexibility. If the corrective teacher is scheduled to be in the room at 10:30, then the classroom teacher would need to adhere to that schedule. The corrective specialist in Gelzheiser and Meyers' study also found that when there were only one or two corrective students in a class, it was a more economical use of time to see students from several classes in a small group on a pull-out basis.

Working collaboratively also demands new skills and new attitudes. Professionals need to learn to plan and work together and to create a coherent program, even when they have very different ideas about how reading and writing should be taught.

### Exemplary Teaching: Working with Other Professionals

How might a *Title I* teacher revamp her program so that it becomes a pull-in rather than a pull-out model? Standerford (1993), a *Title I* teacher, offers an outstanding example.

Realizing that her *Title I* students weren't making the gains that they seemed capable of, Standerford started searching for reasons. Skill and drill hadn't worked. Skill instruction was isolated from sufficient opportunities for meaningful application. Moving to a more holistic program that featured cooperative grouping didn't work either. The thirty minutes a day allocated to the fifth-graders in the *Title I* program just didn't allow for extended exploration. Besides, since all the students were performing on a low level, they couldn't help each other. Being stereotyped as *Title I* participants, the students had low expectations for themselves, as did their teachers.

Meanwhile, back in the classroom, Cindy W., the fifth-grade teacher, was pleased with the progress her better students were making in her holistic approach but was concerned about the lowest-achieving students. They simply weren't making adequate progress. The two teachers joined forces. As a result of collaborative planning, they constructed a program in which both worked in Cindy W's classroom. Their aim was to "develop all students into successful communicators" (p. 43). To achieve that aim, they provide whatever support was necessary.

As the two planned the program, Standerford's role was to make suggestions that would enable *Title I* students to complete assignments. The two teachers had already decided on cooperative grouping so that the more able students could help the less able ones. Standerford helped make up individual assignments that capitalized on the strengths of the *Title I* students. For instance, *Title I* students were adept at discussing stories but had difficulty composing summaries. The more proficient writers in the group helped the *Title I* students translate their oral summaries into written ones.

Standerford also devised teaching techniques that would enable *Title I* students to compensate for their weaknesses. For instance, if students had difficulty reading a selection, the difficult parts of the selection or the whole selection was read to them. All students were provided with expert direct instruction in effective reading and writing strategies and then given whatever support was necessary to enable them to apply the strategies. With two teachers in the class and the mix of able and less able students in each group, there was far more support than there had been.

As a result of the collaborative program, both students' expectations of themselves and teachers' expectations of students rose. Rising expectations were accompanied by enhanced self-esteem and improved performance in reading comprehension and writing.

## Components of a Corrective Program

Although the corrective program should be an integral part of the regular program, it should also have certain key elements. These elements are explored in the following section.

### Goals

**Goal:** general statement of what students are expected to learn.

A clear statement of **goals** is the first step in creating an effective program. A statement of philosophy is also helpful. From the statement of general goals should flow specific **objectives.**

Successful programs have overall goals and specific objectives and concrete ways of determining whether goals and objectives have been met. For instance, the overall goal of Reading Recovery is to help students who are falling behind in reading to catch up with their peers. More specifically, the objective is to accelerate students' progress so that after about twelve to twenty weeks of one-to-one instruction, they will have attained the same level of proficiency as their peers. In addition, they will have a self-extending system. They will be able to read well enough so that they can make progress on their own.

One source of goals/objectives is the *English Language Arts Standards* (NCTE, IRA, 1996).

The Boulder Project, an early intervention program that is used with small groups of first graders who are having difficulty learning to read, also has a specific objective. The objective is that children will be able to read at least on a primer level (Hiebert, 1994). More specifically, it was hoped that children would be able to read *A Kiss for Little Bear* (Minarik, 1957), a favorite children's book, by the end of the school year.

More complex and extensive than Reading Recovery or the Boulder Project, Success for All, a program designed for all students in grades kindergarten through three, has as its overall goal improved performance in reading and writing by disadvantaged elementary school students. It intends to ensure, through prevention and intensive intervention, the success of every child. Success for All is a program that "refuses to accept the idea than even a single child will fail to learn to read" (Slavin, Madden, Karweit, & Dolan, 1994, p. 126). The program also hopes to halt retention of students and reduce the number placed in special education.

These broad goals are translated into a series of assessments. Student reading achievement is measured as is retention rate and numbers of students tracked into special education.

### Selecting Students

A major practical concern of intervention programs is selecting pupils who need special help and scheduling instruction. A basic principle of selection is to choose those students who have the greatest need. In some circumstances, laws and regulations govern the selection process. Students are chosen for an LD class on the basis of discrepancy guidelines. There is a discrepancy between potential and achievement. For Title I students, standards of achievement are typically used. In the past, students falling below a certain cut-off point—the twenty-third percentile of a standardized reading test, for example—were chosen for Title I programs. Current Title I regulations call for using assessment measures that are aligned with standards established by the states. Under this plan, students who fail to meet criteria set by the state are selected for Title I programs. Reading Recovery and a number of other early intervention programs simply select the lowest-achieving students. This might be the lowest-achieving 20 percent or the neediest three students in a class.

As noted in Chapter 1, both methods of selection have their advantages and disadvantages. Using a discrepancy formula eliminates students who are low achievers in reading because they are lacking in ability. However, given the fallibility of tests of cognitive ability, there is a high probability that some students who score low on intelligence tests have more ability than is indicated. In addition, poor readers, who are cut off from reading, a major source of vocabulary development and information, score lower on IQ tests, especially those that rely heavily on verbal areas. On the other hand, using an arbitrary cutoff score denies help to bright underachievers who are reading on or close to grade level, but because of their above-average ability, should be reading beyond grade level. And what about the students who score just slightly above the cutoff score? Shouldn't they be given some help? As a practical matter, it is helpful to consider both factors: discrepancy and low achievement. Having some measure of a student's cognitive ability or language development is helpful when making selections, as long as that information is used flexibly. It is also important to consider whether the student's difficulties are interfering with his ability to function with literacy tasks in and out of school.

Although you want to be flexible when choosing students for corrective help, it is important to have criteria. You may wish to consult with the administration, teachers, and parents and incorporate their suggestions when setting criteria for selection. One selection consideration includes choosing younger versus older pupils. The idea of intervening early so that students aren't trapped into corrective classes year after year is appealing. But you also have to provide for older students.

> Because of the fallibility of tests and other assessment instruments, it is wise to use more than one selection device.

> Take care when interpreting measures used with students who have not had an equal opportunity to learn. As McGill-Franzen (1994) notes, the role of prior knowledge or experience on assessment devices is "often grossly underrated" (p. 19).

### *Screening Devices*

There are numerous assessment devices that can be used to select students for a program. The selection devices chosen will depend on the goals of the program, the philosophy of reading, and the corrective or intervention procedures. A program that emphasizes letter–sound relationships will probably include a measure of phonics. One that includes writing will probably assess writing. A program that chooses the lowest-achieving students regardless of cognitive ability will not require a measure of aptitude. On the other hand, those that rely on a discrepancy formula will need some measure of ability. Some selection devices that are frequently used include the following.

- Norm Referenced Tests
- Informal Reading Inventories
- Group Reading Inventories
- Criterion-referenced Tests
- Observation
- Writing Samples or Portfolios
- Teacher Recommendations

Tests of oral reading, phonemic awareness, alphabet knowledge, phonics, or other skills and strategies might also be used to select students for a program.

### *Multiple Selection Devices*

Although group tests, whether norm-referenced or criterion-referenced, might be used as a screening device to identify students who might need intervention or a corrective program, they should not be used as the sole selection device. Group tests, because of the guessing factor, can provide erroneous information for individuals. Portfolios, observations, and individual tests, together with recommendations by professionals, should also be used in the selection process.

### *Mandated Selection*

Increasingly, reading specialists are involved in programs that are governed by state and federal laws. In addition to providing funding for programs and services that benefit low-achieving readers and writers, these laws also specify aspects of the selection process, testing program, and the design and delivery of services. Major legislation that affects corrective reading and writing are the Individuals with Disabilities Act of 1990 and Title I provisions, which are described in Chapter 1. In addition, there are state-mandated competency tests. According to a recent survey, forty-five of the fifty states conduct some form of statewide reading assessment (Afflerbach, 1990). In some areas, the tests are used to flag students who may need corrective instruction in reading and writing. And in some instances, passing on to the next grade or earning a high school diploma is dependent upon exceeding the test's cutoff score. Test scores are also used in this way in many local school districts and in individual schools. Tests used to make critical decisions of this type are often known as **high stakes tests.**

> Although most state competency tests use multiple-choice assessments there is a growing use of instruments that require students to construct a written response.

> A **high stakes test** is one in which the results are used to make a critical decision about a student, i.e., passing on to the next grade, graduating.

> The corrective strand of the program should be coordinated with the school's language arts curriculum. Strategies taught through corrective instruction should be those that the student can apply in his regular classroom.

## *Curriculum*

The curriculum for a corrective program should reflect the school's philosophy of reading, goals, the nature of the program, and the students' needs. The curriculum should also be balanced and mesh with what is being done in the classroom. Although the specific needs of the student or group should be addressed, the program should not be too narrow. For instance, if a child has difficulty with word identification, there should be an emphasis on word level skills and strategies. However, these need to be applied within the context of real reading, lest you create a competent decoder who fails to read for meaning or dislikes reading. Too broad a program, on the other hand, might result in one that is unfocused and so is ineffective.

## *Instructional Approaches*

The core of an intervention or corrective program is the instructional approach. The program planner has many decisions to make. Will the program use direct instruction? Will it use holistic approaches? Or will it use some type of combination of the two? Will there be an emphasis on application of skills and strategies? Will voluntary reading be fostered? Will specialized word-learning techniques, such as VAKT, be used with students who have severe reading problems? Will process writing be a part of the program? Will a highly structured writing approach, such as CSIW, be used? The instructional activities should fit in with the philosophy and overall goals of the program. Above all, the instructional components should also consider the strengths and needs of the students.

## *Instructional Schedule*

Scheduling students for fewer than two sessions a week is probably not worthwhile. There would be a lack of continuity and too much forgetting because of the lapse of time between sessions. Five sessions a week is ideal, but may be impractical if there are a large number of students who need help.

For a program to make a difference, a significant amount of time is needed. Based on an analysis of a number of studies, Guthrie, Seifert, and Kline (1978) concluded that a minimum of fifty hours of corrective instruction is required for sustained gains. In the *Boulder Project* (Hiebert, 1994) and *Early Intervention in Reading* (Taylor, Strait, & Medo, 1994), two corrective programs for at-risk first-graders, many students needed a full year before showing adequate progress, and about one in four needed a second year of extra help.

## *Typical Corrective Session*

Time is limited in a corrective class, so it is important to have sessions that are well planned and energetic. The typical session lasts from thirty to fifty minutes and might include three to seven or even more students. A daily session might include: review of past material, introduction or extension of a skill or strategy, reading of a new selection, discussion and extension of the selection, and writing, if time allows. There might also be time for reading of a selection by the teacher or an activity chosen by the student.

**Review of Past Material.** Review of past material might include the rereading of a familiar story or discussion of at-home reading. Another possibility is to have students read a poem or brief passage that incorporates a word pattern previously taught, vocabulary words, or a comprehension strategy previously introduced.

**Introduction or Extension of a Strategy.** The strategy can be a word recognition one (using context or analogies or structural analysis) or a comprehension or study strategy.

**Reading of a New Selection.** A new selection is introduced using the directed reading activity, directed reading-thinking activity, KWL Plus or some other technique. The newly taught strategy is applied in the selection. The selection is discussed and extended.

**Related Writing.** As time allows writing is used to support reading. The writing may be a summary, a graphic organizer, a response, a letter to the author, a journal entry, and so forth.

**Personal Choice.** The final activity, which might last as little as five minutes, should be some activity that brings satisfaction to the learner. It could be listening to a story read orally, a crossword puzzle of pattern words, a brief computer program, a photo essay, reading of jokes or riddles, or even singing a song. In addition to being satisfying and enjoyable, the activities should support the students' literacy learning.

## *Discontinuing Students*

After students have been discontinued, meet with them periodically to make sure that they are having success and are able to apply strategies they learned.

According to Harris and Sipay (1990), one practice that can negate the effects of a corrective reading program is setting arbitrary time limits for corrective instruction with the result that students are discontinued from the program too soon. Harris and Sipay (1990) suggest using two criteria to determine if students are ready to be discontinued: Is the student able to meet the reading demands of the regular classroom? Does the student read voluntarily? If the reading demands of the classroom are too great, the student may be overwhelmed, unless given extra help. If the student does not read on her or his own, improvement may cease.

## *Organizational Patterns*

How should low-achieving readers be organized for instruction? One-on-one teaching? Small group? Whole class with supplementary instruction? The organizational pattern to be followed depends upon the nature of the student's difficulty, the resources available, and the policies and philosophy of the local school district.

### *One-on-One and Small-Group Instruction*

The question of how many is too many in a corrective group depends on the severity of the students' difficulties. The greater the needs, the smaller the group should be.

As can be seen from the dramatic results achieved by *Reading Recovery,* one-to-one tutoring by expert teachers results in the most effective instruction. While one-on-one instruction works best for the neediest students, it is not always possible to supply because of resource limitations. The next best organization pattern is the small group. In one study *Title I* professionals teaching small groups found three to be a workable number. "When there were more than three children with low-entry literacy levels, it was difficult to maintain appropriate levels of feedback and involvement" (Hiebert, 1994, p. 102). However, in a study of a supplementary program for low-achieving first-graders, teachers were able to work successfully with five to seven students (Taylor, Strait, & Medo, 1994). In a review of studies of successful corrective programs, Guthrie, Seifert, and Kline (1978) found that the ratio of students to teacher was no higher than four to one. Apparently as ratios grow higher, the teacher's efforts are stretched too thin. Based on the research, then, three to four would seem to be the optimum number for small group instruction

**Modification:** adapting classroom instruction to assist students with special needs. A modification might entail giving a student extra help with hard words.

### *Modifications and Additional Assistance within the Regular Classroom*

An organizational pattern that is growing in popularity, especially where inclusion is being implemented, is whole class instruction accompanied by **modification** and assistance for those who need it. Problem readers and writers are taught as members of the whole class.

Whenever possible, reading and writing time should be maximized. Ideally, low-progress students should have the benefit of regular class and supplementary programs.

However, their assignments might be modified to compensate for difficulties they are having. In addition, they may be given extra help. If, for instance, the class is preparing to write a piece explaining the steps in a process, all students participate in the discussion of possible topics and the demonstration of ways of explaining the process. However, students with serious writing problems might be given additional assistance in the form of think sheets that provide needed structure for writing about a process. A specialist might also be on hand to offer guidance. If the class is reading a selection from *The Rainbow People* (Yep, 1992) and this is well beyond the capabilities of several problem readers, they might listen to the stories on tape. However, they participate in the class discussion of the stories. (See the section on Grouping on p. 496.)

### *Supplementary Instruction*

One way of preventing students from falling behind is to provide supplementary instruction. In *Early Intervention in Reading,* a program for first-graders who need additional assistance, the classroom teacher provides supplementary reading instruction to the lowest five to seven pupils in her class. The instruction lasts for twenty minutes a day and is in addition to seventy to ninety minutes of instruction in the regular reading program. Students chosen may or may not receive *Title I* or special education instruction (Taylor, Strait, & Medo, 1994).

### *Need for an Extended Program*

Although prevention is preferable to remediation, there is a need for specialized reading and writing instruction throughout all the grades. Moreover, as students pass through the grades and the demands of reading change, different types of reading or writing difficulties may surface. The student who had a word identification problem that was successfully remediated in grade one may evidence a comprehension difficulty in grade three or four when the comprehension of informational text of a more technical nature is required. In addition, students whose reading and writing abilities were adequate in the elementary grades, may encounter difficulties in secondary school. The corrective reading/writing program must be a multifaceted one so that it can meet a variety of demands.

## *Pacing*

**Pacing:** rate at which instruction is provided, and the rate at which students are guided through materials.

Pacing is crucial in a program of remediation. **Pacing** is the rate at which students are introduced to new learning and move through materials. The ideal is to accelerate students' progress so that they can catch up with their classmates and so profit from instruction in the regular program. Having caught up, they should not need corrective services, except perhaps for some follow-up or short-term intervention from time to time. Energized teaching, careful sequencing of tasks, not wasting time on activities that have little or no payoff, and promoting independence so that students can extend their learning promote accelerated progress. Involving parents and emphasizing out-of-school reading helps, too (Goldenberg, 1994).

### *A Word of Caution*

Ironically, students most in need of an accelerated pace are often the ones who are provided with a slower moving program in which expectations are set low (McGill-Franzen, 1994).

Accelerated pacing does not mean pushing children beyond their limits or exerting undue pressure. Students' progress should be monitored to make sure that the pace is appropriate. As Harris and Sipay (1990) note:

> *Instructional pacing, and thereby content coverage, should be adjusted to the rate at which the students can assimilate the learnings. Sufficient time must be allowed to absorb and master the material. (p. 111)*

## *Appropriate Materials*

Because they are reading below grade level or perhaps not reading at all, low-achieving readers frequently encounter materials that are too difficult for them. A variety of materials on the appropriate level of difficulty and maturity are an essential component of any corrective or intervention program. Some questions to be asked when considering materials for a corrective program include the following: Will commercially created materials be used? If so, which ones? Will trade books be used? Do the teachers have access to high-interest, low-reading materials for their below-level readers? Do classroom and school libraries have an ample supply of interesting, easy-to-read materials? What kinds of materials are used with low-achieving readers in the content-area classes? Is full use being made of technology? Are students becoming technologically literate? Is adaptive technology being used to assist low-achieving readers and writers?

## *Monitoring*

A key element in successful programs is monitoring of progress. In addition to the use of ongoing monitoring devices, Success for All conducts more formal assessments every eight weeks. Using curriculum-based measures specifically designed for the program, assessments are used to determine who needs tutoring, to change reading groups, to indicate needed changes in programs, and to determine other needs, such as the need for a hearing check or family intervention. The essential ingredient in a monitoring program is making changes when they are needed.

Students in low groups are often given fewer higher-level questions, fewer prompts to assist them in answering questions, and less wait time (Randencich, Beers, & Schumm, 1993).

## *Grouping*

Overall, homogenous grouping has a detrimental effect on low-achieving students (Barr & Dreeben, 1991). Students in the low class or low group are given less attention by the teacher, are less involved in classroom activities, and are given less instructional time (Rist, 1970). They spend less time on reading and are frequently interrupted by other class members (McDermott, 1976). They read fewer pages, are given more concrete assignments, and are more likely to read orally than silently, which means that accurate pronunciation of printed words is likely to be stressed rather than comprehension (Allington, 1984).

### *Whole Class Instruction*

Because of the possible stigma of grouping and the importance of having low-achieving students interact with others in the class, many teachers have turned to whole-class teaching when appropriate. Whole-class teaching also makes efficient use of time. Discussing rules and routines, reading orally to the class, shared reading, and process writing are natural opportunities for whole-class teaching. Some teachers have also experimented with having the whole class read the same selections, either in basals or children's books (Cunningham, Hall, & Defee, 1991). In this scheme all students read a core text together. Through developing background and vocabulary and activating schema, the teacher prepares the whole class to read and may also read part of the selection orally. Students read the selection either as a whole group or by breaking up into small groups. The best readers might read the selection independently, but average and poor readers might be given additional assistance by the teacher. The poorest readers might listen to a taped version, perhaps on earphones, or listen to the teacher read it aloud. (If everyone is given the option of listening to the selection on earphones, this reduces the possibility that listening to a taped version will be a stigma.)

One form of whole-class grouping is to regroup several classes according to reading ability. This procedure has been used effectively in Success for All (Slavin et al., 1994).

The students can regroup for a whole-class discussion of the selection. However, if these students were given differentiated assignments, they might meet in small groups to discuss these. Skills or strategies can also be taught to the class as a whole.

If the gap between the students' reading ability and the difficulty of the material is not too great and the teacher provides additional assistance, then whole group reading is workable. Otherwise, alternative solutions or procedures should be considered. It is imperative that low-achieving readers have ample opportunity to read material that is on their instructional level.

**Two-tier instruction** includes low-achieving readers in whole class instruction but they are also given supplementary instruction and materials geared to their specific needs.

Radencich (1995) suggests the use of **two-tier** instruction for low-achieving readers. The low-achieving readers participate with the whole class in the discussion of a selection that is on grade level. The low-achieving readers have the selection read to them or listen to it on tape. However, they also receive instruction with texts on their instructional level and are given appropriate skills instruction. The books on their level might complement the theme of the material that the whole class is reading or listening to. Cooperative learning and literature circles also work well with low-achieving readers, as do reading workshops.

**Cooperative learning:** form of classroom organization in which students work together to complete learning activities.

**Literature circle:** classroom activity in which a group of students meet to discuss books they are reading.

In **reading workshop,** which is a form of individualized reading, students choose their own books and read at their own pace. Using dialog journals, the students respond to their reading and carry on a written conversation about their reading with their teacher (Atwell, 1987). Conferences may be held to discuss books, monitor students' progress, and provide on-the-spot instruction if needed. If individual conferences are too time-consuming, then group conferences can be held. During conferences, the teacher notes common needs and at the appropriate time provides whole-class instruction if the entire class seems to need

**Reading workshop:** students choose their own books, respond to their reading in a dialog journal, and meet individually or in groups with the teacher to discuss their reading.

Through teacher modeling and role playing, a program known as Book Club emphasizes teaching students techniques for improving the quality of their literary discussions (Raphael & McMahon, 1994).

the skill. Or the teacher assembles an ad hoc group composed of those students who apparently need instruction in the skill. Reading workshop is an excellent way of providing low-achieving readers with appropriate level materials and personalized instruction. Individualized and small group instruction works especially well when an inclusion model is being implemented and several professionals are working in the classroom simultaneously.

Parents of low-achieving readers should be involved in every step of the process. They can supply information about the student's strengths and needs that otherwise might be unrevealed to the school.

## *Involving Parents*

Reading disabilities, especially serious ones, can be a mystery to parents. They don't understand why their child, who is competent in other areas, has difficulty with reading and writing. They may wonder if their child has mental disabilities, is lazy, or is not trying. Of course, these feelings and attitudes rub off on the child and compound the student's difficulties. Instead of being a safe haven, the home reinforces the negative feedback that the student may be getting from his school activities.

Parents need to know the nature of their child's difficulty. It's helpful if they are informed that many bright children have reading difficulties. There should be an ongoing dialog between the parents and the school to inform the parents of the student's progress, enlist the parents' help, and answer questions. If because of illness, death, divorce, neglect, or some other difficulty, it is not possible to involve parents, then the substitute caregiver or a willing relative should be involved (Comer, 1988).

### *Parental Support*

Working with a disabled reader can be slow and intense and sometimes frustrating. These students may need a great deal of repetition and often show no sign today of what they seemed to know yesterday. Progress can be painstakingly slow. However, corrective specialists take great satisfaction in small achievements. Parents may not have this capacity and may even become visibly upset by their youngster's difficulties. Lacking training and objectivity, they may not be well equipped to teach their children. However, they can help in other essential ways. First of all, they can provide love and support and see to it that the child comes to school well rested, fed, and with all the necessary equipment. They can also supply encouragement. Knowing that their youngster, who had a serious word learning problem, would have difficulty in school, the parents of one reading disabled youngster played up his strengths. They enrolled him in arts and crafts and sports activities—areas in which he showed ability—so that he could experience success. These parents also took their child on visits to museums, zoos and nature exhibits and encouraged him to watch educational shows on TV so that he would have a well developed background of experience. Bringing a wealth of knowledge to the printed page, the youngster was able to make maximum use of context clues.

## *Intergenerational Literacy*

One special way of working with parents who have problems with reading and writing is by helping them with their own literacy difficulties so they can better help their children. Parents who are not proficient readers and writers may not realize the essential role they play in the literacy development of their children and so may fail to support their children's literacy learning efforts. In recent years there has been a movement to make literacy learning a family affair.

**Intergenerational literacy:** efforts to build the literacy of older family members and to show them ways to support the literacy of younger members. Also refers to the literacy heritage passed on to younger members.

An **intergenerational literacy** program can take many forms. Parents and children may attend sessions held after school or during the summer. The parents and children may be given separate programs, or the program might be coordinated in such a way that the parents spend some of the time working directly with their children. In other versions, just the parents attend sessions, but they are taught reading and writing skills, which they pass on to their children. Learning how to read on a basic level, parents are then able to read storybooks to their children or help out with homework. In a third version, parents are taught ways to foster their children's reading and writing skills by reading to them, talking with them, or supervising homework. As they learn ways to help their children, their own literacy skills improve. Whatever form it takes, the goal of intergenerational literacy is to improve the skills of both parents and children.

**Family literacy:** all the types of reading and writing in which a family engages, as well as attempts to foster increased ability in reading and writing within the family.

**Family literacy,** which has a somewhat broader meaning than intergenerational literacy, has as its overall goal, the sharing of reading and writing by a family. Although concerned with helping children become proficient readers and writers, it also sees as one of its major goals the transmission of the family's culture from one generation to the next. In one family literacy program, for instance, parents met to write stories about their experiences that they would then share with their children (Akroyd, 1995).

Parents may need extensive guidance in the use of techniques to help foster their children's literacy development. For instance, while working with parents from diverse cultures, Paratore (1995) found that it wasn't enough to provide parents with storybooks and demonstrations on how to read to children. The parents needed many opportunities to observe read-aloud sessions as well as opportunities to practice reading aloud and discuss their read-aloud sessions.

## *Leadership*

An effective program of remediation and intervention requires leadership. Support from the administration is essential. However, the program also needs expert day-to-day guidance. In helping staff work with low-achieving readers and writers, the literacy specialist can provide assistance in a number of ways. Ideally, decisions would be made in collaboration with the staff, perhaps in the form of a reading committee. The staff should work together on the following:

- Construction of a mission statement and goals for the intervention/corrective program.
- Selection of students needing additional help.
- Construction of curriculum for low-achieving readers.
- Selection of approaches and techniques to be used.
- Selection of materials.
- Construction of a parental involvement component.

- Providing instructional suggestions and program changes for individual students and groups.
- Construction or selection of monitoring and assessment components.
- Construction of a professional development component.
- Decisions about when students are ready to be discontinued.
- Coordination of the efforts of all professionals.

## *Working with the Administration*

Working with the administration is crucial. In virtually every study of effective schools, administrative support is a critical element (Hoffman, 1991). Your first order of business is to discuss your program with the key administrators. They'll be more likely to support your program if they understand it, and it makes sense to them. When you meet with administrators, be prepared to answer any questions that they have. Make sure that you're able to explain your program clearly, have a valid rationale for your program, and can buttress your claims with research or achievement results. Also be aware of any other schools in the area that might have similar programs. Once you initiate a program, be sure to document students' performance.

## *Professional Development*

The most essential element in any program of remediation and assessment is the quality of instruction. Successful programs provide ongoing professional development, including follow-up, active supervision, and feedback. They also have a clearly stated approach, philosophy, and a full description of instructional procedures. When the change in a corrective program is significant, then the inservice should be substantial. Many of the exemplary procedures and programs discussed in this text took months or even years to implement fully. Even relatively minor changes should be given adequate time and attention. An introduction of a new procedure should be accompanied by follow-up sessions, a plan for its gradual implementation, feedback, and coaching (Radencich, Beers, & Schumm, 1993).

In addition to formal inservice sessions, make use of informal ways of spreading the word. Share books and videos with staff. Explore ideas in informal conversations and in study groups. Encourage attendance at local and national conferences and arrange for teachers to visit model classes and model programs. Also encourage staff to become professionally active. *Reading Recovery* and whole language teachers are sustained in their growth by highly active networks.

## *Volunteer Tutors*

While there is no substitute for one-on-one instruction by highly trained professionals, volunteer tutoring can achieve remarkable results and may be the best alternative when funds are lacking. According to an extensive review of the research by Cohen, Kulik, and Kulik (1982), one-on-one tutoring works better than small group instruction. What's more, when older low achieving readers tutored younger low achieving readers, the tutors often improved as much as or even more than the tutees. In a recent study, the following factors were felt to be the foundation for effective tutoring (Juel, 1991, 1994).

- Caring, supportive attitude. Tutors showed that they cared. Many also were able to empathize with their students because they themselves remembered struggling with reading and writing when they were in the primary grades.
- Teaching the system. The tutors showed students how words are deciphered, how comprehension is achieved. They helped them gain insight into the process, the "tricks of the trade."
- Breaking down word recognition and spelling into small steps. Tutors dealt with individual sounds and letters so the students could see how words were composed.
- Reinforcement. Tutors provide ample verbal and nonverbal praise and affirmation.

Tutoring programs work best when the tutors are trained and provided with ongoing support and professional supervision. The tutors need to know that they are on the right track and that their efforts are paying off. They also need praise and affirmation.

## *Evaluation*

Each student needs to be evaluated in terms of the goals established for her or him. Students may spend years in a corrective program and make little progress. When students make limited progress, then the situation needs to be examined and changed.

Programs should also undergo periodic evaluation. Programs need to be evaluated in terms of their overall goals and objectives. If one goal is to increase in-class corrective instruction, then that should be assessed. If another goal is to set up an early intervention program to help the lowest achieving 20 percent of first-graders, then that should be assessed too.

Data gathered for evaluation should be broad-based. The Boulder Project, for example, used a variety of assessment devices. Teacher comments about students' performance on book reading, journal writing, and writing of rhyming words were compiled daily. Performance assessment measures of reading and writing were administered at the beginning of the year and at the end of each quarter. Students were also assessed on an informal reading inventory, and writing samples were obtained. To test knowledge of phonics and spelling, students were assessed on graded reading and spelling tests. Norm-referenced test results were also used because they were administered to all students in the district.

Gathering data is only part of evaluation. The data is then used to make a judgment about the effectiveness of the reading program. The question to be asked is: To what extent were the goals of the program met? Once a judgment has been made, the next step in the evaluation program is to make necessary changes. If the intervention or corrective program isn't reaching enough students or fails to remediate a high proportion of them, then the program needs to be analyzed and revamped.

Goals, student selection, curriculum, instructional approaches, instructional schedule, organizational patterns, pacing, materials, monitoring, grouping, involving parents, leadership, professional development, and evaluation are essential elements in a corrective program (the components of an effective literacy program are listed in Table 18-1). Above all else, a successful program for low-achieving readers and writers requires caring, well-trained professionals, the firm belief that low-achieving readers and writers can learn, and a willingness to affirm and build upon the unique gifts that each student possesses.

**TABLE 18-1 Components of an Effective Program**

Goals
- Clearly stated
- Based on a statement of philosophy
- Translated into specific objectives

Selection of Students
- Based on discrepancy between achievement and potential
- Based on failure to achieve a set standard
- Based on a variety of selection devices

Organization
- Uses one-to-one instruction
- Uses small group instruction
- Makes provision for students who need extended instruction
- Attempts to implement an inclusion model

Pacing
- Accelerates students' progress
- Proceeds at a rate that is challenging but not overwhelming
- Promotes out-of-school reading

Monitoring
- Monitors progress on an ongoing basis
- Uses several devices for monitoring
- Adjusts program as necessary

Grouping
- Uses various grouping patterns
- Does not use patterns that stigmatize low achieving readers
- Uses cooperative grouping

Involving Parents
- Explains program to parents
- Keeps parents informed of child's progress
- Involve parents in supporting the child's efforts

Leadership
- A designated person or group is responsible for planning, supervising, and monitoring the program.

Professional Development
- Provision is made for ongoing inservice

Volunteers
- Parents and other volunteers from the community tutor students or act as aides
- Volunteers are instructed, supervised, and affirmed

Evaluation
- Program is evaluated in terms of its goals
- Evaluation is broad-based and uses many sources of assessment information
- Evaluation is used to improve the program

## *Minicase Study*

Trudy Walp offers an outstanding example of how a corrective reading teacher adopted a partial inclusion model. When Trudy Walp became a corrective reading teacher in 1982, the program she inherited was a pullout program consisting of skill and drill. The first thing Trudy did was to shift instruction from drill on isolated skills to teaching skills and strategies in the context of reading literature. She used a skills-through-application rather than a skills-to-application approach. As students read literary selections, they learned and applied the strategies needed to comprehend and appreciate the selections (Walp & Walmsley, 1995).

Later, with the assistance of Sean Walmsley, she constructed a strong core language arts program that offered all students challenging content and opportunities to engage in higher level thinking. The best corrective program will fail unless it is supported by a strong regular program. As Walp and Walmsley commented, "No matter how good a corrective program is, without a strong core curriculum, there will always be limits on the progress that children can make. What is gained from a superb corrective program may well be lost on the children's return to a meager core curriculum" (1995, p. 181).

Over time, Walp began working with problem readers in their classrooms. Within the classroom, Trudy provided instruction, held reading and writing conferences, and observed her students. She also met weekly with the classroom teachers.

Although Walp continued to meet with some corrective pupils in both the classroom and the resource room, now she was much better able to adapt instruction to the needs noted in their classrooms. If a student got behind in his classroom session in the morning, she could help him catch up or reteach a strategy that was poorly understood. Instead of being determined by a chart of skills, now the program was based on the students' needs. Because the corrective and core programs supported each other, the students received the maximum benefit. As Walp and Walmsley (1995) commented, "The lines between the regular and remedial programs quickly became blurred and have remained so ever since" (p. 186). As a result of the reconstruction and coordination of the school's language arts programs, between 92 and 100 percent of the school's students pass both the state reading and writing tests. In fact, since 1988, the results of the writing assessment have only fallen below 100 percent passing once. Impressive results for an impressive program.

## *Summary*

Remediation is changing. Currently there are movements toward more holistic approaches and inclusive instruction within the regular classroom. There is also a call for closer cooperation among all professionals working with low-achieving readers and writers.

Specialized corrective instruction is provided primarily by the reading specialist, Title I teacher, and LD teacher. The role of the reading specialist is changing. Although a primary responsibility is remediation, the role is changing to that of consultant who works closely with the classroom teacher and other specialists.

Components of a remedial reading/writing program include goals, student selection, curriculum, instructional approaches, instructional schedule, organizational patterns, pacing, materials, monitoring, grouping, involving parents, leadership, professional development, and evaluation. Goals should be clearly expressed and based on a statement of the overall philosophy of the program. Students needing assistance are generally selected on the basis of a discrepancy between potential achievement and/or failure to reach a certain level of achievement. Because of the possibility that any one test or other assessment device might yield erroneous results, students should be selected on the basis of several assessment devices.

The curriculum for a program for low-achieving readers and writers should be broad-based but should mesh with the school's overall curriculum. The daily instructional schedule should include provision for instruction, guided practice, and independent application and should feature varied activities. Students can be discontinued from the program when they are able to meet the demands of the regular classroom and are reading on their own.

Although one-on-one remedial instruction is highly effective, small group intervention, if carefully planned, can also achieve significant results. A current trend is to instruct problem readers in the context of the whole group. Modifications and additional assistance are provided as needed. While short-term intervention succeeds with most students, a small percentage will need extensive, long-term assistance. Programs that are properly paced are more successful.

Appropriate materials and wide reading are essential elements in a successful program. Ongoing monitoring so that appropriate adjustments can be made is also an important ingredient. Although there are many ways of grouping students, heterogeneous and cooperative grouping foster increased achievement in low-achieving readers and writers. Whole class instruction, if used, should be supplemented with small-group instruction or reading or writing workshop or some other form of individualization.

Parents should be informed of any difficulties their children are experiencing in acquiring literacy skills. They should also be involved in supporting their children's efforts.

Leadership and professional development are also important components of an effective program. An often untapped source of additional assistance is the volunteer tutor. Tutors should be trained, supervised, and affirmed.

Programs should be evaluated in terms of their goals. Evaluation should include consideration of a variety of assessment information and should lead to improvement of the program.

## *Application Activities*

1. Observe a successful early intervention or remedial program in your locality. What are the outstanding features of the program?

2. Read one or more of the following, which contain information about a number of early intervention programs. What are some similarities in the programs? What are some differences? What do the programs suggest about early intervention?

   Hiebert, E. H. & Taylor, B. M. (Eds.), (1994). *Getting reading right from the start.* Boston: Allyn & Bacon.

   Pikulski, J. J. (1994). Preventing reading failure: A review of five effective programs. *The Reading Teacher, 48,* pp. 30–39.

   Tierney, R. J., Readence, J. E., & Dishner, E. K. (1995). Intervention programs for "at risk" students." In Tierney, R. J., Readence, J. E., & Dishner, E. K. (Eds.), *Reading strategies and practices* (4th ed.) (pp. 410–440). Boston: Allyn & Bacon.

3. Create a list of suggestions in a resource booklet that can be given to parents whose children are enrolled in an intervention or corrective program. Focus on providing ways in which parents can affirm their children and support their efforts in nonthreatening ways.

4. Plan a corrective session. Using the framework for a daily schedule described in the chapter, make any adaptations that you feel are necessary. If possible, teach the lesson and evaluate its effectiveness.

# Appendix A

# *Informal Assessment Measures*

Name of Student ____________________________ Date ____________________

Grade ____________

***Word Learning Test***

Directions: Ask the student to read the following words until she or he misses at least seven of them, or use seven words that the student missed on a word lists or similar test. Write these words on cards and teach them to the student. Follow the instructions contained on the next page.

both ____________________
few ____________________
much ____________________
eight ____________________
think ____________________
great ____________________
year ____________________
found ____________________
large ____________________
sure ____________________
learn ____________________
group ____________________
word ____________________
come ____________________
front ____________________
hold ____________________
gone ____________________
talk ____________________
dark ____________________
warm ____________________

## *Teaching Presentation*

Present the seven words chosen to be test words. Hold the word so that the student can see it readily. After you say it, have the student say it. Shuffle the word cards and present them in the same way a second time.

## *Testing Trials*

Present each word and ask the student to read it. If the student gives a correct response, say, "Yes, that's correct. The word is ________." If the student gives a wrong response, say, "No, that is not correct. The word is ________." Put the correct responses in a separate pile. Note the correct responses on the Learning Trials sheet. Do not record incorrect responses. Shuffle all the cards after each trial. Continue presenting testing trials until the student gets all the words correct on two consecutive trials or until the student has had ten learning trials. If the student has not gotten all seven words within ten trials, note the number correct. To check long-term retrieval, give a single test trial one hour later and twenty-four hours later.

Name of Student ____________________________ Date ________________________

Examiner ________________________________

*Learning Trials*

| Word | 1 | 2 | 3 | 4 | 5 | 6 | 7 | 8 | 9 | 10 |
|---|---|---|---|---|---|---|---|---|---|---|
| 1. | | | | | | | | | | |
| 2. | | | | | | | | | | |
| 3. | | | | | | | | | | |
| 4. | | | | | | | | | | |
| 5. | | | | | | | | | | |
| 6. | | | | | | | | | | |
| 7. | | | | | | | | | | |

*Results*

Immediate: Words known ________ Number of trials ________

At end of 60 minutes: Words known ________ Number of trials ________

Next day: Words known ________ Number of trials ________

Symbols: Correct on first test- ✓ Correct on first retest (60 minutes later)- **X**

Correct on second retest (24 hours later)- **0**

Comments ______________________________________________

______________________________________________________

______________________________________________________

______________________________________________________

Name ________________________ Total number correct ____________

Date ________________ Estimated Level ______________

# Word Pattern Survey

| | | | |
|---|---|---|---|
| 1. go ______ | 16. drop ______ | 31. chain ______ | 46. park ______ |
| 2. me ______ | 17. jump ______ | 32. speak ______ | 47. purse ______ |
| 3. see ______ | 18. sand ______ | 33. slide ______ | 48. clear ______ |
| 4. I ______ | 19. ship ______ | 34. toast ______ | 49. storm ______ |
| 5. no ______ | 20. lunch ______ | 35. blind ______ | 50. large ______ |
| 6. hat ______ | 21. game ______ | 36. plane ______ | 51. tall ______ |
| 7. wet ______ | 22. tree ______ | 37. steel ______ | 52. cook ______ |
| 8. sit ______ | 23. wide ______ | 38. drive ______ | 53. town ______ |
| 9. hop ______ | 24. road ______ | 39. broke ______ | 54. join ______ |
| 10. fun ______ | 25. use ______ | 40. price ______ | 55. should ______ |
| 11. ran ______ | 26. goat ______ | 41. barn ______ | 56. grew ______ |
| 12. men ______ | 27. save ______ | 42. chair ______ | 57. house ______ |
| 13. win ______ | 28. wheel ______ | 43. store ______ | 58. crawl ______ |
| 14. got ______ | 29. mine ______ | 44. turn ______ | 59. broom ______ |
| 15. bug ______ | 30. cute ______ | 45. deer ______ | 60. pound ______ |

**Directions: Give one copy of the Survey to the student and keep one for marking. Mark each response + or – . If possible, write down each incorrect response for later analysis. Start with the first item for all pupils. Say to the student, "I am going to ask you to read a list of words to me. Some of the words may be hard for you, but read as many as you can." Stop when the student gets five in a row wrong. The Survey tests three levels. Each level has twenty items as follows: 1–20: easy long-vowel and short-vowel patterns (*Book A*), 21–40: long-vowel patterns (*Book B*), 41-60: r-vowel and other-vowel patterns: /aw/, /oo/, /oo/, /ow/, /oy/, (*Book C*). Students are proficient at a level if they get 80% or more correct at that level. Students should be instructed at a level if they get more than 4 out of 20 wrong at that level.**

---

**Word Pattern Survey**

Name ______________________ Score ______________________

Date ______________________

# SYLLABLE SURVEY

1. sunup ______
2. inside ______
3. ago ______
4. open ______
5. under ______
6. farmer ______
7. finish ______
8. mistake ______
9. thunder ______
10. morning ______
11. reward ______
12. famous ______
13. mumble ______
14. spider ______
15. chicken ______
16. rocket ______
17. magnet ______
18. distant ______
19. prevent ______
20. museum ______
21. several ______
22. building ______
23. probably ______
24. modern ______
25. monument ______
26. opposite ______
27. message ______
28. success ______
29. struggle ______
30. repeat ______
31. recognize ______
32. survive ______
33. appreciate ______
34. antelope ______
35. creature ______
36. audience ______
37. pleasant ______
38. spaghetti ______
39. information ______
40. voyage ______
41. confusion ______
42. neighborhood ______
43. studio ______
44. allowance ______
45. microphone ______
46. auditorium ______
47. available ______
48. disappointment ______
49. bulletin ______
50. moisture ______

**Directions: Give one copy of the Survey to the student and keep one for marking. Mark each response + or – . If possible, write down each incorrect response for later analysis. Start with the first item for all pupils. Say to the student, "I am going to ask you to read a list of words. Some of the words may be hard for you, but read as many as you can." Stop when the student gets five in a row wrong. A score of 45 or above indicates that the student is able to decode multisyllabic words and doesn't need to work in Book D. A score between 40 and 44 indicates some weakness in decoding multisyllabic words. A score below 40 indicates a definite need for instruction and practice in decoding multisyllabic words. A score of 5 or below suggests that the student may be deficient in basic decoding skills. Give the Word Pattern Survey.**

**Syllable Survey**

From the *Teacher's Guide for Word Building Book D* by T. Gunning, 1994. New York: Phoenix Learning Resources. Reprinted by permission of Galvin Publications.

# LETTERS

Name ______________________________________________Date ____________

Uppercase score _____ /10 Lowercase score ____/10

**Circle the letter that your teacher says.**

| | | | | | |
|---|---|---|---|---|---|
| A. | | O | X | R | U |
| 1. | | N | S | D | C |
| 2. | | I | T | A | P |
| 3. | | B | J | V | Z |
| 4. | | W | G | K | R |
| 5. | | X | M | H | U |
| 6. | | E | O | F | L |
| 7. | | Y | Q | B | T |
| 8. | | S | R | E | C |
| 9. | | I | G | X | Z |
| 10. | | P | W | H | K |
| 11. | | n | s | d | c |
| 12. | | i | t | a | p |
| 13. | | b | j | v | z |
| 14. | | w | g | k | r |
| 15. | | x | m | h | u |
| 16. | | e | o | f | l |
| 17. | | y | q | b | t |
| 18. | | s | e | r | c |
| 19. | | i | g | x | z |
| 20. | | p | w | h | k |

**Letters**

From the *Teacher's Guide for Word Building: Beginnings* by T. Gunning, 1994. New York: Phoenix Learning Resources. Reprinted by permission of Galvin Publications.

# RHYMING

Name____________________ Date______ _______ Score ________ /10

**In each row, say the name of the first picture. Then find the picture whose name rhymes with the name of the first picture. Draw a ring around the picture that has the rhyming name.**

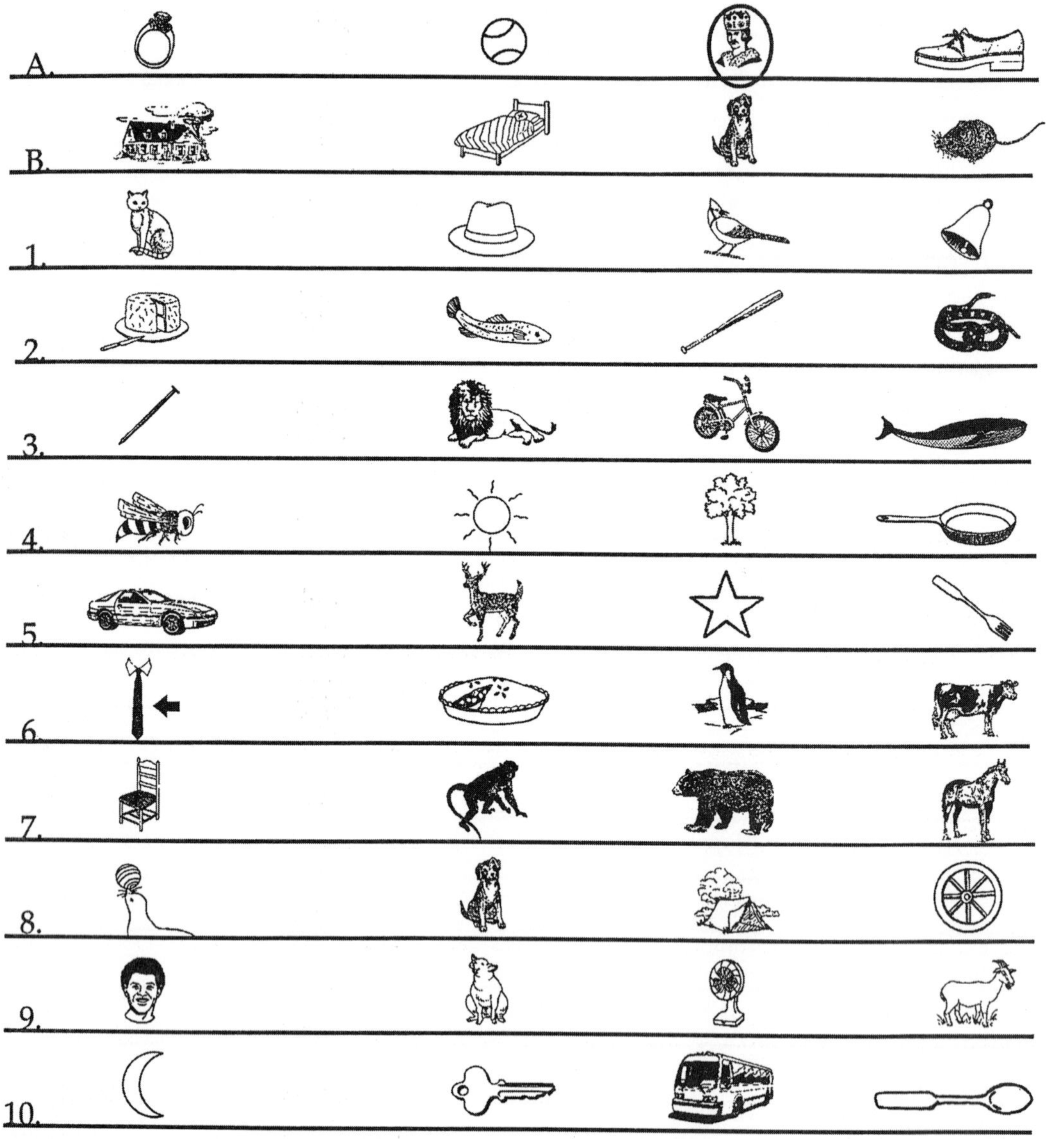

A.

B.

1.

2.

3.

4.

5.

6.

7.

8.

9.

10.

**Rhyming**

From the *Teacher's Guide for Word Building: Beginnings* by T. Gunning, 1994. New York: Phoenix Learning Resources. Reprinted by permission of Galvin Publications.

# BEGINNING SOUNDS

Name ______________________________ Date__________ Score _____/10

**In each row, say the name of the first picture. Then find the picture whose name begins with the same sound. Draw a ring around the picture whose name begins with the same sound as the first one.**

A.

B.

1.

2.

3.

4.

5.

6.

7.

8.

9.

10.

**Beginning Sounds**

From the *Teacher's Guide for Word Building: Beginnings* by T. Gunning, 1994. New York: Phoenix Learning Resources. Reprinted by permission of Galvin Publications.

# BEGINNING CONSONANT CORRESPONDENCES

Name ______________________________ Date ____________

Score ____________ /20 Items missed ______________________

**Circle the letter or letters that spell the first sound of the name of the picture.**

| | | | | | |
|---|---|---|---|---|---|
| A. | | r | b | (z) | f |
| B. | | l | c | g | y |
| 1. | | y | b | m | k |
| 2. | | j | z | g | s |
| 3. | | c | w | n | b |
| 4. | | d | r | v | t |
| 5. | | p | f | h | z |
| 6. | | t | h | k | x |
| 7. | | l | j | s | w |
| 8. | | n | f | r | g |

| | | | | | |
|---|---|---|---|---|---|
| 9. |  | t | f | d | s |
| 10. |  | k | l | z | m |
| 11. |  | p | w | r | d |
| 12. |  | y | c | f | g |
| 13. |  | d | l | c | r |
| 14. |  | w | r | c | n |
| 15. |  | b | t | j | f |
| 16. |  | p | y | h | l |
| 17. |  | wh | th | ch | sh |
| 18. |  | th | ch | sh | wh |
| 19. | 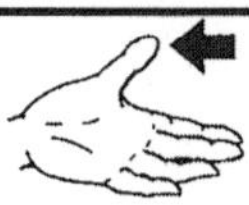 | th | sh | ch | wh |
| 20. |  | ch | th | wh | sh |

**Beginning Consonant Correspondences** *Continued*

From the *Teacher's Guide for Word Building: Beginnings* by T. Gunning, 1994. New York: Phoenix Learning Resources. Reprinted by permission of Galvin Publications.

# Appendix B

# High-Interest, Low-Readability Books

| Title | Publisher | Reading Level | Interest Level |
|---|---|---|---|
| *High-Interest, Low-Readability Series for Younger Students* | | | |
| *African American Biography Series*<br>Features brief biographies of a variety of African Americans. | Enslow | 3 | 3–5 |
| *Amanda and Oliver Pig Series*<br>Tales of growing up in a warm, loving family. | Dial | 1–2 | 1–3 |
| *Amelia Bedelia Series*<br>Because she takes figurative language literally, Amelia Bedelia is always engaged in humorous situations. | Harper | 1–2 | 1–3 |
| *Arthur Series*<br>Arthur, the chimp, experiences the joys and difficulties of childhood. | Harper | 1–2 | 1–3 |
| *Boxcar Children Mysteries*<br>Having made their home in a boxcar, the Aldens solve a variety of mysteries. | | 2 | 2–5 |
| *Cam Jansen Detective Series*<br>Cam solves a variety of mysteries. | Penguin | 2 | 2–4 |
| *Commander Toad Series*<br>Humorous adventures in space. | Putnam | 2 | 2–4 |
| Fox Series<br>Although a wily creature, Fox usually ends up being outfoxed in good-humored fashion. | Dial, Penguin | 1 | 1–3 |
| *Henry and Mudge* Series<br>Young boy enjoys his oversized dog. | Bradbury | 1 | 1–3 |
| *Kids of Polk Street School*<br>Elementary school youngsters have a series of adventures as they encounter the problems of growing up. | Dell | 2–3 | 2–4 |

| Title | Publisher | Reading Level | Interest Level |
|---|---|---|---|
| *Magic School Bus Series*<br>Ms. Frizzle uses a magic school bus to take her class on unusual but scientifically informative field trips. | Scholastic | 3 | 3–5 |
| *Max Series*<br>With his flying umbrella, Max is a very unusual but funny detective. | Harper | 1–2 | 1–3 |
| *Morris Series*<br>A lovable moose, Morris becomes involved in a series of humorous escapades. | Harper | 1 | 1–3 |
| *Nate the Great Detective Series*<br>Making judicious use of clues, Nate finds missing objects and solves other everyday mysteries. | Dell | 2 | 2–4 |
| *Rookie Biography Series*<br>Basic, easy-to-read biographies of a variety of noteworthy individuals. | Children's Press | 2 | 2–4 |
| *Rookie Read-About Science Series*<br>Brief, well-illustrated explorations of varied science topics. | Children's Press | 1–2 | 1–3 |
| *Troll Easy-to-Read Mysteries*<br>Mysteries solved include finding missing animals and lost objects. | Troll | 2 | 2–4 |

| Title | Publisher | Reading Level | Interest Level |
|---|---|---|---|
| *High-Interest, Low-Readability Series for Older Students* | | | |
| *Adventures*<br>Features a variety of exciting adventures in 32-page paperback format. | Steck-Vaughn | 3 | 6–12 |
| *BesTellers®*<br>Features a variety of tales of mystery, suspense, and adventure involving young adults. | Globe/Fearon | 1–4 | 9–12 |
| *Brains and Parker McGoohan*<br>Teens travel in time machine to meet famous scientists of the past. | High Noon | 3 | 6–12 |
| *Double Fastbacks*<br>Features 54 64-page fast-paced novels dealing with romance, mystery, crime, sports, horror, spies, and strange occurrences. Some fastbacks are accompanied by tapes. | Globe/Fearon | 4–5 | 9–12 |
| *The Ecology Kidds Series*<br>Dr. Kidd and her teenage twins solve ecology mysteries. | High Noon | 2 | 5–10 |
| *Encounters Series*<br>Adventure series deals with a variety of problems teens deal with: drugs, running away, and work. | EMC Publishing | 3–4 | 8–12 |
| *Fastbacks*<br>Features 74 32-page fast-paced novels dealing with romance, mystery, crime, sports, horror, science fiction, and spies. | Globe/Fearon | 4–5 | 9–12 |

| | | | |
|---|---|---|---|
| *Fearon's Amazing Adventures*<br>Features eight novels that tell tales of escape and survival. | Globe/Fearon | 3 | 7–12 |
| *Fearon's Flights of Fantasy*<br>Features eight novels that transport readers to other times and other places. | Globe/Fearon | 3 | 9–12 |
| *Fearon's Freedom Fighters*<br>Includes 80-page biographies of M. L. King, Nelson Mandela, Cesar Chávez, Fannie Hammer, and Malcolm X. | Globe/Fearon | 3–4 | 7–12 |
| *High Adventures*<br>Features a series of ten intriguing adventures. | High Noon | 3–4 | 6–12 |
| *History's Mysteries*<br>Features the disappearance of Amelia Earhart, the Roanoke mystery, and other famous mysteries of the past. | Crestwood House/ Simon & Schuster | 5–6 | 4–8+ |
| *Incredible Histories*<br>Includes such high interest topics as famous hoaxes, haunted castles, missing treasure, and impossible quests. | Crestwood House/ Simon & Schuster | 5–6 | 4–8+ |
| *The Kirkwood Kids*<br>Middle school youngsters have a series of adventures. | Perfection Learning | 3–4 | 4–7 |
| *Meridian Books*<br>Teens experience a series of mysteries and adventures. | High Noon | 3–4 | 7–12 |
| *Movie Monsters*<br>Monster movie scripts are rewritten. | Crestwood House/ Simon & Schuster | 3–5 | 4–8+ |
| *The Mystery of . . .*<br>Features Bigfoot, the Loch Ness Monster, and other famous real-life mysteries. | Crestwood House/ Simon & Schuster | 5–6 | 4–8+ |
| *Mysteries*<br>Features a variety of modern-day mysteries in 32-page paperback format. | Steck-Vaughn | 2–3 | 6–12 |
| *Passages Novels*<br>Middle school youngsters encounter variety of conflicts in a series of mysteries and adventures by Ann Schraff. | Perfection Learning | 3–4, 5–6 | 6–8 |
| *Perspectives*<br>Includes twenty tales of adventure. | High Noon | 3–4 | 6–12 |
| *Postcards from America*<br>Four teens have adventures as they visit cultural landmarks in America. | High Noon | 2 | 5–9+ |
| *Postcards from Europe*<br>Four teens have adventures as they visit cultural landmarks in Europe. | High Noon | 2 | 5–9+ |
| *Postcards from South America*<br>Four teens have adventures as they visit cultural landmarks in South America. | High Noon | 2 | 5–9+ |
| *Reading Success Paperbacks*<br>Features Bill Cosby, Michael Jordan, and other celebrities. | High Noon | 3–4 | 6–12 |

| | | | |
|---|---|---|---|
| *The Riddle Street Mystery Series*<br>Meg, a reporter, and Tom, a photographer, team up to solve mysteries. | High Noon | 1 | 4–8+ |
| *Science Fiction*<br>Features a variety of science fiction tales in 32-page paperback format. | Steck-Vaughn | 4 | 6–12 |
| *The Scoreboard Series*<br>High schoolers overcome obstacles in five major sports. | High Noon | 2 | 7–12 |
| *Silverleaf Novels*<br>Middle school students encounter stepparents, divorce, and difficulties with friends and teachers. | Perfection Learning | 3.5 | 4–7 |
| *Sports Immortals*<br>Features Babe Ruth, Jackie Robinson, Babe Didrickson, and other sports greats from the past. | Crestwood House/ Simon & Schuster | 5 | 5–10+ |
| *SporTellers®*<br>Young athletes encounter obstacles. | Globe/Fearon | 2–3 | 9–12 |
| *Star Trek: The Next Generation®*<br>Recounts sci-fi adventures based on the TV series. | Globe/Fearon | 3–4 | 8–12 |
| *Tom and Ricky Mystery Series*<br>Two fourteen-year-olds solve a variety of mysteries. Series features nine five-book sets. Some of the titles are available in Spanish and English. | High Noon | 1–2 | 4–8+ |
| *Uptown, Downtown Series*<br>Vesey, a high schooler, encounters a series of difficulties and adventures in an urban setting. | Globe/Fearon | 2–3 | 9–12 |

| Book's Author, Year and Title | No. of Pages | Reading Level | Interest Level |
|---|---|---|---|
| *High-Interest, Low-Readability Books for Younger Students* | | | |
| Blume, Judy. (1971). *Freckle Juice.*<br>Andrew uses a "secret formula" to acquire freckles. | 40 | 3 | 3–4 |
| Brenner, B. (1978). *Wagon Wheels.*<br>Two African American boys head west. | 32 | 2 | 2–4 |
| Cole, Joanna (1986). *Hungry, Hungry Sharks.*<br>Provides interesting information about sharks. | 48 | 2 | 2–4+ |
| Hayward, L. (1988). *Hello, House!*<br>Brer Rabbit tricks fox. | 32 | 1 | 1–3 |
| Ingoglia, Gina (1992). *Awesome Animals.*<br>Portrays the flying snake, vampire bat, and other intriguing animals. | 48 | 2–3 | 2–4+ |
| Kessler, Leonard. (1982). *Old Turtle's Baseball Stories.*<br>Old Turtle spins some amazing baseball yarns. | 55 | 1 | 1–3 |
| McKie, Roy (1979). *The Joke Book.*<br>Features a number of knock-knock and other jokes. | 48 | 2 | 3–4+ |
| Milton, Joyce. (1985). *Dinosaur Days.*<br>Portrays major dinosaurs and discusses their disappearance. | 48 | 1 | 1–3 |

| Book's Author, Year and Title | No. of Pages | Reading Level | Interest Level |
|---|---|---|---|
| O'Connor, Jane. (1986). *The Teeny Tiny Woman.* A ghost retrieves a bone taken from the top of its grave. | 32 | 1 | 3 |
| Parish, Peggy. (1974). *Dinosaur Time.* Describes the major dinosaurs in very simple language. | 32 | 1 | 1–3 |
| Recht, Lucille. (1991). *Dinosaur Babies.* Explains how baby dinosaurs grew up and how they were cared for. | 32 | 1 | 1–3 |
| Stadler, J. (1988). *Cat at Bat.* Comic drawings illustrate a series of humorous rhymes. | 30 | 1 | 1–3 |
| Stadler, J. (1991). *Cat at Bat is Back.* Sequel to Cat at Bat. | 30 | 1 | 1–3 |
| Stadler, J. (1984). *Hooray for Snail.* A slow base runner, Snail has to hit the ball to the moon to get a home run. | 32 | 1 | 1–3 |

| Book's Author, Year and Title | No. of Pages | Reading Level | Interest Level |
|---|---|---|---|
| *High-Interest, Low-Readability Books for Older Students* | | | |
| Avi. (1980). *Man from the Sky.* A young boy aids in the capture of a thief who parachutes from the sky. | 40 | 2 | 4–6+ |
| Berends, Polly. (1973). *The Case of the Elevator Duck.* Gilbert tracks down the owner of a duck left on an elevator in a housing project. | 54 | 3 | 4–6+ |
| Bunting, Eve. (1984). *Someone Is Hiding on Alcatraz Island.* Danny hides from gang members. | 40 | 3 | 5–8+ |
| Dolan, Edward. (1983). *Great Mysteries of the Air.* Recounts strange disappearances and other mysteries. | 127 | 4 | 4–6+ |
| Gutman, Bill (1988). *Smitty.* Smitty, an outstanding high school female basketball player, struggles against the system as she plays for the boys' team. | 78 | 4 | 7–12 |
| Gutman, Bill (1988). *Rookie Summer.* Bobbie has a difficult time handling the pressures of the big leagues. | 78 | 4 | 7–12 |
| Kehret, Peg. (1988). *The Winner.* Bart helps rescue his kidnapped girl friend. | 78 | 4 | 7–12 |
| Platt, Kin. (1981). *Dracula, Go Home!* Larry notices that one of the guests at his aunt's inn looks like Dracula. | 87 | 2 | 4–7+ |
| Shea, George (1992). *Amazing Rescues.* Rescued are a girl grabbed by an alligator, an unconscious skydiver, and a child trapped in a well. | 48 | 3 | 7+ |
| Wulffson, Don. (1989). *More Incredible True Adventures.* The roof of a jet is ripped off in mid-flight, a camper is attacked by a grizzly, and similar true adventures are dramatically portrayed. | 111 | 4 | 4–8+ |

# Appendix C

# Sample Assessment Report

***Reading Report***

| | |
|---|---|
| Student: | James Lawlor (Not his real name) |
| Evaluator: | Thomas G. Gunning, Ed.D. |
| Dates of Evaluation: | 5–1-97, 5–2-97 |
| Student's Birthdate: | 4–20–87 |
| School: | P. T. Barnum Elementary School<br>501 North St.<br>South Haven, CT |
| Grade: | 3 |
| Parents: | Mildred and Frank Lawlor |
| Address: | 127 Whale St.<br>South Haven, CT |
| Phone: | 123–4567 |

## *Reason for Referral*

James Lawlor is a ten-year-old, third-grade student at the P. T. Barnum School in South Haven, Connecticut. James was referred for testing by Mr. Alvarez his teacher. Mr. Alvarez is concerned because James is struggling with both reading and writing and is operating well below grade level.

## *Observations*

During the two-day test period, James was very cooperative and worked very hard on the many tasks that were presented to him. He never said or showed that he was either tired or bored with the tests. In fact on some of the tests that had to be ended because of a time limit, James expressed a desire to continue. On other tasks that were concluded because he had missed a number of items, James said that he wanted to try again or study the items so that he could do better.

James also frequently inquired about his performance on a number of the tests. He asked such questions as: "How am I doing? How many did I get right? Did I fail that test?" Although the frequent inquiring about performance suggests a certain amount of anxiety, James did not exhibit any overt signs of feeling anxious, except on those tests which demanded reading. On the silent reading selections of the *Basic Reading Inventory,* for instance, James's performance was accompanied by a great deal of lip movement, audible vocalization, and finger pointing. These signs of anxiety were present even when the material being read was well within James' capacity.

Of all the tests that were given, James seemed to enjoy most the one that required him to put blocks together to form a series of increasingly complex designs and the one that entailed putting a puzzle together. These tests were a part of the *Weschler Intelligence Scale for Children.* James' best performance was on that part of the *Weschler Intelligence Scale for Children* that required him to explain what he would do in certain social situations and which asked him to explain why certain social rules and conditions were necessary. His poorest performance was on a test that entailed connecting a series of numbers with their corresponding symbols.

James's favorite subject in school is math. He likes math because it is "easy." He liked reading least of all, and he feels that he does "okay" in reading. He said that he feels that some words are long, the books have too many hard words, and are boring. He feels that reading would be easier if he knew the words. James doesn't have a favorite book or author and doesn't read at home. James's favorite activities are playing sports and building models. He plays on little league baseball and midget football teams.

James wants to be a builder when he grows up. He said it would be fun to build houses. He understands that this occupation demands training and the ability to follow instructions. James' mother said that his brothers and he have helped their father with a number of projects and that James is a good worker.

## *Case History*

A case history was obtained from Mrs. Mildred Lawlor, James' mother, who was openly cooperative and responsive to all questioning. The Lawlor family includes: fifteen-year-old John, thirteen-year-old Lawrence, ten-year-old James, Mrs. Mildred Lawlor, and Mr. Frank Lawlor. The family appears to be closely knit and cooperative. As an example, while the father has been recuperating from injuries resulting from work, the three boys have been cooking meals and taking care of minor repairs under the father's direction. Mrs. Lawlor is employed full-time as a practical nurse. Mrs. Lawlor noted throughout the course of the interview that John's maturational development seemed to lag behind that of her other children almost from the very beginning. She cited that James sat by himself at the age of 11-½ months, walked at 2 years, and talked at 2-½ years. At the present time, however, she believes that James exhibits physical coordination skills which surpass those of his brothers when they were at this age. He especially enjoys participation in team sports such as baseball, basketball, and football.

## *School History*

James' formal education began at the age of 5-½ when he attended kindergarten in the South Haven Public Schools. Because James was still not reading at the end of first grade, he repeated the grade. During his second year in first grade, James was given help twice a week by the school's *Chapter 1* teacher. Assistance continued throughout second grade. James is not currently being given any additional assistance, except that provided by his classroom teacher. James' current teacher reports that James is cooperative and works hard, but lately has been beginning to show signs of avoidance when asked to read and write. Mr. Alvarez reports that James becomes restless during reading time, often asks to leave the room, and can't seem to focus on the selection the group is reading.

## *Classroom Observations*

James is in a class in which reading of basals is combined with the reading of trade books. Because James and several other students would have difficulty reading the third-grade basal on their own, they follow along as the teacher reads the selection to them. Meanwhile, the other class members read the basal on their own. For a twenty-minute period each day, the classroom teacher also provides special instruction and materials for James and the other students in his group. They are given material that they can read on their own and additional instruction in decoding strategies.

Because this group has a limited store of words that they can recognize immediately, the teacher is currently supplying instruction in this area. The words that the teacher presents are drawn from a children's book that the students are about to read. The books used with this group are easier than the basal reader. However, even in this group James is struggling. He is much slower to learn the new words and forgets them more easily. Although James was able to correctly read each of the new words when they were presented on the blackboard, he stumbled over them when he encountered them in the selection. The teacher told James that "he knew the word" and reminded James that they had just studied it, but that didn't help James. When James missed a word, the teacher suggested that he use context; but there were so many words in the selection that James didn't know, he was unable to use context.

After the lesson, the teacher requested a conference with the observer. He confessed to being baffled by James. He couldn't understand why the techniques he was using weren't meeting with success. He was especially distressed because James seemed to forget words so quickly. The observer and teacher discussed James' difficulty remembering printed words and decided to use a word building approach because James didn't seem to do well with a sight approach. It was also decided to teach James pronounceable word–part and analogy strategies in addition to context strategies and to give James easier materials.

A follow-up observation revealed that the recommendations seemed to be working. Even in the easier book, James had to struggle with some of the words, but, because he knew most of the words, he was better able to use context. He also seemed more confident and more willing to take risks. According to the teacher, James also found the pronounceable word–part and analogy strategies to be helpful. As the teacher explained, James no longer had to rely solely on memory, which often failed him. During the session, James was able to decode the word *chimney* by reading the pronounceable word part *im,* adding *ch* to make *chim,* and then using context to figure that the word must be *chimney.*"

## *Assessment Results*

### *Physical*

The *Keystone Telebinocular* was administered by the school nurse in order to assess James's visual functioning. James is functioning within the normal limits. The *Maco Audiometer* was used as a screening device to measure James' hearing capacity. The results seem to indicate that his capacity to hear is within the normal range.

James was given a physical at the walk-in clinic at South Haven General Hospital. James had been complaining of stomach pains. Unable to find a physical cause, the examining physician suggested that James might be experiencing stress but has scheduled a follow-up exam. Other than complaints of stomach distress, James is apparently in good health.

### *Academic Aptitude*

The *Weschler Intelligence Scale for Children Revised* (WISC-R) was administered by the school psychologist in preparation for a conference on James' reading difficulty. *The Weschler Intelligence Scale for Children Revised* is an individually administered intelligence test which consists of a series of verbal sub-tests and a series of performance subtests. The verbal section of the test is subdivided into five areas that are designed to measure the child's ability to deal with verbal tasks in a variety of situations. The performance section, which also contains five subtests, assesses the child's ability to function in situations which are less verbal in nature. James's overall score on the *WISC-R* test fell within the average range. His score on the verbal section was much higher than his score on the performance part and indicates that he is "bright normal." James did particularly well on verbal subtests that required him to define words, use social judgment, and use his general fund of knowledge. However, he had difficulty reciting a series of numbers forwards and backwards. His score on the performance section indicates that he is "average." However, James scored well below average on the subtest that measured his ability to make new associations and to work rapidly and accurately by requiring him to connect a series of numbers with their corresponding symbols.

### *Memory*

The Word Sequences and Design Sequences subtest of the *Detroit Test of Learning Aptitude* (Third Edition) were administered in order to assess James' ability to pay attention, concentrate, and use auditory or visual memory to remember a series of words or designs. Although James did somewhat better on the tasks requiring him to remember a series of designs, his performance on both tasks was well below his expected level of achievement. Performance was similar to his below-average ability to recite numbers forwards and backwards on the *WISC-R.*

### *Rapid Automatized Naming*

A portion of the *Rapid Automatized Naming Tests* (R. A. N.) was administered in order to assess how fast and how accurately James could name a series of letters and numbers. On the letters and numbers subtests, James' performance was similar to that of the average five-year-old. The results suggest a slowness in and lack of automaticity in recognizing and naming letters and numbers.

### *Reading*

The Word Lists portion of the *Basic Reading Inventory,* 6th ed., was administered with the following results:

| Grade Level | Flash Score | Untimed Score |
|---|---|---|
| Preprimer | 75 | 85 |
| Primer | 60 | 75 |
| First | 30 | 40 |
| Second | | |
| Third | | |
| Fourth | | |
| Fifth | | |

The results of the Graded Words List of the *Basic Reading Inventory,* sixth ed., indicate that James' ability to recognize words immediately, without taking time to figure them out, is adequate only at the preprimer (beginning first grade) level. When given time to figure out words that he wasn't able to recognize immediately, James was only able to read five additional words correctly. James was able to figure out three-letter words that began with a single consonant and ended with a single consonant (*top, pet, hen, met*) but had difficulty with words that began with two or more consonants (truck) or which had complex vowel spellings (*brave, hurry, front*).

The passages section of The *Basic Reading Inventory* was also administered. The *Basic Reading Inventory* is an individual reading test. It is designed to indicate the level of reading material a student can profitably handle with instruction in a classroom or small group setting. It also indicates the level of material that a student can read without any assistance, and the level of material that would be very difficult for him to handle, even with assistance. The *Basic Reading Inventory* also gives information about the student's oral reading, his ability to analyze and sound out words in context, and his ability to understand what he had read. The passages portion of the *Basic Reading Inventory* yielded the following results:

| Reading Levels | Grade |
|---|---|
| Independent | Preprimer |
| Instructional | Primer |
| Frustration | First |
| Hearing Capacity | Fifth |

According to the results of this test, James can read preprimer (beginning first-grade) material without any assistance. His comprehension and ability to read the words are nearly perfect at this level. However, because he had difficulty reading several of the words in the selection at the primer (middle first-grade) level, James would need the teacher's assistance with material at this level. James missed so many words at the end of first-grade level that this material would be too difficult for him even with the teacher's help.

Even at the easiest level, James' oral reading was slow and laborious. During silent reading James moved his lips and vocalized several of the words. As the selections grew more difficult, his vocalizations became more frequent and more audible. James seemed to recognize few words automatically and needed time to attempt to sound out most of the words. However, he was attempting to read for meaning. Often, when he misread a high frequency word such as *when* or *are,* he would self-correct his miscue (word misread) when he saw that it didn't fit the sense of the sentence. When James' miscues were analyzed, most fit the context. However, often the miscue was graphically quite different from the expected response. James was using context but failed to integrate his use of context with phonics cues. Because of his apparently weak deciphering skills, he was overrelying on context.

James' comprehension of the selections that he read was perfect. However, because of deficient decoding skills, he was restricted to first-grade material. When selections were read to him, James was able to comprehend material on a fifth-grade level. This suggests that if James had adequate decoding skills, he would be able to read fifth-grade level material.

### *Writing*

Writing was assessed by examining James' portfolio and asking him to write a letter telling about himself. James has written on a variety of topics, but the content of his written pieces lacks elaboration. For instance, in his letter he told that he works with his father on Saturdays but didn't tell what kinds of things he did. James also has difficulty with format and mechanics. He didn't use standard letter form and did not capitalize names or use end punctuation consistently. He also was reluctant to write any word that he couldn't spell.

### *Phonics*

The Word Pattern Survey was administered in order to assess James' ability to use phonics to decipher words. James had no difficulty reading three-letter, short-vowel patterns (wet, sit, hop, fun) but had problems with long-vowel patterns (game, road, wheel). He also had difficulty with words that contained consonant clusters at the beginning or end of the word (drop, jump).

### *Word Learning*

Because James had significant difficulty reading printed words, a number of additional tests and procedures were used to obtain further information in this area.

**Assisted Testing of Words List** After the Words Lists subtest was completed, portions of the subtest were readministered under assisted testing conditions. James was given another opportunity to read some of the easier words that he had missed. If he missed a word again, he was given assistance. The idea was to see how much help and what kind of help he would need in order to be able to read the words. For instance, James was able to read the *il* and *en* in *children* when the teacher asked him if there were any parts of the word he could read. After pronouncing *il* and *en* in *children,* he was able, with a little coaching, to construct the word *children.* Given this same kind of assistance, James was also able to read *silver* and *smell.*

**Word Learning Test** The Word Learning Test was given to assess James' ability to learn to read new words. In this test, the student is presented seven words that were previously missed. Each word is printed on a card and shown to the student, who is asked to say the word. If he is unable to read the word or misreads it, the examiner tells the student the word. After all seven words have been presented, they are shuffled and presented again. After ten trials, James knew just four of the words. The next day James knew just one of the words. His performance was similar to that of other students who have serious word learning problems.

**Visual-Auditory Learning Subtest** The Visual-Auditory Learning subtest of the *Woodcock-Johnson Cognitive Abilities Battery* was administered. This subtest assesses the student's ability to link spoken words with printed symbols. This task is similar to what is required when a student learns sight words. James' performance was equal to that of the average four-year-old.

### *Spelling*

According to the Elementary Spelling Inventory, James is operating on the early within word pattern stage. James is able to spell regular short-vowel words such as *hat, pet, hit, lot,* and *cut* correctly and is ready to learn long-vowel patterns, such as, *late, made, hope, boat, bean.*

## *Additional Testing*

### *Trial Teaching*

Seeing that James did poorly on the Word Learning Test, which presented words in sight word style, James was taught seven words using a word building approach in which the student builds words by adding a consonant to the vowel portion of the word (g + ate). For a period of fifteen minutes, magnetic letters and other devices were used to help James learn the words. Several sentences using the words were constructed so that James could see the words in context. At the end of fifteen minutes, James was able to read all seven of the words. The next day, after a brief review, James was able to read all seven again.

### *Summary*

James appears to have at least average academic ability. His ability to define words and use social judgment and general knowledge suggest that his true academic ability might be above average. In addition, he is able to understand fifth-grade level material when it is read to him. This suggests that his ability to comprehend language is equal to that of the average fifth grader. This is the level of reading that James might be expected to achieve if he were not held back by poorly developed decoding skills. However, James did have difficulty with tasks that involve paying attention and concentrating and remembering a series of numbers, words, or pictures. James also was slow in naming letters and numbers. James' poorest performances was on those tests that required him to associate printed words or wordlike symbols with spoken words or associate numbers with symbols. Apparently because of poor memory and underlying processing abilities, James has a significant difficulty learning to read words. Learning new words is a struggle for him, and he soon forgets them. However, James does do better when a phonics rather than a sight approach is used.

Insofar as his reading ability is concerned, James is able to read preprimer (beginning first-grade) material on his own. However, he needs assistance with any reading selections that are on a primer (middle first-grade) level. Reading material on an ending first grade level and beyond is, at this time, so taxing for James that he would not be able to adequately handle it. However, when material is read to James, he is able to understand selections on the fifth grade level. James is reading well below his capacity. James' spelling and writing are also well below grade level and significantly below James' capacity.

James' low level of achievement in reading is apparently caused by his lack of a store of words that he recognizes instantly or at sight, his limited knowledge of phonics or word patterns, and his lack of strategies that he might use to figure out hard words.

***Recommendations***

Because James seems to learn best through a sounding-out approach, a systematic program of phonics should be taught. The program known as Word Building is recommended because James had some success with this in his trial teaching lesson. In Word Building, the student learns patterns by assembling them: adding *b* + *ake* to construct *bake, c* + *ake* to make *cake* and so on. James should also be taught a series of strategies for deciphering hard words. These strategies should include looking for parts of the word he can say and then using known parts to build the word, or thinking of a known word that is like the hard word, or using context to figure out the word.

James also needs to be given reading material that is on his level. Books that have too many unknown words are discouraging and don't provide James with the opportunity to apply his reading skills. In fact, James needs as much opportunity as possible to read books and other materials that are easy for him. In addition to showing him that reading need not be a struggle, reading easy books will provide practice recognizing words so that the speed and ease with which he reads improves. Because James expressed an interest in animals and sports, he might enjoy books such as the following, which are on a primer (middle first-grade) level:

*Kick Pass and Run.* Leonard Kessler.
*Oliver.* Syd Hoff.
*A Dog Named Sam.* Janice Poland.
*Old Turtle's Riddle and Joke Book.* Leonard Kessler.
*The Day the Teacher Went Bananas.* James Howe.
*Dinosaur Time.* Peggy Parish.
*If the Dinosaurs Came Back.* Bernard Most.

Games might also be used to reinforce James' ability to decode vowel patterns. One possible choice is Road Racer (Curriculum Associates). Puzzles, riddles, songs, verses and poems that incorporate patterns should also be motivating.

Writing might also be used to reinforce James' word-analysis skills. Because James spelling ability is limited, he should be encouraged to use invented spelling so that he can give full expression to his ideas. He would also profit from the language experience approach in which he discusses an experience, dictates a story, and then reads the dictated story. This technique can also be used to explore topics in which James is interested. The teacher or an aide can read aloud to James books and articles that are too difficult for James to read on his own. The information is discussed and then summarized in an experience story. Also take judicious advantage of tape-recorded books, talking software, electronic talking dictionaries, and other technology that might assist James with reading and writing tasks that otherwise would be too difficult for him.

Because of his low level of reading ability, James is restricted in the range of books that he can read. In order to continue building James' excellent background of knowledge, James should be read to in the classroom and at home. Another way of building on James's excellent background of information is to involve him in activities that don't require reading and writing. In class discussions, for instance, make it a point to call on James. Also encourage James to engage in art, sports, and other activities that don't require reading and writing so that he experiences a sense of achievement.

Parents can help by focusing on the things that James does well. They should encourage him to engage in activities that he enjoys, such as playing sports and helping his father. Parents might also continue to read to James and provide books that are on his reading level and in which he is interested. Parents should continue to build his background of information by taking him to the zoo, museums, and other places and discussing topics of interest with him.

# References

## Professional Works


Aasved, H. (1989). Eye examinations. In H. Gjessing & B. Karlsen (Eds.), *A longitudinal study of dyslexia* (pp. 192–209). New York: Springer-Verlag.

Abrams, J. C. (1988). A dynamic-developmental approach to reading and related learning disabilities. In S. M. Glazer, L. W. Searfoss, & L. M. Gentile (Eds.), *Reexamining reading diagnosis: New trends and procedures* (pp. 29–47). Newark, DE: International Reading Association.

Abrams, J. C. (1991). The affective component: Emotional needs of individuals with reading and related learning disorders. *Reading, Writing, and Learning Disabilities, 7,* 171–182.

Adams, M. J. (1990). *Beginning to read: Thinking and learning about print.* Cambridge: MIT Press.

Adoption Guidelines Project (1991). Comprehension I: The directed reading lesson. In *Adoption Guidelines Project: A guide to selecting basal readers.* Urbana, IL: Center for the Study of Reading.

Afflerbach, P. (1990). The influence of prior knowledge on expert readers' main idea construction strategies. *Reading Research Quarterly, 25,* 31–46.

Akroyd, S. (1995). Forming a parent reading-writing class: Connecting cultures one pen at a time. *The Reading Teacher, 48,* 580–584.

Alegria, J. & Morais, J. (1991). Segmental analysis and reading acquisition. In L. Rieben & C. A. Perfetti (Eds.), *Learning to read: Basic research and its implications* (pp. 135–148). Hillsdale, NJ: Lawrence Erlbaum Associates.

Allen, J., Michalove, B., Shockley, B. (1993). *Engaging children: Community and chaos in the lives of young literacy learners.* Portsmouth, NH: Heinemann.

Allen, V. G. (1994). Selecting materials for the reading instruction of ESL children. In K. Spangerberg-Urbschart & R. Pritchard (Eds.), *Kids come in all languages: Reading instruction for ESL students* (pp. 108–131). Newark, DE: International Reading Association.

Alley, G. & Deshler, D. (1979). *Teaching the learning disabled adolescent: Strategies and methods.* Denver, CO: Love.

Allington, R. L. (1983). The reading instruction provided readers of differing reading ability. *Elementary School Journal, 83,* 548–559.

Allington, R. L. (1984). Oral reading. In P. D. Pearson, R. Barr, M. L. Kamil, & P. Mosenthal (Eds.), *Handbook of reading research* (pp. 829–863). New York: Longman.

Allington, R. L. (1994). The schools we have: The schools we need. *The Reading Teacher, 48,* 14–29.

Allington, R. L. (1995). Literacy lessons in the elementary schools: Yesterday, today, and tomorrow. In R. A. Allington & S. A. Walmsley (Eds.), *Rethinking literacy in America's elementary schools* (pp. 1–15). New York: Teachers College Press.

Allington, R. L. & Shake, M. C. (1986). Remedial reading: Achieving curricular congruence in classroom and clinic. *The Reading Teacher, 39,* 648–654.

Alvermann, D. C., Bridge, C. A., Schmidt, B. A., Searfoss, L. W., Winograd, P., & Paris, S. G., (1989). *Heath Reading.* Lexington, MA: D. C. Heath.

Alvermann, D. C. & Hague, S. A. (1989). Comprehension of counterintuitive science text: Effects of prior knowledge and text structure. *Journal of Educational Research, 82,* 198–202.

American Academy of Opthomology, (1984, 1990). *Vision.* Chicago.

American Psychiatric Association (1994). *Diagnostic and Statistical Manual of Mental Disorders* (4th ed.). Washington, DC: Author.

Anderson, R. C. (1990, May). Microanalysis of classroom reading instruction. Paper presented at the Annual Conference on Reading Research, Atlanta, GA.

Anderson, R. C. (1996). Research foundations to support wide reading. In V. Greaney (Ed.), *Promoting reading in developing countries* (pp. 55–77). Newark, DE: International Reading Association.

Anderson, R. C., Hiebert, E. H., Scott, J. A., & Wilkerson, I. A. G. (1985). *Becoming a nation of readers: The report of the commission on reading.* Washington, DC: National Institute of Education.

Anderson, R. C., Wilson, P. T., & Fielding, L. G. (1988). Growth in reading and how children spend their time outside of school. *Reading Research Quarterly, 23,* 285–303.

Anderson, T. H. (1980). Study strategies and adjunct aids. In R. J. Spiro, B. C. Bruce, & W. F. Brewer (Eds.), *Theoretical issues in reading comprehension* (pp. 483–502). Hillsdale, NJ: Erlbaum.

Anderson, V. & Henne, R. (1993). *Collaborative, integrated reading and writing strategy instruction.* Paper presented at the annual meeting of the National Reading Conference, Charleston, SC.

Anderson, V. & Roit, M. (1993). Planning and implementing collaborative strategy instruction for delayed readers in grades 6–10. *The Elementary School Journal, 94,* 121–137.

Anyon, J. (1980). Social class and the hidden curriculum of work. *Journal of Education, 162*(1), 67–92.

Applebee, A. N., Langer, J. A., & Mullis, I. V. S. (1988). *Who reads best? Factors related to reading achievement in grades 3, 7, and 11.* Princeton, NJ: Educational Testing Service.

Armbruster, B. B. (1991). Framing: A technique for improving learning from science texts. In C. M. Santa & D. C. Alvermann (Eds.), *Science learning: Processes and applications* (pp. 104–113). Newark, DE: International Reading Association.

Armbruster, B. B. & Anderson, T. H. (1981). *Content area textbooks* (Tech. Rep. No. 23). Champaign, IL: University of Illinois, Center for the Study of Reading.

Armstrong, T. (1996). ADD Does it really exist? *Phi Delta Kappan, 77,* 424–428.

Askov, E. N. (1991). Teaching study skills. In B. L. Hayes (Ed.), *Effective strategies for teaching reading* (pp. 84–102). Boston: Allyn & Bacon.

Atwell, N. (1987). *In the middle.* Portsmouth, NH: Boynton/Cook.

Atwell, N. (Ed.). (1990). *Coming to know: Writing to learn in the intermediate grades.* Portsmouth, NH: Heinemann.

Au, K. H., Mason, J. M., & Scheu, J. A. (1995) *Literacy instruction for today.* New York: HarperCollins,

Ayres, S. (1912). *Ayres Scale for Measuring Handwriting.* Princeton, NJ: Educational Testing Service.

Baddeley, A. D. (1986). *Working memory.* Oxford: Oxford University Press.

Baddeley, A. D. (1992). Working memory. *Science, 255,* 556–559.

Bader, L. A. (1994). *Bader Reading and Language Inventory* (2nd ed.). New York: Longman.

Bader, L. A. & Wiesendanger, K. O. (1986). University based reading clinics: Practices and procedures. *The Reading Teacher, 39,* 698–702.

Bain, A. M. (1991). Handwriting disorders. In A. M. Bain, L. L. Bailet, L. C. Moats (Eds.), *Written language disorders: Theory into practice* (pp. 43–64). Austin, TX: Pro-Ed.

Baker, L. & Brown, A. L. (1984). Megacognitive skills and reading. In P. D. Pearson, R. Barr, M. L. Kamil, & P. Mosenthal (Eds.), *Handbook of reading research* (pp. 353–394). New York: Longman.

Bandura, A. (1977). Self-efficacy: Toward a unifying theory of behavioral change. *Psychological Review, 84,* 191–215,

Barba, R. H. (1995). *Science in the multicultural classroom: A guide to teaching and learning.* Boston: Allyn & Bacon.

Barnes, B, L. (1996–1997). But teacher you went right on: A perspective on Reading Recovery. *The Reading Teacher, 50,* 284–292.

Barnes, W. G. W. (1989). Word sorting: The cultivation of rules for spelling in English. *Reading Psychology, 10,* 293–307.

Bartoli, J. & Botel, M. (1988). *Reading/learning disability: An ecological approach.* New York: Teachers College Press.

Barr, R. & Dreeben, R. (1991). Grouping students for reading instruction. In R. Barr, M. L. Kamil, P. Mosenthal, & P. D. Pearson (Eds.), *Handbook of reading research,* Volume II (pp. 885–910). New York: Longman.

Barr, R., Wogman, S., Blachowicz, C. L. Z., & Sadow, M. W. (1996). *Reading diagnosis for teachers: An instructional approach.* New York: Longman.

Barron, R. F. (1969). The use of vocabulary as an advance organizer. In H. L. Herber & P. L. Sanders (Eds.), *Research in reading in the content areas: First year report.* (pp. 29–39). Syracuse, NY: Syracuse University Reading and Language Arts Center.

Barron, R. F. (1979). Research for classroom teachers: Recent developments on the use of the structured overview as an advanced organizer. In H. L. Herber & J. D. Riley (Eds.), *Research in reading in the content areas: Fourth report* (pp. 171–176). Syracuse, NY: Syracuse University Reading and Language Arts Center.

Barstow, B. & Riggle, J. (1995). *Beyond picture books: A guide to first readers.* (2nd ed.). New York: Bowker.

Bartlet, D. & Shapiro, M. B. (1956). Investigation and treatment of a reading disability in a dull child with severe psychological disturbances. *British Journal of Educational Psychology, 26,* 180–190.

Baumann, J. F. (1986). The direct instruction of main idea comprehension ability. In J. F. Baumann (Ed.), *Teaching main idea comprehension* (pp. 133–178). Newark, DE: International Reading Association.

Baumann J. F. (1989). *Reading assessment: An instructional decision-making perspective.* Columbus, OH: Merrill.

Baumann, J. F. & Kameenui, E. J. (1991). Research on vocabulary instruction: Ode to Voltaire. In J. Flood, J. M. Jensen, D. Lapp, & J. R. Squire (Eds.), *Handbook of research on teaching the English language arts* (pp. 604–632). New York: Macmillan.

Baumann, J. F. & Serra, J. K. (1984). The frequency and placement of main ideas in children's social studies textbooks: A modified replication of Braddock's research on topic sentences. *Journal of Reading Behavior, 16,* 27–40.

Bear, D. R. (1995). *Word study: A developmental perspective based on spelling stages.* Paper presented at the annual meeting of the International Reading Association, Anaheim.

Bear, D. R., Invernizzi, M., Johnston, F., & Templeton, S. (1996). *Words their way: Word study for phonics, vocabulary, and spelling instruction.* Upper Saddle River, NJ: Merrill.

Beck, I. L. & McKeown, M. G. (1991). Conditions of vocabulary acquisition. In R. Barr, M. L. Kamil, P. Mosenthal, & P. D. Pearson (Eds.), *Handbook of Reading Research,* Volume II, (pp. 789–814). New York: Longman.

Beck, I. L., McKeown, M. G., & Omanson, R. C. (1987). The effects and uses of diverse vocabulary instructional techniques. In M. G. McKeown & M. E. Curtis (Eds.), *The nature of vocabulary acquisition* (pp. 147–163). Hillsdale, NJ: Lawrence Erlbaum.

Beck, I. L., Omanson, R. C., & McKeown, M. G. (1982). An instructional redesign of reading lessons: Effects on comprehension. *Reading Research Quarterly, 17,* 462–481.

Berkowitz, S. J. (1986). Effects of instruction in text organization on sixth-grade students' memory for expository text. *Reading Research Quarterly, 21,* 161–178.

Bereiter, C. & Scardamalia, M. (1982). From conversation to composition: The role of instruction in a developmental process. In R. Glass (Ed.), *Advances in instructional psychology,* Volume 2 (pp. 1–64). Hillsdale, NJ: Lawrence Erlbaum.

Berliner, D. C. (1981). Academic learning time and reading achievement. In J. T. Guthrie (Ed.), *Comprehension and teaching: Research reviews* (pp. 203–226). Newark, DE: International Reading Association.

Berres, F. & Eyer, J. T. (1970). Cases from full-time remedial students, John. In A. J. Harris (Ed.), *Casebook on reading disability* (pp. 25–47). New York: David McKay.

Betts, E. A. (1946). *Foundations of reading instruction.* New York: American Book Company.

Beverstock, C. (1991). *Your child's vision is important.* Newark, DE: International Reading Association.

Biemiller, A. (1970). The development of the use of graphic and contextual information as children learn to read. *Reading Research Quarterly, 6,* 75–96.

Biemiller, A. (1977–1978). Relationships between oral reading rates for letters, words, and simple text in the development of reading achievement. *Reading Research Quarterly, 13,* 223–253.

Biemiller, A. (1994). Some observations on acquiring and using reading skill in elementary schools. In C. K. Kinzer & D. J. Leu (Eds.), *Multidimensional aspects of literacy research, theory, and practice. Forty-third Yearbook of the National Reading Conference.* (pp. 209–216). Chicago, IL: National Reading Conference.

Blachowicz, C. L. Z. (1986). Making connections: Alternatives to the vocabulary notebook. *Journal of Reading, 29,* 643–649.

Blaine, M. (1986). Giants of the city. In J. Stanchfield and T. Gunning (Eds.), *Wings (New Directions in Reading)* (pp. 162–169). Boston: Houghton Mifflin.

Bloodgood, J. & Broaddus, K. (1994, May). *Working with severe reading problems: Remediation.* Paper presented at the annual meeting of the International Reading Association, Toronto.

Bloom, B. (Ed.). (1957). *Taxonomy of educational objectives.* New York: McKay.

Bloom, F. E. & Lazerson, A. (1988). *Brain, mind, and behavior* (2nd ed.). New York: W. H. Freeman.

Bond, G. L., Tinker, M. A., Wasson, B. B., & Wasson, J. B. (1994). *Reading difficulties: Their diagnosis and correction* (7th ed.). Boston: Allyn & Bacon.

Bos, C. S. & Vaugh, S. (1994). *Strategies for teaching students with learning and behavior problems.* (3rd ed.). Boston: Allyn & Bacon.

Bradley, L. & Bryant, P. (1985). *Children's reading problems.* Oxford: Basil Blackwell.

Bradley, J. M. & Thalgoot, M. R. (1987). Reducing reading anxiety. *Academic Therapy, 22,* 349–358.

Brady, S. A. (1986). Short-term memory, phonological processing, and reading ability. *Annals of Dyslexia, 36,* 138–153.

Brady, S. A. (1991). The role of working memory in reading disability. In S. A. Brady & D. P. Shankweiler (Eds.), *Phonological processes in literacy: A tribute to Isabelle Y. Liberman* (pp. 129–151). Hillsdale, NJ: Lawrence Erlbaum Associates.

Bransford, J. D. (1994). Schema activation and schema acquisition: Comments on Richard C. Anderson's remarks. In R. B. Ruddell, M. R. Ruddell, & H. Singer (Eds.), *Theoretical models and processes of reading* (4th ed.), (pp. 483–495). Newark, DE: International Reading Association.

Breitmeyer, B. G. (1993). Sustained (P) and transient (M) channels in vision: A review and implications for reading. In D. M. Willows, R. S. Kruk, & E. Corcos (Eds.), *Visual processes in reading and reading disabilities* (pp. 95–110). Hillsdale, NJ: Lawrence Erlbaum.

Bricklin, P. M. (1991). The concept of "self as learner:" Its critical role in the diagnosis and treatment of children with reading disabilities. *Reading, Writing, and Learning Disabilities, 7,* 201–217.

Bridge, C. A., Winograd, P. N., & Haley, D. (1983). Using predictable materials vs. preprimers to teach beginning sight words. *The Reading Teacher, 36,* 884–891.

Bristow, P. S., Pikulski, J. J., & Pelosi, P. L. (1983). A comparison of five estimates of reading instructional level. *The Reading Teacher, 37,* 273–279.

Broaddus, K. & Bloodgood, J. (1994). *Working with severe reading problems: Diagnosis.* Paper presented at the annual conference of the International Reading Association, Toronto.

Brown, A. L. & Day, J. D. (1983). Macrorules for summarizing text: The development of expertise. *Journal of Verbal Learning and Verbal Behavior, 22*(1), 1–14.

Brown, A. L. & Palincsar, A. (1985). *Reciprocal teaching of comprehension strategies: A natural history of one program for enhancing learning* (Tech. Rep. No. 334). Champaign, IL: University of Illinois, Center for the Study of Reading.

Brown, A. L. & Palinscar, A. S. (1986). Interactive teaching to promote independent learning from text. *The Reading Teacher, 39,* 771–777.

Bruner, J. S. (1986). *Actual minds, possible worlds.* Cambridge, MA: Harvard University Press.

Bruner, J. S. (1978). The role of dialogue in language acquisition. In A. Sinclair, R. J. Jarvelle, & W. J. M. Leveet (Eds.), *The child's conception of language* (pp. 92–101). New York: Springer.

Bryant, N. D., Kelly, M. S., Hathaway, K., & Rubin, E. (1981). *A summary of directions for the "LD-Efficient" teaching manual.* New York: Research Institute for the study of Learning Disabilities, Teachers College, Columbia University.

Bryant, P. E. & Bradley, L. (1980). *Processes in spelling.* (pp. 355–370). London: Academic Press.

Burcham, B., Carlson, L., & Milich, R. (1993). Promising school-based practices for students with attention deficit disorder. *Exceptional Children, 60,* 174–180.

Bush, C. & Huebner, M. (1979). *Strategies for reading in the elementary school.* New York: Macmillan.

Butkowsky, I. S. & Willows, D. M. (1980). Cognitive-motivational characteristics of children varying in reading ability: Evidence for learned helplessness in poor readers. *Journal of Educational Psychology, 72,* 408–422.

Cairney, T. H. (1990). *Teaching reading comprehension: Meaning makers at work.* Philadelphia: Open University Press.

Calkins, L. M. (1994). *The art of teaching writing* (2nd ed.) Portsmouth, NH: Heinemann.

Calkins, L. M. & Harwayne, S. (1991). *Living between the lines.* Portsmouth, NH: Heinemann.

Cantrell, R. J. (1997). K-W-L learning journals: A way to encourage reflection. *Journal of Reading, 40,* 392–393.

Carbo, M., Dunn, R., & Dunn, K. (1986, 1991). *Teaching students to read through their individual learning styles.* Boston: Allyn & Bacon.

Cardarilli, A. F. (1988). The influence of reinspection on students' IRI results. *The Reading Teacher, 41,* 664–667.

Carigan-Belleville, L. (1989). Jason's story: Motivating the reluctant student to write. *English Journal, 78,* 57–60.

Carlson, N. R. (1993). *Psychology: The science of behavior* (4th ed.). Boston: Allyn & Bacon.

Carnine, D., Kameenui, E. J., & Coyle, G. (1984). Utilization of contextual information in determining the meaning of unfamiliar words. *Reading Research Quarterly, 19,* 188–204.

Carnegie Corporation (1994). *Starting points: Meeting the needs of our youngest children.* New York: Author.

Carr, E. M. (1985). The vocabulary overview guide: A metacognitive strategy to improve vocabulary, comprehension and retention. *Journal of Reading, 28,* 684–689.

Carroll, J. B. (1977). Developmental parameters in reading comprehension. In J. T. Guthrie (Ed.), *Cognition, curriculum and comprehension* (pp. 1–15). Newark, DE: International Reading Association.

Carver, R. P. (1990). *Reading rate: A review of research and theory.* San Diego, CA: Academic Press.

Carver, R. P. (1992). Reading rate: Theory, research, and practical implications. *Journal of Reading, 36,* 84–95.

Casbergue, R. M. & Greene, J. F. (1988). Persistent misconceptions about sensory perception and reading disability. *Journal of Reading, 31,* 196–203.

Caverly, D. C. & Orlando, V. P. (1991). Textbook study strategies. In D. C. Caverly & V. P. Orlando (Eds.), *Teaching reading and study strategies at the college level* (pp. 86–165). Newark, DE: International Reading Association.

Celano, M. P. & Geller, R. J. (1993). Learning, school performance, and children with asthma: How much at risk? *Journal of Learning Disabilities, 26,* 23–37.

Chall, J. S. (1988). The beginning years. In B. L. Zakaluk & S. J. Samuels (Eds.), *Readability: Its past, present, and future* (pp. 2–13). Newark, DE: International Reading Association.

Chall, J. S., Bissex, G. L., Conard, S. S., & Harris-Sharples, S. H. (1996). *Qualitative assessment of text difficulty: A practical guide for teachers and writers.* Cambridge, MA: Brookline.

Chall, J. S. & Conard, S. S. (1991). *Should textbooks challenge students? The case for easier or harder books.* New York: Teacher's College Press.

Chall, J. S. & Dale, E. (1995). *Readability revisited: The new Dale-Chall Readability Formula.* Cambridge, MA: Brookline.

Chall, J. S., Jacobs, V. A., & Baldwin, L. E. (1990). *The reading crisis: Why poor children fall behind.* Cambridge: Harvard University Press.

Chamot, A. U. & O'Malley, J. M. (1994). Instructional approaches and teaching procedures. In K. Spangenberg-Urbschat & R. Pritchard (Eds.), *Kids come in all languages: Reading instruction for ESL students* (pp. 82–107). Newwark, DE: International Reading Association.

Chin, C. A. & Brewer, W. F. (1993). The role of anomalous data in knowledge acquisition: A theoretical framework and implications for science instruction. *Review of Educational Research, 63,* 1–49.

Cho, K. S. & Krashen, S. (1994). Acquisition of vocabulary from the Sweet Valley Kids series: Adult ESL acquisition. *Journal of Reading, 37,* 662–667.

Chomsky, C. (1978). When you still can't read in third grade: After decoding, what? In S. J. Samuels (Ed.), *What research has to say about reading instruction* (pp. 13–30). Newark, DE: International Reading Association.

Clark, D. B. (1988). *Dyslexia: Theory and practice of remedial instruction.* Parkton, MD: York Press.

Clay, M. M. (1985). *The early detection of reading difficulties* (3rd ed.). Auckland, NZ: Heinemann.

Clay, M. M. (1991a). *Becoming literate: The construction of inner control.* Portsmouth, NH: Heinemann.

Clay, M. M. (1991b). Reading recovery surprises. In D. E. DeFord, C. A. Lyons, & G. S. Pinnell (Eds.), *Bridges to literacy: Learning from Reading Recovery* (pp. 55–74). Portsmouth, NH: Heinemann.

Clay, M. M. (1991c). Introducing a new story book to young readers. *The Reading Teacher, 45,* 264–272.

Clay, M. M. (1993a). *An observation survey of early literacy achievement.* Portsmouth, NH: Heinemann.

Clay, M. M. (1993b). *Reading Recovery: A Guidebook for teachers in training.* Portsmouth, NH: Heinemann.

Cohen, A. S. (1974–75). Oral reading errors of first grade children taught by a code emphasis approach. *Reading Research Quarterly, 10,* 616–650.

Cohen, P. A., Kulik, J. A., & Kulik, C. (1982). Educational outcomes of tutoring: A meta-analysis of findings. *American Educational Research Journal, 19,* 237–248.

Colvin, R. J. & Root, J. H. (1982). *Reading evaluation—adult diagnosis: A test for assessing adult student reading needs and progress.* Syracuse, NY: Literacy Volunteers of New York.

Comer, J. P. (1988). *Maggie's American dream: The life and times of a black family.* New York: New American Library.

Comfort, R. L. (1994). Understanding and appreciating the ADHD child in the classroom. In C. Weaver (Ed.), *Success at Last: Helping students with AD(H)D achieve their potential* (pp. 63–74). Portsmouth, NH: Heinemann.

Conoley, J. C., & Impara, J. C. (1995) (Eds.). *The twelfth mental measurements yearbook.* Lincoln, NE: University of Nebraska Press.

Cook, D. M. (1986). *A guide to curriculum planning in reading.* Madison, WI: Wisconsin Department of Public Instruction.

Cook, L. K. & Mayer, R. E. (1983). Reading strategies training for meaningful learning from prose. In M. Pressley & J. Levin (Eds.), *Cognitive strategies research: Educational applications* (pp. 87–131). New York: Springer-Verlag.

Cooper, P. D. (1996, May). Intervention literacy instruction for hard-to-teach students in grades 3–6. Paper presented at the annual meeting of the International Reading Association, New Orleans.

Cudd, E. T. & Roberts, L. (1989). Using writing to enhance content area learning in the primary grades. *The Reading Teacher, 42,* 392–404.

Cummins, J. (1994). The acquisition of English as a second language. In K. Spangenberg-Urbschat & R. Pritchard (Eds.), *Kids come in all languages: Reading instruction for all ESL students* (pp. 36–62). Newark, DE: International Reading Association.

Cunningham, A. E. & Stanovich, K. E. (1991). Tracking the unique effects of print exposure in children: Associations with vocabulary, general knowledge, and spelling. *Journal of Educational Psychology, 83,* 264–274.

Cunningham, J. W. & Foster, E. O. (1978). The ivory tower connection: A case study. *The Reading Teacher, 31,* 365–369.

Cunningham, P. M. (1978). Decoding polysyllabic words: An alternative strategy. *Journal of Reading, 21,* 608–614.

Cunningham, P. M. (1979). A comparison/contrast theory of mediated word identification. *The Reading Teacher, 32,* 774–778.

Cunningham, P. M., Hall, D. P., & Defee, M. (1991). Non-ability grouped, multi-level instruction: A year in a first-grade classroom. *The Reading Teacher, 44,* 566–571.

Cunningham, P. M. (1988). When all else fails. . . . *The Reading Teacher, 41,* 800–805.

Cunningham, P. M. (1991). *Phonics they use: Words for reading and writing.* New York: HarperCollins.

Cunningham, P. M. & Allington, R. L. (1994). *Classrooms that work: They can all read and write.* Boston: HarperCollins.

Cunningham, P. M. & Cunningham, J. W. (1992). Making words: Enhancing the invented spelling-decoding connection. *The Reading Teacher, 46,* 106–115.

Dale, E. & Chall, J. (1948). *A formula for predicting readability.* Columbus, OH: Bureau of Educational Research, Ohio State University.

Dale, E. & O'Rourke, J. (1971). *Techniques of teaching vocabulary.* Chicago: Field.

Dale, E. & O'Rourke, J. (1976). *The living word vocabulary, The words we know: A national vocabulary inventory.* Chicago, IL: Field Enterprises.

Daneman, M. & Carpenter, P. A. (1980). Individual differences in working memory and in reading. *Journal of Verbal Learning and Verbal Behavior, 19,* 450–466.

Deford, D. E., Lyons, C. A., & Pinnell, G. S. (1991). Introduction. In D. E. DeFord, C. A. Lyons, G. S. Pinnell (Eds.), *Bridges to literacy: Learning from*

*Reading Recovery* (pp. 1–8). Portsmouth, NH: Heinemann.

Denckla, M. B. & Ruddell, R. B. (1976). Naming of object drawings by dyslexic and other learning disabled youngsters. *Brain and language, 3,* 1–16.

Dickinson, D. K. & Smith, M. W. (1994). Long-term effects of preschool teachers' book reading on low-income children's vocabulary and story comprehension. *Reading Research Quarterly, 29,* 104–122.

Dixon, R. C., Carnine, D., & Kameenui, E. (1994). Tools for teaching diverse learners: Using scaffolding to teach writing. *Educational Leadership,* 100–101.

Dole, J. A., Brown, K. J., & Trathen, W. (1996). The effect of strategy instruction on the comprehension performance of at-risk students. *Reading Research Quarterly, 31,* 62–88.

Donavin, D. P. (Ed.). (1992). *Best of the best for children.* New York: Random House.

Duffelmeyer, F. A., Baum, D. D., & Meekley, D. J. (1987). Maximizing reader-text confrontation with an extended anticipation guide. *Journal of Reading, 31,* 146–150.

Duffy, G. G. & Roehler, L. R. (1987). Improving reading instruction through the use of responsive elaboration. *The Reading Teacher, 40,* 514–520.

Duin, A. H. & Graves, M. F. (1987). Intensive vocabulary instruction as a prewriting technique. *Reading Research Quarterly, 22,* 311–330.

Dunkfield, C. (1991). Maintaining the integrity of a promising program: The base of reading recovery. In D. E. Deford, C. A. Lyon, & G. S. Pinnell (Eds.), *Bridges to literacy: Learning from Reading Recovery* (pp. 37–53). Portsmouth, NH: Heinemann.

Dunn, L. M. & Dunn, L. M. (1981). *Peabody Picture Vocabulary Test* (Rev.). Circle Pines, MN: American Guidance Service.

Durrell, D. & Catterson, J. (1980). *Durrell analysis of reading difficulty.* San Antonio, TX: Psychological Corporation.

Dykman, R. A. & Ackerman, P. T. (1991). Attention deficit disorder and specific reading disability: Separate but often overlapping disorders. *Journal of Learning Disabilities, 24,* 96–103.

Dyson, A. H. & Freedman, S. W. (1991). Writing. In J. Flood, J. M. Jensen, D. Lapp, & J. R. Squire (Eds.), *Handbook of research on teaching the English language arts* (pp. 754–774). New York: Macmillan.

Early, M. & Sawyer, D. J. (1984). *Reading to learn in grades 5 to 12.* New York: Harcourt Brace Jovanovich.

Education Department of Western Australia (1994). *First steps: Spelling resource book.* Melbourne, Australia: Longman.

Ehri, L. C. (1994). Development of the ability to read words: Update. In R. B. Ruddell, M. R. Ruddell, & H. Singer (Eds.), *Theoretical models and processes of reading* (4th ed.), (pp. 323–358). Newark, DE: International Reading Association.

Ehri, L. C. (1992). Reconceptualizing the development of sight word reading and its relationship to reading. In P. B. Gough, L. C. Ehri, & R. Treiman (Eds.), *Reading acquisition* (pp. 107–143). Hillsdale, NJ: Lawrence Erlbaum.

Ehri, L. C. & Robbins, C. (1992). Beginners need some decoding skill to read words by analogy. *Reading Research Quarterly, 27,* 12–26.

Ehri, L. C. (1983). A critique of five studies related to letter–name knowledge and learning to read. In L. M. Gentile, M. L. Kamil., & J. S. Blanchard (Eds.), *Reading research revisited* (pp. 143–153). Columbus, OH: Merrill.

Elkonin, D. B. (1973). Reading in the USSR. In J. Downing (Ed.), *Comparative reading* (pp. 551–579). New York: Macmillan.

Ekwall, E. E. & Shanker, J. L. (1988). *Diagnosis and remediation of the disabled reader.* Boston: Allyn & Bacon.

Elley, W. B. (1989). Vocabulary acquisition from listening to stories. *Reading Research Quarterly, 24,* 174–187.

Englert, C. S. & Hiebert, E. H. (1985). Children's developing awareness of text structures in expository materials. *Journal of Educational Psychology, 76,* 65–75.

Englert, C. S., Raphael, T. E., Anderson, L. M., Anthony, H. M., Fear, K. L., & Gregg, S. L. (1988). A case for writing intervention: Strategies for writing informational text. *Learning Disabilities Focus, 8,* 98–113.

Esler, W. K. & Esler, M. K. (1989). *Teaching elementary science* (5th ed.). Belmont, CA: Wadsworth.

Enz, B. (1989, May). *The 90 percent success solution.* Paper presented at the International Reading Association Annual Convention, New Orleans.

Estes, T. & Vaughn, J. (1985). *Reading and learning in the content classroom* (2nd ed.). Boston: Allyn & Bacon.

Farnan, N., Flood, J., & Lapp, D. (1994). Motivating high-risk learners to think and act as writers. In K. D. Wood & B. Algozzine (Eds.), *Teaching reading to high-risk readers* (pp. 291–314). Boston: Allyn & Bacon.

Farnham-Diggory, S. (1992). *The learning-disabled child.* Cambridge, MA: Harvard University Press.

Farr, R. & Carey, R. F. (1986). *Reading: What can be measured?* Newark, DE: International Reading Association.

Farr, R. & Farr, B. (1990). *Integrated assessment.* San Antonio, TX: Psychological Corporation.

Fernald, G. M. (1943). *Remedial techniques in basic school subjects.* New York: McGraw-Hill.

Fernald, G. M. & Keller, H. B. (1921). Effects of kinesthetic factor in development of word recognition, *Journal of Educational Research, 4,* 355–377.

Feurstein, R., Rand, Y., & Hoffman, M. B. (1979). *The dynamic assessment of retarded performers: The Learning Potential Assessment Device, theory, instruments, and techniques.* Baltimore: University Park Press.

Fielding, L. G. (1996). Choice makes reading instruction child centered. In C. Roller (Ed.), *Variability, not disability: Struggling readers in a workshop classroom* (pp. 43–55). Newark, DE: International Reading Association.

Fielding, L. G. & Roller, C. (1992). Making difficult books accessible and easy books acceptable. *The Reading Teacher, 45,* 678–685.

Fielding, L. G., Wilson, P. T., & Anderson, R. C. (1986). A new focus on free reading: The role of trade books in reading instruction. In T. E. Raphael (Ed.), *The contexts of school-based literacy* (pp. 149–160). New York: Random House.

Filmore, L. W. & Valdez, C. (1986). Teaching bilingual learners. In M. E. Wittrock (Ed.). *Handbook of research on teaching* (pp. 648–685). New York: Macmillan.

Fitzgerald, J. A. (1951). *A basic life spelling vocabulary.* Milwaukee, WI: Bruce Publishing.

Fitzgerald, J. & Spiegel, D. (1983). Enhancing children's reading comprehension through instruction in narrative structure. *Journal of Reading Behavior, 15,* 1–17.

Five, C. L. (1992). *Special voices.* Portsmouth, NH: Heinemann.

Fountas, I. C. & Pinnell, G. S. (1996). *Guided reading: Good first teaching for all children.* Portsmouth, NH: Heinemann.

Franklin Electronic Publishers (1991–1992). *User's manual.* Mt. Holly, NJ.

Frazier, M. K. (1995). Caution: Students on board the Internet. *Educational Leadership, 53* (2), 26–27.

Freppon, P. A. (1994). Understanding the nature of reading and writing difficulties: An alternative view. *Reading and Writing Quarterly: Overcoming Learning Difficulties, 10,* 227–238.

Fry, E. B. (1977a). *Elementary reading instruction.* New York: McGraw-Hill.

Fry, E. B. (1977b). Fry's readability graph: Clarifications, validity, and extension to level 17. *Journal of Reading, 21,* 242–252.

Fry, E. B., Kress, J. E., & Fountoukidis, D. L. (1993). *The reading teacher's book of lists* (3rd ed). Englewood Cliffs, NJ: Prentice Hall.

Fusaro, J. (1988). Applying statistical rigor to a validation study of the Fry Readability Graph. *Reading Research and Instruction, 28,* 44–48.

Gallo, D. R. (1985). Teachers as reading researchers. In C. N. Hedley & A. N. Baratta (Eds.), *Contexts of reading* (pp. 185–199). Norwood, NJ: Ablex.

Galvin, G. A. (1981). Uses and abuses of the *WISC-R* with the learning disabled. *Journal of Learning Disabilities, 14,* 326–329.

Gambrell, L. B. & Bales, R. J. (1986). Mental imagery and the comprehension monitoring performance of fourth- and fifth-grade poor readers. *Reading Research Quarterly, 21,* 454–464.

Gambrell, L. B., Wilson, R. M., & Gantt, W. N. (1981). Classroom observations of good and poor readers. *Journal of Educational Research, 24,* 400–404.

Ganske, K. (1993). *Developmental spelling analysis: A qualitative measure for assessment and instructional planning.* Barboursville, VA: Author.

Garcia, G. E. (1991). Factors influencing the English reading test performance of Spanish speaking Hispanic children. *Reading Research Quarterly, 26,* 371–392.

Garcia, G. E., Pearson, P. D., & Jiminez, R. T. (1994). *The At-risk situation: A synthesis of reading research.* Champaign, IL: Center for the Study of Reading, University of Illinois.

Gardner, H. (1983). *Frames of mind: The theory of multiple intelligences.* New York: Basic Books.

Garner, R. (1994). Metacognition and executive control. In R. B. Ruddell, M. R. Ruddell, & H. Singer (Eds.), *Theoretical models and processes of reading* (4th ed.), (pp. 715–732). Newark, DE: International Reading Association.

Garner, R. & Reis, R. (1981). Monitoring and resolving comprehension obstacles: An investigation of spontaneous text lookbacks among upper-grade good and poor comprehenders. *Reading Research Quarterly, 16,* 569–582.

Garnett, K. (1986). Telling tales: Narratives and learning disabled children. *Topics in Language Disorders, 6*(2), 44–52.

Gaskins, R. W., Gaskins, J. C., & Gaskins, I. W. (1991). A decoding program for poor readers and the rest of the class, too! *Language Arts, 63,* 213–225.

Gaskins, I. W., Ehri, L. C., Cress, C., O'Hara, C., & Donnelly, K. (1996–1997). Procedures for word learning: Making discoveries about words. *The Reading Teacher, 50,* 312–327.

Gates, A. I. (1931). *Interest and ability in reading.* New York: MacMillan.

Gaudrey, E. & Spielberger, C. D. (1971). *Anxiety and educational achievement.* Sydney, AUS: John Wiley & Sons.

Gelzheiser, L. M. & Meyers, J. (1990). Special and remedial education in the classroom: Theme and variation. *Reading, Writing, and Learning Disabilities, 6,* 419–436.

Gentile, L. M. & McMillan, M. M. (1987). *Stress and reading difficulties: Research, assessment, intervention.* Newark, DE: International Reading Association.

Gentry, J. R. (1997). *My kid can't spell.* Portsmouth, NH: Heinemann.

Gentry, J. R. & Gillet, J. W. (1993). *Teaching kids to spell.* Portsmouth, NH: Heinemann.

German, D. J. (1992). Word-finding intervention for children and adoelscents. *Topics in Language Disorders, 13*(1), 33–50.

Gersten, R. & Jiminez, R. T. (1994). A delicate balance: Enhancing literature instruction for students of English as a second language. *The Reading Teacher, 47,* 438–449.

Gesell, A. (1925). *The mental growth of the pre-school child.* New York: Macmillan.

Gibson, E. J. & Levin, H. (1974). *The psychology of reading.* Cambridge: MIT Press.

Gibson, E. J., Gibson, J. J., Pick, A. D., & Osser, H. (1962). A developmental study of the discrimination of letter-like forms. *Journal of Comparative and Physiological Psychology, 55,* 897–906.

Gillett, J. W. & Temple, C. (1994). *Understanding reading problems: Assessment and instruction* (4th ed.). New York: HarperCollins.

Gillingham, A. & Stillman, B. (1936). *Remedial training for children with specific disability in reading, spelling, and penmanship.* New York: Sackett & Wilhelms.

Gillingham, A. & Stillman, B. (1960, 1983). *Remedial training for children with specific disability in reading, writing, and penmanship* (7th ed.). Cambridge, MA: Educators Publishing Service.

Glass, G. G. (1976). *Glass analysis for decoding only, teacher's guide.* Garden City, NY: Easier to Learn.

Glass, G. G. & Burton, E. H. (1973). How do they decode? Verbalizations and observed behaviors of successful decoders. *Education, 94,* 58–65.

Glazer, S. M. (1991). Behaviors reflecting emotional involvements during reading and writing activities. *Reading, Writing, and Learning Disabilities, 7,* 219–231.

Gluskho, R. J. (1979). The organization and activation of orthographic knowledge in reading aloud. *Journal of Experimental Psychology: Human Perception and Performance, 5,* 674–691.

Gold, J. & Fleisher, L. S. (1986). Comprehension breakdown with inductively organized text: Differences between average and disabled readers. *Remedial and Special Education, 7,* 26–32.

Goldenberg, C. (1994). Promoting early literacy development among Spanish-speaking children: Lessons from two studies. In E. H. Hiebert & B. M. Taylor (Eds.), *Getting reading right from the start* (pp. 171–200). Boston: Allyn & Bacon.

Goodman, K. S. (1974). Miscue analysis: Theory and reality in reading. In J. E. Merritt (Ed.), *New horizons in reading* (pp. 15–26). Newark, DE: International Reading Association.

Goodman, K. S. (1994). Reading, writing, and written texts: A transactional sociopsycholinguistic view. In R. B. Ruddell, M. R. Ruddell, & H. Singer (Eds.), *Theoretical models and processes of reading* (4th ed.), (pp. 1093–1130). Newark, DE: International Reading Association.

Goodman, K. S. (1982). Revaluing readers and reading. In D. K. Reid, W. P. Hresko, & Y. M. Goodman (Eds.), *Topics in learning disabilities, 1* (No. 4), 87–93.

Goodman, K. S. (1984). Unity in reading. In A. C. Purves & O. Niles (Eds.), *Becoming readers in a complex society, 83rd yearbook of the National Society for the Study of Education,* Part 1 (pp. 79–114). Chicago: National Society for the Study of Education.

Goodman, K. S. & Goodman, Y. S (1978). *Reading of American children whose dialect is a stable rural dialect of English or a language other than English.* Detroit: Wayne State University Press (ERIC Document Reproduction Service No. ED 182-465).

Goodman, K. M. (1992). Through the miscue window. In K. S. Goodman, L. B. Bird, & Y. M. Goodman (Eds.), *The whole language catalog: Supplement on authentic assessment* (pp. 20–21). Santa Rosa, CA: American School Publications.

Goodman, Y. M. & Marek, A. M. (1996). *Retrospective miscue analysis: Revaluing readers and reading.* Katonah, NY: Richard C. Owen.

Goodman, Y. M., Watson, D. J., & Burke, C. L. (1987). *Reading miscue inventory: Alternative procedures.* New York: Richard C. Owen.

Gordon, C. J. (1990). Contexts for expository text structure use. *Reading research and instruction, 29*(2), 55–72.

Gordon, W. C. (1989). *Learning and memory.* Belmont, CA: Brook/Cole.

Goswami, U. (1986). Children's use of analogy in learning to read: A developmental study. *Journal of Experimental Child Psychology, 42,* 73–83.

Goswami, U. (1988). Orthographic analogies and reading development. *Quarterly Journal of Experimental Psychology, 40,* 239–268.

Goswami, U. & Bryant, P. (1990). *Phonological skills and learning to read.* Hillsdale, N.J.: Lawrence Erlbaum Associates.

Gough, P. B. & Hillinger, M. L. (1980). Learning to read: An unnatural act. *Bulletin of the Orton Society, 30,* 179–196.

Gough, P. B., Juel, C., & Griffith, P. L. (1992). Reading, spelling, and the orthographic cipher. In P. B. Gough, L. C. Ehri, & R. Treiman (Eds.), *Reading Acquistion* (pp. 35–48). Hillsdale, NJ: Lawrence Erlbaum Associates.

Gough, P. B. & Walsh, M. A., (1991). Chinese, Phoenicians, and the orthographic ciper of English. In S. A. Brady & D. P. Shankweiler (Eds.), *Phonological processes in literacy: A tribute to Isabelle Y. Liberman* (pp. 199–210). Hillsdale, NJ: Lawrence Erlbaum Associates.

Graham, S. & Harris, K. R. (1993). Teaching writing strategies to students with learning disabilities: Issues and recommendations. In L. J. Meltzer (Ed.), *Strategy assessment and instruction for students with learning disabilities: From theory to practice* (pp. 271–292). Austin, TX: PRO-ED.

Graves, D. H. (1982). Break the welfare cycle: Let writers choose their topics. *Forum, 5,* 7–11.

Graves, D. H. (1983). *Writing: Teachers and children at work.* Exeter, NH: Heinemann.

Graves, D. H. (1975). Examination of the writing processes of seven-year-old children. *Research in the Teaching of English, 9,* 221–241.

Graves, D. H. (1991). All children can write. In S. Stives (Ed.), *With promise: Redefining reading and writing to "special" students* (pp. 115–125). Portsmouth, NH: Heinemann.

Graves, M. F. & Slater, W. H. (1996). Vocabulary instruction in content areas. In D. Lapp, J. Flood, & N. Farnan (Eds.), *Content area reading and learning instructional strategies* (pp. 261–275). Boston: Allyn & Bacon.

Gunning, T. (1975). *A comparison of word attack skills derived from a phonological analysis of frequently used words drawn from a juvenile corpus and an adult corpus.* Unpublished doctoral dissertation, Temple University, Philadelphia.

Gunning, T. (1982). Wrong level test: Wrong information. *The Reading Teacher, 35,* 902–905.

Gunning, T. (1988a, May). *Decoding behavior of good and poor second grade students.* Paper presented at the annual meeting of the International Reading Association, Toronto.

Gunning, T. (1988b). *Teaching phonics and other word attack skills.* Springfield, IL: Charles C Thomas.

Gunning, T. (1994a). *Word Building: Beginnings.* New York: Phoenix Learning Systems.

Gunning, T. (1994b). *Word Building: Book D.* New York: Phoenix Learning Systems.

Gunning, T. (1995). Word building: A strategic approach to the teaching of phonics. *The Reading Teacher, 48,* 484–488.

Gunning, T. (1996). *Creating reading instruction for all children* (2nd ed.). Boston: Allyn & Bacon.

Gunning, T. (1998). *Best books for beginning readers.* Boston: Allyn & Bacon.

Guthrie, J. T., Seifert, M., & Kline, L. W. (1978). Clues from research on programs for poor readers. In S. J. Samuels (Ed.), *What research has to say about reading instruction* (pp. 1–12). Newark, DE: International Reading Association.

Halsey, S. & Morris, E. (1977). *Macmillan beginning dictionary.* New York: Macmillan.

Hammond, W. D. (1995, December). *From homophones to roots: Word study that emphasized the spelling-meaning connection.* Paper presented at the annual meeting of the National Reading Conference, New Orleans, LA.

Hansen, J. (1987). *When writers read.* Portsmouth, NH: Heinemann.

Hansen, J. & Hubbard, R. (1984). Poor readers can draw inferences. *The Reading Teacher, 37,* 586–589.

Hansen, J. & Pearson, P. D. (1980). *The effects of inference training and practice on young children's comprehension* (Tech. Rep. No. 166). Urbana, IL: University of Illinois, Center for the Study of Reading.

Hansen, J. & Pearson, P. D. (1982). *Improving the inferential comprehension of good and poor fourth-grade readers* (Rep. No. CSR-TR-235). Urbana, IL: University of Illinois, Center for the Study of Reading. (ERIC Document Reproduction No. ED 215–312)

Hardy, M., Stennett, R. G. F., & Smythe, P. C. (1973). Word attack: How do they figure them out? *Elementary English, 50,* 99–102.

Harris, A. J. & Jacobson, M. D. (1980). A comparison of the Fry, Spache, and Harris-Jacobson readability formulas for primary grades. *The Reading Teacher, 33,* 920–923.

Harris, A. J. & Sipay, E. R. (1985). *How to increase reading ability* (8th ed.). New York: Longman.

Harris, A. J. & Sipay, E. R. (1990). *How to increase reading ability* (9th ed.). New York: Longman.

Harris, K. R. & Graham, S. (1992). *Helping young writers master the craft: Strategy instruction and self-regulation in the writing process.* Cambridge, MA: Brookline Books.

Harste, J. C., Short, K. G., & Burke, C. (1988). *Creating classrooms for authors: The reading-writing connection.* Portsmouth, NH: Heinemann.

Haywood, H. C. (1993, November). *Interactive assessment: Assessment of learning potential, school learning, and adaptive behavior.* Paper presented at the Ninth Annual Learning Disorders Conference, Cambridge, MA.

Haywood, H. C., Brown, A. L., & Wingenfield, S. (1990). Dynamic approaches to psychoeducational assessment. *School Psychology Review, 19,* 411–422.

Head, M. H. & Readence, J. E. (1986). Anticipation guides: Meaning through prediction. In E. K. Deshner, T. W. Bean, J. E. Readence, & D. W. Moore (Eds.), *Reading in the content areas* (2nd ed.) (pp. 229–234). Dubuque, IA: Kendall/Hunt.

Heiman, M. & Slomianko, J. (1986). *Methods of inquiry.* Cambridge, MA: Learning Associates.

Hembree, R. (1988). Correlates, causes, effects, and treatment of test anxiety. *Review of Educational Research, 20,* 415–421.

Henderson, E. H. (1990). *Teaching spelling.* Boston: Houghton Mifflin.

Henderson, E. H. & Templeton, S. (1986). A developmental perspective of formal spelling instruction through alphabet, pattern, and meaning. *Elementary School Journal, 86,* 305–316.

Henk, W. A. & Melnick, S. A. (1995). The Reader Self-Perception Scale (RSPS): A new tool for measuring how children feel about themselves as readers. *The Reading Teacher, 48,* 470–482.

Herber, H. L. (1978). *Teaching reading in content areas* (2nd ed.). Englewood Cliffs, NJ: Prentice-Hall.

Herber, H. L. (1992). Foreword. In K. D. Wood, D. Lapp, & J. Flood (Eds.), *Guiding readers through text: A review of study guides* (pp. v-vi). Newark: DE: International Reading Association.

Herber, H. L. & Herber, J. N. (1993). *Teaching in content areas with reading, writing, and reasoning.* Boston: Allyn & Bacon.

Herman, P. A., Anderson, R. C., Pearson, P. D., & Nagy, W. E. (1987). Incidental acquisition of word meanings from expositions with varied text features. *Reading Research Quarterly, 22,* 263–284.

Hidi, S. A. & Anderson, V. (1986). Producing written summaries: Task demands, cognitive operations, and implications for instruction. *Review of Educational Research, 56,* 473–493.

Hiebert, E. H. (1996). Creating and sustaining a love of literature . . . And the ability to read it. In M. F. Graves, P. van den Broek, & B. M. Taylor (Eds.), *The first R: Every child's right to read* (pp. 15–36). Newark, DE: International Reading Association.

Hiebert, E. H. (1994). A small-group literacy intervention with Chapter 1 students. In E. H. Hiebert & B. M. Taylor (Eds.), *Getting reading right from the start* (pp. 85–106). Boston: Allyn & Bacon.

Hiebert, E. H. & Taylor, B. M. (1994). Interventions and the restructring of American literacy instruction. In E. H. Hiebert & B. M. Taylor (Eds.), *Getting reading right from the start* (pp. 201–217). Boston: Allyn & Bacon.

Hiebert, E. H., Valencia, S., & Afflerbach, P. P. (1994). Definitions and perspectives. In S. Valencia, P. P. Afflerbach, & E. H. Hiebert (Eds.), *Authentic reading assessment: Practices and possibilities* (6–21). Newark, DE: International Reading Association.

Hodges, F. E. (1991). The conventions of writing. In J. Flood, J. M. Jensen, D. Lapp, & J. R. Squire (Eds.), *Handbook of research on teaching the English language arts* (pp. 775–786). New York: Macmillan.

Hoffman, J. V. (1991). Teacher and school effects in learning to read. In R. Barr, M. L. Kamil, P. Mosenthal, & P. D. Pearson (Eds.), *Handbook of reading research,* Volume II (pp. 911–950). New York: Longman.

Hoffman, J. V., McCarthy, S. J., Abbott, J., Christian, C., Corman, L., & Curry, C. (1994). So what's new in the new basals? A focus on first grade. *Journal of Reading Behavior, 26,* 47–73.

Hoffman, L. (1993, October). *Using readers' theater in the general English classroom: Motivating reluctant readers and writers.* Paper presented at the annnual meeting of the Connecticut Reading Association, Waterbury.

Holliday, W. G. (1991). Helping students learn effectively from science text. In C. M. Santa & D. E. Alvermann (Eds.), *Science learning: Processes and applications* (pp. 38–47). Newark, DE: International Reading Association.

Holmes, B. C. (1987). Children's inferences with print and pictures. *Journal of Educational Psychology, 79,* 14–18.

Homa, L. L. (Ed.). (1996). *The elementary school library collection* (20th ed.). Williamsport, PA: Brodart.

Horowitz, R. (1985). Text patterns. *Journal of Reading, 28,* 534–542.

Hudgahl, K. (1993). Functional brain asymmetry, dyslexia, and immune disorders. In A. M. Galbruda (Ed.), *Dyslexia and development: Neurological aspects of extra-ordinary brains* (pp. 133–154). Cambridge, MA: Harvard University Press.

Hulme, C. (1981). *Reading retardation and multi-sensory teaching.* London: Routledge & Kegan Paul.

Hulme, C. & MacKenzie, S. (1992). *Working memory and severe learning difficulties.* Hillsdale, NJ.: Lawrence Erlbaum Associates.

Hyman, R. T. (1978). *Strategic questioning.* Englewood Cliffs, NJ: Prentice-Hall.

Idol, L. (1988). G. M. Fernald (Ed.) (1943). *Remedial techniques in basic school subjects.* Austin, TX: PRO-ED.

Ilg, F. & Ames, L. B. (1965). *School readiness.* New York: Harper & Row.

Invernizzi, M., Abouzeid, M., & Gill, J. T. (1994). Using students' invented spellings as a guide for spelling instruction that emphasizes word study. *The Elementary School Journal, 95,* 155–167.

Irwin, P. A. & Mitchell, J. N. (1983). A procedure for assessing the richness of retellings. *Journal of Reading, 26,* 391–396.

Iverson, S. & Tunmer, W. W. (1993). Phonological processing skills and the Reading Recovery program. *Journal of Educational Psychology, 85* (1), 112–126.

Jackson, M. D. (1980). Further evidence for a relationship between memory access and reading ability. *Journal of Verbal Learning and Verbal Behavior, 19,* 683–694.

Jenkins, J. R., Matlock, B., & Slocum, T. A. (1989). Approaches to vocabulary instruction. *Reading Research Quarterly, 24,* 215–235.

Jett-Simpson, M. (1981). Writing stories using model structures: The circle story. *Language Arts, 58,* 293–299.

Jobe, F. W. (1976). *Screening vision in schools.* Newark, DE: International Reading Association.

Johns, J. L. (1994). *Basic reading inventory* (6th ed.). Dubuque, IA: Kendall/Hunt.

Johnson, D. (1993). *Diagnostic teaching: Implications for intervention.* Paper presented at the Ninth Annual Learning Disabilities Conference, Cambridge, MA.

Johnson, D. J. & Myklebust, H. (1967). *Learning disabilities: Educational principles and practices.* New York: Grune & Stratton.

Johnson, D. W. & Johnson, R. T. (1994). *Learning together and alone: Cooperative, competitive, and individualistic learning* (4th ed.). Boston: Allyn & Bacon.

Johnson, M. S. (1957). Factors related to disability in reading. *Journal of Experimental Eduation, 26,* 1–26.

Johnson, M. S. (1966). Tracing and kinesthetic techniques. In J. Money (Ed.), *The disabled reader: Education of the dyslexic child* (pp. 147–160). Baltimore: The Johns Hopkins Press.

Johnson, M. S. & Kress, R. A. (1966). *Eliminating learning problems in reading disability cases.* Unpublished paper, Temple University, Philadelphia.

Johnson, M. S., Kress, R. A., & Pikulski, J. J. (1987). *Informal reading inventories* (2nd ed.). Newark, DE: International Reading Association.

Johnston, F., Juel, C., & Invernizzi, M. (1995). *Guidelines for volunteer tutors of emergent and early readers.* Charlottesville, VA: Authors, University of Virginia.

Johnston, P. H. (1992). *Constructive evaluation of literate activity.* New York: Longman.

Johnston, P. & Allington, R. (1991). Remediation. In R. Barr, M. L. Kamil, P. Mosenthal, & P. D. Pearson (Eds.), *Handbook of reading research,* Volume II (pp. 984–1012). New York: Longman.

Joint Task Force on Assessment (1994). *Standards for the assessment of reading and writing.* Newark, DE: International Reading Association & Urbana, IL: National Council of Teachers of English.

Jongsma, E. (1980). *Cloze instruction research: A second look.* Newark, DE: International Reading Association.

Joshua, S. & Dupin, J. J. (1987). Taking into account student conceptions in instructional strategy: An example in physics. *Cognition and Instruction, 4,* 117–135.

Juel, C. (1988). Learning to read and write: A longitudinal study of fifty-four children from first through fourth grade. *Journal of Educational Psychology, 80,* 437–447.

Juel, C. (1991). Cross-age tutoring between student athletes and at-risk children. *The Reading Teacher, 45,* 178–186.

Juel, C. (1994). *Learning to read and write in one elementary school.* New York: Springer-Verlag.

Juel, C., Griffith, P. L., & Gough, P. B. (1986). Acquisition of literacy: A longitudinal study of children in first and second grade. *Journal of Educational Psychology, 78,* 243–255.

Kephart, N. C. (1966). *The slow learner in the classroom* (2nd ed.). Columbus, OH: Merrill.

Khan, A. U. (1988). *Clinical disorders of memory.* New York: Plenum.

Kibby, M. (1995). *Practical steps for informing literacy instruction: A diagnostic decision-making model.* Newark, DE: International Reading Association.

Killgallon, P. A. (1942). *A study of relationships among certain pupil adjustments in language situations.* Unpublished doctoral disseration, Pennsylvania State University.

Kimmel, S. & MacGinitie, W. H. (1984). Identifying children who use a perseverative text processing strategy. *Reading Research Quarterly, 19,* 162–172.

Kincaid, J. P., Fishburne, R., Rogers, R. L., & Chissom, B. S. (1975). *Derivation of new readability formulas (Automated Readability Index, Fog Count, and Flesch Reading Ease formula) for Navy enlisted personnel (Branch Report 8–75),* Chief of Naval Training, Millington, TN.

Kinder, D., Bursuck, B., & Epstein, M. (1992). An evaluation of history textbooks. *The Journal of Special Education, 25,* 472–491.

Kirsch, I. S. & Jungeblut, A. (1986). *Literacy: Profiles of young adults.* Princeton, NJ: Educational Testing Service.

Kletzien, S. B. (1991). Strategy use by good and poor comprehenders reading expository text of differing levels. *Reading Research Quarterly, 26,* 67–86.

Kletzien, S. B. & Bednar, M. R. (1988). A framework for reader autonomy: An integrated perspective. *Journal of Reading, 32,* 30–33.

Krashen, S. (1996). *Effective second language acquisition.* Torrance, CA: The Education Centre.

Kresse, E. C. (1984). Using reading as a thinking process to solve math story problems. *Journal of Reading, 27,* 598–601.

Lake, J. H. (1973). The influence of wait-time on the verbal dimensions of student inquiry behavior. *Dissertation Abstracts International, 34,* 6476A. (University Microfilms No. 74–08866).

Langer, J. A. (1981). From theory to practice: A prereading plan. *Journal of Reading, 25,* 152–156.

Langer, J. A., Applebee, A. N., Mullis, I. V. S., & Foentsch, M. A. (1990). *Learning to read in our nation's schools: Instruction and achievement in 1988 at grades 4, 8, and 12.* Princeton, NJ: Educational Testing Service.

Lapp, D. & Flood, J. (1992). *Teaching reading to every child* (3rd ed.). New York: Macmillan.

Learning Media (1991). *Reading in junior classes.* Wellington, NZ: Ministry of Education.

Learning Media (1994). *Books for Ready to Read classrooms.* Katonah, NY: Richard C. Owen.

Lerner, J. W. (1989). *Learning disabilities: Theories, diagnosis, and teaching strategies* (5th ed.). Boston: Allyn & Bacon.

Lerner, J. (1991, May). *New issues and trends in instruction for disabled readers.* Paper presented at the International Reading Association Convention, Las Vegas.

Leslie, L. & Caldwell, J. A. (1995). *Qualitative reading inventory* (2nd ed.) Glenview, IL: Scott, Foresman/Little Brown Higher Education.

Levin, J. R. et al. (1984). A comparison of semantic and mnemonic-based vocabulary-learning strategies. *Reading Psychology, 5*(2), 1–15.

Levin, J. R. (1993). Mnemonic strategies and classroom learning: A twenty-year report card. *The Elementary School Journal, 94,* 235–244.

Lewin, T. (1996). Study of welfare families warns of problems for schoolchildren. *The New York Times,* February 29, 1996, p. A14.

Liberman, A. M. & Mattingly, I. G. (1989). A specialization for speech perception. *Science, 243,* 489–494.

Liberman, I. Y. & Shankweiler, D. (1991). Phonology and beginning reading: A tutorial. In L. Rieben & C. A. Perfetti (Eds.), *Learning to read: Basic research and its implications* (pp. 3–18). Hillsdale, NJ: Lawrence Erlbaum Associates.

Liberman, I. Y., Shankweiler, D., Fischer, F. W., & Carter, B. (1974). Explicit syllable and phoneme segmentation in the young child. *Journal of Experimental Child Psychology, 18,* 201–212.

Lindamood, C. H. & Lindamood, P. C. (1975). *The A.D.D. program: Auditory discrimination in depth.* Allen, TX: DLM Teaching Resources.

Linden, M. & Wittrock, M. C. (1981). The teaching of reading comprehension according to the model of generative learning. *Reading Research Quarterly, 17,* 44–57.

Lipson, M. Y. (1984). Some unexpected issues in prior knowledge and comprehension. *The Reading Teacher, 37,* 760–764.

Lipson, M. Y. & Wixson, K. K. (1991). *Assessment and instruction of reading disability: An interactive approach.* New York: HarperCollins.

Lipson, M. Y. & Wixson, K. K. (1997). *Assessment and instruction of reading and writing disability: An interactive approach* (2nd ed.). New York: Longman.

Loudon, B. & Arthur, G. (1940). An application of the Fernald method to an extreme case of reading disability. *Elementary School Journal, 40,* 599–606.

Lovegrove, W. J. & Williams, M. C. (1993). Visual temporal processing deficits in specific reading disability. In D. M. Willows, R. S. Kruk, & E. Corcos (Eds.), *Visual processes in reading and reading disabilities* (pp. 311–329). Hillsdale, NJ: Lawrence Erlbaum Associates.

Lovitt, T. C., Rudsit, J., Jenkins, J., Pious, C., & Benedetti, D. (1986). Adapting science materials for general and learning disabled seventh graders. *Remedial and Special Education, 7* (1), 31–39.

Luria, A. R. (1970). The functional organization of the brain. *Science, 153,* 66–78.

Lyons, C. (1995, December). *An analysis of the literacy behaviors of hard to accelerate Reading Recovery students.* Paper presented at the annual meeting of the National Reading Conference, New Orleans, LA.

Lyons, C. A. & Beaver, J. (1995). Reducing retention and learning disability placement through Reading Recovery: An educationally sound, cost-effective choice. In R. A. Allington & S. A. Walmsley (Eds.), *Rethinking literacy in America's elementary schools* (pp. 116–136). New York: Teachers College Press.

Maclean, M., Bryant, P., & Bradley, L. (1987). Rhymes, nursery rhymes, and reading in early childhood. *Merrill-Palmer Quarterly, 33,* 255–281.

McArthur, T. (Ed.) (1992). *The Oxford Companion to the English language.* New York: Oxford University Press.

McAlexander, P. J., Dobie, A. B., & Gregg, N. (1992). *Beyond the "sp" label: Improving the spelling of learning disabled and basic writers.* Urbana, IL: National Council of Teachers of English.

McBurnett, K., Lahey, B. B., & Pfiffner, L. J. (1993). Diagnosis of attention deficit disorders in DSMV-IV: Scientific basis and implications for education. *Exceptional Children, 60,* 108–117.

McCarrier, A. (1995, May). *Linking practice and theory, overview.* Paper presented at the annual meeting of the International Reading Association, Anaheim.

McCormick, S. (1987). *Remedial and clinical reading instruction.* Columbus, OH: Merrill.

McCormick, S. (1992). Disabled readers' erroneous responses to inferential comprehension questions. *Reading Research Quarterly, 27,* 54–93.

McCormick, S. (1994). A nonreader becomes a reader: A case study of literacy acquisition by a severely disabled reader. *Reading Research Quarterly, 29,* 157–176.

McCormick, S. (1995). *Instructing students who have literacy problems* (2nd ed.). Englewood Cliffs, NJ: Prentice-Hall.

McCracken, R. A. (1971). Initiating sustained silent reading. *Journal of Reading, 14,* 521–524, 582–583.

McCracken, R. A. (1991). Eleven best ideas for reading teachers. In E. Fry (Ed.), *Ten best ideas for reading teachers* (pp. 90–91). Menlo Park, CA: Addison-Wesley.

McDermott, R. (1976). *Kids make sense: An ethnographic account of the interactional management of success and failure in one first-grade classroom.* Unpublished doctoral dissertation, Stanford University, Stanford, CA.

McGill-Franzen, A. (1994). Compensatory and special education: Is there accountability for learning and belief in children's potential. In E. H. Hiebert & B. M. Taylor (Eds.), *Getting reading right from the start* (pp. 13–35). Boston: Allyn & Bacon.

McGill-Franzen, A. & Allington, R. L. (1991). Every child's right: Literacy. *The Reading Teacher, 45,* 86–90.

MacGinitie, W. & MacGinitie, R. (1989). *Manual for scoring and interpretation of the Gates-MacGinitie reading tests* (3rd ed.). Chicago: Riverside.

McGinley, W. J. & Denner, P. R. (1987). Story impressions: A prereading/writing activity. *Journal of Reading, 31,* 248–253.

McKenna, M. C. & Kerr, D. J. (May, 1990). Measuring attitude toward reading: A new tool for teachers. *The Reading Teacher, 43,* 626–639.

McKenna, M. C. & Robinson, R. D. (1993). *Teaching through text: A content literacy approach to content area reading.* New York: Longman.

McKeown, M. G. (1993). Creating effective definitions for young word learners. *Reading Research Quarterly, 28,* 16–32.

Maclean, M., Bryant, P., & Bradley, L. (1987). Rhymes, nursery rhymes, and reading in early childhood. *Merrill-Palmer Quarterly, 33,* 255–281.

McNamara, T. P., Miller, D. L., & Bransford, J. D. (1991). Mental models and reading comprehension. In R. Barr, M. L. Kamil, P. Mosenthal, & P. D. Pearson (Eds.), *Handbook of reading research,* Volume II (pp. 490–511). New York: Longman.

Manelis, L. & Yekorich, F. R. (1976). Repetitions of propositional arguments in sentences. *Journal of Verbal Learning and Verbal Behavior, 15,* 301–312.

Manning, G. L. & Manning, M. (1984). What models of recreational reading make a difference? *Reading World, 23,* 375–380.

Manzo, A. V. (1969). The ReQuest procedure. *Journal of Reading, 13,* 123–126.

Manzo, A. V. & Manzo, U. C. (1993). *Literacy disorders: Holistic diagnosis and remediation.* Fort Worth, TX: Harcourt Brace Jovanovich.

Manzo, A. V. & Manzo, U. C. (1995). *Teaching children to be literate: A reflective approach.* New York: Holt, Rinehart and Winston.

Maria, K. (1990). *Reading comprehension instruction: Issues and strategies.* Parkton, MD: York Press.

Maria, K. & MacGinitie, W. (1987). Learning from texts that refute the reader's prior knowledge. *Reading Research and Instruction, 26,* 222–238.

Martin, M. (1995, May). *Spelling in the kindergarten.* Paper presented at the annual meeting of the International Reading Association, Anaheim.

Mason, J. M. & Au, K. H. (1990). *Reading instruction for today* (2nd ed.). Glenview, IL: Scott, Foresman.

Mastropieri, M. A. & Scruggs, T. E. (1991). *Strategies for learning mneomonically.* Cambridge, MA: Brookline Books.

Mastropierei, M. A. & Scruggs, T. E. (1994). Text verus hands-on science curriculum: Implications for students with disabilities. *Remedial and special education, 15*(2), 72–85.

Maxworthy, A. G. (1993). Do study guides improve text comprehension? *Reading Horizons, 34,* 137–150.

Medley, D. M. (1977). *Teacher competence and teacher effectiveness: A review of process-product research.* Washington, DC: American Association of Colleges for Teacher Education.

Mellor, B. & Simons, M. (1991). As we see it: An interview with Kenneth S. & Yetta M. Goodman. In K. S. Goodman, L. B. Bird, & Y. M. Goodman. (Eds.), *The whole language catalog* (pp. 100–101). Santa Rosa, CA: American School Publishers.

Meltzer, L. (1993). *Assessment of learning disabilities: The challenge of evaluating the cognitive strategies and processes underlying learning.* Paper presented at the Ninth Annual Learning Disorders Conference, Cambridge, MA.

Memory, D. M. & Moore, D. W. (1992). Three time-honored approaches to study: An update. In E. K. Dishner, T. W. Bean, J. E. Readence, & D. W. Moore (Eds.), *Reading in the content areas: Improving classroom instruction* (3rd ed.) (pp. 326–340). Dubuque, IA: Kendall/Hunt.

Menyuk, P. (1991). Linguistics and teaching the language arts. In J. Flood, J. M. Jensen, D. Lapp, & J. R. Squire (Eds.), *Handbook of research on teaching the English language arts* (pp. 24–29). New York: Macmillan.

Meyen, E. L. & Skrtic, T. M. (1988). *Exceptional children and youth: An introduction.* Denver, CO: Love.

Meyer, C. A. (1978). Reviewing the literature on Fernald's technique of remedial reading. *The Reading Teacher, 31,* 614–619.

Meyer, L. A. (1991). Are science textbooks considerate? In C. M. Santa & D. E. Alvermann (Eds.), *Science learning: Process and applications* (pp. 28–37). Newark, DE: International Reading Association.

Meyer, B. J. F., Brandt, D., & Bluth, G. (1980). Use of top-level structure in text: Key for reading comprehension of ninth-grade students. *Reading Research Quarterly, 16,* 72–103.

Meyer, B. J. F. & Rice, G. E. (1984). The structure of text. In P. D. Pearson, R. Barr, M. L. Kamil, & P. Mosenthal (Eds.), *Handbook of reading research* (pp. 319–351). New York: Longman.

Meyers, J. B., Gelzheiser, L., & Yelich, G. (1991). Do pull-in programs foster teacher collaboration? *Remedial and Special Education, 12,* 7–15.

Miller, G. A. (1956). The magical number seven plus or minus two: Some limits on our capacity for processing information. *Psychological Review, 63,* 81–97.

Mish, F. C. (1993). *Webster's tenth new collegiate dictionary.* Springfield, MA: Merriam-Webster.

Moffett, J. (1982). *Teaching the universe of discourse.* Portsmouth, NH: Boynton/Cook.

Moll, L. C. (1988). Some key issues in teaching Latino students. *Language Arts, 65,* 465–472.

Montessori, M. (1964). *The Montessori method* (A. E. George, trans.). Cambridge, MA: Robert Bentley.

Moore, B. H. & Caldwell, H. (1991). Drama and drawing for narrative writing in primary grades. *Journal of Educational Research, 87,* 100–110.

Moore, D. W. & Moore, S. A. (1986). Possible sentences. In E. K. Dishner, T. W. Bean, J. E. Readence, & D. W. Moore (Eds.), *Reading in the content areas: Improving classroom instruction* (2nd ed.). (pp. 174–179). Dubuque, IA: Kendall/Hunt.

Moore, D. W. & Readence, J. E. (1984). A quantitative and qualitative review of graphic organizer research. *Journal of Educational Research, 78,* 11–17.

Moore, D. W., Readence, J. E., & Rickelman, R. J. (1989). *Prereading activities for content area reading and learning* (2nd ed.). Newark, DE: International Reading Association.

Morris, D. (1992). Concept of word: A pivotal understanding in the learning-to-read process. In S. Templeton & D. R. Bear (Eds.), *Development of orthogrpahic knowledge and the foundations of literacy: A memorial festschrift for Edmund H. Henderson* (pp. 53–77). Hillsdale, NJ: Lawrence Erlbaum Associates.

Morrow, L. M. (1994). *Literacy development in the early years* (2nd ed.). Boston: Allyn & Bacon.

Mullis, I. V. S. & Jenkins, L. B. (1990). *The reading report card, 1971–1988.* Princeton, NJ: Educational Testing Service.

Mullis, I. V. S., Campbell, J. R., & Farstrup, A. E. (1993). *Executive summary of the NAEP 1992 reading report card for the nation and the states.* Princeton, NJ: Educational Testing Service.

Murray, B. A., Stahl, S. A., & Inez, M. G. (1993, December). *Developing phonological awareness through alphabet books.* Paper presented at the annual meeting of the National Reading Conference, Charleston, SC.

Murray, D. M. (1989). *Expecting the unexpected: Teaching myself—and others—to read and write.* Portsmouth, NH: Boynton/Cook.

Muth, K. D. (1987). Teachers' connective questions: Prompting students to organize ideas. *Journal of Reading, 31,* 254–259.

Myers, J. & Lytle, S. (1986). Assessment of the learning process. *Exceptional Children, 53,* 138–144.

Nagy, W. E. (1988). *Teaching vocabulary to improve reading comprehension.* Newark, DE: International Reading Association.

Nagy, W. E. & Anderson, R. C. (1984). How many words are there in printed English? *Reading Research Quarterly, 19,* 304–330.

Nagy, W. E. & Herman, P. A. (1987). Breadth and depth of vocabulary knowledge: Implications for acquisition and instruction. In M. G. McKeown & M. E. Curtis (Eds.), *The nature of vocabulary acquisition* (pp. 19–35). Hillsdale, NJ: Lawrence Erlbaum.

National Assessment of Educational Progress (1986). *The reading report card, Progress toward excellence in our schools: Trends in reading over four national assessments, 1971–1984.* Princeton, NJ: Educational Testing Service.

National Council of Teachers of English/ International Reading Association (1996). *Standards for the English language arts.* Urbana, IL: National Council of Teachers of English.

Neville, D. (1965). The relationships between reading skills and intelligence test scores. *The Reading Teacher, 18,* 257–262.

Offman, W. & Shaevitz, M. (1962). The kinesthetic method in remedial reading. *Journal of Experimental Education, 31,* 317–320.

Ogle, D. M. (1989). The know, want to know, learn strategy. In K. D. Muth (Ed.), *Children's comprehension of text* (pp. 205–223). Newark, DE: International Reading Association.

Olivares, R. (1993). Using the newspaper to teach ESL learners. Newark, DE: International Reading Association.

Olson, J. L. (1987). Drawing to write. *School Arts, 87*(1), 25–27.

O'Mara, D. W. (1981). The process of reading mathematics. *Journal of Reading, 25,* 22–30.

Orton, S. T. (1937). *Reading, writing, and speech problems in children.* New York: Norton.

Orton, J. (1966). The Orton-Gillingham approach. In J. Money, *The disabled reader: Education of the dyslexic child* (pp. 119–145). Baltimore: The Johns Hopkins Press.

O'Rourke, J. P. (1974). *Toward a science of vocabulary development.* The Hague: Mouton.

Palincsar, A. S. & Brown, A. L. (1986). Interactive teaching to promote independent learning from text. *The Reading Teacher, 39,* 771–777.

Palincsar, A. S. & Klenk, L. (1992). Fostering literacy learning in supportive contexts. *Journal of Learning Disabilities, 25,* 211–225, 229.

Palincsar, A. S., Winn, J., David, Y., Snyder, B., & Stevens, D. (1993). Approaches to strategic reading instruction reflecting different assumptions regarding teaching and learning. In L. J. Meltzer (Ed.), *Strategy assessment and instruction for students with learning disabilities: From theory to practice* (pp. 247–292). Austin, TX: PRO-ED.

Paratore, J. R. (1995). Implementing an intergenerational literacy project: Lessons learned. In L. M. Morrow (Ed.), *Family literacy: Connections in schools and communities* (pp. 37–53). Newark, DE: International Reading Association.

Paris, S. G. (1991). Assessment and remediation of metacognitive aspects of children's reading comprehension. *Topics in Language Disorders, 12*(1), 32–50.

Paris, S. G. & Myers, M. (1981). Comprehension strategies of good and poor readers. *Journal of Reading Behavior, 13,* 5–22.

Paris, S. G., Wasik, B. A., & Turner, J. C. (1991). The development of strategic readers. In R. Barr, M. L. Kamil, P. Mosenthal, & P. D. Pearson (Eds.), *Handbook of reading research,* Volume II (pp. 609–640). New York: Longman.

Paris, S. G., Cross, D. R., & Lipson, M. Y. (1984). Informed strategies for learning: A program to improve children's reading awareness and comprehension. *Journal of Educational Psychology, 76,* 1239–1252.

Paris, S. G. & Okra, E. (1986). Children's reading strategies, metacognition, and motivation. *Developmental Review, 6,* 25–56.

Pauk, W. (1984). The new SQ3R. *Reading World, 23,* 386–387.

Pauk, W. (1989). *How to study in college* (4th ed.). Boston: Houghton Mifflin.

Paul, T. D. (1996). *Patterns of reading practice.* Madison, WI: Institute for Academic Excellence.

Pearson, P. D. (1986, November). *What research has to say about comprehension.* Paper presented at the quarterly meeting of the Connecticut Association for Reading Research, New Britain, CT.

Pearson, P. D. & Gallagher, M. C. (1983). The instruction of reading comprehension. *Contemporary Educational Psychology, 8,* 317–345.

Pearson, P. D. & Johnson, D. D. (1978). *Teaching reading comprehension.* New York: Holt, Rinehart & Winston.

Peha, J. M. (1995). How K–12 teachers are using computer networks. *Educational Leadership, 53*(2), 18–25.

Perfetti, C. A. (1992). The representation problem in reading acquisition. In P. B. Gough, L. C. Ehri, & R. Treiman (Eds.), *Reading Acquisition* (pp. 145–174). Hillsdale, NJ: Lawrence Erlbaum Associates.

Perfetti, C. A., Beck, I., Bell, L., & Hughes, C. (1988). Phonemic knowledge and learning to read are reciprocal: A longitudinal study of first grade children. In K. E. Stanovich (Ed.), *Children's reading and the development of phonological awareness* (39–75). Detroit: Wayne State University.

Peters, C. (1979). The effect of systematic restructuring of material upon the comprehension process. *Reading Research Quarterly, 11,* 87–110.

Peterson, B. (1991). Selecting books for beginning readers. In D. E. DeFord, C. A. Lyons, & G. S. Pinnell (Eds.), *Bridges to literacy: Learning from Reading Recovery* (pp. 111–138). Portsmouth, NH: Heinemann.

Philliber, W. W., Spillman, R. E., & King, R. E. (1996). Consequences of family literacy programs for adults and children: Some preliminary findings. *Journal of Adolescent and Adult Literacy, 39,* 558–565.

Phillips, L. M. (1988). Young readers' inference strategies in reading comprehension. *Cognition and Instruction, 5*(3), 193–222.

Pickary, J. A. (1949) An adult nonreader. In W. S. Gray (Ed.), *Classroom techniques in improving reading. Supplementary Educational Monographs,* No. 69 (pp. 115–117). Chicago: University of Chicago Press.

Pikulski, J. J. (1994). Preventing reading failure: A review of five effective programs. *The Reading Teacher, 48,* 30–39.

Pilla, M. L. (1989). *The best: High/low books for reluctant readers.* Englewood, CO: Libraries Unlimited.

Pinnell, G. S. & McCarrier, A. (1994). Interactive writing: A transition tool for assisting children in learning to read and write. In E. H. Hiebert & B. M. Taylor (Eds.), *Getting reading right from the start* (pp. 149–170). Boston: Allyn & Bacon.

Pittelman, S. D., Heimlich, J. E., Berglund, R. L., & French, M. P. (1991). *Semantic feature analysis: Classroom applications.* Newark, DE: International Reading Association.

Powell, W. R. (1971). The validity of the instructional reading level. In R. E. Leibert (Ed.), *Diagnostic viewpoints in reading* (pp.121–133). Newark, DE: International Reading Association.

Pressley, M. (1977). Imagery and children's learning: Putting the picture in developmental perspective. *Review of Educational Research, 47,* 585–622.

Pressley, M., Borkowski, J. G., Forrest-Pressley, D., Gaskins, I. W., & Wile, D. (1993). Closing thoughts on strategy instruction for individuals with learning disabilities: The good information-processing perspective. In L. Meltzer (Ed.), *Strategy assessment and instruction for students with learning disabilities: From theory to practice* (pp. 355–377). Austin, TX: PRO-ED.

Pressley, M., Johnson, C. J., Symons, S., McGoldrick, J. A., & Kurita, J. A. (1989). Strategies that improve children's memory and comprehension of what is read. *Elementary School Journal, 89,* 3–32.

Probst, R. (1988). Dialogue with a text. *English Journal, 77*(1), 32–38.

Project CRISS (1993). *Evidence of effectiveness.* Kalispell, MT: Author.

Radencich, M. C., Beers, P. G., & Schumm, J. S. (1993). *A handbook for the K–12 resource specialist.* Boston: Allyn & Bacon.

Radencich, M. C. (1995). *Administration and supervision of the reading/writing program.* Boston: Allyn & Bacon.

Raphael, T. E. (1984). Teaching learners about sources of information for answering questions. *The Reading Teacher, 28,* 303–311.

Raphael, T. E. (1986). Teaching question answer relationships, revisited. *The Reading Teacher, 39,* 516–522.

Raphael, T. E. & Englert, C. S. (1990). Writing and reading: Partners in constructive meaning. *The Reading Teacher, 43,* 388–400.

Raphael, T. E., Englert, C. S., & Kirschner, B. W. (1989). Acquisition of expository writing skills. In J. M. Mason (Ed.), *Reading and writing connections* (pp. 261–290). Boston: Allyn & Bacon.

Raphael, T. E. & McMahon, S. I. (1994). Book Club: An alternative framework for reading instruction. *The Reading Teacher, 48,* 102–116.

Rasinski, T. & Padak, N. (1996). *Holistic reading strategies: Teaching children who find reading difficult.* Englewood Cliffs, NJ: Merrill.

Ratner, N. B. (1993). Atypical language development. In J. B. Berko (Ed.), *The development of language* (pp. 325–368). New York: Macmillan.

Rayner, K. & Pollatsek, A. (1989). *The psychology of reading.* Englewood Cliffs, NJ: Prentice-Hall.

Read, C. (1971). Pre-school children's knowledge of English phonology. *Harvard Educational Review, 41,* 1–34.

Rhodes, L. K. & Dudley-Marling, C. (1988). *Readers and writers with a difference: A holistic approach to teaching learning disabled and remedial students.* Portsmouth, NH: Heinemann.

Rhodes, L. K. & Nathenson-Mejia, S. (1992). Anecdotal records: A powerful tool for ongoing literacy assessment. *The Reading Teacher, 45,* 502–509.

Riccio, C. A. & Hynd, G. W. (1996). Neuroanatomical and neurophysiological aspects of dyslexia. *Topics in Language Disorders, 16,* 1–13.

Richardson, J. S. & Morgan, R. F. (1997). *Reading to learn in the content areas* (3rd ed.). Belmont, CA: Wadsworth.

Richek, M. A., Caldwell, J. S., Jennings, J. H., & Lerner, J. W. (1996). *Reading problems: Assessment and teaching strategies* (3rd ed.). Boston: Allyn & Bacon.

Richek, M. A., List, L. K., & Lerner, J. W. (1989). *Reading problems: Assessment and teaching strategies* (2nd ed.). Boston: Allyn & Bacon.

Richek, M. A. & McTague, B. K. (1988). The "Curious George" strategy for students with reading problems. *The Reading Teacher, 42,* 220–226.

Richgels, D. J. & Hansen, R. (1984). Gloss: Helping students apply both skills and strategies in reading content texts. *Journal of Reading, 27,* 312–317.

Rist, R. (1970). Student social class and teacher expectations: The self-fulfilling prophecy in ghetto education. *Harvard Educational Review, 40,* 411–451.

Robeck, M. C. & Wallace, R. R. (1990). *The psychology of reading: An interdisciplinary approach* (2nd ed.). Hillsdale, NJ: Erlbaum.

Robinson, F. P. (1970). *Effective study* (4th ed.). New York: Harper & Row.

Roller, C. (1996). *Variability, not disability: Struggling readers in a workshop classroom.* Newark, DE: International Reading Association.

Rosen, G. D., Sherman, G. F., & Galbunda, A. M. (1993). Dyslexia and brain pathology: Experimental animal models. In A. M. Galbunda (Ed.), *Dyslexia and development, Neurobiological aspects of extra-ordinary brains* (pp. 89–111). Cambridge, MA: Harvard University Press.

Rosenberger, P. B. (1992). Dyslexia—Is it a disease? *The New England Journal of Medicine, 326*(3), 192–193.

Rosenblatt, L. M. (1978). *The reader, the text, and the poem: The transactional theory of the literary work.* Carbondale, IL: Southern Illinois University Press.

Rosenblatt, L. M. (1994). The transactional theory of reading and writing. In R. B. Ruddell, M. R. Ruddell, & H. Singer (Eds.), *Theoretical models and processes of reading* (4th ed.), (pp. 1057–1092). Newark, DE: International Reading Association.

Roswell, F. G. & Natchez, G. (1989). *Reading disability: A human approach to evaluation and treatment of reading and writing difficulties* (4th ed.). New York: Basic Books.

Roswell, F. G. & Chall, J. S. (1992). *Trial teaching strategies teacher's manual.* Chicago, IL: Riverside.

Roswell, F. G. & Chall, J. S. (1994). *Creating successful readers: A practical guide to testing and teaching at all levels.* Chicago, IL: Riverside.

Rosner, J. (1975). *Helping children overcome learning difficulties.* New York: Walker.

Rosner, S., Abrams, J., Daniels, P., & Schiffman, G. (1981). Dealing with the reading needs of the learning disabled child. *Journal of Learning Disabilities, 14,* 436–448.

Roth, K. J. (1991). Reading science texts for conceptual change. In C. M. Santa & D. E. Alvermann (Eds.), *Science learning: Process and applications* (pp. 48–63). Newark, DE: International Reading Association.

Routman, R. (1991). *Invitations: Changing as teachers and learners K–12.* Portsmouth, NH: Heinemann.

Rowe, M. B. (1969). Science, silence, and sanctions. *Science for Children, 6*(6), 11–13.

Rowell, C. G. (1992). *Assessment and correction in elementary language arts.* Boston: Allyn & Bacon.

Ruddell, M. R. (1994). Vocabulary knowledge and comprehension: A comprehension-process view of complex literacy relationships. In R. B. Ruddell, M. R. Ruddell, & H. Singer (Eds.), *Theoretical models and processes of reading* (4th ed.), (pp. 414–447). Newark, DE: International Reading Association.

Ruddell, M. R. (1996). Engaging students' interest and willing participation in subject area learning. In D. Lapp, J. Flood, & N. Farnan (Eds.), *Content area reading and learning: Instructional strategies* (pp. 95–110). Boston: Allyn & Bacon.

Ruddell, R. B. (1978). Developing comprehension abilities: Implications from research for an instructional framework. In S. J. Samuels (Ed.), *What research has to say about reading instruction* (pp. 108–120). Newark, DE: International Reading Association.

Ruddell, R. B. & Ruddell, M. R. (1995). *Teaching children to read and write: Becoming an influential teacher.* Boston: Allyn & Bacon.

Rumelhart, D. E. (1980). Schemata: The building blocks of cognition. In R. J. Spiro, B. C. Bruce, & W. F. Bruner (Eds.), *Theoretical issues in reading comprehension* (pp. 33–58). Hillsdale, NJ: Lawrence Erlbaum.

Rumelhart, D. E. (1985). Toward an interactive model of reading. In H. Singer & R. B. Ruddell (Eds.), *Theoretical models and processes of reading* (3rd ed.) (pp. 722–750). Newark, DE: International Reading Association.

Rusnak, G. (1994, May). *Instructional conversations in the writing process.* Paper presented at the annual reading conference of the International Reading Association, Toronto.

Rutherford, F. J. & Ahlgren, A. (1990). *Science for all Americans.* New York: Oxford University Press.

Ryder, R. J. & Graves, M. (1996–97). Using the Internet to enhance students' reading, writing, and information-gathering skills. *Journal of Reading, 40,* 244–254.

Rye, J. (1982). *Cloze procedure and the teaching of reading.* London: Heinemann.

Sack, K. (December 31, 1995). 84-year-old finds the joy of reading a good book. *The New York Times,* p. 16.

Sadowski, M. (1983). An exploratory study of the relationship between reported imagery and the comprehension and recall of a story. *Reading Research Quarterly, 19,* 110–123.

Sadowski, M. (1985). The natural use of imagery in story comprehension and recall: Replication and extension. *Reading Research Quarterly, 20,* 658–667.

Sadowski, M., Goetz, E. T., & Fritz, J. B. (1993). Impact of concreteness on comprehensibility, interest, and memory for text: Implications for dual coding theory and text design. *Journal of Educational Psychology, 85,* 291–304.

Salvia, J. & Ysseldyke, J. E. (1988). *Assessment in special and remedial education* (4th ed.). Boston: Houghton Mifflin.

Samuels, S. J. (1979). The method of repeated reading. *The Reading Teacher, 32,* 403–408.

Samuels, S. J. (1994). Toward a theory of automatic information processing in reading revisited. In R. B. Ruddell, M. R. Ruddell, & H. Singer (Eds.), *Theoretical models and processes of reading* (4th ed.), (pp. 816–837). Newark, DE: International Reading Association.

Santa, C. M. (1976–1977). Spelling patterns and the development of flexible word recognition strategies. *Reading Research Quarterly, 12,* 125–144.

Santa, C. M. (1988). *Reading opportunities in literature.* Unpublished manuscript.

Santa, C. M., Abrams, J., & Santa, J. L. (1979). Effects of notetaking and studying on the retention of prose. *Journal of Reading Behavior, 11,* 247–260.

Santa, C. M., Havens, L. T., & Maycumber, E. M. (1996). *Creating independence through student-owned strategies* (2nd ed.). Dubuque, IA: Kendall/ Hunt.

Sawyer, D. J. (1987). *TALS Test of Awareness of Language Segments.* Rockville, MD: Aspen.

Sawyer, D. J. (1985). *Language problems observed in poor readers.* Boston: College Hill Press.

Sawyer, D. J. (1988). Studies of the effects of teaching auditory segmenting skills within the reading program. In Masland & Masland (Eds.), *Preschool prevention of reading failure* (pp. 121–142). Parkton, MD: York Press.

Schlagal, R. (1992). Patterns of orthographic development in the intermediate grades. In S. Templeton & D. Bear (Eds.), *Development of orthographic knowledge and the foundations of literacy: A memorial Festschrift for Edmund H. Henderson* (pp. 31–52). Hillsdale, NJ: Lawrence Erlbaum.

Schumm, J. (1997, May). *Planning for inclusion.* Paper presented at the annual meeting of the International Reading Association, Atlanta.

Schumm, J. S., Vaughn, S., & Leavell, A. G. (1994). Planning pyramid: A framework for planning for diverse student needs during content area instruction. *The Reading Teacher, 47,* 608–615.

Schunk, D. H. (1989). Self-efficacy and cognitive achievement: Implications for students with learning problems. *Journal of Learning Disabilities, 22,* 14–22.

Schunk, D. H. & Rice, J. H. (1987). Enhancing comprehension skill and self-efficacy with strategy value information. *Journal of Reading Behavior, 19,* 285–302.

Schunk, D. H. & Rice, J. M. (1993). Strategy fading and progress feedback: Effects on self-efficacy and comprehension among students receiving remedial services. *The Journal of Special Education, 27,* 257–273.

Seligman, M. E. P. (1975). *Helplessness.* San Francisco: W. H. Freeman.

Senechal, M. & Cornell, E. J. (1993). Vocabulary acquisition through shared reading experiences. *Reading Research Quarterly, 28,* 360–374.

Shand, M. (1993). *The role of vocabulary in developmental reading disabilities* (Tech. Rep. No. 576). Urbana, IL: Center for the Study of Reading.

Shankweiler, D., Crain, S., Brady, S., & Macaruso, P. (1992). Identifying the causes of reading disability. In P. B. Gough, L. C. Ehri, & R. Treiman (Eds.), *Reading acquisition* (pp. 275–305). Hillsdale, NJ: Lawrence Erlbaum Associates.

Shefelbine, J. L. (1990). Student factors related to variability in learning word meanings from context. *Journal of Reading Behavior, 22,* 71–97.

Shanahan, T., Mulhern, M., & Rodriguez-Brown, F. (1995). Project FLAME: Lessons learned from a family literacy program for linguistic minority families. *The Reading Teacher, 48,* 586–593.

Shany, M. T. & Biemiller, A. (1995). Assisted reading practice: Effects on performance for poor readers in grades 3 and 4. *Reading Research Quarterly, 30,* 382–395.

Sharan, S. (1985). Cooperative learning and the multiethnic classroom. In R. Slavin, S. Sharan, R. Hertz-Lazarowitz, & R. Schmuck (Eds.), *Learning to cooperate, cooperating to learn* (pp. 255–267). New York: Plenum Press.

Shaywitz, S. E. & Shaywitz, B. A. (1993). Learning disabilites and attention deficits in the school setting. In L. Meltzer (Ed.), *Strategy assessment and instruction for students with learning disabilities: From theory to practice* (pp. 221–241). Austin, TX: PRO-ED.

Silvaroli, N. J. (1994). *Classroom Reading Inventory.* Madison, WI: Brown & Benchmark.

Simmons, J. (1990). Portfolios as large-scale assessment. *Language Arts, 67,* 262–268.

Simon, H. A. (1986). The role of attention in cognition. In S. L. Friedman, K. A. Klivington, & R. W. Peterson (Eds.), *The brain, cognition, and education* (pp. 105–115). Orlando, FL: Academic Press.

Simonsen, S. (1996). Identifying and teaching text structures in content area classrooms. In D. Lapp, J. Flood, & N. Farnan (Eds.), *Content area reading and learning instructional strategies* (pp. 59–73). Boston: Allyn & Bacon.

Simpson, E. (1979). *Reversals: A personal account of victory over dyslexia.* Boston: Houghton Mifflin.

Simpson, M. L. (1992). PORPE: A study strategy for learning in the content areas. In E. K. Dishner, T. W. Bean, J. E. Readence, & D. W. Moore (Eds.), *Reading in the content areas: Improving classroom instruction* (3rd ed.) (pp. 340–348). Dubuque, IA: Kendall/Hunt.

Simpson, M. L. (1986). PORPE: A writing strategy for studying and learning in the content areas. *Journal of Reading, 29,* 407–414.

Simpson, S. B., Swanson, J. M., & Kunkel, K. (1992). The impact of an intensive multisensory reading program on a population of learning-disabled delinquents. *Annals of Dyslexia, 42,* 54–67.

Singer, H. (1977). IQ is and is not related to reading. In S. Wanat (Ed.), *Issues in evaluating reading.* Arlington, VA: Center for Applied Linguistics, 43–55.

Slater, W. H., Graves, M. F., & Piche, G. L. (1985). Effects of structural organizers on ninth grade students' comprehension and recall of four patterns of expository text. *Reading Research Quarterly, 20,* 189–202.

Slavin, R. E. (1990). *Cooperative learning: Theory, research, and practice.* Englewood Cliffs, NJ: Prentice-Hall.

Slavin, R. E., Madden, N. A., Karweit, N. L., & Dolan, L. (1990). Success for All: First year outcomes of a comprehensive plan for reforming urban education. *American Educational Research Journal, 27,* 255–278.

Slavin, R. E., Madden, N. A., Karweit, N. L., Dolan, L. J., & Wasik, B. A. (1994). Success for all: Getting reading right the first time. In E. H. Hiebert & B. M. Taylor (Eds.), *Getting reading right from the start* (pp. 125–147). Boston: Allyn & Bacon.

Slingerland, B. H. (1971). *A multi-sensory approach to language arts for specific language disability children: A guide for primary teachers.* Cambridge, MA: Educators Publishing Service.

Smith, C. R. (1994). *Learning disabilities: The interaction of learner, task, and setting* (2nd ed.). Boston: Allyn & Bacon.

Smith, F. (1988). *Understanding reading: A psycholinguistic analysis of reading and learning to read.* Hillsdale, NJ: Lawrence Erlbaum.

Smith, M. K. (1941). Measurement of the size of general English vocabulary through the elementary grades and high school. *General Psychological Monographs, 24,* 311–345.

Smith, P. L. & Tompkins, G. E. (1988). Structured notetaking: A new strategy for content area readers. *Journal of Reading, 32,* 46–53.

Smith-Burke, M. T. & Jaggar, A. M. (1994). Implementing Reading Recovery in New York: Insights from the first two years. In E. H. Hiebert & B. M. Taylor (Eds.), *Getting reading right from the start* (63–84). Boston: Allyn & Bacon.

Snyder, L. S. & Godley, D. (1992). Assessment of word-finding disorders in children and adolescents. *Topics in Language Disorders, 13,* 15–32.

Spangenberg-Urbschat, K. & Pritchard, R. (1994). Meeting the challenge of diversity. In K. Spangenberg-Urbschat & R. Pritchard (Eds.), *Kids come in all languages: Reading instruction for ESL students* (pp. 1–5). Newwark, DE: International Reading Association.

Spear-Swerling, L. & Sternberg, R. J. (1994). The road not taken: An integrative theoretical model of reading disability. *Journal of Learning Disabilities, 27,* 91–103, 122.

Spear-Swerling, L. & Sternberg, R. J. (1996). *Off track: When poor readers become "learning disabled."* Boulder, CO: Westview Press.

Spring, C. & French, L. (1990). Identifying children with specific reading disabilities from listening and reading discrepancy scores. *Journal of Learning Disabilities, 23,* 53–58.

Stahl, S. A. (1986). Three principles of effective vocabulary instruction. *Journal of Reading, 29,* 662–668.

Stahl, S. A. & Fairbanks, M. M. (1986). The effects of vocabulary instruction: A model-based meta-analysis. *Review of Educational Research, 56,* 72–110.

Stahl, S. A. & Kapinus, B. A. (1991). Possible sentences: Predicting word meanings to teach content area vocabulary. *The Reading Teacher, 45,* 36–43.

Standerford, N. S. (1993). Where have all the sparrows gone? Rethinking Chapter 1 services. *Reading Research and Instruction, 33,* 38–57.

Stanovich, K. E. (1986). Matthew effects in reading: Some consequences of individual differences in the acquisition of literacy. *Reading Research Quarterly, 21,* 360–407.

Stanovich, K. E. (1991). Discrepancy defintions of reading disability: Has intelligence led us astray? *Reading Research Quarterly, 26,* 7–29.

Stanovich, K. E. (1992). Speculations on the causes and consequences of individual differences in early reading acquisition. In P. B. Gough, L. C. Ehri, & R. Treiman (Eds.), *Reading acquisition* (pp. 307–342). Hillsdale, NJ: Lawrence Erlbaum Associates.

Stanovich, K. E. & Siegel, L. S. (1994). Phenotypic performance profile of children with reading disabilities: A regression-based test of the phonological-core variable-difference model. *Journal of Educational Psychology, 86,* 24–53.

Stauffer, R. G. (1969). *Directing reading maturity as a cognitive process.* New York: Harper & Row.

Sternberg, R. J. (1985). *Beyond IQ: A triarchic theory of intelligence.* Cambridge, Eng.: Cambridge University Press.

Sternberg, R. J. (1987). Most vocabulary is learned from context. In M. G. McKeown & M. E. Curtis (Eds.), *The nature of vocabulary acquisition* (pp. 89–105). Hillsdale, NJ: Lawrence Erlbaum.

Stewart, R. A. & Cross, T. L. (1991). The effect of marginal glosses on reading comprehension and retention. *Journal of Reading, 35,* 4–12.

Stewart, R. A. & Cross, T. L. (1993). A field test of five forms of marginal gloss study guides: An ecological study. *Reading Psychology, 14,* 113–139.

Stewig, J. W. & Nordberg, B. (1995). *Exploring language arts in the elementary classroom.* Belmont, WA: Wadsworth.

Sticht, T. G. & James, J. H. (1984). Listening and reading. In P. D. Pearson, R. Barr, M. L. Kamil, & P. Mosenthal (Eds.), *Handbook of reading research* (pp. 293–317). New York: Longman.

Stoll, D. R. (1994). *Magazines for kids and teens.* Newark, DE: International Reading Association.

Story House (1996). *Story House book catlalog.* Charlotteville, NY: Author.

Sulzby, E. (1989). Assessment of writing and of children's language while writing. In L. Morrow & J. Smith (Eds.), *The role of assessment and measurement in early literacy instruction* (pp. 83–109). Englewood Cliffs, NJ: Prentice-Hall.

Sulzby, E. & Barnhart, J. (1992). The development of academic competence: All our children emerge as writers and readers. In J. W. Irwin & M. A. Doyle (Eds.), *Reading/writing connections: Learning from research* (pp. 120–144). Newark, DE: International Reading Association.

Taba, H. (1965). The teaching of thinking. *Elementary English, 42,* 534–542.

Taba, H. (1967). *Teacher's handbook for elementary social studies.* Reading, MA: Addison-Wesley.

Tallal, P. (1976). Auditory perceptual factors in language and learning disabilities. In R. Knight & D. Bakker (Eds.), *The neuropsychology of learning disabilities* (pp. 315–325). Baltimore: University Park Press.

Tallal, P., Miller, S. L., Bedi, G., Byma, G., Wang, X., & Nagarajan, S. S. (1996). Language comprehension in language learning-impaired children with acoustically modified speech. *Science, 271,* 81–84

Taylor, B. M. (1992, May). *Early intervention in reading: Supplemental instruction for low achieving readers provided by first grade teachers.* Paper presented at the annual meeting of the International Reading Association, Orlando, FL.

Taylor, B. M., Harris, L. A., & Pearson, P. D. (1988). *Reading difficulties: Instruction and assessment.* New York: Random House.

Taylor, B. M. (1982). A summarizing strategy to improve middle grade students' reading and writing skills. *The Reading Teacher, 36,* 202–205.

Taylor, B. M. & Hiebert, E. H. (1994). Early literacy interventions: Aims and issues. In E. H. Hiebert & B. M. Taylor (Eds.), *Getting reading right from the start* (pp. 3–35). Boston: Allyn & Bacon.

Taylor, B. M., Strait, J., & Medo, M. A. (1994). Early intervention in reading: Supplemental instruction for groups of low-achieving students provided by first-grade teachers. In E. H. Hiebert & B. M. Taylor (Eds.), *Getting reading right from the start* (pp. 85–106). Boston: Allyn & Bacon.

Taylor, D. & Dorsey-Gaines, C. (1988). *Growing up literate, learning from inner-city families.* Portsmouth, NH: Heinemann.

Taylor, K. K. (1986). Summary writing by young children. *Reading Research Quarterly, 21,* 193–208.

Temple, C., Nathan, R., Temple, F., & Burris, N. A. (1993). *The beginnings of writing* (3rd ed.). Boston: Allyn & Bacon.

Thames, D. G. & Reeves, C. K. (1994, May). *Preventing the progression of negative attitudes among poor readers.* Paper presented at the annual meeting of the International Reading Association, Toronto.

Thorndike, R. L. & Hagen, E. P. (1977). *Measurement and evaluation in psychology and education* (4th ed.). New York: Wiley.

Tierney, R. J., Readence, J. E., & Dishner, E. K. (1995). *Reading strategies and practices: A compendium* (4th ed.). Boston: Allyn & Bacon.

Title 1 of Improving America's Schools Act of 1994, Sec. 101.

Tofig, D. (1994, October 22). School software puts reading on the menu. *The Hartford Courant,* p. 36.

Tompkins, G. E. & Hoskisson, K. (1991). *Language arts: Content and teaching strategies.* New York: Merrill (Macmillan).

Tonjes, M. J. (1991). *Secondary reading, writing, and learning.* Boston: Allyn & Bacon.

Torgesen, J. K. (1990). Studies of children with learning disabilities who perform poorly on memory span tasks. In J. K. Torgesen (Ed.), *Cognitive and behavioral characteristics of children with learning disabilities,* 41–57. Austin, TX: PRO-ED.

Torgesen, J. (1994). *Research-based approach to prevention of reading disabilities.* Paper presented at the New York Branch of the Orton Dyslexia Society, twenty-first annual conference, Language & Medical Symposia on Dyslexia, New York.

Torgesen, J. K. & Hecht, S. A. (1996). Preventing and remediating reading disabilities: Instructional variables that make a difference for special students. In M. F. Graves, P. van den Broek, & B. M. Taylor (Eds.). *The first R: Every child's right to read* (pp. 160–188). Newark, DE: International Reading Association.

TASA (Touchstone Applied Science Associates) (1990). *Degrees of Reading Power.* Brewster, NY: Author.

TASA (Touchstone Applied Science Associates) (1994). *Readability of Textbooks* (10th ed.). Brewster: New York: Author.

TASA (Touchstone Applied Science Associates) (1996a). *DRP BookLink.* Brewster: New York: Author.

TASA (Touchstone Applied Science Associates) (1996b). The DRP Scale of Readability. In Touchstone Applied Science Associates, *Readability of textbooks* (10th ed.) (pp. 7–9). Brewster, NY: Author.

TASA (Touchstone Applied Science Associates) (1996c). *Readability of Textbooks in a Series* (10th ed.). Brewster: New York: Author.

Trachtenburg, P. (1990). Using children's literature to enhance phonics instruction. *The Reading Teacher, 43,* 648–654.

Trathen, W. (1995). *What is the effect of children's orthographic knowledge on their ability to learn and retain new orthographic structures?* Paper presented at the 45th annual meeting of the National Reading Conference, New Orleans.

Traub, N. & Bloom, F. (1975). *Recipe for reading.* Cambridge, MA: Educators Publishing Service.

Tremain, R. (1992). The role of intrasyllabic units in learning to read and spell. In P. B. Gough, L. C. Ehri, & R. Tremain (Eds.), *Reading acquisition* (pp. 65–106). Hillsdale, NJ: Lawrence Erlbaum Associates.

Turbill, J. (1982). *No better way to teach writing!* Rozelle, Australia: Primary English Teaching Association.

Vacca, R. T. & Vacca, J. L. (1986). *Content area reading* (2nd ed.). Boston: Little, Brown.

Vellutino, F. R. (1987). Dyslexia, *Scientific America, 256*(3), 34–41.

Vellutino, F. R. & Denckla, M. B. (1991). Cognitive and neuropsychological foundations of word identification in poor and normally developing readers. In R. Barr, M. L. Kamil, P. Mosenthal, & P. D. Pearson (Eds.), *Handbook of reading research* (pp. 571–608). New York: Longman.

Vellutino, F. R. & Scanlon, D. M. (1988). Phonological coding: Phonological awareness and reading ability: Evidence from a longitudinal and experimental study (pp. 77–119). In K. Stanovich (Ed.), *Children's reading and the development of phonological awareness.* Detroit, MI: Wayne State University Press.

Vellutino, F. R., Scanlon, D. M., Sipay, E. R., Small, S. G., Pratt, R., Chen, R., & Denckla, M. B. (1996). Cognitive profiles of difficult-to-remediate and readily remediated poor readers: Early intervention as a vehicle for distinguishing between cognitive and experiential deficits as basic causes of specific reading disability. *Journal of Educational Psychology, 88,* 601–638.

Venezky, R. L. (1965). *A study of English spelling-to-sound correspondences on historical principles.* Unpublished doctoral dissertation, Stanford University, Stanford, CA.

Vygotsky, L. S. (1962). *Thought and language.* Cambridge, MA: MIT Press.

Vygotsky, L. S. (1978). *Mind and society: The development of higher psychological processes.* Cambridge, MA: MIT Press.

Wade, S. E. & Reynolds, R. (1989). Developing metacognitive awareness. *Journal of Reading, 33,* 6–14.

Wade, S. E. (1990). Using think-alouds to assess comprehension. *The Reading Teacher, 43,* 442–451.

Walker, B. G. (1992). *Diagnostic teaching of reading: Techniques for instruction and assessment* (2nd ed.). New York: Macmillan.

Walmsley, S. A. & Allington, R. L. (1995). Redefining and reforming instructional support programs for at-risk students. In R. A. Allington & S. A. Walmsley (Eds.), *Rethinking literacy in America's elementary schools* (pp. 19–44). New York: Teachers College Press.

Walp, T. P. & Walmsley, S. A. (1995). Scoring well on tests or becoming genuinely literate: Rethinking remediation in a small rural school. In R. A. Allington & S. A. Walmsley (Eds.), *Rethinking literacy in America's elementary schools* (pp. 177–196). New York: Teachers College Press.

Wark, D. M. & Flippo, R. F. (1991). Preparing for and taking tests. In R. F. Flippo & D. C. Caverly (Eds.), *Teaching reading and study strategies at the college level* (pp. 294–338). Newark, DE: International Reading Association.

Watson, A. J. (1984). Cognitive development and units of print in early reading. In J. Downing & R. Valten (Eds.), *Language awareness and learning to read* (pp. 93–118). New York: Springer-Verlag.

Watson, C. & Willows, D. M. (1993). Evidence for a visual-processing-deficit subtype among disabled readers. In D. M. Willows, R. S. Kruk, & E. Corcos (Eds.), *Visual processes in reading and reading disabilities* (pp. 287–309). Hillsdale, NJ: Lawrence Erlbaum.

Weaver, B. M. (1992). *Defining literacy levels.* Charlotteville, NY: Story House.

Weaver, C. (1994a). *Reading process and practice* (2nd ed.). Portsmouth, NH: Heinemann.

Weaver, C. (1994b). Understanding and educating students with attention deficit hyperactivity disorders: Toward a system-theory and whole language perspective. In C. Weaver (Ed.), *Success at Last: Helping students with AD(H)D achieve their potential.* Portsmouth, NH: Heinemann.

Wechsler, D. (1974). *Manual for the Wechsler Intelligence Scale for Children—Revised.* Cleveland: The Psychological Corporation.

Weinstein, C. & Mayer, R. (1986). The teaching of learning strategies. In M. C. Wittrock (Ed.), *Handbook of research on teaching* (pp. 315–327). New York: Macmillan.

Weisberg, R. & Balajthy, E. (1990). Improving disabled readers' summarization and recognition of expository text structure. In N. D. Padak, T. V. Rasinki, & J. Logan (Eds.), *Challenges in reading* (pp. 141–151). Provo: UT: College Reading Association.

West, R. F., Stanovich, K. E., & Mitchell, H. R. (1993). Reading in the real world and its correlates. *Reading Research Quarterly, 28,* 34–50.

White, T. G., Power, M. A., & White, S. (1989). Morphological analysis: Implications for teaching and understanding vocabulary growth. *Reading Research Quarterly, 24,* 283–304.

White, T. G., Sowell, J., & Yanagihara, A. (1989). Teaching elementary students to use word-part clues. *The Reading Teacher, 42,* 302–308.

Wigfield, A. & Asher, S. R. (1984). Social and motivational influences on reading. In P. D. Pearson,

R. Barr, M. L. Kamil, & P. Mosenthal (Eds.), *Handbook of reading research,* Volume II (pp. 423–452). New York: Longman.

Wiig, E. H. (1994). The role of language in learning disabilites. In A. J. Capute, P. J. Accardo, & B. K. Shapiro (Eds.), *Learning disabilites spectrum: AD, ADHD, & LD* (pp. 111–131). Baltimore: York Press.

Wiig, E. H. & Semel, E. M. (1976). *Language disabilities in children and adolescents.* Columbus, OH: Merrill.

Wiig, E. H. & Semel, E. M. (1984). *Language assessment and intervention for the learning disabled* (2nd ed.). Columbus, OH: Merrill.

Williams, P. L., Reese, C. M., Campbell, J. R., Mazzeo, J., & Phillips, G. W. (1995). *1994 NAEP Reading, A first look: Findings from the National Assessment of Education Progress.* Washington, DC: Office of Educational Research and Improvement, U.S. Department of Education.

Willows, D. M., Kruk, R. S., & Corcos, E. (1993). Are there differences between disabled and normal readers in their processing of visual information? In D. M. Willows, R. S. Kruk, & E. Corcos (Eds.), *Visual processes in reading and reading disabilities* (pp. 265–285). Hillsdale, NJ: Lawrence Erlbaum.

Wilson, M. M. (1979). The processing strategies of average and below average readers answering factual and inferential questions of three equivalent passages. *Journal of Reading Behavior, 11,* 235–245.

Wilson, P. (1992). Among nonreaders: Voluntary reading, reading achievement, and the development of reading habits. In C. Temple & P. Collins (Eds)., *Stories and readers: New perspectives on literature in the elementary classroom* (pp. 157–169). Norwood, MA: Christopher-Gordon.

Winograd, P. N. (1984). Strategic difficulties in summarizing text. *Reading Research Quarterly, 19,* 404–425.

Winograd, P. N. & Smith, L. A. (1987). Improving the climate of reading comprehension instruction. *The Reading Teacher, 41,* 304–310.

Winograd, P., Lipson, K. K., & Wixson, M. Y. (1989). *Improving basal reading instruction.* New York: Teachers College Press.

Wixon, K. K. & Lipson, M. Y. (1991). Perspectives on reading disability research. In R. Barr, M. L. Kamil, P. Mosenthal, & P. D. Pearson (Eds.), *Handbook of reading research,* Volume II (pp. 539–570). New York: Longman.

Wolf, M. A. (1991). Naming speed and reading: The contribution of the cognitive neusosciences. *Reading Research Quarterly, 26,* 123–141.

Wolf, M. A. & Goodglass, H. (1986). Dyslexia, dysnomia, and lexical retrieval. *Brain and Language, 28,* 154–168.

Wolman-Bonilla, J. (1989). Reading journals: Invitations to participate in literature. *The Reading Teacher, 43,* 112–120.

Wood, F. P. (1994). *Cortical activation patterns in normal reading and dyslexia: PET and ERP.* Paper presented at the New York Branch of the Orton Dyslexic Society Annual Conference, Language and Medical Symposia on Dyslexia, New York.

Wood, K. D. (1984). Probable passages: A writing strategy. *The Reading Teacher, 37,* 496–499.

Wood, K. D., Lapp, D., & Flood, J. (1992). *Guiding readers through text: A review of study guides.* Newark: DE: International Reading Association.

Yopp, H. K. (1995). A test for assessing phonemic awareness in young children. *The Reading Teacher, 49,* 20–29.

Ysseldyke, S. (1988). *Assessment in special and remedial education.* (4th ed.). Boston: Houghton Mifflin.

Zentall, S. S. (1993). Research on the educational implications of attention deficit hyperactivity disorder. *Exceptional Children, 60,* 143–153.

Zeno, S. M., Ivens, S. H., Millard, R. T., Duvvuri (1995). *The educator's word frequency guide.* Brewster, NY: Touchstone Applied Science Associates.

Zutell, J. (1979). Spelling strategies of primary school children and their relationship to Piaget's concept of decentration. *Research in the Teaching of English, 13,* 69–80.

## Children's Books and School Textbooks

Abbye, S. & Donahue, B. C. (1991). *Our country's geography.* Austin, TX: Steck-Vaughn.

Bains, R. (1993). *Thurgood Marshall: Fight for justice.* Mahwah, NJ: Troll.

Baldwin, D. & Lister, C. (1984). *Your senses.* New York: Bookwright Press.

Blaine, M. (1986). Giants of the city. In J. Stanchfield and T. Gunning (Eds.), *Wings (New Directions in Reading)* (pp. 162–169). Boston: Houghton Mifflin.

Berends, P. B. (1973). *The case of the elevator duck.* New York: Random House.

Bledsoe, L. J. (1988). *Biology: The kingdom of life.* Castro Valley, CA: Quercus.

Bledsoe, L. J. (1990). *Fearon's biology.* Paramus, NJ: Globe Fearon.

Bledsoe, L. J. (1994). *Fearon's general science* (2nd ed.). Paramus, NJ: Globe Fearon.

Brenner, M. (1994). *Abe Lincoln's hat.* New York: Random House.

Brenner, M. (1978). *Wagon wheels.* New York: HarperCollins.

Brown, C. (1989). *Big Red Barn.* New York: Greenwillow.

Brown, C. (1995). *Tractor.* New York: Greenwillow.

Bulla, R. C. (1987). *The chalk box kid.* New York: Random House.

Carle, E. (1987). *Have you seen my cat?* New York: Scholastic.

Cameron, P. (1990). *Donna, A helping hand.* Hayward, CA: Alemany Press.

Carroll, L. (1969). *Alice in wonderland* and *Through the looking glass.* Chicago: Children's Press.

Chardiet, B. (1994). *Something is coming.* New York: Puffin Books.

Cole, J. (1986). *Hungry, hungry sharks.* New York: Random House.

Cowley, J. (1980). *The hungry giant.* Bothell, WA: The Wright Group.

Curtis, N. & Greenland, P. (1992). *I wonder how tires are made.* Minneapolis, MN: Lerner.

Degen, B. (1983). *Jamberry.* New York: Harper.

Domanska, J. (1969). *The turnip.* New York: Macmillan.

Ehlert, L. (1987). *Growing vegetable soup.* Orlando, FL: Harcourt.

Folsom, M. & Folsom, M. (1986). *Easy as pie.* Boston: Houghton Mifflin.

Fulghum, R. (1992). *Writers' voices: Selected from It Was on Fire When I Lay Down on It.* New York: Literacy Volunteers of New York City.

Gág, W. (1928). *Millions of cats.* New York: Coward.

Garten, J. (1964). *The alphabet tale.* New York: Random House.

Geisel, T. S. (Dr. Seuss). (1958). *The cat in the hat.* New York: Random House.

Geisel, T. S. (Dr. Seuss). (1974). *There's a wocket in my pocket.* New York: Beginner.

Gelman, R. G. (1977). *More spaghetti I say.* New York: Scholastic.

Godall, J. (1992). *Writers' voices: Selected from In the Shadow of Man.* New York: Literacy Volunteers of New York City.

Gottlieb, J. S. (1991). *The wonders of science: The human body.* Austin, TX: Steck-Vaughn.

Greenfield, E. (1978). *Honey, I love and other poems.* New York: Harper.

Gutelle, A. (1990). *Baseball's best.* New York: Random House.

Haskins, J. (1991) *Outward dreams: Black inventors and their inventions.* New York: Crowell.

Hill, E. (1986). *Spot goes to the circus.* New York: Putnam.

Hopkins, L. B. (1984). *Surprises.* New York: Harper.

Hopkins, L. B. (1987). *More surprises.* New York: Harper.

Issacesen-Bright, B. & Holland, M. (1986). *No, no, Joan!* New York: Willowwisp.

Kimmel, E. A. (1992). *Anansi goes fishing.* New York: Holiday House.

King, W. & Napp, J. (1989). *Our nation's history.* Circle Pines, MN: American Guidance Services.

Kuskin, K. (1992). *Soap soup and other verses.* New York: HarperCollins.

Leedy, L. (1992). *Blastoff to earth: A look at geography.* NY: Holiday House.

Lefkowitz, W. (1990). *Fearon's United States geography.* Belmont, CA: Globe Fearon.

Lionni, L. (1959). *Little blue and little yellow.* New York: Astor-Honor.

Littledale, F. (1975). *The boy who cried wolf.* New York: Scholastic.

Lowery, L. & Lorbiecki, M. (1993). *Earthwise at home.* Minneapolis: Carolrhoda Books.

Marshall, J. (1990). *Fox be nimble.* New York: Penguin.

Martin, B., Jr. (1983). *Brown bear, brown bear, what do you see?* New York: Holt.

McKissack, P. C. (1983). *Who is who?* Chicago: Children's Press.

McMullen, K. (1989). *Dinosaur hunters.* New York: Random House.

McMurty, L. (1992). *Writers' voices: Selected from Lonesome Dove.* New York: Literacy Volunteers of New York City.

Milton, J. (1985). *Dinosaur days.* New York: Random House.

Minarik, E. H. (1958). *A kiss for little bear.* New York: Harper.

Morris, A. (1992). *Tools.* New York: Lothrop, Lee & Shepard.

Morris, R. A. (1975). *Dolphins.* New York: Harper.

Nentl, J. A. (1983). *Big rigs.* New York: Crestwood House.

Parish, P. (1974). *Dinosaur time.* New York: Harper.

Penner, L. R. (1991). *Dinosaur babies.* New York: Random House.

Potter, B. (1908). *The tale of Peter Rabbit.* London: Warne.

Reef, C. (1991). *Ellis Island.* New York: Dillon Press.

Robart, R. (1986). *The cake that Mack ate.* Boston: Little, Brown.

Rosen, S. (1987). *Biology workshop.* Upper Saddle Brook, NJ: Globe/Fearon.

Sattler, H. R. (1993). *The earliest Americans.* New York: Clarion Books.

Schade, S. (1992). *Toad on the road.* New York: Random House.

Schade, S. (1994). *Railroad toad.* New York: Random House.

Shaw, N. (1986). *Sheep in a jeep.* Boston: Houghton Mifflin.

Scott, (1993). *A picture book of reptiles and amphibians.* Mahwah, NJ: Troll.

Shea, G. (1992). Amazing rescue underground. In G. Shea, *Amazing rescues* (pp. 28–48). New York; Random House.

Steele, P. (1990a). *Pocket facts: Insects.* New York: Crestwood House.

Steele, P. (1990b). *Pocket facts: Wild animals.* New York: Crestwood House.

Steele, P. (1991). *Pocket facts: Birds.* New York: Crestwood House.

Stewart, G. (1989). *Timelines 1930s.* New York: Crestwood House.

Stott, C. (1991). *Observing the sky.* Mahwah, NJ: Troll.

Tan, A. (1992). *Writers' voices: Selected from The Joy Luck Club.* New York: Literacy Volunteers of New York City.

Torres, L. (1993). *Subway Sparrow.* New York: Farrar, Straus, & Giroux.

Viorst, J. (1972). *Alexander and the terrible, horrible, no good, very bad day.* New York: Atheneum.

Walker, A. (1992). *Writers' voices: Selected from The Temple of My Familiar.* New York: Literacy Volunteers of New York City.

Wildsmith, B. (1982). *Cat on the mat.* New York: Oxford University Press.

Wiseman, B. (1959). *Morris and Boris.* New York: Harper.

Yep, L. (1989). *The rainbow people.* New York: Harper.

# Index